Revolution and Democracy in Tunisia

Revolution and Democracy in Tunisia

A Century of Protestscapes

Larbi Sadiki
and
Layla Saleh

Great Clarendon Street, Oxford, OX2 6DP,
United Kingdom

Oxford University Press is a department of the University of Oxford.
It furthers the University's objective of excellence in research, scholarship,
and education by publishing worldwide. Oxford is a registered trade mark of
Oxford University Press in the UK and in certain other countries

© Larbi Sadiki and Layla Saleh 2024

The moral rights of the author have been asserted

All rights reserved. No part of this publication may be reproduced, stored in
a retrieval system, or transmitted, in any form or by any means, without the
prior permission in writing of Oxford University Press, or as expressly permitted
by law, by licence or under terms agreed with the appropriate reprographics
rights organization. Enquiries concerning reproduction outside the scope of the
above should be sent to the Rights Department, Oxford University Press, at the
address above

You must not circulate this work in any other form
and you must impose this same condition on any acquirer

Published in the United States of America by Oxford University Press
198 Madison Avenue, New York, NY 10016, United States of America

British Library Cataloguing in Publication Data

Data available

Library of Congress Control Number: 2023916669

ISBN 9780192863997

DOI: 10.1093/oso/9780192863997.001.0001

Printed and bound by
CPI Group (UK) Ltd, Croydon, CR0 4YY

Links to third party websites are provided by Oxford in good faith and
for information only. Oxford disclaims any responsibility for the materials
contained in any third party website referenced in this work.

For all those who have—across time and space—revolted to make 'Tunis Al-Tha'irah', *an iconic and centennial moral flame*

Contents

List of Figures	x
List of Tables	xi
Preface	xii
List of Abbreviations	xx

1. Trace of a Revolution: Tunisia's "Missing People" in Time and Space — 1
  Introduction — 2
  Protest, Revolution, and Peoplehood — 2
  Angles and Approaches — 4
  Conversations with "Metropolitan Revolution" — 5
  "Protestscapes": Frames of Rebellious Flows and "Free Play" of the Un-free — 15
  Interdisciplinary Revolution — 16
  Revolution against Epistemic Injustice — 16
  Protest and Revolution: Postcolonial Readings — 18
  "Knowing" Revolution — 25
  Interpreting Peoplehood and Revolution — 26
  Outline of the Book — 30
  References — 31

2. Tunisian Protestscapes: The Clamor of Peoplehood — 37
  Introduction — 38
  Conceptualizing Peoplehood — 38
  Agency — 43
  Affect — 44
  Cognition — 46
  Postcolonial "One-Dimensionality" — 50
  The Post-independence Crucible: From Resistance to Counterrevolution — 52
  Synchrony and Diachrony — 53
  Demotic and Insurgent Protestscapes — 56
  A Four-Pronged Approach to Protestscapes — 60
  Intersectional Being(s) — 62
  Genius Mázes — 63
  Protest and Positionality — 66
  Tunisian Protest: Re-Ontologizing Struggles — 67
  A Sociology of Tunisia's "Protest Momentum/Ethos" — 72
  Protest as Counter-Logos — 73
  Conclusion — 78
  References — 78

3. Striking Back: A Century of UGTT and Workers' Syndicalism — 88
Introduction — 89
Early History: The General League for Tunisian Labor — 90
UGTT Beginnings — 96
Characterizing Tunisian Syndicalism — 100
Protest Confrontations: Tunisia's "Black Thursday" — 104
The 1984 Bread Riots — 121
Conclusion — 124
References — 126

4. Dissent of the Mind: 100 Years of Student Activism — 130
Introduction — 130
Situating the Student Protestscape — 131
Forgotten Struggles — 133
Gafsa: Memories and Musings — 135
Freed Spaces: The University as *Mantiqah Muharrarah* — 138
The Student–Teacher Learning Loop — 142
Generative Events — 151
A More "Separate" Union: Islamist Students' Resistance and Representation — 162
Student "Logoi" and Social Imaginaries — 165
Student Social Imaginaries and Becomings — 169
Ideology and Protest in Speech — 174
Gender-ed Spaces — 176
Conclusion — 180
References — 181

5. Miners' Voices: Revolution in Miniature in the Phosphate Basin — 188
Introduction — 189
The Revolutionary South — 190
Alienating the Periphery: Regional Underdevelopment — 191
Spatialized Unruliness — 193
The Phosphate Curse — 194
The 1980 Gafsa Revolt — 198
Sparking Rebellion in 2008 — 199
Mutiny of the Miners: January–June 2008 — 201
Counter-Narratives of Revolt — 207
Sensory Rebellion and Becoming — 209
A Convergence of Activisms — 211
Mobilizing beyond the Phosphate Basin — 213
Conclusion — 222
References — 223

6. Becoming in Diachrony: The Revolution of 2011 — 229
Introduction — 230
Revolutionary Diachrony as "Carnival" — 231
(Southern) Revolutionary Launch — 238
Compounded Suffering — 242
A Revolution in Travel — 245

	Contemporaneous Revolutionary Narratives	255
	Gendering Revolutionary Diachrony	257
	"Occupy" Kasbah	261
	Conclusion	269
	References	271
7.	**"Kamour": A Periphery Uprising**	**276**
	Introduction	277
	The Kamour Protestscape	279
	Notable Features	282
	"We Are Tunisians, Too": Affect and Precept of *Hogra*	285
	Counter-*Hogra*	288
	Protesting (under) Democracy	297
	Cognizing "*Al-Rakh La*"	303
	Conclusion	306
	References	307
8.	**Tunisia's Ultras: The "Freeplay" of Resistance**	**312**
	Introduction	313
	Charting the Ultras Protestscape	314
	Staging Protest … Pre- to Post-Revolution	317
	Tunisia's "Ultras Culture"	323
	Visualizing Peoplehood?	325
	Inaugurating a Resistance Competency	329
	Ultras as Identity and Belonging	332
	Protest Practices	336
	Singing and Choreographing Protest	341
	T'allam 'Oum (Learn to Swim)	346
	Conclusion	350
	References	352
9.	**Conclusion: Taming the Revolution?**	**356**
	Tunisia in Revolt	357
	Demos and Rebirth in Protestscapes	358
	Convergence of Theories	359
	From Post-colony to Post-Structure	361
	Embodied Knowledge and Dis-Embodied People	361
	Revolutionary Becomings	362
	Taming the Revolution	363
	Dictator's Learning Curve	364
	Safeguarding the Revolution	367
	Protest: Learning "Counter-Democracy"	369
	Branching out of Revolution	371
	"Useless to Revolt?"	375
	References	377

Index   380

List of Figures

2.1	Revolution and Peoplehood Concept Map	39
2.2	Researching Protestscapes	61
2.3	Synchrony–Diachrony in Tunisia's Revolutionary Élan, 1864–Present	70
4.1	Schooling Protest Generations: Student–Teacher Learning Loop	144
9.1	A Branching of the 2011 Revolution	373

List of Tables

1.1	Metropolitan Revolution and the Arab World	8
1.2	Postcolonialism and Post-Colonialism	19
1.3	Uprising of Words	23
3.1	UGTT Congresses and Leadership, 1946–2022	106
3.2	Discursive Convergence with UGTT: Political Opposition in 1978	120
3.3	Unpacking Social Acting and En-Acting in 1984	122
4.1	Diachrony of Student Protestscape	152
4.2	Social Imaginaries and Ideologies of Student Protestscape Tendencies (1963–1991)	172
5.1	Slogans of the Phosphate Basin Uprising	206
5.2	Civil Society Mobilization in the 2008 Uprising	214
5.3	Linguistic Features of Criminal Charges against 2008 Uprising Protestors	219
6.1	Old and New Protest Geographies	233
6.2	Revolution Timeline (2008–2011)	239
7.1	The Language of Kamour	284
8.1	Language of the Ultras	315
8.2	Geographic and Club Distribution of Tunisia's Ultras	319

Preface

Ibn Khaldun, Tunisia's traveling man of letters and politics, was no stranger to revolt.[1] Family pedigree converged with participant-observation to sharpen his astute readings of attempts to unseat power and foment political change. Kurayb was an ancestor who instigated a revolt against the Umayyad reign in Al-Andalus, enabling him to rule Seville for at least ten years. Ibn Khaldun's great grandfather Abu Bakr met his demise during a revolt staged by Ibn Abi Umarah in the late 13th century opposing the Hafsids of Tunis. During Ibn Khaldun's own lifetime, revolt raged against Barquq in Egypt. Because he wrote critically against him, Ibn Khaldun was barred from his position as professor and Maliki judge when Barquq emerged victorious. Somehow, Ibn Khaldun convinced the ruler of Egypt to restore these positions to him. Soon after, revolt reared its head again, this time against Barquq's son Faraj. We hear of this insurrection in the sociologist's autobiography.[2] Ibn Khaldun narrates his eventful journey to Damascus, and his encounter with the conquering Tatar Timur alongside Faraj at the behest of the Egyptian ruler who was planning to confront Timur's pillaging of the Islamic East. During their stop in Gaza, news broke that a revolt (thawrah) was brewing in Egypt. Faraj quickly changed direction, apprehensive of a wide-scale uprising (intifadah) by the locals. Ibn Khaldun carried on to Damascus, where he dazzled Timur with his erudition. Working through part flattery and part scholarly services (a meticulous description of the Maghreb, including his own Tunisia or Ifriqiyyah), he convinced Timur to spare his life and that of others. Not, however, before Ibn Khaldun bore painful witness to the razing of ancient Damascus, including its Great Mosque.

In its various enactments, revolt, then, boasts a long pedigree of Arab scholarly observation and interest. The political and personal turbulence to which Ibn Khaldun was witness springs to life in centuries-old historiography and sociology. Historians such as Al-Jabarti[3] and Ahmad ibn Abi Diyaf,[4] did not preclude rebellion and revolt in their great narrations. The characters, exploits, and hardships of revolt have been documented for posterity in their great tomes. One such figure mentioned by Ibn

---

[1] This vignette draws on Rosenthal's biographical introduction to his translation of Ibn Khaldun (b. 1332–1406). See Ibn Khaldun. 1958. *The Muqaddimah: An Introduction to History, V. I.* Trans. Franz Rosenthal. New York: Pantheon Books (xxxiii–lxii).

[2] See Ibn Khaldun's autobiography (1979, 407–428), *Al-Ta'rif bi Ibn Khaldun wa Rihlatihi Gharban wa Sharqan*. Beirut: Dar Al-Kitab al-Lubnani *li Al-Tiba'ah* wa Al-Nashr.

[3] Al-Jabarti, Abdulrahman. 2003 [1880]. *'Aja'ib Al-Athar fi Al-Tarajim Wa Al-Akhbar* [History of Egypt]. Cairo: Maktabat Madbuli.

[4] Ibn Abi Diyaf, Ahmad. 1990. *Ithaf Ahl Al-Zaman Bi Akhbar Muluk Tunis Wa 'Ahd Al-Aman*, [A History of Rulers of Tunis and the Fundamental Pact]. Ed. Riyad Al-Marzouki. Tunis: Al-Dar Al-Tunisiyyah li Al-Nashr.

Khaldun[5] is legendary Al-Jaziyah Al-Hilaliyyah (Zaziyah in Tunisian parlance). The story of this courageous, larger than life figure from the eleventh century would be (re)narrated and mythologized in Arab oral history.[6] Her iconic image adorns countless homes and beckons tourists from shopkeepers' stalls in the Tunis *souq*. She is immortalized not just by Ibn Khaldun, but in the epic *(Sirah)* of Banu Hilal. The story of how they settled in Tunisia has traveled by mouth and pen, westward in space and forward in time, like the tribe that is its subject. Forced to endure a migration (*taghribah*) from the Arabian Hijaz to the Levant, the Banu Hilal wound their way through Egypt, and westward to the Maghreb's land of verdure, Ifriqiyyah, as Tunisia was then known. Leading this migration to "the land that was not barren, where water flows abundantly," was Al-Jaziyah. Possessing one third of Banu Hilal's political counsel, this formidable woman lived unconventionally, rebelliously, leaving her husband (the Sharif of Makkah) and child behind, to help her tribe find succor after seven years of drought. She traded comfort and luxury for the dangers and coarseness of a desert journey. Banu Hilal's combat and victory over Zanati Khalifah who ruled Tunisia, allowing the tribe to settle in this land of plenty, is fabled. A skilled horsewoman, a brave warrior, an eloquent poet, a sagacious politician, Al-Jaziyah in all her oral and written versions is indelible in the collective memory of Tunisians. She is a founding mother, a wellspring of Bedouin identity and values, a symbol of gallantry, unity, loyalty, and mutiny.

Sirat Banu Hilal offers a glimpse of Arab and Tunisian rebelliousness of spirit and determination in action. In this vein, we seek through this book to re-ontologize Tunisian protest and revolution. The story dramatizes Al-Jaziyah, a woman of grit, imagination, and courage, an intrepid personality with a cause. She mobilized agency, affect, and cognition to overturn a barren, un-dignified existence for her tribe. Moving from Arabia to Tunisia through all kind of stops (synchronies) along the way, Al-Jaziyah's journey is one of hardship and struggle, combat and politics. A major showdown with Zanata would decree eternal life, rebirth after death for Al-Jaziyah and Banu Hilal in a myth that would shape a consciousness of identity, and selfhood and solidarity. The trans-spatial, trans-temporal terrain of Banu Hilal's migration has become for us a metaphor of Tunisia's revolution, a journey in time and space that we seek to piece together retroactively in the diverse, partial, and situated protestscapes we chart in the following chapters. Embodied in the roving person of Al-Jaziyah is the potent agency of protest, embedded in the telling and (re)writing of the mythology and historiography of Tunisia. Hers is a narrative of literal and figurative de-territorialization and re-territorialization. It is a story of how people sow the seeds of self-defense, renewal, and self-reproduction in word and deed, often at great personal sacrifice.

There is no one rendition of Al-Jaziyah, no agreed-upon chronicle of her life or those surrounding her like Abu Zaid Al-Hilali. Such an elusive and intriguing

---

[5] See Chapter VI, Section 59 of Ibn Khaldun's *Kitab Al-'Ibar* [Book of Lessons].
[6] See for instance, Mohamed Al-Marzouki. 1988. *Al-Jaziyah Al-Hilaliyyah: Qissah Min Al-Turath Al-Sha'bi*. [Al-Jaziyah Al-Hilaliyyah: An Epic from Folk Tradition] Tunis: Al-Dar Al-Tunisiyyah Li Al-Nashr.

historical figure is fitting inspiration for our own daunting but invigorating journey in writing this book. What does it really mean to add to the canon of revolution, neither single nor fixed, but multi-faceted like the stories of humanity itself? One stubborn notion has informed our enterprise: there are no "exemplary" people who have forged the template for revolution. The world is not populated, historically or currently, by passive peoples (e.g. Arabs, in Orientalist imaginaries), to be contrasted with active counterparts, whether they be French or American or Russian. While our book launches the stories of Tunisia's revolution in 1864, with the revolt of Ali Ben Ghedhahem, Al-Jaziyah, romanticized as she is, hints at older figures and struggles across the arc of Tunisian experiences. In fact, Tunisian history brims with protest and revolt, as recounted by Ibn Khaldun and Ibn Abi Diyaf.

Writing this book was for us an imperative, pressing undertaking. As the 2011 "Arab Spring" revolutions took off from Tunisia and leapt across the region, as they reached highs (democratic transition) and lows (coups and power grabs), one epistemological implication became clear. The idea of revolution, as emblematized in classic texts on the topic—and their endless re-workings—could not remain untouched. Freedom and dignity for Tunisian and Arab publics is a worthy quest, its appreciation integral to writing revolution through research and scholarship. Delinking research from identification with (and even participation in) human aspirations and postcolonial strivings for emancipation, is simply not possible from where we stand. Critical knowledge-making implies continuous questioning, of our own assumptions and those of others. Our investigation would center on how Tunisians enacted an ongoing, arduous process of *demos-making* that bears traces of the past, and leaves its imprint on the future.

To juxtapose Tunisia and revolution is to re-ontologize the filters of peoplehood in the service of emancipatory impulses, in time and space. The interpretation presented here breathes life into protestscapes with a strong accent on specificity: situated protest. These protestscapes may not appear to be related to other world revolutions. However, such emancipatory impulses are not entirely unrelated to recorded stories of struggles throughout history. Within protestscapes, the need to invent agency, rediscover affect, and renew cognition can only occur through revolutionary identities, bearers of aspirations of a dignified, free, and audacious community. A community that reconstitutes itself through historic struggles, disobedience, disruption—"dissensus"—to unbind its members from the adversity of absence as people. Writing and knowing Tunisia's revolution through protestscapes, the book showcases ways to glimpse acts of rebellion across 150 years, synchronically and diachronically. It becomes possible to historically situate social doing; locate sites of contesting unjust power; and animate text and context with the agentic, affective, and cognitive reflexes that pulsate with emancipatory responses to misrule. Revolutions and revolutionaries unnerve and disturb the powers-that-be, in Tunisia as elsewhere. After independence, "revolution" fades into insignificance. It denotes lawlessness. Rebels and any "cause celèbre" exit theory and practice. Even the *fellaga*, the anti-colonial freedom fighters, becomes unsuited as a word to a world which is discomposed into "a-territory"—that is, de-territorialized. The term manifests its search for territory—re-territorialization—in social doing, acts, and enactments of rebellion, refusing omission in affect and cognition. It fails to bow to postcolonial authoritarian logics and orders and to relinquish the right to have rights. The utility of protestscapes partly lies in peoplehood's self-constituting histories and spaces, and the exercise of unruly power to resist being neutered and purged in post-independence Tunisia.

Moreover, postcolonialism's critical consciousness of the complicity between scholar and politician, energizes our "writing back" of Tunisian protest and revolution. Protest is a practical medium of resistance, against both the *colon* and the authoritarian, neo/internal colonizer. Turning our attention to real-world resistance, we try to unhinge that complicity. The canonized texts and theories of imported "-isms" of the ex-*colons*, from nationalism to democracy, condition even postcolonial theorists. Our focus on protest and its practicalities as an expression of peoplehood entails a critical cross-referencing of local ideational/experiential knowledge and what we call "metropolitan revolution." Spotlighting resistance by emphasizing local knowledge, know-how, strategies of doing politics, learning, *acting*, and *en-acting* peoplehood is a way to disrupt and decenter Eurocentric protest and revolutionary theory. Even postcolonialists have not fully delved into the agents of those cultures they seem to be championing, at least in the Arab world. Deconstructing dominant cultural representations can be a stepping-stone to critical engagement—narration and re-narration—of the lived experiences of the formerly colonized. Postcolonialism can straddle investigations of both the "objective history of the subaltern" as well as the "subjective experience of … colonialism".[7] Of course, cognition of the "objective" is grounded in the subjectivity of perceptions that construct variegated and diverging dimensions of *multiple* realities which are neither single nor fixed, as postmodernism's provocations maintain. The point is that we seek to examine iterations of practical resistance muffled by metropolitan revolution, in conjunction with the agency, affect, and cognition of such acts and en-actments. We turn to experiences that have not yet been sufficiently narrativized in academia, with special reference to Tunisia. We attempt this through a form of subversive knowledge-practice. Identities engendered by resistance to colonialism in the Arab setting entail commonalities with other postcolonial conditions as well as regional specificities. Laying out localized protest to be investigated sheds light on how resisters could become oppressors (Bourguiba). The attendant situatedness colors both socio-historical-political *happenings* and their *analysis*, as we attempt to "write back." The authenticity of identity that has predominated postcolonial Arab academia for decades, or "new" nationalisms, tends to skip over the people's revolts, focusing instead on ideological polarities or the state and its elites. Our practice of a "people's history" zooms in

---

[7] Young, Robert J.C. 2016. *Postcolonialism: An Historical Introduction, Anniversary Edition*. Oxford: Wiley, p. 398.

on bottom-up struggle, instead of what can be a postcolonial abstraction of real-life struggle and resistance.

To do this, our interviews include oral history testimonies. These offer telling snippets that help illuminate the travails of peoplehood-in-becoming. We filter, read, interpret, and present these first-hand accounts thus. Oral history allows sightings of remembered and memorialized perceptions, feelings, sensibilities, and overall meaning-making. It is paramount to a bottom-up reconstruction of protestscapes. However, our pursuit of epistemic justice renders the situated remembrances (oral history) of high-level and rank-and-file activists vital but incomplete. Interviews, however numerous, are not enough for a thorough, decolonial investigation of a phenomenon as intricately complex as revolution. The seriousness with which we regard the indigenous field of knowledge necessitates meticulous treatment of Tunisian historical and sociological scholarship. We cannot cast aside local knowledge-making. Neither are we the first native Arabic speakers to ponder the unfolding and significance of revolution. As social scientists hailing from the region but writing in English, our positionality enables a mediating function between the making and writing of revolution, between the (re)construction and translation of knowledge. The social acts and en-actments of peoplehood that accumulate in revolution acquire layers of meaning and significance through their (re)narrations by indigenous, postcolonial, and Western social scientists. We thus attempt to absorb, interrogate, and build on the work of our Tunisian and Arab colleagues. This we do against the backdrop of a critique of Western metropolitan revolution (Chapter 1), also deploying other Western concepts (e.g. from critical and democratic theory to poststructuralism). This fruitful, contemplative, labor-intensive, intertextual foray lifts the veil on our own critical rendering of Tunisian protest and revolution.

Readers will note that the book attempts to capture how multi-dimensional affect, often prompted by visual and sensory cues, permeates the political, including protest and revolution. For example, rapper EL General's *Rayes Lebled* was a message to a dictator by a young indignant. It gives scathing, relatable musical expression to the *hogra* (contempt for the state, a "dog"-like life) of Tunisians mired in everyday "humiliation," "suffering," and "injustices"—a "dead people." People forced to rummage through trash for sustenance are constantly "trod" down by the ubiquitous boot of authoritarian domination and coercion. The song was part of the mesh of affect that entangled feeling, intellect, and protestors with the moment of peoplehood via revolution. A flash of technologically mediated rage, an affective medium of rebellious and revolutionary peoplehood, it went viral in Tunisia and across the Arab Spring geography. The hip-hop song seemed to give voice to the impassioned masses who felt the power of the moment and the medium, of a drive so fervid in the genius of making music and revolution. Thus peoplehood, riding the wavelength of rebellion, was catapulted into presence through revolution that traveled from Tunisia throughout the region. Other examples of affective triggers include images such as that of Mohamed Bouazizi's body going up in flames, the almost satirical photo of Ben Ali visiting him in the hospital, and crowds congregating in Habib Bourguiba

Avenue. Such images can jolt viewers into recalculating their affective radar. *Does fear of the state always paralyze?* Perhaps not. In this way, the revolution becomes a point of no return through the performance and actualization (acting and en-acting) of peoplehood through protest. The affective power of the state to subdue through fear is reversed by action, cognition, and affect outside its control. The state loses the plot, beginning perhaps at the affective level. For emboldened forms of demos, there is no going back to the "first republic" of pre-2011 Tunisia. Affect and its reversals perpetually carry a call to action.

The study of protest and revolution inevitably treads familiar territory. "Metropolitan revolution," more or less, occupies a privileged place by pioneering the study of Western revolution. The attempt to study Tunisia's revolution pushes the boundaries beyond the reigning wisdom on Arab revolutions. It opens up a forum to re-ontologize hidden or under-examined forces, voices, and discourses whose own "truths" fill in gaps in dominant versions of knowledge-making, polity, identity, history, and society. In this vein, the book's six protestscapes open up undisclosed narratives in a way that renders hidden struggles and their unsung heroes in a new light and scholarly sensibility—both vivid and partial. This approach weakens the authoritative knowledge assumed by claimants of power in authoritarian settings. Their empassioned drive to reproduce their stranglehold over power equates with passionate dogged resolve to reproduce versions of knowledge that offer uncontested control over word and world. Epistemologically, our use of protestscapes enables a reliving of the contest over meaning and imaginary, word and world, self and other, and subject and object. The tension is what postcolonial Tunisian politics has sought to suppress as if to save a newly forming post-independent demos from itself. Tension is the stuff of politics. By bringing to life the tense conversations, the acts and en-actments of self-constituting *demoi* and *logoi*, protestscapes capture partial, fractured, and contested subjectivities seeking reconstitution as emancipated beings and people. This epistemic enterprise is thus geared towards the interpretation of situated protest and the experience of domination that are partially constitutive of both subject and object under authoritarian power relations, in both colony and postcolony. In Tunisia's case, knowing revolution through protestscapes steeped in intersecting synchronies and diachronies of revolt contributes to revising a quasi-Faustian bargain which credits some constestants of power (Bourguiba included) with "sublime struggle" (*al-jihad al-akbar*) and discredits others for standing in the tribunal of history as agents of disorder. From this perspective, writing Tunisia's revolution benefits histories, conversations, imaginaries, and struggles in the periphery and in precarity due to authoritarian domination. The significance of the book lies in catalyzing critical knowledge of political transformation by accounting for agentic, affective, and cognitive registers mobilized in favor of both revolution and the status quo.

Demonstrating and illustrating these claims has required interrogating the canon of "metropolitan revolution," identifying its silences as a departure point for "speaking back." This invigorating endeavor has also meant marshaling extensive evidence across disciplines, methods, and texts—in an attempt not just to dream, but also to *do* the epistemology of revolution otherwise. Questioning and revisiting the ghosts and myths of revolution, emblematized by the Bastille or Independence Hall, has proven an exhilarating research venture. We have also had to resist the temptation of romanticizing Tunisia's own storied revolution, confronting its contradictions and fragmentations entangled in the emancipatory verve of its peoplehood and rebirth. This we have attempted through an excavation of situated struggles within the locale of aesthetics and politics.

A brief note on translation and transliteration is in order. We have adopted a very simple transliteration schema following the Library of Congress system, except for words with commonly used Tunisian spelling. We use no diphthongs and minimalist diacritics. Our text features two types of apostrophe:

Al-Niha'i uses *the hamza:* ' ء whilst *'asabiyyah* uses the ع '. We have translated book titles in abbreviated form. Most newspaper article titles are in the bare transliterated form in consideration of a fast-mounting word count. In some instances (for instance, the conclusion), newspaper article titles also include a translation given their substance significance, temporally and textually. Unless otherwise specificied, all translations of both written and spoken texts are our own.

Researching and writing this book has been a delightfully challenging epistemological experience. We would like to thank a number of Tunisian academics for their abundant moral support: Rachida Tlili Sellouati, Raoudha Ben Othman, Chaker Houki, Moncef Khaddar, Noureddine Jebnoun, and Amor Boubakri. We are also grateful to Abdelhamid Ben Rabeh, Lotfi Zitoun, and Mohamed Larbi. This book would not have been possible without the generosity of our interlocutors—many of whom prefer not to be named—who shared their time and experiences with us. Thanks are also due to the Tunisian National Archives, the Zitouna University library and the archives of the General Union of Tunisian Workers (UGTT), for allowing us access to rich repositories of newspapers, magazines, and other publications. The Tamimi Foundation offers an extensive collection of references invaluable to the study of Tunisia's recent history. Our aspiration of centering the local and the indigenous was further facilitated by the always well-informed, helpful, and patient proprietors and staff of Librairie Al-Kitab, a beautiful and peaceful intellectual oasis amidst the hubbub of Habib Bourguiba Avenue. We extend to them endless gratitude for recommending and finding dozens of books over the last few years. Thanks also to Librairie Bouslama, near Bab Bhar, and the Ibn Manzur bookshop in Gafsa, a great source for works on Tunisia's South. Outside Tunisia, we would like to express appreciation to our colleagues at the SHAPEDEM-EU Project, in particular Andrea Gawrich, Elena Korosteleva, Michelle Pace, and Daniela Huber. Their palpable excitement about this book nudged us along as we scrambled to revise its many chapters. We would also like to recognize Lucia Sorbera, chair of the University of Sydney's Department of Arabic Languages and Cultures, where Larbi Sadiki has been an Honorary Associate, as well as John Keane at the University's Department of Politics. We take this opportunity to thank Mansour Nasasra of the University of Exeter and BGU Beersheba, in addition to Muntasir Alhamad, Haitham Sarhan, and Ali Alshawi at Qatar University, for their encouragement and friendship. Thanks to Abdallah Saeed and Vedi Hadiz at the University of Melbourne, David Lee at the University of New South Wales, George Lawson at the ANU, and Beverley Milton-Edwards at Queen's University Belfast, for their warm collegiality. Andrea Khalil of CUNY (also editor of *The Journal of North African* Studies) has been an incredibly supportive colleague. From Japan, Keiko Sakai and Kiichi Fujiwara at Chiba University, and Erina Iwasaki at Sophia University have kept our spirit of intellectual adventure going. Thanks are due to Tarik M. Yousef and the Middle East Council on Global Affairs for their support through a Senior Fellowship. Mohammed Kirat at the American University in the Emirates has been an excellent friend and colleague. At Oxford University, Laurence Whitehead of Nuffield College and Louise Fawcett of St. Catherine's College have long been generous with their interest and encouragement. Thanks is due to Jason Prevost for supporting our work on protest over the past few years. At Oxford University Press, we would like to thank Dominic Byatt for enthusiastically engaging new ideas, for shepherding this entire project, and for his enormous patience. Vicki Sunter has been a wonderful production editor, and Karthiga Ramu ably guided us through edits and proofreading. We are grateful to anonymous reviewers who provided invaluable feedback which we sought to incorporate at the various stages of drafting and revising. Two-year old Tayeb Sadiki has been our constant companion throughout the enjoyable labor of writing this book. All shortcomings and mistakes are, of course, our own.

List of Abbreviations

AFTURD	Tunisian Women's Association for Research and Development
ATFD	Tunisian Association of Democratic Women
BOP	Public Order Brigade
CPG	Gafsa Phosphate and Chemical Company
CPR	Congress for the Republic Party
CPS	Personal Status Code
CREDIF	Center for Research, Studies, Documentation and Information on Women
GEAST	Working Group for Socialist Studies and Work
LTDH	Tunisian League of Human Rights
MTI	Islamic Tendency Movement
PDP	Progressive Democratic Party
POCT	Tunisian Communist Workers' Party
RCD	Democratic Constitutional Rally: Ben Ali's party
UGET	General Tunisian Students' Union
UGTE	General Tunisian Union of Students
UNFT	National Union of Tunisian Women
UGTT	Tunisian General Labor Union
UTICA	Tunisian Union of Industry, Commerce, and Artisans
WATAD	Democratic Patriots' Unified Party (Arabic acronym for *Al-Wataniyyun Al-Dimuqratiyyun*)

1
Trace of a Revolution

Tunisia's "Missing People" in Time and Space

Al-Jallaz cemetery[1] *adorns a hilltop overlooking the capital Tunis. For centuries, Tunisians had buried their loved ones according to Muslim rites, in un-demarcated plots passed down along generations. When news spread of plans to formally register the cemetery under ownership of the Tunis municipality in fall 1911, residents were "astonished." How could a city own the communal Muslim property of Al-Jallaz? Who had authorized the pilfering of age-old property belonging to locals? Rights, identity, and dignity were at stake. Colonial menace threatened proud tradition and sacred ownership. Affect of anger and anxiety drove the agency to demonstrate in protest against the policy. Here "the winds of revolution blew" through the city. Tunisians plastered stone walls with written announcements. To protect their property rights, to offset their "religious sentiment that had been deeply" hurt, they would protest. As throngs congregated at the cemetery gates, Tunis's mayor (Shaykh Al-Madinah) retracted his plan. The French colons had already grasped the threat posed by the masses' critical consciousness of refusal. The cognition of a people struggling to become scared them. They blocked access to the cemetery. Undeterred, the crowds demanded entry. Police called in the army. Altercations erupted, and Tunisians pelted stones at French soldiers, some of whom fired their weapons. Casualties began to fall and blood trickled through the streets. The killing of a 12 year-old boy, Rabeh ben Amor Deglah, by a stealthy Italian sniper shooting from the rooftops was another provocation. The crowds' agency, affect and cognition mingled together. Cold-blooded murder was a dangerous escalation they would not accept. The cemetery forgotten, an all-out battle broke out between the Tunisians and Italians. The Battle of Jallaz was neither the first nor the last flare-up of anti-colonial popular resistance. Tunisians were socially acting and en-acting their peoplehood-in-becoming.*

---

[1] This account draws on reporting by Ali Bach Hamba (1876–1918) (in El-Douggui 1999, 193–195). Of Ottoman origin, the *Sadiqiyyah* (Sadiki College) and French-educated journalist, attorney, and Tunisian nationalist politician who headed the Young Tunisians founded the newspaper *Le Tunisien*, until he was exiled by the French to Istanbul, his property later confiscated (see El-Douggui 1999, 233–235). The quotation marks indicate excerpts from Hamba's original article published two days after the events.

2 Trace of a Revolution: Tunisia's "Missing People" in Time and Space

Introduction

Tunisia's politics is steeped in a history of protest and revolution. One thread that connects its antiquity and modernity is an imaginary of rebellion that makes and remakes polity, dynasty, republic, identity, city, and people in pre- and post-colony, a morality of protest. It is as if society and intellect welcome revolt, rather than shun it. Revolt and resistance make frequent appearances in the historiography and civilization ('umran) of Ibn Khaldun, Tunisia's best-known thinker. This book seeks to distill the specificities of Tunisia's long revolutionary élan, favoring the longue durée, from the 1860s to the present. Such an élan yields an insight, still calling for scholarly attention, which combines synchrony and diachrony in the writing of Tunisia's revolution. Inquiry into revolution is far from being an intelligible field. The genealogies of this body of knowledge are varied and rich. Mapping out the field, this book investigates Tunisia's 2011 revolution. It deliberately sidesteps plotlines tracing Tunisia as a regional "anomaly" (Masri 2017) or "exception" (e.g. Othman 2018).[2] The book finds both correspondence and divergence between different stories of protest and revolution, across boundaries of time and space. It critically integrates and engages with the concepts and theories traceable to the knowledge corpus, attending to this conversation of words and worlds of revolution. In so doing, it partly interprets practical, cognitive, normative, and discursive comparability and incomparability, against the backdrop of Tunisian protest happenings since 1864. Thus, the book brings to the fore the utility and limitations of studying revolutions with lineages that appear to be culturally, contextually, and politically incompatible or incommensurable.

This chapter introduces the book's main aims and arguments. First, Tunisia's revolution must be studied over the longue durée. Through various "protestscapes," it brings to life socio-political activism, within a framework of dynamic reciprocity of time (synchrony) and space (diachrony). Second, the agentic, affective, and cognitive dimensions of peoplehood unravel through protest. Third, peoplehood and revolution co-construct one another in a "twin ferment." Further setting the stage for the book, the chapter critically engages the corpus of Western revolutionary theory. We call this canon the "metropolitan revolution," highlighting its contributions and shortcomings when applied to the postcolonial Arab setting. Next, the chapter positions the book's investigation as an interdisciplinary endeavor and a postcolonial corrective to reigning "epistemic injustice" in research on Arab revolution. The chapter maps out the book's ontological moorings, explaining its interpretivist epistemology and methodology. Finally, it closes with an overview of the book's chapters.

Protest, Revolution, and Peoplehood

The book re-narrates Tunisia's postcolonial politics through the prism of historical key protests. Beginning with the "crucible" of Tunisian constitutionalism (1861)

[2] For a different view, see Filiu (2011).

and anti-monarchical revolt (Ali Ben Ghedhahem, 1864–5), it offers "frames" to re-conceptualize the dynamics of change and the key shifts they engendered in relations between rulers and ruled. It untangles encounters between bottom-up activism/movement (*hirak*) and revolution (*thawrah*). Such historicization delves into an interpretation of "history from below" (Thompson 1963) with respect to Tunisia's revolution. It is not just the Bourguibas and Ben Alis who are consequential in the country's politics and history. Contrary to the Orientalist reigning wisdom of passive citizens, the analysis posits protest as contests of power and civic engagement at the center of a chief argument: the postcolonial state has atrophied in Tunisia, but society has not, as has been in evidence since the 1960s. We argue that modern-day Tunisia's revolution and politics are marked by "cyclical" struggles. Over the decades, an explicitly counter-revolutionary statecraft of a "one-dimensional" (linear, singular, and antithetical to change, à la Marcuse) brand of citizenship tussled with a recalcitrant society. We re-present Tunisia as a "paradoxical" polity, in which postcolonial values and ideals of "constitutionalism," "freedom," "order," and "justice" seem to have come up against the hard realities of "two-dimensionality" (values vs. their implementation). The antinomies and contradictions of acquiescence and resistance, quietism and struggle, state and society, *beldi-afaqi* (coastal–interior), north–south, and colonialism and anti-colonialism bespeak the official transcript of a fixed Tunisian nationalist kernel. The book catalogues the onset of protests in the 1960s with the rejection of cooperatives, through the 2011 "Arab Spring" revolution, and since. The Tunisia we depict here is one not devoid of an active citizenry; their collective memories and imaginaries are stamped by trials of anti-colonial and anti-dictatorial rebellion.

This book aims to serve as a "corrective" of sorts—to limited, fractional examinations of Tunisian politics. Beyond a deconstruction of Eurocentric perspectives and blind spots, it is an attempt to "reconstruct" Tunisian protest, revolt, and peoplehood. We aim for a "restitution," via protestscapes, of evolving *demoi*, determining their self-presence, across time and space. We delve into revolution both as an assemblage of power and as a historical depository inscribing a partial *demos* into peoplehood. Here we invoke the Derridean absence–presence duality of language, in a search for the "missing people" across Tunisia's modern history. Traces of the "missing" will lead us to the assertion of presence as peoplehood, unambiguous in the 2011 revolution, as we set out to show. Tunisia's revolution did not begin in 2010; nor did its rebellious peoplehood. Both, we argue, have been over a century and a half in the making. This book offers a novel, holistic exploration of revolution as "situated protest" in the country. It posits a "double articulation" of revolution and peoplehood that feed into each other in a twin ferment. Put another way, protest makes peoplehood, and peoplehood makes protest. To this end, we ask: How does peoplehood relate to bottom-up struggles against domination and authoritarianism? How can we conceptualize the linkages and "threads" between contemporary spurts of popular contention and those that pre-date the postcolonial Tunisian state? In so doing, the book interweaves the acts and enactments of rebellion into agency, affect, and cognition determining peoplehood.

Angles and Approaches

Protest is an inherently interconnected social activity. It speaks to concerns of the human condition through text in context, in word and world, in thought and practice, and across fixed and evolving histories. The interconnectedness of the inquiry into protest highlights how it shapes forms of identity and *demos* within specific protestscapes and how these, in turn, inform struggle and protest.

Four inter-related lines of inquiry frame the book. *First*, it places the "politics of the people" front and center. Turning the analytical lens downward, it prioritizes the experiences and perspectives of "the people" twice marginalized: by *colons* and dictators, and by social scientists writing about Tunisian postcolonial political development, Bourguibist nation-building, or Ben Ali's façade liberalization. Through disaggregation and contextualization, we attempt to illustrate that bottom-up forces are neither incidental nor coincidental, but that they are central and habitual, involving actors who precipitate processes of political change. Empirically, we show how forms of partial *demos* come into being. Collectivities such as the General Union of Tunisian Workers (UGTT) and the student movement, Gafsa miners and Sidi Bouzid's indignants, ultras and *Tansiqiyyat al-Kamour*, are drivers of change from below. This makes them accessible to "measurement" and interdisciplinary analysis. Normatively, a critical theory (Frankfurt school, postcolonial, feminist) focussed on "the people" resonates with emancipatory claims from the protestors and rebels. A common moral flame evokes signs of unruly objections to harsh taxation or oppressive hikes in the price of bread, and demands the "employment, freedom, and national dignity" mantras of 2010–2011. This approach contributes to the conceptual and theoretical development of notions of peoplehood, leaning to the agentic without neglecting the structural, elitist, or statist.

Second, we argue that protest and revolution erupt and re-erupt against the backdrop of counterrevolution in Tunisia. Reversing the revolution–counterrevolution dialectic, we suggest that postcolonial nationalism since formal independence from the French in 1956, under the auspices of Bourguibism, essentially sought to rein in "the people." That is, in the immediate aftermath of the revolution against the French, the postcolonial Tunisian state's self-conscious regimen of progressive modernization and development in effect sought to demobilize society and shrink those spaces where autonomous forces or ideologies that could nurture rival power centers might thrive. The book re-reads the postcolonial nationalist epoch as one seeking to abort the same revolutionary impetus that had fought the French for freedom and self-determination. Yet this "counterrevolution" (adapted from Marcuse 1972) was never total. Various rebellious sectors of society—demoi in various protestscapes—consistently disrupted (1960s … 1978, 1984, 2008) any "counter-revolution" through protest. They sought to carve out a margin of self-expression, social justice, and the latitude to fall out of line with The Leader's (*al-za'im's*) leanings. Counterrevolution was thus interspersed by outbursts of bottom-up resistance, by student movements, labor unions, football fans, phosphate miners, and more, cresting in the revolution of 2011.

Third, we demonstrate that Tunisia boasts over 150 years of a revolutionary élan (*madd thawri*), characterized by ongoing "chains" of protests, from Ben Ghedhahem (1864) to the Jallaz uprising (1911) to the postcolonial protest activity mentioned above. To unpack this élan, we take an approach that is simultaneously synchronic and diachronic, exploring situated protest happenings *within* the longue durée—a panoramic portrait of protest. We seek to uncover "traces" of morally-imbued agentic, affective, and cognitive practices and imaginaries etched into constitutions and re-constitutions of peoplehood in postcolonial Tunisia.

Fourth, we bring the debate on revolution back to the perennial question of democracy and democratization. We suggest that in the years since 2011, a "taming" of the revolution surfaces through institution-building and implementation of democratization. It is as though the ballot box encapsulates attempts (2011, 2014, 2018, 2019, 2022–3) to dampen bottom-up revolutionary vigor. Whether the paraphernalia of procedural democracy placates Tunisia's disaffected, has been a pressing question. Through protest and riot, the country's subalterns, hailing from the under-developed *afaqi* hinterland, the "misery belts" of its major cities, and its ranks of unemployed university graduates, push back against the new post-2011 political establishment. We caution against an analytical "double teleology" of democratization-consolidation twinned with revolution-democratization. Kais Saied's 2021 power grab seems to confirm this hunch.

Conversations with "Metropolitan Revolution"

This section critically reviews the corpus of revolutionary theory. Developed in mostly Western economic (capitalist, industrializing) and political (democratizing) contexts, a reconsideration of "metropolitan revolution" can clear the way for a deep and thoughtful examination of the Tunisian revolution. When it comes to the Arab Middle East, scholars interrogating the how, why, and direction of socio-political change—the stuff of revolution—confront manifold analytical challenges. Immersion in knowledge built on Western experiences rendered "universal," is no simple undertaking. For the critical and reflexive researcher, it implies redoubled attention in knowledge-practice to the lived experiences, immaterial and material, of postcolonials in Tunisia and elsewhere. Intersecting layers of political imaginaries, aspirations, frustrations, outlooks, repression, and deprivation, structural and otherwise, all beckon. Tunisians engage the self and other at multiple levels within and without state and society. We do not purport to offer here a comprehensive survey of revolution research, ably rehearsed elsewhere (Goldstone 2001; Lawson 2016). Instead, through a critical lens, we seek to identify the relevance and/or suitability to Arab states and societies. Our engagement with "metropolitan revolution" thus attends to vestiges of Orientalism and more importantly, exclusions and silences pertaining to the Arab region.

"Great" Western Blind Spots

Western social science on revolution is not devoid of generalizations and assertions with an Orientalist hue. De Tocqueville's (1856, 27), disparaging remarks on "Islamism" (presumably referring to Islam) and Brinton's (1938, 249) comments on the formidability of "the prodding god ... Allah" even in comparison to Marx are examples. Even Eric Hobsbawm (1962, 144–145) invokes old Orientalist tropes, commenting on "oriental despot" Mohamed Ali of Egypt. More substantively, Huntington (1968) typologizes revolutions in culturalist terms. Eastern revolutions are anti-colonial and violent; they are rural and tend to precede state collapse (Huntington 1968, ch. 5). Even more explicitly, Eisenstadt (1978) attempts to explain "civilizational" differences in revolutionary propensities and processes. For him a seemingly timeless "Islamic" civilization is not predisposed to revolution. The civilizational barometer renders Western Europeans more amenable to modernization via revolution than "Islamic" peoples (Eisenstadt 1978, 134–151). Even revisionists accounts of revolution by feminists do not entirely fend off the lures of neo-Orientalism. Sheila Rowbotham(1974, 244–245) attends to "masculine bias," frankly admitting that Western bias may linger. Assertions of religious-based "subordination" and insufficient "enlightenmen[t]" by the Prophet Mohamed as to the status of women (1974, 241) without much evidence from local sources, feature in her discussion of Algeria. Writing of women revolutionaries in Yemen, Molyneux and co-authors (1979) caution against a Western yardstick. Nonetheless, their analysis does not seem to challenge the view of Islamic tradition as oppressive (1979, 7).

More glaring in "metropolitan revolution" is a relative negligence of non-Western and specifically Arab experiences. Modern social science scholarship on the topic is built on the analysis of "great revolutions" (e.g. Brinton 1938), the launching pad for subsequent "generations" of revolutionary theory (Goldstone 2001). Despite a nuanced recognition of the dangers of generalization across geo-cultural contexts, Moore (1966, 160–161, xiii), too, focuses on large countries with greater agency. Skocpol (1979, 3–5) self-consciously limits her cases to the "rare" cases of social revolutions in France, Russia, and China. These are swift and dramatic transformations that upturn and overhaul not only the distribution of political power, but also class, economic relations, and political ideologies. She does note, however, that anticolonial variants as in Mexico or Vietnam require further study (Skocpol 1979, 287–293). Similarly, Tilly does not deny his exclusive examination of Western cases shaped by particular socio-economic and political factors. His conclusions, he admits (1978, 10), may "apply only to the modern urban-industrial world."

Uncritical adoption of "metropolitan revolution" may thus circumscribe alternative (non-industrializing) routes to revolution. The Arab world appears beleaguered by a status on the periphery. Paradoxically, revolt and revolution arguably animate the imaginaries of Arab publics. Well-known to area specialists, Sherif Hussein's Revolt (1916–18), the Great Syrian Revolt (1925–27), and anti-colonial revolutions from Mashreq to Maghreb (1940s–1960s) shape the contours of the modern Middle East. Yet with the notable exception of Algeria,[3] Arab revolution seem to barely register on the radar of disciplinary social science. This pattern provokes us to question the generalizability or applicability of concepts and models from Moore to Tilly. In no way does it discount the wealth of empirical and analytical arguments revolutionary theories offer. Yet, we contend that metropolitan revolution cannot be convincingly transposed through additive considerations of non-Western cases. A careful, critical reading, summarized in Table 1.1, can help to identify transferability as well as limits for the understudied Arab region.

Industrialization and Modernization as Rupture?

In the Arab world, industrialization and the spread of capitalism were not the "big bang" precipitating various rebellions or revolution, as in Moore's (1966) and Hobsbawm's (1962) macro-historical accounts of great revolutions. Hobsbawm (1962), for instance, recounts the "dual revolution" in Europe from the late eighteenth century to the middle of the nineteenth century. England's Industrial Revolution and the French Revolution forever transformed the continent and the world. Marxian-inspired class conflict, between the landed aristocracy and peasantry, is Moore's causal story. Instead, colonialism and its traumas have been the major turning point of socio-political-economic and cultural change in a country like Tunisia. They comprise, we suggest, the earth-shattering "rupture" fomenting socio-economic and political change, including revolt "from below" at various junctures. This does not mean that capitalism does not play a role in the long-term and cumulative marginalization or sub-alternization of Tunisia's underclasses. Class dynamics are not feudal-turned-industrial, however. Tunisia as a "peripheral capitalist" economy features asymmetries entrenched in the global capitalist economy, one reason for perpetual under-development (Alavi 1982).[4] Colonialism deepened existing *beldi/afaqi* cleavages pandering to the interests of ruling elites. These cleavages did not abate with formal independence, but were neglected or exacerbated by the policies of postcolonial ruling elites from Bourguiba to Ben Ali. Thus, the existing divisions took new forms via peripheral development and crony capitalism (Amin 1997). Multinational corporations concentrated in Tunisia's coastal areas, for instance. Thus, intersecting interests between power-holders and national-international relations of productions persist, from pre- to post-colonial times. Here is a more complicated tangle of power and distributional dynamics than Moore's or Hobsbawm's rural or urban classes reeling from industrialization in France or England.

---

[3] Algeria's war for independence from France features in some comparative studies of "Third World" anti-colonial revolutions; see also Foran (2005, 91–104). The Palestinian *intifadah* also makes an appearance (Teitelbaum and Kostiner 1991; Robinson 1997).

[4] Combining peripheral dependency, culture, regime type, Foran argues "that the Third World needs its own theory" of (non)revolution (Foran 2005, 15).

Table 1.1 Metropolitan Revolution and the Arab World

Focus	Theorists/Scholars	Notion of "The People"	Critique/Limitations	Transferability to Tunis/AW?
Moral Impetus (Freedom/Emancipation)	De Tocqueville, Arendt, Bailyn	Drivers of change: ideas + practice	French ethnocentrism "men of letters": elitism	Protest and revolution as emancipatory practice: moral flame
Modernization-related structuralism: class conflict, states, international dynamics. Macro-historical	Moore, Skocpol	– People/class immutable – Agency to peasants (Moore and Skocpol) – Favors structure over agency (Skocpol)	– Purely class-based analysis does not carry into 21st century (Moore) – Downplaying popular agency (Skocpol)	– Arab structures differ from Western and/or modernizing models – Ongoing revolutions: too early for outcome-based analysis – Revolution as violence – International dimension: Arab dependency
Two-pronged revolution (industrialization/modernization and French constitutionalism) as historical rupture that spreads across Europe	Hobsbawm	"The people" excluded from early capitalist revolution: poor demand rights – "Bandits" as "prepolitical" groups with agency but limited political consciousness	Admittedly very specific to Western experience	– First "rupture" is colonialism, then 2011 – Different underlying economic and social structures: e.g. peripheral capitalism not industrial revolution
Relative deprivation: grievances	Gurr	Engine of rebellion and revolution. Psychological factors explain mobilization	Downplays other structural factors. Rigid behavioralism	Deprivation prevalent. Affect is one link between marginalization and protest

Theme	Author	Description	Context / Critique	Arab world relevance
Collective action: mobilization, organization, interests, and opportunity interact as groups compete	Tilly	Groups make claims and become power contenders who mobilize and compete with existing state power-holders	Western industrializing, state-centered context; Does control of resources, organization determine outcome? Loss/gain model may not adequately explain less organized protest, or immaterial "resources"	Conflict, possible violence between state/society; Collective action as continuum where greatest impact is revolution; Protest as part of "repertoire"; Historical experiences matter; State-building (later than West) and collective action/protest/revolution may *coincide* in Arab world; How well-defined are "groups" such as "the people," or their interests?
"Third World," often anti-colonial	Goodwin Goldstone	Active role for rural peasants; Violent uprisings (sometimes professionalized) against colonial power	Cold War + colonial context no longer apply; Arab states ignored except for Algeria, sometimes Palestine	- Historically: anti-colonial revolutions across Arab world in 1940s–1960s - 2011 wave against domestic authoritarianism, initially relatively peaceful
(Post)Communist: China and USRR: political and/or economic elite reforms lead to "societal revolutions" + state decay; Linkage to democratic transitions	Minxin Pei, Vaclav Havel	"Autonomous" and organized societal forces can capitalize most on elite-led openings; Level of development (literacy, urbanization, etc.) indicative of society's role: "social mobilization profile"	- Echoes teleological transitology/modernization theory (development and democracy) - State capacity + reform sequencing significant - Bipolar system no longer structures international hierarchy	- Communist factor and "dual reforms" not applicable to Arab world - Popular mobilization not precipitated by elite reforms in 2011 Arab uprisings that rebuffed the "modernization theory" narrative - Society's "rising up" has analog in Arab uprisings (not sectorial or merely class-based)
Contentious politics: "collective political struggles" from strikes to revolutions	McAdam, Tarrow, and Tilly	Popular mobilization vis-à-vis government; "Relational": links actors and structures, defying institutional/non-institutional boundaries	Broad approach that similarly analyzes a wide range of dissimilar kinds of socio-political change regardless of context; "Causal" explanations via mechanisms seem contingent on how episodes are delineated, compared	Attention to "contingency" and "context"; Fluid enough to account for structural, historical, cultural specificities of Arab world; Interest in bottom-up agency; "Political opportunity structures" may not help explain contention in Arab authoritarian regimes

Hence, Western modernization's template of standard political-economic elevation of groups to "people" with rising living standards and political rights plays out differently in *(post)colonial* settings such as Tunisia. The bottom-up wresting of power, resources, and substantive recognition entails forms of resistance to national *and* international structures of domination.

Statist, Structuralist Limitations

Thus, international structures matter for the modernization-related dimensions of revolution. In her massive and enduringly influential tome, Skocpol (1979) analyzes structures of the state and of the international system as they play out against changes in class structures. She very self-consciously favors structure over agency of the masses, refuting "voluntaristic" or "purposive" accounts (or shades thereof) of revolution, espoused by Gurr, Tilly, and others (Skocpol 1979, 15–18). Skocpol thus sees the state before "the people." Revolution from above does not always carry over so well in the (postcolonial) Arab region. Tellingly, Skocpol's (1979) statist paradigm that deliberately overlooked "the people" faced important challenges outside the West. The "surprise" of the Iranian revolution spurred Skocpol (1982) to revise her purely state/society structuralist explanations of revolutions. Ideational and religious/cultural factors (Shi'ism and bazarism) could help to account for a revolution that was "made" from below against the Shah (Skocpol 1982). Building off Skocpol, Goodwin's (2001) comparative examination of Third World revolutions in the twentieth century remains "state-centered," even as it examines "peripheral states" across Central America, East Asia, and Eastern Europe. (He mentions Algeria in passing.) Similarly, musing over the Third World revolutions proliferating in the twentieth century, Goodwin and Skocpol (1989) offer a structuralist explanation revolving around state, military, and relations with society and its classes. In fact, they note that Middle East states are "probably too powerful and ruthless to be toppled by armed struggle" (Goodwin and Skocpol 1989, 497). No wonder, then, that the 2011 Arab Spring was such a shock to Goodwin (2011) and others!

A major limitation of statist metropolitan revolution, then, is its relative dismissal of "the people" as drivers of change. This book takes a different approach, centralizing "people" and peoplehood in Tunisian protest and revolution. Our analysis, further, is not *only* historical. Tunisia's is a revolution still in the making. Nevertheless, the historical-comparative approach of Moore, Hobsbawm, and Skocpol does offer some nuggets of analytical transferability to Tunisia. The longue durée is necessary. Also, despite Hermassi's (1976, 212) complaints of over-emphasis, violence seems to closely accompany revolution across time and space. Counter-revolution, whether by a class (Moore), monarchs (Hobsbawm), or the "state" (Skocpol) is also a persistent feature of revolutions. The historical trajectory of decolonization, as we will later argue, feeds into both revolutionary and counterrevolutionary dynamics in Tunisia. Moreover, structural arrangements (and shifts) inform the people's agency, as befits our focus.

Mobilization and Contention

Theories of collective violence, collective action, and contentious politics challenge structuralist and statist frameworks. Gurr, Tilly, and others hold violence to be salient to revolution and other forms and modes of political action. This group of scholars emphasizes popular grievances (relative deprivation theory) or political processes (Tilly and Tarrow) over more or less deterministic structure. Ted Gurr's psychological-cognitive account proposes that "the greater the intensity of deprivation, the greater the magnitude of violence" (1971, 9). Thus, "political violence" (or its *threat*) against the state, ranges from "turmoil," "conspiracy," and "internal war": civil war and revolution fall into the last category (1971, 11). The notion of deprivation, *hirman* in its Arabic rendition, is doubtless significant for the story of Arab and Tunisian revolt and peoplehood.[5] So are the emotional/affective and solidarity dimensions of Gurr's framework. However, Gurr's (2016, 157–158) considerations of varying propensities toward violence in cultural terms (Black vs. White Americans, Southern Europeans vs. Scandinavians, etc.) raise questions of culturalist bias. His somewhat politicized framing of the inquiry is couched in a Cold War or War on Terror view to scoping out potential "political violence," as if to "tame" unruly Third World publics (e.g. Gurr 2016, vii–xi).

For Tilly (1978, 177–188), violent and nonviolent collective action intersect, even when the violence is usually wrought by the state. Tilly's (1978) concept of "collective action" thus allows us to consider a spectrum of (Western) contentious politics from demonstrations and strikes, all the way to revolutions. These all contest power under the auspices of the modern state. They comprise culturally-learned "contentious repertoires" (Tilly 1993). Further, Tilly's (1978, 228) appreciation for context including historical experiences and trajectories is resonant even outside his Western scope. Unlike the structuralists and like Gurr, he allots people extensive agency. However, for Tilly (1978, 9), "the people" are mostly concretely defined (not new) groups. His initially rationalist model of interests, mobilization, power, and opportunity/threat, varying based on structural changes such as industrialization and state-building, seems too neat to account for bottom-up unruliness and peoplehood. Tilly does not seem initially interested in immaterial resources and interests that may be important drivers of politics "from below," particularly in postcolonial settings. Are revolutions that constitute and are constituted by "peoplehood" merely a struggle over power and resources vis-à-vis the state? We will argue: no. Tilly adds a category to Moore's and Skocpol's "political outcomes." He avoids an all-or-nothing approach. "Revolutionary situations" are characterized by competing claims on the state ("multiple sovereignty"), while "revolutionary outcomes" are where power-holders are unseated and replaced (Tilly 1978, 189–194). Such tidy categories, however, may belie the complexities and messiness of revolutions-in-the-making. (Does Tunisia's "revolutionary outcome" with the departure of Ben Ali still stand after Kais Saied's 2021 power grab?)

---

[5] He considers his approach vindicated by the Arab Spring (Gurr 2016 [1971], xiii–xvi).

The "contentious politics" school, with its origins in investigations of Western protest movements in the 1960s and 1970s—but "aim[ing] to go beyond" those historical-cultural contexts (McAdam, Tarrow, and Tilly 2001, 14)—takes this propensity further. It examines the blurring of "institutionalized and non-institutionalized politics" in a "relational approach" that diverts from the age-old structure–agency dichotomy (McAdam et al. 2001, xvii–7). Scholars of contentious politics thus keep an eye on how people organize, and the "mechanisms" through which they make claims on government to realize interests. This "process approach" casts itself as more fluid and flexible, taking into account identities and "framing" dynamics than in the earlier "resource mobilization" school in social movement theory (McAdam et al. 2001, 15–16). For McAdam and colleagues, "revolution," then, is a "macro-process" comprised of sequentially specific mechanisms amenable to comparison (McAdam et al. 2001, 196–198). This approach is geared toward causal explanations, shot through with "contingency and context" (McAdam et al. 2001, 223–225). The authors are correct to argue "revolutions are not A Single Thing" (McAdam et al. 2001, 226). However, "contentious politics" may limit scholars interested in the longer-term dynamics of socio-political change. Different kinds of questions relate to the longue durée of revolution and making of peoplehood in Tunisia. Pre- and post-colonial politico-economic structures, power asymmetries, popular consciousness, and resistance against domination, are difficult to bracket into the "episodes" of the contentious politics. "Contentious politics" does not do justice to the breadth and depth of Tunisian political change.

Even with a more comparative outlook, gaps arise in contentious politics empirics and analysis when considering the Arab world. Classic cases (McAdam et al. 2001) include: India, Italy, Kenya, China, Philippines, Nicaragua, South Africa, the Soviet Union, Spain, Sweden, Mexico, the US, and France. In a later edition, Tilly and Tarrow (2006) still seem to downplay the Arab region. Expanding the range of cases, they include "composite" Israel-Palestine (a case of "civil war") to investigate the contentious politics of Israeli settlers (Tilly and Tarrow 2006, 165), and the "lethal conflict" in Sudan (Tilly and Tarrow 2006, 135–136, 141–143). As Tilly notes, "social movements" (the precursor to "contentious politics") formed in specifically Western democratizing settings. They "parallel and feed on electoral politics," a mode of voter "pressure" on elected officials and parties (Tilly 1993, 275). It is appropriate to note differences in political organizations and power distribution between colonial and postcolonial Arab states and their Western counterparts (*colons*, in fact!). Commenting on an expanding comparative stockpile of contentious politics studies, McAdam, Tarrow, and Tilly (2009) confirm that democratization conditions it in important ways. "Political opportunity structures" facilitate the development of social movements (McAdam et al. 2009, 279). What of mobilizing and organizing within dictatorial regimes, without the benefit of the said structures—as in the 2008 Gafsa phosphate uprising in Tunisia? Originating in the Western "collective action" school, contentious politics theorizing seems ill-equipped to account for bottom-up mobilization that does not simply look to the state for cues as to opportunities. It does not extend easily to less organized groundswells of activism and mobilization.

In their critique of political process theory, Goodwin and Jasper (2004, 27) caution against universalizing models of social movement processes. Some movements are not necessarily making claims on the state but on wider social norms or understandings, mandating attention to identitarian and emotional factors (Goodwin and Jasper 2004, 9–11). Such analytical complications are welcome. Yet, Arab cases seldom seem to feature in studies of social movements (Jenkins and Klandermans 1995) or contentious politics before 2011.[6]

The concept "contentious politics" may allow us the analytical range required to span histories and modes of politics from below, to protest and revolution and back. It potentially frees us from the obligation of precisely pinpointing the beginning and ends of "revolution" and its political outcomes. Yet even if "contentious politics" or Gurr-type "mobilization" subsumes revolution, we prefer to retain the latter term. Revolution, we will argue, spills into peoplehood. This label is laden with political and normative implications that resonate in scholarly, political, and popular discourse. "Revolution" implies specific types of claims and change related to social justice and dignity. More importantly, in this book we are not searching for generalizable logics and workings of particular mechanisms and their causal sequencing. Instead, we glean Tunisia's political history and present for recurring bouts of bottom-up calls for political change, harbingers of democratization (Sadiki 2000), eventually culminating in revolution and peoplehood.

Nonviolence and Bottom-Up Protest

"Metropolitan revolution" took a new turn after the watershed political changes of 1989 and in context-bound investigations. Cold War bipolarity and ideology, in addition to Eastern and Central European geography, do not extend to the Arab world. However, the 1989 post-communist revolutions or "refolutions" (Ash 1990; Goodwin 2001), partly "from below," introduced the empirical and analytical element of (relatively) peaceful organizing in the "Second World" (Goodwin 1994, 591). Pei's focus on 'societal revolutions' in tandem with elite reforms in the USSR and China bears echoes of modernization theory" (1994, 44–45). Certain groups of people (the educated and urbanized), who have the "social mobilization profile," collectively move to demand change and political power (Pei 1994, 52–58). The Arab Spring profile, however, defies this expectation. Tunisia's own revolution was ignited in Sidi Bouzid, by impoverished, marginalized populations—*later* joined by middle-class urban dwellers.

More philosophical interventions on the post-1989 events express strongly normative outlooks that resonate with the 2011 "Arab Spring" revolutions. Czechoslovakia's Vaclav Havel (1985), for instance, summoned an "existential revolution" springing from society itself, electrified by the "power of the powerless" people seeking

---

[6] Exceptions include some interest in Islamists (Wickham 2002) and political opposition movements (Albrecht 2010).

freedom. Havel narrates the advent of people power as above all a moral, nonviolent struggle (Havel et al. 1985, 23–96). In Poland, Adam Michnik (1985) similarly wrote of a "strategy for social resistance" through an "organized society," exemplified by coalitional formations such as Solidarity. Like the American (Arendt 1990) and French (de Tocqueville 1856) revolutions, popular movements resisting communist rule invoke emancipatory claims and (more explicitly) democratic dreams. Explorations of nonviolence highlight the morality and effectiveness of nonviolence by withdrawing obedience to rulers (e.g. Gene Sharp 1973). The "pragmatic choice" of nonviolence thus bolsters civil society and can facilitate democratization; violence is ill-advised (Ackerman and Duvall 2000, 3–7). Gee (2011), who catches the Egyptian revolution just in time, explains that nonviolent "counterpower" in its ideational, economic, and physical forms, bespeaks untold potential. Proponents of "civil resistance" Chenoweth and Stephan (2012) deploy quantitative, large-n analysis to conclude that nonviolent action is more "legitimate" and thus "successful" than violent collective action in removing dictators and facilitating democratic transitions. Scholarship on nonviolent or civil resistance thus rubs elbows with "metropolitan revolution." Inaugurated before the 2011 revolutions, its emphases on people power (Carter 2013), nonviolent protest, and democratization are salient to the ironically overlooked Arab setting.

Over the past decade or so, research attending to the 2011 revolutions has yet to fill gaps skipped over by metropolitan revolution. It is easy to observe a lack of attention to indigenous scholarship and a dearth of Arabic sources. Some scholars delve into Western revolutionary theory, emphasizing larger global analytical frames such as historical sociology (Lawson 2019, 226–259). Investigating Egypt, Mona El-Ghobashy (2021) digs into familiar "metropolitan revolution" territory in her *Bread and Freedom*. She opts for Tilly's concept of "revolutionary situation" falling short of a "revolutionary outcome" or lasting democratic transition. Moreover, few works have dealt exclusively or in-depth with Tunisia's revolution that launched regional revolt. Comparative volumes (e.g. Kienle and Sika 2015) take up traditional themes from the military to authoritarian resilience to political transition, with little context-sensitive theorizing about the revolutions (e.g. Lynch 2014). Theories of revolution are given short shrift in scholarship on Tunisia. For instance, Azmi Bishara's (2012) book, unlike Hermassi's (2023, 7–22) attempt at a "balanced" narrative, is a misreading that romanticizes "the glorious revolution" (*al-thawrah al-majidah*). Explanations of the Arab Spring revolutions more generally, while representing fine attempts, are also wanting. For example, it is not clear how the "nonmovements" inherent in "street politics" of urban populations heaving under neoliberalism transformed into revolt by 2011, albeit without ideological muster (Bayat 2017). New scholarship must challenge metropolitan revolution's silences. This is not to detract from the eminent "repertoires of revolution" depicted from Moore to Tarrow. Revolutions are not only *made* (by people), but *written* in narratives colored by context, tinted with the situated-ness of knowledge and knowledge-maker. The research scene is ripe for theoretical innovation paired with meticulous, indigenously-rooted empirical investigations. The time has come, we contend, for writing Tunisia's revolution *from below*.

"Protestscapes": Frames of Rebellious Flows and "Free Play" of the Un-free

If Tunisians never rebelled and never dissented about the values of being and conditions of rule, revolutio-scapes, resistance-scapes, rebel-scapes and dissent-scapes could never have been constructed across time and space. These revolutioscapes, rebelscapes, dissentscapes (*thawrah*-scapes, so to speak), flow from century-old argumentative, disputative, discursive, insurrectionary and demotic competencies and struggles. We use them here interchangeably with the term "protestscapes". These, resistancescapes facilitate understanding of situated protest, as in synchronic protest (at a specific point of time) and diachronic protest (through history). Thus, rebelscapes capture how resistance-specific social doing has implications for revolution qua world-transforming emancipatory movements of de-territorialization and re-territorialization. They probe the clamor of peoplehood and rebirth under colonial and postcolonial domination.

Offering a rejoinder to "metropolitan revolution," we examine six protestscapes[7] across Tunisia's modern history. As we elaborate in Chapter 2, protestscapes arise from three forms of activity at the core of revolutionary continuity. Affect, agency, and cognition dynamically interact as indignants socially act and en-act continuous protest, reconstructing new ideas about self-group identity, also re-thinking and re-discovering norms, morals, practices and imaginaries. Thus, new constructs blend with the old. Protests were socialized and routinized, from nationalist myths to socio-political status, to re-adapt or subvert pre-constructed notions and imaginings of self-group, rights, obligations, and entitlements, to support the reconstruction of affect, experiences, practices, and knowledge of life-worlds. This is integral to cumulative processes of de-territorialization and re-territorialization, the dislodging and transplanting of discourses and practices, defining revolutionary moments. Partial and situated (Haraway 1988), protestcapes re-appropriate the "inherited" repository of self and group knowing, recasting it in a momentum of resistance and a spiral of collective revolutionary engagement. This brand of plural and relational engagement transforms the revolutionary experience and the social learning that comes with it. Protestors' flows of social doing, affect, and free play of imaginaries and perspectives melt into the crucible of *hirak*. They allow for a build-up of know-how and assimilation of the craft, maybe even the art, of protest. The iterative social acting and en-acting of revolution is critical in order to sustain struggles and the operation of protestscape emotions, experience, and imagination. What distinguishes protestscapes is not only the question of "what is" (*al-wadʿ al-qaʾim*), but

---

[7] For different usage, see Eagelton (2022, 334–336) and Sorg (2019, 4)

also "what should be" and "what could be." These are the core of the imagination of hope and becoming that drive revolutionary commitment.

Interdisciplinary Revolution

Interdisciplinarity is one crucial point of departure for exploring protestscapes. Scholars who once so possessively divided the world into neat compartments are today refashioning knowledge production, by re-assembling the disciplinary pieces of the jigsaw puzzle of scholarly investigation across the social sciences and humanities (Weingart 2000, 25–42). Revolution is itself interdisciplinary, involving diverse disciplines and histories. Revolution is plural, another claim advanced here. This is due to the wide variety of theories and experiences, spanning diverse temporal and spatial contexts. Hence, the use of interdisciplinarity is warranted in our book's examination of revolution in the Tunisian context. The analysis attempts to mediate the "journey" of concepts and theories in a way that allows us to parse the problematic under investigation. This "conversational," "dialogic," or "integrative" approach is intended to maximize intertextuality/intersubjectivity. In theoretical terms, we conceive of revolution here as indeterminate, plural, transcultural, trans-historical, and socially and intellectually relational. Moreover, we concretize its study by embedding it in Tunisian historicity. From this standpoint, as a problematic it warrants study using multiple "interactions" (Maasen 2000), between and within political science, history, linguistics, and sociology. Drawing on these disciplines, we piece together conceptual and theoretical capacities, permitting "intersections" of meanings and of analytical tools. This is intended to strengthen a firm grip on the competition over meaning and knowledge-making as well as over power resources or "capitals" (Bourdieu 1986), among forces and discourses locked in revolutionary settings of tension, pressures, or conflicting socio-political balances. The interrelatedness of meanings, in scholarly terms, and the interpenetration of situated revolutions, as social relations in terms of experience, call for conversations about concepts, epistemologies, and ontologies. Thus, the analysis does not only consider the (pre-2011) reticence for Arab revolution. It also seeks to locate subject and object, structure and agent, consensus and conflict over power, interest, meaning, value, norms, rights, and identity through disciplinary suffusion. The interdisciplinarity pursued here is designed to provide a rich interpretation of revolution in Tunisia. It also addresses epistemic silences—along the lines of what Fricker (2007) calls "epistemic injustice".

Revolution against Epistemic Injustice

Even if Fricker's construct seems reductionist (Maitra 2010, 195–211), by leaving out colonialism, its utility speaks to notions of interrogating marginalizing knowledge-making. In this vein, resistance to Euro-American renditions of revolution gestures towards tackling "epistemic injustice." In response to the prevalence of metropolitan revolution's findings drawn on Western and "great" trajectories, the present work examines a case study from the Arab setting. Epistemic injustice is a useful construct dealing with issues that cohere with reflections on knowledge–power dyads. The mutually constitutive nature of both knowledge and power, subject and object, in power relations involving knowing has been amply rehearsed (Foucault 1978).

By implicating the construct of epistemic injustice in the investigation, the aim is twofold: enacting indigenous knowledge practices by rediscovering the local corpus of knowledge; and disrupting existing knowledge-making derived from metropolitan revolution, and specific (Western) politics, including US monitoring of insurrectionary activities worldwide (Wolin 1973, 343–358). The scholarly disruption attempted here, while it borrows concepts and theories from the likes of Moore and Tilly, aims not to dismiss the Western corpus of knowledge on world revolutions, including American, French, Russian, and Chinese. Rather, it assumes a kind of decentering of knowledge practices, displacing Euro-centric narratives of history as the final arbiters of all things revolution. Therefore, the use of the concept of epistemic injustice is one way of ensuring scholarly "interactions" and "intersections," dialogically. Invoking epistemic injustice is also a way to horizontally plug into discussion of Arab revolution. We do so within what is an established field of study of revolution marred by Western ideological entanglements and biases (Wolin 1973, 343–345). This carries the potential to inhibit discursive formations grounding discussion of revolution in non-Western settings within neocolonial power structures, both ideational and material.

The significance of Fricker's (2007, 17–21) concept lies in the unequal power relationship, privileging a single center and source of knowledge. At its core lies the idea of demoting agency, that is, the "capacity" of an "other" (alterity in general, race, gender, class) as a "knower." Epistemic injustice is due to not sharing one's knowing, a disadvantage of consequence for inclusiveness, in social, political, economic, and ideational terms (Fricker 2007, 44–46). Where Fricker is potent is in the correlation between her "disadvantage condition" and epistemic absence, absence as a voice, as a mind, as a knower in relation to fellow citizens in a given society. Fricker's epistemic injustice thus translates into all types of inequity within society, including material inequity. Its vicious circle results in the reproduction of exclusion, and attendant disempowerment. Fricker's construct ties up smoothly with José Medina's (2013) concept of "epistemic justice." Epistemic justice is embedded within a theory that normatively grounds scholarship, in inclusive, rather than exclusive or exclusivist, knowledge-making, part and parcel of an "epistemology of resistance." What Medina seeks to normativize is an epistemic ethic of humility towards learning. This approach may allow the subalterns, the voiceless, or the powerless to learn and account for the oppressor's worldviews or knowing. Thus obtains the ethic of "metalucidity," that is, embracing "regulative principles of *epistemic friction*" (Medina 2013, 29), whereby opposition between conflicting imaginaries and standpoints mediates knowledge practices founded on intertextuality, intersection among approaches of knowledge production and subjectivities. Medina's variant adds a critical edge to Fricker's construct, toning down the excesses of self-image in any knowledge–power equation, such as those pitting the colonized against the colonizer. It is of use here as a critique against the impulses of disciplinary knowledge-making. It helps to pitch our argument in favor of interdisciplinarity, in which epistemic friction opens up cross-disciplinary pollination. Fricker's and Medina's concepts are viewed in this book as integral to the reconceptualization of authorial positionality/word in relation to power/world, given the interconnectedness in the chain of knowledge-production *qua* resistance.

Protest and Revolution: Postcolonial Readings

In addition to epistemic in/justice, postcolonialism rings salient to our investigation. Postcolonialism interrogates Western knowledge making and its constitutive canon (social sciences, art, literature, etc.) for the reproduction of power relations entrenched in the colonizer's superiority over the colonized. It frames one's critical standpoint vis-à-vis knowledge-making in the context of the colonizer—colonized opposition. What is at issue is more than the civility of the European and un-civility of the colonized other. Table 1.2 outlines a sample of major theorists, critiques, and literary voices of postcolonialism that are relevant to our inquiry. Dualistic representations are an entry point. Critique of the category "Orient" by Said (1978) and others illustrates a use of language that reproduces notions of Western cultures and peoples' superiority through East/West binaries. These binaries can also be racialized, as Black/White corresponds to colonized/colonizer with implications for psyches and selfhoods (Fanon 1952). Power–knowledge complicity is inescapable, a platform for European hegemony over the colonized (Viswanathan 1989). Tunisian postcolonial theorist Albert Memmi (2003 [1957], 96–99)suggests that, seeking "legitimacy" for his "usurpation," the colonizer highlights the "demerits" of the colonized while accentuating his own "eminent merits" such that the colonizer and colonized are ever "irretrievably in opposition". It is no surprise that the figure of the acquiescent Oriental, of placid publics that were "Orientalizable," colonizable—externally, by Europeans, then internally, by postcolonial leaders from Bourguiba to Nasser—looms large. It largely crowds out interest and attention to acts of resistance that we seek to re-insert into the social science of Tunisian (and Arab) peoplehood and revolution.

Orientalist discourse, of course, can be riddled with contradictions. On the one hand, Muslims and Arabs are stereotyped and generalized as passive (Said 1994, 108–109, 138, 311). Some Orientalists have posited that Arabs are incapable of imagining, let alone carrying out, revolution (Said 1978, 314). On the other hand, Orientalism features designations of Arabs as violent in language and practice (Said 1994, 287, 307). How can passive peoples and societies be violent? The discrepancy is puzzling. Muslim societies are wracked by "irrationality, violence, and injustice" inviting English imperialism and imposition of the rule of law, according to reams of British writings (Kerr 2008, 198–207). Some have tried to periodize these paradoxical representations, Quinn identifying passivity as a European construction of the Orient

Table 1.2 Postcolonialism and Post-Colonialism

	Author	Text	Designation
	Fanon, 1952	*Black Skin, White Masks*	Essentializing race in colonist knowledge/politics of identification and constructions (of blackness) founded on implacable binary of colonizer (zone of Being) and colonized (zone of non-Being)
	Edward Said, 1978, 1994	*Orientalism; Culture and Imperialism*	Orientalism as knowledge-practice creating East/West binaries that justify and legitimate colonialism; imperial domination was not without resistance
	Gauri Viswanathan, 1989	*Masks of Conquest: Literary Studies and British Rule in India*	Colonizer's strategies of power and knowledge mask hegemony over, exploit the colonized
	Salman Rushdie, 1999	*Imaginary Homelands*	Cultural dislocation and hybridity of exilic identity; past and nation of the colonized are ostensibly *imbricated* into the texture of the present and the colonizer's world and language
	Homi Bhabha, 1994	*The Location of Culture*	Potentiality for negotiating colonizer–colonized polarity and reconstituting new subjectivities in a liminal, "third" or "interstitial space"
THEORY	Stuart Hall and Paul du Gay, 1996	*Questions of Cultural Identity*	Fluid view of identities as sites and processes of "becoming" where subject meets discursive structures; identities are power-laced and constantly in flux within unbreakable referentiality between self/other
	Arjun Appadurai, 1996	*Modernity at Large: Cultural Dimensions of Globalization*	Imagining of postnational identity, subjectivity and locality embedded in politico-cultural and socio-economic globality
	Gayatri Spivak 1987; 1999	*In Other Worlds; A Critique of Postcolonial Reason*	Mutuality between "verbal" and "social texts" and counter-readings; global capitalism as a form of neocolonialism; insufficiency of a simple "reversal" of West/non-West binaries; "Third Worldism" can create new forms of material and immaterial domination and subalternity; yet, "native informant" role (e.g. "poorest *woman* of the South") can become site of resistance via critical re-interpretation
	Bill Ashcroft, 2007	*Postcolonial Studies: Key Concepts*	Hybridization *qua* transcultural shifts of domination mediated by "cross-breeding" and "cross-pollination" between colonizer and colonized

Continued

Table 1.2 *Continued*

	Author	Text	Designation
	Ella Shohat, 1992	"Notes On the Postcolonial"	Interrogates "ahistoric[ity]" of term and "multiplicity of positionalities," diluting opposition between colonizer and colonized and importance of resistance; concerned over depoliticizing wrongs of colonization
	Anne McClintock, 1992	"The Angel of Progress: Pitfalls of the Term Post-colonialism"	Criticizes "post" in post-colonialism for non-nuanced account of "beneficiaries (the ex-colonizers)" and "the casualties (the ex-colonized)" of colonialism; objects to ahistorical "axis of time" whereby cultures of the colonized are not "positively" defined within their histories, on their own terms, but according to "linear, European time"
CRITIQUES	Aijaz Ahmad, 1997	"Postcolonial Theory and the 'Post'-Condition"	"Telling discrepancy" between postcoloniality as near-universal condition and postcolonial theory designed by narrow circle of elites; "anti-colonial" is trampled in concepts such as hybridity (e.g. Bhabha); excessive focus on narrative and language to the neglect of more substantive empirics
	Neil Lazarus, 2011	"What Postcolonial Theory Doesn't Say"	"Blind spot" in postcolonial theory that neglects forced incorporation into world capitalism as central dynamic of colonialism; theory "essentialize[s]" the West
	Tayib Salih, 1969	*Season of Migration to the North*	Lasting impact of violence of uneven colonizer-colonized power relations and identity crisis amidst contradictions between precolonial, colonial, and decolonial subjectivities, overlaid with personal-political tension
LITERATURE	Arundhati Roy, 1997	*The God of Small Things*	Multilayered subalternity and "othering" in the context of ambivalent identity via Anglophile cultural molding
	John Maxwell Coatzee, 1999	*Disgrace*	Double colonization, silence, and marginalization of the colonized (esp. women) transpires from collusion of empire and patriarchy

from the seventeenth century onward (2008, 161). This image has been replaced since the 1970s or so with the portrayal of Islam (and by extension, Muslims) as a "global political-militant presence" menacing in its violence and tendency towards "extremism" (Quinn 2008, 164–165).

Silenced Histories

These inconsistencies arise not from clashing interpretations of empirical evidence, but from the *absence* of such empirical explorations in the first place. (Orientalist, Euro-centric) "regimes of truth," to employ a Foucauldian concept, create and determine the "place" of the subaltern. Discourse, whether written or unwritten, explicit or hidden, creates identity. Subjectivity flows from discursive formations. What concerns us is the distinction between the revolution of the by-and-large rational civilized, and the non-revolution of the West's Others—a distinction between agentic *people* and passive *non-people*. Constructing this discursive (non)representation involves playing on the difference between who is revolutionary and who is not, in turn reflecting how (West/East) power relations are mapped out, and the *Other's* location within that scheme. That is to say, silence reigns regarding revolution and revolutions of the "other" world and its absent "missing people." Taking potentially multiple forms, "silence," as Foucault notes, involves "the things one declines to say, or is forbidden to name" (Foucault 1978, 27). "Metropolitan revolution" is thus in a way complicit in schemes of Western modernity. Silence on protest/revolutionary practices and experiences is a tool of domination, a way to subjugate the Other. In one set of well-known rejoinders, the Subaltern Studies collective sought to reverse the effacement of non-elite Indians in colonial history. These scholars "acknowledg[ed] the peasant as the maker of his own rebellion," in possession of a formidable political consciousness (Guha 1999, 4). Not without pitfalls, including too much "indifference to … the subjectivity of … woman" Spivak (1987, 216), the project was nonetheless an admirable set of historiographical interventions. Sharing their affinity for the "subaltern," we orient the present work toward counteracting a kind of "metropolitan silence" dovetailing with epistemic injustice, on Arab protest and revolution. The *making* and the *narrating* of history—and politics—thus intertwine. Our turn to history from below is, following Trouillot (1995, 27), one such attempt to "deconstruct these silences" in Tunisian history. A panoply of historical and contemporary empirical evidence becomes readily visible when one *chooses* to look for it. In such an undertaking, we pick up on echoes of those who were *not* silent.

Decolonizing Revolution?

Thus, one primary aim of our multilayered text is to open up space for subalterns or locals who have always spoken about their own struggles (à la Spivak 1987). We take their voices into account as we research protest and revolution. Postcolonialism as an optic enables the interrogation of linkages between circles of knowledge and circles of power. It lends critical texture to our study of Tunisian revolution. We have critiqued dominant (read: cultural) representations or erasures of metropolitan revolution. Moreover, self/other binarisms *and* attempts to overcome subsequent, inevitable entanglements carry over from postcolonial theory into the investigation of revolution. Colonialism's chokehold may have been formally loosened in Tunisia by 1956. Yet the domination of the *colon* soon gave way to the hegemonizing project of Bourguiba's (and then Ben Ali's) state: its institutions, bureaucracies, national and cultural development projects. Dissent was stifled in attempts to eradicate difference and instill deference to one-partyism. A kind of "double colonization," a double exploitation, a double estrangement—terms and states of being adopted and adapted from the postcolonial corpus—have been at play in postcolonial, authoritarian, and even post-revolutionary Tunisian politics. The potential for and existence of pushback from the margins as outlined in postcolonial theory is additionally instructive. The "twin ferment" of peoplehood/revolution, showcased in our protestscapes, explores practices of resistance by the (formerly colonized) subalterns in an intertextual, interpretive analysis.

Uprising of Words and Worlds

With a postcolonial bent, this book critically engages with key concepts from the corpus of knowledge on protest and revolutions. It stresses the importance of interplays between language (Arabic-English-French) and "power" (revolutionary and protest activities, ideas, etc.). This text thus reflects a range of "dialogue" or "conversation" with theoretical frameworks, paradigms, methodologies, and methodological questions. We blend these together through an argumentative analytical style that fleshes out areas of silence and absence as far as Arab revolution is concerned. The book "writes" Tunisian revolution by unhinging existing meaning-making and the rich signage that comes with it. Hence, this book emphasizes the linkages between argumentation, evidence, and critical reflection. We aim to construct a kind of analytic "toolkit" that builds on the erudition of classic narratives of revolution, augmented by a postcolonial/decolonizing sophistication.

Here, we build on the protest and revolution lexicon to localize and indigenize concepts through dialogic meaning-making. The list displayed in Table 1.3 thus incorporates conceptual and theoretical elements from the vast literature on revolutions. We elaborate our eclectic and innovative conceptualizations in Chapter 2. Thus, following Tilly (1978), the concept of revolution includes the notion of radical change of political power arrangements. At the same time, our treatment leaves room for the socio-economic emphasis of revolution (Moore 1966; Skocpol 1979) alongside deep-rooted political change. Without adopting the rigidity of protest "cycles" and "episodes," our conceptualizations of protest and uprisings are informed by Tilly's (1978) contentious politics and popular mobilization, in addition to his later work with McAdam and Tarrow (see McAdam, Tarrow, and Tilly 2009; Tilly and Tarrow 2015). We thus borrow from Tilly and Tarrow's work on contentious politics to conceptualize protest. Yet we go further.

Table 1.3 Uprising of Words

Arabic Term	English Translation	Meaning-in-Context	Variations and Iterations
THAWRAH	Revolution	(Attempts to) overhaul, violently or peacefully, the political and/or economic system throughout Tunisian history, with a strong emancipatory, bottom-up element Open-ended, dramatic happenings in extended contests with counter-revolution	Against the Bey (e.g. Ali Ben Ghedhahem 1864) Against the French (1954–6) Against Ben Ali's regime (2010–2011)
AL-THAWRAH AL-MUDADDAH	Counter-revolution	In constant dialectic with Tunisian revolution's various historical renditions. It can *precede* as well as *succeed* revolution: the state's attempts to rein in "the people" as active political agents via postcolonial nationalism Occupation of the state to penetrate and dominate society, preempting gains of independence (from colonialism or authoritarianism) Contains seeds of its own "emptying," prompting intermittent protest and other forms of resistance	Post-independence nationalism (1956) and "taming the revolution" (2011–)
IHTIJAJ	Protest	Bottom-up claim-making against the state or powers-that-be A form of mediation (by "appearing" in public space) in the absence of (established) democracy because people feel mis-, under-, or not represented May be more or less organized/spontaneous	Intersperses Tunisian history over 150 years, from the 1860s "crucible" to 2011, disrupting state-society, ruler-ruled relations Quasi-permanent" since 2011
INTIFADAH	Uprising	Larger-scale protest episodes, including across Tunisia's geography Connotations of righteous outcries against injustice	*Intifadat al-Khubz* (bread uprising, 1984) *Intifadat al-hawd al-manjimi* (phosphate basin uprising, 2008)
	Protestscape	Relational iteration of protest activity as a cognitive, affective, agentic assemblage that feeds into identity, memory, learning; extended "moment" in protest milieu synchrony along the diachrony of Tunisia's revolutionary élan.	Students, unions, phosphate basin, 2011 revolution, Kamour, football ultras

Continued

Table 1.3 Continued

Arabic Term	English Translation	Meaning-in-Context	Variations and Iterations
AL-MADD AL-THAWRI	Revolutionary élan	Ongoing chain of protests, pre-colonial to postcolonial (post)revolutionary: intermittent struggles (with reversals) by Tunisia's subalterns against domination Longue durée of protest activity that leaves "traces" (affective, cognitive, agentic) contributing to Tunisian peoplehood	Ali Ben Ghedahem (1864), Jallaz (1911), anti-colonial (1956), bread riots (1978–84/5), phosphate basin, anti-authoritarian (2010–2011), post-revolutionary (2011–present)
AL-SHA'B	The People	Members of the Tunisian polity who through social acting, feeling, thinking, and being recognize one another, are recognized by the state, and exercise sovereignty	Deferred, constant individual-collective becoming Term de-territorialized and re-territorialized to counteract its disingenuous appropriation by political leaders (Bourguiba, Ben Ali)
AL-HIRAK	Peoplehood	Diachronically and synchronically accumulating, socially acted and en-acted struggles against authoritarianism, domination, or exclusion Reclaiming of the "people" status that culminates via revolution	2010–2011 revolution was the "crowning" of peoplehood-in-becoming for decades Disparate conceptions contributed to events of July 25 and their reception

Protest (*ihtijaj*), is more than a medium. It is a vernacular for the marginals. Perhaps a vernacular, which pastiches the portraits of life in the doldrums. Its locutions, expressions, and idioms tramp in the alleys of misery, pulsating with the innate affect of both resistance and worthlessness, darkened by the dimming light of oppressive and unjust nationalism, and yet morally enflamed with self-consciousness and cognition for socially acting and enacting freer subjectivities. Further adapting Arendt's (1958, 1963) "revolutionary élan", our longue durée orientation considers Tunisia's 2011 revolution within the context of over a century and a half of bottom-up struggles forming a "protest chain." We posit a Marcusian counter-revolution as *preceding* the 2011 revolution via postcolonial nationalism that attempts to rein in the people. With a nod to its narrative aspects, we additionally account for the embodied, affective, argumentative, agentic, and cognitive elements of peoplehood (Sadiki 2015) (Chapter 2).

Moreover, the terms rendered in Arabic as *thawrah*, *intifadah*, *al-sha'b*, *intifada*, and *hirak* point to actual usage in written and spoken discourse. The point is not simply that these are Arabic translations of their English-language conceptual counterparts of revolution, protest, the people, uprising, and popular mobilization, respectively. Instead these transliterated Arabic terms flash with changing meanings across the various "texts" we analyze over the course of the book's nine chapters. True to interpretivist form, the concepts shown and defined above heave under the weight of power contests (e.g. protestors vs. the state). The terms are certainly steeped in their local Tunisian context. We employ these terms throughout the book to explicate the Tunisian experiences with protest and revolution as well as the links and commonalities with other similar-yet-different revolutionary milieus. In turn, this analytic enterprise is itself an exercise and manifestation of knowledge–power dynamics as we "rise up" with our own writing of revolution. The very emphasis and insistence on the localized lexicon enhances what we hope is critical and innovative knowledge-making on protest, revolution, peoplehood, and even democratization.

"Knowing" Revolution

One approach to writing Tunisian revolution is to put forth a provocative "story" that correlates with the dynamic of political words, worlds, actors, and contexts. Tunisia's millennial history of continuous statehood[8] and peoplehood is punctuated by stress intervals and times of crisis. Strengthening the book's story of revolution is the weaving of an interpretivist trace throughout, accounting for forces and discourses integral to construction of revolution. These include the cultural, the economic, and the socio-political, to deliver a well-rounded account of Tunisia's revolutionary élan. We assign indeterminacy to a multimodal approach that avoids sharp boundaries

---

[8] The Aghlabid dynasty lasted from 800 to 909 CE, followed by the Fatimids, 909–1171 CE. The Hafsyds ruled Tunisia (known as *Ifriqiyyah*) from 1229 to 1574 CE. The Muradid Dynasty ceded power to the Husaynid dynasty in 1705 CE. Husaynid Beys ruled Tunisia until the founding of the Republic, by Habib Bourguiba, in 1957.

between past and present, fact and affect, synchrony and diachrony, agency and structure, and local and global. Revolution is conceived of as a historical chain of cumulatively interacting links of motion and emotion, actor and action, the normative and the descriptive. One assumption underpinning the analysis is that revolution and peoplehood, in their "journey" through history, not only articulate one another, but also affirm their mutually reinforcing social construction. This double ontology (nature of reality) about the existence of peoplehood and revolution is novel. This is because, peoplehood and revolution are implicated in ongoing reification with material and immaterial contemporaneous realities. Authors of revolution, from Marx to Moore and beyond, partake in such construction. How authors write or do revolution may reflect epochal realities. The research we draw on and the evidence we marshal for our own construction of Tunisia's revolution seeks to connect the past with all that the present offers in terms of epistemology (nature of knowledge, what can be known) and methodology (strategy of knowing "what should be" vs. "what is").

The book's research on the interlacement of revolution and peoplehood is grounded in questions that articulate interrelated trajectories:

1) The ontological question: What is the nature of revolution and of peoplehood? What words (texts, theories, concepts, and paradigms, etc.) help explain their existence?
2) The epistemological question: How do we go about knowing both revolution and polyvalent peoplehood in the Tunisian context? How does "protestscape" mediate the writing of protest and peoplehood? How does it account for the flow between synchrony and diachrony?
3) The (people's) historical question: What cumulatively interlocking processes and histories explain revolutionary change and the (re)birth of peoplehood?

Intertextually and syncretically, we deploy texts and conceptual frameworks spanning diverse disciplines. The tapestry of concepts is woven into a text that pluralizes data sources and methods. This approach puts into dialogue, as well as into tension, diverse words and worlds, together not apart, dictating against a straight-line trajectory of analysis. It panders to assumptions of both peoplehood and revolution as fluid socio-political dynamics, defying fixity and singularity. The approach also challenges the cause–effect tradition by favoring an outlook in which author, text, context, and subject are active participants in the construction of revolution. All are stationed within relational, plural and dynamic realities, as well as those of the peoples who construct them, and are constructed by them.

Interpreting Peoplehood and Revolution

Seeking to understand such a revolutionary élan, we favor the longue durée as a depository of socio-political impact on the making of peoplehood. We trace this dynamic back to the "crucible" of the 1850s–1860s. The synchrony–diachrony lens

(Chapter 2) helps this line of argumentation. We examine attendant agentic norms and matching insurrectionary and mobilizational activisms and struggles. Ours is an interpretivist—contextualized, reflexive, hermeneutically-leaning (Yanow and Schwartz-Schea 2015; see also Alvesson and Sköldberg 2009)—rather than positivist methodology. Its underlying approach stems from the observation that explanations given so far of Tunisia's revolution are insufficient, given to quasi-experimentation and "romanticization."

We thus seek to "write" indeterminacy into Tunisia's revolution. This is an attempt to relativize revolution and re-center peoplehood through a protestscape lens in the Tunisian setting. It resists the wholesale transposition of revolutionary paradigms (mobilization, contentious politics, structural changes of industrialization and state-building, etc.) without adequate bottom-up consideration of local context, history, and politics. Indeterminacy here is about providing evidence-based interpretations of protests and revolution in the Tunisian setting that veer away from answers to fixed or singular knowing or knowable claims. Instead, we attempt to develop a more capacious, multi-modal account of revolution, drawing on qualitative methods that factor in interpretations of peoplehood formation. Hence, our analysis seeks to untangle the story of Tunisia's revolution by a *re*interpretation of the imbrication of subject, object, time, and space, synchrony and diachrony. This is a means to dissect the complexities of a dual revolutionary transformation of self and society.

Intertextuality

Intertextuality is our approach to the interdisciplinarity elaborated above, also feeding into a "triangulation" of concepts/theories, methods, and sources. It further suits our emphasis on indeterminacy. For Kristeva (1980), intertextuality involves a certain relationality between social and written/spoken "systems of signs," that is, where various texts "intersect" directly or indirectly at various levels of both word (other written texts) and world ("historical and social" texts) (Kristeva 1980, 36–37). No text exists in isolation of either spoken/published discourses or the socio-cultural-historical positions in which they are situated. Interpretation of the "text" of Tunisia's protest and revolution—ideas, memories, affect, experiences, and narratives thereof—requires attention to these social-textual systems and an attempt to unpack the relations and transmutations therein. For our analysis, we mean by "intertextuality" the mixing of diverse data and evidence comprising a patchwork of narratives that we aim to explicate. This includes historical and archival texts, interviews, social media, and Western secondary sources. We forage through this rich and varied source material, pinpointing silences, vocalizing voices "from below," threading them with indigenous and "outside" accounts to (re)construct and recalibrate an admittedly complex medley of narratives.

We utilize an intertextual approach in stitching together first, our conceptual/theoretical framework. Second, we intertextually comb through five sets of texts, comprising mostly primary and some secondary data in three languages (English, Arabic, and French):

1. **Interviews and oral history:** testimonials (*shahadat*) (Arabic): 300 or so interviews with activists and witnesses to various protest "moments" from the 1970s onwards, as well as oral history transcripts collected and collated by Tunisians, including the Tamimi Foundation.
2. **Archival material:** (mostly Arabic, some French): from (semi)official and opposition newspapers including *Al-'Amal, Al-Sabah, Al-Ra'i, Al-Sha'b, Al-Mawqif, Al-Mustaqbal, Al-Tariq Al-Jadid*, and *Elchourouk*.
3. **Online sources:** newspaper and opinion articles, social media posts (e.g. Facebook), and videos (e.g. YouTube), comprising "bottom-up" documentation and *constructions* of the 2010–2011 revolution and the political-socio-economic environment since then.
4. **Tunisian historiography and sociological scholarship:** (Arabic, and some French): books and articles on history and politics contributing to an analysis of history as (indigenous) narrative and knowledge-making.
5. **(Western) secondary source material:** (mostly English, some French) on Tunisian politics, history, protest, and revolution—a corpus in which we identify "silences" and against which we measure the necessary extent of the "corrective" which our book undertakes.

Oral History

Proceeding in triangulation with the plethora of other written sources mentioned above, we engage in a threefold use of this method (particularly in Chapters 3 and 4). First, our interview material is one form "oral history" evidence, what Gluck (1977, 5) refers to as "topical" interviews regarding a particular theme. A second form we utilize is the public or published testimonies available online, part of the "digital revolution in oral history" (Thomson 2007, 68). This material includes sample sessions convened by the Truth and Dignity Commission (2011–2018) and other media outlets. The public platforming of historical parleys with dictatorship, of involvement in protest, transforms personal, individual memories into shared, collective memory-making. Counter-memory rebutting and revising official accounts of hegemonic counter-revolution, Bourguiba to Ben Ali, gets a more widely circulated hearing, as it were. Third are published transcripts of testimonials (*shahadat*) by activists and policymakers. These are a rich and valuable resource untapped in Western scholarship. As social scientists, our eyes and ears are on the agentic, affective, and cognitive cogs whirring in the human machinery of protest. This is paramount to a bottom-up reconstruction of what we call "situated protest."

Thick Description

Augmenting our intertextual treatment is a quasi-"thick description." We present evidence from our various sources to transcend a reductive analysis of the staging of protests as merely performative or purely functional acts. This qualitative, ethnographic method places primacy on seeing cultures from within their own context, beginning with documenting detailed notes about social action (Geertz 1973). Interpretation is key (Schwandt 2001). Denzin (1989, 83–85) elaborates that thick description provides "detail, context, emotion, and the webs of social relationships that join persons to one another." We tap into his fivefold framework that contributes to understanding our dual socio-political phenomenon of peoplehood-revolution. This involves at various intervals in our synchronic–diachronic "plotting":

a) The *interactional*: concerning relationships and meanings of protest, people(hood), and revolution;
b) the *situational*, attending to the temporal-spatial context of social doing;
c) the *biographical*, focusing on the who of (in our case) protest and revolution;
d) the *relational*: joining the dots between actors and processes, charting the "travel" of ideas and practices; and,
e) the *historical*, where we note and counteract the "silencing" of history.

Hence, the interpretation of thick descriptions helps to unlock characters and protagonists, capturing subjects, to help see the unseen, or that which is not explicitly or coherently articulated in a given scenario (historical or contemporary). We apply this brand of interpretivism to events we observe firsthand as well as historical/archival texts—"read" intertextually, ethnographically—*thickly*.

(Critical and Multi-Modal) Discourse Analysis

Our interpretivist, intertextual methodology sustains a pointed interest in language and meaning-making. More concretely, our three dimensions of peoplehood (agentic, affective, cognitive) serve as rough units of analysis along which to understand and interpret our data. In addition to "thick description," we also subject our diverse groups of texts, both spoken (interviews, recordings, videos) and written (archival data, official documents, secondary sources) to discourse analysis. Grasping the emancipatory calling and the historical becoming of peoplehood within protestscapes lends itself to deconstructing socio-political and socially situated narratives. In this vein, investigating the extent to which meanings given to the three dimensions of peoplehood reveals practices and identities (Gee 1999) of protest. Critical discourse analysis (CDA) adopts the "critical" label in its slant towards power asymmetries (van Dijk 2009). In this case, between the (non)people and the authoritarian/counterrevolutionary state. Paired with interdisciplinarity, discourse analysis augments the triangulation that embraces a mixture of empirical observations, theories, methods, and background information (Reisigl and Wodak 2009, 89; see also Fairclough 2012). It facilitates examination of the linguistic, meaning-making aspects of power contests relevant to the making of peoplehood and revolution and even struggles on behalf of democracy. We also make use of multi-modal discourse analysis (Kress 2011) as a valuable supplement to traditional CDA. This allows for investigations of *embodied* discourses and practices across space and time in music, films, online content, in addition to conventional written and spoken text. Taken together, these methodologies and the ontologies and epistemologies they indicate provide a nuanced, polyvocal, textured understanding of Tunisia's peoplehood-in-becoming. In this way, we shun fixity and tackle head-on indeterminacy in the writing of revolution.

Outline of the Book

Chapter 2 lays out our theoretical framework of socially acted and en-acted peoplehood and its agentic, affective, and cognitive elements. Protest is where and how a people become. As an epistemology of researching revolution, protestscapes frame the crux of the book's empirical investigation. As evanescent moments, protestscapes aid in the dis-assembling of situated, partial components of Tunisia's revolution. The analysis links resistance and social acting and enacting to the rise of peoplehood, the nemesis of "counterrevolution," which marked the onset of postcolonial state-building and nationalism immediately after independence.

Chapter 3 outlines the anatomy of a hundred years of a syndicalist tradition, our first protestscape. Spanning anticolonial and postcolonial spatialities and temporalities, this protestscape investigates the General Union of Tunisian Workers' (UGTT) as a formidable anti-systemic force leading the "insurrectionary politics" of the 1970s onwards. The chapter traces the buildup, execution, and fallout of popular protest in the 1978 General Strike ("Black Thursday") and the bread riots of 1984. Broaching syndicalism of a different kind, Chapter 4 focusses on student "ruly and unruly"activism in the 1960s–1980s. It contextualizes these struggles, linking them to social, political, and intellectual dynamics. The analysis ascribes the brand of dissent spreading across university campuses to a capacity for translating heightened political awareness into sustained, polyphonous dissent. It links social acting and en-acting of protest to pluralist "ideologies," social imaginaries, and speech acts.

The materiality of protestscapes mired in deprivation and marginalization is on full display in Chapter 5. It turns to Gafsa and the towns making up the mining workforce in the phosphate basin in 2008. Against a longstanding tradition of anti-colonial and postcolonial resistance, the chapter examines the politics around organizing social doing, and the framing of speech acts around social justice. The protestscape highlights how the 2008 protests exemplify contests over material and distributional goods and resources. Picking up where the phosphate uprising left off, Chapter 6 explores the "acme" of protestscapes, Tunisia's 2011 revolution, from Sidi Bouzid protests to Ben Ali's departure and the Kasbah 1 and 2 sit-ins. As an apex of rebelscapes, the revolution derives its historical uniqueness and solemnity (with its freedom and dignity motto) from diachronic fruition: a crossing point of spatiality and temporality. Time and space collapse as counter-memories, learned protest competencies, deepening socio-economic marginalization, and political exclusion all come to a head. Diverse and situated protestscapes converge into a Bakhtinian-type "carnival" upturning dominant power relations and patterns of meaning-making. The analysis concretizes the strategies and experiences of nationwide popular protest in which human suffering and sacrifice loom large, in an indeterminate revolution— perhaps à la Babeuf, none other than a "precursor" of revolutionary times (Rose 1978).

Chapter 7 delves into the Kamour movement protestscape erupting years after the 2011 revolution. The chapter explores enduring questions of spatial justice and the perpetuation of marginalization under democratization through examining a youth-led movement demanding a local share of oil wealth in Tataouine province. The chapter lays out the Kamour's organization, demands, strategies, and identity-markers, dwelling on its "normative learning." Our final protestscape in Chapter 8 concerns the anti-systemic force that is Tunisia's "ultras" football fans. Defying the "pre" and "post" labels, the motor of young super-fans' rebelliousness runs strong over a decade after the revolution against Ben Ali. The analysis focusses particularly on protest and spectacle, including songs and choreographies. The *T'allam 'Oum* campaign demonstrates conflict with police over the last few years. The Conclusion (Chapter 9) reiterates the theoretical and empirical contributions of our "decolonizing" foray into Tunisian revolutions. Emphasizing the ontological, epistemological, and methodological value of protestscapes, it also takes up the relationship between protest and democracy.

References

Ackerman, Peter and Jack Duvall. 2000. *A Force More Powerful: A Century of Nonviolent Conflict*. New York: St. Martin's Press.

Ahmad, Aijaz. 1997. "Postcolonial Theory and the 'Post'-Condition." *Socialist Register* 33: 353–381.

Alavi, Hamza. 1982. "The Structure of Peripheral Capitalism." In *Introduction to the Sociology of "Developing Societies"*, edited by Hamza Alavi and Teodor Shanin. London: Macmillan, 172–192.

Alvesson, Mats and Kaj Sköldberg. 2009. *Reflexive Methodology: New Vistas for Qualitative Research*. London: Sage.

Amin, Samir. 1997. *Capitalism in the Age of Globalization: The Management of Contemporary Society*. London: Zed Books.

Appadurai, Arjun. 1996. *Modernity at Large: Cultural Dimensions of Globalization*. Minnesota: University of Minnesota Press.

Arendt, Hannah. 1958. *The Human Condition*. Chicago: University of Chicago Press.

Arendt, H. 1990 [1963]. *On Revolution*. London and New York: Penguin Books.

Ash, Timothy Garton. 1990. *The Magic Lantern: The Revolution of '89 Witnessed in Warsaw, Budapest, Berlin and Prague*. New York: Random House.

Ashcroft, Bill. 2007. *Postcolonial Studies: Key Concepts*. London: Routledge.

Bayat, Asef. 2017. *Revolution without Revolutionaries: Making Sense of the Arab Spring*. Stanford: Stanford University Press.

Bhabha, Homi. 1994 [2004]. *The Location of Culture*. London and New York: Routledge.

Bishara, Azmi. 2012. *Al-Thawrah al-Tunisiyyah al-Majidah: Bunya al-Thawrah wa suririyyatah* [The Diary of a Resplendent Revolution in the Making]. Doha: Arab Center for Research and Policy Studies.

Bourdieu, Pierre. 1986. "The Forms of Capital." In *Handbook of Theory and Research for the Sociology of Education*, edited by J. G. Richardson. New York: Greenwood Press, 241–258.

Brinton, Crane. 1938. *The Anatomy of Revolution*. New York: W.W. Norton and Company.

Carter, April. 2013. "People Power Since 1980: Examining Reasons for its Spread, Success and Failure." *Sicherheit und Frieden* (S+F)/*Security and Peace* 31(3): 145–150.

Chenoweth, Erica and Maria J. Stephan. 2012. *Why Civil Resistance Works: The Strategic Logic of Nonviolent Conflict*. Cambridge: Cambridge University Press.

Coatzee, J. M. 1999. *Disgrace*. New York: Viking.

Denzin, Norman K. 1989. *Interpretive Interactionism*. London: SAGE.

De Tocqueville, Alexis. 1856. *The Old Regime and the Revolutions*, trans. John Bonner. New York: Harper and Brothers.

Eagleton, Jennifer. 2022. *Discursive Change in Hong Kong: Sociopolitical Dynamics, Metaphor, and One Country, Two Systems*. Lanham: Lexington Books.

Eisenstadt, S. N. 1978. *Revolution and the Transformation of Societies: A Comparative Study of Civilizations*. New York: The Free Press.

El-Douggui, Noureddine, ed. 1999. *Harakat Al-Shabab Al-Tunisi* [The Tunisian Youth Movement]. Tunis: Al-Ma'had Al-A'la li Tarikh Al-Harakah Al-Wataniyyah.

El-Ghobashy, Mona. 2021. *Bread and Freedom: Egypt's Revolutionary Situation*. Stanford: Stanford University Press.

Fairclough, Norman. 2012. "Critical Discourse Analysis." In *The Routledge Handbook of Discourse Analysis*, edited by J. P. Gee and M. Handford. New York: Routledge, 9–20.

Fanon, Frantz. 1952. *Black Skin, White Masks*. New York: Grove Press.

Filiu, Jean-Pierre. 2011. *The Arab Revolution: Ten Lessons from the Democratic Uprising*. Oxford: Oxford University Press.

Foran, John. 2005. *Taking Power: On the Origins of Third World Revolutions*. Cambridge: Cambridge University Press.

Foucault, Michel. 1978. *The History of Sexuality, Vol. 1*, Trans. Robert Hurley. New York: Pantheon Books.

Fricker, Miranda. 2007. *Epistemic Injustice: Power and the Ethics of Knowing*. Oxford: Oxford University Press.

Gee, J. P. 1999. *An Introduction to Discourse Analysis: Theory and Method*. Abingdon: Routledge.

Gee, Tim. 2011. *Counterpower: Making Change Happen*. Oxford: New Internationalist Publications.

Geertz, Clifford, Ed. 1973. *The Interpretation of Cultures*. New York: Basic Books

Gluck, Sherna. 1977. "What's So Special about Women? Women's Oral History." *Frontiers: A Journal of Women Studies* 2(2): 3–17.

Goldstone, Jack A. 2001. "Toward a Fourth Generation of Revolutionary Theory." Annual Review of Political Science 4: 139–187.

Goodwin, Jeff. 1994. "Old Regimes and Revolutions in the Second and Third Worlds: A Comparative Perspective." *Social Science History* 18(4): 575–604.

Goodwin, Jeff. 2001. *No Other Way Out: States and Revolutionary Movements, 1945–1991*. Cambridge: Cambridge University Press.

Goodwin, Jeff. 2011. "Debate: Why We Were Surprised (Again) by the Arab Spring." *Swiss Political Science Review* 17(4): 452–456.

Goodwin, Jeff and James M. Jasper, eds. 2004. *Rethinking Social Movements: Structure, Meaning, and Emotion*. Lanham, MD: Rowman and Littlefield.

Goodwin, Jeff and Theda Skocpol. 1989. "Explaining Revolutions in the Contemporary Third World." *Politics and Society* 17(4): 489–509.

Guha, Ranajit. 1999 [1983]. *Elementary Aspects of Peasant Insurgency in Colonial India*. Durham, NC: Duke University Press.

Gurr, Ted. 2016 (1971). *Why Men Rebel: Fortieth Anniversary Paperback Edition*. London and New York: Routledge.

Hall, Stuart and Paul Du Gay. 1996. *Questions of Cultural Identity*. London: SAGE.

Haraway, Donna. 1988. "Situated Knowledges: The Science Question in Feminism and the Privilege of Partial Perspective." *Feminist Studies* 14(3): 575–599.

Havel, Vaclav, et al. 1985. *The Power of the Powerless: Citizens Against the State*. London: M. E. Sharpe.

Hermassi, Abdellatif. 2023. *Tunis Al-Thawrah Wal-Mihnah: Muqarabah min Manthur 'Ilm Al-Ijtima'Al-Siyasi* [Tunis of Revolution and Woe: A Political Sociology Approach]. Tunis: Sotumedia.

Hermassi, Elbaki. 1976. "Toward a Comparative Study of Revolutions." *Comparative Studies in Society and History* 18(2): 211–235.

Hobsbawm, Eric. 1959. *Primitive Rebels*. New York: W. W. Norton.

Hobsbawm, Eric. 1962. *The Age of Revolution: 1789–1848*. New York: Vintage Books.

Huntington, Samuel. 1968. *Political Order in Changing Societies*. New Haven: Yale University Press.

Jenkins, Craig and Bert Klandermans. 1995. *The Politics of Social Protest: Comparative Perspectives on States and Social Movements*. Minneapolis: University of Minnesota Press.

Kerr, Douglas. 2008. *Eastern Figures: Orient and Empire in British Writing*. Hong Kong: Hong Kong University Press.

Kienle, Eberhard and Nadine Sika, eds. 2015. *The Arab Uprisings: Transforming and Challenging State Power*. London: I.B. Tauris.

Kress, G. 2011. "Multimodal Discourse Analysis." In *The Routledge Handbook of Discourse Analysis*, edited by J. P. Gee and M. Handford. London: Routledge, 35–50.

Kristeva, Julia. 1980. *Desire in Language: A Semiotic Approach to Literature and Art*, Ed. Leon S. Roudiez. New York: Columbia University Press.

Lacroix, Stéphane and Jean-PIerre, Filiu. 2018. *Revisiting the Arab Uprisings: The Politics of a Revolutionary Moment*. Oxford: Oxford University Press.

Lawson, George. 2016. "Within and Beyond the 'Fourth Generation' of Revolutionary Theory." *Sociological Theory* 34(2): 106–127.

Lawson, George. 2019. *Anatomies of Revolution*. Cambridge: Cambridge University Press.

Lazarus, Neil. 2011. "What Postcolonial Theory Doesn't Say." *Race & Class* 53(1): 3–27.

Lynch, Marc, Ed. 2014. *The Arab Uprisings Explained: New Contentious Politics in the Middle East*. New York: Columbia University Press.

Maasen, Sabine. 2000. "Inducing Interdisciplinarity: Irresistible Infliction? The Example of a Research Group at the Center for Interdisciplinary Research (ZiF), Bielefeld, Germany." In *Practising Interdisciplinarity*, edited by Peter Weingart and Nico Stehr. Toronto: University of Toronto Press, 173–193.

McAdam, Doug, Sidney Tarrow, and Charles Tilly. 2001. *Dynamics of Contention*. Cambridge: Cambridge University Press.

McAdam, Doug, Sidney Tarrow, and Charles Tilly. 2009. "Comparative Perspectives on Contentious Politics." In *Comparative Politics: Rationality, Culture and Structure*, 2nd edn, edited by Mark Irving Lichbach and Alan S. Zuckerman. Cambridge: Cambridge University Press, 260–290.

Maitra, Ishani. 2010. "The Nature of Epistemic Injustice." *Philosophical Books*, 51(4): 195–211.

Marcuse, Herbert. 1972. *Counterrevolution and Revolt*. Boston: Beacon Press.

Masri, Safwan. 2017. *Tunisia: An Arab Anomaly*. Columbia: Columbia University Press.

Medina, José. 2013. *The Epistemology of Resistance: Gender and Racial Oppression, Epistemic Injustice, and the Social Imagination*. New York: Oxford University Press.

Memmi, Albert. 2003 [1957]. *The Colonizer and the Colonized*. London: Earthscan Publications.

McClintock, Anne. 1992. "The Angel of Progress: Pitfalls of the Term 'Post-Colonialism.'" *Social Text* (31/32): 84–98.

Michnik, Adam. 1985. *Letters from Prison and Other Essays*, Trans. Maya Latynski. Berkeley: University of California Press.

Molyneux, Maxine, Aida Yafai, Aisha Mohsen, and Noor Ba'abbadd. 1979. "Women and Revolution in the People's Democratic Republic of Yemen." *Feminist Review* 1(1): 4–20.

Moore, Barrington Jr. 1966. *Social Origins of Dictatorship and Democracy: Lord and Peasant in the Making of the Modern World.* Boston: Beacon Press.

Othman, Farhat. 2018. *L'Exception Tunisi: I-slam: Islam Postmoderne vs. tradition judeo-chretienne.* Tunis: Arabesque.

Pei, Minxin. 1994. *From Reform to Revolution: The Demise of Communism in China and the Soviet Union.* Cambridge, MA: Harvard University Press.

Quinn, Frederick. 2008. *The Sum of All Heresies: The Image of Islam in Western Thought.* Oxford: Oxford University Press.

Reisigl, M. and R. Wodak. 2009. "The Discourse-Historical Approach (DHA)." In *Methods of Critical Discourse Analysis.* 2nd edn, R. Wodak, and M. Meyer, . London: SAGE, 87–121.

Robinson, Glenn E. 1997. *Building a Palestinian State: The Incomplete Revolution.* Indianapolis: Indiana University Press.

Rose, Robert R. 1978. *Gracchus Babeuf: The First Revolutionary Communist.* California: Stanford University Press.

Rowbotham, Sheila. 1974. *Women, Resistance and Revolution: A History of Women and Revolution in the Modern World.* New York: Vintage Books.

Roy, Arundhati. 1997. *The God of Small Things.* New York: Random House.

Rushdie, Salman 1999. *Imaginary Homelands.* New York: Penguin.

Sadiki, Larbi. 2000. "Popular Uprisings and Arab Democratization." *International Journal of Middle East Studies* 32(1): 71–95.

Sadiki, Larbi. 2015. "Unruliness through Space and Time: Reconstructing 'Peoplehood' in the Arab Spring." In *Routledge Handbook of the Arab Spring: Rethinking Democratization.* London: Routledge, xxv–xxxi.

Said, Edward W. 1978. *Orientalism.* New York: Vintage.

Said, Edward W. 1994. *Culture and Imperialism.* New York: Vintage.

Salih, Al-Tayyib. 1966. *Mawsim al-Hijra ila al-Shamal* [Season of Migration to the North]. Beirut: Dar Al-'Awdah.

Schwandt, Thomas A. 2001. *Dictionary of Qualitative Inquiry*, 2nd edn. London: SAGE.

Sharp, Gene. 1973. *The Dynamics of Nonviolent Action.* Boston: Porter Sargent.

Shohat, Ella 1992. "Notes on the 'post-colonial.'" *Social Text* (31/32): 99–113.

Skocpol, Theda. 1979. *States and Social Revolutions: A Comparative Analysis of France, Russia, and China.* Cambridge: Cambridge University Press.

Skocpol, Theda. 1982. "Rentier State and Shi'a Islam in the Iranian Revolution." *Theory and Society* 11(3): 265–283.

Sorg, Christoph. 2019. *Disrupting Debt and Austerity: Resistance Against Debt Since the Southern Debt Crisis.* Hamilton: McMaster University. https://altausterity.mcmaster.ca/documents/sorg-berlin-paper-to-post.pdf

Spivak, Gayatri Chakavorty. 1987. *In Other Worlds: Essays in Cultural Politics.* New York and London: Methuen.

Teitelbaum, Joshua and Jospeh Kostiner. 1991. "The West Bank and Gaza: The PLO and the Intifada." In *Revolutions of the Late Twentieth Century*, edited by Jack A.

Goldstone, Ted Robert Gurr, and Farrokh Moshiri. Boulder, Co: Westview Press, 298–324.

Thompson, E. P. 1963. *The Making of the English Working Class*. New York: Vintage Books.

Thomson, Alistair. 2007. "Four Paradigm Transformations in Oral History." *The Oral History Review* 34(1): 49–70.

Tilly, Charles. 1978. *From Mobilization to Revolution*. New York: Random House.

Tilly, Charles. 1993. "Contentious Repertoires in Great Britain, 1758–1834." *Social Science History* 17(2): 253–280.

Tilly, Charles and Sidney Tarrow. 2006. *Contentious Politics*. Boulder: Paradigm Publishers.

Tilly, Charles and Sidney Tarrow. 2015. *Contentious Politics*, 2nd edn. Oxford: Oxford University Press.

Trouillot, Michel-Rolph. 1995. *Silencing the Past: Power and the Production of History*. Boston: Beacon Press.

Van Dijk, T. A. 2009. *Society & Discourse: How Social Contexts Influence Text & Talk*. Cambridge: Cambridge University Press.

Viswanathan, Gauri. 1989. *Masks of Conquest: Literary Study and British Rule in India*. New York: Columbia University Press.

Weingart, Peter. 2000. "Interdisciplinarity: The Paradoxical Discourse." In *Practising Interdisciplinarity*, edited by Peter Weingart and Nico Stehr. Toronto: University of Toronto Press, 25–42.

Weingart, Peter and Nico Stehr. 2000. "Concluding Comments." In *Practising Interdisciplinarity* edited by Peter Weingart and Nico Stehr. Toronto: University of Toronto Press, 270–272.

Wickham, Carrie. 2002. *Mobilizing Islam: Religion, Activism, and Political Change in Egypt*. New York: Columbia University Press.

Wolin, Sheldon S. 1973. "The Politics of the Study of Revolution." *Comparative Politics* 5(3): 343–358.

Yanow, Dvora and Peregrine Schwartz-Shea. 2015. *Interpretation and Method: Empirical Research and the Interpretive Turn*, 2nd edn. Armonk and London: M.E. Sharpe.

2
Tunisian Protestscapes

The Clamor of Peoplehood

"Bey al-Ummah" (the people's Bey) was no palace-dweller. Ali Ben Ghedhahem[1] of the Majir tribe was a learned man, son of a judge. In 1864, he led a rebellion protesting a backbreaking tax (majba) hike (from 36 to 72 riyals) decreed by Mohamed Sadiq Bey. Tunisia's ruler floundered under the influence of the Mamluk Grand Vizier Khaznadar, infamous for his taxing frenzy. Meanwhile, the French, English and Italians greedily eyed and vied for control of a Tunisia already sinking in foreign debt. A skilled horseman and charismatic orator who moved hearts and rallied followers, Ben Ghedhahem triggered tribal solidarity that flowed from Majir to Jlass to H'mammah and others, Westward and Northward. He called for 'isyan, *disobedience, against the new law that taxed the poor to finance the (deeply indebted)[2] rich and powerful. Ben Ghedhahem coaxed previously warring tribes into new alliances, coaching them to wield rage against injustice like defensive armor. "The fence that protects us is that we are oppressed," he declared.[3] The largest and most sustained revolt in Tunisia's modern history tore across the Beylicate from South to Sahel. Coordinating tribes forcefully reclaimed money stolen from them by Khaznadar's tax-men. Rallying under a common cry against injustice the tribes in revolt alighted fitnah* (unrest) *unseemly to the likes of court historian Ahmad Ibn Abi Diyaf. Schisms shattered the tribal coalition. Ben Ghedhahem's downfall would be trust in the mediation of a fellow Sufi* shaykh. *Captured in 1866, Ben Ghedhahem faced public humiliation. Onlookers spit in his face as he was trotted out in the Bardo palace courtyard. His final destination was the Karrakah prison. There he died alone soon after (October 10, 1867), in the cold stone fortress that to this day mournfully watches over the tourist-friendly town Halq Al-Wad* (La Goulette), *near the capital. The ugliness of his death was a warning to anyone who braved mutiny. The flouted promise of an aborted revolution* (thawrah) *was not buried with Ben Ghedhahem. The idea of rebellion carried over in the praxis, ethos, and imaginary of protest. Ben Ghedhahem was killed but not dead.*

---

[1] This vignette draws on Ibn Abi Diyaf (1990, 139–199) and Perkins (2014 34–36). For a recent discussion of Ben Ghedhahem's revolt and its echoes in the 2011 revolution, when Thala and Kasserine protestors proclaimed "victory by the grandsons of Ben Ghedhahem" see Al-Nabli (2021).

[2] By 1863, the Bey reportedly owed France sixty million francs (McKay 1945, 376–377).

[3] Ibn Abi Diyaf (1990 141).

Introduction

This chapter establishes the centrality of peoplehood to revolution, which is further suggested by the idea that in Tunisia the (multi-faceted, contestable) people were "missing" or "not found" up to the 2011 revolution. It opens with a concept map of (Tunisian and Arab) revolution and peoplehood, incorporating the rich litany of concepts comprising our theoretical framework. It conceptualizes peoplehood as interrelated agentic, affective, and cognitive struggles, a becoming through social doing crowned by the 2011 revolution. We then dwell on protest's "building-blocks" of revolution, their interaction and connection across time and space, through act and affect, by forms of demos and attendant discourses, in both colony and post-colony.

The resulting resistance through which peoplehood is acted and en-acted flies in the face of "one-dimensionality" and counterrevolution (Marcuse) engineered by colons and dictators alike. It is the agonistic, cumulative practice through which peoplehood is forged. Here we introduce a conceptual center-piece running through the book: *protestscapes*. Protestscapes as mini "case studies" of social doing contribute to understanding the patterns of revolutionary transformation, synchronic and diachronic, in Tunisia. The chapter closes with a representative "mapping" of the North African country's historical and representative rebelscapes, inaugurated by the crucible of Ali Ben Ghedhahem's revolution portrayed in the vignette above.

Conceptualizing Peoplehood

Having critically scrutinized the gaps left by "metropolitan revolution" in the Introduction, in this chapter we present our own conceptualization and theoretical framework. Deeply entangled in the unfolding of revolution is the notion of peoplehood (see Figure 2.1). The two feed into each other through what we consider a "double articulation." (Contra Skocpol), we argue that it is people who make revolutions, shaped by and shaping historically contingent economic, social, and power structures. Specifically, our interest is not in the "potent but hazy" concept of "the people" (Canovan 2008, 353). Rather, we explore peoplehood-in-becoming, or the transit from "non-people" to "people" through resistance and struggle, and its relation to revolution and protest. In "rare cases," popular mobilization rises to the fabled agency and authority attached to the people, becoming kindling for the continually-burning fire of myths (Canovan 2008, 359). We suggest that neither sacrosanct legal texts (Ackerman 1991) nor stories (Smith 2003) alone make peoplehood. The conception of peoplehood we offer in this book expresses the embodiment of a consciousness that is given life by an impulse to revolt against injustice, to socially act and en-act emancipatory aspirations. Hence, acts of protest play out synchronically (spatially) and accumulate diachronically (temporally) within a revolutionary élan at once fed by and inculcating (self–other) understandings of peoplehood. Tunisian peoplehood is the consummation of a century and a half of resistance and bottom-up struggle, in

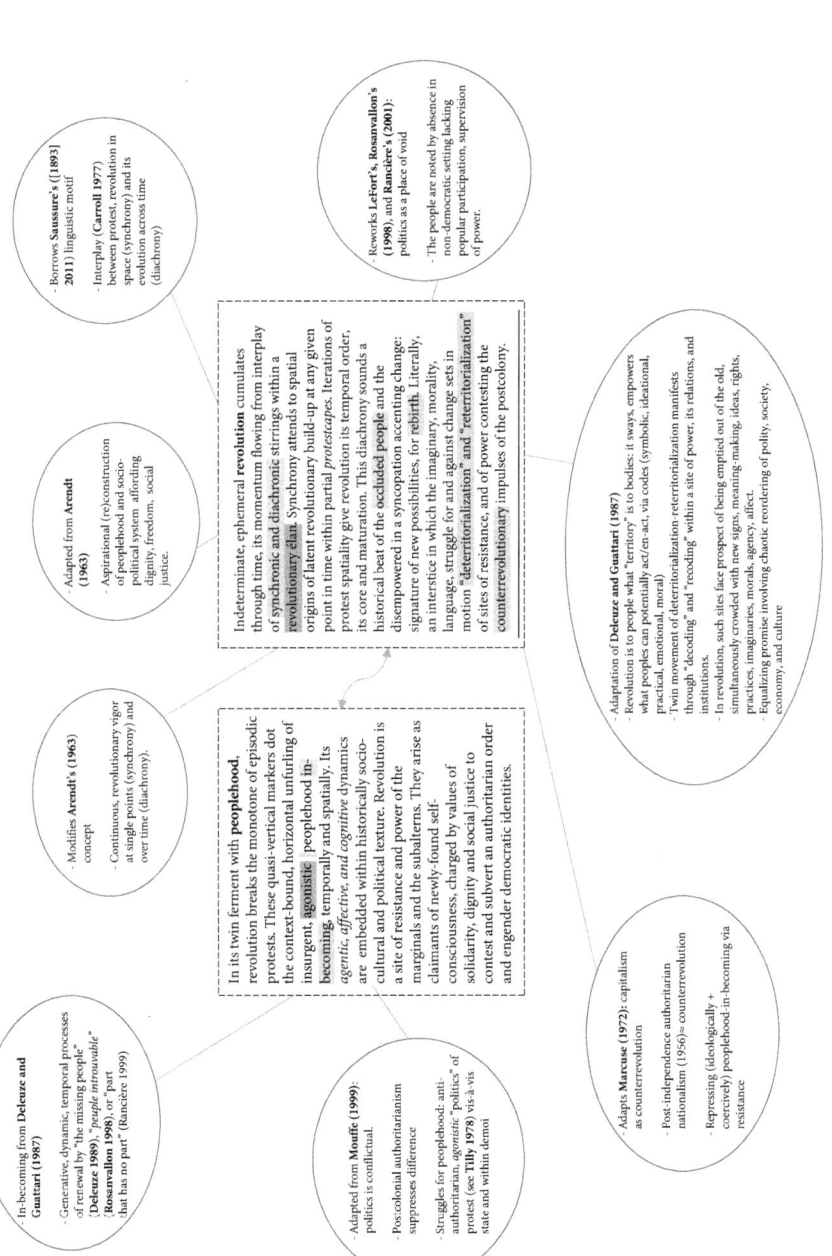

Figure 2.1 Revolution and Peoplehood Concept Map

turn colored by Tunisia's own political pedigree of constitutionalism (even if aborted or bypassed after Khayr Al-Din).[4]

"Missing" and "Absent" People

Our delineation of peoplehood in Arabic as *hirak* denotes movement (from *harakah*). Both national and international discourses enliven the bottom-up "groundswell" of protest that strikes back against the authoritarian state (Sadiki 2016). A catena of actions spell the spatio-temporally multi-sited social acts and enactments that actualize the people. Peoplehood thus comprises the agentic, affective, and cognitive struggles against (colonial, then authoritarian) domination, spanning social imaginaries (*mikhyal*) and repertoires of experiences (*makhzun*). The crowning moment is the fortuitous blooming of the diachronically accruing revolutionary élan in the synchrony of the 2011 revolution. Here we draw briefly on Gilles Deleuze in theorizing how a "people" comes into being. Deleuze's (1989) concept of the "missing" people refers to "a becoming." This becoming is actualized by people who "invent themselves . . . in new conditions of struggle" (1989, 217). Tunisian politics, from the heyday of subjects (*ra'iyyah*) under the Beylicate through the French mandate and into the one-party reigns of Bourguiba and Ben Ali, is marked by the absence of the people. Yet, this "missing"-ness of Tunisia's "non-people," was neither totalizing nor absolute. Persistent spurts of protest and resistance are exemplified by iconic figures (e.g. Ben Ghedhahem) and collectivities (e.g. UGTT). Rosanvallon's (1998) concept, "le peuple introuvable", is similarly appropriate. Rendered here as the "absent" and "occluded people," it presents some correspondence with Deleuze's "missing people." The people are epistemically silenced and politically dis-authorized. Rosanvallon's critique of (neoliberal) models of democracy points to the vanishing will of the people, almost a democratic fiction nowadays. Intellectually, the concept of the people is central to the nomenclature of political science. Partly, the idea of the people is a kind of absent referent in concepts such as nationalism, the nation-state, democracy, and sovereignty. This harks back to Derrida's puzzle in the metaphysics of presence about the absence–presence duality in meaning. Literally, we confront an incongruity of a lexical and cognitive usage the referent of which, the people, is a construction that is socially de-constructed. That is, a quasi-disembodied body. The term "people," in Tunisia, and almost invariably, across the Arab political geography, produces mental images of absence, not presence, and emptiness, not crowdedness. Rosanvallon (1998) proceeds with the French political trope that wonders who occupies the void when the king dies. For our purposes, the king is not dead but is reincarnated. Tunisia's Mohamed El-Amin Bey was replaced by Bourguiba in 1957. The postcolonial leader went on to decree the "death" of the people.

---

[4] Minister under Tunisian reformer Mohamed Bey (ruler from 1855–1859), who promulgated in 1857 the Fundamental Pact (*'ahd al-aman*). The pact was documented by beylical clerk/ "chancellor" and court historian Ahmed Ibn Abi Diyaf. See Carl Brown's (2005, 1–32, 131–136) translation and opening commentary.

Peoplehood's Becomings

The book's protestscapes (below) scope out self-propelled attempts at Arendtian "rebirth" for and by the people. In these synchronies, we discern the seeds of peoplehood as becomings. Our corrective narrative of Tunisia's peoplehood follows the twisting pathways in which Deleuze's "missing people" find and construct themselves, mandating that the powers they displace find them, too. Even the Arendtian perspective views "becoming a people," too as "an ongoing practice" (Zakin 2020, 53). Aiding us in explaining the becomings of peoplehood is another Deleuzian concept: deterritorialization that goes hand-in-hand with reterritorialization. Deleuze and Guattari write, "Revolution is absolute deterritorializaiton even to the point where this calls for a new earth, a new people. ... Absolute deterritorialization does not take place without reterritorialization" (1994, 101). These two authors explore this as they define philosophy by reference to its journey from Greece to modern-day capitalism. Relevant to their purposes is how deterritorialization denotes movement and change, involving "freeing" from a dominant system of percept, affect and concept: "A composite sensation, made up of percepts and affects, deterritorializes the system of opinion that brought together dominant perceptions and affections within a natural, historical and social milieu" (Deleuze and Guattari 1994, 196–7). Hence, deterritorialization refers to a kind of "deframing" of a dominant system, "break[ing] it open," resulting in a "freeing [of] all the sensations," be they emotional, ideational, spatial, or temporal … (1994, 197). Becomings/becoming, whether "sensory" or "conceptual," concern the notion that new percepts, concepts, and affects are possible and multiple, mediated by repeated movement of deteritorialization-reterritorialization, engendering new lives, new forms, new sensations, which are never fixed but are caught up in flows of intensity, making shifts and displacements and transformation permanent (Deleuze and Guattari 1994, 177).

Our use of the deterritorialization/reterritorialization duo here resonates with LeFort's notion of "the locus of power becom[ing] an empty place" (quoted in Sadiki 2004, 65). The French philosopher's recasting of democracy as an ethos stripped of singular assertions of power twins with the indeterminacy comprising its core. Democracy is disembodied, or "disentangled" from a (single) body, its resultant void spelling possibility for endless power contests (Sadiki 2004, 64–66). The gist of authoritarian rule is to use a mix of rhetoric and other instruments to delay this operation, emptying the place of power. This marks out the notion of deterritorialization. Such exclusionary politics does not represent the people. Instead, deterritorialization provides the impulse to turn the place of power into a void. *Re*territorialization, in response, refers here to re-instituting the people as sovereign. Hence, revolution partakes of two important moments. One is the invention of the moment of deterritorialization. This involves protesting against an authoritarian body politic ('sovereign king') as a means of contesting delegitimized power. The second moment of reterritorialization, as the creativity of protestors (agentically, affectively, cognitively) to give motion to building capacity to emancipated peoplehood ('sovereign people'). Equality is the benchmark of deterritorialization and reterritorialization - revolution. A revolution lives and dies by its promise to be an equalizer - a moment of rebirth.

A revolution's equalizing capacity- at least in theory - lies in a historic beginning in which peoples are empowered to co-evolve with kings equally. Implicit in the processes of deterritorialization and reterritorialization (integral to our definition of revolution) is an ontology of becoming people, and being free and dignified. In the context of postcolonial authoritarianism, attempts to empty out the center of power are incomplete. They peaked in the 2011 revolution, when the 'king's' stand-in (Ben Ali) fled the country. The ever-deferred ideal was forged by fits and starts throughout Tunisia's postcolonial history. The notion of the people existed as a value, from Farhet Hached's speeches to Bourguiba's usurpation. In Tunisia, the discourse of the "general will," whatever it means (realized through elections or reliable opinion polls) is absent. It is a Euro-American neologism with no Arab parallel. Instead, it is social doing, acts and en-actments, that puts this conceptual exemplar into practice, reterritorializing "the people" in struggles of becoming.

Embodied Performances and Appearances

Peoplehood in our conception is more than simply a discourse or a set of ideas. A *performative* angle resides in its social acting, making its en-acting (actualization) possible. For Tilly (2008), *performances*, made up of "actions and interactions," are ingredients of contention that come together to comprise "learned" *repertoires* (2008, 12–17). Others have investigated the symbolic and identitarian dimensions and connotations of performance in protest, including through music (e.g. Juris 2014) and re-appropriated symbolism (e.g. Casquete 2016). Arab Springers including Tunisians re-claimed *space* (public squares and mosques) and *time* (the religious Friday to organize and mobilize) from the authoritarian state (Sadiki 2015a). They thus drew upon what Tarrow (2013, 17–18) calls, with a narrower reference to language, nodal points with "symbolic resonance". That is, a re-ordering of time and space in a manner that "intertextually" references their recognizable and identifiable cultural-religious meanings.

Peoplehood's performativity thus extends to the collective insistence that I and we exist. The very moment of its acting and en-acting flows from the "right to have rights," in Arendt's (2000 [1948]) terms. For Judith Butler (2015), this is the right to a "livable life," shielded from the vulnerability of "precarity." Arendt and Butler draw our attention to rights in the collective sense. Through her focus on the plight of the stateless and the "rightless," Arendt exhibits the depth of belonging to a political community. Indeed, it would be inadequate to consider the "freedom" and "dignity" demanded by raging and raucous protestors as an entreaty for mere individuals, cut off from one another. Emancipation catalyzes the collective "we the people" that is "transversal to class, gender, and race" (Arditi 2020, 22). Revolutionaries from Sidi Bouzid to Habib Bourguiba Avenue, self-consciously in mind, body, and expression, urged *al-sha'b yurid* (the people want/will/vow). Neoliberal obsessions (normative or epistemological) with individual rights (Butler 2015, 15–20) do not measure up to the challenge of understanding peoplehood. Bourdieu's notion of relationality stitching together structure and agency, *field* and *habitus*, is apropos. "What exist in the social world are relations," not among individual people and their awareness of one another, but "objective relations" "configur[ing]" "fields" or positions of power (Bourdieu and Wacquant 1992, 97). This strikes at least a slight chord with the contentious politics school (McAdam, Tarrow, and Tilly 2001; Tilly and Tarrow 2006) and some scholars of revolution (Lawson 2019) who assume a relational analytic posture. Our inclusion of the cultural-social bases of peoplehood (see also Skocpol 1982; Ashraf 1988) also reflects relationality.

Through social acting and en-acting peoplehood, (non)people reverse postcolonial patterns that monopolize narratives and the development of state and society in the Arab world. In their own version of McAdam's (1982, 108–116) emotionally-charged "cognitive liberation", Tunisians come to a shared consciousness (*wa'y*) of deprived rights and a will to change them. They do so in the *embodied* manifestations of peoplehood, that are part of its performative nature. Public assemblies where sizable crowds gather ring with both *linguistic* and *bodily performativity* surpassing simply the discursive (Butler 2015, 9). Participants in assemblies re-claim the "right to appear" or the "bodily demand for a more livable set of lives" as well as recognition (Butler 2015, 24–26). Recognition of equality among (diverse) partners in performance, a theme Arendt and Butler take up, is insufficient when solely imagined or cognized. It requires the exercise of politics, for Arendt through speech and action—"acting in concert" (Arendt 1958, 162). Put another way, peoplehood necessarily involves the "networks …. of mutual recognition" comprising Bourdieu's (1992, 119) view of social capital in the broadest and deepest sense. These unfurl over time. Ben Ghedhahem's 1864 revolt, the Jallaz uprising of 1911, the 1938 "Tunisian parliament" demonstrations, the bread riots of 1978, the 2008 Gafsa uprising, Sidi Bouzid and Tunis in 2010–11, are notches in the collective imaginary-practice dialectic strengthening links of "mutual recognition." The agency, affect, and cognition of peoplehood crests in enunciated and embodied revolution.

Agency

Expressed performatively, the three dimensions of peoplehood (agency, affect, and cognition) are not mutually exclusive, and may reinforce one another. These conceptual constituents will be our units of analysis within dissentscapes, as we parse the "twin ferment" of Tunisia's peoplehood-revolution. Peoplehood necessarily speaks to the deliberate and purposeful actions of agents. Even, that is, as the discourses and practices of the aspiring "people" yield often unpredictable consequences, relationally encountering the labyrinth of ideational, historical, political, and socio-economic *structural* contexts. Not unlike Scott's (1976, 4–10) focus on peasant action in revolution or the contentious politics school, with its emphasis on the "contingent" nature of claim-making and mobilization, we zoom in on agents who socially act and en-act, perform and appear in, peoplehood.[5] Agency can be embodied, enunciated, internalized, externalized, or otherwise. In his *Argumentative Indian*, Amartya Sen

---

[5] Without attempting generalizable models that are too rigid for our interpretivist take. See Figure 2.2.

(2005, 6–9) maintains that traditions and contemporary practices of argumentation are conducive to democracy and the realization of social equality. Argumentative "voice,"[6] the expression and working through of alternative viewpoints, possibilities, and solutions to trenchant problems, is evident in the literary corpus (e.g. Bhagavad Gita) of ancient Indian civilization.[7] Elites do not and should not monopolize argumentation (2005, xiii). Nor should Western culture or history (2005, xv). Here, Sen implies the need for agentic interference. A push for rights and challenges to the *status quo* by those on the "bottom rungs" of the power ladder is necessary, to paraphrase Enloe (1996). Tolerance and acceptance, translated in modern systems into "political equality," often does not "translat[e]" into social and economic equality (Sen 2005, 36). Too many are left behind, wading through the bog of deprivation. Dignity, in all its pressing inseparability from freedom, is wanting. Severance of the link between the tolerance of argumentation (political equality) and social justice (socioeconomic parity), however, is not definitive. Much can be done, notes Sen, to chip against existing circumstances and demand the fulfillment of rights.

A kind of embodied argumentation, to wed Butler with Sen, features in the agency of repeated protests against excessive taxation (Ben Ghedhahem rebellion 1864), colonial interference in religious rites (Jallaz protest 1911, as in the opening vignette), and the slashing of food subsidies under the International Monetary Fund (IMF), seen as the hidden hand of crony capitalism in the margins (bread riots, 1984). The argumentative-ness of Tunisia's protest momentum/ethos (*zakham ihtijaji*) helps to cultivate peoplehood through resistance, which culminated in the 2011 revolution and persisted afterward, as we argue throughout the book. People are not acted upon through an inevitable teleological momentum. We do not subscribe to Rosa Luxemburg's (2008 [1905]) implication that protests (including failed and repressed protest campaigns) are almost rehearsals activated by the historical inevitability of revolutionary movement, as in Marx's understanding of class conflict. Instead, arguing, performing, and appearing, Tunisians carry the "inner dimension" of revolt (Kristeva 2014, 2) outward, refusing their "non-people" status. They insist on their rights as people vis-à-vis state domination and injustice. The moment of peoplehood does not simply *arrive*, with people taken in by the tide of revolution. Peoplehood is, rather, hammered out by indignant "non-people" abnegating their relegation.

Affect

Rebelling against (colonial or authoritarian) domination, social acts and en-actments of peoplehood involve intense embodied emotions.[8] Feelings of affect are mediated through the body in contact with its material/immaterial surroundings and the

---

[6] See also Hirschman's (1970) more economic concept

[7] Islamic history has its own analogues in intellectual disputation as *jadal* (see Miller 1985) or *munzarat*, "dialogues across difference with" the Greeks, the Indians, the Chinese (Sadiki 2004, 387) in masterpieces penned by the likes of Al-Farabi. On Khayr Al-Din's modernizing recommendations informed by knowledge of European political systems, see Abu-Lughod (1976, 24).

[8] Our relational perspective exceeds "micro-politics" accounts that astutely identify the centrality of emotion to individual protest (e.g. Pearlman 2013).

materiality of repression, domination, and deprivation. We propose that affect is pivotal to peoplehood and revolution. Influenced by Deleuze and Guattari (1987), affect theory regards affect as bi-directional: affecting and being affected at the level of embodied feelings in flows or "encounters" among material and immaterial bodies. "Bodies, minds, and social settings" interpenetrate, which makes the "social and the somatic" inextricable (Protevi 2009). The study of affect and Deleuzian "becomings" extends beyond explications and deconstructions of language to examine power dynamics (Gregg and Seigworth 2010, 3–19; see also Massumi 2010). The sociality of affect renders it almost socio-culturally constructed (Ahmed 2010, 41–42; see also Hutchison 2016). Affect underlies an "aesthetic" notion of politics as sensory and experiential, as we elaborate in the section on Rancière below. Necessarily political, affect carries the perennial possibility of counter-power: "moving, acting, perceiving, thinking that decide their own form as they enact themselves" in "affirmative, primary resistance" to the "power-over" of domination (Evans and Massumi 2017). It is well-suited for the study of protest (Ayata and Harders 2024). Social movement (e.g. Gould 2010) and contentious politics scholars acknowledge the impact of "heightened emotion" facilitating the mobilization of contention (Aminzade and McAdam 2001, 17). In this way we avoid inflated expectations of a "beefed-up agency," unhelpful and unrealistic for analysis, where "everything rests on agency's shoulders" (Stewart 2007, 59). Affect opens an analytical window to examining indignants' standing on the cusp of change and creating their own transformations, *becoming* through revolt against the dominant power. An affective radar picks up the socially active and en-active, not passive, in history not out of history. Relationally, it cultivates bonds linking into solidarity. Affect brings the marginal out of hiding and into the public space for the purposes of de-alienation, the right to have rights, to share in deterritorialization and reterritoralization, as an implicit ontology of becoming, being and self-making.

Hogra

Both positive and negative affect shape the contours of peoplehood. One noteworthy, negative indigenous affect is *hogra*. Deriving from *ihtiqar*, or contempt/humiliation, this is a common term in the contemporary Maghrebi (Algerian, Moroccan, and Tunisian) political lexicon. It connotes an amalgamation of feelings spanning "injustice, indignation, resentment, humiliation [and] oppression" in everyday encounters with state domination and control (Saadi 2021). Mounting feelings of injustice fuel contempt, a turning away from the misery-inducing state. Yet far from a recipe for complacency, *hogra* can become a call to action, propelling an embodied "striking back" of resistance (Lacchab and Yachoulti 2018). Tunisia's *maghorin* (oppressed and experiencing *hogra*), then, are the country's indignants.[9] Sometimes, *hogra's* intensities can be spatialized, as in Gafsa (Chapter 5) and Tataouine (Chapter 7).

---

[9] Recalling 2011 youth protest in Spain and Greece (Charnock et al. 2011, 4–5).

W.E.B. Dubois' (1903, 4–10) notion of "double consciousness" speaks to the *hogra* of Tunisian non-people denied their (postcolonial) freedom and dignity. Time and again, they are addressed (by political elites, educators, etc.) as *al-shaʻb* while the term rings hollow in the lives of those living under authoritarianism or in destitution. They suffer the *absence* of true peoplehood that enshrines individual and collective worth and participation. As DuBois (1903, 3) indicates, there is a physicality to this "sensation" of double consciousness, which entails the "two warring ideals in one dark body, whose dogged strength alone keeps it from being torn asunder." Resistance emerges to the overpowering bifurcation and cleaving creep of feeling excluded and rejected by the state. This kind of alienation, belonging but not belonging, has an accumulating effect. The "double" of this consciousness would recede had the will to live in dignity and freedom been entirely stamped out. State domination is never total. People carve out spaces of defiance even in the authoritarian polity. *Hogra* may impel the will to peoplehood.

Solidarity

Alongside *hogra*, brighter affective hues color Tunisians' struggles toward a "livable life." Solidarity (*tadamun* or *luhmah* in Arabic) stands out as a cornerstone of peoplehood. Durkheim (1960, 105–106) has written of the "collective consciousness" of norm-pervaded solidarity, a "pursuit of collective end[s]" among people that "links the individual with society" towards a kind of "harmon[y]." In fact, scholars of revolution have long recognized conceded solidarity as an adhesive for revolt (e.g. among peasants in Moore 1967, 475–479; Skocpol 1979, 115–116, 126–127), for eventually "self-sustaining" protest rebellion (Gurr 2016, xvi). Tarrow (2011, 11, 266) considers solidarity to reflect "common purpose," identity, and meaning-related "consensus." Solidarity is "the palpable sense of 'weness,'" or group belonging and rough cohesion, that is "emotionally intoxicating and socially connective" (Aminzade and McAdam 2001, 43). This group feeling (Ibn Khaldun's *ʻasabiyyah*) engendered by experiences of *hogra*, for instance, can in turn spur collective resistance against the authoritarian state. Clare Hemmings' (2012) "affective dissonance," the disjuncture between expectations and experiences, is germane here. Such dissonance becomes the affective departure for enacting change and "knowing differently" (2012, 151). For protestors, this entails alternative possibilities for life as a full-fledged, engaged people adorned with dignity and rights. Advancing from affective dissonance to action is not automatic, but must summon "a mutual recognition," as well as "affective solidarity" (Hemmings 2012, 157). It is not simply through shared suffering, but through an embodied desire to protest and reverse such anguished hardship, that people can construct resistance in solidarity, and solidarity in resistance.

Cognition

Both the agentic and affective feed into *cognitive* expressions of peoplehood. These constructivist acquisitions regarding self–other (society–state) interactions and social learning seek to mediate connections between inherited and new ideas and ideals. The interaction of past and present, memory and contemporaneous history, mobilizes all kinds of resources (affective and agentic) for re-matching and organizing word and world. What we propose as a *cognitive ontology of peoplehood-in-becoming* opens up horizons for self-knowing. The social acting and en-acting of peoplehood unfolds not only through affective resources, including "auto-affection" as "self-presence" in the manner of Derrida (Lawlor 2009), re-internalizing feelings of self-appreciation (reversing *hogra*). It prompts the exploration of one's social environment through solidarity, collaboration, and interaction with people, symbols, values, ideas, and norms (freedom, dignity, social justice). Crucial to this cognitive aspect is the (embodied and spatialized) reterritorialization of ideals (e.g. *al-sha'b*). In protest, people open up public squares (Tripp 2015) and civic lyceums or "gymnasiums" (Sadiki 2011), attempting to give form to the idea of *the people*.

Contentious politics scholars have perceptively recognized *potential* triggers of claim-making against the state, grounded in citizens' mental assessments of their experiences. McAdam, Tarrow, and Tilly's (2001, 25–26) "cognitive mechanisms," for instance, "operate through alternations of individual and collective perception" of the situation(s) at hand. Writers on protest social psychology have sought to explicate its emotional and cognitive individual (Gurr 2016) and group features (e.g. Van Stekelenburg and Klandermans 2013, 893–894). Cognition also contains an element of collective "counter-memory" that disputes or modifies dominant (historical) narratives by the state (Wheedon and Jordan 2012, 150–151). In Tunisia, exclusion and silencing proceeded in tandem with state-building and nation-building and attendant (e.g. Bourguibist) myths. Tunisians rebut and insist on their existence and presence as *people* with a "right to have rights." Bottom-up, people-led re-calibrations of peoplehood bloom, as identity, meaning-making, and representations of self-other.

Peoplehood's cognitive side touches on feminist "consciousness-raising" (see Sowards and Renegar 2004). Sarachild (1973) comments on this feminist praxis through which women shared their trials and tribulations as a first step to collectively understanding the sources, processes, and actors continually oppressing them. Paulo Freire's (1999 [1970], 1–54) well-known "pedagogy of the oppressed" and its "critical consciousness" speaks to similar points. The journey towards "liberation" by the oppressed is a "struggle." It is not a one-time endeavor, Freire insists, but a repeated, "dialectical" pursuit of learning. In other words, bottom-up, self-other understandings of the pitfalls and afflictions of non-peoplehood spur action to resist, to change, to hit back. We can add to Freire's account of a protracted struggle that setbacks (e.g. "Black Thursday" in 1978) intersperse the continuities of acting and en-acting peoplehood. They are almost a "rest" and a recharge before defiant, unruly indignants assert their political selfhood as *people* anew. There is no struggle without sacrifices. Martyrs and the missing are more than just footnotes along the path to peoplehood. Their memorialization is part of a cognitive ontology. Protests (sometimes irregularly) punctuate the revolutionary–counterrevolutionary milieu prior to and after 2011 Tunisia.

Protest as Agonism

The synchronies of protest dot the diachrony of revolution, as shown in Figure 2.2. Why and how is it that accumulating assertions of peoplehood (in-becoming) render themselves as practice, embodied emotion, and oppositional thought of protest? Pondering this question prompts consideration of Arab politics as such. We suggested earlier in Chapter 1 that Euro-American paradigms of metropolitan revolution do not quite fit the Arab setting whose socio-political-cultural domains are not framed in a capitalist, democratizing, "liberal" trajectory. Tunisian specificity of time, place, culture, and experience ground our argument that protest as (ongoing) social doing, lending itself to diachronic–synchronic investigation, relates to "the political" itself. This calls for enunciating an ontology of Tunisian/Arab politics.

We find analytical purchase in the originally Nietzschean rendition of the Greek concept of *agon*. This alternatively political or cultural notion of contest, is possibly a "sublimated form [of] potentially destructive passions and affects," a "taming of aggressiveness" (Lemm 2015, e13–15). This feature of Greek social life paradoxically enabled Greek community-making, according to Nietzsche's various interpreters (Lemm 2015). Resulting tensions between individuals and collectives, unity and competition, carried over into (Western) modernity that drew Nietzsche's scathing, nihilistic critiques (Lemm 2015). Chantal Mouffe has famously picked up this concept of *agon* in her theorizing on radical democracy. Mouffe (1999) proposes an "agonistic pluralism" that parts ways with what she considers the unrealistic idealism of "deliberative" conceptions of democracy. Habermasian attempts to construct, both theoretically and practically, an "ideal speech situation," a communicative action platform for open, rational, inclusive, rule-bounded debate where the better argument wins, are off the mark (Mouffe 1999, 749–752). "Rational consensus," she continues, is no more than a "dream," couched in a "fantasy" ignoring "power and antagonism" (Mouffe 1999, 750–752). Here, Mouffe differentiates between "the political," which for her is "the dimension of antagonism that is inherent in all human society," and "politics." The latter concerns the "practices, discourses, and institutions" that administer and manage "the political," to "domesticate its hostility" (Mouffe 1999, 754). In other words, for Mouffe it is conflict that irrefutably defines human existence and relations. Politics is thus necessarily conflictual, antagonistic. The challenge of radical democracy is for her enacting an "agonistic pluralism" that acknowledges this conflict. It is to transform "antagonism" into an "agonism" that turns "enem[ies]" into "adversar[ies]" with whom we disagree but only within mutual recognition and a few "ethico-political principles" (Mouffe 1999, 755–756). Disagreement does not disappear—it cannot, and should not. Difference is as close to a socio-political "fact" as a poststructuralist can vouch for. Conflict remains, but she reins it in through a democratic moral-institutional framework.

We take ontological cues from Mouffe, maintaining that for Tunisians and Arabs "the political" is by nature conflictual. For our analysis, we remain in Mouffe's "political" territory. In these anti/postcolonial societies and states, "politics" remains mired in the authoritarian. The democratic horizon opened up only in 2011. Center, periphery, margin, interior, colonizer, colonized, state, society, rural, urban, tribe, ideology, have, have-not—are all locked into various patterns of conflictual relations that have defined and continue to define "the political" in the Arab setting. In these non-democratic, authoritarian locales, conflict and (ant)agonism run deep, creating fissures about what *politics* should be, how political community should be imagined, what participation and citizenship mean. Power and distributional disparities are rampant, giving rise to such conflict. Ibn Khaldun's prismatic concept of *'asabiyyah*, in fact, involves taming other *'asabiyyat*. The political history of Arabs is one of repeated attempts to *tame*, rather than accommodate, conflict. Monarchs, state-builders, and any number of elites seek to avert the discordant unrest (*fitnah*) instigated by multitudes, rebels, revolutions, and peoplehood.

Against this background, we can understand the (anti)politics of *protest* as a sort of agonism, reflecting underlying conflicts and even "conflicting ontologies" (Wight 2006) constituting the political. True to our critique of (Western) theories of protest and revolution, we put forth an alternative understanding. Putatively emancipated publics that confront misery and marginalization are not always given to the aesthetics of postcolonial state politics. They may not be amenable to patriotism, nationalism, unified identity, and rationality underpinning newly independent states and their membership. People need not be rational or loyal when they are actually struggling for survival. Nationalist canticles do not always echo in the hearts and minds of the excluded, the repressed, and the deprived. This dynamic begets the agonistic posture that materializes as protest. Arab protest, we suggest, is in this way distinct from the "claim-making" on the state (Tilly 1978). The polity itself, Tilly's (democratic) state and its apparatuses, the (industrialized, capitalist) economy, do not form Tunisia's structural scaffolding. Arab-side, protest is not, therefore, an *alternative, extra-parliamentary* version of politics. It is (a form of) politics itself, emanating from "the political" that is at its heart conflictual. Protest as the original and perpetual political contest: this is the specifically Arab variant that we conceive of here. It is the (often-fragmented) people's rejoinder, their assertion of presence, voice, demands, rights, in perpetual struggles against domination. Agonistic protest additionally involves mediation grasped from below, performances of acted and enacted self-representation. Hannah Pitkin (1967, 81) suggests that "representation always means that something absent is made present in some sense, although not literally present". Hence, representation is "'standing-for' something absent" whether regarded descriptively or symbolically (1967, 84). What she regards as a "standing-for" transmogrified under the postcolonial Arab state. Under authoritarianism, an abundance of patronizing, top-down claims (by the president and his coterie, the military, other elites, etc.) regarding "the people" chased out and nearly erased the thing being stood for, the people. In this sense, protest is a kind of bottom-up, popular mediation, marked by appearing in public spaces where democracy is absent. The people feel mis-represented, under-represented, or in the most extreme case, *not represented*. They move to represent themselves, directly, practicing presence in "lyceums" of public protest. At the dawn of independence, people were still inhaling the air of (deferred) freedom and independence. As counter revolution (below) wore on, high-minded rhetoric was no longer enough. Losing steam, it suffocated the aspirant "people" who were rendered once again, "non-people." A rejigging of agency, affect, and cognition was in order. This suggestion flies in the face of (Orientalist) generalizations of Arab popular acquiescence. Agonistic protest is resistance.

Postcolonial "One-Dimensionality"

In exploring the resistance of protest and revolution, a turn to the Frankfurt School helps to illuminate how Tunisia's postcolonial regime kept peoplehood's becomings' at bay. Having just wrested their freedom from French rule, mobilized, self-sacrificing, and battle-hardened Tunisians were riding high, skating along the route to peoplehood. Emancipation seemed within reach, with all its political, socio-economic, and cultural trappings. How did the new state contain this accretion of sentient peoplehood, and with it full-fledged liberation? A consideration of *global* structural (economic-political-cultural) developments lays some groundwork. We borrow from Kellner's introduction about Herbert Marcuse's (2002 [1964]) critical social theory in *One-Dimensional Man*. This text situates what we deem Bourguiba's "counterrevolutionary" nationalism within a mushrooming capitalism tussling with its alter-ego, socialism. Marcuse is concerned, like his compatriot Frankfurt critical theorists, with how capitalist consumption and production render dissent and opposition null. Individuals and groups are integrated into dominant capitalist-based modes of thinking and behavior. Marcuse's critique harks back to the Enlightenment paradox: seventeenth- and eighteenth-century liberal European thinking arrived to engender progress, but ended up fomenting methods of social control. However, control was never total. Summarizing the book's most important outputs, Kellner (in Marcuse 2002, xxxiv) notes that critique of "contemporary social theory and politics" includes "forms of both domination and resistance." To an extent, our book, too, tackles both domination and resistance. Our "corrective" attempt at epistemic (in)justice investigates popular resistance to authoritarianism.

The problems of both capitalism and socialism afflict the under-developed parts of the globe, Marcuse contends. He projects that "backward areas" such as Egypt and India "are likely to succumb" to a brand of "neo-colonialism" or a variously a "terroristic system of primary accumulation" (Marcuse 2002, 49–50). Yet Marcuse finds the prospect of total revolution unlikely, given the hegemony of both Eastern and Western blocs (2002, 50–51). Thus, formerly colonized societies face the daunting prospect of reincarnated colonialism on the path to industrialization and social-material advancement. There is no likely escape from one-dimensionality. Marcuse also writes of "totalitarian social control" stemming from technology. Recurring patterns of domination and social control stamp the praxis of peripheral capitalism and subsequently failed local development (see also Bousnina 2019). The idea of the "one-dimensional man" is striking. It hints at a new radicalism and possibilities of changing the system through struggle. Particularly, the "Great Refusal" of state oppression rings true in the Tunisian context. Marcuse helps to demonstrate "what was wrong with the system," exerting impact on the student movement, "exhilarated when the Great Refusal was being acted out on a grand scale" (Kellner in Marcuse 2002, xxxvi). A student of Marcuse in 1968, Angela Davis (2019) recalls his enthusiasm for the student movement as a theory-practice fusion gesturing toward "new possibilities of emancipation."

Also relevant to the Tunisian and Arab settings is Marcuse's concept of "false needs." Elaborating, he writes, "'False' are those which are superimposed upon the individual by particular social interests in his oppression; the needs which perpetuate toil, aggressiveness, misery, and injustice" (Marcuse 2002, 7). People are fixated on conformism and consumption, trapped into the status quo, precluding a capacity or even desire for dissent. False needs are almost an illusory "happiness." Herein lies the paradox of affluent society: through "overdevelopment," people become part of a system that is oppressive (Marcuse 2002, 246). For our purposes, independence from the French is the shift from social progress to control—the Arab world's "Enlightenment" moment, applying Marcuse's analysis. Integration of thought into the vagaries of a term such as *Bourguibism* itself has created extensive problems. Tunisians are hard-pressed to find the means of transcending allegiance to ideology and a charismatic leader (the Supreme Combatant). When they do, polarization within their own society arises to harangue them. It is almost an internalization of Bourguiba's famed declaration that, "Out of the dust of individuals, of a magma of tribes, of sub-tribes, all bent under the yoke of resignation and fatalism, I created a people of citizens" (June 1973 speech before the International Labor Organization; see also Krayyim 2000, 17). ("The dust of individuals" is the same phrase by which the French colonizers referred to Tunisians, according to Al-Taimoumi (2023, 134).)

Furthermore, the ideology of the "one-dimensional man," where the masses buy into a particular forward-looking worldview, is the precursor to the repressive practices of Marcuse's counterrevolution. Policing, education, and bureaucratized development become systems of oppression and control. We adapt this concept, positing that "one-dimensional thought" deepened or set in place counterrevolution. "False needs" in the postcolonial Tunisian context relate to the reproduction of the state. Sacrifice and submissiveness to the state becomes social control. Control by consumerism, industrial society, and "technological rationality" are somewhat subtle structures built into people's production, consumption, and work practices. In authoritarian societies, social control manifests in ideology, unregulated policing, military bureaucracy, the arts, school curricula, labor relations, sports, the sciences, architecture, the media, etc. Moreover, Arab counterrevolution distorted society and even communication, truncated into transmission from the state to the rest. Such suffocation prevented the rise of a quasi-Habermasian "public sphere," a shared space where society's individuals and collectivities come together to express diverse views and arguments. The management of authoritarianism and single-party rule, including "Neo-Destour[10] hegemony" (Ashford 1965, 218), also feature a manipulation of

---

[10] It began its long career in 1912 as the Destour or Constitution, created by former Sadiki college alumni, civil and intellectual activists, led at the time by the Young Tunisians of Ali Bash Hamba. In June 1920 Sheikh Abdelaziz Tha'alibi formalized it as a political party: the Tunisia Free Constitutional Party

the public: unity, development, progress, espoused by Bourguibists and others. In peripheral contexts, society was dependent on the state, which did not allow material or immaterial initiative. This would be uniformity as "conformity," which Marcuse rejects. Tunisia's peoplehood was in peril; it had to be (re)invented.

The Post-independence Crucible: From Resistance to Counterrevolution

Compounded ideological-coercive control sets the stage for counterrevolution in Tunisia after independence from the French in 1956, a "revolution" that remained imponderable. Tunisians saw little of the glow of emancipation from colonialism that was to descend on their newly independent country. Protest and revolution erupt and re-erupt, we argue, against the backdrop of counterrevolution. Reversing the revolution–counterrevolution dialectic, we suggest that postcolonial nationalism since formal independence, under the auspices of Bourguibism, essentially sought to constrain "the people." The book re-reads the postcolonial nationalist epoch as one seeking to abort the same revolutionary impetus that had fought the French for freedom and self-determination. Marcuse writes of counterrevolution as "fear of revolution" whereby "capitalism reorganizes itself to meet the threat of a revolution." Revolution would threaten capitalism's political-economic hegemony (Marcuse 1972, 1–2). Marcuse's (1972) counterrevolution refers to capitalism, namely, being "preventive." It is underpinned by a system that blocks any attempts at revolution, even via the implements of the state, be they democratic, authoritarian, or ultimately fascist. In our portrayal, counterrevolution smothers *precursors to* revolution.

In the immediate wake of independence, the false needs of "one-dimensional" control converged with nationalism. This dangerous duo served as counterrevolution that sought to reverse any gains or potential for *peoplehood* among Tunisians. For a brief moment, revolutionary figures, including those struggling alongside Bourguiba from Farhet Hached to Habib Achour, among others, had led and mobilized anti-colonial resistance by the people. Just as the "self-consciousness" of becoming *people* shimmered upon 1956 independence, the state made reprisals. Under Bourguiba[11] and then Ben Ali's socio-political control (Hibou 2017, 97–123), the increasingly authoritarian polity sought to nip in the bud any stirrings of peoplehood among unionists, students, ideological foes, or collectivities claiming para-state ideas (e.g. tribal, *al-'urush*). Thus, in our conception, counterrevolution *precedes* revolution, lashing out against mobilization of Tunisia's various rebelscapes (discussed

(TFCP). Bourguiba renewed it as his Neo-Destour (1934–64), and again as the Destour Socialist Party (1964–88). Its last version was Zinelabidine Ben Ali's Democratic Constitutional Rally, banned in 2011, after the revolution.

[11] For authoritarian structures of the Bourguiba regime and the personality cult, see Charfi (2015, 47–57)

below). We reverse the cycle of revolution–counterrevolution analytical and empirical trajectories, stressing its non-linearity. As we propose in the following chapters, post-independence corporatist-authoritarian (Ehteshami and Murphy 1996) nationalism emerged as the new "occupier" of the state. It sought to penetrate society; and it dominated every space. Thus, Bourguibism (Perkins 2014, 135–159) and, to an extent, its self-reproducing security-political-economic apparatuses preempted the gains of independence. The new occupier seized power by constituting and instituting power qua authority to contain rival forms of demos that were developing, "flattening" their potential to speak back at the occupier. That is, it flattened their skills to question power, to protest and contest it. Instauration of state–society relations that rested on indivisible and uncontested power did freeze peoplehood's "becoming." The new occupier turned back the clock on emancipation, dimming the glow of the "revolution" of independence.

Yet this rendering of Marcuse's (1972) "counterrevolution" was, like social control, never total. Through protest, various rebellious sectors of society consistently disrupted (1960s … 1978, 1984) the state's counterrevolutionary wiles. Dissidents chiseled out spaces—including forms of demos within protestscapes—of self-expression, social justice, and the latitude to fall out of line with the regime's leanings. Labor strikes and what some dubbed the "spring" of the 2008 phosphate basin uprising, progenitor of "infectious protest" (Guessoumi 2015, 106–117) for instance, were noteworthy. Counterrevolution was thus punctuated by surges of agonistic, bottom-up resistance, socially acted and en-acted by student movements, labor unions, football fans, and phosphate miners, etc. that peaked in the revolution of 2011. In fact, counterrevolution helped to sow the seeds of the 2011 revolution.

Synchrony and Diachrony

We have argued how the agentic, affective, and cognitive social acts and en-actments of Tunisian peoplehood, rebelling against Bourguiba's counterrevolution, played out as discrete moments while accumulating peoplehood momentum. We turn to synchrony and diachrony. The co-mingling of time and space has vexed linguists before it confounded philosophers and social scientists. Derived from Saussure's theory of linguistics, synchrony is De Saussure's "relation between simultaneous events" while diachrony "is an event" (quoted in Ricoeur 1989, 32). Working through the tradition of both Saussure and Sartre, structuralist anthropologist Levi-Strauss's (1966 [1962]) appreciation for synchrony (space) exceeds that of diachrony (time) without denial of a place for the latter in understanding the world. Diachrony as emblematized by the discipline of history never satisfactorily fulfills the urge to account for any particular phenomenon. Historical "events," distilled as dates, are purposively chosen by the historian in such a fragmentary manner as befits the narrative being told and its emphasis. Thus, history as diachronic telling is only "partial," a deliberate picking and choosing to fend off the "chaos" of any "truly total history" (Levi-Strauss 1966, 256–257). In contrast, Levi-Strauss is more partial to synchronic parsing delineating a "multitude of individual psychic movements" oriented in the "physical or chemical order"—that is, space (1966, 257). He specifically points to revolutions and wars as examples that are illustrative of this kind of analysis where synchrony must reign.

On the other hand, David Carroll (1977) is critical of structuralist (and possibly post-structuralist) stances prioritizing either time or space in writing-reading (see also Ricoeur 1989, 43–52). Here Ricoeur and Carroll break with the Structuralists. Ricoeur's quest takes him to the proposition that language is "neither structure nor event" (neither synchrony nor diachrony) but the perpetual "conversion of one into the other in discourse" (Ricoeur 1989, 89). Ricoeur puts it another way: in his hermeneutic approach, "synchrony of speech envelops the diachrony of language" (1989, 248). Granted, our analysis is not linguistic. We transplant these originally Saussurian concepts to social science—as Levi-Strauss does in the cases of history and anthropology. Like Ricoeur (1989), Carroll is averse to singularly synchronic scrutiny as it pertains to the writing and reading of texts. In order to avoid "monolithic" orderings, of "either a fully enclosed unified space or a continuous, evolutionary temporal order," he argues that the two must be engaged simultaneously (Carroll 1977, 801). Such an analytic orientation, continues Carroll, is as relevant to literary analysis as it is to history. (For us, its significance pertains to writing revolution.) There is no "origin," no single reality of identity or experience or chronologically unfolding events. Instead, a "chaotic plurality, [a] disorder, [is] inscribed in the space of experience" (Carroll 1977, 802). The task of the author—whether novelist, or social scientist—is to eschew finalities in narration. In turn, the burden of acknowledging the lack of closure in any one text falls to the reader. Explaining the intertwinement between synchrony (space) and diachrony (time), Carroll employs a number of metaphors (language/painting, sound/sight) borrowed from structuralism and post-structuralism. He notes that the dynamic between the two is "not simple, causal, or preformative but one in which one term continually undermines, takes the place of, and adds to the other" (Carroll 1977, 805).

In postmodern, poststructuralist fashion, we too propose the Tunisian revolution, *and* our investigation of it, as a "text." As Carroll (1977, 806) reminds us, this view of a text is "non-finalized" and "complex," "non-reducible to any present, spatial or temporal." The subsequent mandate for interpreting such a text is a "dual strategy" of "reading" that "looks at discourse" and "listen[s] to painting." Put another way, it requires interchangeably utilizing strategies attending to both synchrony and diachrony, space and time in the "present of writing" (Carroll 1977, 805–6). The appeal of such dual reasoning as Carroll's was not lost even on the structualists. Levi-Strauss admits that the "savage mind" dips into both synchronic and diachronic modes, as illustrated by Australian tribes (Reynolds 2004, 186). He validates the "savage mind" and native (non-European) ways of knowing as credible and coherent. He is not dismissive of this form of knowledge and its toolkits for grasping the world. As Ricoeur elaborates, Levi-Strauss upholds "mythical" thought via the figure of the bricoleur who makes use of the tools available to him and "forms a structure from the remains and the debris of events" (Ricoeur 1989, 42–45). The anthropologist refuses to attach himself to either of the two poles, ultimately retaining the "*primacy* of synchrony" (1989, 43, emphasis added). If Levi-Strauss underscores the importance of both synchrony and diachrony but values the former at least slightly more, Ricoeur and Carroll decline to choose one over the other. It is with the latter camp that we align ourselves. What does this mean for understanding, and for writing, Tunisia's revolution?

Tunisia in Synchrony and Diachrony

The *synchronic* events of 2010–11 tend to dominate the telling of Tunisia's recent political history. Overlooked or subsumed is the longue durée of Tunisian resistance and protest history. Yet as our book seeks to illustrate, 2011 was only a revolution because of earlier spatialized-temporalized protests signified by dates, among many, such as 1864, 1911, 1938, 1969, 1978, 1980, 1984, 2008, etc. The agency, affect, and cognition of peoplehood-in-becoming did not build up in *linear* fashion, but through the struggles and defeats of Tunisia's subalterns. Al-Taimoumi comments on an uprising pressure, *al-ihtiqan al-intifadi*, preceding the revolution. Tunisians sharpened their protest sophistication through methods acquired from the 1990s into 2008, he suggests. These range from strikes, sit-ins, pamphlet printing and dissemination, protest graffiti, anti-regime articles published (less dangerously) from abroad, faculty boycotts of exams, hunger strikes, to anti-regime signs waved by soccer fans in the face of President Ben Ali, spectating in the stadium (Al-Taimoumi 2013, 179–180).

Moreover, 2011 was not the endpoint of either Tunisian peoplehood (the people permanently found) or revolution (freedom and dignity achieved). The uprising (and attendant coup) of July 25, 2021 signals wildly here. As Carroll indicates, synchronic renderings are not "totalizing," only "fragmentary," and thus excessively artificial. Snapshots, whether as scholarly texts (political science representations of Tunisians or Arabs), or as particular moments (the happenings of 2010–11) are far from self-explanatory. They are broken off from the larger background of diachrony. Hence, synchrony poses another problem. By situating it in space, it amounts not only to a "reduction" but also to a "repression of" all else, including "cultural others" (Carroll 1977, 818). As stand-ins for synchrony, portraits for instance are images frozen in time themselves "the image of [European] self ... project[ed] as universal to all men and women" (Carroll 1977, 816). Taking this line of critique seriously, we extricate our inquiry from the exclusive synchrony of scholarly representation and meaning-making. We part ways with metropolitan revolution that takes Western (industrializing, democratizing) trajectories as their undisputed origin. Rather than a portrait, our explication resembles more the "collage" of which Carrol writes; it is "inter-textua[l]" and complicated (Carroll 1977, 818). This book is an attempt at a contextualized, localized narrating of Tunisian revolution on its own terms. Investigating it thus, we are letting in the "Other" (Carroll 1977, 818)—relieving "other-ized" (Arabs, Muslims, subalterns) from the exile to which they were relegated by metropolitan revolution's mightiest pens. Tunisia's revolution must therefore be *written* self-referentially. The Other is reclaimed as Self and Self/Other are forever bound together.

In the same way as the approach in our entire book, we are considering both synchrony and diachrony:

- First, by seeing the ontological treatment of Tunisian revolution as (a chain of) empirical happenings bearing the "traces" of an accumulating revolutionary milieu and an accumulating peoplehood;
- Second, epistemologically and methodologically, in (re)presenting scholarship, or writing Tunisian protest and revolution liberated from the Carroll's "European constructs of himself," in this case metropolitan revolution. We thus conceive and interrogate revolution and its writing both diachronically and synchronically: neither one substituting or subsuming the other. In so doing, our "reading"(/writing) too is limited and only partial.

Thus, what Carroll calls "histoire" (history as events and history as telling, in novels) self-reflexively admits its own incompleteness, the impossibility of "captur[ing] what is (or what was) exactly as it is" (Carroll 1977, 823–824). That is a futile task for any narrative. We do not claim this book to be the final word. Instead, we vie with other "readings"/writings for analytic and scholarly credibility by presenting abundant evidence filtered through our novel and critical conceptualizations of revolution and peoplehood. We can only offer our version of Tunisia's revolution.

Demotic and Insurgent Protestscapes

We explore Tunisia's revolution and peoplehood through the novel concept of "protestscape." In the Tunisian setting, "protestscape" captures a compelling people–power interplay. At the heart of the concept lies a transformative–constitutive versatility. Just as protest constitutes a medium of people-as-power (peoplehood), people-as-power undergirds the incremental transition of protestors across time and space from non-people to peoplehood. In so doing, dissentscape relates to the wider question of how protest, synchronically and diachronically, adds nuance and meaning to the overall agentic, affective, and cognitive churnings of peoplehood. This trajectory aids in grasping historically-grounded, largely under-represented dimensions of emancipatory, creative politics, the epitome of which are bottom-up activisms. Just as protest was deployed in the past to resist colonialism, it is appropriated in the postcolonial context to resist authoritarian nationalism. Protest empowers postcolonial civic identity. Observable dissentscapes re-ontologize that insurgent identity. They depict how it unfurls spatially and temporally in its singularities and collectivities. A kind of political "ecphrasis," with reflective and expressive description of the public squares and theatres of protest, with attendant scenes of artistry of fighting back—via words, slogans, poetry, music, chants, marches—reveals hidden stories of resistance by "non-people" in solidarity. In solidarity, they summon the agency to transgress rigid boundaries of authoritarian rule to socially act and en-act their long and arduous transition into becomings of peoplehood. Hence, "lines of escape" from "non-people-ness," the "missing people," are drawn in space and across time via protest. Through quasi-ecphrastic representation of protest, protestscapes "re-stage" struggles which commingle personal and group experiences, colonial and postcolonial meaning-making, and original and contemporary interpretations. Even if slogans, music, poetry, marches, and dances—staged within various protestscapes— approximate forms of "art" elevated to meet the goals of all kinds of moral protest, the point made about them does not solely concern aesthetics. Protests occasion violence, and involve life-changing sacrifices. People put their lives on the line, risking death, incarceration, and torture for a cause. Causes may vary but overall they tend to imbibe moral stands that endeavor to question and resist a hegemon, a consciousness, and all forms of singularity, material and intellectual. The operative term here is consciousness. Unhinging hegemony is, in a Deleuzian sense, to deterritorialize and reterritorialize consciousness. Thus are sown the seeds of revolution, reversal of political, legal, intellectual, cultural, and material estrangement from peoplehood.

Protestscape is, thus, an approach, a toolkit for reconstructing protest, ruly or unruly. As with the study of revolution as a whole, regional specificity warrants special consideration. The contention throughout this book is that Tunisian (and Arab) protest erupted again and again as a form of volatile popular participation in the (post)colonial polity. In Tunisia before 2011, there was no democracy, no sustained contests over power. The upshot has been a sort of "rebellious society," a civil society in-becoming rather than formalized, state-sanctioned domain of neat, licensed, freely operating NGOs and voluntary associations. Several implications arise. We choose to dwell on renditions that downplay both individual and collective level motivators for protest. Political un-freedom and socio-economic destitution converge for "non-people", as we have argued. Socially acting and en-acting peoplehood through protest is a mode of (informal, agonistic) politics to assert and demand recognition, equality, distribution, and regular, substantive participation in an authoritarian setting. Akin to Poland's "paradigmatic status" for research on postcommunist transitions (Ekiert and Kubik 2001, 3), Tunisia's protest and revolutionary scene is similarly "paradigmatic" for the region. That is one impetus for our situated dissection of Tunisia's myriad protestscapes, as one way to re-ontologize protest and forgotten struggles.

From Pre- to Postcolonial

Thus, we examine a kind of "re-socialization" of protest as agonistic practice in authoritarian settings or hybrid regimes. Rather than trickling in from Western models as some scholars (Dalton et al. 2010) seem to assume, protest has an evident history in Tunisia, predating even Bourguiba and Ben Ali's iron rule. Marginalization and deprivation have recurrently stood out as a salient feature of socially acted-en-acted protest. Protest spaces have often been a bastion of have-nots, congregations of the deprived, with little or no access to power: Rancière's (2001, 1–10) "the part of those who have no part [le compte des incomptés]," or "that part that has no part" (1999, 49–50). The significance of this concept for re-ontologizing the hidden, uncounted, discounted, unfound, missing identities, their feelings, toil, resistance, voice and uprising within Tunisia's protestscapes cohere with doubts Rancière harbors vis-à-vis democracy's production of social orders and of the logics of instauring political community.

In his "Ten Theses of Politics" Rancière's (2001, 1–10) critical social theory adds a creative edge to the way, in our case, one can re-ontologize the subjectivities and identities that populate Tunisia's spatiality and temporality of rebelscapes for over one hundred years. From the angle of Rancière's post-political re-reading, notions of power, consensus, democracy, people, community, and protest are reconstructed critically. Power is not reduced to an exercise the end of which is the social production of influence, for example; power as in "the distribution of positions between the one who exercises it and the one subject to it" (Rancière 2001; see also Ranciere 2010).) Rather, power is relational, having an ontological facet having to do with the conception of ruling (arche) and the constitution of political identities. That is, the people counted and discounted when accounting for democracy, community, and citizenship, etc. Rancière opens new avenues for provocatively interrogating practices of politics and democracy, noting the rupture to both. He favors dissensus—as opposed to consensus—as the arena of active and subversive politics. Here lies one relevance of dissensus to protest. Within dissensus, the French philosopher locates the "essence of politics" that manifests via "dissensual subjectification" through which difference is revealed, rather than suppressed (Rancière 2001). The reigning ruling regime that Rancière questions is that of consensual management of the social order. The practice of consensus, on behalf of democracy, routinizes a social order bereft of democracy and of an inquisitive public space. This management of consensus is realized through a "police" logic or order that designs the social order in the name of inclusion and consensus via the "distribution of the sensible" (Rancière 2001). The upshot is the production of inclusions: "parts," that are counted and integrated within political community; and exclusions, "parts" that are uncounted and/or marginalized. This policing and partitioning of the social order is reproduced owing to parallel imagining of politics sustained by structures of affect, senses, and feelings. Nonetheless, this part-ing and partitioning looms large in Rancière's critique of the calculus of modern politics. It derives from a quasi-quantification of community: "a count of community 'parts,' which is always a false count, a double count, or a miscount" (Rancière 1999, 2). The miscounting of the people, as it were, is not only anti-political, it is also a negation of the potentiality of a *demos*—made up of the uncounted and miscounted. Rancière stresses the notion of a void—the fluidity of politics, its indeterminacy. Contra to Greek philosophers such as Plato, Rancière empties the center (King) and rejects natural rights to rule. Thus, turning rule, or arche, to an-archy, blowing wide open the public space and horizon of political imaginary to include "the part that has no part," the demos. Hence, "the … void refers to an-archy, to the absence of an entitlement to rule that constitutes the very nature of the political space; ... the void is caused by the 'dis-incorporation' of the king's two bodies—the human and divine body" (Rancière 2001, 1–10).

Rancière's "distribution of the sensible" strikes a chord with the management of postcolonial regimes (under Bourguiba and then Ben Ali). The partitioning, whether executed along regional or ideological lines, involved drawing "red lines" to designate what is doable in the public space, who is counted in and who is counted out, and what emotions, discourses, values, ideas, and social activities are to be or not to be acknowledged. Distribution of the sensible and the police order underpinning it spell the "end of politics" according to Rancière, entrenching consensus as the name of the democratic game with its multiple polarities: the seen and unseen, the speak-able and unspeak-able, that is, the unidentifiable—"the part that has no part." In Tunisia, the postcolonial "police" order's distribution of the sensible closed public space, emasculating civil and political societies of plural social doing and activity. The "part that has no part," Tunisia's postcolonial "subalterns", grew stubborn in the struggle for rights, crafting enduring networks of oppositional forces and discourses and social imaginaries as the basis for social acting and en-acting, social doing and protest. It is "the part that has no part" that does embody, within dissensus, opposition to the dominant partitioning order and the struggle to disrupt the practices of inequity and exclusion. Rancière holds that politics is primarily "intervention upon the visible and sayable"; "configuration of its proper space"; "disclos[ure] [of] the world of its subjects and operations"; and "manifestation of dissensus" (Rancière 2001, 1–10). The reconfiguration of the distribution of the sensible—be it "spaces, times ..."[12] (Rancière 2004, 12) or other forms of power or empowering feelings—is assigned to "the part that has no part." Dissensus may be viewed as simultaneously disruptive to the dominant order privileging the counted, the rich, or the elites and constitutive of demotic public space, and of the people qua citizens. As put by Rancière, "Politics ... consists in transforming this space of ['police' and absence] into a space for the appearance of a subject: i.e., the people, the workers, the citizens: It consists in refiguring the space, of what there is to do there, what is to be seen or named therein" (Rancière 2001, 1–10). One key observation is in order here. In the context of protest, the arrival of the "part that has no part" on the public scene as a visible, audible, and insurgent form of demos, demos in-becoming or as plurality of logoi and demoi is a function of speech—the demotic test: Spivak's subalterns speaking or not speaking. That is a relevant question for actualizing dissensus, whether via protest or some other form of insurgent social doing. It is about demotic agency summoned by "the part that has no part." Through demotic agency, in our protestscapes, "the part that has no part" crafts the logos or logoi with which to refashion politics: "politics exists when the natural order of domination is interrupted by the institution of a part of those who have no part" Rancière 1999, 11). This is a reversal of the prior position

---

[12] A definition of the "distribution of the sensible" refers to: "...who can have a share in what is common to the community based on what they do and on the time and space in which this activity is performed" (Rancière 2004, 12).

of voiceless-ness. Under the police order, so to speak, "'the people'" is the name, the form of subjectification, of this immemorial and perennial wrong through which the social order is symbolized by dooming the majority of speaking beings to the night of silence or to the animal noise of voices expressing pleasure or pain" (Rancière 1999, 22). This is because "the difference is marked precisely in the logos that separates the discursive articulation of a grievance from the phonic articulation of a groan" (Rancière 1999, 2). Thus, in the various protestscapes we present via six mini-cases, "the part that has no part" emerges insurgent in the struggle to find itself, carve out a margin of existence, craft appearance and speak back, via acquisition of a logos/logoi. Those logoi, as in our interpretations throughout the book, struggle to speak truth to power through a grammar of social justice and alternative imagining of politics and of political community. As Rancière avers, through logos, the formerly miscounted, dis-counted, or uncounted—or the "missing"—come to count via logos/logoi and speech by virtue of proving their appearance, their presence by being "capable of enunciating what is just" (Rancière 1999, 23).

Students, syndicalists, women, and other groups, take on the state through protests in somewhat distinct protest cultures. We showcase them by examining their respective protestscapes. As we demonstrate later in this chapter, Tunisia's diachronic protests that dot the time/space continuum of its revolutionary milieu have been precolonial, colonial, postcolonial, and post-revolutionary. The mixed dynamics of protest depict a *prismatic* situation, as our protestscapes will show. Protests are thus not just a form of popular participation. They are also tests of the regime, contests over power, and demands for access to power that democracy would have afforded and authoritarianism did not. In the absence of democratic representation, protests can be thought of as forms of demos, formerly "the part that has no part," crafting logoi, speech to scrutinize power-holders under single party rule.

Moreover, protests have not simply fizzled out since the 2011 elections. Harkening back to a history of constitutionalism in the country, from 1861 to 1959 (Bouguerra 2012b), the democratic constitution of 2014 did not dampen the protest impetus (see Chapters 6–7). Regional comparisons can be instructive if not necessarily predictive. Ekiert and Kubik (2001, 7) trace an inverse relationship between a divided, fragile party system and state institutions, on the one hand, and expanding "contentious-ness of civil society" that helped consolidate new Polish democracy. Thus, our protestscapes also include post-revolutionary synchronies: recent phosphate mining activism, Kamour, and the ultras, also hinting at political disaffection building up to July 25, 2021.

A Four-Pronged Approach to Protestscapes

Protestscape thus unravels through an interdisciplinary lens, as shown in Figure 2.2. It "visualizes" in order to see the multi-dimensionality of protest. This "visualization" is mediated through a focus on imaginary, versus imagery of, for instance Lynch's

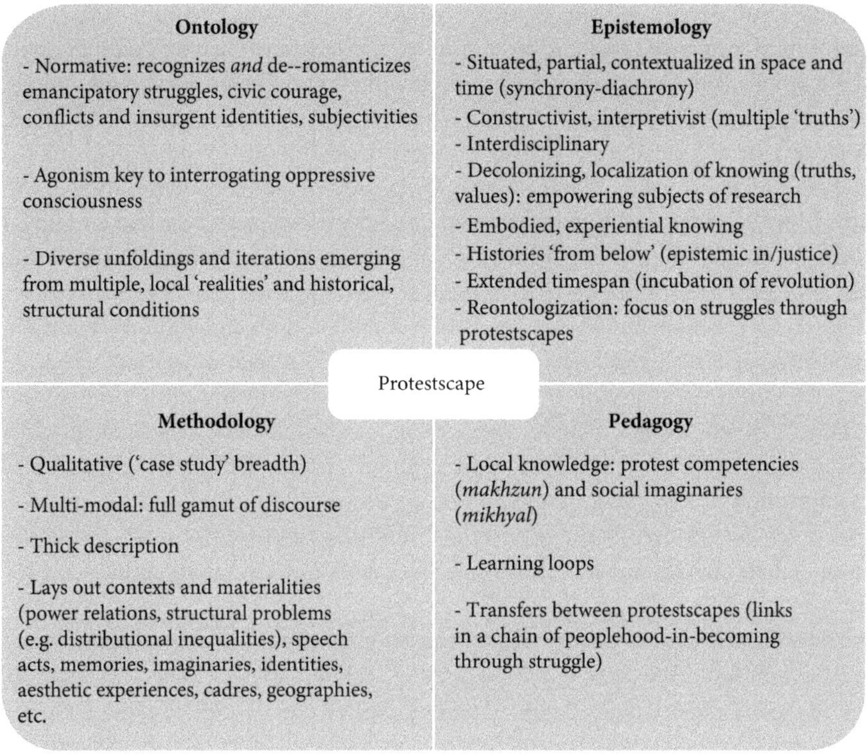

Ontology - Normative: recognizes *and* de-romanticizes emancipatory struggles, civic courage, conflicts and insurgent identities, subjectivities - Agonism key to interrogating oppressive consciousness - Diverse unfoldings and iterations emerging from multiple, local 'realities' and historical, structural conditions	**Epistemology** - Situated, partial, contextualized in space and time (synchrony-diachrony) - Constructivist, interpretivist (multiple 'truths') - Interdisciplinary - Decolonizing, localization of knowing (truths, values): empowering subjects of research - Embodied, experiential knowing - Histories 'from below' (epistemic in/justice) - Extended timespan (incubation of revolution) - Reontologization: focus on struggles through protestscapes
Methodology - Qualitative ('case study' breadth) - Multi-modal: full gamut of discourse - Thick description - Lays out contexts and materialities (power relations, structural problems (e.g. distributional inequalities), speech acts, memories, imaginaries, identities, aesthetic experiences, cadres, geographies, etc.	**Pedagogy** - Local knowledge: protest competencies (*makhzun*) and social imaginaries (*mikhyal*) - Learning loops - Transfers between protestscapes (links in a chain of peoplehood-in-becoming through struggle)

Protestscape

Figure 2.2 Researching Protestscapes

(1960) "imageability of the city." We study protest through the use of a fourfold knowledge trajectory:

1 The protestscape *historicizes* protest via longue durée, tracing continuous and discontinuous temporal characteristics. Such an historical perspective allows the depiction of spatial frames, archive portraits of protestscape (synchrony) through selected segments of time. The segments are dots calling for connection, giving insight into the longitudinal view of change in protestscape across time (diachrony).

2 The protestscape *localizes* protest, from within. It maps out the "design" of power and counter-power relations. Here, the protestscape uses another type of segmentation, spatial. The geographies of protest have internal dynamics and specificities. The protestscape captures spatial-political peripheries and edges within national layouts cluttered by histories of misery and neglect on which endless pictures of marginalization and attendant affects of solidarity, community, identity, human worth, anger, and rebellion are set out. Study of the protestscape of Tunisia's southern regions, for instance, reveals the bewildering antinomies of center and margin, hierarchies of power from north to south, haves and have-nots, people and non-people, and configurations of spatial justice/injustice. Nothing like the locale visualizes the spatiality of protestscape in its entirety, seen (material/practical) and un-seen (immaterial/ideational/emotional).

3 The protestscape re-*ontologizes* those lives, emphasizing the human face, *qua* peoplehood, immersed in a socio-political web of resistance against multiple injustices and struggles for the right to have rights, for a share of the homeland's riches, no matter how modest. It is not just the historical exhaustion of endless "blood, toil, sweat and tears." The allure of writing Tunisia's revolution lies in re-ontologizing the co-evolution of kings (dictators) and peoples (protestors) under conditions of domination, un-freedom, and inequality. Re-ontologization aims to keep the embodied selves, individuals and groupings, whose spiritedness has spawned age-old struggles and protests, from remaining muted or 'missing'. It does not keep enactment of resistance (agency) and embodiment of peoplehood (affect, cognition) separated. Authoritarian orders and logics have effaced both from state transcripts of nation and state-building. Worse, they ontologized protestors as disorderly, mob-like, and seditious. By embedding peoples in protestscapes and embodying them in their acts and en-actments of insurbodintion to power and wording, worlding and self-reformulation of free being, re-ontologization as an epistemology and pedagogy of protest seeks to relearn constructions of Tunisian protestors, not from above, but through their own discourses. In doing so, the exercise aids in interrogating accepted interpretations.

4 The protestscape *reconceptualizes* protest via interpretivist and critical (Frankfurt School, feminist, postcolonial) prisms. The luminaries Horkheimer, Adorno, and Marcuse, the original Frankfurt School theorists in 1930s Germany, critiqued capitalist societies in unabashedly political interventions (Jay 1973), reinvigorated by the 1990s (Kellner 1989). In postmodern guise, critical theory may help to galvanize democratic selfhoods (Carlson and Apple 1998). Its emancipatory thrust echoes in our conception of partial and situated protestscapes (explained below) that attempts to stamp the analysis with diversity, without shunning specificity, allowing for disagreement but also for conversation with "metropolitan revolution." In so doing, it affirms the changing nature of protest and revolution, rejecting single and fixed blueprints for their representation. It integrates critique as a broad church of "takes," reinterpreting the connections and nuances between them and their conceptual frameworks, whilst problematizing "reality," and its socio-economic and/or textual construction. Rather than adopting a fixed notion of reality, our take is antifoundationalist in its "confluence" of constructivist and critical theory paradigms (Lincoln and Guba 2018, 237–238).

Intersectional Being(s)

How do we characterize the Tunisian peoplehood aspirants that rebelscapes reveal? We propose an intersectional understanding, adapting feminist conceptualizations. Attending to power disparities and socio-political exclusion of "different kinds of difference" (Yuval-Davis 2006, 199–200) lends complexity to postcolonial Tunisian *intersectionality*. Moreover, forms of domination may have distinct "logics." Just as there is no "universal 'woman'" who is exploited, discriminated against, deprived of socio-political rights (Nash 2008, 3), there is no universal "non-people" even within a single country. The "non-people" struggling within "peoplehood-in-becoming" are identifiable by more than simple social markers (gender, race, class) or demographic groupings (women, youth, working-class unemployed). Compounded faces of downtrodden-ness emerge, enabling us to pin down issues fomenting protest. Ruly and unruly "agonism", the stirrings of peoplehood-in-becoming, manifest in protest. They involve bread, region, tribe, economic deprivation, bitter, aggrieved historical memories, or any combination thereof. Deferred livelihoods, dashed aspirations to freedom and dignity, chip away at self-worth until notions of self-hood acquire the shape and texture of the missing job at the *kubbaniyyah* (the slang word for the phosphate company in the Gafsa region) or the *vana* (an oil pump in the local Tataouine parlance). Deprivation, socio-political exclusion, spatialized "multiple" marginalization, all augment uncounted-ness in specific sectors within specific sub-cultures in postcolonial Tunisia.

This composite intersectionality is not uniform throughout the country. Considering "differences between" (Nash 2008, 12) disenfranchised, deprived, and/or marginalized Tunisians, illuminates variations and patterns across the different protestscapes. The resultant nuanced analysis further helps to explicate their coalescence in the 2011 revolution. Each protestscape we feature interrogates a unique intersectional mélange. It explores different collectivities (students, unionists, peripherals, football fans) that cognize, feel, socially act and en-act peoplehood-in-becoming, through protest in particular ways within the diachrony of Tunisia's revolutionary milieu. A kind of division of solidarity labor across sectors (Al-Tamimi 2002) crystallizes. Protestscape in this regards is a mode of analysis for understanding the politics, semantics, and contextual atmospherics of concretizing "being." That is, closing the gap not just of postcolonial expectations. Additionally and more importantly, protestscape swaps constitutionally and legally "idealized" forms of identities of "perfect" citizenship with "real," even if imperfect, subjectivities with unfulfilled rights to freedom and dignity. This is reminiscent of the known dualisms found in the philosophy of Plato and Aristotle (Bolton 1975): mind versus body, being versus becoming, ideational versus material, essence versus representation, and abstract versus actual existence. Plato's foundationalism posits in the *Timaeus* a polarity between "that which is always *becoming* and never is" as a subordinate shadow of the "really real" of being, timeless essence "which always *is* and has no becoming" (Bolton 1975, 67, emphasis added). By considering peoplehood, protestscape facilitates interpretations where *change* does not detract from existence and reality is not single but plural.

Genius Mázes

Protestscape thus spotlights the intersectionality of Tunisia's (non)-people. It also embeds and is embedded within the so-called "genius loci," the spirit of the locale (Norberg-Schulz 1963, 1979). This concept implies identitarian consequences for existence, but also, imagining/re-imagining, of community for deterritorialization and reterritorialization. Architecture is more than material structures. Norberg-Schulz (1979, 5) conceptualizes *genius loci as* "the concrete reality man has to face and come to terms with in his daily life." The physicality and spatiality of natural and built place ("environment") is rendered meaningful through perceptual-psychological encounters of "identification" and "orientation," further shaped (but not determined) by socio-economics and history (Norberg-Schulz 1979, 5–20). Architecture as a normative undertaking should both "visualize the genius loci" and "create meaningful places" in which human beings can "dwell," he contends (Norberg-Schulz 1979, 5). Places derive meaningfulness as identity markers (Hull et al 1993). Specific "place icons," from parks to churches in the vicinity of homes, radiate notions from values (e.g. endurance); personal history (specific events or traditions); emotions (pride, attachment); distinctive characters (landmarks); groups (family or community); to people's fit with their environment (shelter, safety) (Hull et al 1993, 112–114).

If Norberg-Shculz (1979, 6) angles Heidegger's *being-in-the-world* towards place and phenomenologically excavates the structures, relations, and experiences therein, we tilt such being towards *the people*. As place, space, and locale reproduce and are reproduced by a populace, Norberg-Schulz's concept may be refashioned as "genius mázes" (μάζες—masses, populace, people). It is not just the place but also the populace who make it and design its ideals, ideas, abstractions, physical form, and substance. The protestscape heaves with human relations, enveloping the full gamut of antinomies and synergies. These arise from assigning meaning, value, sign, particularity, and commonality, with identitarian resonances and contentions, dominant and hidden histories, and experiences of bond formation and fragmentation. People can inject places and spaces with *new* meaningfulness, inverting the original intents of presidents for life. In the 2011 revolution, protestors transformed Habib Bourguiba Avenue into the site of paralysis-inducing civic action. Tunisia's indignants redesigned the tree-lined boulevard, home to the Interior Ministry, as a "gymnasium" for civic action. From there, they "purged the state" and flexed their once-atrophied democratic muscles (Sadiki 2011).

Constructivism

The interpretivist bent of protestscapes draws from psychologist and social constructivist Lev Vygotsky's work (e.g. 1986). He probes the thought/language dyad as the crux of socially mediated human consciousness. Not unlike our multivalent conception of peoplehood, Vygotsky posits that in the "system of meaning" that is thought/language and individual/social symbiosis, "the affective and the intellectual unite," such that ideas contain within them emotive traces, or "transmuted affective attitude[s]" (Vygotsky 1986, 10). He postulates a constant back-and-forth between "social speech" and "inner speech." Thoughts must be put into words: inner or external (social) speech (Vygotsky 1986, 249–250). Parallel to Vygotsky's "process" of language/thought evolution, the self-consciousness of peoplehood blossoms only relationally through social interaction that then ricochets back to individual protestors/people. Internalization (individual) and externalization (collective) of peoplehood's agency, affect, and cognition, its discourses and practices, are mutually reinforcing. In this way, peoplehood-in-becoming is a constructivist endeavor. Moreover, inner and written speech is necessary for the "dialogue" of Vygotsky's social or oral speech to take place (Vygotsky 1986, 240–245). In our running metaphor (development of language as the becoming of peoplehood), the outward performances, the social acts and en-actments of peoplehood, reinforce and are reinforced by an internal budding of self-consciousness. I am a part of the people, and I will do, feel, think, and become. Acting in concert, in the spirit of Arendt, the "I"s become "We"s: we the people-through-protest.

"Partial" Knowledge

Protestscapes have a restorative aspect to them. They reconstruct protests and contribute interpretations—critical versions of and reflections on past subversionary activisms, thus expanding the empirical re-reading of politics by indignants *qua* subalterns. In this vein, dissentscapes have the potential to address glaring omissions in history, politics, and sociology, etc. . . . This forces thinking about the nature of knowledge production under authoritarianism. It incentivizes epistemology to look deep into the knowledge "reservoir" of politics or history with a view to relearning the facts of life, of the reality of protest and protestors. The crux of this exercise then is to contribute contextualized knowledge. Haraway (1991, 183–201) termed it "situated knowledges." This restorative research exercise is not about evaluation or validation of scientific knowledge. Loose criteria geared towards situated knowledge integral to an epistemology of protest ought to obey basic conditions. These include the pluralizing of authors, disciplines, data, and voices from within a given locale, incorporating temporal and spatial variation. This inflects protestscapes with a healthy degree of indeterminacy.

Situated knowledge with its leitmotif of "vision" equips protestscapes to see the unseen bias, specifically denaturalizing the received wisdom of an account of politics or history devoid of the state's others and subalterns—"the part of those who have no part," à la Rancière. The resulting critical knowledge production is mediated as fluid, indeterminate, partial, and contingent. This speaks to Haraway's concept of "critical positioning" (Haraway 1988, 586) and "critical vision" (Haraway 1994, 62). The stress on partial, contingent, and dynamic knowledge within situated knowledges—without any pretensions of out-and-out "objectivity"—enables grappling with the complex problem of protest. It is one problem which demands answers in order to rebuild, from primary evidence, a pertinent and credible genre of situated protest. Relatedly, relearning Tunisian protest and revolution resonates with Haraway's (1994, 62) idea of "materialized refiguration" aimed at reconstructing knowledge. Thus, the deftness of situated knowledge benefits, first, from the seeing–unseeing paradox inherent in Haraway's "vision" metaphor. Second, Haraway's situated knowledges as a lens enables multiple and fluid "standpoints" (Haraway 1988, 586), resisting any modicum of single truth. Therefore, situated protest not only embraces Haraway's (1988, 590), mantra of "location" and "position," but also seeks to relearn without any pretentions of a "God-trick" (1988, 584) portrait. That is, we present each protestscape as "embodied knowledge" that reflects "view[s] from somewhere," not "nowhere," limited and partial rather than totalizing and definitive. Each protestscape emits a specific brilliance cut from the angle of its location in the larger "gemstone" of Tunisian protest and revolution. Laying out these protestscapes side-by-side, we seek to trace their respectively distinctive glimmers as well as the meeting-points of overlapping rays.

Protest and Positionality

Rebelscape as a focused study of protest within a specific context cannot be, however, a neutral undertaking. It attempts to normativize the unmasking of practices and representations (Hall 1997) of injustice, domination, marginalization, authoritarianism, racism, sexism, and Orientalisms in postcolonial contexts. These "isms" all combine in denying credence and respect to marginals in the practice and in the study of politics, and the social sciences more generally. "Epistemic justice" and the "pedagogy of freedom" help to interpret injustices that continue to shape power relations in Tunisia. They empower the analyst to assume a reflexive (Lincoln and Guba 2018, 246–247) positionality that commits to refashion knowledge-making as emancipation-conscious. They name and rename the word and world of power relations and the socio-political atmospherics that condition them. In this sense, we adopt a form of "participatory action research" (Kemmis and McTaggart 2000): reflexive, deliberate, *intellectual* participation and action linking theory to practice.

The notion of contested knowledge is not cultivated under authoritarian regimes, such as in postcolonial Tunisia. An aversion to speaking and writing back under such regimes renders imperative "situated knowledges" (the use of term in the plural is Haraway's) approach. The chasms between Bourguibists and Youssefists (Oualdi 2022) or between the Destour Party and the left proved to define the brand of singular politics in contemporary Tunisia. Yet they are notable for their omission. Authoritarianism prevented not only the creation of pluralist politics and institutions, but also autonomous and free scientific inquiry. In particular, the control of word, text, author, and all knowledge production was literally the death knell for a partial historical rendition. Specifically, foreclosing the knowledge production that could account for the dyads, oppositions, struggles, and activisms that enlivened the country's politics, not to mention its historical record.

We locate ourselves as researchers who are scholar-inhabitants of a setting (an epistemic community) in which we seek to write back and *rewrite* Tunisian and Arab revolution. The impulse to indigenize (Viergever 1999) and decolonize imaginaries (Pieterse and Parekh 1995) of revolution colors the enterprise. It follows that positionality can take on a type of self/other awareness to counteract domination via interpretation and (de/re)construction of narratives. An introspective notion of positionality (e.g. Richter-Devroe 2018, introduction) is relevant here. Critical epistemology aims at emancipation. It seeks to trace and mirror the emancipation of "demanding democracy under authoritarianism" (Arditi 2020, 22). Our "insider" (Arab and Arabic-speaking) status does indeed contract some of the distance separating us from our research interlocutors. The protection of Western passports does not, however, dull the memories (experiential or inherited) of struggles for freedom and dignity, against repression and deprivation. We are biased toward the marginalized, the excluded, the downtrodden: against domination colonial, postcolonial, or even "post-revolutionary." That is our understanding and practice of positionality in this context.

Tunisian Protest: Re-Ontologizing Struggles

Tunisia's History from Below

Thus far the chapter has introduced the agentic, affective, and cognitive moorings of our peoplehood-revolution framework, studied through protestscapes. We turn now to a brief excursion into Tunisia's synchronic–diachronic protests reaching back into its colonial history. Dhouib (2017) presents a historical-sociological survey to assist an understanding and interpretation of what might be termed a culture of protest in Tunisia. The term *al-mughayyabun* (the occluded) is one refrain in quasi-subaltern study of farmers' and other protests, including medieval uprisings prior to the 1864 rebellion.[13] Popular revolts in medieval Tunisia were not infrequent. They involved rebellions by peasants. But they were of much wider scope, including learned scholars and judges. However, the pre-1864 history of revolt is not within the remit of this book. Throughout Tunisian history, chaos, autonomy, tribe, and religion interact within an oral culture (see Al-Taieb 2009). Political activism came late to the South of "inherited rebellion" (Dhouib 2017, 58), partly because of its distinct political sub-culture. Dhouib draws on an archive of "unwritten sources," including audiovisual documents and what is "etched into the archive of hearts" or memorized and transmitted orally. This is partly because in colonial Tunisia, "oral narratives" were a dominant mode of historiography (Dhouib 2017, 9). Tunisia had its own indigenizing revisionist movement in the 1970s, in the "National Research Program" (PNR in French acronyms) that revamped the country's nationalist history, leading up to the High Institute for Contemporary Tunisian History in 1990. Thus, Dhouib takes upon himself the task of "excavating and unearthing" Tunisian "subterranean" history alongside and complementary to the "formal" history of the nationalist movement (Dhouib 2017, 10). (For instance, nationalist movement clashes in the 1930s.)

---

[13] See the chapter: Hassan, Mohamed. 1999. *Harakat Al- 'Ammah Bi-Mudun Ifriqiyyah fi Al- 'Ahd Al-Hafsi* [Popular Movements [Revolts] in Tunisian Cities in the Hafsid Era]. In *Al-Mughayyabun fi Tarikh Tunis Al-Ijtima'i* [The Occluded in Tunisia's Social History], Ed. Hadi Al-Taimoumi. Carthage: Bayt Al-Hikmah, pp. 225–266.

What he describes as a "democratization of history" (Dhouib 2017, 37), we consider a kind of decolonization of knowledge from hegemonic narratives of colon, dictator, and Orientalist in equal measure.

Similarly, Al-Taimoumi (2015, 16) expresses interest in Tunisia's "'silent' heroes," Farashish style, as a rejoinder to the "urban bias" of Tunisian historiography. History from below aims to rectify epistemic injustice. Scouring Tunisia's historical struggles through this mini-portrait of the South creates a working hypothesis "tested" through our protestscapes and their culmination in the 2011 revolution. Namely, Southern "protest culture" diffused and blended with Saheli nationalist syndicalism and mobilization. From "below," then, this final section of the chapter briefly maps out samples from Tunisia's history of synchronic–diachronic protest. When talking repositories of rebellion, across time and space, iconic figures driving popular struggle—Ali Ben Ghedhahem in 1864, or Ali Belhaouane and Khadija Tabbal, a female leader, among the organizers of the April 8 and 9, 1938 mass demonstrations demanding a Tunisian parliament[14]—feature as precursors of modern-day protestors. On those fateful days, recently resigned Neo-Destour official Dr. Mahmoud Al-Materi gave a speech to the 10,000 strong crowd, with the hope of calming the throngs and preventing a blood bath by the French. Protestors, including women, held up signs declaring "Tunisian Rule," "Down with Fascism," "Long live Tunisia," and "We Demand a Tunisian Parliament" (Al-Tawili 2021, 53). Al-Materi, after being summoned by French official Guillon, clashed with Ali Belhaouane and Habib Bourguiba, more gung-ho about confrontation, to the demise of those martyred on April 9 (see Al-Tawili 2021, 49–58). Also reportedly present were 300 women, including Bachira ben M'rad (Inkyfada 2021). Anti-colonial protest had never really abated. Youth strikes surfaced in 1912, for instance in the February anti-tramway protest by the Young Tunisians.[15] They hung posters calling for a boycot of the French rail company, objecting to its callous running over of pedestrians in cars that sped too quickly across "narrow streets" teeming with people (Al-Shaibi 2015, 66–67). The momentum was unstoppable. In April 1922, nationalist protests and a strike were organized in support of Ahmed Bey, whose statements in support of the party had been distorted in the (French-backed) press (Jellab 1992). The Bey and even the Neo-Destour, who the next day expressed a newfound pliability in their negotiations with France, disappointing the masses (Jellab 1992, 244–245). Yet these retractions do not reduce the significance of the popular protests that had encircled the city and marched to Marsa (see Jellab's map on page 236).

---

[14] In his 1970 novella *Mihfadhat Al-Samar* (Spiny Rush Wallet) Bechir Khraief (1917–1983) takes up the theme of anti-French resistance and the mass movement behind demands against French discrimination and for a Tunisian parliament and independence. He describes how protests departed from different suburbs (e.g. Helfaouin and Rahmet Al-Ghanam), meeting in central Tunis's Embassy Square. On the 8th of April 1938 the day of reckoning, people's "faces [were] lit with enthusiasm", scouts and youth groups, students and teachers from Zaytuna and Sadiqiyyah, mobilized people in the streets and squares (2006 [1970], 86). In parallel, colonial forces sought to disperse the crowds. Khraief stresses the significance of dignity (*karamah*) which sometimes supersedes rights (*huquq*) (1970, 92).
[15] Founded by Ali Bach Hamba and with Béchir Sfar in 1907.

The Revolutionary Century

Protests against price hikes in 1925 and sundry other mobilizations displayed popular anger at mis-rule by the French colons (and perhaps other European imperialists, under what Lewis (2014) calls "divided rule") in a grinding struggle to expel them. An account of past protests does more than simply draw a timeline back into the historical recesses of an anti-colonial blur. Historical protests manifest the kernels of a kind of social learning in the design and passing on of protest modes. Temporally and spatially protestscapes intersect, building up a protest competency that cascades from one generation to the next, one site and one protestscape into another. Social acting and en-acting elevates protest to an intergenerational art in a dynamism that spills across space and time. What we conceive of here as protest competency encompasses the inherited repository (*makhzun*) of human and normative capital. This stock of competencies and its attendant norms, morals, sacrifices, tenacity, resilience, solidarities, and memories has agentic, affective, and cognitive elements and implications. Studying protestscapes is an attempt to visualize not just the public display of protests, but also what is hidden from performative view (e.g. emotions, memories). Examining protest is more than seeing: it is also accounting for the "unseen."

There is nothing submissive in Tunisia's long history of struggle, hinted at in Figure 2.3. It brims with inherited and learned protest traditions. The resulting repositories are the terrains in which Tunisian protestors staged uprisings, and honed resistance, against local and external oppressors. It was this *intifadah* ethos that helped pave the way for the 2011 revolution,[16] according to Yadh Ben Achour (2018, 231). These uprisings featured the likes of Ali Bach Hamba, Rachid Sfar, Misbah Jarbou in the past, and leaders of the phosphate basin and Kamour protestors in contemporary times. The resulting blows administered against the archaic and corrupt Bey system in 1864 or against the French in 1911 (the Jallaz protests) did not shake the orders of human subjugation to their foundations. But they remain indelibly etched in the Tunisian psyche, fodder for an expanding protest competency. The Jallaz (or *Zallaj*) protests recounted in the book's opening vignette, for example, denounced a new cemetery which touched sensitive identitarian nerves as colonialism encroached on Tunisia (Shibani 2005).[17] The Jallaz protest campaign also involved petitions and newspaper articles in the name of the *ra'iyyah* (sometimes up to 55 pages!), resisting double taxation by the Bey and the French (Yahya and Marzouki 1974, 15–16). One of many swirling rumors (see Lewis 2009) was that the reviled tramway company, which employed only Italians, was going to build a track through cemetery lines (Yahya and Marzouki 1974, 19). Mosques, particularly Zaytuna, *al-jami' al-a'zam*, were springboards of protests for youth eager to defend an Arabo-Islamic identity

---

[16] The climactic protestscape of 2011 was not an intellectual revolution per se. However, some Tunisian activists developed a specific conceptual lexicon. The journal *Perspectives* is worthy of study (Bouguerra 2019), attending to topics relating to resistance and protest, signaling a history imbued with leftist ideologies and imaginaries.

[17] A conflict that Bourguiba reincarnated, appropriating the *awqaf* (Islamic endowments) under state control (see Shibani 2009).

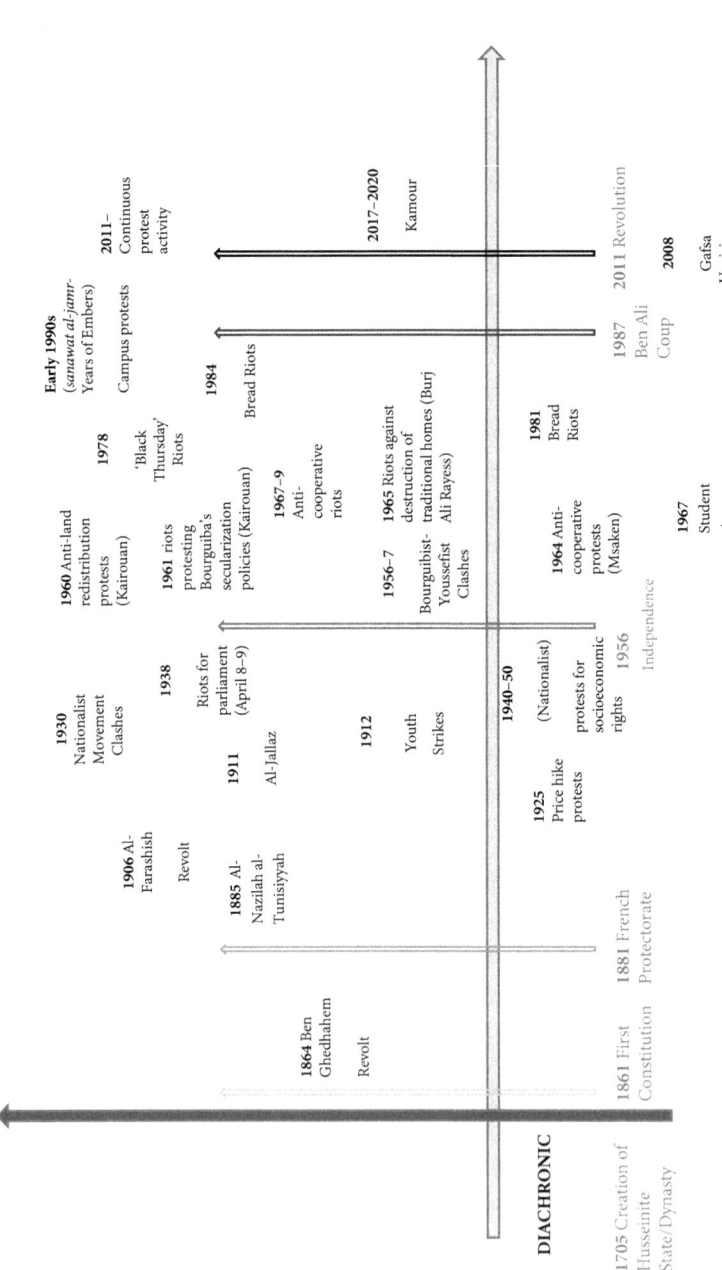

Figure 2.3 Synchrony–Diachrony in Tunisia's Revolutionary Élan, 1864–Present

against cultural imperialism (Yahya and Marzouki 1974, 20–21). Like other anti-colonial synchronic protestscapes, the "battle of Jallaz" embodies a "multi-faceted popular resistance," no less than a "political uprising" aimed at expelling foreign occupation (Yahya and Marzouki 1974, 11–12). Even the early Bourguiba narrated it as a permanent memory moment informing his own early political consciousness (Yahya and Marzouki 1974, 7). Such historical feats of resistance were engraved onto Tunisian memory and nourished modern-day agency, affect, and cognition within the occupiers of the public squares. Acquired protest competencies stretch into ongoing struggles throughout the North African country. Diachronically accumulating, adapted, and disseminated through social learning, this cross-pollination etched a "protest ethos" (which we will take up shortly), into a sprouting and germinating self-consciousness of peoplehood.

Tunisia's Protest Crucible

Tunisia's synchronic–diachronic revolutionary élan exploded in what we regard as the *crucible* of the nineteenth century. The crucible is a metaphor for a kind of "zeitgeist" in which the dynamism of the times, as figures or events, and the affect that conditioned mood and intellect drove a spirit of dramatic change, ruly and unruly, positive and negative, internal and external. As Tunisia was sitting on the cusp of cascading change, the politics of the mid-1800s was turbulent, replete with villains (Khaznadar, General Zarrouq) and heroes (Ahmed Bey) (Brown 1974), Ben Ghedhahem). Events and characters, plotting to amass power or topple it within a decaying order were being sucked into the vortex of insecurity from lurking perils, local rebels, and external colonists, and the influx of new ideas, conservative and reformist. Tunisia's crucible was an era replete with modernizing intellectual and political elites rolling out *Nahdah* (Arab renaissance) (Ibn Achour 2000) and reformist thinking (Al-Imam 2010) from above. From below, the marginalized burst out in popular uprisings. A multiplicity of social and political forces and movements and ideas were boiling in the resulting "cauldron." In a sense, Tunisia's crucible was an *assemblage* (Sadiki 2020, 50–59) of rippling ideas and actors, of rippling material and immaterial forces. A new intellectual momentum, a dizzying distribution of newspapers, a rumbling youth's civic activism (El-Douggui 1999 9–15), all bubbled in the transformative propulsion of an Arab renaissance. Women's associations (Rahmuni 1998, 112–113) included the Tunisian Islamic Women's Union founded by Bachira ben M'rad, espousing the mantra "educate women if you aim for splendor and dignity" (Al-Tawili 2021, 117–123). Tunis was a hub (Al-Tawwati 2003) in this broader Arab reawakening. Coffeehouses buzzed with the creativity and curiosity of a new cultural-political literati (Al-Bakkoush 2010). Urban and cultural development pronounced a civility for the times.

The crucible was not all genteel urbanity, however. Harbingers of the violence, economic exploitation, and attempted cultural eradication of an impending colonialism also sprang up in the late nineteenth century. The Bey's indebtedness, in fact, was the gateway to the avarice of French imperialism landing in Tunisia. Within this assemblage, affect (rage, anxiety, aspiration) "flowed," in the manner of Deleuze and Guattari (1987), between "bodies" that were structural, material, cultural-intellectual, and socio-political. Ali Ben Ghedhahem's revolt did not appear unprompted. Neither was the gamble of revolt resolved in 1864. Rather, the assemblage of popular motivations, grievances, dreams, and demands, stirring in the mixing pot of transforming structural orders, was tested but ultimately deferred with Ben Ghedhahem's defeat. Yet the revolt lingered in popular folklore memory, protest competency, and accumulating *hogra* all kick-started in Tunisia's crucible. A series of synchronic rehearsals would mark Tunisia's postcolonial history of protestscapes, almost re-enacting Ali Ben Ghedhahem's of 1864. The day of reckoning arrived in the revolution of 2010–11. Put another way, the crucible was a tri-partite inferno of elite political modernization, budding intellectual and civic innovation, and external encroachment. Out of this conflagration arose the bottom-up unruliness of 1864. The 1881 resistance (Wazarat al-Ta'lim al-'Ali 1986) flared up not long after. The rest is a living history of protest and revolt.

A Sociology of Tunisia's "Protest Momentum/Ethos"

Some patterns become evident across the diachrony of Tunisian protest. From the *fellaga* (anti-colonial guerillas) to Youssefists (followers of oppositionist Salah ben Youssef whose "sedition" is decried in nationalist narratives (Sayyah 1979, 381–414)), Tunisia's South was a fountainhead of resistance. These subalterns had long been written out of Tunisia's annals of history, despite pioneering protest against the French and after. In the South, the nationalist movement was late to bloom (Dhouib 2017, 90). The South(east) was a stronghold for Salah Ben Youssef, who drove into Tunisia's Deep South in a black car adorned with a Tunisian flag, to set up party "cells" there (Dhouib 2017, 91). Indeed, even desert Tataouine was politicized, as associations sprung up among Zaytuna-educated residents in 1937, including the Dwiri Destourian Collective, the Wargimi Youth (both named for tribes in the region), and the Destouri Union for the Tunisian South (Dhouib 2017, 92). The South rallied the resistance cry to oust the French invaders, including the revolution that led to independence between 1954–56. Led by heroic figures such as sniper-savvy Misbah Al-Jarbou, the armed resistance against the French was possibly launched in Medenine in 1952 (Dhouib 2017, 95–97). The *fellaga* organized themselves into relatively autonomous units of four to twelve people they called "*isabat*" (literally, gangs), usually bound by tribal ties (Dhouib 2017, 97). The initiation of new members included a prayer of two Muslim *rak'at* (the prayer unit cycle), accompanied by an oath not to "betray the revolution" (Dhouib 2017, 98). As we recount in Chapter 7, the *fellaga* were later disarmed, and demilitarized by Bourguiba following an agreement with the French. The intransigent "new *fellaga*" regrouped within the Youssefist movement (Al-Turki 2011). During 1956–57 Youssefists clashed with Bourguiba's forces, crushed by the two-pronged repression of the French and the new Bourguiba-led Tunisian state (Dhouib 2017, 174–175).

Even long before (Southerner) Ali Ben Ghedahem led a revolution against excessive taxation in 1864, the moorings of revolt were evident in Tunisia. Piracy meant socio-political actors expanded their horizons, as Dhouib (2017, 55–58) narrates. They were no longer mainly engaged in tribal raids and coalitions, among other internal matters. With the start of piracy from Tunisia's ports, engagements expanded into the surrounding Mediterranean maritime environs. Bandits were seeking new riches and power to exploit. However, after the ill-fated 1864 rebellion (and Ben Ghedhahem's killing), the basis for the seeds for country's protest (including the 1867 Kroumirs' rebellion) were being sown closer to home, in the southern and central arid regions. In the lead-up to colonization in 1881, and the years and the decades that followed, Southerners made the most of knowledge of terrain and launched raids, allowing them to take on the powers that be, in some cases with catastrophic naiveté. The southern fighter who obeyed values of honor, courage, piety and self-sacrifice, could not be successful in the face of mechanized colons or a brand of Francophile, elite-led and organized politics. The southern rebel hailed from an inhospitable environment, matched by tough communities and hard norms. What nature furnished in austerity, had to be replenished by the cunning of survival, and a latent rebellious instinct.

One important interpretation of Southern resistance is what we consider the diachrony of Tunisia's dissentscapes not being simply an additive compilation of synchronies. Rather, an underlying protest sociology or protest culture stitches together the synchronies, forged in the iron-fire of the 1860s–1881 crucible. A historical excursion thus affirms our *longue durée* approach. It further gels with our theorizing about how agency, affect, and cognition—including solidarities in which tribe, autonomy, religion, and chaos combine—carry over across time and throughout the geographic-political-social spaces from Tunisia's desert to its *Sahel*. Shared histories, legacies, remembrances, and struggles against colon and dictator alike are bequeathed, inherited, and learned through collective experiences and memories. So are conflictual, agonistic relations and postures. Tunisian protests are not incidental happenstances littering dusty history books. They are living, breathing, dynamic expressions of simmering unruliness and a historically-honed propensity for collective rebellion by the have-nots and the downtrodden, the subalterns and the deprived. In the ensuing protestscapes we try to recreate and refashion through scholarly narrative the crossroads at which memory and action meet. That is, the social imaginary (*mikhyal*) of memory and counter-memory entangles with the accumulating, intersectional experiences (*makhzun*) of protest competencies (see Sadiki 2015b). We pull the past back into the present and even Tunisia's post-revolutionary future, which will in turn become past. Protestscapes are the synchronic signposts along the trudging path of Tunisia's revolutionary milieu.

Protest as Counter-Logos

This historically-minded interpretation also rebuts some popular narratives that dominate both public discourse and scholarly tomes. One common storyline, for instance, follows the metrics of modernization to erect a pantheon to Bourguiba. The first president's state-building, his postcolonial nationalist project (Tlili 1974) that fashioned schools, built roads, and lit up Tunisia's 'darkness' with electricity and compulsory education, is unduly credited for emancipatory gains. Bourguiba's modernizing salvation is rendered almost a continuation of his campaign against the French colonizer. As though he himself liberated the country from the French. Dhouib (2017, 59) stresses that it was the illiterate among the country's Southerners who first rebelled and revolted against the colonial encroachment in 1881. Led by the storied figures of *al-muqawimin*, armed resistance (Ben Hammad 2004) in the early years of French occupation also took shape in the 1885 "Tunisian Miasma" or *Al-Nazilah-al-Tunisiyyah*.[18] Later, this anti-colonial resistance crossed borders in a trans-Maghrebi turn (Ben Faraj 2006). It temporarily united North Africans (Egyptians, Tunisians, Libyans) to fight the French in a common revolution steered by the "Committee for the Liberation of North Africa" between 1951 and 1954, partly fomented by the pan-Arabist fervor of the times (Dhouib 2017, 80–81). Primarily, "resistance movements were a [cause] of those illiterate [people]," declares Dhouib (2017, 38). That is, the country's earliest rebels and freedom fighters, were uneducated, poor, and tribal.

Another notable bout of anti-colonial resistance was (Southern) Kasserine's Farashish Revolt in 1906. Since the advent of colonialism, Kasserine has been plugged into the Tunisian "crucible," staging a geographically-rooted protestscape in its own right. The South accumulated its own protest competency (*ahliat al-ihtijaj*), built into recurring sites of resistance and struggle with interlocking dimensions (colonial, regional, tribal, socio-economic). Countryside farmers inhabiting the margins exemplified a kind of subalternity completely "silence[d]" in Tunisian history (Al-Taimoumi 2015, 16), suffering from politicized and spatialized barrenness in the hinterlands or *"Tunis al-a'maq"*. Paradoxically, what Al-Taimoumi (2015, 7) calls *al-zakham al-intifadi* (verging on an ethos of protest), elsewhere *al-indifa' al-ihtijaji* (protest drive) (Al-Taimoumi 2023, 154), becomes through iterative practice the means of survival for the region and its people. It transforms into a form of protest competency in which the region "invests" to ameliorate its laggardness, send messages to rulers, and interrogate uneven power relations. Led by the Farashish tribe, the 1906 uprising was primarily anti-colonial, but related also to the French manipulation of local sources of subsistence, due to forced quasi-sharecropping and confiscation of land (Al-Taimoumi 2015, 107). The political and the economic have historically been entwined. Farashish became a name synonymous with rebellion, dubbed the "seriously subversive tribe" by the French, alluding to their insurrection (Al-Taimoumi 2015, 14). The label is akin to Bourguiba's *agent provocateur*,

---

[18] According to author Shaykh Mohamed Al-Sanussi, the crux of the case involves a number of grievances: heavy taxes and hikes in food prices and water. The protectorate favored settler and European employees over Tunisians, especially the Beldis of Tunis. The protest action taken included a petition signed by 3000 people. Neither Ali Bey and his Grand Vizier nor the French administration met the demands of the protestors, many of whom were blacklisted, exiled, imprisoned, etc. See Al-Sanussi, Mohamed. 1976. *Al-Nazilah Al-Tunisiyyah* [The Tunisian Miasma] Tunis: Al-Dar Al-Tunisiyyah li Al-Nashr.

a term picked up in various articulations by even post-2011 politicians. In historical and contemporary settings, Tunisian politics is dredged in elite semiotics trying to expel subalterns from the "people" deserving of recognition. This in turn engenders agentic, affective, and cognitive tones of self/Other understandings—a self-fulfilling prophecy that foments further rebellion. It is no coincidence that a little over 100 years later, the 2010–11 revolution was launched in impoverished Sidi Bouzid (UGTT 2010a), lit up next in Kasserine, before tearing through the entire republic.

Digging into oral archives and other "silenced" repositories, then, has an important historiographic purpose: piecing together a counter-history elided in formal nationalist mythologies of Bourguiba's grand exploits, or of a cohesive, monolithic "people." The earliest seedlings of Tunisian protest, rebellion, and revolution appear to have been planted not by the educated, Francophile bourgeoisie stratum. Rather, it was the have-nots of the marginalized South and interior, with their traditional ways of being in society and the world, who faced off against the encroaching French. Without falling into an essentializing trap, we note the similar Southern flare of the 2010–11 conflagration. Mohammad Bouazizi's self-immolation in the destitute governorate of Sidi Bouzid is by now well-known (Henry 2015, 3–4). The modes and nodes of modernity seem far removed from a Tunisian "protest personality" (to re-appropriate Khaddoumah's (2012) notion of the "Tunisian personality"). History from below speaks in protest tongues. In both South and Coast, Tunisian protest is complex, rich, varied, intersectional, and multi-vocal—thus we weave a protestscape tapestry in the coming chapters.

Protest Pluralism: Generative Conflict?

In demography, tribes and clans make and break alliances, while Arabs and Berbers co-mingle (Dhouib 2017, 49–51) while generating (relatively minimal) residual tensions. Regionally, the North (Tunis, home to the *Beldis*) stands out from the marginalized, exploited Interior (*al-dakhil*) and South (*al-Janub*), drought-stricken for decades (Dhouib 2017, 84), home to the *Afaqis*. Tunisia's much-vaunted syndicalism, even if not quite approaching an animosity, was at least *plural* and diverse: workers, students, women. Figures such as Farhet Hached led politicized workers from 1948 onwards. In a nearly continuous protestscape, students protested and went on strike against French rule from the 1930s (Dhouib 2017, 89–90), rioted in 1968 (Chegrouche 1984),[19] and faced off in leftist/Islamist campus organizations in the early 1990s under Ben Ali.

---

[19] By the time the "transnationalism" Hendrickson (2012) charts burgeoned in 1968, Tunisia's student movement had already proven its mettle through a decades-long history of confronting the ruling powers. Earlier, Ben Youssef (2006) explored transnational (France–Tunisia) student linkages in the colonial and early postcolonial periods.

Leftist activism had long been brewing even outside campuses, an indication of sometimes *interpenetrating* protestscapes. Moreover, elite political activism was also formidable. Its significance lies as much in gradually developing political openings and eventually, a democratic sensibility, as it does in building protest competency. Historically, "palace elites" who supported the Bey to some extent sought to mold politics with restraints on absolute power. We find that this recurs in postcolonial times. Even elites that served Bourguiba quite well, displayed this dynamic with regular frequency (Al-Ahmar 2011, 38). Communists (e.g. Al-Hammami 1988) granted Bourguiba what is known in the Tunisian political lexicon as critical endorsement (*al-musanadah al-naqdiyyah*), conditional on some modicum of reform that would account for the demands of the working and deprived classes, in order to hamper liberalizing policies (Bouguerra 2019, 71). In the 1980s, as Al-Troodi (2016) implies, the activism (*harakiyyah*) of Bourguiba's opposition (Al-Mistiri 2011) paid off. It chipped into the Trojan horse of Tunisian power. Bourguiba's Destour party was suddenly factionalized and consequently, pluralized. The upshot was the creation of new democratic currents, including leftist-leaning ones. Thus, protest was not fruitless, even if it was repressed with bloodshed. Incremental dynamism and political changes ate away at the ruling regime, in a "twin crisis" of government and opposition (Al-Troodi 2016, 68–77). During this last period of Bourguiba's rule, a tepid consensus about the "utility" of democratic choice was crystallized in Tunisian politics for the first time—through collective action (Al-Troodi 2016, 76). These kinds of *values-shifting* acts and en-actments would reveal their importance later, most clearly in the 2010–11 revolution. Moreover, we glean from Al-Troodi's account that the question of democracy in Tunisia was founded on both political and social grounds. This is a specificity that has come to mark Tunisia's democratic transition and its backsliding since July 2021.

Women organized and protested, including in the National Women's Union (see Al-Tamimi 2007). Intersectional collectivities organized in movements demanding "the right to have rights" in some form, mobilizing for membership in the "people" in their respective (sometimes overlapping) protestscapes. In turn, each group confronted attempts at cooptation by Bourguiba or later Ben Ali. (The months-long 2008 phosphate basin uprising where protestors demanded jobs (UGTT 2010b) and fairer hiring practices, was shut down, with some activists killed.) Part of the long-standing grievances over regional underdevelopment and unemployment persisted, as identified by the UGTT (2010b) slightly before the 2011 revolution. As the postcolonial state-builder, Bourguiba had no tolerance for a diversity that would challenge his singular role: one ideology, one leader, one party, one opinion. The refusal to be subsumed under Bourguibism, their peoplehood aspirations held in abeyance by *al-mujahid al-akbar*, materialized in protest. In a Rancière-type paradox, conflict has been democratically generative. Authoritarian attempts to crush pluralism thus precipitated conflictual responses. In turn, this conflict which manifested in protest has been instrumental in Tunisia's sputtering itinerary toward democratization. Liberalization followed the 1981 and 1984 bread riots, a popular refusal of subsidies being withdrawn from this lifeline staple (Sadiki 2000). A recurring theme of suffering flecked with deprivation (Jaballah 2020, 135–142) runs through the past and present history of Tunisian protest. Ben Achour (2018, 223) cites an instance of what he calls popular disaffection (*al-istiyaa' al-sha'bi*), clearly visible in the declarations of the diaspora opposition in 2003 and 2005. The subsequent *agon* is key to understanding Tunisia's peoplehood, pounded into becoming through the transformative versatility of rebelscapes.

Bourguibism and Protest Provocation

A historical reading of Bourguiba's rule further enriches our understanding of the protestscape complex. Specifically, his counterrevolution paved the way for protests. Objections to Ahmed ben Salah's (Ben Salah 1980) cooperative scheme flared, for instance, in Msaken in 1964. Farmers engaged in civic disobedience against a cooperative law forcing them to merge their olive groves and to diversify their crops (Bouguerra 2012a 73–74). Objections to land confiscation and the President's secularization policies incited similar eruptions in Kairouan in 1960–61. We read this Rancière-like syndrome of "dissensus"-type politics, in a conflict-charged field that catalyzed liberation with a kind of emancipatory ethos, as part of an embedded culture of protest. This same dynamic was mis-read by the new Bourguiba establishment as a potential rival for the center of power. So, it clamped down on those peripheral spaces where dissenting opinions were expressed, where the calisthenics of a budding peoplehood played out. The center–periphery dialectic is central to this picture. Tunisian protest was founded upon a multiplicity of voices, forces, struggles, and actors, united even if intermittently by the common struggle against the French. This multivalence is a riposte to the Orientalist trope of passive Arabs, or Arabs who have been timelessly submissive to dictatorship. Hence, one of the ironies of Tunisia's postcolonial reality is how monist political practice came to prevail. Even Youssefist ideology, a facet of pluralist intellect, was sublimated.

We argue here that across Tunisia's revolutionary milieu, we can observe the transformation from anti-colonial agency, affect (solidarity) and cognition to stirrings of anti-authoritarian peoplehood through protest. Pre-nationalist (pre-independence) political identities thrived because of pluralism, but died as the state killed off this very pluralism. Tribal identities were forcibly subdued in a top-down nationalist identity project (Boutalib 2002). However, such suppression *triggered* protest: voices previously gagged, silenced, sidelined, and excluded found a way to revive themselves in forceful comebacks. These were the stirrings of becoming. The state thought it had pre-empted all opposition, argumentation, and sub-national expressions of ideology and identity, demands and declarations. Yet this variously manifesting unruliness repeats throughout Tunisia's postcolonial history in new or old guises to challenge authority, domination, and singular rule. Snuffed-out difference helps to mobilize protest.

Conclusion

If people make revolutions, peoplehood is forged through social agentic, affective, and cognitive acts and en-actments of people-in-becoming. *Protest* is the performative practice through which the tools, capabilities, and imaginaries of "non-people" agonistically challenge dominant and oppressive powers. This chapter has presented the core concept of *protestscape* as a means of observing and analyzing events, environments, attitudes, dispositions, and behaviors of protests within their localized spatio-temporal settings, demands, and repertoires. With epistemological creativity, the concept captures how protest is rooted in situated knowledge. While conceptualization speaks to specific spatio-temporal settings, it aspires to add an edge to the analysis of protest with the potential to interpret the phenomenon more generally. Each dissentscape, we have suggested, stands as a synchrony sliding along the diachrony of Tunisia's modern history. The past melts into the present and projects into the future through a concatenation of memory, identity, locality, and power struggles in claims both general and specific. From the 1860s crucible to the 2011 revolution, our brief dive into Tunisian historiography has showcased the continuity of protest, further suggesting the acquisition of protest competencies. The following chapters will delve into particular Tunisian protestscapes in detail. They present six situated concretizations of how "the people" variously learnt to exhibit their peoplehood resolve, as it were. The protestscapes do not just enter into the Tunisian archive of protest as praxis, emotion, intellect, history, and demotic agency. They record the plurality of the phenomenon at hand, speaking back to "police" orders and logics of authoritarianism as well as to academic omission, namely, metropolitan revolution.

References

Abu-Lughod, Ibrahim. 1976. "The Islamic Influence on Khayr al-Din of Tunis." In *Essays on Islamic Civilization: Presented to Niyazi Berkes*, edited by Donald Presgrave Little. Leiden: Brill, 9–24.

Ackerman, Bruce. 1991. *We the People, Vol. 1: Foundations*. Cambridge, MA: Belknap Press of Harvard University Press.

Ahmed, Sara. 2010. "Happy Objects." In The Affect Theory Reader, edited by Melissa Gregg and Gregory J. Seigworth. Durham and London: Duke University Press, 29–51.

Al-Ahmar, Al-Mouldi. 2011. *Fi al-Thawrah: Min Manthur "Ilm Ijtimaa" Siyasi* [On Revolution: A Political Sociology Approach]. Tunis and Libya.

Al-Bakkoush, Samir. 2010. *Al-Maqha Al-Siyasi fi Tunis min Khilal Al-Jam'iyyat al-Thaqafiyyah (1936–1952)* [Political Coffeehouses in Tunisia]. Tunis: Markaz Al-Nashr Al-Jami'i.

El-Douggui. 1999. *Harakat al-Shabab Al-Tunisi* [The Young Tunisians Movement]. Tunis: Jam'iat Tunis Al-Ula.

Al-Hammami, Hamma. 1988. *Qira'ah fi al-Harakah al-Naqabiyyah al-Tunisiyyah*. Tunis.

Al-Imam, Rashad. 2010. *Al-Tafkir al-Islahi fi Tunis fi al-Qurn al-Tasi' 'Ashar ila Sudur Qanun 'Ahd al-Aman* [Reformist Thought in Tunisia]. Tunis: Dar Sahnun lil-Nashr wal-Tawzi'.

Al-Mistiri, Ahmad. 2011. *Shahadah li al-Tarikh* [A Historical Testimony]. Tunis: Dar al-Janub li al-Nashr.

Al-Nabli, Yasin. 2021. *Ali Ben Ghedhahem: Hamil Alam Al-Qaba'il Alladhi Saqata fil Montasef.* October, 6, https://bit.ly/3x3ZvdK

Al-Shaibi, Mohammad Lutfi. 2015. *Al-Harakah al-Wataniyyah al-Tunisiyyah wa al-Mas'alah Al-'Ummaliyyah-al-Naqabiyyah* [Tunisian Nationalist Movement and the Labor Question], Part I: 1894–1925, 2nd edn. Manouba: Markaz al-Nashr al-Jami'i.

Al-Taieb, Mahmood. 2009. *Al-Suluk Al-Siyasi li Al-Qabilah fi Tunis fi Al-'ahd Al-hadith: Awlad el-Saied bayna al-Walaa wa al-Muqawamah: 'A'ilat bin al-Wa'ir Namood-hajan (1864–1881)* [Tribal Political Behavior in Tunisia]. Tunis: Kuliyyat al-Ulum al-Insaniyyah wal Ijtima'iyyah.

Al-Taimoumi, Al-Hadi. 2013. *Khid'at al-Istibdad al-Na'im: 23 Sanah min Hukm Ben Ali* [Sham Soft Despotism]. Sfax: Dar Mohamed Ali li al-Nashr.

Al-Taimoumi, Al-Hadi. 2011. *Intifadat Al-Kasserine: Thala 1906* [The Kasserine Uprising]. Tunis: Dar Mohamed Ali.

Al-Taimoumi, Al-Hadi. 2023. *Kaifa Sara Al-Tunisiyyuna Tunisiyyin* [How did the Tunisians become Tunisians?], 6th Edition. Sfax: Dar Mohamed Ali.

Al-Tamimi, Abdeljalil, ed. 2002. *A'mal al-Mu'tamar al-'Alami al-Awwal Hawla Farhat Hacchad: Al-Harakah Al-'Ummaliyyah Wa Al-Nidal Al-Watani* [Proceedings of the First Intl. Conference on Farhat Hached]. Zaghouan: Mu'assassat Al-Tamimi lil Bahth al-'Ilmi Wa Al-Ma'lumat.

Al-Tamimi, Abdeljalil, ed. 2007. *Al-Mu'tamar Al-Alami Al-Sabi' 'Ashar li Muntada al-Fikr al-Mu'asir Hawla Dawr al-Mar'ah Al-Magharibiyyah fi Harakat Tahrir Bina' al-Dawlah al-Wataniyyah* [Conference on Maghrebi Women in Liberation]. Zaghouan.

Al-Tawili, Ahmad. 2021. *Zu'ama' Khalidun fi Tarikh al-Harakah Al-Wataniyyah* [Immortal Leaders of the Nationalist Movement]. Tunis: Al-Magharibiyyah li Al-Tiba'ah Wa Al-Nashr.

Al-Tawwati, Mustafa. 2003. *Tunis al-Nahida: Min Al-Tajdid ila al-Tahdith fi Al-Qarnayn al-Khamis 'Ashar wa Tis'ata 'Ashar Miladi* [Renaissance Tunisia]. Tunis: Dar Al-Ma'rifah.

Al-Troodi, Al-Hashmi. 2016. *Al-Mashhad al-Siyasi fi Tunis: 1960–2015, Reading 1: Fi al-Bahth 'an Kutlah Tarikhiyyah Jadidah*, ed. Mohamed al-affas. Sfax: Dar Mohamed Ali lil-nashr.

Al-Turki, Arusiyyah. 2011. *Al-Harakah Al-Yusifiyyah fi Tunis: 1955–56* [The Youssefist Movement]. Sfax: Maktabat Alaaeddin.

Aminzade, Ron and Doug McAdam. 2001. "Emotions and Contentious Politics." In *Silence and Voice in the Study of Contentious Politics*, edited by Ronald R. Aminzade, Jack A. Goldstone, Doug McAdam, Elizabeth J. Perry, William H. Sewell Jr., Sidney Tarrow, and Charles Tilly. Cambridge: Cambridge University Press, 14–50.

Ayata, Bilgin and Cijla Harders. 2024. *The Affective Dynamics of Mass Protests: Midān Moments and Political Transformation in Egypt and Turkey.* London: Routledge.

Arditi, Benjamin. 2020. "Politics, Shamelessness and the People of Ressentiment." In *Constituent Power: Law, Popular Rule and Politics*, edited by Matilda Arvidsson, Leila Brännström, and Panu Minniken. Edinburgh: Edinburgh University Press, 8–23.

Arendt, Hannah. 1958. *The Human Condition.* Chicago: University of Chicago Press.

Arendt, Hannah. 2000 [1948] "The Perplexities of the Rights of Man." In *The Portable Hannah Arendt*, edited by Peter Baehr. New York: Penguin Books, 31–45.

Arendt, Hannah. 1963. *On Revolution.* New York: Viking Press.

Ashford, Douglas E. 1965. "Neo-Destour Leadership and the 'Confiscated Revolution.'" *World Politics* 17(2): 215–231.

Ashraf, Ahmad. 1988. "Bazaar-Mosque Alliance: The Social Basis of Revolts and Revolutions." *Politics, Culture, and Society* 1(4): 538–567.

Ben Achour, Yadh. 2018. *Tunis: Thawrah fi Bilad al-Islam* [Tunisia: Revolution in the Land of Islam], tr. Fathi bin Al-Hajj Yahya. Tunis: Ma'had Tunis li al-Tarjamah and Ceres.

Ben Faraj, Moncef. 2006. *Malhamat al-Nidal al-Tunisi-al-Jaza'iri min Khilal Ahdath Saqiyat Sidi Yousuf* [The Epic of Tunisian-Algerian Struggle]. Tunis: Matba'at al-Maghrib li Al-Nashr.

Ben Hammad, Hamadi. 2004. *Rijalat min Zaman Al-Kifah* [Men from the Age of Struggle]. Tunis: Elif-Manshurat al-Mutawassit.

Ben Salah, Ahmed. 1980. *Tunis: Al-Tanmiyah wa al-Mujtama' wa al-Siyasah: Hiwar Mark Nirfan* [Development, Society, and Politics]. Beirut: Dar al-Kalimah li al-Nashr.

Ben Youssef, Adil. 2006. *Al-Nukhbah al-'Asriyyah al-Tunisiyyah: Talabat al-Jami'at al-Faransiyyah, 1880–1956* [Tunisia's Modern Elite]. Tunis: Dar al-Mizan lil-Nashr.

Bolton, Robert. 1975. "Plato's Distinction between Being and Becoming." *The Review of Metaphysics* 29(1): 66–95.

Bouguerra, Abdeljalil. 2012a. *Al-Nizam al-Bourguibi…Al-Su'ud wa Al- Inhidar: 1956–1987 [Bourguiba's Regime]: Dirasah Tarikhiyyah.* Tunis: Dar Afaq.

Bouguerra, Abdeljalil. 2012b. *Al-Majlis al-Qawmi al-Ta'sisi al-Tunisi: Al-Wiladah al-'Asirah li Dustour June 1959* [The Tunisian National Constituent Assembly]. Tunis: Dar Afaq.

Bouguerra, Abdeljalil. 2019. *Fusool min Tarikh Al-Yasar Al-Tunisi: Al-Shiyu'iyyun wa Perspective wa al-Intizam al-Bourguibi 1963–1981* [Chapters in the History of the Tunisian Left]. Tunis: Dar Afaq-Perspective li al-Nashr wa al-Buhuth.

Bourdieu, Pierre and Loic J.D. Wacquant. 1992. *An Invitation to Reflexive Sociology.* Chicago: University of Chicago Press.

Bousnina, Adel. 2019. *La Tunisie peripherique oubliee. Essai sur le développement local, la marginalisation et les disparités territoriales.* Paris: L'Harmattan.

Boutalib, Mohammad Najib. 2002. *Al-Qabilah al-Tunisiyyah Bayna al-Taghayyur wa Al-Istimrar: Al-Janub Al-sharqi min al-Indimaj al-Qabali ila al-Indimaj al-Watani*

[Tunisian Tribes: Change and Continuity]. Tunis: Kuliyyat al-Ulum al-Insaniyyah wal Ijtima'iyyah.

Brown, L. Carl. 1974. *The Tunisia of Ahmad Bey: 1837–1855.* Princeton, NJ: Princeton University Press.

Brown, L. Carl (Trans). 2005. Consult Them in the Matter: A NInetheenth-Century Islamic Argument for Constitutional Government. Fayettville: The University of Arkansas Press.

Butler, Judith. 2015. *Notes Toward a Performative Theory of Assembly.* Cambridge, MA: Harvard University Press.

Canovan, Margaret. 2008. "The People." In *The Oxford Handbook of Political Theory*, edited by John S. Dryzek, Bonnie Honig, and Anne Phillips. Oxford: Oxford University Press, 349–362.

Carlson, Dennis and Michael Apple, eds. 1998. *Power/Knowledge/Pedagogy: The Meaning of Democratic Education in Unsettling Times.* Boulder, CO: Westview.

Carroll, David. 1977. "Diachrony and Synchrony in Histoire." MLN 92(4): 797–824.

Casquete, Jesus. 2016. "Symbols in Movement: The Calendar and Symbolic Vampirism in Radical Basque Nationalism." In *Regarding Tilly: Conflict, Power, and Collective Action*, edited by Maria J. Funes. Lanham: University Press of Americam, 197–220.

Charfi, Mohamed. 2015. *Mon Combat pour les Lumières.* Tunis: Éditions Elyzad.

Charnock, Greig., Purcell, Thomas., and Ribera-Fumaz, Ramon. 2012. ¡Indígnate!: The 2011 popular protests and the limits to democracy in Spain. Capital & Class, 36(1): 3–11.

Chegrouche, Tahar. 1984. *Le Mouvement Etudiant Tunisen 1961–1981: Genèse d'une Intellengentsia.* Paris 7: DES Sciences Sociales.

Dalton, Russel, Alix Van Sickle, and Steven Weldon. 2010. "The Individual–Institutional Nexus of Protest Behaviour." *British Journal of Political Science* 40(1): 51–73.

Davis, Anglea. 2019. "Angela Davis on Protest, 1968, and Her Old Teacher, Herbert Marcuse." *Literary Hub*, 3 April, https://lithub.com/angela-davis-on-protest-1968-and-her-old-teacher-herbert-marcuse/

Deleuze, Gilles. 1989. *Cinema 2: The Time Image.* Minneapolis: University of Minnesota Press.

Deleuze, Gilles and Felix Guattari. 1987. *A Thousand Plateaus*, Trans. Brian Massumi. Minneapolis: University of Minnesota Press.

Deleuze, Gilles and Félix Guattari, 1994. *What is Philosophy?* Trans. H. Tomlinson and G. Burchell. New York: Columbia University Press.

Dhouib, Mohamed. 2017. *Al-Fallaga wa al-Yusfiyyah min Khilal al-Masadir al-Shafawiyyah* [Fallagah and Youssefists through Oral Sources]. Tunis: Sotumedia.

Dubois, W.E.B. 1903. The Souls of Black Folk: Essays and Sketches. Chicago: A.C. McClurg and Co.

Durkheim, Emile. 1960 [1933, 1893] *The Division of Labor in Society*, Trans. George Simpson. New York: The Macmillan Company.

Ehteshami, Anoushiravan and Emma C. Murphy. 1996. "Transformation of the Corporatist State in the Middle East." *Third World Quarterly* 17(4): 753–772.

Ekiert, Gregorz and Jan Kubik. 2001. *Rebellious Civil Society: Popular Protest and Democratic Consolidation in Poland, 1989–1993*. Ann Arbor: University of Michigan Press.

Enloe, Cynthia. 1996. "Margins, Silences, and Bottom Rungs: How to Overcome the Underestimation of Power in the Study of International Relations." In *International Theory: Positivism and Beyond*, edited by Steven Smith, Ken Booth, and Marysia Zalewski. Cambridge: Cambridge University Press, 186–202

Evans, Brad and Brian Massumi. 2017. "Histories of Violence: Affect, Power, Violence— The Political is Not Personal." Los Angeles Review of Books, November 13, https://bit.ly/44CmeO8

Freire, Paulo. 1999 [1970]. *Pedagogy of the Oppressed: New Revised 20th Anniversary Edition*. Trans. Myra Bergman Ramos. New York: Continuum.

Gould, Deborah. 2010. "On Affect and Protest." In *Political Emotions*, edited by Janet Staiger, Ann Cvetkovich,and Ann Reynolds. London: Routledge, Chapter 1.

Gregg, Melissa and Gregory Seigworth, eds. 2010. *The Affect Reader*. Durham and London: Duke University Press.

Guessoumi, Al-Mouldi. 2015. *Mujtama' Al-Thawrah* [Revolutionary Society]. Tunis: Al-Sharikah al-Tunisiyyah li al-Nashr wa Tanmiyat Funoun al-Rasm.

Gurr, Ted. 2016 [1971]. *Why Men Rebel: Fortieth Anniversary Paperback Edition*. London and New York: Routledge.

Hall, Stuart, ed., 1997. *Representation: Cultural Representations and Signifying Practices*. London: Sage.

El-Douggui, Noureddine, ed. 1999. *Harakat Al-Shabab Al-Tunisi* [The Tunisian Youth Movement]. Tunis: Al-Ma'had Al-A'la li Tarikh Al-Harakah Al-Wataniyyah.

Haraway, Donna. 1988. "Situated Knowledges: The Science Question in Feminism and the Privilege of Partial Perspective." *Feminist Studies* 14(3): 575–599.

Haraway, Donna. 1991. *Simians, Cyborgs and Women: The Reinvention of Nature*. London & NY: Routledge.

Haraway, Donna. 1994. "A Game of Cat's Cradle: Science Studies, Feminist Theory, Cultural Studies." Configurations 2(1): 59–71.

Hemmings, Clare. 2012. "Affective Solidarity: Feminist Reflexivity and Political Transformation." *Feminist Theory* 13(2): 147–161.

Hendrickson, Burleigh. 2012. "March 1968: Practicing Transnational Activism from Tunis to Paris." *International Journal of Middle East Studies* 44(4): 775–774.

Henry, Clement M. 2015. "In Appreciation of Zghal and Tunisian Civil Society." Middle East *Insights 126*: Middle East Institute: National University of Singapore. https://bit.ly/38r1C34

Hibou, Beatrice. 2017. *The Political Economy of Domination*, Trans. Andrew Brown. Cham: Palgrave Macmillan.

Hirschman, Albert. 1970. *Exit, Voice, and Loyalty: Responses to Decline in Firms, Organizations, and States.* Cambridge, MA: Harvard University Press.

Hull IV, R., M. Lam, and G. Vigo. 1993. "Place identity: Symbols of self in the urban fabric." *Landscape and Urban Planning* 28: 109–120.

Hutchison, Emma. 2016. *Affective Communities in World Politics: Collective Emotions After Trauma.* Cambridge: Cambridge University Press.

Ibn Abi Diyaf, Ahmad. 1990. *Ithaf Ahl Al-Zaman Bi Akhbar Muluk Tunis Wa 'Ahd Al-Aman,* Vol. 5, edited by Riyad Al-Marzouki. Tunis: Al-Dar Al-Tunisiyyah lil Nashr.

Ibn Abi Diyaf, Ahmad. 2005. *Consult them in the Matter: A Nineteenth-Century Islamic Argument for Constitutional Government,* trans. Carl L. Brown. Fayetteville: University of Arkansas Press.

Ibn Achour, Mohammad Al-fadil. 2000. *A'lam al-Fikr wa Arkan Al-Nahda bi Al-Maghrib al-Arabi* [Intellectual Luminaries and Renaissance Pillars]. Tunis: Markaz Al-Nashr Al-Jami'i.

Inkyfada. 2021. *Khafaya min Al-Tarikh*: 9 april 1938: *Sawt al-Ghadab Did al-Isti'mar.* https://bit.ly/3LZm4pw

Jaballah, Soufyan. 2020. "*Nidal Al-Huquq al-Iqtisadiyyah wa al-Ijtima'iyyah fi Tunis: Fardu Kifayah* [Economic and Social Struggles in Tunisia]." In ' *Arajin Al-Ghadab: Kitabat Siyassiyyah Mujaddidah,* edited by Fouad Ghirbali, Mohammad Rami Abd Almoula, and Soufian Jaballah, Tunis: *Mots Passants,* 135–142.

Jay, Martin. 1973. *The Dialectical Imagination: A History of the Frankfurt School and the Institute of Social Research 1923–1950.* Boston, MA: Little Brown.

Jellab, Alhedi. 1992. "*Azmat Avril 1922: Madhahir Al-Taharruk Al-Sha'bi Wal Jamahiri: Al-Ma'ani Wal Dalalat.*" *Les Cahiers de Tunisie,* No. 159–160: 225–263.

Juris, Jeffrey S. 2014. "Embodying Protest: Culture and Performance within Social Movements." In *Conceptualizing Culture in Social Movement Research,* edited by Britta Baumgarten, Priska Daphi, and Peter Ulrich. Basingstoke: Palgrave Macmillan, 227–247.

Kellner, Doug. 1989. *Critical Theory, Marxism, and Modernity.* Baltimore, MD: Johns Hopkins University Press.

Kemmis, S. and R. McTaggart, 2000. "Participatory action research." In *Handbook of qualitative research,* edited by N. K. Denzin and Y. S. Lincoln. Thousand Oaks, CA: Sage, 567–605

Khaddoumah, Farid. 2012. *Al-Shakhsiyah al-Tunisiyyah baina al-Tarikh wa al-Siyasah* [The Tunisian Personality]. Tunis: Manshourat Karim al-Sharif.

Khraief, Bechir. 2006. *Al-A'mal Al-Kamilah* [The Complete Works], Vol. 3. Tunis: Dar Al-Janub.

Krayyim, Mustafa. 2000. "*Ta'ammulat fi Shakhsiyyat Bourguiba* [Reflections on Bourguiba's Personality]." In *Al-Habib Bourguiba wa Insha' al-Dawlah Wataniyyah: Qira'at 'Ilmiyyah lil Bourguibiyyah,* edited by Al-Tamimi, Abdeljalil. Zaghouan: Mu'assasat Al-Tamimi lil Bahth al-Ilmi wal Ma'lumat, 12–20.

Kristeva, Julia. 2014. "New Forms of Revolt." *Journal of French and Francophone Philosophy*. XXII(2): 1–19.

Lachhab, Mohamed and Mohamed Yachoulti. 2018. "Moroccan Women's Resistance to Al-Hogra in the Aftermaths of Arab Spring: Patterns and Outcomes." *Feminist Research* 2(1): 34–40.

Lawlor, Leonard. 2009. "Auto-Affection and Becoming (Part I)." Environmental Philosophy 6(1): 1–20.

Lawson, George. 2019. *Anatomies of Revolution*. Cambridge: Cambridge University Press.

Lemm, Vanessa. 2015. "Review: Nietzche's agon for Politics?" *Contemporary Political Theory* 14, e12–317. https://doi.org/10.1057/cpt.2014.3

Levi-Strauss, Claude. 1966 [1962]. *The Savage Mind*. London: Weidenfeld and Nicolson.

Lewis, Mary Dewhurst. 2009. "Necropoles and Nationality: Land Rights, Burial Rites and the Development of Tunisian National Consciousness in the 1930s." *Past and Present* 209: 105–141.

Lewis, Mary Dewhurst. 2014. *Sovereignty and Empire in French Tunisia: 1881–1938*. Berkeley and Los Angeles: University of California Press.

Lincoln, Y. S. and E. G. Guba, 2018. "Paradigmatic Controversies, Contradictions, and Emerging Confluences. In *Handbook of Qualitative Research*, edited by N. K. Denzin and Y. S. Lincoln. Fifth Edition Thousand Oaks, CA: Sage, 213–263.

Luxemburg, Rosa. 2008 [1905]. "The Mass Strike." In *The Essential Rosa Luxemburg; Reform or Revolution and the Mass Strike*, edited by Helen Scott. Chicago: Haymarket Books.

Lynch, Kelvin. 1960. *The Image of the City*. Cambridge MA, The M.I.T Press.

McAdam, Doug. 1982. *Political Process and the Development of Black Insurgency*. Chicago: University of Chicago Press.

McAdam, Doug, Sidney Tarrow, and Charles Tilly. 2001. *Dynamics of Contention*. Cambridge: Cambridge University Press.

McKay, Donald Vernon. 1945. "The French in Tunisia." *Geographical Review* 35(3): 368–390.

Marcuse, Herbert. 1972. *Counterrevolution and Revolt*. Boston, MA: Beacon Press.

Marcuse, Herbert. 2002 [1964]. *One-Dimensional Man: Studies in the Ideology of Advanced Industrial Society*. London and New York: Routledge.

Massumi, Brian. 2010. "The Future Birth of the Affective Fact: The Political Ontology of Threat." In *The Affect Theory Reader*, edited by Melissa Gregg and Gregory Seigworth. Durham, NC and London: Duke University Press, 52–70.

Miller, Larry Benjamin. 1985. *Islamic Disputation Theory: The Uses and Rules of Argument in Medieval Islam*. Springer.

Moore, Barrington Jr. 1967. *Social Origins of Dictatorship and Democracy: Lord and Peasant in the Making of the Modern World*. Boston, MA: Beacon Press.

Mouffe, Chantal. 1999. "Deliberative Democracy or Agonistic Pluralism?" *Social Research* 66(3): 745–758.
Nash, Jennifer C. 2008. "Re-thinking Intersectionality." *Feminist Review* 89(1): 1–15.
Norberg-Schulz, Christian. 1963. *Intentions in Architecture*. Oslo: Universitetsforlaget.
Norberg-Schulz, Christian. 1979. *Genius Loci: Towards a Phenomenology of Architecture*. New York: Rizzoli.
Oualdi, M'hamed. 2022. *Salah Ben Youssef Et Les Youssefistes: Au Tourant De L'IndépendanceTunisienne 1955–1956*. Tunis: Cérès Editions.
Pearlman, Wendy. 2013. "Emotions and the Microfoundations of the Arab Uprisings." *Perspectives on Politics* 11(2): 387–409.
Perkins, Kenneth. 2014. *A History of Modern Tunisia*, 2nd edn. Cambridge: Cambridge University Press.
Pieterse, Jan N. and Bhikhu Parekh. 1995. "Shifting Imaginaries: Decolonization, Internal Decolonization, and Postcoloniality." In *The decolonialization of imagination: Culture, knowledge, and power*, edited by J. Pieterse and B. Parekh. Atlantic Highlands, NJ: Zed, 1–19.
Pitkin, Hannah. 1967. *The Concept of Representation*. Berkeley and Los Angeles: University of California Press.
Protevi, John. 2009. *Political Affect: Connecting the Social and the Somatic*. Mineapolis, MN: University of Minnesota Press.
Rahmuni, Sai'dah. 1998. "Al-Jamʻiyyat al-Nisa'iyyah fi Tunis: Al-Ikhtilaf wal Indimaj." *Al-Mustaqbal Al-Arabi* 21(231): 112–127.
Rancière, Jacques. 1999. *Disagreement: Politics & Philosophy*. Minneapolis: University of Minnesota Press.
Rancière, Jacques. 2001. "Ten Theses on Politics." *Theory and Event* 5(3): 1–10.
Rancière, Jacques. 2004. *The Politics of Aesthetics*. London: Continuum Press.
Rancière, Jacques. 2010. *Dissensus: On Politics and Aesthetics*. New York: Bloomsbury.
Reynolds, Ann. 2004. *Robert Smithson: Learning from New Jersey and Elsewhere*. Cambridge, MA: MIT Press.
Richter-Devroe, Sophie. 2018. Women's Political Activism in Palestine: Peacebuilding, Resistance, and Survival. Springfield: University of Illinois Press.
Ricoeur, Paul. 1989. *The Conflict of Interpretations: Essays in Hermeneutics*, edited by Don Ihde. London: The Athlone Press.
Rosanvallon, Pierre. 1998. *Le Peuple Introuvable*. Paris: Gallimard.
Saadi, Meryem. 2021. "Al Hogra." *Decolonizing Architecture: Advanced Studies*. https://www.daas.academy/research/al-hogra-%D8%A7%D9%84%D8%AD%D9%83%D8%B1%D8%A9/, accessed June 3 2021.
Sadiki, Larbi. 2000. "Popular Uprisings and Arab Democratization." International Journal of Middle East Studies 32(1): 71–95.
Sadiki, Larbi. 2004. *The Search for Arab Democracy: Discourses and Counter-Discourses*. New York: Columbia University Press.

Sadiki, Larbi. 2011. "Egypt and Tunisia: Regime Failure and the 'Gymnasiums' of Civic Empowerment." September, 1, *Middle East Institute*, https://bit.ly/3uyP8O4

Sadiki, Larbi. 2015a. "Unruliness through Space and Time: Reconstructing 'Peoplehood' in the Arab Spring." In *Routledge Handbook of the Arab Spring: Rethinking Democratization*. London: Routledge, xxv–xxxi.

Sadiki, Larbi. 2015b. "Towards a 'Democratic Knowledge' Turn? Knowledge Production in the Age of the Arab Spring." *The Journal of North African Studies* 20(5): 702–721.

Sadiki, Larbi. 2016. "The Arab Spring: The People in IR." In *International Relations of the Middle East*, 4th edn, edited by Louise Fawcett. Oxford: Oxford University Press, 325–355.

Sadiki, Larbi. 2020. "Middle of Where? East of What? Simulated Postcoloniality's Assemblages, Rhizomes, and Simulacra." In *Routledge Handbook of Middle East Politics: Interdisciplinary Inscriptions*, edited by Larbi Sadiki. London: Routledge, 21–69.

Sarachild, Kathie. 1973. "Consciousness-Raising: A Radical Weapon." First National Conference of Stewardesses for Women's Rights, New York City, March 12. https://vrrws.serioussotters.com/wp-content/uploads/2021/03/Feminist-Revolution-Consciousness-Raising-A-Radical-Weapon-Kathie-Sarachild.pdf

Saussure, Ferdinand de. 1986 [1893], Trans. Roy Harris. *Course in General Linguistics*. Chicago: Open Court, 75–98.

Sayyah, Mohamed, ed. 1972. *Histoire Du Mouvement National Tunisien: Pour Preparer la Troisieme Epreuve: Le Neo-Destour Brise le Silence 1944/49*. Tunis: CDN.

Sayyah, Mohamed, ed. 1979. *Histoire Du Mouvement National Tunisien: Pour Preparer la Troisieme Epreuve 1952–1956: L'independence*. Tunis: Dar el-Amal.

Scott, James C. 1976. *The Moral Economy of the Peasant: Rebellion and Subsistence in Southeast Asia*. New Haven, CT: Yale University Press.

Sen, Amartya. 2005. *The Argumentative Indian: Writings on Indian History, Culture and Identity*. New York: Penguin.

Shibani, Benbalghaith. 2005. *Jam'iyyat al-Awqaf wal Isti'mar al-Tunisi fi Tunis: 1914–1943*. Sfax: Maktabat Alaeddin.

Shibani, Benbalghaith. 2009. *Bourguiba wal Awqaf*. Sfax: Maktabat Alaeddin.

Skocpol, Theda. 1979. States and Social Revolutions: A Comparative Analysis of France, Russia, and China. Cambridge: Cambridge University Press.

Skocpol, Theda. 1982. "Rentier State and Shi'a Islam in the Iranian Revolution." *Theory and Society* 11(3): 265–283.

Smith, Rogers. 2003. *Stories of Peoplehood: The Politics and Morals of Political Membership*. Cambridge: Cambridge University Press.

Stacey K. Sowards & Valerie R. Renegar. 2004. The rhetorical functions of consciousness-raising in third wave feminism, Communication Studies, 55(4): 535–552.

Stewart, Kathleen. 2007. *Ordinary Affects*. Durham, NC: Duke University Press.

Tarrow, Sidney. 2011. *Power in Movement: Social Movements and Contentious Politics*. Revised and updated 3rd edn. Cambridge: Cambridge University Press.

Tarrow, Sidney. 2013. *The Language of Contention: Revolution in Words 1688–2012*. Cambridge: Cambridge University Press.
Tilly, Charles. 1978. *From Mobilization to Revolution*. New York: Random House.
Tilly, Charles. 2008. *Contentious Performances*. Cambridge: Cambridge University Press.
Tilly, Charles and Sidney Tarrow. 2006. *Contentious Politics*. Boulder, CO: Paradigm Publishers.
Tlili, Béchir. 1974. *A propos de la formation du fait national et de l'idéologie nationaliste en Tunisie: Un colloque sur l' « Identité Culturelle et la Conscience Nationale »*, *Les Cahiers de Tunisie*, No. 87–88: 237–271.
Tripp, Charles. 2015. *Battlefields of the Republic: The Struggle for Public Space in Tunisia*. LSE Middle East Centre Paper Series 13.
UGTT. 2010a. *Al-Tanmiyah al-Jihawiyyah bi Wilayet Sidi Bouzid: Bayna al-Waqi' al-Mukabbad wal Imkaniyyat al-Wa'idah*. Tunis: UGTT.
UGTT. 2010b. *Al-Tashghil wal Tanmiyah bi Wilayat Gafsa: Al-Waqi' wal Afaq*. Tunis: UGTT.
Van Stekelenburg, Jacquelien and Bert Klandermans. 2013. "The Social Psychology of Protest." *Current Sociology Review* 61 (5–6): 886–905.
Viergever, M. 1999. "Indigenous Knowledge: An Interpretation of Views from Indigenous Peoples." In *What is indigenous knowledge? Voices from the academy*, edited by L. Semali and J. L. Kincheloe. Bristol: Falmer, 333–343.
Vygotsky, Lev. 1986. *Thought and Language*, Trans. Alex Kozulin. Cambridge, MA: The MIT Press.
Wazarat al-Ta'lim al-'Ali wal Bahth al-'Ilmi. 1986. *Rudood al-Fi'l 'Ala al-Ihtilal Al-Faransi lil Bilad al-Tunisiyyah fi Sanat 1881*. Tunis: Al-Markaz Al-Qawmi Al-Jami'I lil Tawthiq al-'Ilmi wal Taqani.
Wheedon, Chris and Glenn Jordan. 2012. "Collective Memory: Theory and Politics." *Social Semiotics* 22(2): 143–153.
Wight, Colin. 2006. *Agents, Structures, and International Relations: Politics as Ontology*. Cambridge: Cambridge University Press.
Yahya, Al-Jailani bin al Hajj and Mohammad Marzouki. 1974. *Ma'rakat al-Zallaj: 1911*. Tunis: Al-Sharikah al-Tunisiyyah li al-Tawzi'.
Yuval-Davis, Nira. 2006. "Intersectionality and Feminist Politics." *European Journal of Women's Studies* 13(3): 193–209.
Zakin, Emily. 2020. "Public Space, Public Time: Constitution and the Relay of Authority in Arendt's 'On Revolution.'" In *Constituent Power: Law, Popular Rule and Politics*, edited by Matilda Arvidsson, Leila Brännström, and Panu Minniken. Edinburgh: Edinburgh University Press, 43–60.

3
Striking Back

A Century of UGTT and Workers' Syndicalism

Mohamed Ali Al-Hammi was a brash man. His bold ideas were too big for Tunisia, as his comrade and friend (fellow "reformist" thinker) Tahar Haddad fondly remembers. He was a man on a mission. Freedom and dignity was within the grasp of the Tunisian people (sha'b). Sharper political consciousness, organization, and hard work were the key. Always on the move from meeting to meeting, Al-Hammi lived simply. He slept little and ate even less, munching on olives and bread on his way to and fro. Acute sensitivity to the suffering of the poor, the desolation of the unemployed, led him to focus on the plight of laborers. Solidarity, cooperation, and independence of organized workers were vital to wresting the fate of the Tunisian people from the French. A people's man, Al-Hammi lent a ready ear to workers who poured out to him their many woes. He was not afraid to experiment. The Association of Tunisian Economic Cooperation, the traders' guild he created, was short-lived. His attention zeroed in on French unions. Within them, Tunisian workers suffered the double consciousness of racism and humiliation atop exploitation by French mining, railroad, and other companies. After working with dock-workers to organize, coordinate, negotiate, and strike, Al-Hammi would settle on his life project: the establishment of a Tunisian union. In 1924, he and a loyal following founded the General League for Tunisian Labor. It was embattled from the start. The colons chafed at the prospect of an autonomous Tunisian body. Hounded by the French, betrayed by his fellow countrymen in the Free Destour party, Al-Hammi and his comrades were arrested and prosecuted. The League was shut down. As architect of the first organized, systematic indigenous union work, Al-Hammi was exiled, forced on a boat to Italy. After a tragic demise not unlike Ali Ben Ghedhahem before him, Al-Hammi gained iconicity status in years to come. The nationalist liberation movement elevated his standing as a nationalist symbol. His gaunt-faced image graces UGTT headquarters, (previously) housed in Tunis's Mohamed Ali Square.[1] His memory continues to animate syndicalists and countless Tunisians energetically pursuing dignity and freedom.

---

[1] This vignette draws on Tahar Haddad's account of his friend Al-Hammi (Haddad 2015, especially 147–150), as well as nationalist politician Mohieddine Alqlibi's remarks in Alqasantini (2012, 169–170).

Introduction

This chapter launches the investigation into Tunisia's diverse yet interconnected protestscapes, focalizing the Union Générale Tunisienne du Travail (UGTT). Boasting a storied history, the union's origins and development are interwoven with Tunisia's anti-colonial then postcolonial state- and nation-building. A veritable subgenre of Tunisian history and politics exploring the union has sprung up over the past decade or so. The complex organization of rich pedigree has garnered extensive interest, sometimes comparative (e.g. Beinin 2015; Churchill 2016), by scholars and observers (Omri 2015; Adouani and Ben Sedrine 2018). Our focus on the UGTT is thus deliberately narrow. The puzzle of this protestscape concerns the role of unions in organizing and mobilizing protests for nearly a century. How does protest journey through the colonial era into the Tunisia of the late 1970s and 1980s? We argue that the UGTT (and its predecessor, the General League for Tunisian Labor, noted in the vignette) engages in two-fold mobilization: first, against the coloniality of the French, then against single-party rule and the corporatist, *dirigiste* politics forming the scaffolding of Bourguiba's counterrevolution. In this sense, the union has been a force of contrepouvoir against the shifting stages of political domination in Tunisia: external and internal occupation and colonization. Second and relatedly, the UGTT mobilized against First Minister Hedi Nouira's (1970–80) open-door policy (Gamaoun 2019, 40–61) and by extension, against the coloniality of neoliberalism within the periphery. In so doing, the union resisted the intrusive and hegemonic role of international financial institutions (e.g. the IMF) in Tunisian economic and development policy. A further complication in the protestscape is the dual cooperation–confrontation dynamic between the UGTT and the state. Movement between power-holders and publics, state and society, is one defining feature of the union since its early inception.

By the 1970s, a sort of insurrectionary politics cropped up in the new postcolonial state. Workers' protests took center-stage. This dissent gained steam as Ahmed Ben Salah's (himself a former UGTT Secretary General)[2] "cooperatives" (*ta'adudiyyat*) development scheme shattered, abruptly shut down by Bourguiba in 1969 (see Gamaoun 2019, 30–39). Tunisia's protest ethos and momentum (*al-zakham al-ihtijaji*) solidified in this period. As value-laden practice, this momentum coached workers and other downtrodden Tunisians into resistance against worsening socio-economic conditions. Such social acting and en-acting took a leaf from the book of the collective memory and social imaginary (*mikhyal*) of their forebears. These included the *fellaga* resistance fighters, and fellow anti-colonial union militants led by Mohamed Ali Al-Hammi. Laborers in agriculture, mining, and other sectors organized and mobilized in the face of quasi-state retrenchment from welfare programs and subsidies. Such cuts affected the price of bread and the employment, housing, and education of Tunisians. The UGTT radicalized its posture vis-à-vis the state, mobilizing its expanding "reservoir" of members. It activated a history of solidarity

---

[2] Born January 13, 1926; died September 16, 2020: architect of planned economy until 1969.

and commitment to social justice, rejecting Nouira's liberalizing policy offensive. An array of subaltern voices and forces rose up to challenge state economic management and political singularity. Protests are thus relevant in the inventory of social groups faced with marginalization.

The chapter begins with the early anti-colonial history of the labor movement and the General League for Tunisian Labor. It then moves to unionist involvement in the nationalist movement, as the UGTT, into independence in 1956. Drawing on this history and focus group interviews with unionists, the chapter highlights features of Tunisia's syndicalism. Next, the chapter sets the scene for the insurrectionary politics of the 1970s. Cooptation slowly moves into confrontation between the UGTT and the postcolonial state, against the backdrop of a weakening Destour Socialist Party and a leader (*za'im*) losing his appeal. A rivalry of (male) charismatic 'legitimacies' (Bourguiba vs. UGTT head Habib Achour) heightened tensions. It is within this setting that the build-up to the union's General Strike of 1978 unfolded, one centerpiece of this chapter. Brutal state repression would be a stain on Bourguiba's political record and legacy, further straining relations with the UGTT. The chapter then turns to a second major episode of popular protest, the bread riots of 1984. It traces the aftermath as Bourguiba took vengeance on protestors and the UGTT alike, coopting its leadership for years. The chapter's conclusion touches on the pendulous taming-resistance dynamic into the Ben Ali era, from key Congresses to spurts of protest by UGTT local and regional members. Throughout this tumultuous history, we show how people's social acting and en-acting fortified growing protest competencies and demotic agency. Tunisia's masses marshalled and honed the agency, affect, and cognition of a people learning to resist, beginning to become. It is not for nothing that the UGTT is synonymous with protest.

Before that, we recount the origins and history of Tunisia's labor movement.

Early History: The General League for Tunisian Labor

Al-Hammi's Dream

Tunisia's anti-colonial struggles for independence won in 1956 are a kind of lodestar illuminating and legitimating founding myths. Prominent in the history of its nationalist movement (*al-harakah al-wataniyyah*) are larger-than-life figures. These include self-styled "Supreme Commander" (*al-mujahid al-akbar*) Habib Bourguiba, but also UGTT founder Farhat Hached (chief of the Tunisian Office for National Liberation 1953) and before him, Mohamed Ali Al-Hammi (1890–1928). It was not always this way. When reformist intellectual-activist Tahar Haddad[3] wrote his history of Tunisia's labor movement, *Al-'Ummal al-Tunisiyyun wa Zuhur Al-Harakah*

---

[3] Also embraced as Tunisia's pioneering champion of women's rights for his 1899 book *Imra'atuna fi Al-Shari'ah wa Al-Mujtama'* (Our Woman in Religious Law and Society) and namesake of the Tahar Haddad Club where Tunisia's contemporary feminist movement was born (Chapter 4).

Al-Naqabiyyah (Tunisian Workers and the Genesis of the Syndicalist Movement) in 1927, his friend Mohamed Ali Al-Hammi had been exiled shortly before. The French were cracking down on workers' protests demanding fairer treatment and pay. It was in this hostile setting that Haddad set out to vindicate Al-Hammi's legacy (see Al-Mukni's forward in Haddad 2015, 7–8). In exquisitely detailed narrative style, he recorded for posterity Al-Hammi's audacious dream of Tunisian emancipation and renaissance. Haddad sketches how Tunisia's first labor movement was born out of conflict with the colonizers. In the union rebelscape as in others, agonism characterizes the origins and the pit stops of peoplehood-in-becoming. As they face the violence and humiliation (*hogra*) of colonial domination, Tunisians' social acting and en-acting is confrontational rather than collegial. Experiences of numbing and intolerant *hogra* shaped more than one generation. Years later, nationalist and later union leader Habib Achour drove home the point. He recalled the "humiliation" Tunisians had weathered under the French, prompting them to "reclaim [their] dignity" (quoted in Al-Haddad 2011, 83).

The Zaytuna-educated Haddad was remarkably well-versed in the transforming economic system of the time. Himself a southerner of poor means, empathy with the plight of agricultural and industrial workers shines through his narrative. This affective identification complements Al-Hammi's avant-garde and revolutionary class consciousness. Haddad tells of workers' misery. Sharecroppers (*khammasah*) were so downtrodden that the term was hurled as a colloquial insult, a linguistic reflection of social denigration (*hogra*) (Haddad 2015, 25–26). In small industries, small apprentices (*sani'*, mostly children), day workers (*gilfah*), then bosses (*m'allim*) formed a hierarchical triad (Haddad 2015, 26). Haddad dwells on how economically unprepared rural and urban Tunisian workers were for the onslaught of French colonialism. With little sovereignty, working without guilds, they were unable to economically modernize (Haddad 2015, 27–33). Tunisians were forced to work for French mega-projects in mining and railroads, or earn day wages sharecropping. A new elite intelligentsia formed literary salons, but remained distanced from the people (*'ammat al-sha'b*) (Haddad 2015, 39–40). Haddad even flags Al-Hammi's idea of cooperatives (*ta'adud*) for mutual support and protection (2015, 38), three decades before Ahmed Ben Salah would institute the system in Tunisia. Haddad's (2015, 41) use of the term bespeaks an early cognition of Tunisians as a people set against the illegitimate government that felt no pressure from civil society. We see here the seedlings of democratic thought and aspirations in early Tunisian syndicalism, part of the progressive reformist thinking of the day. Haddad (2015, 41) notes the establishment of the Free Destour party in 1920, the "first role to which the people elevated after its acquiescent slumber." Still, the constitutional party did little to rescue the downtrodden (*al-shu 'ub al-mustad'afah*—a term he used over fifty years before it was popularized in the Iranian revolution!). Organizing was necessary to command respect from the dominating powers (2015, 42). Thus, Haddad frames Al-Hammi's union project, which he eagerly joined, as a complement to the emancipatory political enterprise of the burgeoning nationalist movement. This duality between political and economic wings of organized militancy or activism, would run through the country's state- and nation-building, into (anti)authoritarian politics and post-2011 democratization.

Workers Strike Back

How, then, did this union movement develop into such a formidable force in Tunisian society and politics? Enter Mohamed Ali Al-Hammi. After a 15-year absence, he returned to Tunisia with a head full of new ideas eagerly lapped up in Europe. He set off to put his studies in political economy from Berlin to good use. Exposure to German, Russian, and Ottoman discourses and practices (Al-Shaybi 2015a, 133–137) sharpened Al-Hammi's conceptions of student and labor organization. His words and Haddad's own commentary are imbued with Marxist-sounding ideas about class consciousness, revolution, and emancipation. Al-Hammi's thought met practice. His extended encounter with the dockworkers (*'amalat al-rasa'if*) was a significant milestone. These laborers who toiled under precarious conditions in Tunisian ports had protested before, in the 8-day strike in May 1904 (Al-Taimoumi 2021, 159). Haddad tells how these examples of misery personified were not without a striking (known at the time as *i'tisab*, now called *idrab*) history. Without organization, however, they had no group to protect them (Haddad 2015, 59). Striking in August 1924 to demand wage increases and staging a 23-day sit-in, the dock workers consulted with Al-Hammi (Haddad 2015, 58–60). Their new mentor coached them into presenting written demands, organizing committees, and engaging in negotiations (Haddad 2015, 61–62). From Al-Hammi, says Haddad, the strikers learned the steadfastness and forbearance (*tahammul*) engendered by workers coordinating their resistance. He planted in them an ILO-type consciousness of working laws and international standards (Haddad 2015, 66–70). When the Minister was not responsive, they published the "Red Statement" (*Al-Balagh al-Ahmar*) in the newspaper *Al-Nahdah*. The dock workers addressed the people (*al-sha'b*) directly, explaining how they had used "legitimate methods to defend our right to life," in pleas that fell on deaf ears, against the repressive "trickery" of colonial administration. They declared a willingness to seek their "children's sustenance even if that leads to us losing our life," entreating the people "to stand with us against the … enemies of humanity" starving them and their families (Haddad 2015, 71–72). Al-Hammi was a worthy teacher, in Haddad's telling. We have narrated this episode in some detail to highlight budding protest competencies that combine agentic, affective, and cognitive discourse and practice. These the workers acquired through a didactic learning process. The agency of moving to strike, sit-in, demand, and negotiate stems from a cognition of rights (to sustenance, security, freedom) transgressed. Self–other (colonized–colonizer) perceptions further underlie this cognition. The workers saw themselves as members of a people (*sha'b*), comrades in arms against French violence and exploitation. Affective appeals (starving workers and children) and practice (solidarity between similarly suffering workers) enhanced the agency and cognition of these laborers as they learned how to protest in concert.

The General League Forms

The dock-workers' story was a prelude to Al-Hammi's venture to form a Tunisian union. Conflict with the French union led by Durrell heaves with colonizer/colonized tensions. A new Tunisian movement incited "separatism" where there should be unity, Durrell proclaimed (Haddad 2015, 123–124). Redoubling Durrell's efforts, Haddad recalls, Léon Jouhaux[4] arrived in Tunisia in 1924 to block attempts at forming a local union (see also Beling 1964, 553). Justifying the "Tunisification" of syndicalism, Haddad, Al-Hammi, and others insisted on "autonomy" (*istiqlaliyyah*) (Haddad 2015, 126–129). Union autonomy was part of the quest for comprehensive independence. Here, too, Al-Hammi laid the groundwork for a UGTT preoccupation (independence) that would last into the postcolonial period. By the end of October 1924, Al-Hammi and others announced the formation of their General League for French Labor in the *Al-Zahra* newspaper. Its creation was a necessity due to worker exploitation, lack of competitiveness, and violations of even French syndicalist law, they asserted. The statement argued for the legal legitimacy of the new body, to be guided by the same principles as French unions, similarly connected to international union federations (Haddad 2015, 130–131). Some in the Destour Party[5] expressed support (Haddad 2015, 133). In a meeting with workers, Al-Hammi exhorted the workers to defy the (French) skeptics' expectations: "We have proven that we are capable men, who can do whatever [other] men of the world do" (Haddad 2015, 133–134). He thus cognizes the workers as a collective of competent resisters with deliberate agency, throwing off the double consciousness of colonizer/colonized inferiority. Civic skill-building was also in evidence. The birth of the union in 1924 was "the result of ongoing dialogue," notes Haddad (2015, 137). The League elected a temporary executive committee (Haddad 2015, 145). Its by-laws (Haddad 2015, 160–165) outlined an organization inclusive of faiths and cultures, defending the "material and moral rights" of workers "using all possible methods." Roughly democratic in operation, its leadership would be elected through an annual congress, with sectoral and regional representation. Membership fees would render it self-sufficient. There is no reference to political parties, confirming Al-Hammi's vision of an independent union. The logo needed to signal the climb out of misery and *hogra*, explains Haddad. The founding of the League was almost a rebirth and reclaiming of a long-lost dignity. In the words of one worker at the time, its establishment represented a rupture with the past, from "the misery and slavery of the worker [to] the new age in which the doors of happiness and freedom are opened to the laborer …" (quoted in Al-Shaybi 2015b, 61). Evidently Al-Hammi's and Haddad's fervor was matched by the celebratory affect of member workers. For its crucial logo, the League leadership settled on a sketch of a male worker breaking free of chains,

---

[4] Representative of the French General Confederation of Labor, branch of the Communist World Federation of Trade Unions. His decades of union work, including contributions to the establishment of the International Labor Organization (ILO), earned him a Nobel Peace Prize in 1951.

[5] The party would transform into the Neo-Destour upon the exceptional Congress of March 1934, convened in Ksar Hellal (Al-Shaybi 2015b, 227)

framed by the slogan "freedom is in the union." The scythe and other work tools and the bundle of wheat signify freedom, hard work, strength, and hope, also indicating different sectors (Haddad 2015, 164–165).

The League was formally launched at a rousing and packed Congress in Tunis's Harir hotel, eagerly attended by 3,000 new unionists from Sfax (Haddad 2015, 186–187). Shortly thereafter, the French—who had attempted to ban the meeting—arrested Al-Hammi and other League leaders. They were charged with conspiring against France, including through preparing to call for a general strike. Fed by politicized "communist" ideas, the unionists were exhibiting "sectarianism," out of control "eruption" (*hayajan*), and creating chaos (Al-Shaybi 2015b, 63). (Bourguiba and Ben Ali would inherit this oppressive reterritorialization of mass protest as criminal mutiny, as we will show.) That the French targeted the League for its independent streak was no surprise. The plot twist came with the position of the Destour. Refusing to bow to its tutelage, Al-Hammi and his comrades did not heed the Party's directives to avoid labor confrontation with the French (Al-Mahjoubi 2015, 99). This seems to have been the impetus for the Destour's betrayal of Al-Hammi and the remaining League leadership. The Party scrambled to extricate itself from any role in the League's founding, exhorting Tunisian workers to join the (French) Confederation of Workers' Unions even as Al-Hammi and his comrades withered away in prison (Al-Shaybi 2015b, 68). Left to face the French alone, Al-Hammi and Mokhtari were exiled for ten years. Their comrades were sentenced to five years. All save one, whose appeal delayed his exile, were shipped off to Italy on November 28, 1925 (Haddad 2015, 212). In a blow to Tunisian resistance, the French outlawed the freedom of assembly and expression (journalism) on January 29, 1926 (Al-Shaybi 2015b, 76). Ironically, the French may have inadvertently buttressed the link between protest and anti-colonial resistance. If the *colon* outlaws protest, then any protest, under any organizing body, is literally rendered a mode of resistance!

Al-Hammi was a pioneer of shared and organized syndicalism. The reason is threefold. First, his syndicalism of the 1920s centered around connectivity. Struggle within unions is a form of collective organized social doing. The dockworkers lacked the group dynamic to give them unity of purpose and direction, much less the collective structuring of unionized solidarity, that is, communal agency. As Al-Hammi told the crowd gathered at the Harir hotel, "no attention was paid to the dockworkers until they organized in an independent body" (Haddad 2015, 189). This organized dynamic is what frames resistance as a matter of intersubjectivity. Herein lies the second aspect of Al-Hammi's syndicalism: unionizing powerless workers via bonding and binding of separate individual experiential realities into a dynamic sociality. A specialized language was one medium of establishing, communicating, and maintaining newfound social ties among workers. Al-Hammi introduced them to a new vocabulary that named—and thus created possibilities for—worker resistance through social acting and en-acting. Strike (*i'tisab*), negotiations (*mufahamah*), and secretary general (*naqib*, union leader) were just some of the terms in this new union lexicon (see Al-Mukni's forward in Haddad 2015, 8). It is this sociality, which enlivens minds and impassions hearts to mutually defend rights and resist injustice. By foregrounding the sociality of shared exploitation and the materiality of the colonial condition, Al-Hammi's syndicalism implicates cognition. He frequently uses the word "people" (*sha'b*) as well as workers *(al-'ummal)*, conveying a class consciousness within an assertive consciousness of Tunisians as a people. Workers, "the absolute majority of the people," are the most "miserable" and "victim[ized]" among them (in Haddad 2015, 187). Tunisians are no different. European workers had advanced through knowledge-making and institution-building, organizing and mobilizing to protect workers. Tunisians as members of the "East" lagged behind, says Al-Hammi, but they could not submit to their lot (Haddad 2015, 188). With their links to the colonial metropole, French unions only reinforced the exploitation, exclusion, and humiliation of Tunisian workers. Forming the League was a matter of urgency. A way out of "misery" (a word he and Haddad repeat incessantly throughout the book) was achievable through such a joint project. Workers could thus break the reigning "silence" in which workers in the "Tunisian nation" were submerged (Haddad 2015, 189). Unionizing in the colonial contest is a forum and medium for group self-definition and self-understanding. It attempts to reconfigure the power relations of socio-economic and political coloniality of the "missing people" (Deleuze) or the "uncounted" (Rancière), a category of colonized Tunisian workers, imperiled by subalternity and quasi-erased by the big business and capitalist interests of the French colons.

Al-Hammi's tragic end parallels the demise of his revolutionary predecessor Ali Ben Ghedhahem, who died alone in the Karrakah prison (its ruins still standing today in La Goulette) after leading an (armed) popular revolt in the 1860s. The short lives of Tunisia's rebels end badly. Yet dwelling on the brevity of the General League's career would not do justice to the turning point its founding signifies. Cognizing Tunisians as a "people" struggling for emancipation and social justice, inculcating protest competencies at the heart of a new syndicalism, insisting on independence even from Tunisian ruling powers, the League's legacy breathes life into the country's turbulent syndicalism decades later.

Revivals and Re-Creations

Even after Al-Hammi's dark fate, Tunisian protests continued despite the French ban of 1929. It is difficult to overstate the ubiquity of protest as a mode of anti-colonial resistance. Here, boundaries between political and social demands melted away. In November 1934, a 10,000-person strong protest in Kairouan, for instance, objected to the colonial ban on the Neo-Destour party as well as the crackdowns on freedom of expression (Al-Shaybi 2015b, 240). Miners, dockworkers, and agricultural workers continued to strike between 1936 and 1937 (Al-Shaybi 2015b, 272). Rising star Habib Bourguiba organized a demonstration of 6,000 on January 31, 1937, promising to continue mobilizing "the people" to pressure the French for reforms (Al-Shaybi 2015b, 277). Moreover, Tunisian anti-colonial resistance revived the organizational imaginary and skillset that Al-Hammi had taught and modeled a decade earlier.

Divided by sector and region, unions were missing an umbrella association. By March 16, 1937, the cart workers' (*karartiyyah*) union convened a meeting to form a preparatory committee aiming to restore the General League (Al-Shaybi 2015b, 279). It briefly came to life again under Belqasem Qennawi in 1937 (Al-Shaybi 2015b, 482). A meeting in January 1938 drew enthusiastic workers from the Gafsa (Metlaoui, Medhila, Umm Larayes, Redeyef) mines, builders, bakeries and orange juice sellers, restaurant owners, seed farmers, and agricultural students from Bizerte and Tunis (Al-Shaybi 2015b, 374). History would be repeated, in an adaptation of the Neo-Destour's impulse for control. The Congress was derailed and coopted by the party's Hedi Nouira, former student leader and future Prime Minister, in January 1938 (see Al-Mahjoubi 2015 153, 153–155). This was despite Neo-Destour leader Habib Bourguiba having publicly supported the League's second iteration. Bourguiba published articles in the *Al-'Amal* newspaper vociferously defending the League against the "malice, baseness, and violence" of French defamation (see Al-Mahjoubi 2015, 147–151).

Even absent an independent general union, however, Tunisian workers' strikes and protests continued, with the Neo-Destour party fully involved. Tunisians from the interior (*dawakhil*) joined those in the capital, undertaking civil disobedience, refusing to pay taxes or serve their military conscriptions, and striking from school under the likes of Ali Belhouane, known as *za'im al-shabab* (youth leader) (Al-Shaybi 2015b, 386–391).[6] Tensions arose in the Neo-Destour between Habib Bourguiba, Salah ben Youssef, and Salman ben Salman, radicals who pushed for escalation against the French. The likes of Habib Al-Materi, Elbehri Guiga, and Tahar Sfar took a more moderate position (Al-Shaybi 2015b, 482). Sfar, for instance, was concerned by the "threat to the Tunisian people" posed by confrontations such as the April 1938 protests for a sovereign parliament (Al-Shaybi 2015b, 386–393). Apparently a fan, Bourguiba would almost imitate Al-Hammi. In March 1933, Bourguiba called for a confederation of unions that would ward off "fragmentation," because "on their own, they cannot wage the great battle" for life and freedom (Al-Shaybi 2015b, 400).

UGTT Beginnings

These snapshots do not attempt a holistic rendering of Tunisia's anti-colonial movement. Rather, our brief "concretization" has showcased the centrality of union dissent that mingled with anti-colonial popular mobilization. Resistance against the *colons* was multi-dimensional. Moreover, strains between political (party) and socio-economic (union) activism would ebb and flow for decades to come (Mnassar 1992). Farhat Hached, born in the Kerkennah islands and working for a transport company in Sfax, had only an elementary education. He was an upstart laborer expelled for his union work. Like Al-Hammi, he was a charismatic man with a (socialist) leaning; that is, "a refusal to drag labor unions into the political domain" (Al-Mahjoubi 2015,

---

[6] A leader of the anti-colonial struggle who led the April 9, 1938 demonstration that called for the creation of a Tunisian parliament (1909–1958).

99). As the UGTT officially tells it, Tunisians bristled at the racism and unequal pay within the French unions. Founding the Union of Independent Unions in the South in November 1944, Hached traveled northward to merge it with unions there. Thus was the UGTT was born in January 1946 (Al-Mahjoubi 2015, 98–99). Its purpose was to "achieve the goal for which Mohamed Ali was working, [which was] creating a national, independent union organization." In the same Khaldounia[7] hall where Al-Hammi and his comrades had gathered, the first Congress elected Hached Secretary General.[8] The "demands-based" (*matlabiyyah*) union concerned itself primarily with "improving the material conditions of workers," leaning toward a "separation" from the formal political domain (Al-Mahjoubi 2015, 99). Still, Al-Taimoumi (2021) emphasizes the conspicuous role of the UGTT in the political project of national independence. The French came to view the union as a threat. The anti-colonial nationalist movement had gained momentum (Al-Taimoumi 2021, 160).

Union vs. Party?

Farhat Hached favored union independence, explaining why the Neo-Destour did not attend the UGTT's founding meeting. He later relaxed this condition somewhat. By 1949, the UGTT "prioritized nationalist [anti-colonial] activism" (Al-Mahjoubi 2015, 102). It was not only the leadership that embraced "national" militancy over "workers" struggles. Rank and file unionists joined the armed struggle against the French and waged "political strikes." Organized white collar workers (*al-muwazafin*) exhibited a more mature "national consciousness" than their blue-collar (*al-'ummal*) counterparts, who served a mediating role between the Neo-Destour Party leadership and the working class (Al-Mahjobui 2015, 103). Formalizing the party/union duality in the heat of anti-colonial battle, in 1952 Hached served a brief stint as head of the Neo-Destour while Bourguiba was in exile. He continued in this role until he was assassinated in December 1954 by the "Red Hand," a French secret service organization (Al-Mahjoubi 2015, 103). Thereafter, says Al-Mahjoubi, the "alliance" of rough parity between the party and the union intensified into a "marriage" (Al-Mahjoubi 2015, 104–105). Unionists were loyal to Bourguiba, siding with him in his legendary conflict[9] with Salah ben Youssef (see also Klibi 2014, 52–53). Ben Youssef's vision and strategy differed from Bourguiba's, as he objected to the gradualism of "internal autonomy" (*al-istiqlal al-dakhili*) that would precede Tunisia's full independence in 1956 (Al-Tawili 2021, 61–68).

Ensuring UGTT allegiance in the mythical saga against Ben Youssef and his adherents was no small feat. Popular support for Ben Youssef and his opposition

---

[7] Khaldounia was founded in 1896 by Sadiki College alumni. Its precincts were historically used to organize many huge syndicalist and nationalist gatherings, including anti-colonial meetings.
[8] *Kaifa Ta'assasa Al-Ittihad Al-'Amm Al-Tunisi li al-Shughl?* In *Al-Sha'b*, January 21, 1977, p. 9.
[9] Habib Achour has suggested that Farhat Hached lent towards Ben Youssef, not Bourguiba. See *Al-Habib Achour Yatahaddath 'An Kitabihi li "Al-Shuruk,"* in *Alchourouk*, December 19, 1989.

to the independence agreements was performed in protests especially in the interior and South (Jendouba, Tataouinee, Kasserine, and Tozeur) in 1955 (Al-Tawili 2021, 97–98). Bourguiba moved to expel Youssefists, ideationally and practically, in his construction of the Tunisian people "*al-ummah al-tunisiyyah*," through monopolizing new institutions, circulating state propaganda (e.g. *Al-'Amal* or *L'Action* newspaper), and an armed offensive (Manser 2007, 66–74). He kept the union ever closer. Ahmed Ben Salah's entry into the UGTT leadership, and his socialist-cooperative vision for the Neo-Destour party, buttressed this "marriage." The party endorsed the UGTT's socio-economic program in its 1955 Sfax Congress (where Ben Youssef was expelled from the Neo-Destour), also appointing two UGTT leaders (Ahmed Tlili and Abdallah Farhat) to its Political Bureau. Independence was announced in 1956, an occasion for Bourguiba to further reward union loyalists. He named four of them ministers in his new government.

Yet balances of power are never stable. Bourguiba's victory over Ben Salah diminished his dependence on the UGTT's support. He moved to swallow it up within the Party apparatus. This "containment" strategy (Al-Mahjoubi 2015, 105) was institutionalized in the 1956 UGTT Congress. The union asserted itself as an important player in state-building, through its (mobilizable) worker membership and its socio-economic and educational research and proposed policies (e.g. UGTT 1951; see also Klibi 2014, 133–134). Domination over the UGTT was a decisive counterrevolutionary strike. Yet Bourguiba could never fully overpower the union. Waxing and waning conflicts ensued. The President would by turns cajole or target UGTT personnel who vocalized opposition to the party's domination. Divide and conquer was one strategy. The President suggested to Habib Ashour, his anti-colonial comrade but a staunch advocate of union independence, to split from the UGTT and form a new union. (That did not work.) Ben Salah, head of the UGTT for a time, was recruited as a "super-minister" to Bourguiba's government. His work for the International Federation of Free Unions exposed him to European development models, especially Swedish cooperatives (Al-Mahjoubi 2015, 58–59). Perhaps he failed in recalibrating syndicalism and development to the local setting. Tunisification of syndicalism apparently had its limits. As Bourguiba's minister he would later enact his grand cooperative scheme. Almost overnight, Bourguiba nationalized agricultural land in 1964 (Klibi 2014; 131–132, 147–149) in a hugely unpopular program that would just as abruptly end in 1969. The oppositional line was most markedly expressed by Habib Achour. Bourguiba would not tolerate such insubordination. Achour's opposition to the devaluation of the dinar in 1965, which he saw as harmful to workers, put him in Bourguiba's crosshairs. He was jailed, shaking up a turbulent relationship with the President which would become legendary. By extension, the party's relationship with the union would oscillate between cooptation/cooperation and confrontation. Underlying this tumultuous dynamic was the continuation of the battle for independence, from both party and colon, which Al-Hammi had launched for the union. The stakes were high in the post-independence state. The UGTT asserted itself as a still-formidable force, for instance in its "nationalist" general strike on November 23, 1956 (Al-Awwadi 2022, p. 9).

Hached's Struggle for Workers and Peoplehood

The elite power plays between union and party, Secretary General and President recounted above, did not tarnish founder Farhat Hached's luminous image in the Tunisian social imaginary. Hached did not live long enough to enjoy the fruits of the anti-colonial struggle. Yet he did reap reputational benefits that outlived his short time on earth. Just as there is a Tunisian "cult of Bourguiba," there may also be a "cult of Hached." Comrade (and later Socialist Democratic Party opposition leader) Ahmed Mestiri described him decades later as a man of "sincerity and truthfulness," slow to anger, never raising his voice, keen on the "idea that union freedoms and public freedoms are inseparable."[10] Perhaps one reason why everyone loves Hached is his moving profession of love for the people, expressed in his famous article in 1951 in the newspaper *Al-Hurriyah*. Titled "I love you, oh people" (*uhibbuka ya sha'b*), in it Hached addresses Tunisians he cognizes as a "people." His words overflow with affect—love, solidarity, admiration, encouragement. "I love you, O people of Tunisia, tested by and testing time, such that you were known for courage and sincerity, patience and persistence," he declares. Hached loved the (Tunisian) people in all their classes, professions, contradictions, arguments, and behaviors. He enjoined them to unity and steadfastness against "the enemy" (the French). The occasion was a brutal French crackdown on an agricultural strike in Enfidha (Sousse province). In this tragedy, historically commemorated by the UGTT,[11] five workers, including a pregnant woman, were killed (Othman 2012). Such a painful loss would beget the indomitable anger of determination, says Hached. His closing words cement the tie between union protest and anti-colonial resistance:

> The strikers fell in Enfidha so the nation (*ummah*) stood up in its entirety, calling for vengeance, and responses echoed from every direction, and the strikers in Zaghaoun and Enfidha were arrested, too, so the entire working class cried out, and the Tunisian people with it, as one [person], in a day that history witnesses as a day of pride and memories that will not be erased. … And if you [people] remain that way, united, by God you will not be defeated at all!
> (Hached, Nov. 26, 1950; see UGTT 2023, 68–69)

The working class is the Tunisian people, the people the working class, Hached seems to say. Revenge for laborers' murder will translate into deeper insistence, further coordination, more strikes and fighting back against the colonizer. A written/read "speech act" par excellence, Hached's article is a battle cry to rally the troops. Protesting laborers are almost indistinguishable from armed *fellaga* fighters. Tunisians are a people arisen, says Hached. It is as if the revolt makes them a people. For the colonized, peoplehood is forged in struggle and confrontation, antagonism (vis-à-vis the colonizing other) and agonism (among Tunisians themselves). Foremost among the

---

[10] *Fi Dhikra Hached: Ma Ahwaja Tunis Al-Yawm Ila Farhat Hached Wa Amthalihi*, in *Al-Mustaqbal* December 1, 1980, p. 3.
[11] *Waqi'at Enfidah … Ramzun Barizun fi Al-Nidal Al-'Ummali*, in *Al-Sha'b*, November 25, 1977, p. 3.

instruments and modalities of a peoplehood-in-becoming is the thought-practice, the social acting and en-acting, of protest. This Farhat Hached understood and conveyed. Carrying on Al-Hammi's legacy through the UGTT, he settled through word and deed the close kinship between union and party, the political and socio-economic, freedom and dignity.

Characterizing Tunisian Syndicalism

The above sections have outlined the early history of Tunisia's labor movement. Before we move to the insurrectionary politics of the 1970s–1980s, a few comments on Tunisian syndicalism are in order. *First* is the anti-colonial, emancipatory genesis of the country's unions. From the two iterations of Al-Hammi's league to the UGTT, Tunisian unions emerged out of generative conflicts with the colons (and their unions). Geared at two parallel objectives, the country's syndicalism sought to defend Tunisian workers' rights while gaining autonomy from the French. Autonomy and independence thus became driving values in the practice of Tunisian syndicalism. Furthermore, the UGTT (and its predecessor's) long resistance pedigree has earned them pride of place and abundant legitimacy as a national force and movement. The UGTT and its heroes loom large in the self-affirming Tunisian social imaginary, as the discussion of Farhat Hached above indicates (and later 2008 and 2011 protest slogans confirm). *Second*, the Tunisification of unions was an underlying tenet and pursuit of Al-Hammi, then Hached. This kind of (anti/postcolonial, Arabo-Islamic) localization of European syndicalism did not discount transnational connections and adaptations. Al-Hammi's, Hached's, and Ahmed Ben Salah's connections to international unions, including the American Federation of Labor (Disney 1978, 12), nurtured an almost syncretic learning. Such ideas and practices (from the Arabized union lexicon to international labor laws and standards) would nurture protest competencies that would in turn be adopted by Tunisian workers and broader masses, as the later protestscapes will demonstrate. *Third*, syndicalism was a brand of hands-on struggle generally devoid of ideologues. Al-Taimoumi (2021, 162–163) notes that Tunisian unionists swung between various types of "syndicalist thought": "corporatist," "revolutionary" (against party domination), and "worker-ist" (viewing the party as a vehicle for achieving labor demands). These diverging inclinations may not be so cleanly discernible. What is clear is that the UGTT was not able to sustain any "revolutionary" syndicalism outside the main episodes of confrontation (Al-Hammi in 1924, Achour in 1978 and 1984) explored in this chapter. Equally evident is that the union and its leaders generally did not espouse a specific body of thought or comprehensive worldview that an ideology or social imaginary would offer (see Chapter 4). Table 3.1 lists the Secretary Generals who have overseen the UGTT since its founding. Each ascribed to a kind of puritanical syndicalism, all nominally Destourian (i.e. espousing the ruling party's ideology) except for independent leftist Taieb Baccouche. Rank and file or regional members could hold more pronounced ideological tendencies, such as the Democratic Union Meeting

(Al-Liqaa' Al-Democrati Al-Naqabi) of the late 2000s.[12] However, these leanings (which may reflect internal power struggles) were not adopted by the national leadership (*al-naqabah al-markaziyyah*).

Fourth, the UGTT to some extent displayed in practice a kind of quasi-centralized, corporatist governance despite persistent rhetoric of "democracy." Tensions between local, regional, and national UGTT members and bodies, especially evident in the 2008 uprising (Chapter 6) and 2011 revolution (Chapter 7) may thus manifest the problematic of internal representation and democracy. Relatedly, the UGTT leadership is decidedly male-dominated. An enormous female membership does not trickle up to national decision-making structures. Historically, patriarchal governance is not an uncommon feature of syndicalism worldwide (Hartmann 1976, 155–167). Gradual awareness of women's exclusion occasionally peeks out of *Al-Sha'b*'s articles.[13] Under pressure from women activists, including former members of the student movement who created the Tahar Haddad club (Chapter 4), the UGTT formed a women's committee by the early 1980s. Its gendered power-sharing impact has been arguably limited, however, with some calling for quotas (Mahfoudh 2018, 72–73). In 2017, Na'imah Hammami became the first female member of the Executive Committee since Sharifah Mas'adi's term in 1949 (Hamdi 2017).

Fifth and finally, although an important *contrepouvoir* force in Tunisian society and politics, for the most part the UGTT did not directly contest formal politics. The cooperative/confrontational dynamic with the President and ruling party translated into on-and-off acceptance of formal political positions within the party or government, as noted above. Ahmed Ben Salah's aspiration for a socialist workers' party was short-lived (Al-Mahjoubi 2015, 62–64). At the 16th Congress in December 1984, when Taieb Baccouche proposed turning the UGTT into a workers' party, uproar ensued. The idea was so unpopular that Baccouche withdrew the suggestion (Belhoula 2015, 173). The crux of the UGTT's power instead lies in its ability to mobilize its large reservoir (*makhzun*) of would-be protestors. It was this socio-political leverage that Bourguiba and Ben Ali both sought to curtail, never with complete success. And it is this kind of counter-power capacity that is of interest to us. The uncounted (the sum of missing and "peuple introuvable") constructed their own politics. They planted speech acts, protest, and cadres, all illuminated by an emancipatory social imaginary, into Tunisia's tumultuous political setting. One forum within which they did so was the UGTT. Away from formal state institutions, Tunisia's "uncounted" cleared their own space and acted within it. The crisis-ridden context of Bourguiba's flailing rule and fragmented party (Ashford 1965, 220–229) conditioned them, but they too created another context elevating protest, not party wrangling or ministerial projects, into a (counter) power to be reckoned with. Credit for the unmistakable imprint of protest in Tunisia's politics is due in large part to the UGTT.

---

[12] See for instance, *"Alchourouk" Tanshur Nass Al-Ardiyyah Al-Naqabiyyah Al-Jadidah li al- Liqaa' Al-Naqabi*, in *Alchourouk*, January 1, 2011.

[13] For instance, for a report on a female unionists' attendance of a Swedish panel on enhancing female unionist presence and representation, from choice of meeting venue to overcoming prohibitive traditions to re-socialization towards gender equality, see *Min Ajli Tashrik Akthar li al-Mar'ah fi Al-'Amal Al-Naqabi*, in *Al-Sha'b*, November 4, 1977, p. 11.

Insiders' Views on Syndicalism and Protest

As described above, Tunisia's unionists have longstanding syndicalist traditions and values. A focus group with six unionists from the Gafsa UGTT branch offers important empirical clues to further understand the lived imaginaries and experiences of Tunisian syndicalism.[14] They view Tunisia's brand of syndicalism as steeped in a history of fighting "*al-istiʿmar*" (colonialism) and "*al-istiʿmar al-jadid*" (neocolonialism). The conversation explored the use of protest in the history of the UGTT. They agree on this definition of social doing under the rubric of "*al-nidal al-naqabi*" (syndicalist struggle). For them, this congruence between syndicalism and anti-colonial activism is what makes struggle within unions revolutionary. They all agree that understanding the symbiosis between syndicalism and nationalist liberation is an important context for socialization into protest. According to a member of the group: "struggle via protest against the colons and then against the post-colonial regimes is the midwife of Tunisian syndicalism." They stress that given the anti-colonial context of the rise of syndicalism, protest remains instilled as a legitimate form of activism. One observation from the group was the historic legitimacy assigned to protest during the fight for national liberation up to the 1950s that came under attack after independence. Protestors felt somewhat "shamed" by the state. Another interviewee noted the following: "Protests and protestors from our union or students were given pejorative names. This particularly arose from the threat to regime stability during times of crisis, such as in 1978, 1984 and the phosphate basin protests of 2008." There is an interplay of historic and contemporary factors in the signage intended in derogatory appellations used by postcolonial regimes and their propaganda machines. Such words seek to defame, and have an etymological meaning of manifest negativity. Protestors are described by references with a semantic content of "enmity" to patriotism, order, dialogue, and overall morality. The modes of signification include the use of "conspirators" and "anarchists" (*fawdawiyyun*), amongst other terms that seek to delegitimize protest and protestors. These exhibit stress on deviance and on anti-social behavior.

This quasi-semiotic formulation of propaganda and the use of naming and shaming belonged to the inventory of the authoritarian state's self–other denigration of all opposition under both Bourguiba and Ben Ali. Reference to *fellaga*, for example, another word that is at once expressive of communal acceptance in the cultural repository and imaginary and of deviancy (immediately after independence in 1956), was appropriated when equalizing between the protestors in 1978, 1984, 2008, and 2010–11 and those who resisted colonialism—Mohamed Daghbeji, Bechir ben Sdira, and Lazhar Shraiti. It is a recognition that valorizes a norm—emancipatory social doing—and restores to memory a transcendent ethos of self-sacrifice, freedom, and rights-seeking agency. Thus is shaped "*iradat al-hayat*" (the will to live), as one respondent underscores a point by reference to Tunisia's

---

[14] Focus group interviews with unionists, October 26, 2022, Gafsa.

revolutionary poet, Chebbi. This constitutes part and parcel of the consciousness of the transcendent exuberance of peoplehood-in-becoming. One respondent argues that protest as a value was entrenched in the early activism of Tunisian syndicalism's founding fathers: "Since the inception of syndicates by Mohamed Ali al-Hammi in 1925 and Farhat Hached since 1946, workers followed in the footsteps of those inspiring heroes who branded the trade union movement to be from the outset revolutionary." He adds, "Mohamed Ali pioneered picket lines, organized strikes, negotiation with employers for increased wages and labor rights in the 1920s. His League of Tunisian Workers invented activist traditions that remain legendary in the history of our country's labor movement."

These early starts by Al-Hammi are lodged in the collective memory of syndicalist publics in Tunisia. A fellow focus group participant notes that it was through protests and strikes that Hached and others left the Confédèration Genérale du Travail (CGT) to create unions across Tunisia that were eventually unified in 1946 into today's UGTT. He was its first General Secretary after "a historic and democratic founding congress." That "second birth" of Tunisian syndicalism, as another interviewee put it, "established the idea of independence (*istiqlal*) from France and autonomy from government (*istiqlaliyyah*)." The group values the fact that the 2014 constitution upholds the right to strike and protest. Since independence, the UGTT has had to manage obstinate regimes whose aim was to tame the union and make it play "second fiddle" to the state. Political clashes flared up between the two periodically (nearly every decade) as a result. Use of protest recurs when bargain politics fails. Normatively, the focus group is of the view that the UGTT leadership and workers have fought many battles with the postcolonial state. In addition to maintaining autonomy, these battles are "to stay intact as a coherent and solidaristic body in order to be able to carry out its activism for the benefit of Tunisian workers," as one put it. For this reason, the protests are innumerable. The control the state sought in order to keep syndicalists in check mostly "radicalized" rather than contained the UGTT. Even under Ben Ali during the 2008 phosphate basin uprising, the UGTT found ways via regional and local activisms to evade state control. Moreover, the union's use of protest is underpinned by key values. These values have shaped its politics since independence as explained by one interviewee: "political struggle without contesting politics, adopting bargain politics with the state but without sacrificing the principle of autonomy, committing to collective action and social justice along a socialist vision for Tunisia's development, and honoring the legacy of struggle for independence and workers' rights."

A pedagogic mission within the UGTT supports this agenda, as the focus group participants pointed out. There is a "department of syndicalist training and acculturation" (*qism al-takwin wa al-tathqif al-naqabi*). It instills the right to protest and strike but within legal and moral boundaries that do not harm the public or the state. Amongst the learning imparted there is an emphasis on:

- social and political engagement within syndicalist parameters, i.e. advocacy work on behalf of workers;
- dedication to moral and professional conduct of syndicalist activism;

- a high sense of autonomy;
- social, cultural, and political awareness;
- social activism and engagement in the pursuit of workers' rights;
- and political engagement nationally and internationally.

Protest Confrontations: Tunisia's "Black Thursday"

Setting the Scene

The previous section drew on both historical material and interviews to glean basic features of Tunisian syndicalism, past and present. Protest stands out as a key instrument in the unionist toolkit. Leadership and rank-and-file members deploy protest to both challenge authoritarianism and to assert the "right to have rights," political and socio-economic. This section traces the deepening friction between the UGTT and the President/party from the smaller 1977 strikes into the General Strike of 1978 and its aftermath. Thus, this protestscape re-ontologizes subjectivities in time, space, and in activism that breathed life into anti-authoritarian civic engagement and overall demotic agency. In the postcolonial era, it was the General Strike of January 1978 that re-authorized, as it were, such (ant)agonistic social acting and en-acting of peoplehood. With long-time regime irritant Habib Achour at the helm, the UGTT departed from the relative "harmony" (*tanaghum*) between union and party/Bourguiba that prevailed from 1970 to 1977 (Al-Haddad 2011, 85–86). Bourguiba could be just as vicious with loyalists as with oppositionists. In a huge turn-around, "super-minister" Ben Salah was sacked and tried in the State Security Court for "high treason" (Manser 2007, 133). Authorizing Achour's comeback as head of the union in the wake of this fantastic cooperative collapse may have been a strategic error for Bourguiba.

The second half of the empirical investigation of the union dissentscape rests chiefly on a critical discourse analysis of union primary documents, namely its mouthpiece (*lisan*), *Al-Shaʿb* in 1977–78 and coverage by other (state and opposition) newspapers. Initially a monthly magazine launched in 1969, *Al-Shaʿb* was converted into a weekly newspaper in January 1976 (Al-Asali 2018). We thus treat the publication as co-extensive with official positions, or centrally-sanctioned debates, within this heavyweight (sometimes oppositional) syndicalist group. Like reams of other publications, *Al-Shaʿb* features more than third-party reporting on issues of social, political, or economic interest. Within the newspaper's broadsheets, the UGTT disseminates coverage of events (meetings, strikes, formation of new unions), but also its Congress documents, political manifestos, and leaders' speeches. Disseminating *Al-Shaʿb* is an integral mode of UGTT self-reproduction, self/other identification, communication, recruitment, and mobilization. The "dialectical" CDA approach between "orders of discourse," actors, and behaviors (Fairclough 2012, 9–14) squares with our view as to the relationality of protestscapes and thus revolution. Interpreting textual and non-textual circumstances, events, historicity, power struggles, and political/policy developments (Carvalho 2008) is thus precisely the aim of the remaining analysis below. Specifically, our attention is on the UGTT's published discourse to understand the vacillations and transitions in its positions vis-à-vis the Destour party and the corporatist Bourguibist state. We zero in on "critical discourse moments," where (published media) language and the word and world-making they both create and reflect, feature a departure from dominant discursive strategies and frames (Carvalho 2008, 166–167). These critical discourse moments correspond to major "critical protest moments" in the UGTT's long history, particularly 1978 and 1984.

Our detailed sojourn into the events of 1977–78, from mounting state–union tension to general strike and violent state response, is due to their immense significance. This first major anti-state revolt of the postcolonial era was a distressing challenge to Bourguiba and his increasingly divided party. After the defections of the 1971 Monastir party Congress, the Destour party was being pulled apart by competing "wings" in the wake of the cooperatives debacle (Al-Haddad 2011, 76–77, 391). Tussling between "hawks" (Nouira, Mohamed Sayyah, Abdullah Farhat) and "doves" (the President's wife Wasila ben Ammar, Mohamed Al-Naser, Tahar Belkhodja and Ahmed Bennour, some of whom would resign their posts) was well-known.[15] That this rebellion took the form of protest (strikes, demonstrations) led by the UGTT, as its détente with Bourguiba and the party crumbled, exemplifies the agonistic nature of Tunisia's peoplehood in-becoming, its social acts and en-actments. The account below is far from a granular description of events. Rather, we pick up on the agentic, affective, and cognitive discursive markers of burgeoning resistance through protest indicating a peoplehood-in-becoming. Two interrelated themes emerge. *First* is the stock of values constructing the union's self-identification and self-understanding (see Table 3.1). An anti-colonial pedigree, a mandate to defend workers' and Tunisian rights and dignity, a close-knit organic relationship with the people, and an explicitly demotic orientation characterize Al-Hammi's and Hached's brainchild. *Second* is the UGTT's insistence on the legitimacy of strikes as a mode of resistance. This argument is crucial in the union's narrative contest with state media and officials. The strike was bloodily put down, of course. Habib Achour and his leading comrades were arrested and tried, the UGTT leadership hastily replaced until Bourguiba released them after the attempted Gafsa coup in 1980 (Belhoula 2015, 163). However, we contend that lasting protest competencies carried through into the 1984 bread riots sparked by secondary school youth just a few years later.

The UGTT: The 'Clamor of Being'[16] for All Tunisians

Gearing up for the great confrontation, all through 1977 the pages of *Al-Shaʿb* were buzzing with reports of meetings and strikes, including "warning strikes," by unions across sectors. They included workers in academia, finance, medicine, railroads, steel, the post office, forestry, tourism, regional meetings, agriculture, garments and

---

[15] Interview with Abdelmajid Sahraoui, UGTT leader and last surviving adherent of Achour, with whom he served a prison sentence in 1978, October 26, 2022.
[16] This sub-title is inspired by the phrase "…a single clamor of Being for all beings" by Gilles Deleuze (1994, 378).

Table 3.1 UGTT Congresses and Leadership, 1946–2022

Congress	(Condensed) Slogan	Year	Chosen Secretary General (SG)	SG Ideology/political affiliation
1	Independence	Jan. 1946	Farhat Hached	Neo-Destour
2	Unity and Struggle	Dec. 1947	Farhat Hached	Neo-Destour
3	None	April 1949	Farhat Hached	Neo-Destour
4	The National Cause and Social Struggle	March 1951	Farhat Hached	Neo-Destour
5	Social Justice	July 1954	Ahmed ben Salah	(Socialist-leaning) Neo-Destour
6	Freedom and Progress	Sept. 1956	Ahmed ben Salah	(Socialist-leaning) Neo-Destour
7	Unity	September 1957	Ahmed Tlili	Neo-Destour
8	Tunisian Solidarity	April 1960	Ahmed Tlili	Neo-Destour
9	Justice and Democracy	March 1963	Habib Achour	Neo-Destour
10	(Exceptional Congress)	July 1965	Bechir ben Lagha	Destour
11	Administration and Production	August 1969	Bechir ben Lagha	Destour
12	Unity, Discipline, and Trust	May 1970	Habib Achour	Destour
13	Sincerity in Work	March 1973	Habib Achour	Destour
14	Freedom and Progress	March 1977	Habib Achour	Destour
15	(Exceptional Congress)	April 1981	Taieb Baccouche	Independent Leftist
16	Struggle, Dignity, and Independence	Dec. 1984	Habib Achour	Destour
17	Reconciliation	April 1989	Ismail Sahbani	Destour
18	Solidarity for the Future	Dec. 1993	Ismail Sahbani	Destour
19	Social Balance	Feb. 1999	Ismail Sahbani	Destour
20	(Exceptional)	Feb. 2002	Abdelslam Jrad	Destour
21	Independence, Democracy, Unity Steadfastness Struggle, Progress	Dec. 2006	Abdelslam Jrad	Destour
22	I Love You, O People	Dec. 2011	Houcine Abassi	"Achour-ite"
23	Allegiance to Tunisia, Loyalty to the Martyrs, and Sincerity to the Workers	January 2017	Noureddine Tabboubi	"Achour-ite"
24	(Exceptional Congress) Agency, Steadfastness, Progress	2020	Noureddine Tabboubi	
25	We cling to the independence of our decision … we triumph for Tunisia of freedom, democracy and social justice	Feb. 2022	Noureddine Tabboubi	Achour-ite

Source: Compiled from Al-Haddad (2011), Belhoula (2015), *Al-Sha'b* Newspaper, and UGTT (2023, 14–18).

textiles, animal husbandry, education, and mines. Regional and local offices met and selected leaders. New union chapters were announced. National political happenings featured in detail, such as a full-six-page transcription of discussions over the state budget in Parliament (*Majlis Al-Ummah*).[17] Union updates from around the world, including in the International Confederation of Free Unions, also landed in the newspaper.[18] Secretary General Habib Achour headlined most front pages, at times (before the crisis peaked in fall 1977), alongside President Habib Bourguiba.[19] The terminology of "trust" in the UGTT recurred, as pledged by different unions.[20]

Before, into, and after the crisis climax on January 26, 1978, commemorations of the Union's founding took up space (and doubtless, intense preparation). Keeping alive the memory of the "leader *(za'im)* of eternal mention, the martyr Farhat Hached" was serious business.[21] Routinized on both the anniversary of his assassination and the UGTT's founding, this guided memorialization fed into the socialization of union members. *Al-Sha'b* re-published old articles penned by Hached for *Al-Hurriyyah* newspaper during the anti-colonial struggle.[22] "Our path is a straight path," he expounded. Steadfastness in the union struggle, "not caring about the barking of dogs," working within the "truth" to achieve practical successes, is a must. An issue a quarter century after his murder, strained at the seams with famous personalities' quotes about Hached, legends about his anti-colonial struggles, and his life story. An attempt to discern a referential body of thought from his discourses and practices is particularly noteworthy. This rough intellectualization of Hached gleaned main ideas such as "union independence," as well as "social justice, democracy, and freedom." Development of the latter was cut short by his untimely death, but his words from the piece "I love you, O people," indicate a demotic sensibility, the short article maintained. Hached's exhortations to involvement in public affairs, constant critique, "defense of different theories," and argumentation were some key (democratic) behaviors the legendary unionist espoused.[23] In this kind of discussion, the UGTT continually (re)constructed the cult of Hached, a central axis of its organizational myth-making. Moreover, such commentary helps to engrain particular values and principles (democracy, syndicalist struggle, social justice, public monitoring of power-holders) as central tenets to be cognized by its members.

The UGTT thus exhibits an agency of didactic socialization (*takwin* or *tarbiyah*) to reproduce its own distinct identity, buttressing the values-based protest competencies its members acquire. This point comes to the fore amidst worker anger against the assassination plot (recounted below). The UGTT "represents the nationalist tendency that works hard to center social justice and create democratic traditions far

---

[17] *Munaqashat Mizaniyyat 'Am 1977*, in *Al-Sha'b*, January 7, 1977, pp. 12–17.
[18] For instance, *Al-Sha'b*, January. 7, 1977, p. 24
[19] *Al-Ra'is Ya'ud Al-Yawm*, in *Al-Sha'b*, January 14, 1977, p. 1.
[20] *Fi Al-Mu'tamar Al-Ta'sisi li Naqabatihim* in *Al-Sha'b*, January 14, 1977, p. 2.
[21] *Al-Sha'b*, January 14, 1977, p. 1.
[22] *Tariquna Huwa Al-Tariq Al-Mustaqim*, in *Al-Sha'b*, December 2, 1977, p. 2.
[23] *Al-Fikr Al-Hachedi min Khilal Nidalihi*, in *Al-Sha'b*, December 2, 1977, p. 7.

from discrimination or membership in any political direction."[24] The pedagogical rings through here, as does the emphasis on the national interest of the people and democratic coaching. Threading together past and present, the newspaper's lengthy reflections on Hached lend historical credence to the mobilization of the union's rank and file. His mustachioed image graces the cover of the same December 1977 special issue. Underneath, he poses the provocative (headline) question: "does [the person] who does not defend their dignity deserve life?"[25] It is an anti-colonial rendered post-colonial insubordination and dare, for worker and citizen alike to rise up and seize their dignity from those who have unlawfully impounded it. Is it the government, the President and Party, against whom citizens must "defend their dignity"? The implied connection is difficult to miss. The UGTT's founding anniversary was another occasion to reiterate its mission. In January 1977, the union framed its goals as "social justice," or "building a society [free of] exploiting human beings," doing away with social inequalities to attain a "life of dignity and peace." The second goal was democracy: "the freedom of elections that is the basis of union work, and it is the freedom of discussion and [different] opinions and expression in wider society." The third goal was "freedom of the individual and the group" made possible through social justice.[26] In addition to its transmission through the mouthpiece of *Al-Sha'b*, this kind of normative, didactic commitment is quasi-institutionalized. "Schools" to train and socialize union workers popped up across the country. For instance, the Sfax branch announced two three-month courses with union history, structures, roles, professional problems, contracts, and social solidarity funds in January 1979.[27]

Such training could tilt toward politicized objectives. A lecture on the UGTT's training program highlighted the accent put on "progress, secularism, planning" aided by "logic and ... rationality." This outlook undergirded the "the courageous corrective stance" of the union, in reference to the (coopted) new leadership replacing Achour and his Executive Committee the year before. Training required a "change in mindset and ways of thinking," echoing Bourguiba's own language of the "jihad" for development and modernization.[28]

In both its historical and contemporary reporting, the UGTT consistently wears the mantle of worker protector, by extension champion of the people. Some spaces enjoy a special stature. That is, they comprise an important constituency for the UGTT. Speaking to workers in his five-day visit to phosphate miners in Gafsa, Achour invoked the "strength of the organic and spiritual link between the heroic miners in that region of fighters (*mantiqah mujahidah*)" and the UGTT.[29] This relationship was "revered" for the workers there. In turn, laborers complained about working and living conditions, including shoddy housing and water

---

[24] *Murasalat Gafsa*, in *Al-Sha'b*, November 25, 1977, p. 6.
[25] *Hal Yastahiq Al-Hayat Man La Yudafi' 'An Karamatihi?* in *Al-Sha'b*, December 2, 1977, p. 1.
[26] *Al-Ittihad Al-'Amm Al-Tunisi li Al-Shughl, Mabadi'uhu wa Ahdafuhu*, in *Al-Sha'b*, January 21, 1977, p. 9.
[27] *Ba'th Madrasah li Al-Takwin Al-Naqabi Wa Al-Tathqif Al-'Ummali bi Sfax*, in *Al-Sha'b*, Jan. 12, 1979, p. 9
[28] *Muhadarat Al-Akh Mohamed Ali Al-Shili*, in *Al-Sha'b*, Dec. 12, 1979, p. 14
[29] *Khamsat Ayyam Ma'a 'Ummal Manajim Al-Fusfat fi Gafsa*, in *Al-Sha'b*, Jan. 28, 1977, p. 4

scarcity. (Miner–union entanglements would be significant to the 2008 uprising: see Chapter 5.)

All worker-peoples are implicated in government plans and policies. Inside and outside of mining country, the conflict with the state that spiraled into "Black Thursday" originated in part from demands for pay raises. "Our demands are not unreasonable and aim only to improve the condition of workers," Achour declared to his Executive Committee, in the midst of ongoing negotiations surrounding the national compact the year before.[30] With its demographic and geographic reach expanding southward, the union easily claims a popular depth, perhaps rivaling only that of state institutions. In 1977, for instance, a new UGTT regional headquarters in Sidi Bouzid was in the works.[31] Defending workers and Tunisians were union efforts pursued for the "public good," through the "rule of law."[32] Visions of emancipation fittingly beamed postcolonial disaffection. Workers in a French-owned garment factory in Hammam-Lif complained of a "colonial mentality" that "humiliates (*tahtaqir*, from the *hogra* of double consciousness) the workers and stomps on their rights."[33] Humiliation by the colons is not a thing of the past. It grated on Tunisians even more in the decades after formal independence. Self–other identification intersects along class, state–society, and colonizer–colonized delineations. Worker exploitation mimicked the dynamics at which Al-Hammi, Hached, and even Achour had balked in the three decades of Tunisia's nationalist movement.

Syndicalist Resistance under Habib Achour

Through this backdrop of normative identity- and claim-making, *Al-Sha'b* made for riveting reading as the General Strike approached. Achour's visits to Libya exacerbated the strife between him and the President.[34] Bourguiba's own relationship with Muammar Ghadafi was tense after the 1974 "union" between the two countries fell flat. Respective supporters and constituencies of the two "Habibs" took this political squabble seriously. Proximate causes for the crisis include alleged attempts to assassinate Habib Achour. As the story goes, a man appeared in the Sousse Kasr Hotel, and announced, brandishing his gun, that he would kill Achour with this same weapon that he had used to kill Salah Ben Youssef in 1961.[35] The provocation was great indeed. (Bourguiba propagandist Mohamed Sayyah (2012, 165) would later deny the plausibility of the entire assassination threat). A red-lettered headline screamed "Overflowing Workers' Protest Against Terrorism and Assassination Intentions," above pictures of large gatherings.[36] Emotive language conjured the affect of loyalty and love, combined with the agency of existentialist determination. It

---

[30] *Al-Sha'b,* January 7, 1977, p. 1.
[31] *Al-Akh Habib Ashour Qariban fi Sidi Bouzid,* in *Al-Sha'b,* January 7, 1977, p. 1.
[32] *Fi Mu'tamar Al-Ittihad Al-Mahalli li Al-Shughl bi Al-Hammamet,* in *Al-Sha'b,* November 4, 1977, p. 3.
[33] *Fi Ma'mal Bonanville Lelgir bi Hammam Al-Anf,* in *Al-Sha'b,* November 25, 1977, p. 9.
[34] As recounted later by deposed Minister Tahar Belkhodja, for instance in *Ahdath "Al-Khamis Al-Aswad" bi Tunis: Talaq Damawi Baina Al-Sultah Wa Ittihad Al-Shughl,* in *Al-Tunisiyyah,* January 26, 2013.
[35] Interview with Abdelmajid Sahraoui, October 26, 2022.
[36] *Al-Sha'b,* November 11, 1977, p. 1.

also touched upon the cognition of refusing injustice and exhibiting collective self-presence. "Once again, workers have proven their consciousness—once again they have proven their attachment to the UGTT and its SG, once again they have proven that the principles for which the great Hached and caravans of workers, believers in the authentic union message were martyred ... in the path of truth and social justice and freedom and democracy ..." The diatribe was a daring portrait challenging "envious" naysayers.

This sensational incident came after state violence against workers in Ksar Hellal (Qasr Hilal). In an unforgivable affront, the army had put down a garment factory strike that had surged into a town-wide uprising in Monastir.[37] "Outright lies" and press "clownery" were compounded by government backtracking from promises to raise wages. Against this escalating tension came the "frank declaration of the intention to assassinate their secretary general." This was an "egregious attack on the feelings of the workers and their futures." Assassination contradicted the "principles upon which the workers in the UGTT were raised," especially since the workers considered Achour "an example...of struggle and sincerity towards workers' causes and the people's interest."[38] Democracy too was under fire, as an academic unionist saw it: the assassination threats sought to abort "all action aimed at creating a democratic life in the country."[39] The appeals to workers' and peoples' affect of adulation and devotion seemed to parallel talk of Habib Bourguiba as the Supreme Combatant. "We are soldiers to protect the Union and its Secretary General."[40] The emotional overload does not detract from the outcry's cognitive content. Insistence on workers'/people's rights, the refusal of attacks on persons and dignity, and the celebration of agentic "striking back" transform this potentially catastrophic event into an occasion to develop and display the social acting and en-acting of peoplehood in the works.

UGTT denouncements against the state are principled. "We refuse absolutely that workers' blood is spilled," claims Achour to his Executive Office meeting.[41] Still, the UGTT leadership exhorts its rank and file to discipline. Adherence to syndicalist protocols was imperative. Affective responses must be guided before they were unleashed. The Executive Office thus advised all workers to "hold onto their nerves and abstain from any spontaneous" moves. When on strike, they were not to descend into any "chaotic action" nor respond to "provocations" from any side.[42] Protest competencies themselves contain a normative component that values life. Unionists were to shun unfettered unruliness that could endanger people and property, as well as the UGTT's claims about the legitimacy of strikes. The union prided itself on the "complete discipline" of workers on strike, as in Sousse workers' denunciation of the

---

[37] See *Min Tarikh Al-Ittihad Al-'Amm Al-Tunisi li Al-Shughl: Azmat Sanat 1979* (Al-Halaqah Al-Thaniyah 'Ashr), in *Al-Sha'b*, March 6, 2010. Bourguiba reportedly exclaimed that Ksar Hellal, fabled as the birthplace of the Neo-Destour in 1934, was now synonymous with "destruction and spreading chaos"—a bottom-up reterritorialization of symbolism in official history narratives.
[38] *Kalimat Al-Ittihad: Ilama Tazal Al-Bilad Dahiyyat Al-Akhta'!* in *Al-Sha'b*, November 11, 1977, p. 1.
[39] *Itar Naqabat Al-Ta'lim Al-'Ali Wa Al-Bahth Al-'Ilmi*, in *Al-Sha'b*, November 11, 1977, p. 8.
[40] *'Ummal Al-Dawahi Al-Janubiyyah Yudribun*, in *Al-Sha'b*, November 11, 1977, p. 11.
[41] *Al-Sha'b*, November 11, 1977, p. 2.
[42] *Nida' li Al-Shaghalin min Al-Maktab Al-Tanfidhi li Al-Ittihad*, in *Al-Sha'b*, November 11, 1977, p. 2.

assassination attempt.[43] The provinces all rose up: Sfax, Kerkennah, Sousse, Tunis, Medenine, Kef, Bizerte, Beja, and more. Escalation was unavoidable. A week later, the union issued "A Call to Rectify the Situation before it's too Late,"[44] above an enormous picture of Sousse protests, objecting to new arrests. Achour mustered the union's people power once again, counting on the backing of Tunisians: "the people know the truth and support the union."[45] Its ranks on the march, the UGTT clung to its "principles in defending workers and country and freedoms and democracy." This was so "the people remain free and in good health." The UGTT became almost a stand-in for the people, sentry and soldier of freedom and independence, dignity and prosperity. Strikes were "successful," spreading to all sectors.[46] In a formal statement, the union's Administrative Body was blunt, condemning the "intentions to spread terrorism and preparation for murder."[47] Across regions and sectors (construction, postal work, education, health), support and solidarity ensued.[48] Thus, standing up to the state was cast as "counter-terrorism and protecting the country," alongside condemnations of media propaganda seeking to dupe the people.[49]

Walking away from the National Compact

(Threats of) state violence materialized in a period of strained relations with the UGTT. The 1977 National Compact between Nouira's government and the union generated immense controversy. Initially, it was celebrated by the UGTT. This landmark agreement codified the Prime Minister's neoliberal policies as Tunisia drew back from Ben Salah's cooperatives scheme. Wage increases might buy union quietism, at once promising increased production. Such was the reasoning, at least. "General raise in wages," announced the front page of the January 21, 1977 issue.[50] Agricultural and industrial workers would receive a 33 percent pay rise, and 10–11 dinar increase for public and private sector workers. These were "satisfying results for all workers and [white collar] employees," Achour explained. Al-Haddad notes, however, that the UGTT rank-and-file did not unanimously accept the compact. Leftists in particular considered the agreement for which they claim Achour did not consult them as caving in to capitalist imperialism. Achour's rejoinder was that the prerogative to strike remained in the hands of the workers, who could object to price increases and inflation. This they did mightily, through all of 1977 (see Al-Haddad 2011, 77–84). Like a president touring his country to promote his political agenda, Habib Achour visited the provinces to drum up enthusiasm for the social compact. He traveled to Gafsa and Sidi Bouzid, explaining its terms. "Our goal is to reach the standing of European workers," he promised. A comparative outlook impatient with

---

[43] *Al-Sha'b,* November 11, 1977, p. 3.
[44] *Al-Sha'b,* November 18, 1977, pp. 1–2.
[45] *Ijtima' Al-Hai'ah al-Idariyyah li Al-Ittihad Al-'Amm,* in *Al-Sha'b,* November 18, 1977, p. 3.
[46] *Al-Sha'b,* November 18, 1977, p. 4.
[47] *Fi La'ihat Al-Hai'ah Al-Idariyyah li Al-Ittihad* in *Al-Sha'b,* November 18, 1977, p. 5.
[48] *Al-Sha'b,* November 18, 1977, pp. 6–8.
[49] *Murasalat Sfax,* in *Al-Sha'b,* November 18, 1977, p. 18.
[50] *Al-Sha'b,* January 21, 1977, pp. 1–2.

Tunisia's sluggish economic development thus lent an aspirational benchmark on which he rested the union's participation in the compact.[51] A small column that ran in 1977 was the front page "Union Report," which would forecast, weather-like, union mobilization. On this occasion, "the strike clouds retreated" after the announcement, a fitting gift on the UGTT's 31st anniversary.[52]

Yet the agreement would quickly go awry. UGTT workers did not refrain from strikes. The government in turn set loose militias and police. A November editorial laid out the reasons for abandoning the social compact of 1977. The justifications are moral and reasoned. A convergence of three crises had fomented conflict with the state: a rise in prices, the Ksar Hellal events where striking workers were attacked (October), and the assassination threats to Achour discussed above (November) shook the "trust between the UGTT and the political authorities in the country."[53] Thus, the necessary conditions for the social compact were not fulfilled, particularly given the government's "mismanagement" (*su' tasarruf*). Moreover, legally enshrined rights for particular sectors (mines, agriculture, petroleum) were in question. Workers were confused over this insistence on the "law" in letter but not spirit or action, the editorial explained. As the 1977 social compact fell through and the UGTT was increasingly under attack, the union argumentatively elaborated how and why it had veered towards escalation with the government.[54] The national newspaper *Al-Sabah* re-published the article that had run in *Al-Sha'b*, signaling the importance of the conflict to a national audience. "Clarity" of language and stance pointed to a departure of sorts from earlier maneuverings that had avoided confrontation. "The government's behavior these days" was problematic, descending into violence and domination. In contrast, the UGTT stuck to its values-based mission to ensure "happiness and material and moral dignity and the continual development (take-off) of" human beings. Rising prices and frequent job expulsions necessitated union action.

Its main tool was protest: "use of the strike is more than a basic choice … not open to discussion." Thus, while the union had sincerely "welcomed" the January 19, 1977 agreement, its mandate to defend the "rights" of workers and Tunisians required a stand against rising prices. Moreover, the UGTT chafed at government demonization of its leaders, all under the pretext of "national unity" (*al-wihdah al-qawmiyyah*). Here, more explicitly political conflict comes into view. If distributional rights were foremost among the union's goals, its independent streak comes in a close second. The two were intertwined. The union would not allow a rerun of the 1965–69 takeover by the government that weakened the organization into an "instrument to subjugate their workers and lose [take away] their rights." Exacerbating the problem was the government "heading towards violence and intransigence (*tasallub*)." Party militias' (*firqat al-nizam al-'amm*) attacks on workers would not be tolerated. The article noted that even Bourguiba was beleaguered by ministerial resignations. A

---

[51] *Al-Akh Habib Achour Yaltaqi bi Al-'Ummal fi Sidi Bouzid wa Gafsa, Al-Sha'b*, in January 28, 1977, p. 1.
[52] *Al-Nashrah Al-Naqabiyyah, Al-Sha'b*, January 21, 1977, p.1.
[53] *Kalimat Al-Ittihad, Al-Sha'b*, November 25, 1977, p. 1.
[54] *Idha Kunna Nuridu Al-Wuduh, Al-Sabah*, January 7, 1978, p. 3.

party Political Bureau shakeup reflected his unease. (Earlier, the UGTT had praised the mass exodus from the Cabinet, including Interior Minister Tahar Belkhodja, as a "responsible position for the sake of democracy and against violence and bloodshed."[55]) Easing the public into the strike, the reasonable-sounding text reminded readers and the government that the union was "the only popular organization before which the tyranny of French colonialism was unable [to triumph] with its land, water, and air weapons." Anti-colonial pedigree and pursuant popular legitimacy aided the union's argument. The UGTT brandished its hefty weight and resistance experience. Creating some drama, the article closed by declaring that its legislative-type National Council (*Majlis Watani*) would decide on its exact course of action. Institutions were important in publicized UGTT protocol.

The Legitimacy of Strikes

Crucial to the social acting and en-acting of union protest in 1977 and afterwards was a publicly-directed assertion of the strikes' legitimacy. This argumentation strategy reflected and propagated the UGTT's normative self-conceptions. Moreover, this defense exposed the government's campaign against a brewing General Strike as a move to disarm the union of its main source of leverage, itself a union right. Emphasizing morality rather than political ambition, Achour insisted, "we are not pursuers of power." Instead, he proposed that the union should "improve the [public] perception of a strike."[56] Achour assured workers that the General Strike would be "only 24 hours in consideration of the public good."[57] International support was forthcoming.[58] Otto Christiansen, head of International Confederation of Free Unions noted in a visit to Tunisia, "strikes are the only expression unions own to make their voice heard."[59] (This external solidarity would carry through to Achour and his comrade's incarceration.[60] They would not live out their sentences, due to Bourguiba's pardons in 1981 as part of a liberalizing streak after the failed coup in Gafsa. Granted permission to visit Achour in prison, Christiansen and Oscar Vatter opined after the visit that he and the other unionists were "innocent."[61])

Strikes were also a venerable UGTT tradition. Hached had himself sanctioned this right in 1947. By striking, "the working class [shows] its readiness to seriously

---

[55] *Al-Wuzara' Al-Mustaqillun, Al-Sha'b,* December 30, 1977, p. 2.
[56] *Al-Akh Al-Habib Achour li Jaridat Al-Jazirah Al-Su'udiyyah,* in *Al-Sha'b,* December 23, 1977, p. 1.
[57] *Fi Ijtima' 'Ummal Al-Sikak Al-Hadidiyyah bi Tunis,* in *Al-Sha'b,* December 23, 1977, p. 1.
[58] Additionally, futile attempts at intercession and mediation by the Palestinian Liberation Organization indicated the Union's closeness to the foremost regional cause (Palestine) and its leadership. In its battle with the state, the UGTT boasted the declared support of American unions, in addition to international ones. *Abu Iyad fi Dar Al-Ittihad and Jami'at Al-Naqabat Al-Amrikiyyah fi Barqiyyah ila Al-Ittihad,* in *Al-Sha'b,* December 16, 1977, p. 1.
[59] *Al-Amin Al-'Amm li Jami'at Al-Naqabat Al-Hurrah Yaqul fi Nadwa Sahafiyyah,* in *Al-Sabah,* January 25, 1978, p. 4.
[60] Achour and Abdelrazzak Gherbal were sentenced to 10 years hard labor, 8 and 6 years respectively for other comrades. See *Al-Hukm Al-Sadir 'Ala Al-Mutawarritin fi Hawadith 26 Janfi,* in *Al-'Amal,* October 11, 1978, p. 6. They would not live out their sentences, as Bourguiba's 1980/1981 liberalizing streak after the 1980 Gafsa uprising included prison pardons.
[61] *Al-Naqabiyyun Al-Mu'taqalun Abriya',* in *Al-Ra'i,* February 23, 1978.

defend its interest, and to wrest its seized rights" to live a "dignified life" fully (quoted in Ben Salah, 2013, 91–92). The UGTT was thus true to form when, in 1977, *Al-Sha'b* had explained that phosphate miners' and petroleum transporters' strikes were "legitimate" in the face of "administrative delays" for years without "real concern" from their respective companies.[62] Thus, workers surmised that "strikes were the only instrument through which they could achieve their demands," precisely as Christiansen had stated. This was especially so, since workers felt "belittlement" and "humiliation" (*ihtiqar* or *hogra*), their "human dignity" injured. Moreover, ignoring workers' demands floods them with "the feeling that they are victims, which they refuse." Importantly, strikes fall under the umbrella of historically "national" syndicalism work: "Syndicalist work since our country was formed has always born a nationalist stamp … and educating the unionist is a correct and difficult education for he is a nationalist who places the interest of the nation and the worker on equal footing."[63] The stress on pedagogy is unmistakable. Within the ranks and the institutions of the UGTT, unionists undergo a values-based education rooted in nationalist feeling. It is thus that protest competencies, for good of worker and country, are developed, as corroborated by the focus group above. A week later, these strikes were declared a "success": worker demands were being considered in the province.[64] The newspaper also defended the democratic procedure through which a Sousse strike was decided, as the union seethed from media attacks.[65] Was not the union "national organization" that is "free and independent" as stated in the constitution? Why the controversy over strikes, the sarcastic letter implied.

Of Infiltrators and Mischief-Makers: The State's Narrative

The union's case before the public was at odds with the government narrative. Dismissal of union demands explains why the union was at such pains to demonstrate the legitimacy and moral urgency of its claims and protest modes of action. A party committee addressed the president following the UGTT's National Council decision to advance with the General Strike.[66] It condemned the decision on grounds of "chaos" by those with "destructive inclinations" and had opted for "rebellion" against the president who stood for "democratic institutions" and socio-economic progress. A contest over memories and re-territorialization appeared. Farhat Hached worked from "authentic union principles." This crew, the party admonished, was a deviation from his model and legacy. Indicating a battle for the rank-and-file unionists, it praised those members who withstood the calls for rebellion. Shortly thereafter,[67] the party invoked the Tunisian people's debt to its liberators, that is, Bourguiba and the Neo-Destour. It entreated Tunisians, now a "free, independence, unified,

[62] *Tahiyyat Al-Sha'b*, in *Al-Sha'b*, November 4, 1977, p. 1.
[63] *Al-Hay'ah Al-Idariyyah li Jami'at Al-Naql Tuqarrir*, in *Al-Sha'b*, November 4, 1977, p. 4.
[64] *Al-Katib Al-'Amm li Al-Ittihad Al-Jihawi li Al-Shughl bi Gafsa*, November 11, 1977, p. 13.
[65] *Risalah min Sousse: Limadha Al-Idrab?* In *Al-Sha'b*, November 18, 1977, p. 21.
[66] *Lajnat Al-Tansiq Al-Hizbi bi Al-'Asimah: Barqiyyah ila al-Ra'is*, in *Al-Sabah*, January 13, 1978, p. 2.
[67] *Bayan Lajnat Al-Tansiq Al-Hizbi fi Tunis*, in *Al-Sabah*, January 15, 1978, p. 4.

coherent nation," currently waging the "greater struggle (*jihad*) ... to emerge from backwardness, [for] comprehensive development, [for] pride and dignified living." Do not let the "chaotic elements" of the UGTT, whose national council had confirmed the insidious plans to destroy the "pillars of the state," sway you, the statement warned. Union insurrection threatened these gains achieved thanks to the "wise leadership of the supreme combatant Habib Bourguiba" under the government of Hedi Nouira. This propagandistic party take presented a choice between modern progress (Bourguiba–Nouira) and unruly regression (the UGTT).

Retreating into defensiveness, Prime Minister Hedi Nouira insisted on the participatory nature of decision-making as government worked contractually through a "social compact."[68] Thus he expressed incredulity that parties (i.e. UGTT) would ungratefully "renege" on the agreement reached early the previous year "between a night and a day." Disconcerted by Achour's resignation (from the party's political bureau), he cautioned that this action could incite "confusion" among partisans. The decision was irresponsible. As matters came to a head, the President himself declared war on the UGTT. Bourguiba was prepared to "stand against the vandals" and the "mischief-makers"; Ba'athists and communists "st[ood] behind" the UGTT Secretary General.[69] This government narrative was one of infiltrators who had poisoned the UGTT, turning it against party and nation. It set the tone for the repression to come.

Right on schedule, state-allied media reports attacked a security officer "dragged into UGTT headquarters," darkly implicating the union and justifying in advance a brutality framed as defensive.[70] Hence, the government held that it was fending off unruly "attempts to dominate" the party and "national organizations" such as the UGTT. It nominally assured its commitment to the "right to strike."[71] Striking appeared to be almost a sacred practice that could not be publicly or formally retracted even by a government in attack mode. Given its anti-colonial deployment, it was as though the right to strike was so deeply entrenched in the social imaginary, Tunisians' cognition of themselves as a people, that to challenge strikes as such would diminish the party's Destourian credibility. Also, attempting more positive propaganda, the high profile Destour official Mohamed Sayyah said that the party "calls for love and brotherhood and harmony."[72] Others present at the meeting decried the "political color" of the strike, grounds for disputing its validity.

The Union's Counter-Offensive

The union's response to this media salvo was vehement. A form of narrative agency complemented the discourse and practice of protest. In fact, the UGTT newspaper *Al-Sha'b* adopted a "new editorial line" during this crisis, engaging in a narrative

---

[68] *Tunis La Tamurru bi Azmah Siyasiyyah bal bi Tasaddu' fi Al-Saff Al-Qawmi*, in *Al-Sabah*, January 21, 1978, pp. 2–3.
[69] *Al-Ra'is: Musta'iddin li Al-Wuquf fi Wajh Al-Mukharribin*, in *Al-Sabah*, January 22, 1978, p. 2.
[70] *I'tida' 'Ala Ba'd A'wan Al-Amn*, in *Al-Sabah*, January 22, 1978.
[71] *Ashghal Al-Lajnah Al-Markaziyyah li Al-Hizb*, in *Al-Sabah*, January 22, 1978, p. 2.
[72] *Al-Sayyah Yajtami' bi Ru'asa' Al-Sha'b fi Wilayat Tunis*, in *Al-Sabah*, January 26, 1978, p. 2.

play-by-play with official accounts (Belhoula 2015, 123). Unionized media workers called for *Al-Sha'b*'s opening column to be published in the official news agency.[73] Taking the media and political battle to an international audience, Habib Achour affirmed that the union demands were of a "social and economic hue."[74] Refuting rumors, he added that the UGTT had no political aspirations. Rather, the face-off was "to defend the freedom of the union" especially since the cabinet reshuffle. At this point, he was careful not to completely sever ties with the party, to whose "lofty principles" he was still "attached." Achour also went on a European tour to clarify the Ittihad's "true position" to international unions amidst the government onslaught.[75] Activating transnational labor connections central to its cosmopolitan self-image, he sought and signaled external solidarity with the union. To a great extent, the unfolding national theatrics were a narrative contest. Again, the union's Executive Committee declared its commitment to "the principle of work and dialogue to reform matters."[76] The government, on the other hand, which "dominate[d] public media outlets," was guilty of demonizing the UGTT and of issuing a call to vigilante violence. A few days before the strike, Achour struck a more personal tone. His words hinted at a clash of personalities that was the subtext of the whole conflict. He lashed out against the defamation campaign attributing the UGTT's planned strike to the Secretary General's ambition to take Bourguiba's place as president.[77] Achour renounced this tactic as "incitement to murder." Summoning the affective nostalgia of anti-colonial loyalty and sacrifice, he clarified a few "historical truths" for Tunisians, recounting how he saved Bourguiba's life in March 1945 on his way to Egypt. Over two nights, the current President hid in Achour's house, for which the latter was arrested by the French. We are "authentic citizens," proclaimed Achour, unlike party newcomers who could potentially betray Bourguiba in a heartbeat.

Its reputation was essential to the UGTT's counter-narrative. For example, Habib Achour maintained the moral high ground against calumnious critics of the government and its propagandists. "We want for them what is good, and they want for us [the] hangman's noose," was the dramatic contrast he drew between the two. Theirs was the goodwill of "the working masses," he stated.[78] At the same time, the UGTT drew a line in the sand to separate itself from the increasingly hawkish government. Against creeping state militarization, the union conveyed an expansive notion of human security ("political and social security").[79] The disparity between the union and the government was unambiguous. The state should stand on pillars of "brotherhood and solidarity not bloodshed," it suggested. The union presented an understanding of order which was "not achieved through the police but through

---

[73] *Fi Ijtima' Al-Hay'ah Al-Idariyyah li Al-Naqabah Al-'Ammah li Al-Thaqafah Wa Al-I'lam*, in *Al-Sha'b*, November 18, 1977, p. 24.
[74] *Al-Habib 'Achour Yu 'alliq fi Bruxel 'ala Ashghal Al-Majlis Al-Qawmi*, in *Al-Sabah*, January 15, 1978.
[75] *'Ada Achour min Uruba*, in *Al-Sabah*, January 18, 1978, p. 3.
[76] *Ijtima' Al-Maktab Al-Tanfidhi li Al-Ittihad*, in *Al-Sabah*, January 15, 1978, p. 4.
[77] *Al-Habib Achour: Ba'd Al-Haqa'iq Al-Tarikhiyyah*, in *Al-Sabah*, January 21, 1978.
[78] *Kalimat Al-Ittihad*, in *Al-Sha'b*, December 9, 1977, p. 1.
[79] *Al-Amn fi Mafhumihi Al-Rafi' Huwa Al-Amn Al-Siyasi wa Al-Ijtima'i*, in *Al-Sha'b*, December 30, 1977.

effective political means." The message was a denouncement of increasing state securitization, in contradistinction to the UGTT's values of rights, democracy, and socio-economic emancipation. "Democracy is not [merely] talk," the union added.[80] It reiterated concerns over changes in the Interior Ministry and Head of Security, "a step towards harshness." This indicated the union's defiance. Regional unions also chimed in. The agency to fight back is always an option, the UGTT said through its various institutional bodies. "We resisted colonialism … and will resist every rigidity whatever its source."[81] It drew once again on its anti-colonial credentials in a veiled threat as a response to the new hawkish government. State security looked alarmingly "military," it noted. The media was "falsified," and "nationalism" itself was at stake. These critiques surpassed simple socio-economic demands, ascending to a daring political critique by the union.

The General Strike

The escalating confrontation reached fever pitch on the eve of the announced strike. In (presumably party militia) attacks on UGTT headquarters in the regions, for example Kairouan, the government again showed its violent hand.[82] The ensuing strike engulfed the capital, with parallel strikes in the regions, for instance the industrial capital Sfax.[83] The brutality of the army and police shocked Tunisians. Officials admitted to 40 deaths and 325 injured, later driving up the number to 46.[84] It was likely much higher. The opposition Socialist Democrats pressed the Prime Minister's office to release the actual numbers.[85] In the aftermath, the Tunis governor paid a visit to affected neighborhoods (Bab Bhar, Sidi Bechir, Bab Souika).[86] Prime Minister Hedi Nouira insisted that "the government didn't prohibit the strike on Thursday … but took necessary measures to protect security." He callously rebuffed notions that the state of emergency was a "siege" or excessive "militarization."[87] Its words defying its deeds, the government still publicly spoke of the right to strike as untouchable. State retaliation did not stop at the immediate violence. In a repeat of his 1965 incarceration, Habib Achour was arrested from his house in Al-Menzah on January 28, 1978.[88] Others were arrested and charged with blocking traffic, light violent attacks,

---

[80] *Nala 'Ummal Al-Manajim Matalibahum Al-Mulihhah … fa Ulghiya Al-Idrab,* in *Al-Sha'b,* December 30, 1977, p. 1.
[81] *Al-Naqbiyyun fi Ijtima' Al-Hay'ah Al-Idariyyah li Al-Ittihad Al-Jihawi,* in *Al-Sha'b,* December 30, 1977.
[82] *Muhajamat Maqarr Al-Ittihad Al-Jihawi li Al-Shughl bi Al-Kairouan,* in *Al-Sabah,* January 25, 1978.
[83] *Al-Idrab Al-'Amm fi Sfax,* in *Al-Sabah,* January 26, 1978, p. 3.
[84] *Wazir Al-Dakhiliyyah fi Nadwah Sahafiyyah,* in *Al-Sabah,* January 28, 1978, p. 2 and *Wazarat Al-Sahhah: 'Adad Al-Mawta Ba'da Hawadithi Al-Khamis: 46 Shakhsan,* in *Al-Sabah,* February 2, 1978, p. 2.
[85] *Al-Khabar Muqaddas Wa Al-Ta' liq Hurr,* in *Al-Ra'i,* March 16, 1978, p. 3.
[86] *Al-Wali Ra'is Iqlim Tunis Yazuru Al-Ahya' al-Mutadarrirah min A'mal Al-Takhrib,* in *Al-Sabah,* January 28, 1978.
[87] *Al-Wazir Al-Awwal Yudli bi Tasrih Li Jam' Min Al-Sahafiyyin al-Ajanib,* in *Al-Sabah,* January 29, 1978.
[88] *Iqaf Al-Sayyed Habib Achour and Mahkamat Al-Nahiyah Tanzur fi Qadaya Al-Idtirab Al-Akhirah,* in *Al-Sabah,* January 31, 1978, p. 4.

and assault of public officials.[89] Sentences for lower profile unionists ranged from 15 days to six months.[90] For Achour and his higher-level comrades (defended by a team including the young Radia Nasraoui,[91] who would reappear in 2008 and the 2011 revolution), later sentences would be higher. Addressing parliament, Hedi Nouira noted that "Tunis will live, despite illness and enemies, free, invincible, everlasting." He insisted that the UGTT should return to activity with "legitimacy," further reassuring listeners that democracy "was continuous development." This was not a setback for putative Bourguibist democracy.[92]

The government matched its repression with additional action to curb the union. The UGTT had shown itself to be a formidable counterforce in Bourguiba's increasingly authoritarian regime. Its wings had to be clipped. Reported resignations in the UGTT by those with allegiance to Bourguiba were the beginning.[93] Regional Executive Offices (e.g. Sousse) activated a change of personnel in exceptional congresses, launching a "corrective movement."[94] Not all unionists subscribed to Achour and his supporters' radicalism. The most notable blow came not two weeks after the strike. The Executive Office of UGTT named Tijani Obid as Secretary General until an extraordinary congress on February 25. This action by the Executive Office stripped Achour and "extremist factions" of union status, and also sent a message to the Prime Minister and to the President with "gratitude for his decisive position to rescue the country and the nation and … the workers specifically, from the illness of … discord (*fitnah*)." The new leadership pledged adherence to "national unity," and Bourguibism.[95] Perhaps the swiftness of the (new) UGTT leadership's retreat indicates long-standing internal union tensions. For the moment, the UGTT had been reined in.

The Opposition's Support

Strengthening its democratic credibility, before and after the general strike and crackdown, was the (radicalized) UGTT's connection to the burgeoning political opposition. The likes of Ahmed Mestiri and Hassib ben Ammar had split off from the Destour after the 1971 Monsastir Congress. Mutual promotion and amplification testified to the affinity between the Mestiri-led opposition and the union. The

---

[89] *Al-Mahkamah Tuwasilu Al-Nazara fi Qadiyyat Al-Thalb wa Al-Tajamhur fi Al-Tariq Al-'Amm*, in *Al-Sabah*, February 2, 1978.
[90] *Fi Mahkamat Al-Nahiyah: Ahkam bi Al-Sijn Natijat A'mal Al-Shaghab*, *Al-Sabah*, February 5, 1978.
[91] Radia Nasraoui had also been named to defend some of the accused in the 1980 Gafsa insurrection. See *Qadiyyat Al-'Udwan 'Ala Gafsa*, in *Al-Ra'i*, March 21, 1980, p. 2. Attorneys from the Young Lawyers' Association were also on the team who complained of obstacles against their free and fair defense of the defendants. See *Bayan Min Al-Muhamin Al-Shubban*, in *Al-Ra'i*, June 20, 1980, p. 2.
[92] *Bayan Al-Sayyid Hedi Nouira fi Majlis Al-Ummah*, in *Al-Sabah*, February 1, 1978, p. 2.
[93] *Istiqalat Kathirah Min Al-Ittihad*, in *Al-Sabah*, January 29, 1978.
[94] *Tajdid Al-Maktab Al-Tanfidhi li Al-Ittihad Al-Jihawi li Al-Shughl bi Sousse*, in *Al-Sabah*, January 31, 1978, p. 4.
[95] *Al-Maktab Al-Tanfidhi li Al-Ittihad Al-'Amm Al-Tunisi li Al-Shughl Yuqarrir*, in *Al-Sabah*, February 3, 1978, p. 3.

front page of the December 30, 1977 issue, for instance, featured an advertisement for a new "weekly political newspaper" called *Al-Ra'i*, with clues to some of the article titles.[96] This would be one outlet (alongside student publications explored in the next chapter) inaugurating oppositional media in Tunisia (Qam 'oun 2021, 104–105). *Al-Ra'i* also ran news of nascent civil society forces such as the Tunisian League of Human Rights.[97] As Table 3.2 shows, the new opposition that called for democracy and the rule of law[98] professed positions similar or supportive of UGTT stances. These politicians had expressed skepticism about the procedures and the representativeness of the exceptional Congress.[99] Mestiri wrote of a "chronic crisis" in socio-economic and political domains, necessitating "deep treatment" to avert a fall into "chaos."[100] The newspaper was one face of demotic agency and the struggle for democracy.[101] This opposition inclined towards the UGTT as strikes intensified.[102] The flailing Destour could not save the National Compact, Mestiri, Hassib Ben Ammar, and their colleagues argued.[103] Reflections on the "deep causes" of the crisis suggested that the (1971–77) alliance between two great personalities, the "two Habibs" (Habib (Achour) and Habib (Bourguiba)) had been shaky from the start.[104] At its heart, the 1978 eruption was an indisputable sign that "singular rule inside the party and the country" had failed.

Nearly a month after the 1978 strike, a petition signed by 246 UGTT members ran in *Al-Ra'i*.[105] They called for the release of the imprisoned unionists, the "legitimate leadership" (*al-qiyadah al-shar'iyyah*) and insisted they would proceed within the by-laws and decisions of the previous Congress (1977). These adamant signatories also demanded an end to the state of emergency and formation of a committee to investigate and "assign responsibility" to the bloody events of January 26. Importantly, they would proceed undeterred "within the scope of democratic practices of union rights," implying they would not abide by the exceptional congress that had been so quickly cobbled together. Moreover, they refuted any blame on UGTT rank and file or its leadership for the disastrous events. Preserving the hard-won reputation of strikes, these unionists noted they had avoided strikes in water, gas, electricity, and hospitals, also staying away from protests on main roads. The General Strike

---

[96] *Al-Sha'b*, December 30, 1977, p. 1.
[97] The LTDH expressed reservations about the state crackdown and state of emergency. See *Mawqif Al-Rabitah Al-Tunisiyyah li Al-Difa'i 'An Huquq Al-Insan*, February 16, 1978, p. 3.
[98] *Waznu Al-'Adalah…fi Al-Mizan*, in *Al-Ra'i*, March 9, 1978, pp. 4–5.
[99] *Qabla In'iqad Al-Mu'tamar Al-Istithna'i li Al-Ittihad Al-'Amm Al-Tunisi li Al-Shughl: Tasa'ulat*, in *Al-Ra'i*, p. 4.
[100] *Tariq al-'Unf Tariq Masdud*, in *Al-Ra'i*, December 29, 1977, p. 1.
[101] *Al-Ra'i*, December 29, 1977, p. 1.
[102] *Hal Hiya Qati'ah?* In *Al-Ra'i*, January 12, 1978, p. 1; and *Nida' Ila Al-Ta'aqqul and Mawqifuna*, *Al-Ra'i*, January. 26, 1978, p.1.
[103] *Al-Muraja'ah Aslam Min Al-Taraju' Al-Mutakarrir and Fashal Al-Mithaq Al-Watani*, in *Al-Ra'i*, January 19, 1978, p. 1.
[104] *Hawla Asbab Al-Azmah*, in *Al-Ra'i*, February 16, 1978, p. 1.
[105] *Aswat Hurrah Tunadi bi Al-Ifraj 'An Al-Naqabiyyin wa Bi Raf' Halat Al-Tawari'* in *Al-Ra'i*, February 9, 1978, p. 1.

Table 3.2 Discursive Convergence with UGTT: Political Opposition in 1978

Democratic Socialist language*	Significance	Parallel UGTT language, positions
Goals of "democratic, socialist" country	Ambitions to achieve democracy, social justice neglected since independence	Democracy, social justice are historical values (Al-Hammi, Hached, then Achour)
Wish for "human being [to] have value"	Human dignity sutured to democracy	Dignity of workers and people is a central value
Critique of Bourguiba regime: "rigidity" and "decay" and "terrorism"	Origins of movement is defection from Neo-Destour	Denounces government "rigidity," weakness, and use of violence
"strong and independent workers' organization" [union] is in "national interest"	Support for union against government harassment or prosecution Workers' interest=the people's interest	"Independence" slogan continuously used since Al-Hammi's era
National Compact had "failed"	Initially UGTT-government agreement had failed to foment social equality or de-escalate conflict	Abandons National Compact because government policies (rising prices, attack on union) contradicted its essence
Stands with "freedom and the rule of law," "union freedoms"	Ultimately sides with UGTT in conflict with government	"freedom," individual and collective (union, people) is a central tenet
Denounces "singular rule" of party	Bourguiba's government and party are un-democratic	Union democracy and country-wide democracy are inseparable
Al-Ra'i: a platform for free media expression, a "step towards democracy"	State propaganda is a cornerstone of Bourguiba's un-democratic rule	*Al-Sha'b*: union's platform for free expression during crisis
Skepticism over new UGTT leadership (Sec. Gen. Tijani Obid)	Questions about democratic legitimacy	UGTT petitioners' refusal of "illegitimate" leadership

* Drawn from *Al-Ra'i*'s coverage of the crisis, Dec. 1977–Feb. 1978, especially, *Qabla In'iqad Al-Mu'tamar Al-Istithna'i li-l-Ittihad Al-'Am Al-Tunisi li Al-Shughl: Tasa'ulat, Al-Ra'i*, p. 4; *Tariq al-'Unf Tariq Masdud*, Dec. 29, 1977, p. 1; Dec. 29, 1977, *Hal Hiya Qati'ah?* Jan. 12, 1978, p. 1; *Nida' Ila Al-Ta'aqqul wa Mawqifuna, Al-Ra'i*, Jan. 26, 1978, p.1; *Al-Muraja'ah Aslam Min Al-Taraju' Al-Mutakarrir* and *Fashal Al-Mithaq Al-Watani*, Jan. 19, 1978, p. 1.; *Hawla Asbab Al-Azmah*, Feb. 16, 1978, p. 1; *Aswat Hurrah Tunadi Bi Al-Ifraj 'An Al-Naqabiyyin wa Bi Raf' Halat Al-Tawari'*, Feb. 9, 1978, p. 1; *Min Ajli Istiqrar Haqiqi, Al-Ra'i*, March 9, 1978, p. 1.

was a "success," despite media vilification and government repression. The government bore both immediate (e.g. security violence) and more deep-rooted blame for the events. The whole debacle stemmed from the government's fear of the UGTT. Swelling union numbers, its achievements in securing workers' rights, its internal "democratic opening," had propelled it forward "for the first time since independence" as "representative ... of popular hopes and aspirations." Through this written challenge, the petitioners reached into the Tunisian social imaginary (*mikhyal*), the positive affect, historical-turned-present agency, and cognition of the union as an emancipatory force. Just as it had fought for people's independence against the colons, it was battling for their rights and liberation from the domineering party and president. The petition characteristically upholds the UGTT as both champion and extension of *Al-Sha'b*. Facing off against to the government (and the new UGTT leadership that lacked legitimacy) was the only route for continued struggle. The use of the term "democracy" is striking, a modernizing update to anti-colonial combat waged over two decades earlier. Also noteworthy is the persistent stress on the efficacy and (moral) validity of strikes. Repression would not cow free-spirited unionists seeking to advance people's rights. The government could not confiscate its modus operandi. If the UGTT was a popular advocate, protests (strikes) were its main weapon. Some unionists, at least, would not de-mobilize. The 1984 bread riots would be the next round in the ongoing UGTT–state saga.

The 1984 Bread Riots

In contrast to 1978, the UGTT national leadership did not lead the 1983/1984 bread riots. These sudden events (see Dakhli 2021) were sparked by rioting youths, among the poor and marginalized of Tunisia. Tunisia's Southern periphery, beginning with secondary school students and children in Douz (Kebili province), then Gafsa, then the rest of the country, rose up in a new insurrection: the bread uprising (*intifadat al-khubz*). This they did in response to a sudden skyrocketing of bread and grain prices, part of First/Prime Minister Mohamed Mzali's IMF and World Bank-inflected neoliberal economic agenda. In Gafsa, the Tunisian Human Rights League (LTDH) helped to mobilize a "peaceful demonstration" on January 1, 1984.[106] Protestor violence[107] came up against state repression, not unlike that of Black Thursday six years earlier. Table 3.3 analyzes the agentic, affective, and cognitive connotations of protestors' language. Slogans scrawled on the walls in red declared "popular revolution" and "revolution until victory." Others declared: "With our soul and blood, we sacrifice to you, o people," and "Bread, Freedom, and National Dignity." This protest language would resurface in 2008 (Chapter 5) and the revolution of 2011 (Chapter 6).

From December 27, 1983 until January 6, 1984, when Bourguiba retracted the price increases, protests and riots tore through Tunisia. Looting and violence accompanied the protests. Caught unprepared, the state imposed a state of emergency and a nightly curfew between 6 p.m. and 5 am.[108] The chaos was brief. Crowds erupted in spontaneous celebration at the "Supreme Commander's" announcement through

---

[106] *Al-Khubz…wa Al-Fawda…wal Al-Amn*, in *Al-Ra'i*, January 6, 1984, pp. 2–3.
[107] For instance, *Ahdath Mu'limah fi Gafsa wa Al-Kasserine wa Manatiq Ukhra fi Al-Janub*, in *Al-Sabah*, January 3, 1984.
[108] *Halat Tawari' wa Man' Al-Jawalan Lailan Bikamil Al-Bilad*, in *Al-Ra'i*, January 6, 1984, p. 1.

Table 3.3 Unpacking Social Acting and En-Acting in 1984

	Language*	Translation	Significance
Agency	Wild Al-'Amil wal Fallah Aqwa Minnak Ya Saffah	Son of the worker and the farmer are stronger than you, o killer	Strength of the marginalized comes from just demands that overpower state military might
	Thawrah Hatta Al-Nasr	Revolution until victory	Determination to persist in radical protest until demands are met
Affect	Bil-Ruh Bil-Damm, Nafdik Ya Sha'b	With our soul and blood, we sacrifice to you, o people	Sacrifice to worthy cause of people's dignity
	Ji'anin, Ji'anin, Wil Khubza bi Mi'ah wa Sab'in	We are hungry, hungry, and the bread [loaf] is 170 [milim]	Anger at policy lifting subsidies is unbearable for Tunisia's poor who suffer deprivation
	Ya Bourguiba, Ya Hanin, Rajji' Al-Khubza Bi-Thmanin	O loving Bourguiba, return the [price] of the bread [loaf] to 80 [milim]	Appealing to (putative) loving and fatherly bond between Bourguiba and the people
Cognition	Thawrah Sha'biyyah	Popular Revolution	Cognizing uprising as made by representative of the people
	Khubz, Hurriyyah, Karamah Wataniyyah	Bread, freedom, social justice	Demands of marginalized are pursuit of dignity by (non)people

* These are protest slogans as reported in *Al-Ra'i*, Jan. 6, 1986, pp. 2–3.

his now—famous words, "we return to where we were," *(nirja'u win kunna)*.[109] In flowery language, presidential minions acclaimed the "paternal love" of the President for his "weak children." Bourguiba was keen on "protecting the dignity of the low-income" (by reducing the price hike), at the same time protecting state institutions (by using the army).[110] Not unlike the civil society mobilization that would blossom in defense and advocacy of Gafsa's imprisoned protestors in 2008 (Chapter 5), the work of attorneys and the LTDH would be instrumental in securing an eventual pardon for many of the young people arrested in January.[111] In the midst of the fracas, Habib Achour gave assurances that "the workers did not engage in strikes."[112] In this popular rebellion, the UGTT presented itself as a rational force, displaying the same demotic agency, this time for the greater sake of de-escalation. Decrying the violence of looting, Achour added that responsibility for "destruction and burning" paled in comparison to "firing bullets on protests," and killing protestors. The

[109] *Masirah Sha'biyyah Tilqa'iyyah Dakhmah*, in *Al-'Amal*, January 7, 1984, p. 3.
[110] *Iftitahiyyah*, in *Al-'Amal*, January 7, 1984, p. 1.
[111] *Al-Istijabah…* in *Al-Tariq Al-Jadid*, June 23, 1984
[112] *Al-Khubz…wa Al-Fawda…wa Al-Amn*, in *Al-Ra'i*, January 6, 1984, p. 2.

union had, however, called for a wage increase to offset the near doubling of the price of a baguette (90 to 170 millim) on December 27, 1983.

Some members of the Socialist Democrats (now a licensed opposition party), recognized the wide-ranging nature of this uprising where "the entire people" participated, downplaying the looting. Capitalizing on the opportunity for political critique, the opposition suggested it was the gulf between the (falsely) elected Parliament, now called the Popular Assembly (*Majlis Al-Nuwwab*) and popular aspirations that resulted in this predicament.[113] A week later, above a picture of a protestor raised over the crowd, flashing the victory sign, one headline dubbed the riots a "street revolution."[114] Others stressed that this was the revolt of Tunisia's most marginalized, not a proper revolution since even the students leading it lost control of the crowd and the more privileged classes did not join.[115] The government was culpable above all other parties, answerable to eliminating "the causes of violence" through an overhaul of socio-economic policy.[116] Prices should not have been raised to begin with. Here, the opposition's agency was one of (more or less) objective analysis, its cognition that of problem-solving as an elite acting on behalf of the people. On the other hand, the mutinous youth and their fellow marginalized exhibited the agency (to protest), affect (rage against price increases), and cognition (refusal of state injustice). The union, finally, framed its role as the agency of restraint, animated by the affect of solidarity with Tunisia's poor, and the cognition of social justice driving it to oppose the new policy.

Al-Sha'b's coverage of its 1984 Congress hailed the union's "exceptional position" that facilitated the government's retreat from the grueling bread and grain price hikes.[117] In this sense, the UGTT was attuned to the anti-social welfare meddling of the international financial institutions, whose directives to lift state subsidies had been eagerly taken up by First Minister Mohamed Mzali. On the other hand, perhaps given its ongoing warfare with the government, the UGTT withdrew from this match. Perhaps it "let" Tunisia's downtrodden take the lead. Al-Haddad (2011, 221–222) almost faults the union for overlooking the plight of the most downtrodden (including the unemployed) through its fixation on the working class. Whatever its motives, we suggest that the UGTT's impact is indisputable. Even if it did not directly lead the 1984 *intifadah*, the protest competencies it inculcated among its members, the public argumentation in defense of freedom and dignity through the right to strike, the showdowns with the state in 1978 to which the wider society had paid attention, are not to be treated lightly. Interviewees (including student interviewees who took part; see Chapter 4) furthermore suggest that regional UGTT

---

[113] *Qudiya Al-Amr, fa Man Al-Mas'ul?* in *Al-Mustaqbal*, January 19, 1984, p. 2.
[114] *Thawrat Al-Shari' fi Tunis*, in *Al-Ra'i*, January 13, 1984, p. 1.
[115] *Asda' Al-Zilzal*, in *Al-Ra'i*, January 27, 1984.
[116] *Bayan Al-Maktab Al-Siyasi li Harakat Al-Dimuqratiyyin Al-Ishtirakiyyin*, in *Al-Mustaqbal*, January 11, 1984, pp. 1–2.
[117] *Mawqif Mutamayyiz li Al-Ittihad fi Qadiyyat Ilgha' Al-Da'm*, in *Al-Sha'b*, December 14, 1984, p. 1.

were active in the bread riots. Habib Achour held the official line in an interview with an opposition newspaper. He maintained that neither the national UGTT or regional branches formally called for protest or strikes. If unionists had taken part, they had done so "as individuals" and not on behalf of regional or national UGTT branches.[118] Perhaps the UGTT was simply distributing roles so that the leadership could technically stay above the fray. National and regional administration, gradually established in the union's founding decade (Belhadi 2020), have not been without tension. Most importantly, the situated-ness of this protestscape (as all others) lies in its partial re-ontologizing, its polyphonous components. Formal, institutionalized leadership of protest in Tunisia (through the UGTT, or the student movement) is one part of the equation. Tunisia's have-nots, historically "the part that has no part," its marginalized and excluded, may not be formally embroiled in these often oppositional organizations. This dynamic, the sometimes strained complementarity of more "formalized" syndicalist protest and that of the unaffiliated, will recur in Tunisia's various protestscapes up to and after the revolution itself (2008, 2010–11, 2017 in Kamour).

Conclusion

Achour's UGTT did not take the helm in the 1984 bread riots. However, the union was unable to avert Nouira's "strike" as the government sought to keep it in check through divide-and-conquer strategies (for instance, between "Achour-ites" and so-called "Front-ists" (*Jabhawiyyun* in reference to those (coopted) against him) (Al-Medini, 2019, 69–71). Achour's re-election[119] as Secretary General at the 16th Congress of 1984, celebrated as "a success that dashed the hope of the UGTT's enemies,"[120] likely did it no favors in the eyes of the Prime Minister.

Tunisia's most visible contrepouvoir continued to pump new life into its reservoir of adherents. At least 120,000 new members attended the 1984 Congress, doubling the total number at the 1981 meeting.[121] A report released at the Congress formally attributed responsibility of the January 26, 1978 tragedy to the ruling party. "The people" stood by the UGTT as the party's "fascist" tendencies were exposed.[122] Soon after, a new crisis would erupt in 1985 as the government coopted the UGTT leadership headed by the so-called "Shurafa" (the honourable). After Ben Ali's coup, the new President plotted to further de-fang the union. Along with some initially optimistic opposition parties, the UGTT signed the "National Compact" and participated

---

[118] *Hiwar Ma'a Habib Achour*, in *Al-Ra'i*, January 6, 1984, pp. 4–5.
[119] Taieb Baccouche, voted Secretary General in the exceptional 1981 Congress, and with whom Achour had a tense relationship, offers an unenthused, less complimentary account of the 16th Congress (see Baccouche 2021, 150–155).
[120] *Ahlam A'da' Al-Ittihad*, in *Al-Sha'b*, December 22, 1984, pp. 1–2.
[121] *Al-Mu'tamar Al-Watani Al-Sadis 'Ashar*, in *Al-Sha'b*, December 14, 1984, p. 2.
[122] *Muqtatafat min Al-Taqrir Al-Adabi Qaddamahu Al-Akh Habib Achour*, in *Al-Sha'b*, December 22, 1984, p. 18.

in the pursuant committee of the same name.[123] He instated the lackey Ismail Sahbani (elected to the Executive Office in the 1984 Congress).[124] The notorious Sahbani remained in power until 2000 when he was arrested on corruption charges. In the 2002 Djerba Congress, the tide began to turn toward (cautious) opposition within the UGTT leadership. Abdelslam Jrad was elected in this "democratic" moment, designated a "corrective pathway" (*masar al-tashih*) as Secretary General.[125] Still, the UGTT duly thanked the President for "the nobility of his feelings towards" the union![126]

The UGTT entered into a so-called "associative cooperation" with the President who had achieved international recognition of sorts through the Barcelona Partnership (1995) with the EU. Union relations with the state continued to transform in a globalizing age (Ennaceur 2000). Increasingly neoliberal Ben Ali bound the union within periodic negotiations, avoiding the possibility of overwhelming union protest and pressure (see also Zemni 2013, 137–140). The UGTT even supported the president's much-mocked extension (*tamdid*) of his presidency and his "re-elections" in 2004 and 2009,[127] although not without internal wrangling. This, despite the fact that the union had adopted 2-term limits at the 2002 congress for its own executive office in an indirect message to the President about democratic practice.[128] Yet even Ben Ali did not (could not) quell the impetus for striking. Perhaps he had done a bit of "dictator's learning" (Dobson 2013) himself. Strikes by sectoral or regional unions did take place even during the Ben Ali years.[129] Mohamed Ali Square in which the UGTT national headquarters was nestled, became a kind of "free space" (see Chapter 4) for unionists. There, they could vent their frustrations and criticisms of the regime, even cursing Ben Ali, so long as they remained within the cordoned space.[130] Within the UGTT leadership, figures such as Houcine Abassi[131] exemplified an expanding oppositional trend.

By the time the 2008 phosphate basin (Gafsa) uprising (Chapter 4) erupted, local and regional unionists were well-positioned to wage a full-scale uprising. The national leadership expressed first its tepid, then less so, support in 2008. Rank and file Gafsa unionists lived and breathed the agency, affect, and cognition of Al-Hammi's and Hached's mythical models. The epic battles of 1978 and 1984, too,

---

[123] *Al-Ijtima' Al-Awwal li Al-Majlis Al-A'la li Al-Mithaq Al-Watani*, in *Al-Sha'b*, January 13, 1990, pp. 1, 9.
[124] *A'da' Al-Maktab Al-Tanfidhi Al-Jadid*, in *Al-Sha'b*, December 22, 1984, p. 32.
[125] *Kaifa Tamma Tamhid Al-Tariq li Al-Mu'tamar Al-Isthithna'i?* in *Al-Sha'b*, February 9, 2002, p. 4.
[126] *Al-Akh Al-Amin Al-'Amm li Al-Ittihad fi Mu'tamar Sahafi*, in *Al-Sha'b*, February 16, 2002, p. 3.
[127] See *Ittihad Al-Shughl Yusanid Tarashuh Ben Ali li Al-Fatrah Al-Ri'asiyyah Al-Muqbilah*, in *Alchourouk*, June 18, 2005; and *Musanadat Tarashuh Ben Ali Li-yuwasil Qiyadat Masirat Al-Bilad*, in *Al-Sha'b*, October 24, 2009.
[128] Interview with UGTT Regional Secretary General, July 24, 2022.
[129] See for instance, *Idrabat 'Adidah fi Al-Ufuq*, in *Al-Sha'b*, January 20, 1990, p. 1; *Al-Idrab wa Al-Tahawwul*, February 10, 1990, p. 1; *Ba'da Al-Idrabat Al-Akhira: Matalib Al-Shaghalin: Hal min Hall?* February 17, 1990, in *Al-Sha'b*, p. 1; *Idrabat fi Al-Mawani' Al-Jawwiyyah wa Al-Sahhah*, in *Al-Sha'b*, March 10, 1990, p. 1; *La Li-Darb Hurriyyat Al-'Amal Al-Naqabi fi Al-Qita' Al-Khass*, in *Al-Sha'b*, April 7, 1990, p. 1; *Harakiyyah Naqabiyyah Mukaththafah wa Idrab bi Al-Ma'amil Al-Aliyyah Yawm 19 Fivri*, in *Al-Sha'b*, February 8, 1992, p. 7.
[130] Interview with UGTT regional Secretary General, October 22, 2022.
[131] A Nobel Peace Laureate, as part of the quartet of Tunisian civic bodies that won the award in 2015.

had penetrated the social imaginary of Tunisians who were potentially ready to be rebellious against a dictatorial and impoverishing regime. Hence, the union's outsize presence in the 2011 revolution (Yousfi 2018) was almost a fulfillment of its anti-colonial genesis. Worker resistance to the dictates of global capitalist institutions (Hanieh 2013) has been one notable feature of the 2011 revolution in Tunisia and elsewhere (Alexander and Bassiouny 2014; Talani 2014). Since its contentious origins in 1924, Tunisia's worker movement was always present, openly or latently, in disputes with the state. The UGTT was a backbone of Tunisian peoplehood-in-becoming. It was one unmissable pillar, cementing a "rendezvous," as it were, with Tunisia's 2011 revolutionary diachrony. Perhaps Achour's words at the opening of the 1984 Congress still ring true: "the UGTT is a force of struggle (*munadil*) forever and ever."[132]

References

Adouani, S. and Ben Sedrine, S. 2018. *Trade Unions in Transformation: Trade Union Power and Democratic Transition in Tunisia*. Friedrich Ebert Stiftung.

Al-Asali, Ahmed. 2018. *Ta'rif Mujaz Li Jaridat Al-Sha'b Lisan Al-Ittihad Al-'Amm Al-Tunisi Li Al-Shughl* [Concise Introduction to *AL-Sha'b*: the UGTT Newspaper]. UGTT, March 28, https://www.ugtt.org.tn/?p=4222

Alexander, Anne and Mostafa Bassiouny. 2014. *Bread, Freedom, Social Justice: Workers and the Egyptian Revolution*. London: Zed.

Al-Haddad, Salem. 2011. *Al-Ittihad Al-'Amm Al-Tunisi li Al-Shughl wa Nidham Bourguiba baina Al-Wi'am wa Al-Sidam* [The UGTT and Bourguiba's Regime: Between Accord and Discord]. Part 2. Tunis: Art Typo.

Al-Mahjoubi, Ali. 2015. *Al-Harakah Al-Naqabiyyah Al-Tunisiyyah Al-Shaghilah: Baina Al-Nidal Al-Ijtima'i wa Al-Nidal Al-Siyasi* [The Tunisian Syndicalist Labor Movement: Between Social and Political Struggle]. Aryana: Nadhar.

Manser, Adnan. 2007. *Dawlat Bourguiba: Fusul fi Al-Ideolojiya wa Al-Mumarasah 1956–1970* [Bourguiba's State: Chapters of Ideology and Practice]. Sfax: Dar Amal.

Al-Medini, Tawfiq. 2019. *Al-Ittihad Al-'Amm Al-Tunisi li Al-Shughl: Hizban Mu'aridan* [The UGTT: An Opposition Party]. Tunis: Al-Magharibiyyah li Tiba'at wa Ishhar Al-Kitab.

Alqasantini, Alkrrai. 2012. *Haqiqat Al-'Alaqah Baina Al-Hizb Al-Hurr Al-Destouri Al-Tunisi wa Jami'at 'Umoom Al-'Amalah Al-Tunisiyyah (1924–1925)* [The Truth About the Relationship Between the Tunisian Free Destour Party and the CGTT]. Tunis: University of Manouba.

---

[132] *Najah Al-Mu'tamar…Kalimat Al-Akh Habib Ashour fi Iftitah Al-Mu'tamar*, *Al-Sha'b*, December 16, 1984, p. 4.

Al-Shaybi, Mohamed Lutfi. 2015a. *Al-Harakah Al-Wataniyyah Al-Tunisiyyah wa Al-Mas'alah Al-'Ummalliyyah al-Naqabiyyah* [The Tunisian Nationalist Movement and the Syndicalist Question] *Vol. 1 1894–1925*. Manouba: Markaz Al-Nashr Al-Jami'i.

Al-Shaybi, Mohamed Lutfi. 2015b. *Al-Harakah Al-Wataniyyah Al-Tunisiyyah wal Mas'alah Al-'Ummalliyyah al-Naqabiyyah,* [The Tunisian Nationalist Movement and the Syndicalist Question] *Vol. 2 1925–1943*. Manouba: Markaz Al-Nashr Al-Jami'i.

Al-Taimoumi, Al-Hadi. 2021. *Tarikh Tunis Al-Ijtima'i* [Tunisia's Social History] *1881–1956*. Sfax: Dar Mohamed Ali lil Nashr.

Al-Tawili, Ahmed. 2021. *Baina Bourguiba wa Ibn Youssef* [Between Bourguiba and Ben Youssef]. Tunis: Al-Magharibiyyah lil Tiba'ah Wal Nashr.

Ashford, Douglas. 1965. "Neo-Destour Leadership and the 'Confiscated Revolution,'" *World Politics* 17(2): 215–231.

Baccouche, Taieb. 2021. *Al-Ra'is Al-Habib Bourguiba Kama 'Ariftuhu: Khafaya Alliqa'at Hawla Al-Azmah Al-Naqabiyyah* [President Habib Bourguiba As I Knew Him: Behind the Scenes of Meetings Regarding the Union Crisis]. Tunis: Leaders.

Beinin, Joel. 2015. *Workers and Thieves: Labor Movements and Popular Uprisings in Tunisia and Egypt*. Stanford, CA: Stanford University Press.

Belhadi, Abdelmajid. 2020. *Al-Ittihad Al-'Amm Al-Tunisi li Al-Shughl fi Al-Jihat: Adwa' 'ala Al-Hayakil wa Qadaya Al-'Ummal* [UGTT in the Regions: Spotlight on Structures and Worker Issues] *1946–1957*. Tunis: UGTT.

Belhoula, Almoncef. 2015. *Al-Haqa'iq Al-Makhfiyyah fi Al-Tarikh Al-Mu'asir li Al-Ittihad Al-'Amm Al-Tunisi li Al-Shughl* [The Hidden Truth in the Contemporary History of the UGTT]. Tunis: Al-Magharibiyyah li Tiba 'ah wa Nashr Al-Kitab.

Beling, Willard A. 1964. "W.F.T.U. and Decolonisation: A Tunisian Case Study," *The Journal of Modern African Studies* 2(4): 551–564.

Ben Salah, Ahmed, ed. 2013. *Risalat Al-Ittihad Al-'Amm Al-Tunisi li Al-Shughl* [The Message of the UGTT]. Tunis: Dar Al-Janoub.

Carvalho, Anabela. 2008. "Media(ted) Discourse and Society." *Journalism Studies* 9(2): 161–177.

Churchill, A. 2016. Labor Organization in the Arab Spring: A Comparison of Tunisia and Egypt, Kuwait Program at Sciences and Po, https://www.sciencespo.fr/kuwait-program/wp-content/uploads/2018/05/KSP_Paper_Award_Fall_2016_CHURCHILL_Amie.pdf

Dakhli, Leyla. 2021. "The Fair Value of Bread: Tunisia, December 28, 1983–January 6, 1984." *International Review of Social History* 66(S29): 41–68, doi:10.1017/S0020859021000110

Deleuze, Gilles. 1994. *Difference and Repetition*, Trans. Paul Patton. London: Bloomsbury.

Disney, Nigel. 1978. The Working Class Revolt in Tunisia. MERIP Reports 67: 12–14. Doi:10.2307/3011401

Dobson, William J. 2013. *The Dictator's Learning Curve: Inside the Global Battle for Democracy*. New York: Anchor Books.

Ennaceur, Mohamed. 2000. *Les syndicats et la mondialisation: le cas de la Tunisie.* International Institute of Social Studies: ILO working document.

Fairclough, Norman. 2012. "Critical Discourse Analysis." In *The Routledge Handbook of Discourse Analysis*, Edited by James Paul Gee and Michael Handford. London: Routledge, 9–20.

Gamaoun, Sahraoui. 2019. *Nouira-Bourguiba: Pouvoir, économie et démocratie*, trans. Mohamed Ben Ezzeddine. Tunis: Mim Editions.

Haddad, Tahar. 2015 [1927]. *Al-'Ummal Al-Tunisiyyun wa Zuhur Al-Harakah Al-Naqabiyyah* [Tunisian Workers and the Emergence of the Labor Movement]. Sfax: Dar Samed.

Hamdi, Faten. 2017. *Na'imah Al-Hammami fi Awwal Muqabalah Laha Ba'da Intikhabiha fi Maktab Ittihad Al-Shughl* [Naimah Al-Hammami in Her First Interview After Her Election to the UGTT Office]. January 27, Al-Mufakkirah Al-Qanuniyyah, https://bit.ly/3NMtJtM

Hanieh, Adam. 2013. *Lineages of Revolt: Issues of Contemporary Capitalism in the Middle East.* Chicago: Haymarket Books.

Hartmann, Heidi. 1976. "Capitalism, Patriarchy, and Job Segregation by Sex." *Signs* 1(3): 137–169.

Klibi, Chedli. 2014. *Adwa' min Al-Dhakirah: Habib Bourguiba* [Flashbacks: Habib Bourguiba]. Tunis: Demeter.

Mahfoudh Draoui, Durrah. 2018. *Al-Nisa' Al-Tunisiyyat fi Al-Shughl wa Al-Harakah Al-Naqabiyyah* [Tunisian Women: At Work and in the Labor Movement]. Tunis: Friedrich-Ebert-Stiftung.

Mnassar, Adnan. 1992. *Al-Hizb, Al-Dawlah, Al-Naqabah* [The Party, the State, the Union]. *Les Cahiers de Tunisie* No. 159–160: 7–52.

Omri, Mohamed-Saleh. 2015. "No Ordinary Union: UGTT and the Tunisian Path to Revolution and Transition." *Workers of the World: International Journal on Strikes and Social Conflicts* 1(7): 14–29.

Othman, Farhat. 2012. *Uhibbuka ya Farhat Hubbika li Al-Sha'b.* December 5, Nawaat, https://bit.ly/3WEdympli

Qamoun, Al-Sahrawi. 2021. *Qarn Wa Nisf Min Al-Sahafah fi Tunis* [A Century and Half of Tunisian Journalism]. Tunis: Al-Magharibiyyah li Tiba'at wa Nashr Al-Kitab.

Sayyah, Mohamed. 2012. *Al-Fa'il wa Al-Shahid* [The Agent and Witness]. Tunis: Ceres Editions.

Talani, Leila Simona. 2014. *The Arab Spring in the Global Political Economy.* Basingstoke: Palgrave Macmillan.

Tunisian Office for National Liberation. 1953. *Farhat Hached, Tunisian Labor Leader, Patriot, Martyr.*

UGTT. 2022 [1951]. *Qadaya Ijtima'iyyah fi Tunis* [Social Issues in Tunisia] *(1951)*, edited by Sami Al-Awwadi. Tunis: *Al-Sha'b* Newspaper.

UGTT: Women, Working Youth, Associations, and Constitutional Institutions Section. 2023. *Al-Mujaz fi Al-Intima' Ila Al-Ittihad Al- 'Amm Al-Tunisi li Al-Shughl* [Abridged UGTT Membership Guide.] Tunis: Matba'at Fann Al-Tiba'ah.

Yousfi, Hèla. 2018. *Trade Unions and Arab Revolutions: The Tunisian Case of UGTT*. London: Routledge.

Zemni, Sami. 2013. "From Socio-Economic Protest to National Revolt: The Labor Origins of the Tunisian Revolution." In *The Making of the Tunisian Revolution: Contexts, Architects, Prospects*, edited by Nouri Ghani. Edinburgh: Edinburgh University Press, pp. 127–146.

4
Dissent of the Mind

100 Years of Student Activism

It was a strange feeling. We charged out of the school aimlessly. I felt that motion deep in my veins as a rush [of adrenalin] (hamas). The whole thing happened so fast. Thinking about it now, it was like an optimal form of existence. So strange in a moment of violence or chaos, I felt the power; I felt alive (hassit b'quwwah, hassit hali hayy). Truth be told we never felt this autonomy, breathing freedom amidst crowds of people. Thank God! Several years of schooling did not tame us. Gone were the orderly queues, the silence and the obedience we displayed in classrooms. I saw Si Usama, my Arabic teacher, screaming and waving fists. He too could shout. He joined in when the chants of the national hymn were sung intermittently. I liked seeing him violent, angry, disorderly and uncontrollable. My peers and I never thought he and we could be so similar. Teachers, pupils and ordinary people mostly workers melted into a single human wave. A human wave with loud vocals and violent motion. We poured out our hearts so loudly to lines of security forces blocking our advance towards the municipality. For months and even years we could only whisper the chants and slogans against the regime. What a liberating cacophony (hutaf)! Suddenly simple words shouted in loud chorus scared the regime. Words that once were hidden from our relations and families formed during that protest a chain of connections.[1]

Introduction

Accounts of Tunisia's revolution neglect protests by students, itself a form of demos in-becoming, a "part that has no part," with its demotic agency, aesthetic experiences, social imaginaries, and speech acts. A syncretic approach is needed to put together different components in this mix of activisms, a politics–life conflation, as well as the discursive and extra-discursive threads interwoven into this particular brand of protest. This chapter interpretively triangulates individual (oral history) testimonies and interviews, Tunisian historiographical and sociological sources, newspapers, and other archival documents. It reconstructs a protestscape re-ontologizing the struggles led by students across decades: pre-colonial, colonial, and postcolonial.

---

[1] Excerpt from focus group interview with teacher and unionist on protest from the 1980s, February 6, 2011, Gafsa.

Thus, the analysis seeks to dismantle the assemblage of multi-temporality and multi-spatiality of student protests. In so doing, the dissentscape is a kind of compact repository in which not only do generations of protestors' memories and humanities meet, but so do the interactions, tensions, and the residue of their social acts and en-actments. The emphasis is on their agentic, affective, and cognitive codes and registers. By disentangling and interpreting these codes and registers, the analysis attempts to evince the transmission of knowing, learning, and becoming of a partial demos, a peoplehood across time in space. We do this with special reference to protest from the late 1960s to the 1980s, given their generative and interactive capacities: combative (agency), expressive (affect), knowing and learning (cognitive), and transformative (power relations).

We begin the chapter with a discussion of the significance and features of this rebelscape, the site of "other-ed" students, their struggles deliberately "forgotten" by the state. Next is an analysis of focus group interviews with teachers in the 2011 revolution. This is followed by a background on the century-long student protestscape and its major events. We then introduce the notion of the Tunisian university as a "free space" carved out by activist students. We argue and show through interviews how students developed their protest competencies through a "learning loop" featuring secondary teachers, secondary students, and university students. The chapter then chronicles major events in the student movement, zooming in on consequential developments (1968, Korba (in the governorate of Nabeul) Congress, founding of UGTE) as narrated by former activists. The last section turns to ideological polarization. We suggest that ideological debates within the university reflect a type of "communicative protest": a site of "dissensus" where (imperfect) dialogue and pluralism were practice runs for democratizing politics. Finally, the chapter probes the place of women in students' communicative protest.

Situating the Student Protestscape

Why and how do teachers and pupils rise up and mobilize in protest? As social acts and en-actments of peoplehood, responses to injustice at different points of Tunisia's social tumult, represent a quintessential example of protestscape. Answering this question requires portrayals of "situated protest" via several interpretive frames, tableaux, as it were. These frames adduce a chain of reconstruction from first-hand accounts and their situated agency, affect, cognition, and meaning-making. The chapter illustrates the spatio-temporal situatedness of protest. A synchrony–diachrony interaction mediates the interpretation of protest as a spatial fixture of subversive politics and historical development. This helps to capture the evolution to revolution. The aim is threefold. First, to historicize and re-ontologize teachers' and students' struggles via situated and localized types of protest, by stressing embeddedness (in power relations, time, and space) and interconnectedness (subject and object, word and world, text and context). Second, to grasp dynamics of spatialities and temporalities and the geo-historical becomings of subject (people) and object (protest, revolution). Third, to understand how these becomings affect and are affected by authoritarian materiality with its own apparatuses of reproduction of myth and reality, the state and its others, empowerment and disempowerment, citizens and denizens. The protestscape at hand displays how struggles are imbricated within the power webs of this materiality.

Research on student movements (Entelis 1974) has too often originated in Western settings and experiences, as Gill and DeFronzo (2009) note. They define a student movement as a "relatively organized effort" by a sizeable student cohort, aimed at fomenting or blocking policy-based, institutional, or cultural change through institutional or non-institutional means, or some combination of the two (Gill and DeFronzo 2009, 208). Our approach throughout this book necessitates a framework tailored to Tunisian specificities. This is a notable protestscape within the country's 150 year revolutionary élan, formative in the struggle for peoplehood. The student protestscape is:

1. *Agentic*: involving social acting and en-acting of struggle/resistance for the purposes of de-territorializing and re-territorializing the political, social, cultural, and ideational in post-colonial societies suffering from singular domination by an elite embracing the former colonizers' language, values, system, etc. Acting–en-acting here endeavors to empty the center of power (disowning existing institutions, structures of power, and non-inclusive distribution of power and resources). This syndicalist anti-systemic dissent–protest–ideology manifests as campus mobilization via free spaces. Exclusionary practices spawned these anti-authoritarian students' activisms.
2. *Affective*: speaking to a locale of the former colonized, populating students' struggles. It is framed by both specificity and historicity: relating to (anti)authoritarian postcoloniality. The anti-colonial struggle and the *fellaga* legacy is one powerful contextual lens, with an enduring sensory imprint and identitarian cultural translation, binding action and emotion. This does not preclude sharing in emancipatory values of universalized emotions such as those transpiring from the 1968 student protests (Häberlen 2018).
3. *Cognitive*: interworking struggles, with attendant forms of demos, to reconfigure self and other, within the contours of authoritarian politics, interpreting intersubjectively power relations and power representations, with a view to producing parallel and viable power representations, myths, and modes of engaging the political, by way of dissent and not consent. The student protestscape opens up new horizons of dissenting conceptions of collective anti-systemic politics and of social imaginaries, as part of an historic emancipatory logos. These are ideologically-informed imaginaries and re-imaginings of identity, community, rights, democracy and even religion. They interpenetrate with both agency and affect as students seek to carve out free spaces, from which to socially act and en-act the quest for a free and dignified peoplehood.

An Epistemological/Methodological Note

In the second half of this chapter, we rely on first-hand oral history-type accounts recounted by former student activists. Interpretation helps construct narratives that contribute to "situated knowledges." The self-contradictory relaying of experiences, "self-images," and emotions is not a problem to be averted. Passerini instead suggests we tackle the internal discrepancies head on, placing them within the broader sociopolitical context, structures, and happenings under study (Passerini 1989, 191–192). Seeming internal and external contradictions all illuminate, rather than obscure, important tensions and polarizations. Discomfiting juxtapositions come to the fore at the level of individual encounters and their necessarily reflective narration, maturing over the temporal distance memory offers. In this sense, as Passerini (1989) notes, all the students' "autobiographical memor[ies are] true."

As Gluck (1977) suggests, the work of oral history that dwells on gaps in the written record is a "collaborative" venture between interviewer and interviewee. Oral history can thus fill voids overlooked in social science, to possibly "rectify … bias" permeating dominant histories (Gluck 1977, 4–6). Employing and activating oral history as epistemology and method is a mode of pursuing epistemic justice with respect to Tunisian protest. We seek to establish a perpetuity "denied" (Gluck 1977) in more episodic, reactionary metropolitan revolution. In this way, oral history facilitates "releasing multiple truths into the scholarly environment" (Geiger 1990, 179). There is also a practical side to our (partial) reliance on oral history. Scarce availability of written documents drafted by undercover activists, organizing and mobilizing in the shadow of repressive authoritarianism, seems to have contributed to an often "oral" student protest culture. Daifallah (2016, 18–19) has flagged this challenge, too. Songs, protest slogans, meeting minutes, conferences proceedings, and movement statements have not always survived the fire and brimstone of Bourguiba's and Ben Ali's police states. Forcible confiscation or destruction by choice has rendered movement documentation spotty. Oral history interviews vastly enrich our attempts to visualize, concretize, and re-ontologize the student protestscape.

Forgotten Struggles

Oral history can uncover a great deal. Politics bears the trials and tribulations of power in the face of revolting resisters and heroes' indignations. In the same way, history envelops the silences of the forgotten pains, defeats, and victories of women and men enamored by the quest for freedom. Amongst them, one must count students. They shoulder some of the burden of speaking back and acting against all forms of captivity, to unjust individuals and systems. Thus, students in Tunisia, as elsewhere around the globe, have stories to tell about peoplehood's social acts and en-actments intended to erode or "subvert autocracy" (Zavadskaya and Welzel 2015). Stories abound of unfree people propping up the weight of costly moral and physical struggles. In authoritarian contexts, the memories of resistance and resisters are seldom enacted in the open. Protracted despotism has meant censure, committing many narrations of struggle to public oblivion. That is, to the slaughter-bench of public memory in politics, in arts, in culture, and in history making and unmaking. The adage "to forgive but not to forget" is, however, not just an aphorism. In research, un-thinking oblivion and the erasure of sacrifices and struggles when writing protest is a tall order. To this end, the task warrants invoking, anew, the issue of epistemic injustice (Fricker 2007). The task of un-thinking silence and exclusion in the practice of knowledge-making frames emancipatory epistemology. Here lies an ethic that surpasses the politics of memory. Memorials and memorialization do not on their own yield justice. The restorative value comes through voicing past experiences, or re-learning and re-experiencing the ontologies of past struggles, by subject and by author. Thus, measuring up to addressing, respectively, "testimonial" and "hermeneutical" injustice (Fricker 2007). This undertaking renders the knower's task (subject) a matter of rights to recognition and historical "truth," and the author's interpretivist vocation a medium of scholarly inclusivity and veracity. The mantra of Freire's (1998) "pedagogy of freedom" and Tyson's (2003) "epistemology of emancipation" spring to mind. The crux of the latter is decentering. How researchers frame questions, design methodology, interpret text and re-read polity, society and power relations critically, by going beyond the academic smokescreens of neutrality, are of import if we are to account for the multiplicity versus singularity of experiences. Not overlooking affect when stating facts, we might add, in order to note the relevance of extra-discursive dimensions (Tyson, 2003, pp. 19–28). Tyson's reformulation of knowledge practices for emancipatory purposes as a means to subvert "othering" and domination, material and immaterial, echoes Freire's position. It is a position that denaturalizes knowing that entrenches powerlessness as permanence. Freire's argument is to substitute knowledge-making that reproduces powerlessness with liberating pedagogies founded on contestation of domination, ideational, socio-economic, and political.

This dissentscape does not seek to "compartmentalize" activism and struggle. It tackles epistemic injustice given the "inside" and "outside" significations of "othering"—taking the form of "double" erasure, by self and by other. Student-led protests are misrepresented, in the case of Tunisia relegated to a sphere of silence. Students feature as "*agents provocateurs*," literally trouble-makers in the "official transcript." The state authoritarian bureaucracy preferred sweeping under the carpet known atrocities in the history of the student movement, such as in the 1970s and 1980s. The forced enlisting of students into the army, prolonged incarceration, torture, and killings, under both Bourguiba and Ben Ali, will be returned to later. However, these brands of authoritarianism deliberately structured history-making and with it knowledge-making by editing out from the "his-story" of Tunisian nationalism all facets of the social, cultural, and political life that challenged the authoritarian fixing of power (relations). Authoritarianism's fixing of power entailed the social construction of reality in its entirety: knowledge, history, power, and discourse all call for deconstruction. Their historical significations resulted in incommensurabilities, with their own order of oppression, exclusion, and knowledge practices. Incommensurabilites such as between unfree citizens and their supposedly independent state. As part of these incommensurabilities, a "logic of equivalence," *qua* "simplification of the political space," was the order of the day (Laclau and Mouffe 1985, 130). In terms of meaning-making and signification this logic is one means not only of the supervision of power, but also of inclusion and exclusion, concomitantly. For, when shaped into a "chain of equivalence" (Laclau and Mouffe 1985, 144)—a quasi "us" against "them"-type device—the circle of hegemonic self–other identification and formation is closed. Thus, such a hegemonic chain owes its co-extensiveness to the exclusionary posturing of its unified forces and discourses. In practice, this exclusionary logic of equivalence is to blame for a kind of student activist-as-other-type "subalternity." Within it, students assumed postures and discourses that reified social formations of themselves as the state's "others." The resulting brand of misrepresentation invokes the Althusserian notion of interpellation. The context of interpellation is ideological: capitalist rule routinizing reproduction of itself by interpellating workers into a "reproduction of submission to the ruling ideology" (Althusser 2014 [1970], 236). Almost a case of "students being what the state makes them to be."

Authoritarianism has elevated this "interpellation" of identities to an art form. This is one reason why for decades activist students had been at the receiving end of the stick of "logic of equivalence"—subject to antagonism by the regime, media, opinion, and knowledge-makers. Writing student protest partly moves to a place where some disruption of any past unjust ordering of lives, embellished histories, and knowing becomes possible. That is, it enables a disruption of subjection. If writing protest is one medium for righting wrongs in the realm of social justice, then re-validating the struggles led by generations of students must be charged with a dose of moral courage for seeking to speak back at and subvert authoritarian consciousness. Epistemic in/justice enables equivalence. The gist of the exercise is to return to knowing the multiplicity of political struggles, activisms, and emancipatory identities. Hence, vocalizing silenced and hidden histories is part and parcel of bringing to the fore the situatedness of protest.

Gafsa: Memories and Musings

How do the state's "others" see their own struggles? The articulation of a political position in defense of civil and social rights in impoverished, under-represented, and historically oppressed regions needs no public staging of protest. According to one teacher (Bou Fawzi),[2] reflecting on teachers' role in resistance typical of the heightened rioting in the 1970s to mid-1980s, this articulation was germane to how they mostly silently but, on occasions, vociferously enacted protest as "moral positioning" (*waqfah wataniyyah wa akhlaqiyyah*). According to him, this positioning relates more to morality than politics. Teachers saw first-hand water-less taps, unsafe

---

[2] This section draws on focus group interviews with eight teacher unionists, February 6, 2011, Gafsa.

conditions, overcrowded classrooms, and leaking roofs, all of which prompted outrage. School staff were neck-deep in poor conditions. They had to resort to protest to resolve problems within the precincts of their schools. There was already a surplus of outrage and pent up anger within them. Bou Salim, a witness to the same period of burgeoning schools' rioting, adds that feelings of *ihtiqar* (another term for *hogra*, humiliation and disregard) from the powers that be (*al-hakim*) can never be bottled up for too long. They cascaded over into public protest squares to drive home one key message. As a people, teachers stood up against governments' violations of declaratory policies of equal development and free education. "Those conditions reminded teacher and pupil on a daily basis that they were lesser citizens (*muwatin aqall darajah*) than compatriots in the country's North and the Sahel," according to Bou Salim. Under such settings, protest was a label for struggle (*nidal*) and the state (*al-hukumah*) was almost a word for unjustness. The colonial past and regional setting represented a crucial backdrop against which resistance positioning ensued for teachers in towns like Gafsa. As put succinctly by a seasoned teacher (Bou Abdelqadir) who worked in several southern towns over two decades: "protest comes natural in these parts." The region's past as a hotbed of anti-colonial resistance imbues protestors with multiple forms of self–other definition. None of these outweighs the colonial history, anti-colonial struggle, and regional misery resulting from government neglect. Bou Abdelqadir expresses an idea that operates on three interconnected planes, agentic, affective, and cognitive.

> We continue to live in colonial times even after independence. In our region, anti-colonial heroes (*alabtal illi waqfu didd alisti'mar*) and stories of struggle remain vivid in peoples' memories. Memories of anti-colonial struggle and national pride are dear to people. ... These memories are powerful sentiments. They are reminders of who they were in the past and who they are today: once heroes and freedom fighters (*fellaga*); today, second-class citizens with second-class lives (*hayat darajah thaniah*). They do not wish to be freed from a past they associate with strong will, sacrifice, and respect.

Bou Misbah is another seasoned teacher familiar with the enduring emotions of (post)colonial historicity. He makes a powerful statement that requires elaboration given its relation to the entire mantra of protest ethos. On the one hand, there is an understanding of self and world deriving from the vestigial and laudatory memories and narratives in the south of the much storied anti-colonial resisters, *fellaga* freedom fighters. On the other, there is independence's materiality with its fetishized developmental goods, rights and freedoms that eluded the impoverished regions of the center and the south. It represented a rude awakening to degrading realities, resulting in a lasting sense of disillusionment, invidiously positioning southerners in inferior lives and living standards. What resulted was disabled independence and even belonging, not just the quality of citizenship. This deep divide between past and present, self and other frames not only social, cultural, and political interaction and struggle, but also affect and cognition. In their turn, affect and cognition frame the divide.

> Despite two decades of independence, the realities of the 1970s and 1980s, including the debacle of Ahmed Ben Salah's co-operatives (*alta'adudiyyat*), they felt unfree ... not reassured about the future. ... Their acts of protest were channels of public steadfastness (*sumud sha'bi*). Protest and defiance (*wuquf*) in town itself released teachers and pupils from unfreedom (*'ubudiyyah*—literally slavery, but is rendered here as unfreedom). The unfreedom of our unjust reality, our under-resourced schools, and the feeling of living under [iniquitous structures] (*muqawwimat ghayr 'adilah*).

The above extract is one example of interpreting protest by a category of teachers whose schools suffered from pupils' under-performance and high drop-out rates because of poor resources. For the interlocutors, protest was justified striking back at unfair political administration and oppressive living conditions. Each protest was above all else a definitional moment. Each highlighted difference and differentiation: self–other, citizen–state, and past–present difference, without losing sight of the discrepancies between privilege and disadvantage. The hints in their discourses speak volumes. They travel through temporalities and spatialities, never overlooking the materiality of protest. This they do to unfix power and drain powerlessness out of affect and cognition. Past respect and pride contrast with modern-day emotions of disrespect, effectively *hogra*. Their intuitive and impassioned vocalization of the contexts of protest contrasts positive affect from the past to underscore present negativity. Such negativity is a kind of dialogic device with cognitive meaning-making about the self. Vocalizing it is traversing a distance between epochs of time via emotions of both pride and pain of cognitive authority or confidence in who they were, their yesteryear identities, as if to deny who they are today. Most importantly, to intimate who or what peoples of Gafsa could have been. A heritage of glory all dissolves under the juggernaut of injustice into disadvantage. Injustice is calamitous. It overburdens disadvantaged people's present with unbearable political distortions and uneven power relations in quotidian living. They live a loss of sorts, more or less a state of "cognitive dissonance." Protest is the antidote. People protest to enact who they were and who they could be. As if to relive in the present all that the past symbolizes, in agentic and affective terms. What these veteran teachers' revelations show is that peoplehood, the making of this partial demos, in the context of protest is disjunctive. It flows from a heterogeneity of social acts and en-actments, temporalities and spatialities, peripheral existences. An ever-shifting, fluid affect and cognition are pitted against self and other.

Student Struggles

The resistance witnessed among schools and students (*al-nidal al-talmadhi*, as scholars of Tunisia's student movement call it) features as a mainstay in the organizational scheme of the internal and external worlds of teachers as protestors. It is a site with a plethora of relationships, which are arguably significant to teachers' and pupils' contact with the state, the emotions surrounding it, and into the present. The protest lens offers a perspective to situate uneven power relations, which enhances the reading of indignation and related affect and cognition. These power hierarchies for school communities seem to accentuate regional differences (e.g. south vs north) and dyadic aspects (e.g. justice–injustice polarities). The social acting and en-acting, absorbed as it is in conflicting affect and cognitive self–other portrayals, is self-defining on a moral plane. Three veteran teachers who were active participants in the 1974 school riots in Gafsa concisely summed up the feeling. Protest is the citizens' moral armor (*silah, sayf*, used by two of them) against humiliating and unequal politics. "Teachers and pupils take to the streets fearlessly (*ma ykhafoush*) [of] reprisals by BOP (Brigade d'Ordre Publique)," Bou Rabah states. Another (Bou La'roussi) makes the same point in a rather slanted way: "Many know of oppression, in economics and in politics; they experience inequality directly and so do their children inside their schools. Whilst few in society relatively react against it, teachers rise up. … Moreover, they draw their classes into rioting too." Bou Muhktar says that teachers amassed knowledge about the political system from informal networks. These were made up of other teachers, relatives at university campuses, and local syndicates. Secret pamphlets were circulated widely, passed among teachers, friends and sometimes are shared within the community. "Reprints of banned pamphlets resurface surreptitiously. In many instances, they expressed criticism of the regime more than support of one political current against another, such as the left (*alyasar*) or the trade union movement or the ruling Destour party (*alhizb al-hakim illi tabi' bourguiba wa el-dsatra*)." Bou La'roussi considers that the circulation of information about the state of politics, economics, and repression proved to be useful. Its utility was not so much in delegitimizing the regime because, despite rising opposing and economic woes, Bourguiba remained popular. Instead, "we used the pamphlets (*almanashir*) to mobilize schools and raise their awareness about happenings in Tunisia."

Freed Spaces: The University as *Mantiqah Muharrarah*

University Syndicalism: Early History

The tableaux above hints at an agentic, affective, and cognitive continuity of student-teacher protest, pellucid in the memory of activists. We now turn to conceptualizing the distinctiveness of the student protestscape that catapults the university into a free space. Distinctly present and lively from the time Zaytuna students waged strikes in the early twentieth century (Daifallah 2016, 9), student activism had, by the time of the 2010 revolution, existed for an entire century. Against the ever-present backdrop of anti-French resistance, students have protested since the Zaytuna strike of April 18, 1910 to demand educational reforms and improved subsistence conditions. Resentment against cultural imperialism flared up in protests again in 1928 and then 1936, in Zaytuna secondary school and university students' objections to French language requirements for students and public sector employees (Labyad 2014, 2–4). Varied expressions of protest during the nationalist struggle (1952–54) included statements and telegrams by public sector employees and Zaytuna students, published in *Al-Sabah* newspaper. They railed against student arrests and expulsions by the French fighting to repel Tunisian resistance (Ben Yousef 2004, 8). From Paris, members of the Union of North African students also waged hunger strikes in solidarity with colleagues in Tunisia.[3]

With its militant pedigree, the student protestscape is anchored in a prominent spatial element. It is difficult to overstate how generative the university campus has been to the forging of peoplehood. Many interviewees refer repeatedly to the university as a liberated space or freed zone, *mantiqah muharrarah*. This liberation takes on physical, emotional, intellectual, and ideological qualities—of diminished estrangement. By fits and starts, leftists, Islamists, and nationalist students "freed" the university, as it were, from the occupation of all symbols of state power, including regime-affiliated unionists and sometimes security forces. The onset of leftist activism in the 1960s through the "Perspective" movement by students expelled from the semi-official UGET student union (Bouguerra 2021, 32–33) sought and achieved—at least partially—liberation from political propaganda and party domination. They chased representatives of Bourguiba's Destour party, succeeded by Ben Ali's RCD, out of the university space.

The University of Tunis was hostage to the postcolonial counterrevolution. Even the student union was gripped by the tentacles of the ruling party. The union's building blocks were fashioned in the anti-colonial mobilization involving over 20,000 students between January–April in Tunis, Sfax, Sousse, Bizerte, Kairouan, Gabes, and Mahdia (Ben Shaban 2019, 33–44).). The UGET (French acronym for General Union of Tunisian Students) was "formed" in Tunis but "founded" in Paris by expat Tunisians in 1952–53 (Ben Shaban 2019, 45). Initially working under the cover of secrecy (Ben Shaban 2019, 51), the UGET with Bourguiba's blessing had by 1956 maneuvered the merging (or swallowing up) of the Zaytuna student union—with its Youssefist sympathies (Ben Shaban 2019, 62–67). Years into Tunisia's independence, in the eyes of oppositionists the student syndicate was overrun by loyalist partisans. These student foot-soldiers in Bourguiba's project to eradicate rival affiliations and ideologies, beginning but not ending with traditional Zaytuna-Youssefist adherents, appropriated the union to the exclusion of other "logoi," worldviews, or political leanings. An ensuing political battle played out in the university. Thus, the transformation into a "freed zone" was won through combat—political, ideological, and even physical—waged again partisans and security forces alike. However, university spaces were not off the radar of authoritarian scrutiny and censorship *by default*. The term used by former student activists plays on this distinction: not free (*hurrah*), but freed or liberated (*muharrarah*). It was through protest, as we will show, that such liberation unfolded, during iterative epochs of contestation against authoritarianism.

---

[3] *Al-Sabah*, March 25, 1952, p. 1.

Freeing University Spatiality

We thus posit the sites in which the student protestscape flourished from the 1960s onward as a "freed space." Evans and Boyte (1992) conceptualize "free spaces" as the wellspring of piecemeal democratic change in the United States. They show how blacks, women, and others at different junctures wrested their rights through variable invocation of American Revolutionary republican ideals in these public spaces that lent didactic democratic value to rights-based struggles. Culturally mediated (Polletta 1999), organizational and normative benefits accrue within these free spaces. They are the "sustaining bases of democratic social movements" and "schools for democracy"; "norms of egalitarian exchange, debate, dissent, and openness" (Evans and Boyte 1992, ix). One caveat in our adoption of this concept is the extent to which agonism features to render Tunisian university campuses *manatiq muharrarah*. Within the authoritarian Tunisian setting, it was through resistance and protest that student activists created—as well as socially constructed—these "freed spaces."

Here, too, the "demotic" thrust of student activism must be qualified, distinguished from the institutionalized, constitutionalized context of the US. University freed spaces were thus "schools for democracy" insofar as they were *anti-authoritarian*. The concept of "free spaces" allows for the observation and analysis of a counter-politics. We pry open this potential crack in dominant power and one-party hegemony—Bourguiba's and Ben Ali's counter-revolution. Evans and Boyte rebuff the notion that people succumb to domination entirely: "groups of people in society are never simply or completely 'powerless' ... relatively autonomous popular activity—what can be called 'free spaces'—can be sustained over long periods" (1992, xvii). We suggest that decades of Tunisian student experiences illustrate how within this protestscape, the partial student demos survived and struck back against the power-holders: colons and dictatorial regimes both.

A long history of such resistance beckons. Over the course of a century, Zaytuna students (Daifallah 2020, 14–16) to April 9 College leftists (Qaboos 2020a, 11) to Islamists at various University of Tunis campuses, organized and mobilized against the ruling powers. Their demonstrations, strikes, public meetings, petitions, newspapers, even reported hostage-taking,[4] succeeded in threatening the two successive authoritarian regimes, if not dislodging them altogether. Evans and Boyte (1992, 19) add that "free spaces are never a pure phenomenon" but always intersect and clash with un-free spaces and relations and practices. Students may have never quite emptied out authoritarian power. Yet they militated for a "free, democratic, and representative union," according to one common slogan.[5] Students' syndicalist self-conception was democratic in aspiration, as it was popular in outlook. Their movement was coextensive with the UGTT in defending the "economic, political, and cultural rights" of the "people," as one student put it in a 1980 roundtable debate

---

[4] Islamists abducted the Dean of the College of Sciences, demanding the release of arrested students and withdrawal of security forces from campus; see *Al-Mustaqbal*, March 9, 1981, p. 8.
[5] *Al-Mustaqbal*, December 29, 1980, p. 8.

on ways out of the perpetual crisis. "The student movement is part of the popular movement," spawning "activism for emancipation and democracy," confirmed fellow students.[6] Another leftist student declared, "the student movement is a popular movement" (*harakah jamahiriyyah*)—albeit not inclusive of Islamist students, for him.[7] In a departure from this cognition of student-peoplehood, the unremitting activism of at least two generations helped to erode the authoritarian center. With an emphasis on *the people*, social acting and en-acting of peoplehood-in-becoming by students rings with democratic resonance. Student activism amply supplied the repository of protest competencies by a partial demos. It spilled into other dissentscapes and political opposition movements, doubling as a recruitment mechanism, as we will show.

Pedagogy of Freedom?

When applied to Tunisian students, the concept of freed spaces emphasizes learning. It further recalls Freire's (1998) "pedagogy of the oppressed/freedom." Learning experiences pave the road to freedom, sometimes through contestation and even dialogue with the oppressor. An epistemology of protest and revolution is rooted in political-intellectual brawls, and vice versa. What we have called protest competencies are a repository of skills, adaptations, and norms acquired through experiential, social learning. Transformed by students into free spaces, university campuses became lyceums or gymnasiums of protest (Sadiki 2011). Such pedagogical milestones include events (the "glorious February" of 1972) and junctures in which students participated directly or second-hand, through narrations of counter-memory. The pedagogical emphasis is doubly relevant to our investigation of the student protestscape. First, the *manatiq muharrarah* that were Tunisian campuses became a sort of "haven" carved out through the acquisition of skills and the deployment of civic practices. At the very least, these values were conducive to anti-authoritarian resistance, even if not always precisely democratic. By organizing protests, writing persuasively in newspapers and magazines (their own, but also broader opposition newspapers such as *Al-Ra'i*), holding public meetings, forming and electing committee leaders in deliberately non-hierarchical (even *ad-hoc*) structures, students developed skillsets and norms feeding into resistance, as we demonstrate below. They formed pockets of peoplehood over the diachrony of Tunisia's revolutionary milieu, honing and passing on the agency, affect, and cognition of a microcosmic, partial demos that exploded in the 2011 revolution. Second and interrelatedly, we attempt to showcase the learning that took place within what we call the *student–teacher learning loop* (outlined below) between teachers, high school students, university students, and back.

Freed spaces thus pose a question of the ontology of freedom/resistance. To know obligates students to speak truth to power, to write back. Unique to the student

---

[6] *Al-Mustaqbal*, December 22, 1980, pp. 8–9.
[7] *Al-Mustaqbal*, December 29, 1980, p. 12.

protestscape are the ways in which the pursuit of knowledge is parallel to and tantamount to the pursuit of freedom *qua* freedom. As if the place (campus) cultivated a (freed) space from which and through which students launched their liberation struggles. In the university, they discovered and chiseled a wider horizon to push the boundaries of place to construct their self-presence within a wider space (*fada'*). They were not bound by political rigidity, nor the freezing of learning about possible and viable free ontologies. In a postcolonial authoritarian setting where there was far-reaching state control over society, "people were banned from thinking," as Al-Jellab (2021, 27) puts it. Tunisian politics and society were coercively calcified by the likes of Bourguiba to justify domination and enforce homogeneity. Students resisted such freezing of authoritarian temporalities that foreclosed possibilities for deep and meaningful emancipation. Time thus comes to the fore alongside space. Just as these students sought to empty place (the campus) of state power in order to carve out free space, they took umbrage at dictatorial time. Their protest and other activism exhibited a refusal to be confined by single rule temporality, by quasi predetermined and subject ontology. Here students used knowing to transformatively travel to future possibilities of another time. These were historical moments in which they determine how and what to know *to become* a people enjoying dignity, freedom, and the right to have rights. All this students socially acted and en-acted within freed spaces. They traveled from the space *and time* of unfreedom to freedom, constructing the *mantiqah muharrarah* befitting the monumental undertaking, upholding the dreams and ethos of freedom. Freire's "pedagogy of freedom" takes on a poignant meaning in campuses where the cost of such emancipatory struggles extend to lives stolen by security forces, such as the two students killed on May 8, 1991 (Daifallah 2020, 9). For a dear price, students revolutionized the temporal reality of living under authoritarian structures that occupy space and time. Through protest as resistance, they embarked upon a temporal transition through rioting at the level of selfhood and peoplehood.

The Student–Teacher Learning Loop

After conceptualizing the university as a freed space, we now offer a mini-framework charting the travel of knowing discussed above. The UGTT (Chapter 3) and Tunisia's student protestscapes were the longest-running in the country's revolutionary milieu. An intellectual and empirical conundrum presents itself. Tunisians did not have the benefit of political party membership and activism, to pass the torch from one generation or cohort to another. Colons and authoritarians circumscribed organizational and institutional continuity. What, then, were the threads stitching together a century of student protests? What might be the link between vehemently anti-colonial Zaytuna youth in 1910 and the April 9 College students mobilizing in solidarity with Sidi Bouzid in December–January 2010–11? Bourguibism, and later Ben Ali's "new era," simply did not tolerate fleshed out, fully operational political parties or social movements. Holt's attention to political parties at the forefront of instilling a "critical consciousness" within civil society (2002) is not quite applicable to pre-2011 Tunisia. Cross-country comparisons with other postcolonial or "Third World" locales such as Chile, while partially instructive, nevertheless fall short. Tunisian student protest must be understood within its own (authoritarian and counterrevolutionary) context. Our focus on social and political learning is one key to understanding this puzzle. Student activists could not simply "rekindle previous political networks" or "negotiat[e] new ones across party lines" as did the women who opposed Pinochet's military regime (Chovanec and Bentiez 2008, 47). Even the quasi-movements and embattled, provisional structures that student activists cobbled together between the mid-1960s and early 1990s operated underground (*fi al-sirriyah*).[8]

Yet it would not be accurate to say that the first opposition movement in Tunisia, the Perspectivists (Qabous 2021b, 11) organized without precursors. Rooted in colonial, anti-colonial, and early postcolonial Tunisian history, formative ideational and experiential influences and encounters propelled the thrust of two (perhaps three) generations of student activism. The "student–teacher learning loop" we theorize here (see Figure 4.1) helps explain both the relative continuity of Tunisian protest *and* acquired protest competencies central to our narrative of peoplehood struggles. Student activists would draw on these competencies across the synchronies of protest, some rising in the ranks of political opposition or even (paradoxically) serving within the state bureaucracy.

In our learning loop, we take almost the opposite tack from "institutional learning" arguments championed by scholars such as Rohrschneider (1999). Contrasted with people dwelling in a democracy (West Germany), people living under authoritarianism (East Germany) are less tolerant because they have had no chance to practice political tolerance whilst living in a repressive system that outlawed opposition (Rohrschneider 1999, 2–3). Are people who throw off the shackles of dictatorship inevitably doomed to anti-democratic values, attitudes, and practices? We avoid such a vicious cycle. Institutions predetermine neither macro-level socio-political processes nor micro-level attitudes and behaviors. Instead, the social and political learning we conceptually adopt incorporates discourses, political imaginaries, and affect that are sometimes de/reterritorialized (as in the case of "the people," or "liberation," or "independence"). Institutional constraints under Bourguiba or Ben Ali did not foreclose the possibility of attitudes and practices aspiring towards freedom and tolerance, even democracy. Insofar as peoplehood-honing protest was democratic in its anti-authoritarian thrust, Tunisia's example appears counter-indicative of the institutional learning model. Instead, we view learning in social and political terms. It is constructivist à la Vygotsky's (1986) relation between language and consciousness. Such (oppositional, anti-authoritarian) political learning is a *social process* through which inner and outer, individual and collective, consciousness are braided together through the agency and affect of protest. Students and teachers taught and learned from one another how to resist authoritarianism, intellectually, practically, and even aesthetically. This they often did far from the prying eyes of authoritarian institutions,

---

[8] Interviews with former student activists, July 2022, Tunis.

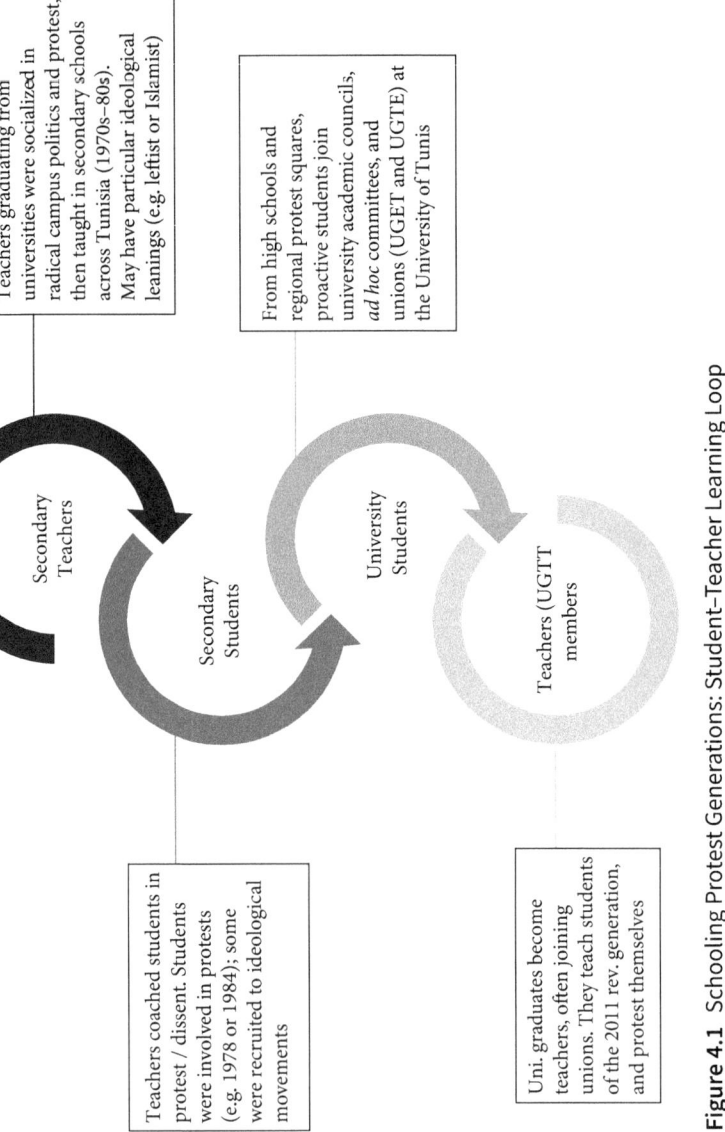

Figure 4.1 Schooling Protest Generations: Student–Teacher Learning Loop

watchmen, and propagandists. Rather than simply emulating and evaluating state institutions (in Rohrschneider's terminology), they subverted those tasked with pedagogy. Protestors "flipped," even if in piecemeal, impermanent fashion, universities into freed spaces.

Learning is not a one-time episode but an ongoing, processual endeavor, constantly refigured within changing contexts and actors. Chovanec and Gonzalez (2009, 231, emphasis added) note the "creating and *recreating*" of knowledge. Learning further accumulates within the repository or (sometimes unwritten) archive of counter-memory. The learning loop thus lends itself to agentic, affective, and cognitive dimensions and manifestations of protest as peoplehood-in-becoming. Contests over power are flecked with entanglements between (official, nationalist) memory that is the one-man Bourguiba show, and militant struggles (*nidalat*) of resistance figures and movements. In her study on women activists opposing the Pinochet dictatorship in Arica, Chile, Chovanec (2009) investigates criss-crossing personal and public identifications, relations, and practices. Once formed, a critical political consciousness must be activated. Among activists, theory imbibed in the family ("accessibility to consciousness") meets practice undertaken in society and polity ("engagement with consciousness") (Chovanec 2009, 75–80). Political learning occurs within this nexus, she argues.

Social and political learning refracts into protest competences through which Tunisian peoplehood struggles are forged. The student learning loop is one distinct, non-linear pathway where the pedagogical and didactic feature. Early family socialization may translate into a kind of ideational intergenerational learning (Chovanec and Benitez 2008, 49). Childhood and teenage political consciousness sprouts from the seeds planted by family stories and histories of feats of resistance, informing the agency, affect, and cognition undergirding the turn to protest-as-peoplehood activism of high school and university students. To various degrees, family histories are significant in activist trajectories (Sorbera 2020), pushing young people to leftist activism by "red diaper babies," for example (Evans 1980, 63, 112).

Our interviewees recounted comparable experiences. The counter-memory of *fellaga*, Youssefists, even sidelined paragons of traditional Islamic learning and identity, filter through personalized memories of family tales. All and sundry seemed keen to demonstrate a resistance link in their family, to Tunisia's insurgent "greats." Sometimes family ties are additionally place-based, that is, localized, rooted in politicized regional identities. "I was part of a family that hated the powers that be (*al-hukm*), [in] a syndicalist region … prone to revolution," says Samir Laabidi. "I am the outcome of a region (*jihah*), and also a family" with resistant activist tendencies, including a grandfather who wrote for Islamic modernist Mohamed Abduh's *Al-ʿUrwa al-Wuthqa*.[9] Mehdi Abdeljawad, calls himself son of the desert (*al-sahra* and *al-badiyah*) and mentions the Youssefists in his extended family.[10] From the city of El Ksour in El Kef, Abdellatif Mekki's father was a Destourian militant, and three of his

---

[9] Interview, August 2, 2022, Tunis.
[10] Interview, July 24, 2022, Tunis.

uncles were resistance fighters, one martyred in combat against the French colons. (He prefers the term *mujahidin* to the *fellaga* label Bourguiba used disparagingly).[11] Family involvement in the anti-colonial struggle breathed a spirit of opposition, sometimes sharpened by a rebellious regional connection, helping steer students toward a path of activism.

Young Tunisians Learn Protest

Family history is one of several threads to follow when deconstructing and assessing the learning loop we posit here. The social learning giving rise to a propensity and practice of protest-as-peoplehood appears also indebted to direct, formal and informal pedagogical encounters in the high school and university setting. Anti-colonial, nationalist, and postcolonial anti-authoritarian resistance poured out from the edifices of secondary education at repeated junctures of Tunisian history. This is more than happy serendipity. Teachers at their secondary schools (*maʿahid*) are one influence interviewees mentioned as they reflected on their involvement in leftist, Islamist, or unaffiliated participation and even the leadership of protests. Secondary schools had long been rife with protests. Demonstrations and sit-ins with sectoral demands (objections to expensive calculators in exams, or Physical Education marks in final scores[12]) were not uncommon. Students published petitions in newspapers decrying an absence of rights, problems with the finals schedule, and low educational standards.[13] National causes also featured. Dalilah Mahfoudh-Jédidi recalls waging an entire month of protest activity (strikes, demonstrations on Bourguiba Avenue) alongside her colleagues in the Nahj Al-Basha high school in February 1972. Their dissidence was in support of the students who had stood up to the Destourian takeover in the Korba UGET congress of 1971 (in Zankah 2020, 65).

The 1984 bread riots loom large in activist recollections. A secondary student at the time, Mehdi Abdeljawad was in the thick of the uprising of December 26 that broke out in Douz that year. "For four or five days, I didn't go home," hiding from the security forces pursuing him. Almost presaging his later efforts to carve out freed spaces within the university, he adds, "Douz was a liberated city from the security [forces] at the time. This experience sculpted my personality ... [it]made me not afraid to give speeches ... especially because protest was about poverty, and high prices." The issues raised by protestors were "close to my environment," he suggests.[14]

Others, too, recalled experiences of dissidence that inaugurated what we consider protest competencies. High school teachers facilitated students stepping out onto the

---

[11] Interview, July 29, 2022, Tunis.
[12] *Al-Mustaqbal*, December 8, 1980, p. 15.
[13] *Al-Mustaqbal*, January 5, 1981, p. 5.
[14] Interview, July 24, 2022, Tunis.

protest field. From the Boys' Secondary School (*Ma'had al-Duhkur*) in Sousse, Ajmi Lourimi and his colleagues filled the ranks of a large protest on the eve of the UGTT "Black Thursday" general strike (January 26, 1978: see Chapter 3). As was their habit, boys from a nearby (polytechnic) high school "used to throw stones at the windows [of our school]," he recalls. They would chant *come out, in manliness! (khruju bir'juliyyah)*, provoking young masculine egos. "Even the administration would open the doors so the people would go out … to protect the windows" and prevent further damage. "Then we went out in the demonstration and orbited the city … there was burning, destruction …" Slogans included *with our lives and blood, we sacrifice for you, O Achour!*, indicating the Secretary General of the UGTT who was at loggerheads with Bourguiba. Lourimi notes a difference in the "level of consciousness" between protesting secondary and university students. "The university students saw Achour as bureaucracy … the left saw the union as bureaucracy. … Since Achour was part of [Bourguiba's] political bureau, he [was to them] part of the system."[15] Here Lourimi highlighted the tension between the rank-and-file UGTT members and the "union bureaucracy," an antagonism that lasted up to the 2011 revolution. Secondary students' agency was undeniable. Their affect (solidarity instead of anger at Achour) and cognition (self/othering vis-à-vis system supporters) lagged behind the university students they would later become.

Like Abdeljawad, Lourimi, and countless others in secondary school, Mohamed Hamrouni participated in major protest event of his time. He recalled a cinematic episode of the 1984 bread riots. The narrative highlights the intensity of agency, affect, and cognition by students in their mid-to-late teens:

> I was [a student] in Carthage Presidential Secondary (*Ma'had Qartaj al-Ri'asi*). … [There was only] a fence between it and the palace. We didn't study … there was a lot of hubbub, and whistling … that famous day, January 4, we didn't attend class … we were in the square. Most students gathered in front of the main entrance at 9 or 10 am … we were next to the [Presidential] palace, only meters [away]. A group of female workers who used to work in a factory came … they carried bread in their hands[16] … 10 or so of them … in their work uniforms. … This inflamed [us] (*hayajan*) … so the students went out and followed the female workers.

Reliving the highly charged moment, Hamrouni continued:

> Here began a big demonstration joining together all the secondary schools in the area. We did a protest tour (*jawlah ihtijajiyyah*) from Carthage to Marsa to Bousilsili neighborhood. … At maybe 3 pm there were tens of thousands in the demonstrations … in Marsa which is a posh area that usually doesn't [protest]. We went to the main road that connects Marsa to Tunis … we blocked the road. … Then matters

---

[15] Interview, July 22, 2022, Tunis.
[16] Part of symbolic protest paraphernalia. The January 18, 1984 cover of *Jeune Afrique* featured a mustached man, arms outstretched above his head, wielding a baguette in his right hand. A statue of Bourguiba on horseback watched over the crowd.

slipped out of our hands .... I think it was crazy ... the [crowd] decided to return to Carthage to try to raid the palace! We went back to Carthage on foot ... we found a group of [security] in front of the palace ... I think the masses didn't realize the danger of what they were doing. ... [The security forces] used tear gas to break up the demonstrations. A group went to Kram and Halq Elwad [La Goullette], the other group went to Sidi Bou Said, that area ... something much worse could have happened, God forbid! We were about 10 meters away from the palace gate ... for us the demonstration was over, when people were split up ...

Hamrouni's 1984 experience was a particularly dramatic instance of social acting and en-acting via protest. Teachers, too, joined the fray. Some of them former student activist themselves, spoke of indirectly nudging students towards norms and values such as freedom and social justice, even when not explicitly preaching politics.[17] Direct ideological coaching could be another source for this kind of social learning. By the time some student activists reached university, they were already deeply entangled in what we call here the learning loop. Often, they were already part of one ideological camp: Islamist, leftist, nationalist. Ajmi Lourimi, Kamal Ben Younes, Mohamed Hamrouni, and others were (lightly) recruited into the Islamic Tendency Movement during secondary school.[18] Mehdi Abdeljawad led a small leftist cohort in southern Douz, where he and his comrades were outnumbered by predominant Islamists and nationalists.[19] Practically speaking, many university students had already waged battle against Bourguiba's security apparatuses, marching in the bread riots or pelting stones on Black Thursday in 1978 a few years earlier. Sometimes, university students protested and waged strikes in support of secondary school protestors. The learning loop thus changed direction in February 1981,[20] when secondary students demanded a seventh year of schooling, and their own union instead of the regime scouts (Daifallah 2020, 460).[21] We suggest here that the agency, affect, and cognition of protest-as-peoplehood is to, a great extent, learned and honed within this pedagogical cycle, this learning loop. The whole bundle of resistance ethos, anti-authoritarian struggle, and skills of organization and mobilization, gathers in these educational combat zones. If family histories, debates, political stances, and aspirations formed the backdrop, high schools were the first stop of practical experience, perhaps ideological indoctrination. In Chovanec's (2009) words, "engaged consciousness" swooped up to lift existing "access to consciousness" into an agonistic, often high-risk, activism. Protest competencies began to take shape.

[17] Interview, August 1, 2022, Tunis.
[18] Interviews, July 22, 2022, Tunis; July 20, 2022, Tunis; September 15, 2022, Tunis.
[19] Interview, July 24, 2022, Tunis.
[20] Some university strikes that year in the College of Arts (Manouba) had to do with student registration rules. See *Al-Mustaqbal*, November 23, 1981, p. 10.
[21] Including female students nationwide. See *Al-Mustaqbal*, March 9, 1981, p. 10.

University Learning

The previous section laid out the "learning loop" as it played out in secondary schools. Learning does not stop in these often overlooked sites of political initiation and a burgeoning protest competency. Most student activism—ideological tussling and embodied protest appearances—took place in the "freed spaces" of university campuses, to which we now turn. Student–professor synergy was important in this learning loop. Some professors, particularly through their Higher Education and Scientific Research Union, supported students' rights to an independent union. They repeatedly called for the activation of democratic processes and dialogue to resolve the crisis with the state, decrying repression of students and student counter-violence.[22] Despite bitter differences, some level of "consensus" emerged in the early 1980s that professors took "positive" stances in favor of students.[23] The (Islamist) UGTE union's University Compact of 1986, considered "strengthening ties between students and professors at both the academic and activist levels" a necessary part of a wider social and political struggle (Article 15, in Al-Thabti 2017, 225). At university, students learned through self-organizing, forming bodies parallel to those of opposition movements in the country. They clashed with the powers-that-be: Destourian partisans in the UGET student union, and the security arms of Bourguiba's or Ben Ali's coercive authoritarianism. They entered into rivalries with "enemy" ideological tendencies on campus (leftists vs. Islamists). However, neither leftists nor Islamists were able to flourish and expand in the manner of the American civil rights or anti-war movements of which Evans (1980) writes, for instance. Too often, members were jailed. Forced conscription to far-flung areas, a world away from the "freed spaces" these activists so carefully carved out, was a particularly pernicious form of retribution for possibly hundreds of students between the late 1960s into the early 1990s. Students including Khamis Al-Shammari (also spelled Khmais Chamari), Salem Labyad, Adil Al-Thabti, Abdelaziz Krichen, Mohsen Marzouq, Nouman Al'ish, and others were exiled to militarized zones in Sousse, Siliana, Gafsa, Gabes, Kelibia, Tataouine, Kbili, Medenine, and Rajim Maatoug (Al-Haidouri 2019).

Veering into Violence

Membership in these underground quasi-movements extracted a steep price from young people. It engrossed students almost totally. Being a committed leftist or Islamist took over one's life. Reading was one cornerstone of ideological self- and group-indoctrination. Marx, Gramsci, Lenin, Trotsky, Sayed Qutb, Malek Bennabi, Mohamed Ghazali, Esmat Saif al-Dawlah, etc. were some key texts that activists imbibed and discussed. Such zealous reading is not, comparatively, uncommon

---

[22] *Al-Mustaqabal*, December 15, 1980, pp. 9, 13.
[23] *Al-Mustaqbal*, January 5, 1981, p. 8.

among activists. British feminists "ate the literature" on Women's Liberation, for instance (Delap 2016, 171). A certain "evangelism" seems to have gripped some Tunisian students. Dedicated and fervent activists even consumed the literature of the "other" side, arming themselves for endless debates.[24] Study circles, newspapers, pamphlets, protests, and committee/union activities occupied these students even more than their formal degree study, in some cases. As Ajmi Lourimi put it, high school students waited impatiently to enroll in university. For them, activism and formal studies were inseparable. They shrank away from becoming part of the complacent, "silent majority," he said. "We didn't conceive that there [could be] studying without struggle (*nidal*)."[25] The upshot was invaluable learning, intellectual and practical. Chovanec and Gonzalez (2009, 230) write of "instrumental (e.g. skills), interpretive (e.g. emotional), and critical (e.g. feminist)" brands of learning in the Chilean anti-authoritarian women's movement of the 1980s. For us, these interrelated forms of learning feed into the agentic, affective, and cognitive dimensions of peoplehood through protest. That is, students' protest competencies formed within interactions of social learning.

The demotic agency inspiring students to carve out and develop these university freed spaces inhered, as we indicated before, in its anti-authoritarian morality and power. However, the learning record is blinkered. Student attitudes and more importantly, practices, were not all civic and democratic. Violence was not an uncommon occurrence, to the distaste of many in Tunisia and even in the diaspora.[26] Students engaged in physical force against security forces or regime-supporting peers, but also colleagues from rival ideological camps. Neither leftists nor Islamists monopolized this embodiment of extreme antagonism. Even within leftist ranks, differences detonated violence, for instance, between Perspectivists and Shu'lah (a precursor to WATAD, Democratic Patriots) in 1979, as Issam Chebbi (now Secretary-General of the Jomhouri Party) recalled (Al-Thabti 2017, 280). Disagreement on strategies (possibilities and modes of convening the 18th extraordinary congress) stemmed from ideological interpretations—as to whether Tunisia was a feudal or distorted capitalist state, for example (Al-Thabti 2017, 280), the nature of "the revolution," and regional causes, primarily Palestine (Chebbi 2022, 58–59). All interviewees noted the violence, without fail. Mehdi Abdeljawad put it bluntly: "We didn't believe in human rights" at the time. "All the tendencies were extremists … exclusionary … imprinted with primitive tribalism [*badawah*]," in this authoritarian epoch.[27] Independent leftist (later ambassador to the UN and Minister under Ben Ali) Samir Laabidi remembered "violent conflict with Islamists, sometimes bloody, very violent. … Groups used to fight. Ideological violence is the worst kind."[28]

---

[24] All former student activist interviewees mentioned this. Interviews, July–August 2022, Tunis.
[25] Interview, July 22, 2022, Tunis.
[26] For instance, students in Algeria complained of partisanship, violence, and "prevention of all democratic debate" by some student groups, *Al-Mustaqbal*, January 12, 1981, p. 4.
[27] Interview, July 24, 2022, Tunis.
[28] Interview, August 2, 2022, Tunis.

Protestors: Catalytic Actors of Political Recruitment and Change

What happened after university? The violence of enthused, politically suffocated students did not blot out the social and political learning acquired through opposition group membership, organization, and mobilization.[29] Another twist in the learning loop opened up in post-university life. Many student activists of the 1980s and early 1990s era would go on to become either teachers themselves, or members in one of the UGTT's many unions (e.g. for secondary teachers), or both (see also Lipset and Altbach 1969). The rapid swelling in the ranks of university graduates in the 2000s, part of Ben Ali's under-researched expansion of higher education,[30] is only part of the story. It is true that sufficient employment positions simply did not exist for these university graduates—of whom Mohamed Bouazizi was of course one. More qualitatively, however, we suggest that the learning loop through which the social learning of protest took place was also at work. Battle-hardened, equipped with their own protest competencies and attendant experiences and memories, student activists who became teachers and UGTT members would, in turn, influence young students of the "Ben Ali generation."[31] Through the intermingling between the student and union protestscapes, the pedagogy of freedom would live on in the classroom of the 1990s and 2000s. Part of this cohort of restive, disenchanted youth, would eventually erupt in protest eventuating in December 2010. Emboldened by their demotic agency and resistance scars, confident in their protest competencies, teachers' unions were early participants in the revolution.

Generative Events

In what major events did the learning loop manifest? This section focuses on important events in Tunisian student activism. A comprehensive chronology of student protest is impossible (see Table 4.1). We focus on developments and experiences consequential for anti-authoritarian resistance within a century-long student protest élan. Protest occurrences derive additional (sometimes varied) meaning-making through the renditions of our interviewees. Former student activists summon the agency, affect, and cognition of their own and others' activisms from the recesses of (humanly fallible) memory. The independence era student union (UGET) indicated above was born in polarization from the very start. Bourguibism/Youssefism, traditional/modern education, Arabo-Islamic/Francophile orientations and antinomies permeating Tunisian society wound their way into student politics as well. Student unity (*al-wihdah al-tullabiyyah*), orchestrated under coercion, was no more than a

---

[29] The ideological vitriol and self/other demonization continue to strain political discourse since the 2011 revolution.
[30] Interview with Rachida Tlili Sellaouti, July 27, 2022, Tunis.
[31] Interviews with Mehdi Abdeljawad, July 24, 2022, Tunis; Mohamed Hamrouni, September 15, 2022, Tunis.

Table 4.1 Diachrony of Student Protestscape

1910	Zaytuna Strikes
1927	Assoc. for N. African Students formed (Paris)
1927–8	Month-long Zaytuna strikes
1936–7	Over 100 days Zaytuna strikes
1952	UGET formed (Paris)
1952	Zaytuna strikes, petitions
1953–4	100+ days Zaytuna strikes
1955	Tunisian Self-Autonomy
1956	Tunisian Independence
1956	Sawt Al-Talib Al-Zaytuni absorbed into UGET
1963	GEAST (Perspectives) formed (Paris)
Feb. 1965	(leftist) student protest: 1st break with Bourguiba
June 1967	Student protests after Six-Day War
March 1968	Student protests (Ben Jennat case)
August 1971	Korba Congress
Feb. 1972	"Glorious February Movement"; petition of 107
1973	Mass arrests of Perspectivists
Jan. 1978	Black Thursday
March 1982	"Manouba massacre": student–student violence
Jan. 1984	Bread riots
1985	Founding congress of UGTE
May 1988	UGET 18th extraordinary congress
Sept. 1988	UGET + UGTE granted licenses
Feb.-May 1990	UGTE strikes and arrests
May 1991	Two UGTE students killed by security
1991	UGTE disbanded by Ben Ali gov't.

counter-revolutionary policy by Bourguiba's Destour. Any organizational structures or civic-political momentum in society had to be subsumed under the single party regime. In this case, it was Sawt al-Talib al-Zaytuni, absorbed by the UGET in 1956.

The students' protestscape reveals continual construction and variation, across colonial and postcolonial spatialities and temporalities, of protest-based social acting and en-acting. A form of internal synchrony–diachrony interplay is illustrated in this evolution. The founding congress of 7–10 July, three years before independence, represented a historical benchmark. Decades of student activism transpired in an instituting moment: the birth of the Union Générale des Etudiants Tunisiens (UGET). Seventeen UGET annual congresses dominated by partisan students, allied with the ruling party, Bourguiba's Socialist Destour Party (formerly Neo-Destour Party), followed. The left, a formidable force with initially Marxist then Maoist leanings, was gaining a presence and power base. The March 1968 student uprising, fondly remembered as Tunisia's 1968 Spring, that is, a precursor of the Paris 1968 student protests, was life-changing as far as the student body-politic was concerned. In September 1968, an ad hoc State Security Court handed down dozens of sentences against the leaders (mostly Perspectivists but also Ba'athists) of the March 1968 protests. August 12–20, 1971 marked another benchmark of quasi-diachronic symbolism. On the back of anti-regime-affiliated UGET domination, at the 18th congress a democratic voting process was sabotaged, preventing the leftists taking the helm of the students' representative body—as noted above (Al-Habbashi, 2020b, 151–176). Protests of the late 1960s and those of the early 1970s (November–December 1971 student strikes; October 28 riots, including a student occupation of the National Office of University Services) were the tip of the iceberg of continuous protests, within the precincts of various Tunis University campuses, and outside in the capital's main arteries.

The academic year 1970–71, according to Al-Habbashi (2020b, 165), saw tension between the regime and the student body reach fever pitch. Protests encompassed both ruly (petitions, negotiations) and unruly (riots including scuffles with security forces stationed across campuses) social doing. Continuous mobilization opposed the Ministry of Education's capping of the number of repeats of failed academic years to two (the so-called "cartridges system" *nizam al-kharatish*—the number of "cartridges" being a reference to the number of repeats and exam re-sits students were allowed), the late dispensation of bursaries, and forced dismissals of student representatives from elected College Councils (Al-Habbashi, 2020b, 165). No list can exhaust the hundreds of protests and protest-instituting events in the decades before the infamous March 1982 outbreak of systematic violence targeting Islamist students at the Manouba campus, causing hundreds of injuries, some very serious (Al-Habbashi, 2020b, 123–124). The litany of spatialities of student protests and brands of activism, involving confrontation and collaboration, had implications for quasi-diachronic change—moments of triumph in the long student protest élan. One milestone event was the April 18–20, 1985 General Conference for Resolve (*Al-Mu'tamar Al-'Amm li al-Hasm*). It marked the birth of the Islamist student syndicate: Union Générale Tunisienne des Etudiants (UGTE). Another event of equal historical stature was a legal sanction decreed in 1988 by the Ben Ali regime of two student unions, the UGET (leftist) and the UGTE (Islamist). Together the spatialities and temporalities provide an insight into the agentic, affective, and cognitive manifestations across decades, both colonial and postcolonial.

Perspectivist Protest

The above section outlined major protests among Tunisian students. We now consider the particularities of student leftist struggles. The experience of significant student protest events varied across ideological groups. The schismatic birth of state-sanctioned student syndicalism enables an understanding of how the well-known leftist opposition movement Perspectives, founded in Paris, developed.[32] Mohamed Charfi (2015)[33] refers to the constitutive years, 1963–64, of "Perspectives."

---

[32] On the genesis of "Perspectives", see Mohamed Charfi (2015, 75–79).
[33] Leftist activist-turned Minister of Education and Higher Education under Ben Ali (1989–94).

He accentuates the utility of "study"—in their "Groupe d'études et d'action socialiste Tunisien" (Working Group for Socialist Studies and Work, or GEAST). Hence the founding of the journal "*Perspectives* 'for a better Tunisia.'" He says it was "purposeful," derivative of the 50 or so founding members' unmistakable "leftist anchorage," "democratic preference," focus on the Tunisian reality, and "Arab" sense of belonging (Charfi 2015, 78). For Charfi, by the end of the academic year 1963–64, "Perspectives" emerged as the "nucleus for a major opposition party" (Charfi 2015, 78). With their Francophile leanings, the leftist Perspectivists/Afaq (later *Al-'Amil Al-Tunisi*) (see Chebbi 2022, 60–67) did not share an ideological affinity with the Zaytuna students who had resisted UGET's grasp. However, their opposition[34] to Bourguiba's singular hold on power did not extend to an embrace of Youssefism. "No to Bourguiba and No to Ben Youssef" was among their slogans. They considered the latter to be a "demagogue," more bourgeois than proletariat farmer, and culturally backward, relative to their Westernized modernism (Bouguerra 2019, 193–194). Even after moving to Tunis, Perspectivist linkages to Paris remained solid. Student-teacher interactions were sometimes a strategic component of the learning loop. Munira Chabuto, who was teaching history in April 9 College during the 1968 events, reminisced that she carried messages from (underground) leftist activists on her visits to Paris and back. In a kind of willful ignorance, "I did not know exactly what I was doing, but I did it" (Chabuto 2021, 96). The Perspectivist magazine appeared initially in French. Its leaders imprisoned, *Perspectives* gradually ceased publication after 25 issues, replaced by *Al-'Amil Al-Tunisi* newspaper, written in the Tunisian dialect. This became the official newspaper of the movement from 1971 (Chebbi 2022, 57–58). Perhaps the Perspectivists sought wider appeal as Pan-Arabist/Nationalist students critical of cultural imperialism, defenders of Arabo-Islamic identity, grew more influential (Labyad and Daifallah 2017).

Such cross-cutting cultural stances reflect the complexities of the "ideological" map of Tunisia's students, discussed later in the chapter. Commonalities with Bourguiba regarding the cultural outlook for a new postcolonial Tunisia were fodder for debate even among Perspectivists. Noureddine ben Khidhr famously described the group as "Bourguiba's illegitimate children," connoting shared ancestry marred by paternal rejection. His reading conflicts with Gilbert Naccache's more radical revolt against pro-US Bourguibism, which for him was imperialism-coddling dictatorship (Abdelsamad 2020, 15–16). The Perspectivists were far from homogenous, a quasi-school of thought that pioneered challenges to Bourguiba and Bourguibism. Al-Thlijani (2018, 3) notes that Marxists and Bourguibists share some common ideological ground on issues of identity. He also points out, however, the cross-pollination of interactions and debates between the Arab Progressive Unitarian (pan-Arabist) students

---

[34] For more on the ideological tenets of "Perspectives", see Charfi (2015). There is a mix of Marxist, Arab-socialist, modernist, and democratic lineage. Charfi notes how they rejected the Marxist distinction between "true democracy" and "radical democracy" (Charfi 2015, 76). Perspectivists have differed among themselves with regard to ideology, despite a conspicuous leftist stamp on thought and praxis. They were "realistic" about Pan-Arabism and, even if they were supportive of Nasser's anti-imperialism, their tack was to valorize Tunisia's "modernist acquisitions" and type of democracy, especially with regard to Bourguiba's "emancipation of women" (Charfi 2015, 76).

and those very Marxist counterparts. The cultural pattern Bourguiba adopted—anti-Islamic or anti-pan Arabist—created a cultural-political "void" for the decade after independence (Al-Thlijani 2018, 42). Rival expressions of identity and belonging were completely excluded. Paradoxically, then, Bourguiba killed off the Youssefists but by doing so (re)created them. The crackdown on Youssefists incited opposition among student groups, for instance, some of whom derived inspiration (and revenge) from repression of a political faction with a distinct understanding of Tunisian identity, a cultural outlook. Hence, Bourguiba's ruling party was not able to maintain a stronghold on student activism for long. A generation that had lived through the independence struggle did not so easily give up the aspiration for emancipation and peoplehood. The dream of a dignified life as a free "people" did not succumb to counter-revolutionary moves without a fight. Students moved to demarcate freed spaces within the university. Former Perspectivist Ezzeddine Hazgui emphasized the riskiness of such an undertaking: "It was hard to go against Bourguiba at the time ... militias of the party were everywhere."[35] Despite Bourguiba's attempts to avoid confrontation among university ranks, tensions emerged early on between the leftists (the Communist party, then Perspectivists) and the Destourians within the UGET. Contests came to a head in election battles for seats in the Union. The slogan "independence of the union" circulated. Students protested, for instance, as early as 1961 (denouncing Bourguiba's "retreat" in the Battle of Bizerte) (Bouguerra 2019, 92–95).

Tunisia's Early 1968: Augurs of a Spring of Dissent

A regional and international consciousness permeated the militancy of Perspectives and other groups. Rebellious students opposed among other things, Bourguiba's closeness to the US, to them an imperial power. One protest took off in the wake of a student's arrest in December 1966, leading to more arrests including Perspective leaders (e.g. Aziz Krichen and Khamis Al-Shammari), in what Bouguerra considers a turning point in budding anti-regime activity (Bouguerra 1993, 53–54). Not unlike other activists of the "Global 1960s" (Klimke and Nolan 2018), students including Perspectivists organized protests. They decried the Vietnam War and the visit of US Vice President Hubert Humphrey to Tunisia in January 1968, as Leila Blili distinctly remembered.[36] Students uttered slogans such as "Go home, Humphrey!" and "They don't buy us with wheat" (Bouguerra 1993, 84). Anti-Zionist student protests also erupted in wake of the June 1967 Arab defeat by Israel. (Every single interviewee mentioned Palestine.[37] This protest cause was "common to all," inciting "competition"

---

[35] Interview, July 26, 2022, Tunis.
[36] Interview, August 1, 2022, Tunis.
[37] The unions also published manifestos supporting the Palestinian resistance (UGTE in 1985) and the Intifada (UGET in 1988, during the extraordinary 18th congress, published in *Utruhat*, Issue 14, p. 48). Still, perceptions of weak Perspectivist positions on Palestine, after its 1967 "Yellow Notebook" that denied the existence of an "Arab nation," (see Chebbi 2022, 56–7), were hard to undo. See Khamis Al-Shammari's defense years later in *Hatta La Yantali Al-Intilaq min Al-Sifr 'Ala Al-Yasar* in *Al-Mustaqbal*, July 20, 1981, p. 9.

in degrees and expressions of support.[38]) Culpability for student rioting and the destruction of property (including that owned by Jews)—"a mistake," laments Ezzeddine Hazgui—was all pinned on Zaytuna student Mohamed ben Jannat. Hazgui put it bluntly: "Bourguiba was looking for a scapegoat ... the reality was [Jannat] just led a protest."[39] His arrest and sentencing prompted further student raucousness in March 1968, months before the world-renowned May 1968 student Spring uprising in Paris (Bouguerra 2019, 100–103). These youth were driven by the twinned affect of "frustration" and "indignation towards the ruling party," that had let down postcolonial hopes (Al-Waʿir 2020, 83). Their rebellion shook the regime. In December 1967, Bourguiba lectured a group of youths about "the necessity of incorporating all youth in public life, such that not a single individual of the [Tunisian] people (*ummah*) remains outside our ranks" (quoted in Al-Habbashi 2020a, 151). Succumbing to Destour control, via the party and the official union, was imperative. Ahmed Ben Salah, Assistant Secretary-General to the Party at the time (himself a former student activist, later a Minister sacked by Bourguiba), literally said so. In the case of any "students who wished to [partake] in a revolution, we invite them to join us in this enjoyable movement that we are waging" (quoted in Al-Habbashi 2020a, 151).

Officials expressed displeasure at student disorderliness that they framed as irrational and unwarranted. The Secretary-General of the ruling Socialist Destour Party decried the "volcano in the university" (quoted in Al-Habbashi 2020a, 151). A booklet distributed by the Party in August 1968 paved the way for the subsequent criminal sentencing of (mostly Perspectivist) student instigators. It denounced them as "clowns" and "inciters of division (*fitnah*)," ungrateful to Bourguiba's project to unify the "Tunisian people" (*al-ummah al-Tunisiyyah*) and falling back on "hatred" between groups and classes. The (blue-covered) handout made a criminal case for laws they had broken, releasing detailed information about the factions involved in the March 1968 events (Communist, Perspective, Baʿathists), including names of key leaders among students and teachers. Blessing a kind of populist vigilantism, it called on "the people" (read: except oppositionists) to "warn all demagogues ... and to purify society from all those who try to incite and exploit emotions of mischief" (*Al-Haqiqah ʿan Al-Fitnah* 1968). The counter-revolutionary discourse was menacing.

Tunisia's version of the "global 1968" was one synchrony within a diachrony of what was already more than half a century old. Aziz (formally Abdelaziz) Krichen, another Perspectivist-turned-sociologist (and politician after 2011), eventually heard about the May 1968 explosion in France from his prison cell. He had been arrested after the March protests in Tunis. "After what we had been subject to [i.e. torture] in national security [holding places]," he recalls, "we viewed the [French May 1968] movement ... with a kind of arrogance" (Krichen 2020, 61). The notion that Perspectivists possessed both brashness and stoic endurance (agency), engendered a

---

[38] Interview with Ajmi Lourimi, July 22, 2022, Tunis.
[39] Interview, July 26, 2022, Tunis.

quiet pride (affect), internalizing their role as regime challengers (cognition). Historians have drawn attention to letters by student inmates to the special State Security Court—denying charges, requesting marriage contracts, and demanding medical care (Al-Tarshini 2020). The purview of affective orientations is itself up for challenge. Heavy with the "burden of pain," their penned words humanize for posterity the young militants (*munadilin*) who seemed puzzled at their treatment by fellow Tunisians. Was "love of country" an emotion reserved only for Bourguiba and his loyalists (Al-Tarshini 2020, 117)?

Korba: Pursuit of the Extraordinary

After the uproar of 1967–68, the 18th UGET Congress at Korba in August 1971 was another major turning point in the student struggle against Bourguiba's creeping authoritarianism. Daifallah (2016, 26) regards it as a cooptation of UGET and by extension, the larger student movement. Here the leftist opposition sought to assert UGET's independence from the ruling party. The disputed outcome, which firmly ensconced Socialist Destour students in the Executive Office and the Political Committee after divisive voting (Chebbi 2022, 54–56) created a crisis known thereafter as the "student representation crisis" (*azmat al-tamthil al-tullabi*). Apart from the Communists, leftists refused to recognize the election results as legitimate, claiming the whole process to have been rigged (Daifallah 2020, 40). Almoncef Chebbi (Ba'athist-turned-Perspectivist student) recalls the "high hopes" that the congress would be an occasion that would "determine the independence of UGET from the party" (Chebbi quoted in Daifallah 2020, 394). Disagreements among the Destourian students prompted an article-by-article revision of the political register up for a vote at the Congress. The three-day Congress stretched out to 10 days. After one group of students left the room for a break, the others quickly voted on the leadership positions, casting aside the regulation [as part of a manifesto that included vision, structure and positions, and by-laws] (*la'ihah*) into which the leftists had painstakingly incorporated their input. Chebbi says that Hedi Nouira (Bourguiba's First Minister) had ordered the Congress wrapped up, and security forces drove out objecting students from the convening area. "What happened was a coup in the fullest sense of the word," he insists (Chebbi quoted in Daifallah 2020, 395). Such declarations of student treason and authoritarianism did not sway Destourian students. Decades later, Habib Al-Shagghal admitted in an interview with *Al-Sha'b* newspaper[40] the Destourian students' internal split in the wake of Ben Salah's sacking and jailing by Bourguiba as the great cooperative experiment failed miserably. He insisted that the Congress was the "most democratic … in the history of the Union" (Al-Shaghall quoted in Daifallah 2020, 395–396).Turbulence in the university thus echoed or reinforced unrest in the upper echelons of power. Two short years after Bourguiba had discarded Ben

---

[40] *Al-Sha'b*, May 15, 2010 (quoted in Daifallah 2020, 396–399).

Salah, the Socialist Destour Party held its Congress in October in Monastir. Bourguiba faced calls for democracy from within his own party, led by Ahmed Mistiri who would later split and form his own Democratic Socialist Party (Al-Habbashi 2020b, 30).

The following February, dissenting students would pen the Petition of 105, reproduced in the magazine *Utruhat* in 1988. A lack of clarity regarding the 104 signatures in the 1988 version (Daifallah 2020, 401) did not cloud the demand issued by the document. These students (whose number represented a majority of those congregating) announced they would "continue the[ir] activism ... until [our organization] becomes a democratic organization that defends its self-standing entity against any political monopolization" (quoted in Daifallah 2020, 403). Note how these opposing students' self-conception as a movement is a *democratic* one.[41] Students as free people should interact democratically, their petition implied. The union should be unencumbered by ministerial directives and operate in accordance with established, transparent procedures. The petition was a declaration of war against the Destour, ushering an intermittent but ongoing protest campaign to plan and eventually hold an "extraordinary congress" in Spring 1988. Thus, students instigated what became known as the Glorious February Movement (*Harakat Fivri al-Majidah*) of 1972, a milestone of direct confrontation and repression spearheaded by the Perspectivists. Objecting to arrests and the sentencing of student comrades Simone Lallouche and Farid ben Chahida, students tried unsuccessfully to hold the 18th Congress, staging strikes, sit-ins, exhorting colleagues in endless speeches (more than 100 spoke in one day, according to *Perspectives*) (1972, Issue 8, quoted in Daifallah 2020, 408–409). The regime responded to such unruliness with mass arrests and violent repression. *Harakat Fivri al-Majidah* became a commemorative and exhortative occasion, provoking continual protest and stirring students to determined anger at the chokehold surrounding them in the university. Islamist students of the UGTE union later nodded to the name, also dubbing their series of protests and strikes in 1990 *Harakat Fivri*, perhaps to invoke the presence of decades of student struggle. In February 1973, opposition students formed ad hoc committees initially tasked with organizing the extraordinary congress (*al-hayakil al-naqabiyyah al-mu'aqqatah*) (see also Chebbi 2022). The Arab Progressive Unitarian students consented to working within these committees as well (Labyad and Daifallah 2017, 66), as did the Islamists (Daifallah 2020, 493). That meeting did not eventuate until 15 years later. The authorities would bide their time in targeting some students. Perspectivist Ezzeddine Hazgui was arrested after protests in which students stood with the Palestinians and Arabs in the October 1973 war. He documented his personal experiences in the prison memoir *My Mother's Glasses* (2018), pieced together from notes he smuggled, wrapped in cigars, to his wife. "We thought that militarily we had triumphed over the police ... this arrogance led to our downfall. We made a tactical mistake, [and] the rope turned to wrap around us" as over 1300 students were arrested.[42]

---

[41] Article 1 of the new 1988 UGET by-laws also described it as "democratic in its organization" (see Daifallah 2020, 540).

[42] Interview, July 26, 2022, Tunis.

Our interviewees all mentioned Korba and the February movement as cataclysmic events in their narration of student protest. Interpretations of its precise importance, however, varied. Samir Laabidi, who helped organize the 18th extraordinary Congress (at long last!) in 1988, explains that it was a watershed moment in student–regime relations. "The regime lost the student movement…the authorities *(sultah)* lost the university."[43] In this reading, the dubious vote launched a new face-off with Bourguiba and his party. Through their objections to Korba, students began to mark out the university as a freed space. Leila Blili described Korba as a critical moment she could not attend because her parents, in accordance with the social conservatism of the age, would not have allowed her to travel so far as Cap Bon in Nabeul *(Al-Watan Al-Qibli)* where it was held.[44] Abdelaziz Tamimi added that students from the Islamic Tendency Movement (MTI) were closely following the "epic" that was the prolonged effort to hold the extraordinary congress. Islamists, who were present in academic councils but had not yet formed their own union, supported some of the slogans and demands of the February Movement. The slogan "popular university, democratic education, a nationalist culture" gelled with their own aspirations.[45] Korba was certainly an inflection point. For Islamists, it marked a new beginning. Intense discussion and research led the MTI students to see the congressional "coup" as an opportunity, not a disaster. Islamist students dubbed it the "Korba exposure," rather than the "Korba coup," as Abdelaziz Tamimi recalls (in Al-Thabti 2017, 248). The turning point alerted all oppositionists to the intimacy between student union and ruling party. So while leftist students "say [1971] was the beginning of the crisis … we [Islamists] say it was the beginning of a détente *(infiraj)*."[46] Leftists and Islamists thus read Korba "against the grain" of the single party line, as it were. Adel Kaaniche, a Destourian (whose name confusingly appears on the signatures Daifallah believes were belatedly tacked onto the Petition of 105, perhaps in error), reiterated the assessment quoted in Al-Shagghal's testimony above. For him, the hubbub over Korba was no more than internal Destourian disagreement spilling outward through the student movement.[47] Not only was Korba democratic. Disgruntled students threw the student union into decades of crisis in their regrettable attempts to hold a "chaotic Congress" in February 1973, his accusatory label for the Glorious February movement (Kaaniche 2021).

The 18th Extraordinary Congress

Thus far, we have re-constructed major milestones (1967–68, Korba 1972–73) in the Tunisian student protestscape. The analysis now turns to activists' assiduous pursuit of the fabled "18th Congress." An insistent agency was powered by the affect (frustration, anger) of transmitted memories of the February Movement.

---

[43] Interview, August 2, 2022, Tunis.
[44] Interview, August 1, 2022, Tunis.
[45] Interview, July 20, 2022, Tunis.
[46] Interview with Ajmi Lourimi, 22 July 2022, Tunis.
[47] Interview, July 31, 2022, Tunis.

A self-consciousness of people thwarted but not defeated infused the ad-hoc committees' operation. Eventually (and perhaps not unrelated to Islamist ascent), student tenacity prevailed. Their pressure was aided by Bourguiba's half-hearted opening overtures (or delay tactics) in the 1980s towards the UGET and the "student crisis,"[48] followed by Ben Ali's "new era." After repeated attempts, leftists were able to organize and convene the 18th extraordinary UGET Congress in 1988.[49] Academic Maher Hanin, a leftist student activist in the 1980s and later a member of the opposition PDP, admits that "we did not…impose it on the authorities, but it was negotiated" on the condition that students "give up the temporary student committees" (in Laroussi 2023, 215). Nevertheless, this social act and en-actment of protest-as-peoplehood shines bright in narrations of the union's history. Held in the College of Law between April 30 and May 2 (Labyad and Daifallah 2017, 66), the long-awaited event took place shortly after Ben Ali's coup. After months in hiding ("I grew a beard," he remembered), Samir Laabidi was proactive in organizing the congress, and was chosen as UGET's Secretary-General. The atmosphere was joyous, injected with a dose of positive affect after the negativity of frustration and thwarted planning. "Hundreds came who had been dreaming of this extraordinary event," some with their children. "They stayed overnight … it was a festival! People came from all the regions … the idea was that we could (re)build, with a large role for the left." In this Congress, where "dreams and nostalgia" ran thick, "UGET made a comeback, and the *sultah* recognized" this, recalled Laabidi.

Both the reclaimed UGTE and the Islamist UGTE were granted licenses in September 1988.[50] In April 1990 their leaders (Laabidi and Abdellatif Mekki, respectively) also gained an audience (separately) with Ben Ali himself to put forward their demands.[51] Convening the congress did not mean the end of struggle, however. The new UGET pointed to the "historical legitimacy" (political document Article 1, Clause 2) of the UGET, the organizational manifestation of anti-colonial student activism (published in Issue 14 of *Utruhat*, pp. 43–45 and 50–52). The new bylaws expressed an aim to "deepen the militant/activist experience of the student movement" (Article 3). The UGET promised to continue the "struggle" for "a popular university and democratic education," resisting security forces trespassing on university campuses. The democratic outlook[52] was similar to the UGTE's "University Compact" (1986), which stresses the "principle of democratic management" and "participation in decision-making" in university structures (Article Three, in Al-Thabti 2017, 222). UGET recounted the names of well-known Tunisian martyrs Fadhel Sassi (shot dead on January 3 by the security forces during the 1984 bread riots), Fethi Fallah, Mohamed Hammani, Kamal Sib'i, and others (Manifesto, Article 2). The UGET was a part of the people who had "paid and still pays with its blood for

---

[48] See for instance, *Fi Malaff Al-Azmah Al-Tullabiyyah, Al-Ra'i*, November 14, 1980, p. 4.
[49] See coverage of the Congress in the Vol. 3, Issue 14 (1988) of the magazine *Utruhat*, under the headline "Accomplishment" *(Al-Injaz)*, pp. 37–54.
[50] *Al-Sabah*, September 18, 1988, p. 1.
[51] Interview with Abdellatif Mekki, July 29, 2022, and Samir Laabidi, August 2, 2022, Tunis.
[52] Calls for more democratic processes even within student syndicalist structures were ongoing. See *Al-Mustaqbal*, November 23, 1981, p. 10.

… national emancipation and realization of comprehensive social justice." National and international solidarity with fellow peoples struggling for liberation (Manifesto, Article 3) revealed the cognition of an aspiring peoplehood, its attainment obstructed by authoritarianism and imperialist capitalism. Resistance against the regime would continue, UGET documents suggested. Yet Ben Ali would unleash his ire on their Islamist colleagues in the coming years.

Intra-Student "Embodied" Protest: Demoi of Discontent

In its successes and setbacks, demotic agency is multi-vocal, sometimes even discordant. The affect of solidarity against authoritarianism can retreat, feeble against the torrent of antagonistic ideological disputes. Not all students cognized themselves as integral to a student-*demos*, or even as militants, in precisely the same way. Institutionalized pluralization may have ultimately weakened student opposition to authoritarianism. While leftists (joined by the Pan-Nationalists/Arabists) toiled to wrest control of UGET by holding the extraordinary Congress, Islamist students ultimately chose a different route. The crisis of student representation[53] from the early 1970s and into the 1980s inspired Islamist students to conduct a historical (re)reading of Tunisia's long-running student movement. Incessant ideological battles and even physical brawls—of which the March 30, 1982 bloody attack on Islamists is the most notorious (see Daifallah 2020, 473–475)—rendered so-called "union pluralism: (*al-ta'addudiyyah al-naqabiyyah*) a perilous game. Islamists referred to it as the "Manouba massacre" (*majzarat Manouba*). Antagonism, not agonism, took hold of polarized student groups.

Violence precluded any sort of collaboration. Contradictions abounded in students' declared preferences and behavior. An aversion to violence and a "belie[f] in democratic conflict" characterized the leftist–Islamist debate over the history of the student movement (in Al-Thabti 2017, 283). Such dialogism could be abandoned with lightning speed, however. In a blunt testimonial, Issam Chebbi admitted to giving the orders to a fragile coalition of leftists (his own Revolutionary Unionists and the WATAD led by "Rida Lenin," (who would for a while become the infamous "advisor" to President Kais Saied)[54] to attack the Islamists. The offensive aimed to thwart Islamist (physical) disruptions of meetings organized by the temporary committees (*al-hayakil al-mu'aqqatah*) from which leftists excluded them, he explained. "The decision to respond to violence against the general meetings and in April 9 College and Manouba, [was] after convening a meeting of the [temporary] committees

---

[53] The opposition Socialist Democrats held a series of roundtables exploring the crisis. See *Ma'idah Mustadirah: I: Asbab wa Mazahir Azmat Al-Jami'ah Al-Tunisiyyah, Al-Mustaqbal*, December 8, 1980, pp. 6–7, 15. Diverse students agreed that state "repression" was to blame, exacerbated by student "fragmentation."

[54] Larbi Sadiki, "Rida 'Lenin' Cheheb Mekki: The ideologue of Tunisia's July 25 power grab?" In *Middle East Institute*, 13 September 2021, https://www.mei.edu/publications/rida-lenin-cheheb-mekki-ideologue-tunisias-july-25-power-grab, (Retrieved: June 10, 2023).

to impose their legitimacy, and to engage in the utmost possible violence if the MTI engaged in even a simple attempt to disrupt the meeting planned in the college [at] Manouba." Insisting that it was WATAD, rather than his own Revolutionary Unionists, who let loose their full force on the Islamists, Chebbi seemed contrite to some extent. Moral wrongdoing was also a tactical error, he suggested: "The [political] authorities] took advantage of the event to propagate [the notion] that the university space was a space of violence, and that was akin to a gift we presented to them." The violence "weakened the left and weakened the student movement in general" (quoted in Al-Thabti 2017, 285–289). Intra-student collaboration gave way to a normatively questionable confrontation where violence reigned. Shared challenges to authoritarianism appeared to have been forgotten in the heat of battle. Even in the re-telling, students traded blame contentiously and narratives did not always line up. Ajmi Lourimi, for instance, attributed accusations that Islamists stabbed a leftist student with a knife to false rumor-mongering, contributing to an escalation of mounting tensions (in Al-Thabti 2017, 293).

In the wake of this "very violent, very ugly" incident, Islamists called for an honor code (Student Compact) "requiring peaceful interactions between students, and dialogue."[55] This "call for mutual respect" gained "us lots of sympathy from [other] students," recalled Mohamed Al-Hamrouni.[56] The left retreated for a time while the MTI was out for "revenge," outing the leftists for their violence among the student body. Leftists refused to adopt the honor code, as Chebbi recounted (in Al-Thabti 2017, 288–289). Even as students developed their protest competencies in opposing the regime, the dialogic sometimes crashed into the violent. From the outset, ideological competition with the leftists had been fierce. Abdelaziz Tamimi recalled negotiating with leftists over the inclusion of Islamists within the temporary committees in the 1970s. His suggestion for an electoral contest was rebuffed, he said, on the grounds that movement lists would expose activist students to dangerous regime scrutiny. A nomination process (ta'ziz) could have been common ground, but "you aren't socialists," Tamimi said he was told (with the caveat: individual leftists like Issam Chebbi "have moderated a great deal since then!").[57] Some—not all—ideological rivalries have dulled with time, as archenemies learned a modicum of inclusiveness and toleration in the trenches and in the democratic experiment of 2011–21.

A More "Separate" Union: Islamist Students' Resistance and Representation

Acrimony among student activists would have major implications, as this section will show. The Islamists were constantly at odds not just ideologically but also organizationally with the leftists. However, their university activism mirrored that of

---

[55] Interview with Abdellatif Mekki, July 29, 2022, Tunis.
[56] Interview with Mohamed Al-Hamrouni, September 15, 2022, Tunis.
[57] Interview with Abdelaziz Tamimi, July 20, 2022, Tunis.

the other trends, for instance in hosting literary and media clubs. A creative agency propelled propagandist innovations, such as the "wall newspaper." Students from the different ideological groupings would hang their posters and newspapers, penned in large print, on campus walls. The Islamists published *Al-Hadath*, devoting alternating issues to politics and cultural matters, respectively. "Whoever reached the wall first, at 4 am" would emerge the winner, explained Mabrouk Korshid, a spokesperson (and a pamphlet drafter) for the Arab Progressive Unitarian movement. "Nobody could take it [the wall] after."[58] This marking of freed space was thus subject to competition. Within this agonistic climate, the Islamists began toying with the notion of a new founding *(ta'sis)* for the student union. In 1980, the Islamists met to share the results of an internal report excavating and assessing Tunisian student history. At the same time, their numbers grew in the university, even as their main opponent, the leftist WATAD was declining.[59] The nature and direction of the student movement was up for grabs, a sort of "conflicting ontologies" of union militancy.

How "freed" was the university space? All of our interviewees averred that Destourian students "were prohibited" from activism in the university. The passive phrase *(mamnu'un min al-'amal)* sidesteps the aggressive agency with which opposition students of all stripes were the ones doing the prohibiting! Still, were the conditions for students' anti-authoritarian resistance possible within the main organization? Islamist students contended with such questions. The actionable conclusion of their study, was that the UGET had always been an implement of the Destourian regime.[60] This historical re-reading was initially shared by some nationalist students, such as the Pan-Arabists with their postcolonial sensibility.[61] Deciding to put the matter to the broader student body, the Islamists took on board a suggestion to hold a vote for either pursuing the 18th extraordinary congress (discussed above), or establishing a new union altogether. Leftist students chose not to participate in what was termed an agentic decisiveness *(al-hasm)*. The congress convened between April 18–20, 1985 declared this definitive moment a necessary "attempt to end the state of non-action and paralysis and incapacity" (Al-Hasm Manifesto 1985, see Daifallah 2020, 503–508). The proposal for *ta'sis*, the manifesto continued, derived from structural problems within the UGET, namely its "distan[ce] from students," the absence of "independence" and a lack of "minimum conditions for democracy." In this situation, "union pluralism" posed a liability. It was no coincidence that this manifesto mirrored the Islamists' own evaluation of the student movement, as theirs was a majority presence at the congress. The by-laws passed at the same Congress for a new UGTE (its name mirroring the workers' union the UGTT) traced a clear line back to the foundations of Tunisia's student protest élan, in Zaytuna students' anti-colonial activism and *Sawt al-Talib Al-Zaytuni* (UGTE Bylaws 1985, see Al-Thabti 2017, 247–253). The new union strove not only to demand student rights through independent organizing, but also to "contribute to the struggles of all segments of the

---

[58] Interview with Mabrouk Korshid, May 6, 2022, Tunis.
[59] Report in *Al-Sabah*, April 20, 1982 (see Daifallah 2020, 477–485).
[60] Interview with Abdelaziz Tamimi, July 20, 2022, Tunis; Interview with Ajmi Lourimi, July 22, 2022, Tunis.
[61] *Al-Mustaqbal*, December 22, 1980, p. 8.

people for the realization of social justice and authorizing public freedoms" (UGTE Bylaws 1985).

Like the UGET in its 18th extraordinary Congress, the UGTE's was a discourse of agency that intermeshed with a cognitive self-consciousness of a people not yet free, not yet living in dignity, resolved to fight for the right to have rights. The putschist Ben Ali initially postured as a conduit of liberal transformation. Yet the licenses bestowed upon the UGTE and the post-18th Congress UGET did not preclude a turn to repression, even in the university campus. Students escalated their protests as Ben Ali bared his fangs. The "February Movement" of 1990 was a set of strikes by UGTE students. They shouted against the silence of the government to their demands (opposing the controversial move of Zaytuna high school and the expulsion of university students in Sfax) (Al-Thabti 2017, 142). Open mobilization during an academic year when the authorities sought to de-politicize the university (re-occupying freed spaces, as it were) was a risky move. It precipitated confrontations with security forces that led to the arrest of several UGTE leaders and an end to the strike by early March (Al-Thabti 2017, 141–146). The moniker "*Harakat Fivri*" was appropriated perhaps "in the absence of an epic in the history of the [UGTE] union and its supporters that matched" the leftist's "Korba" moment (Al-Thabti 2017, 148). Protest acts and en-actments were not universally embraced by "subalterned" students, however. WATAD members denounced such an appropriation of student militant history, particularly since as some read it, the MTI-turned-Ennahda initially welcomed Ben Ali's promises of change. "The Islamists wanted to create for themselves a parallel history."[62] Affect in its worst incarnations (bitter hatred) worked *against* a civic outlook. "We were happy when Ben Ali attacked the Islamists," helping us get "rid of a rival," Abdeljawad admits. "But we were young and stupid."

A UGTE press statement summarized the meeting between the Secretary General (Mekki at the time) and the Tunisian President. It mentioned the "agreement" that security forces would be withdrawn from the university, "starting next year."[63] (The UGTE shared in this demand with their rival union the UGET (Al-Thabti 2017, 154).) However, on May 8, 1991, security forces killed the students Ahmed Al-Omari and Adnan Ben Said, marking the first such campus deaths since (pre-independence)1954 (Daifallah 2020, 9). From Paris, a statement signed two days later by a diverse group of opposition members including Ahmed ben Salah, Rached Ghannouchi, and Mohamed Mzali condemned the "terrorist" violence "against the people and its lively forces" as embodied by students fighting for freedom and democracy.[64] That same year, Ben Ali's government dissolved the UGTE. It was as short-lived as Sawt Al-Talib Al-Zaytuni before it. Only after the revolution was the UGTE was revived, in 2013. The Islamist-leftist animus continues at the time of writing.[65] So does the divisione over student unity (*al-wihdah al-tullabiyyah*). But the roles have been reversed. The leftist UGTE, now led by its first elected female

---

[62] Interview, July 24, 2022, Tunis.
[63] UGTE Press Statement, April 16, 1990, Ennahda Memory archive, https://bit.ly/41CCUDi
[64] Statement, May 10, 1991, Ennahda Memory Archive.
[65] Interviews with two female Ennahda university students, July 27, 2022, Tunis.

Secretary General Warda Atig,[66] is the side opposing "union pluralism" and closeness to the ruling powers (Hamdi 2019), albeit in a different (democratizing) context. More antagonistic than agonistic, such acute conflicts demonstrate the intractability of ideological polarization, discussed below.

Student "Logoi" and Social Imaginaries

After analyzing how significant events showcase the agency, affect, and cognition of student activists, we turn now to a discussion of student anti-authoritarian thought practices. Any conception of students' politics and struggles in Tunisia must account for ideology. The voices, discourses, and forces that inhabited the various university campuses navigated distinct ideological territories. Maybe they tended to inordinately exalt ideologies—including Trotskyism—which vanished even in Russia itself. Two criticisms may be leveled against these ideologies. First, their adherents were at times mistaken in their blind faith in borrowed "isms," vacillating between distortions and confusions of myth and reality (Mannheim, 1936). None of them since 2011 has managed to come close to winning majorities (with the qualified exception of the Islamists), much less win power in their own right. A Trotskyist, oddly enough, was amongst those who contested and won a seat in the country's 2011 elections for the Constituent Assembly. Leftists managed to win seats in various elections but never in huge numbers. Ideologies of the left reverberated from the mid-1960s to the mid-1980s, prevailing in university campuses. Literally, they were the trailblazers of postcolonial campus activism, deftly socializing university students into insurrectionary politics. They did in post-independence what Zaytunis did during the colonial period. "Perspectivists," whose early ideological lineages were Marxist, were "kings" of university politics. They led and sustained dynamic struggles against the Bourguibist state. With the rise of Islamists in the 1980s, their preponderance as quintessential student-rebels began to wane, at university campuses as in national politics. Second, Tunisian ideological groupings failed the test of time for lack of sensitivity to local dynamics. The upshot was fatal dissonance. They took too far the idea of "thinking globally." They could not, as a result, "act locally," with such borrowed doctrinaire "isms." They were inflexible in their adaptation to local problems of injustice and non-development. The intellectual allure of Marx, Trotsky, or even Nasser (for pan-Arabist students) contorted political judgment and perhaps credulous overestimation of "universal truths." The meanings given to ideology's unstable usage, were shaped by context. The word deflationary comes to mind. The signage given to ideology by practitioners eager to make sense of institutional, behavioral, or individual politics does not always mirror scholars' theoretical heuristics (Eagleton, 1991). For starters, students are not states.

---

[66] See, "Warda Atig, première femme à la tête de l'Uget," in *Jeune Afrique*, May 24, 2019, https://www.jeuneafrique.com/778841/economie/tunisie-warda-atig-premiere-femme-a-la-tete-de-luget/, (Retrieved: June 20, 2022).

The Tunisian student movement is older than the national state. Literally, its century-long trajectory of conflating knowledge and protest speaks not just to a merely memetic feature of self-reproduction. It is a vibrant phenomenon enmeshed in Tunisia's colonial and postcolonial socio-political fabric. The "student-rebel" features in this protestscape as an ontological quality. Protest is ingrained in student life *qua* quotidian politics, on and off campus. It is bone-deep. The student deploys protest to reconfigure power relations and to realize identity and positionality. Her/his brand of protest fashions agency, affect, and cognition according to the exigencies of their time and space. The student-rebel (with a cause), in this instance, makes sense of national politics, playing a critical role through the use of ideas/ideology, emotions, and various tools of protest, peaceful and violent. Politics outside the campus provided an additional layer of galvanization, inspiring a flux of ideological isms for students' activism. Through protest over all things political, student-related, and national, emerged contest over identity, history, meaning-making, position vis-à-vis power, religious and political values, the right to have rights, visions of justice, freed space within university precincts, international paradigms of governance, and regimes of oppression. This ontological quality had implications for how to do protest, enabling a kind of epistemology of rebellion. At its core is first and foremost the ethic of navigating, temporally and spatially, the dissentscape along with fellow students. They espouse diametrically opposed visions of identity, ideology, and even morality, at the same time sharing in regime opposition, one chief commonality.

It looks like a mutuality of unlike-minded actors. They share ideals of patriotism justice, emancipation, and motivation for protest itself. Yet students contest one another's interpretation of these as well as the political happenings around them, and the means to supervise power, reform it, or empty the center altogether. Their sets of agentic, affective, and cognitive resources at once equip them to counteract the official transcripts and prejudices of the powers-that-be, and one another's brands of resistance (agentic), registers (affective), and ideas and "ideal speech" (cognitive). United they stand in the face of authoritarian power structures, practices, biases, and attendant coercive apparatuses. Yet, student-rebels harbor their own ideological prejudices. These divide them some of the time, compounding their epistemology of opposition/resistance against regime and fellow students. Other times, confrontation cedes to solidarity and collaboration. There is, in theory, much, by way of common subalternity, shared emancipatory drive, and interpretations of the condition of subjugation, which binds together students' voices, forces, and discourses. Commonality changes over time and space. This will be corroborated by examples of student-rebels who crossed the floor, and tasted positions in power, after resistance against it. Nonetheless, as a terrain of emancipatory endeavor, with twists and shifts in moral sentiments and emotions, practices and ideational constructs, the students' protestscape recognizes the difference of specific ontologies, opening possibilities for dialogic and "communicative protest." This is sufficiently mandated by the normative relatedness (i.e. how emancipatory quests and morality should be engineered) of specific existing ontologies informed and bound up by competing ideologies. Thus, communicative protest where students' activisms are concerned, across time and space, is the enlisting of the sum of diversified and different assemblages of agency, affect, and cognition into a synergy that mediates their joint aspiration for emancipation.

The Struggle over Meaning-making: (De)Contesting Ideology

Before unpacking Tunisian students' competing ideologies, some conceptual clarification is in order. Ideology is an exportable conceptual apparatus. It remains a relevant analytical lens in the hands of social scientists eager to interpret the nexus of ideas/ideals and political practice/behavior (see Bell 1962). Its ubiquity approximates that of political science's keywords—power, democracy, legitimacy, etc. Perhaps it is this ubiquity of usage in the social sciences since Destutt de Tracy's coinage of the term in 1801 (Roucek 1944, 482) that partly accounts for its "semantic promiscuity" (Gerring 1997, 957). Moreover, ideology is steeped in clashing interpretations (Gerring 1997, 957). Roucek's definition sums up conventional understandings. "Ideological construction," he argues, "involves the projection of a certain ideal into the future" (Roucek 1944, 479). He notes its evaluative utility, given ideology's "programs for the future improvement of society ... covertly or overtly scheduled to come about either logically, morally, or from the point of view of 'natural laws'" (Roucek 1944, 479). "Opposing ideologies," in this scheme of thought, are none other than what Marx calls "false ideologies" (Roucek 1944, 479). Gramsci rethought Marxian dogma, injecting ideology with a healthy dosage of agency. Agency that befits revolution-making via empowering consciousness, rejecting dichotomization of the economic base and the superstructure (the realm of morality, ideas, intellectuals and "civil society" (Bobbio 1988, 73–100)). "Ideology ... is the terrain on which men acquire consciousness of themselves," as a rejection of passive "ideological inculcation" (Mouffe 2014, 196). Intellectuals are "purveyors of consciousness" (Gramsci in Bellamy 1994, 14). Mouffe concurs. As she points out, intellectuals are, thus, assigned contradictory roles within social change. On the one hand, they are galvanizers of change (silent revolution via morality, culture, ideas, arts, etc.). On the other, they are defenders/normalizers of the status quo, that is, the hegemony of the capitalist class. Thus unfurls a "war of position," involving "disarticulation and rearticulation" (Mouffe 2014, 197) of ideas to win the hearts and minds of social groups by the antagonistic classes. The fine *Oxford Handbook of Ideologies* edited by Freeden, Sargeant, and Stears confirms Gerring's observations. The editors appreciate the exegetical enterprise that casts ideology as a problematic and a problem, perennially "mutating," according to Freeden, and, thus, drawing disagreements (Freeden et al. 2013). They stress the contested nature of the concept of ideology throughout (Sargent in Freeden et al. 2013, 516–518).

In Tunisia, the student movement since the 1960s has drawn ideological stands and strands that approximated Freeden's notion of "decontested political concepts" the language and meanings of which defined clear-cut ideational and political currents and orientations (Freeden et al. 2013, 113–122). The laboratory in which these ideologies were created was one of fierce contestation of the official Bourguibist dogma, with its own set of decontested concepts (e.g. Tunisian-ness, patriotism, political deference to Bourguiba, secularity, and incrementalism), but bereft of actual political contests over power. Even if "statist" by accounts of students of ideology in Middle Eastern contexts (Amuzegar 1974, 1–9), the vagaries of Bourguibism (or for that matter Nasserism or Baʻathism) unilaterally sought to mold public consciousness, top-down. Propaganda, new cultural patterns, and state intellectuals played a role in such scheming to routinize Bourguibism by more or less, universalizing Bourguiba's own particularities: a predilection for Francophile culture, the imposition of secular politics, an anti-Arabist stance, etc. The resulting distortions are threefold. First, the myths, values, and ideas championed by way of "cultural construction," deployed state resources including propaganda to penetrate society with the full backing of coercive bureaucracies. State officials hardly equated with a class of intellectuals, as in Gramsci's formulation of "cultural hegemony." Second, Bourguiba's state officials lacked the know-how, à la Gramsci, to "manage through the coordination of different and conflicting interests and ideologies" (Stråth in Freeden et al. 2013, 27). Viable conflicting interests and ideologies were proscribed and excluded, including by the use of force. Salah ben Youssef and his followers are a case in point. This is part of a long and troubled history of brutal rule under Bourguiba, often omitted or seldom problematized in Euro-American studies of Tunisia's politics. Western academics treated Bourguiba with a velvet glove. Like any "dominating class," ideological hegemony via Bourguibism (far from being a tight-knit, coherent set of ideas and values) "provided a mask that repressed the social practices of the subordinate class" (Stråth in Freeden et al. 2013, 27). Writing four years before Bourguiba fired his super-Minister Ahmed ben Salah, whose cooperatives policy caused country-wide mutiny (Bouguerra 2019, 107), and thirteen years before the 1978 bread riots, and nineteen years before the 1984 popular revolt and massacre of civilians by the army, Sharabi overstated Tunisia's liberalism. "Tunisia, on the other hand, is a single-party regime with a good deal of state control in economic life. The president, who is also the head of the party, enjoys extensive powers. The liberal character of Tunisia's parliamentary system derives mostly from the fact that the dominant Socialist Destour party reflects in its composition and orientation the various classes and groups that make up Tunisian society" (Sharabi 1965, 485).

Localizing Ideology

Ideology, in our account, benefits from interrogation that carefully weighs new critique. It is not a fixed and deterministic template of thought and praxis. Ideology has traversed terrains of language, culture, time, and space. With its travel, including to the Arab region, its readings have come to reflect enriching revisions. Its Marxian variant is taken to mirror a super-structure, the imagining of norms, laws, morality, and identity. These are assumed to express the capitalist class's hegemonic socio-economic structures and ruling institutions, reproducing favorable hierarchies, interests, and power relations. This Marxian position has long been superseded by more sophisticated accounts of power and additional social and cultural complexities. Gerring avers: "The interests of an ideologue may refer not simply to the material interests of his or her class but, more broadly, to group interests and even to self-interest, and to a set of tangible and intangible interests which include position, status, power, and perquisite" (Gerring 1997, 973). The position of Rancière's "part that has no part," on the margins of power, cannot be underestimated as a rallying force with the potential to subvert power paradigms, striking back at autocrats, speaking truth to power, and writing back. Tunisia's student movement's usage of ideology approximates a kind of "discourse" of dissent and protest. As a discursive formation, ideology carries political lexicons and codes into which the dynamics of knowledge and power are elided. Ideology is contextual. Foucault's "discourse" may be more apt for capturing the naturalizing of hierarchies and power relations of domination and resistance to them than the concept of "ideology." Simply put, "Foucault's framework favor[s] his own conception of power. Knowledge, language, and power are inextricably linked in discourse: power validates certain speech and invalidates others, while knowledge supports power" (Boswell and Hawkins 1999, 353).

Student Social Imaginaries and Becomings

In addition to Foucault, Charles Taylor's (2004) concept of "social imaginary," even if concerned with Western modernity, is a 'lone concept' borrowed to understand the use of ideologies in students' struggles in Tunisia. Taylor's definition of social imaginary includes components that best summarize the "ideologies" that animated campus politics in Tunisia for decades. First, the ontological element, as the imagining of "social existence," is integral to Taylor's notion of social imaginary. Second, the relational or intra-societal component suggests that a social imaginary includes conceptions of how a group's members "fit together with others." Third, there is a normative aspect: "the deeper normative notions and images that underlie ... expectations" (Taylor 2003, 23). Social imaginary, Taylor insists, is about a heightened sense of commonality, in terms of "common understanding" and a "shared sense of legitimacy" (Taylor 2003, 23). Key to our borrowing of "social imaginary" is its communicative, mutual, and constructivist character. It makes the project of constructing community reliant on group and agentic dynamics, which are not predetermined. We invoke the notion of social imaginary to distill how competing ideologies in university campuses dialectically and collaboratively engage one another in deliberation when seeking mutual goals and goods, prioritizing their specific group agendas when they lapse into a mode of confrontation.

Implicating ideology as a relevant component of the evolution of anti-systemic struggles in Tunisia seeks not only to establish the rise of student movement in the realm of knowledge and meaning-making. It also provides the context for appreciating ontological becoming, speaking and writing back against authoritarian domination. That is, how struggles and "logoi" of peoplehood-in-the-making came to exist, to capture how student-rebels learned to project their own conception of "being" onto the political field, in their own terms, words, accounts, imagining, and imaginaries. Students thus position their activisms on a course to resist a system bent on crushing any rival Weltanschauung.

Thus, the intellectual and cultural mapping sought by students in their bid to resist Bourguibism entailed the morphing of the students from passive vessels of state propaganda to active transformers of intellect and culture within the precincts of university campuses and eventual "freed zones." Note that Bourguiba recruited the brightest and most prominent literati (e.g. Mahmoud Messadi, 1911–2004; Mohamed Mzali, 1925–2010; Mohamed Charfi, 1936–2008, etc. ...) to intellectualize his own brand of politics. To paraphrase Gramsci, within the freed zones a kind of dialectics ensued in which competing ideological currents engaged the student body to propagate their own dogmata. Within the zones, Norberg-Schulz's (1979) visualization of "the genius loci" and construction of "meaningful places" in new logoi and forms of demos breathe life into new becomings. First, this drives home anti-Bourguiba ideas as part of an emancipatory struggle against a dictator. Second, it reconfigures power within university campuses in a way that reshapes the student into an agent of a new consciousness of cultural and political reform. Bourguiba recruited the professorate, Zaytuna's doctors of Islam, the literati and the media to reproduce his stranglehold on power. In a Gramscian sense, by projecting into the cultural and intellectual horizon their own ideological "verities" and claims, students opened a "war of position" in Tunisia. A war of ideas and values, some of which (e.g. Communism, Arabism, etc.) Bourguiba had sought since independence to exclude for good from the public domain.

Here the rise in Tunisia of the student movement's rival ideologies to Bourguibist social structures upset the first president's quest to secure total consent—domination. Dissent instead set in. Dissent via ideology has resonance in Freire's *Pedagogy of the Oppressed* (1970). It was a serious and compelling contestation of power that Bourguiba never expected. At its core, dissent equipped the students with a voice that entered into the public domain—a heard voice. It imputed that voice with presence, with existence. Dissent and, by the standards of the 1960s, 1970s, and 1980s, a new brand of radical activism exploded in university campuses in ways that marked a clear undermining of the normalizing politics of consent at the behest of Bourguiba, his Destour Party, and its coordinating committees (*al-lijan al-tanisiqiyyah*). Bourguiba (*al-hakim bi amrih*—the quintessential omnipotent ruler) had machinated and manipulated all the structures of power, creating with one hand only to dispense of it with another, at a whim and with swift execution, when threatened by his own creations. As if Bourguiba in his bid to take over all power in Tunisia used these creations—syndicates, women's groups, the student body itself, regime intellectuals, youth organizations and corporatist bodies—to be his mouthpieces and consent legitimators. Tunisian politics after independence is Bourguibism writ large. His cunning was immaculate as these entities were the means by which he managed, for a while, to sack society in its entirety and make his closest lieutenants (Ahmed ben Salah; Mohamed Mzali, Habib Achour) sign their own political death warrants when policy failed.

The promulgation of alternative social imaginaries began percolating among student activists in the 1960s. Challenges to Bourguiba's project emanated from the university. No sooner had he quashed his political arch-enemy Ben Youssef (and his adherents) than he was bombarded by insurrections from a fast-growing army of militants. The heterogeneous tendencies (leftist, Pan-Arabist, and Islamist) of shifting and quarrelsome students refused the narrowness of Bourguiba's worldview (see Table 4.2). They resented his singular rule. Idealistic and impassioned, these young students carried no weapons but readily spouted and experimented with ideas and words. The 14th UGET Congress in Tabarka, for instance, identified lectures, trips across the country, cinema, theatre, music, sports, and even student journalism as components of a "holistic education" (Regulations on Cultural Affairs, 1966; see Daifallah 2020, 365–369). Students in a sense wanted to liberate "culture," rendering it a free space amenable to the counter-imaginaries and counter-creativity of their *mikhyal*. They sought to break free of top-down enculturation, as by the semi-official UGET or other amplifiers of regime indoctrination. Islamist students introduced "University Week" in which much of the wider student populace participated, as Abdelkarim Harouni recalls (in Al-Thabti 2017, 267–270). They broadened the tools and substance of student activism, disseminating cultural outputs (documentary showings, "engaged music" performances, etc.) to refract *alternative* social imaginaries yearning for and enacting change. As indicated in Table 4.2, student trends adopted overlapping as well as distinct slogans (e.g. "popular university, democratic education, national culture!" or "one Arab nation") that reflected their shared and particular beliefs, demands, and dreams for the future.

Very parsimoniously, Austin's (1962) notion of speech acts explains how in conditions of protest "utterances," namely the vocalization of slogans, chants, speeches, even persecutory or insulting, have performative utility. Thus, Austin is of relevance here in that student protestors are not mobs in a state of "volcanic eruption" or "wielders of violence and chaos" who hurl words unthinkingly (politicians unwilling to engage students in dialogue impute such unpatriotic and sinister motives to their social acting and en-acting via protests). Rather, the cries of protest may be "declarative" of disaffection, frustration, anger, and a desire for better things. More importantly, in line with Austin's theory, they are "performative." Student protestors state words reflective of their social imaginaries and oppositional discourses. That is, as Austin argues, to perform social acts and social action: "an utterance is the performing of an action" (Austin 1962, 6). Do protests constitute "felicity" conditions (Austin 1962, 14) for verbalizing slogans and chants? Performing action via vocalized words in protests would seem to be felicitous, significant as statements of intent of opposing, quarrelling, and acting on insurrectionary declarations. This echoes

Table 4.2 Social Imaginaries and Ideologies of Student Protestscape Tendencies (1963–1991)

	Left	Destour	Pan-Arabist/Nationalist	Islamist
Name	Perspectivists, then POCT Al-Shu'lah, then WATAD	Socialist Destour Party Democratic Destour Rally	Arab Progressive Unitarian Students (Nasserists, Ba'athists, Qaddafists)	Islamic Tendency Movement (MTI), then Ennahda Islamic Left Hizb Al-Tahrir
Tenets	Anti-imperialism Socialism/Marxism Modernism Anti-Bourguibist	Modernism, secularism, gradual action Bourguibist, then Ben Ali loyalist	Pan-Arabism Anti-imperialism, anti-Zionism Against (existing) student representation Anti-party (social action through popular fronts) Anti-Bourguibist	Islamic revival and identity Critical of Westernization
Discursive Symbols of Activism	Freedom Social justice Secularism Modernity Rationality		Arab unity, pan-Arab solidarity, Arab socialism, Palestinian cause, Student unity	Islamic identity Zaytuna pedigree Da'wah
Action/Strategy	Sit-ins, demonstrations, wall murals, music, cinema, newspapers, discussion circles, violence	Regime propaganda Violence	Coalitional (historic bloc) Mass/popular mobilization Sit-ins, demonstrations, wall murals, pamphlets, discussion circles, violence	Sit-ins, demonstrations, wall murals, University Week activities (music, cinema), pamphlets, newspapers, discussion circles, violence
Means of change	Revolutionary	Incremental Coercive	Revolutionary	Gradualist but sometimes more militant than political movement (e.g. 1978)

Civic/Democratic Engagement	Syndicalism Union Congresses and Elections Academic Council Elections	Retreated, excluded from opposition-led unions after Korba (1971)	Syndicalism Union congresses and elections Democratic dialogue for student unity	Syndicalism Union congresses and elections Academic council elections
Slogans	"Popular University, Democratic Education, National Culture" "Organizational and political rupture with the regime" "A Popular, Democratic, Independent Union" Militancy, Independence, Steadfastness, Democracy (UGET) For a Better Tunisia Land, Freedom, National Dignity (WATAD)	Driven out of university 'freed spaces'; no notable slogans during this period	"One Arab nation" "Organizational and political rupture with the regime" "No party, no regression, popular committees"	"We want freedom in the university, as we want it in the country" "Islam is the revolution of the downtrodden" (*mustadʿafīn*) "Secondary students, university students, workers, [all] unite in militancy" Unity, Militancy, Independence (UGTE) For a free student
Publications	*Perspectives* *Al-Shuʿlah* *Al-ʿAmil Al-Tunisi*		Statements, manifestos, press participation	*Al-Hadath*

Rancière's (1999) reference to the role of speech, and logos in the "the discursive articulation" of rights and ideals vital for the construction of "speaking beings" (Rancière 1991) and for wording the world. This extends to revolutionary becomings, involving the twin processes of deterritorialization and reterritorialization enabled by speaking—not mute—dissidents.

Ideology and Protest in Speech

In this context of students defying authoritarianism, Iris Marion Young's notion of "inclusive communicative democracy" is instructive. The minimal democratic-ness of Tunisia's multi-vocal student protestscape, as we explained above, extended as far as its opposition to Bourguiba and Ben Ali's regimes. Young writes about democratic settings where inclusive communication enhances the potential for achieving justice. Here, we sparingly appropriate her concept to scrutinize the dialogism of quarrelling student trends. The ideological contestation these students waged in discussion groups (*halaqat niqash*) was not aimed merely at proselytization. Disagreements, attempts to persuade would-be members, exhortations to mobilize the broader student body in protest or in voting, were all simultaneously (direct or indirect) challenges to singular rule. Critical evaluation of this discursive, dialogic dimension is an avenue to "criticize exclusion" and "to foster inclusion" (Young 2000, 70) on normative grounds. Young's intervention regards not the substance but the form and style of discursive interventions. Substance was important for these hortatory students, of course. The hours they passed reading Marxist, leftist, and nationalist tomes, as told in our interviews, attest to the centrality of the content of arguments. Competing argumentative texts were also hung on university walls, debating for instance the concept of "the state" or "class," as MTI student activist Mehdi Mabrouk recounted (in Al-Thabti 2017, 297). During in-person debates, (UGTE's) Mohamed Hamrouni recalled, "We would use references … someone would bring 4–5 references and put them on the table" to consult during these debates that "would continue for hours, sometimes days."[67] Kamal Ben Younes regarded his time behind bars in Burj Al-Rumi and Tunis prisons in the early 1980s "an opportunity to read [and] discuss these theoretical works."[68]

The attention Young lavishes on the form and style of arguments is equally important, particularly in an environment as highly charged as the student protestscape. To an extent, rival student groups seem have passed the threshold of her "greeting," or public recognition and acknowledgment of one another. Participation in each other's' discussion circles was one sign of such "public acknowledgment" (Young 2000, 57–62) groups and individuals at odds with one another. Some level of grudging mutual respect grew between competing trends who all similarly regarded the

---

[67] Interview, September 15, 2022, Tunis.
[68] Interview, July 20, 2022, Tunis.

Destour students as enemy number one.[69] In this case, the "aim to solve problems" (Young 2000, 61) is not a particular policy proposal but the overarching political problem of dislodging Destourian rule.

Young also brings attention to the stylistic elements of rhetoric. Relevant to our purposes, she singles out affect such as "fear, hope, anger, joy," as well as forms not limited to words. Protests and various "visual media" (Young 2000, 65) should be taken as seriously as debate. Student banners and wall newspapers, in addition to sit-ins and perennial protesting, are examples animated by heightened affect. Anger against the authorities ("imperialist" and "agent" regime were some terms bandied about), and dreaming hopefully to (re)claim the right to have rights recurred in student language. Often, however, the students turn affect on each other. Most extreme is the violence which leaves dialogue far behind. Even short of violence, leftists and Islamists traded sharp barbs. WATAD students referred to Islamists as "backward," "herds," and "obscurantist." One student dubbed them the "rotting right under the leadership of the Muslim Brotherhood."[70] Islamists in their turn called WATAD "regime tools" who engaged in "domineering" and even "terrorist" methods, according to one report.[71] Such affectively suffused language works to exclude, rather than include. Here the "free-ness" of university spaces is patchy. Students covered their ears, so to speak, falling short of an inclusively communicative stance. They did not pass the rhetorical requirement of listening as well as speaking (Young 2000, 70).

Finally, the dialogism of battling student movements makes use of narrative. They told stories to make political points to like-minded "local public" audiences (Young 2000, 73), the wider student population, and the authoritarian regime itself. Magazine articles, union statements, and political manifestos all employ narratives. Both the UGET and UGTE, for instance, placed their activism within the lineage of anticolonial student movements. The UGTE identified Zaytuna students in particular as their militant forebears. They both framed their strikes, sit-ins, and demonstrations as struggles to obtain rights for students, as well as freedom and justice for all Tunisians. That theirs is the people's struggle is an important narrative device. Importantly, Young notes the didactic or pedagogical function of narrative. "The general normative functions of narrative in political communication … refer to teaching and learning" (2000, 77). Speakers strive to "enlarge th[e] social understanding" of others (Young 2000, 77). Students helped to expand the political horizons and imaginaries of colleagues and other Tunisians through both oral and written storytelling: newspapers, magazines, speeches, protest chants. Taken together, public acknowledgment, affective non-verbal rhetoric, and storytelling contributed to student activists' own learning. Iteratively practiced, dialogic protest competencies were thus (at least sometimes) polished. Moreover, these very communicative skills primed activists for future lives in the bureaucracy, underground-then-official parties, and political posts. Well-known Perspectivist Al-Hachemi Al-Troudi cast the UGET as a "school" where

---

[69] Interviews with Mehdi Abdeljawad, July 24, 2022, Tunis; Abdelaziz Tamimi, July 20, 2022, Tunis.
[70] *Al-Mustaqbal*, December 29, 1980, p. 9.
[71] *Al-Sabah*, April 20, 1982.

he and future intellectual and political elites acquired lifelong political skills. He learned "debate and disputation and modes of analysis and inference," alongside persuasive skills, compromise, and "realistic rationality" (Al-Troudi 2016, 41). His comrade Sadok Ben Mhenni[72] elaborated: this "school makes the human being concerned about what [occurs] around him and understand his country and [learn how] to impact it, and [to] sacrifice for the sake of his right to the word" (Ben Mhenni 2016, 113). Like Nejib Chebbi (2022, 34–35) propelled by his own voracious reading in prison, Ben Mhenni (2017) would later collect book donations for inmates, as he explains to a visiting repairman in an opening scene of his own prison memoir. Similarly, Gilbert Naccache narrated poignantly in his moving prison testimony— putrid smells of human waste, swarming bugs, stale air, suffocating basements—not simply to inspire pathos. His "pedagogical ambitions" were an "alternative way of doing politics and communicating my ideas to others," (Naccache 2018 [1982], 125) through writing more eternal than interminable yet fleeting jail sentences. Access to the word—the right to speak—was a freedom snatched by counterrevolutionary authoritarianism. Students learned through their struggles, appreciating the precise freedoms for which they quarreled with the state, at great personal cost. Islamist Munia Brahim, later Ennahda MP, concurred. Her university activism taught her above all "the boldness to express my opinion," oration, and political consciousness, a toolkit to wield in service of the public interest.[73]

Gender-ed Spaces

Within this lively "communicative protest" climate, in university free spaces, what we have called communicative protest, how did females fare with regard to inclusion? The testimonials of six Perspectivist women, politically active first as students in the 1970s, offer some clues to this ambiguous dynamic. Years after the 2011 revolution, these women who had advanced as academics, unionists, and declared feminists, jointly sought to contribute to Tunisia's "collective memory." Amal ben Abba had sworn off the pen for decades, traumatized by her incarceration experience. Prison guards and interrogators "used to force us, under threat, to write [of] our activist path, revealing the names of our comrades," shredding their drafts and making them write anew when not satisfied (Ben Abba in Zankah 2020, 43). The interventions published over 40 years after the event hint at an overlooked repository of experiential protest knowledge, shared through distinctive firsthand accounts. These women wrote back against epistemic injustice. They joined the company of other sidelined female activists around the world, including former IRA prisoners (McCann 2015). An Antigone theme—not unusual in feminist political theory (Holland 1998) and feminist discourse, to summon a figure defying social mores and the law in pursuit

---

[72] Father to departed revolutionary activist Lina Ben Mhenni (see Chapter 6). He passed away in summer 2023.
[73] Interview, September 24, 2022, Tunis.

of emancipation—runs through a volume collated by Tunisian Perspectivist women. The book is the outcome of a workshop held in 2018 where these female comrades reminisced and recounted stories long untold. Zankah (2020) notes that these women were the "first cell of the feminist movement" in Tunisia. They bequeathed a political consciousness and oppositional vitality to a "new generation of feminist activists/militants," the likes of Lina Ben Mhenni (Farhat in Zankah 2020, 9). "Politics girls," as the guards at the Manouba women's prison called them, was a name that stuck.

Affect streams from their narratives. There was the pain and anguish of incarceration (being stripped of clothes, trapped in filth, hosting large rats as neighbors). "Solidarity" brought them close in prison, where they waged hunger strikes demanding medical treatment for an ailing comrade (Mahdfoudh-Jédidi in Zankah 2020, 80). More uplifting affect also fed into individual cognition wrought by collective debates and struggles. The term "dream" recurs as a driving force for these idealistic women. Hailing from a wealthy family in Bardo, Leila Blili jumped at the chance to join leftist activists in her time at the April 9 College. Among these comrades "in this small and diverse world," she found an inner "harmony" (Blili in Zankah 2020, 195). In the wake of the 1968 protests, Tunisia's first post-independence university cohort had high hopes. "The dream of more social and political rights became possible," she remembers. Students' famed *halaqat niqash* glimmered in the eyes of young recruits. "What struck my fancy in that student environment was the free speech [and] deliberation within the discussion circles, and the overflowing enthusiasm sounding from the throats of the male and female activists, until I became one of them," explains Aisha Gallouz, who commenced her studies at the April 9 College in 1971 (Zankah 2020, 160). As they write from the distance of memory, the movement is not above critique for these women. Dalila Mahfoudh-Jédidi muses that the "the activists' imaginary lost its way … and ignored reality, so it brought to life the Soviet then Chinese models in all their glory" (in Zankah 2020, 89). Too much theoretical bickering, not enough praxis.

A Mixed Record

The women activists' narratives indicate some complexities of female Perspectivist participation. On the one hand, they mingled in the same underground cells (*khalaya sirriyyah*) as the males, leading marches, participating in strikes and sit-ins, standing at the front of picket lines. Perspectivist-turned-Workers' Party militant Mohamed Al-Kilani recalled female comrades as instrumental in rebuilding the "network" after the arrest of leaders in 1973–74, "because they were unknown to the police" (Al-Kilani 2020, 95). Some such women were subject to the regime's harsh punitive measures. Like their male counterparts, the six women above (Amal Ben Aba, Dalila Mahdfoudh-Jédidi, Zainab bent Said Al-Sharni, Sassia Al-Rouisi ben Hasan, Aisha Glouz Ben Mansour, and Leila Tamim Blili) were arrested, picked up in the dark of night by security officials in a Volkswagon. Interrogated and tortured in the notorious bowels of the Interior Ministry, they were then transferred to the Manouba women's prison.

On the other hand, *Banat al-Siyasah* also began to etch a critical consciousness *as women*. They stood at a particular "intersection" of "non-people" deprived of free speech, unionist activism, political rights. Some were disadvantaged socially and economically. Initially, feminism was not articulated as such in the 1970s, because as Blili puts it, "there was widespread certainty regarding [equally] sharing the same rights and responsibilities" (in Zankah 2020, 27). Even women defying the imposed narrative fetishizing the liberated "Bourguiban woman" (*al-Mar'ah al-Bourguibia*) did not all agree (Ilahi 2022, 22). Moreover, not all Tunisian women activists embraced every single symbol of Arab feminism. Communist writers in *Al-Tariq Al-Jadid* newspaper seemed unimpressed by Egypt's Nawal Saadawi for instance (Ilahi 2022, 159). Written and spoken debate about women's social and political plights did arise both simultaneously and subsequently to student activism. Tchaïcha and Arfaoui (2017, 2) mark this shift from what they consider a long-standing "women's movement" to a "formidable Tunisian feminist movement" in the mid-1980s. Kallander (2021, 192–195) concludes that while the discourse of the Perspectives group was in line with a paternalist state feminism, Simone Lellouche, Aisha ben Abed, and other female members defied the constraining contours of deportment and political (dis)interest, through rebellion.

Still, campus "freed spaces" may not have been so free for leftist women who felt belittled, marginalized, and objectified. Un-free pockets impelled the creation of *new* freed spaces. Outside the strictures of student organization, some women commenced meetings at Club Tahar Haddad (Tchaïcha and Arfaoui 2017, 63–64) in the old city of Tunis *(al-madinah al-'atiqah)*. Here they would unload, reflect, and "study" the situation of women. Infused by the "spirit of 68" and moved to action after participation in the 1972 February movement, in these female-only freed spaces, women sought to "take [back] the word" (Jrad 2020, 122). Collectively refusing personal and political silencing, they embraced a kind of (intellectual) militancy aimed at transforming social-cultural consciousness towards full inclusion and equality of women. Skepticism lingered over the bourgeois, French-speaking ambience and the absence of working women. Attendees' radical aspirations to freedom ("Emancipation from whom? From men?") also inspired incredulity among some observers.[74] Naysayers notwithstanding, accomplishments included the creation of a Woman's Committee within the highly masculine UGTT (Jrad 2020, 131).

Club Tahar Haddad

Zainab Al-Sharni recalls joining women's discussion groups in 1979. Caught between economic necessity and extended family pressure not to part with her baby daughter, she had reluctantly returned to her teaching job a mere 20 days after giving birth. "Far from the eyes of the police," these gatherings were additional free enclaves, perhaps a

---

[74] *Al-Mustaqbal*, January 5, 1981, pp. 13, 15.

"Tunisified" version of feminist "consciousness-raising" (Evans 1980) of American-British "Women's Liberations." Events at Club Tahar Haddad included lectures and debates on child-rearing, media portrayals of women and girls, and exhibitions of female-authored books.[75] Women shared personal experiences, including "issues relating to bodily freedoms" in a manner that shocked young attorney Bochra Belhadj Hamida. She attended the *halaqat* as a listener when disillusionment by aspects of her student activism set in. Hamida had engaged in smaller rebellions against male comrades who, in her telling, excluded women from some forms of intellectual activism. Tasked with distributing pamphlets, for instance, she refused, "since I did not participate in drafting them."[76] The thrust of the Club Tahar Haddad discussions was that struggles for socio-economic and political rights must run through women's emancipation, in the spirit of the club's namesake, explains Al-Sharni. They organized lectures to this effect (Al-Sharni in Zankah 2020, 115–116). Eventually in the late 1980s, they and others formed the Tunisian Association of Democratic Women (ATFD in the French acronym) and the Association of Tunisian Women for Research on Development (AFTURD) (see Labidi 2007, 9–11). When it came to women, then, a blinkered inclusion/exclusion dynamic characterized leftist student activism. If various ideological trends were at once democratic (dialogic) and undemocratic (exclusionary, sometimes violent) towards other movements, internally a similar gendered unevenness prevailed. In the same pattern we observe among the males, female student leaders would shine in the post-2011 political limelight. Maya Jribi from the Democratic Progressive Party (comrade to the Chebbi brothers) would become an MP before her untimely death. So would Munia Brahim who had been prominent in the student wing of the Islamist MTI (later Ennahda) in the late 1980s. Suad Abdelrahim of Ennahda was elected as the first woman mayor of Tunis (*shaykhat al-madinah*) in 2018. And so on. These trailblazers imparted skills that were picked up by fellow and future female activists across the political spectrum.

Diverging Assessments

Variation in the levels of inclusiveness also comes to the fore. Leftist movements incorporated some women into their ranks, as female comrades (*rafiqat*) stood shoulder-to-shoulder with male comrades (*rifaq*). Perhaps erring on the side of an inclusionary narrative, Mohamed Hamrouni of the Islamist UGTE insisted that "we didn't use to differentiate" between men and women members.[77] Female colleagues used to demonstrate, strike, weather late nights preparing pamphlets and posters, and give speeches, he recalled. Here, Munia Brahim's experience as a student activist departs from that of the Perspectivist women a decade or so earlier. It was in the university, she remembered, that Islamist women transitioned from "social" roles

---

[75] *Al-Mustaqbal*, December 29, 1980, p. 3.
[76] Interview, Monday, September 12, 2022, Tunis.
[77] Interview, Thursday, September 15, 2022, Tunis.

(charity work, religious proselytizing or *da'wah*), to explicit political engagement. Because "we shared the danger," they insisted on advancing to work outside the party, traditionally reserved for males.[78] In modest numbers, these Islamist women blasted through social barriers, partaking in and directing protests, demonstrations, political campaigning, and even leadership within the party. Not all movements featured close interactions between men and women. Mabrouk Korshid of the pan-Arabist/nationalist Arab Progressive Unitarian Students admitted that "we were very extremist" when it came to this issue. Women (the sisters, or *akhawat*) had their own separate cells based in the dorms (see also Labyad and Daifallah 2017, 276). Female leaders would routinely meet with the heads of the male committees, Korshid explains. The leftists and even the Islamists were less rigid about gender segregation, according to him.[79] However insufficient and imperfect, steps taken towards women's inclusion by the student movement enriched protest competencies. Women student activists later veered in the direction of overtly feminist civic-political work (ATFD and ATFURD), or more political futures. Some, like Belhadj Hamida who served as an MP with Nidaa Tunis (2014–2019), straddled both realms. The gender dimension was one way that communicative protest honed anti-authoritarian struggles in the well-worn journey towards peoplehood.

Conclusion

The student-rebel re-ontologized in this protestscape was a new creation and one which intellectualized protest. This agency was defiantly disseminated through magazines such as *Perspectives*, *Al-Shu'lah*, and daring newspaper murals, including *Al-Hadath*. Cognitively, students expanded the horizon of Tunisian self-hood, refusing obeisance to state-led social and political engineering. They granted free rein to their philosophical learning, wielding new ideas in their struggle against authoritarianism. Students creatively borrowed, debated, and syncretized regional and international ideas and ideologies from Marxism and Maoism to Nasserism and Qutb-ism.

Affectively, they lent painful personal suffering to the meaning of political sacrifice. The student-rebel was not *only* rational, but a human being moved and motivated to rebellious action by memories and stories of prisoners' torture and martyrs' blood. Contending ideas about "freedom" itself (socialist, Maoist, Arabist, Islamist) dulled fear and inspired courage. Counter-memories of these embodied struggles permeate Tunisia's political scene. Former student activists who became Tunisia's intelligentsia and political class are among those who have increasingly shared their encounters with the jailer (*jallad*). These candid texts, whether novels by Perspectivist Fethi Belhadj Yahya (2009) and Islamist Samir Sasi (2011), or syncretic genres (novel/memoir) by Gilbert Naccache (2018), have variously documented for the

---

[78] Interview, September 24, 2022, Tunis.
[79] Interview, May 6, 2022, Tunis.

present and for posterity activists' affect and cognition of resistance behind bars. Sadok Ben Mhenni's *The Tomato Thief* humanizes the webs of suffering but also mundane yearnings (e.g. a tomato craving), and the bonds forged, between prison guards and prisoners. Ennahda's Abdelhamid Jlassi's (2016) *The Small Hand ... Does Not Lie*, the first book in his epistolary/testimonial trilogy, takes its title from his wife's final wave to him, urging courage and channeling confidence, as he rode the car to his prison cell. These and other inscriptions contribute Tunisian voices to the Arab "prison literature" genre that flowered after 2011 (Al-Toumi 2020). Perhaps there is more to the tale, then, that in 2011 protestors "broke the barrier of fear!" Perspectivists, Ba'athists, and Islamists all braved the forbidding citadels of Burj Al-Rumi, the dungeons of the Interior Ministry, the barren desert camps of Rajim Maatoug years and years before the revolution finally exploded in 2011. Courage has not been wanting in Tunisian struggles, student-rebels notable among them. Charted in this dissentscape, their agency is almost self-evident. Intellectual daring, transnational connections (with Palestinian, Maghrebi, French, and other students), and censor-eluding improvisation (magazines smuggled in from Paris, newspapers and posters stealthily hung on university walls under the cover of night, underground organization through cells) were deliberate and defiant social acts and en-actments. Here students asserted themselves as a partial demos, as *people,* not Bourguiba's subjects. Setbacks (e.g. prison or security violence) were memorialized and commemorated, but not accepted as defeats. Re-inventing the anti-colonial resistance of their Zaytuna forebears for the postcolonial authoritarian age, students developed impressive protest competencies for nearly three decades. These adamant militants and those they coached in their turn would re-emerge, some in 2008, 2011, and thereafter.

References

Abdelsamad, Hecham. 2020. "68: Al-Usturah Wa Al-Turath." [68: The Legend and Tradition] In *Rabi' Tunis Al-Awwal: 68* [Tunisia's First Spring: 68], edited by Fethi Benhadj Yahya and Hecham Abdelsamad. Tunis: Kalimat 'Abirah, 11–39.

Al-Habbashi, Mohamed Ali. 2020a. *Harakat Al-Mu'aradah wa Al-Muhakamat Al-Siyasiyyah* [Opposition Movements and Political Trials] : *Tunis 1956–1970*. Ariana: Dar Nahnu.

Al-Habbashi, Mohamed Ali. 2020b. *Harakat Al-Mu'aradah Wal-Muhakamat Al-Siyasiyyah* [Opposition Movements and Political Trials]: *Tunis 1970–1980*. Ariana: Dar Nahnu.

Al-Hayduri, Lutfi. 2019. *Al-Tajnid Al-'Iqabi Li Al-Talabah fi Tunis* [Punitive Conscription of Tunisian Students] 1966–1990, *Alchahed,* March 3, https://bit.ly/3SaxKt2

Al-Jellab, Al-Hadi. 2021. In *Ahdath Maris 1968: 'Ashrat Ayyam Hazzat Al-Jami'ah Al-Tunisiyyah* [The Events of March 1968: Ten Days that Shook the Tunisian University], edited by Abdelkarim Qabous. Tunis: Dar Nathar, 25–29.

Al-Kilani, Mohamed. 2020. *Al-Tarikh Al-Mansi: Mudhakkirat Munadil Watani* [Forgotten History: Memoirs of a Veteran National Activist]. Tunis: Kalimat 'Abirah.

Al-Tarshini, Anisah. 2020. "*Muhakamat Majmu'at Afaq 'Ala Daw' Al-Makatib Al-Mursalah Li-Mahkamat Amn Al-Dawlah*," [The Trials of the Afaq Group in Light of Letters Sent to the State Security Court] In *Rabi' Tunis Al-Awwal: 68*, edited by Fethi Belhadj Yahya and Hisham Abdelsamad. Tunis: Kalimat 'Abirah, 105–117.

Al-Thabti, Adel. 2017. *Al-Ittihad Al-'Amm Al-Tunisi Li Al-Talabah: Khalfiyyat Al-Ta'sis Wa-Ma'alat Al-Masar* [The UGTE: Founding Background and Ends of the Journey]. Tunis: Maktabat Tunis Lil-Nashr.

Al-Thlijani, Abulqasem. 2018. *Khulasat Al-Tabayyun fi Nidal Al-Talabah Al-Arab Al-Taqaddumiyyin Wa Al-Wuhdawiyyin Madiyan Wa-Mustaqbalan* [Summary of an Inquiry Into the Arab Progressive and Unitarian Students, Past and Present]. Tunis: Sotumedia.

Althusser, Louis. 2014[1970]. *On the Reproduction of Capitalism: Ideology and Ideological State Apparatuses*. Trans. G.M. Goshgarian. London: Verso.

Al-Toumi, Mohamed. 2020. *Adab Al-Sujun Fi Tunis Ma Ba'da Al-Thawrah: Baina Mihnat Al-Kitabah Wa Kitabat Al-Mihnah* [Prison Literature in Post-Revolution Tunis: Between the Ordeal of Writing and the Writing of the Ordeal. Tunis: Kalimah.

Al-Troudi, Al-Hachemi. 2016. "*Adwa' 'Ala Harakat Perspective.*" [Spotlight on the Perspective Movement] In *Harakat Perspective/ Al-'Amil Al-Tunisi: Al-Tarikh Wa Al-Imtidad* [Perspective/Tunisian Worker Movement: History and Extension]. Sfax: Dar Mohamed Ali, 15–58.

Al-Wa'ir, Muta' Amin. 2020. "Tunis 68: *Al-Harakah Al-Tulabiyyah Wa-Ba'd Tamathulatiha.*" [Some Manifestations of the Student Movemetn] In *Rabi' Tunis Al-Awwal*, edited by Fethi Benhadj Yahya and Hecham Abdelsamad. Tunis: Kalimat 'Abirah, 75–93.

Amuzegar, Jahangir. 1974. "Ideology and Economic Growth in the Middle East." *Middle East Journal* 28(1) (Winter): 1–9.

Austin, John L. 1962. *How to do Things with Words*. Oxford: Oxford University Press.

Belhadj Yahya, Fethi. 2009. *Al-Habs Katthab wa Al-Hayy Yaruh* [Prison Lies and the Living Return]. Tunis: Kalimat 'Abirah. (Mots Passants).

Bell, Daniel. 1962. *The End of Ideology: On the Exhaustion of Political Ideas in the Fifties*. New York: Collier Books.

Bellamy, Richard, ed. 1994. *Antonio Gramsci: Pre-Prison Writings*. Trans. Virginia Cox. Cambridge & New York: Cambridge University Press.

Ben Mhenni, Sadok. 2016. "*Al-Thakirah Makirah Tab'an: Yumkin Laha an Tuhassin Aw An Tufsid Al-Ahdath Kama Tasha.*" [The Guile of Memory: It Can Improve or Ruin an Event as It Wills] In *Harakat Perspective/Al-'Amil Al-Tunisi: Al-Tarikh Wal-Imtidad*. Sfax: Dar Mohamed Ali, 147–156.

Ben Mhenni, Sadok. 2017. *Sariq Al-Tamatim* [The Tomato Thief]. Tunis: Ceres.

Ben Shaban, Abdelrahman. 2019. *Al-Ittihad Al-'Amm Li-Talabat Tunis: Al-Nash'ah Wa Al-Ta'sis Wa Al-'Alaqat* [UGET: Emergence, Founding, and Social Relations] *1952–1957*. Tunis: Nirvana.

Ben Youssef, Adel. 2004. "Musahamat Al-Wasat Al-Madrasi Fi Al-Ma'rakah Al-Taharruriyyah [Contributions of the School Environment to the Battle for Emancipation] (1952–1954)", Part Two. *Rawafed* 9: 8–38.

Bobbio, Norberto. 1988. "Gramsci and the Concept of Civil Society." In *Civil Society and the State* edited by John Keane. London: Verso, 74–100.

Boswell, Terry and Hannah Hawkins. 1999. "Marxist Theories of Ideologies: An Update." *Critical Sociology* 25(2–3): 352–357.

Bouguerra, Abdeljalil. 1993. *Harakat Afaq Perspectives: Min Tarikh Al-Yasar Al-Tunisi* [Perspectives Movements: From the History of Tunisia's Left] *1963–1975*. Tunis: Dar Ceres Lil-Nashr.

Bouguerra, Abdeljalil. 2019. *Fusul Min Tarikh Al-Yasar Al-Tunisi: Al-Shyu'iyyin Wa-Perspective Wa Al-Nizam Al-Bourguibi* [Chapters from the History of Tunisia's Left: Communists, Perspectives, and Bourguiba's Regime]. Tunis: Dar Afaq-Perspective.

Bouguerra, Abdeljalil. 2021. In *Ahdath Maris 1968: 'Ashrat Ayyam Hazzat Al-Jami'ah Al-Tunisiyyah*, edited by Abdelkarim Qabous. Tunis: Dar Nathar, 31–47.

Chabuto, Munirah. 2021. "Mu'tham Qadat Al-Yasar Kanu Min Talabat Kuliyyat 9 Avril. [Most Leftist Leaders were From April 9 College]" In *Ahdath Maris 1968: 'Ashrat Ayyam Hazzat Al-Jami'ah Al-Tunisiyyah*, edited by Abdelkarim Qabous. Tunis: Dar Nathr, 95–97.

Charfi, Mohamed. 2015. *Mon Combat pour les Lumières*. Tunis: Éditions Elyzad.

Chebbi, Ahmed Najib. 2022. *Al-Masirah Wa Al-Masar: Ma Jara wa Ma 'Ara* [The Journey and the Path: What Happened and What I Believe]. Tunis: Mots Passants.

Chovanec, Donna M. 2009. *Between Hope and Despair: Women Learning Politics*. Blackpoint: Fernwood Publishing.

Chovanec, Donna M. and Alexandra Benitez. 2008. "The Penguin Revolution in Chile: Exploring Intergenerational Learning in Social Movements." *Journal of Contemporary Issues in Education* 3(1): 39–5

Chovanec, Donna M. and Hector M. Gonzalez. 2009. "A Participatory Research Approach to Exploring Social Movement Learning in the Chilean Women's Movement." In *Education, Participatory Action Research, and Social Change: International Perspectives*, edited by Dip Kapoor and Steven Jordan. Basingstoke: Palgrave Macmillan, 223–237.

Daifallah, Mohamed. 2016. *Al-Talabah Al-Tunisiyyun Wa-Makhadat Al-Watan fi Muntasaf Al-Qarn Al-'Ishrin* [Tunisian Students and the Nation's Birth Pangs in the Mid-Twentieth Century]. Tunis: Maktabat Tunis.

Daifallah, Mohamed. 2020. *Azminat Al-Harakah Al-Tullabiyyah Al-Tunisiyyah* [Eras of the Tunisian Student Movement]. Tunis: Al-Ma 'had Al-'Ali Li-Tarikh Tunis Al-Mu'asir.

Delap, Lucy. 2016. "Feminist Bookshops, Reading Cultures and the Women's Liberation Movement in Great Britain, c. 1974–2000. *History Workshop Journal* 81(1): 171–196.

Eagleton, Terry. 1991. *Ideology: An Introduction*. London: Verso.

Entelis, John P. 1974. "Ideological Change and an Emerging Counter-Culture in Tunisia." *The Journal of Modern African Studies* 12(4): 543–568.

Evans, Sara M. 1980. *Personal Politics: The Roots of Women's Liberation in the Civil Rights Movement and the New Left*. New York: Vintage.

Evans, Sara M. and Harry C. Boyte. 1992. *Free Spaces: The Sources of Democratic Change in America*. Chicago: The University of Chicago Press.

Freeden, Michael, Lyman T. Sargent, and Marc Stears, eds. 2013. *The Oxford Handbook of Ideologies*. Oxford: Oxford University Press.

Fricker, Miranda. 2007. *Epistemic Injustice: Power and the Ethics of Knowing*. Oxford: Oxford University Press.

Freire, Paulo. 1970. *Pedagogy of the Oppressed*, Trans. Myra Bergman Ramos. New York: Herder and Herder.

Friere, Paulo. 1998. *Pedagogy of Freedom: Ethics, Democracy, and Civic Courage*. New York: Rowman and Littlefield.

Geiger, Susan. 1990. "What's so Feminist About Women's Oral History?" *Journal of Women's History* 2(1): 169–182.

Gerring, John. 1997. "Ideology: A Definitional Analysis." *Political Research Quarterly* 50(4): 957–994.

Gill, Jungyun and James DeFronzon. 2009. "A Comparative Framework for the Analysis of International Student Movements." *Social Movement Studies* 8(3): 203–224.

Gluck, Sherna. 1977. "What's So Special About Women? Women's Oral History." *Frontiers: A Journal of Women's Studies* 2(2): 3–17.

Häberlen, Joachim C. 2018. *The Emotional Politics of the Alternative Left: West Germany, 1968–1984*. Cambridge: Cambridge University Press.

Hamdi, Faten. 2019. *Hiwar Ma' Al-Aminah Al-'Ammah Lil-Ittihad Al-'Am Al-Talabah fi Tunis*, Legal Agenda, June 6, https://bit.ly/3Lx8ScQ

Hazgui, Ezzeddine. 2018. *Nazzarat Ummi* [My Mother's Glasses]. Tunis: Mots Passants.

Holland, Catherine A. 1998. "After *Antigone*: Women, the Past, and the Future of Feminist Political Thought." *American Journal of Political Science* 42(4): 1108–1132.

Ilahi, Sana. 2022. *Al-Muthaqqafat Al-Tunisiyyat Wa Mawaqifuhunna Min Ahamm Al-Tayyarat Al-Fikriyyah Al-Siyasiyyah Ila Sanat 1987* [Tunisian Female Literati and their Positions Regarding the Most Significant Intellectual and Political Trends Until 1987]. Tunis: Self-Published.

Jlassi, Abdelhamid. 2016. *Hasad Al-Ghiyab 1: Al-Yad Al-Saghirah La Takthib* [Harvest of Absence 1: The Small Hand Does Not Lie]. Tunis: Maktabat Tunis.

Jrad, Naila. 2020. "*Fi Al-Bad'i Kanat Al-Kalimah* [In the Beginning, There was the Word]." In *Rabi' Tunis Al-Awwal: 1968*, edited by Fethi Benhadj Yahya and Hecham Abdelsamad. Tunis: Kalimat 'Abirah, 121–134.

Kallander, Amy Aisen. 2021. *Tunisia's Modern Woman: Nation-Building and State Feminism in the Global 1960s.* Cambridge: Cambridge University Press.

Kaaniche, Adel. 2021. *Mu'tamar Korba: Haqa'iq Tahfathuha Al-Thakirah* [The Korkba Congress: Facts Preserved by Memory], Leaders Arabic, August 24, https://bit.ly/3qVBIdm

Klimke, Martin and Mary Nolan. 2018. "Introduction: The Globalization of the Sixties." In *The Routledge Handbook of the Global Sixties: Between Protest and Nation-Building*, edited by Chen Jian, Martin Klimke, Masha Kirasirova, Mary Nolan, Marilyn Young, and Joanna Waley-Cohen. London: Routledge, 1–9.

Krichen, Abdelaziz. 2020 [1968]. Sanat Al-Intifadah Al-'Alamiyyah Li Al-Shabab [1968: Year of the Universal Youth Uprising", In *Rabi' Tunis Al-Awwal: 68*, edited by Fethi Benhadj Yaya and Hecham Abdelsamad. Tunis: Kalimat 'Abirah, 59–71.

Labidi, Lilia. 2007. "The Nature of the Transnational Alliances in Women's Associations in the Maghreb: The Case of AFTURD and ATFD in Tunisia." *Journal of Middle East Women's Studies* 3(1): 6–34.

Labyad, Salem. 2014. *Al-Harakah Al-Tullabiyyah Al-Tunisiyyah: Al-Nash'ah wa Al-Ta'sis Wa-Qadaya Al-Hawiyyah* [The Tunisian Student Movement: Beginnings, Founding, and Identity Issues].

Labyad, Salem and Mohamed Daifallah. 2017. *Al-Talabah Al-'Arab Al-Taqaddumiyyun Al-Wuhdawiyyun: Nash'at Al-Tayyar Al-Qawmi Al-Taqaddumi Wa-Nidalatihi Al-Tarikhiyyah Fi Tunis* [The Arab Progressive Unitarian Students: Emergence of the Progressive Nationalist Tendency and Its Historical Struggles in Tunisia]. Tunis: Sotumedia.

Laclau, Ernest and Chantal Mouffe. 1985. *Hegemony and Socialist Strategy.* London: Verso.

Laroussi, Amri, Editor. 2023. *Harakat Fifri 1972: Al-Dhikhra Al-Khamsun Shahadat Wa Taqyimat Min Tarikh Al-Ittihad Al- 'Am Li-Talabat Tunis* [The February 1972 Movement: Fiftieth Anniversary: Testimonies and Assessments from the History of the UGET]. Sfax: Dar Mohamed Ali Al-Hammi.

Lipset, Martin S. and P. G. Altbach, 1969. *Students in Revolt.* Boston: Beacon.

McCann, Fiona. 2015. "Commitment and Poetic Justice: Irish Republican Women's Prison Writing." *Commonwealth Essays and Studies* 38(1): 57–66.

Mannheim, Karl. 1936. *Ideology and Utopia.* London: Routledge.

Mouffe, Chantal. 2014. "Hegemony and Ideology in Gramsci." In *Gramsci and Marxist Theory*, edited by Chantal Mouffe. Abingdon: Routledge, 168–203.

Naccache, Gilbert. 2018 [1982]. *Cristal.* Tunis: Dar Shammah.

Norberg-Schulz, Christian. 1979. *Genius Loci: Towards a Phenomenology of Architecture.* New York: Rizzoli.

Passerini, Luisa. 1989. "Women's Personal Narratives: Myths, Experiences, and Emotions." In *Interpreting Women's Lives: Feminist Theory and Personal Narrative*, edited by Personal Narratives Group. Indianapolis: Indiana University Press, 189–198.

Polletta, Francesca. 1999. "'Free Spaces' in Collective Action." *Theory and Society* 28(1): 1–38.

Qabous, Abdelkarim. 2021b. *"Al-Haqiqah 'An Al-Fitnah Bi Al-Jami'ah Al-Tunisiyyah 1968* [The Truth About Divisions in the Tunisian University]." In *Ahdath Maris 1968: 'Ashrat Ayyam Hazzat Al-Jami'ah Al-Tunisiyyah*, edited by Abdelkarim QabousTunis: Dar Nathr, 139–178.

Qabous, Abdelkarim. 2021a. In *Ahdath Maris 1968: 'Ashrat Ayyam Hazzat Al-Jami'ah Al-Tunisiyyah*. Tunis: Dar Nathar, 9–19.

Rancière, Jacques. 1991. *The Ignorant Schoolmaster: Five Lessons in Intellectual Emancipation*. Translated by Kristin Ross. Stanford, CA: Stanford University Press.

Rancière, Jacques. 1999. *Disagreement: Politics & Philosophy*. Minneapolis: University of Minnesota Press.

Rohrschneider, Robert. 1999. *Learning Democracy: Democratic and Economic Values in Unified Germany*. Oxford: Oxford University Press.

Roucek, Joseph S. 1944. "A History of the Concept of Ideology." *Journal of the History of Ideas* 5(4): 479–488.

Sadiki, Larbi. 2011. "Egypt and Tunisia: Regime Failure and the 'Gymnasiums' of Civic Empowerment." September, 1, *Middle East Institute*, https://www.mei.edu/publications/egypt-and-tunisia-regime-failure-and-gymnasiums-civic-empowerment

Sadiki, Larbi. 2021. "Rida 'Lenin' Cheheb Mekki: The ideologue of Tunisia's July 25 power grab?" In Middle East Institute, 13 September, https://www.mei.edu/publications/rida-lenin-cheheb-mekki-ideologue-tunisias-july-25-power-grab, (Retrieved: 10 June 2023).

Sargent, Lyman T. 2013. "Ideology and Utopia." In *The Oxford Handbook of Ideologies*, edited by Michael Freeden, Lyman T. Sargent, and Marc Stears. Oxford: Oxford University Press.

Sasi, Semir. 2011. *Burj Al-Rumi: Abwab Al-Mawt* [Burj Al-Rumi: The Gates of Death]. Tunis: Karim Al-Sharif.

Sharabi, Hisham. 1965. "The Transformation of Ideology in the Arab World." *Middle East Journal* 19(4):471–486.

Sorbera, Lucia. 2020. "Gender: Still a Useful Category to Analyze Middle East Political History? A View from Egypt (1919–2019)." In *Routledge Handbook of Middle East Politics: Interdisciplinary Inscriptions*, edited by Larbi Sadiki. London: Routledge, 362–375.

Stråth, Bo. 2013. "Ideology and Conceptual History." In *The Oxford Handbook of Ideologies*, edited by Michael Freeden, Lyman T. Sargent, and Marc Stears. Oxford: Oxford University Press.

Taylor, Charles. 2003. "What is a 'Social Imaginary'?" In *Modern Social Imaginaries*, edited by Dilip P. Gaonkar, Jane Kramer, Benjamin Lee, and Michael Warner. New York: Duke University Press, 23–30.

Taylor, Charles. 2004. *Modern Social Imaginaries*. Durham, NC: Duke University Press.

Tchaïcha, Jane D. and Khedija Arfaoui. 2017. *The Tunisian Women's Rights Movement: From Nascent Activism to Influential Power-broking*. London: Routledge.

Tyson, Cynthia. 2003. "Interrogating Racism in Qualitative Research Methodology," *Counterpoints* 195: 19–28.

Vygotsky, Lev. 1986. *Thought and Language*, Trans. Alex Kozulin. Cambridge, MA: The MIT Press.

Young, Iris Marion. 2000. *Inclusion and Democracy*. Oxford: Oxford University Press.

Zankah, Haifa. 2020. *Banat Al-Siyasah: Sardiyyat Munadilat Perspective-Al- 'Amil Al-Tunisi Fi Al-Sab'iniyyat* [Girls of Politics: Narratives of Perspective/Tunisian Workers Veterans in the Seventies]. Tunis: Zanoobya.

Zavadskaya, Margarita and Christian Welzel. 2015. "Subverting Autocracy: Emancipative Mass Values in Competitive Authoritarian Regimes." *Democratization* 22(6): 1105–1130.

5
Miners' Voices

Revolution in Miniature in the Phosphate Basin

Founded in the late 1970s in Moularès (Arabic: Umm Al-'Arais), Sons of the Mines was a music band of phosphate workers. Refusing to jump through bureaucratic hoops aimed at containing the loose cannon of lyricized popular discontent, they were more or less forced underground.[1] Affect is of course a close companion of music, a defining feature that stimulates emotion while giving voice to cognition. Tunisia's authoritarians tried to monopolize affect itself as expressed through song. Often performing at UGTT headquarters, Sons of the Mines illustrate the striking link between unions and (this time, lyrical) protest. Their ballad-type, mournfully sung words vocalize an intense affective ambivalence. Work in the mines was suffering incarnate. Damus *featured in the band's repertoire. The name conjures up the darkness of caves, the narrow underground tunnels miners dug to unearth the sandy treasure transported by rickety carts.[2] In Ya Damus, Sons of the Mines croon about a dreadful mining accident (Rawai 2019). The year is 1973, the place Moularès. Miners' "faces were yellow," as they planted "a foot in the earth, a foot in the grave." A torrent strikes. "The workers drown, Ali, Ammar, Belqasem, and Suleiman die/The sacrifice (qurban) was not enough, it continued [to take] three more in the same hour." Having stolen the fathers, damus's hunger was sated, "leaving the orphans wailing in their houses." Exasperation prevails at this woeful entanglement with phosphate, source of provision and thief of life and limb. "Our story with you, O Damus, is long/And your strange wonders surpass 'A Thousand and One Nights.'"... Such embodied suffering wraps around another set of feelings: despair and frustration at joblessness. In their song Unemployment Certificate, Sons of the Mines lament, "I have a new poverty certificate, occupation: unemployed/And my mother tells me, my son, wed, like all the men. ... How can I wed, mother, when my earnings are a scandal?!" (Radio Mines 2011). Joblessness was almost an identity forced upon those who yearn for the dignity of earning their living, deprived of starting and supporting families.*

---

[1] Banned from performing at formal festivals and concerts, they performed instead at UGTT and student union headquarters (Al-Khashnawi 2022).

[2] Cheaper surface, "open-pit" methods of extraction were developed by the 1980s (Vatthauer and Weipert-Fenner 2017, 18).

Introduction

This chapter concretizes the phosphate basin uprising (*intifadah*) of 2008. A protestscape in its own right—the most temporally abbreviated in the book—it also set the stage for the revolution to come less than three years later. The Southern mining region of the country is resource-rich but subsistence-poor for its residents. Demonstrations, sit-ins, negotiating committees, hunger strikes, advocacy, and civil society networking were manifestations of the adaptive agency exhibited by activists and their families. These discourses and practices of the "revolutionary south" were often reinforced by the accumulating affect of double consciousness. State negligence and humiliation (*hogra*) deepened into anger and indignation (*takriz*, Tunisian dialect). Negative emotions, experienced as embodied suffering (tear gas, rubber bullets, security batons, incarceration, torture) were softened only by the solidarity of families similarly under siege, and the Committee to Support the Phosphate Basin. Feeling "uncounted," off the radar of a state that preferred to repress and exploit rather than empower and invest, formed the cognition intermingling with the agency and affect of this memorable and remarkable protestscape. We re-ontologize and situate the 2008 revolt within the history and lived experiences of the marginalization and deprivation of the South. The agentic, affective, and cognitive modalities and manifestations of the longest (pre-2011) uprising in Tunisian postcolonial history come to the fore. Moreover, the chapter pays special attention to the ways in which the phosphate basin *intifadah* presaged the revolution to come. That uprising eviscerated the authoritarian apparatus of Ben Ali's state. Its drivers, its intersectional agents that mobilized in concert (unionists, women, youth, attorneys, civil society activists), its coalitional advocacy, even some of its slogans will become familiar by the time we reach Chapter 6 on the 2011 revolution.

Strikes by dark-pit workers speak to an emancipatory pedagogy. The emotional and physical stress gripping a miner's body affects the body-politic of an entire nation and infects other bodies with matching angst, indignation, emotions of defiance in the face of state oppression and feelings of *hogra*. This rebelscape re-ontologizes miners' insurgency in the phosphate basin in 2008. It records not only through the materiality surrounding the social acting and en-acting of insubordinate identities, but also the immateriality of protest through aesthetic experiences and resulting representational manifestations, ranging from music to poetry. The outburst of communal bonds during that momentous protest in 2008 bore witness to historically-situated affective learning. Miners' em-bodied pain transferred to the wider community in the form of revolutionary modes of acting (empowering agency via diverse forms of protest pitting them against authoritarian rule), being (sense of self presence), and knowing (de- and re-territorializing a domineering body politic and its brands of language of power and of consciousness).

The chapter draws on original interviews, newspapers, and other published testimony (e.g. documentary and media appearances) to explore the phosphate basin protestscape. It begins by grounding the uprising in the spatialized marginalization/rebellion dynamic of Tunisia's South, despite Bourguiba's and Ben Ali's lip service to regional development. Parsing the pitfalls of regional underdevelopment through state negligence, the chapter then portrays the misery, deprivation, anger or *hogra* of phosphate miners and those who lived in the region, as well as a musical counterculture. A brief discussion of the 1980 Gafsa insurrection is an interlude prior to the 2008 uprising. We focus on union-led organization/mobilization, affective responses and incitements, the cultivation of solidarity, and the prominence of women in the protestscape. These features of the "phosphate basin events" (*ahdath al-hawd al-manjimi*) would similarly seep into the 2010–11 revolution to erupt soon after.

The Revolutionary South

Tunisia's South (*al-janub*) has long been difficult to dominate. Here, Ibn Khaldun's (1984, 363) peripheries (*atraf*) live up to his assessment, striking back at the center. The country's residents resisted the chokehold of repressive powers, from the French *colons* to Bourguiba to Ben Ali. From 1881, they lived through fierce French colonialism, tasting the violence of direct foreign rule firsthand. Iron walls trapped residents of Medenine, Kebili, and Tataouine, constraining the mobility to which local tribes were accustomed (Al-Mukni 2005, 22). Responding to this onslaught against fluid tribal livelihoods, Southerners defied the French, voting with their feet, as it were. Male Southerners flocked to Tunis in family and chain migration from 1881 to 1914, then during the inter-war period, growing in number to comprise 10 percent of the capital's population (Al-Mukni 2005, 25–26). These new city dwellers did not leave the old ways behind. They reproduced and adapted their close-knit tribal relations to mingle in cafes (e.g. Café Matwiyyah, Café Hamma) and hotels (Al-Mukni 2005, 30). Seasonal travel back South was common in spring-summer: weddings, harvests, and Ramadan festivities beckoned them home. Adapting tribal customs to modern city living, Southerners developed a knack for protest. Refusing the appointment of a new Shaykh, pancake-makers (*ftayriyyah*) closed their shops and demonstrated in Kasbah square, the seat of power. Practicing civic disobedience, they refused to pay their taxes and even swiped the new Shaykh's seal in objection (Al-Mukni 2005, 29). Southerners' reputation for rebelliousness became legendary. The French forcibly expelled Gabes migrants from the capital in the early 1920s, fearing they would stir up union and labor unrest (Al-Mukni 2005, 31). Indeed, "traditional solidarity" has melded with difficult living conditions to spur early union activism among Southerners since the 1920s (Al-Mukni 2005, 36). Well-known names include Tahar Haddad (woman and workers' champion) and Mohamed Ali Al-Hammi (founder of Tunisia' first union, discussed in Chapter 3). The South was the site of numerous anti-colonial battles, home to the famed *fellaga*. In June 1954, a group of *fellaga* blew up a mine in the phosphate basin and captured French explosives stored inside (Al-Yahyaoui 2005, 232). From this occupied military zone, the South's residents led battles, destroyed telephone lines and reservoirs, attacked convoys, protested, demonstrated, and waged sit-ins against the

French (Al-Hannashi 2005, 266–267). Weighed down by repression, poverty, and social-cultural alienation, Southerners in colonial Tunisia mobilized in ways both civic and violent. Spearheading rebellion across the country's revolutionary milieu, these "have-nots" defied rather than succumbed to colonial control. The people of *al-Janub* adapted their modes of unruliness, stubbornly acting and en-acting resistance to hone protest competencies well into the postcolonial counterrevolution and Ben Ali's grand "change" (*al-taghyir*). From Gafsa to Sidi Bouzid, Tunisia's marginals catapulted the country into full-fledged revolution by late 2010. This was no accident.

Alienating the Periphery: Regional Underdevelopment

We have argued repeatedly that Tunisian independence from colonialism paradoxically stymied popular emancipation. Bourguiba activated a counterrevolution that froze Tunisians into "non-people." However, some people were "missing" or "miscounted," as put by Rancière. It is unsurprising that the phosphate basin protestscape, prelude to the 2011 revolution, flared up in the periphery, a spatiality of "the part that has no part." The rebelliousness of Tunisia's downtrodden South, displayed briefly above, cannot be delinked from striated distributional patterns that locked the country into regional inequality. Postcolonial Tunisia has for decades been afflicted by a spatialized, distributional, and exclusionary "multiple marginalization" of its Southern and internal regions (Sadiki 2019). Redemption from the subjugation endured under colonialism continued to elude the south after independence. International and subnational power and resource asymmetries fed into each other. As a developing country, Tunisia became ensnared in skewed "metropolis–satellite" interactions, described by Gunder Frank (1966) as the "development of underdevelopment." Its center exploited capital and resources from the peripheries, blocking any capacity for economic self-sufficiency or self-renewal exacerbating rather than eliminating underdevelopment (Gunder Frank 1966). One Tunisian considers the distributional pattern that historically favored the North and Sahel over the South and Center to be a manifestation of "internal colonialism" (Al-Salehi 2017). As Casanova (1965) suggests, postcolonial structures left by the colons entrenched the colonial classification of society, particularly with respect to property rights, land, and labor. Thus, the continuation of a "dual society," this time characterized by the "exploitation of natives by natives" (Casanova 1965, 27). In the Tunisian context, the concept of *al-mujtama' al-muwazi* echoes Casanova's "dual societies." In this resulting "parallel society," alternative voices and imaginings emerge where the state has fallen short, including through informal economic activity (Guessoumi 2012, 54–60).

Since independence, governments have failed to effectively address multiple marginalization in Tunisia. Discrepancies abound between state declaratory policy and implementation. Particular attention to the country's lagging regions (the Interior and South) featured in Bourguiba's ambitions. He invoked "a serious policy of regional development" (*al-tanmiyah al-jihawiyyah*) as he boasted to the English-speaking world of his vision and accomplishments (Bourguiba 1966). Thus,

Bourguiba's grand narrative was of national "progress" as against what he considered stifling tradition. The move forward would require gradual, rational improvement of individual mindsets, capacities, and productivity, toward complete independence in part through self-sufficiency. For him, the country was engaged in a struggle for "economic liberation" to complement its "political liberation," warding off the "slavery of poverty" and international vulnerability (Bourguiba 1974, 241). Economic development would thus complement hard-won postcolonial independence. In this endeavor, Tunisia was engaged in a "great battle [to] emerge from the yoke of backwardness, ignorance and entitlement" (Bourguiba 1974, 199).

Moreover, a complementarity between citizen and state efforts was central to development success. Equality of opportunity would seem to be the result of equality of responsibility, both guided by the state. Gender parity was also central. On a visit to Zarzis in the South in 1958, Bourguiba commended the emerging prominence of women, exemplified in the National Union of Tunisian Women: "all contribute to the building of the state, from the schoolgirl to the housewife" (Bourguiba 1974, 310). All Tunisians must adopt and enact the trinity of "merit, work ethic, and dedication" at the crux of "human capital," to combine with "material capital" (Bourguiba 1974, 199). So that economic, social, and political advancement could be enjoyed equally by all citizens, the state would step in to offset regional and urban–rural disparities in infrastructure and capital. Bourguiba highlighted special assistance to villages steeped in misery. "Progress [would not be] limited to large cities but encompass [all] the regions, bit by bit" (Bourguiba 1974, 234). Bourguiba directed promises of state development to the South in particular. To counter its deep "thirst," in 1958 he assured residents of projects to dig wells and extract groundwater. He promised tractors, more schools and hospitals, and 400 state-subsidized "modern" houses with running water and electricity to replace huts unfit for dignified living (Bourguiba 1974, 317–319).

Dragging the laggard South and Interior regions forward to progress was arguably part of the cult of Bourguibism that he himself constructed. He failed to bring his attractive promises to fruition. Regional disparities became *more* aggravated. A corporatist, top-down approach positioned the *dirigisme* "providential state" as the sole owner of resources and the pathways to economic and social progress (UGTT 2010, 21). Over-centralization and bureaucratization established "hierarchical" relations with citizenry, further stifling bottom-up, local initiatives (UGTT 2010, 22). In the eyes of some analysts (Bashir 2018, 80) and our interviewees, state neglect of the South was a "deliberate, systematic policy" and a form of 'retribution' against Youssefists, whose stronghold was the South. From independence into the 1960s, socialist-type collectivities spurred mass migration to the richer cities of the North and the Sahel. This promulgated state investment in urban areas, to the neglect of the country's interior and South (Bashir 2018, 88). On the ruins of the cooperative debacle for which Ahmed ben Salah was scapegoated and sacked, Bourguiba made an about-face in his development policy. He caved in to IMF and World Bank pressure that mandated currency devaluation and lower government spending (Vanderwalle 1988, 611). These structural adjustments began in 1986, and were felt keenly in already peripheral regions among which was Gafsa (UGTT 2010, 12–14). Development for the South, the Center-West, and the North-West was a declared program renamed cohesive development (*al-tanmiyah al-mundamijah*) (Bashir 2018). Ben Ali's continued pledge to "comprehensive, just, [and] balanced" national development, through new wells, hospitals, sports clubs, and livestock in Southern Tataouine (Ben Ali 2009), was more empty rhetoric than reparative policy. Compounding the matrix of stark structural inequalities, privatization policies and the 1996 partnership with the EU further *beldi/afaqi* divisions between the coast *(Sahel)* thrust into the world economy, and the "Interior," dependent on handouts from the state (Bashir 2018, 88). The social question is inherent to any account of the rebellious phosphate basin. It is expressed with clarity because of injustice and inequity. Parallel to it, is the rise of civil courage and equal citizenships as supportive leitmotifs.

Spatialized Unruliness

Bourguiba's and Ben Ali's practical indifference to regional development had consequences for Southerners' social doing. Hence, there is a Lefebvrian flavor to rebellion in Tunisia's protest heartland, literally a socio-economic hinterland. The country's landmark political transformations, from the phosphate uprising to the 2011 revolution, have been the result of bottom-up and sustained protest-led collective action and mobilization. This brand of contentious politics resonates with spatialized marginality. The resulting social struggles (2008 phosphate basin, or 2017 in Kamour) engendered new possibilities. Persistence of anomic realities in geographies of deprivation and "uneven development" (Harvey 2006) was heightened at times of rapid revolutionary change in Tunisia by the marginals and the deprived. Lefebvre's concept of "abstract space" is apropos. It is geared towards maximizing control and eradicating differences: "a space of ... growing homogeneity ... where all elements are exchangeable and interchangeable, a police space in which the state tolerates no resistance and no obstacles" (Lefebvre 1979, 293). Embedded within this abstract space are "conflicts which foster ... the production of a space that is *other*" (Lefebvre 1991, 391). The phosphate basin protestors' confrontations with tear gas, violence, incarceration, and even torture by security forces are ready examples.

Thus, weak socio-economic integration, and feelings of dislocation, owing to widening gaps between expectations and the realities of marginalization and regional and individual deprivation, are not at variance with intense protests. Lefebvre notes the power of spaces of protest, activism, and new possibilities, putting forth two interrelated ideas. Space holds emancipatory promise in sites of new becomings: "the street is where movement takes place, the interaction without which the urban life would not exist ..."(Lefebvre 2003, 18). According to this interpretation, the sites of protest (here, Tunisia's Southern periphery) morph into a body politic in which the reproduction of space is mediated by self–other, north–south, *beldi–afaqi*, haves–have-nots, and center–margin dialectics; a body politic *qua* sites of struggle and mobilization. It is animated by dialectics of location and dis-location, integration and disintegration, construction and deconstruction, order and chaos, quietism and resistance against internal and external neoliberal monopolies of extracted resources (oil, gas, phosphate, salt) and the capturing of wealth.[3] Integral to these dialectics are processes fraught with contradictions, within a context of neoliberal economic activity, that drive dynamics of conflictual change and attendant contentious activisms, resulting in new conceptions of rights, identity, and peoplehood.

Tunisia's postcolonial political and economic masters have exercised control with dexterity, managing *Beldi* heartland space for the benefit of foreign industrialization and corporate ventures in several sectors (e.g. energy, tourism) via dirigisme-based regulation (of information, security, trade unions, and wages). Import-substitution-industrialization (ISI) gave way to liberalization, externally (IMF) mandated structural adjustment policies, deficit reductions, and restructuring of public companies geared toward growth from 1986–87 onward (Murphy 1999, 100–111). These economic shifts reified a bifurcated modernization (with *beldi* and north prioritized over *afaqi* and south). This concurs with Lefebvre's critique of the corporate world that whilst managing and reproducing space tends to downsize society, through "subordination" to capitalism's "totalitarian demands" (Lefebvre 1971, 67). In the case of postcolonial societies, it may be termed "capitalism by proxy" (Amin's (1997) "crony capitalism"), mediated by elites populating states, without democratic checks and oversight.

The Phosphate Curse

Tunisia's spatialized lumbering development took extractive form in the governorate of Gafsa, where phosphate was discovered in the late nineteenth century. Under French rule, "La Compagnie des Phosphates et Chemins de Fer de Gafsa" (CPG) (in local slang, "*kubbaniyyah*") was established in 1897, rising as the foremost employer in all of Tunisia (Perkins 2014, 63–66). The company drew workers from the Maghreb and even neighbors across the Mediterranean. In 1920, it employed over a thousand Europeans (mainly French and Italians), and thousands of Libyans, Moroccans, and Libyans (UGTT 2010, 31). The mines were among the first sectors with paid laborers in Tunisia, in a profound cultural shift away from long-reigning agricultural practices. Driven out of their farming lands by the French, Tunisians were forced to take up work such as mining that was physically taxing, low-paid, and often intermittent (Al-Taimoumi 2021, 154–155). Nationalist politician Mohieddine Klibi observed the plight of phosphate workers. Theirs was "the most horrifying state, the most gruesome that a person can see and narrate: naked bodies stained with … dirt extracted from the mines, faces [made] pale by excessive work and insufficient sustenance." He wrote of "torn tents made of burlap sacks" housing miners' families. Barefoot women and children rummaged the surrounding topography for edible

---

[3] Scholars have linked contentious politics to dissatisfaction with neoliberal policies (Della Porta 2017; Zemni 2017).

weeds (in Al-Qasantini 2012, 160). Working in the *damus* (phosphate tunnels) did not create a dignified living. This rock bottom human misery would carry over the decades into the 2008 uprising and even after.

Fittingly, then, phosphate country was also part of the syndicalist heartland. Miners were among the earliest strikers in the first decade of the twentieth century (Al-Shabbi 2015, 42). Despite class and ethnic differences between diverse Maghrebi populations in Gafsa, together they engaged in "anticolonial resistance" which included "resisting the domination (*qahr*) of the phosphate company, thus entrenching the culture of protest" (Al-Tabbabi 2019, 20). Nevertheless, tribal tensions (e.g. Ouled Bouyahya vs. Ouled Sidi Laabid) may have sapped the potential for workers' coordination, delaying the first proper miners' strike until 1920.[4] French *colons* responded to the 1937 miners' strikes in Mdhila and Metlaoui by killing over 20 people and injuring tens of others (Arfaoui 2020, 45–46). The phosphate industry, one face of colonial subjugation by the locals, additionally shook up traditional tribal cultures and ties. Residents and migrant workers adapted quickly and rebelliously. For instance, the union leader (*za'im naqabi*) became almost a replacement for the waning influence of tribal leader (*shaykh*) (Al-Tabbabi 2019, 20). The intermeshing of tribal and worker memberships nudged forward what Al-Tabbabi (2005, 89–91) calls the "victory of the new over the old", that is, modern modes of social organization and loyalty over primordial connections. What is perhaps more likely is that a type of (anti/postcolonial) hybridity, of identities and affiliations, took shape. Tribalism remains significant to hiring and clientelistic practices steeped in corruption, such as the handling (*munawalat*) companies, as our interviews have confirmed (see also Al-Tabbabi 2012, 37).

The most important takeaway from this perfunctory historical foray into the mining region is the centenary of protest, and an attendant resistance culture, predating the outbreak of the 2008 uprising. As also recounted by reformist intellectual and syndicalist thinker Tahar Haddad (see Chapter 2), Mohamed Ali Al-Hammi visited Metlaoui's phosphate workers seeking to recruit them in December 1924. He exhorted them to resist their miserable working conditions and wretched lives, appealing to their human and Islamic sense of pride and dignity: "What is this life you spend in these mines, under dangers of falling [rocks] or immolat[ion] by burning chemicals, or maybe under the tunnels (*admas*) [plural of *damus*]?" He admonished them to create and join a union, as part of an "obligation to life so that life opens its arms to you," (quoted in Al-Mahjoubi 2015, 138–139; see Haddad 2015, 165–179). Issues like working hours, weekends, and holidays were thorny for decades, prompting strikes in Metlaoui and Redeyef for instance in February 1981.[5]

Tunisians and foreigners thus worked together and went on strike through their respective unions. Foreign laborers in the phosphate basin petered out by the later

---

[4] *Azmat Al-Hawd Al-Manjimi … Ma Hiya Hulul Ma'qoolah?* In *Al-Tariq Al-Jadid,* June 21–27, 2008, p. 9.

[5] *Idrabat Qita 'iyyah bi Manajim Gafsa bi-sabab Qarar Wazari Sabiq, Al-Mustaqbal,* February 2, 1981, p. 5.

part of the post-independence cooperative era, such that Tunisians made up 97 percent of the employees by 1968 (UGTT 2010, 32). Housing, electricity, water, and medical treatment were all provided by the phosphate company, eventually nationalized by 1961 (Ghilès and Woertz 2018, 56–57). By 2009, Tunisia ranked as the fifth largest global producer of phosphate (Brahmi and Ghorbel-Zouari 2012, 94). Phosphate has thus been big business from colonial to postcolonial times. Like Latin American counterparts including in Ecuador (Riofrancos 2020), Tunisian society has pushed back against exploitative "extractivism." The structural adjustment policies mentioned above aggravated unemployment and pauperized social welfare services, reducing the phosphate basin communities to the pessimum of marginal existence. Residents at the bottom of Tunisia's "dual society" battled dwindling resources and dire living conditions. In 2007, on the eve of the uprising, official statistics placed the unemployment rate in Gafsa at 20.1 percent, a full six points above the national average (UGTT 2010, 54). The four mining towns heaved under even greater unemployment: 26.7 percent in Redeyef, 28.4 percent in Mdhila, and 38.5 percent in Moularès compared to the 14.1 percent national average (Gobe 2010, 5).

Gafsa, like other Southern provinces, awaited basic infrastructure more than a quarter century after independence. The wretched of El Burj (Burj Al-'Akarimah) in Gafsa bemoaned the lack of clean water. Writing to an opposition newspaper, they beseeched officials to fulfill their broken promises and pave the road to nearby Mdhila.[6] The phosphate industry compounded destitution. Processing the mineral parched the land and the people dwelling in it. For decades, observers had disseminated warnings about water scarcity. Proposals suggested activating local land rights, as well as redirecting land use and CPG personnel efforts to revive agriculture in Gafsa.[7] Environmental damage, from polluted air to dried up water resources, exacerbated the deprivation. Pollution weathered human bodies as well as the physical surroundings. Exposure to phosphate dust, transported in open-air cargo trains, spread respiratory illnesses. Alarmingly high levels of fluoride in local drinking water yellowed and decayed teeth, a visible ailment among residents (Nawaat 2017). The CPG's withdrawal of social services (UGTT 2010, 92) and other cost-reductions in the mining industry (Murphy 1999, 137) thus hit residents hard. Metlaoui, Mdhila, Redeyef, and Moularès were home to the national treasure of phosphate. Maddeningly, the dusty chemical always departed the rocky basin on train tracks built by the French. Sami Tlili's 2011 documentary about the 2008 uprising, *Curse the Father of Phosphate!* (*Yel'an Bou Al-Fusfat*) is thus suitably titled. As Muzafar Laabidi, a young activist in the 2008 uprising summed it up years later in the documentary, "We have nothing . . . we have phosphate that exits every day ..." The vanishing resource is indeed a scourge on local residents. Cultural impoverishment stung, too. As though people in the South do not deserve the enlightened attention of Bourguiba's modernizing project. Unemployed artists and intellectuals languished in cafes. Just one

---

[6] *Burj Al- 'Akarimah: Al-Maa'. .wa Al-Naql?* in *Al-Mustaqbal*, September 14, 1981, p. 12.
[7] *Fallahu Mantiqat Al-Metlawi La Yamlikuna min al-Filaha Illa 'Aqd Milkiyyah!* in *Al-Mustaqbal*, September 21, 1981, p. 6.

cinema with limited child-friendly showings, only one public library with barren shelves, an absence of newspapers except those carried by travelers from the capital. There were no Carthage-type summer festivals for which the coast is famous, all combined to drag Gafsa residents into "intellectual suicide," as one writer described it 25 years after independence.[8]

Counter-Consciousness/Counter-Culture

Marginalization breeds counter-consciousness. Combined immaterial and material desolation make for harsh living. But it is in stark contrast to the relatively privileged lives of Tunisians outside the basin or the South, less susceptible to the double consciousness of state *hogra*. Even an earthquake in September 1981 could not draw the attention of the government to neglected Redeyef. Unregistered by dilapidated weather equipment, the convulsion slipped by both national media and officials.[9] Metlaoui workers petitioned the public over the untrustworthiness of the CPG that had promised (and approved) home loans being granted, only to drag their feet once building had begun.[10] Human injuries were also a recurring issue. For instance, a miner whose leg was broken at work got no time off. He was advised to bribe the doctor (10 dinars which he had to borrow), who finally gave him a sick leave notice for one month.[11] Another worker in Mdhila broke his hand at work, and faced an overwhelming bill of 300 dinars after treatment in Sfax. The company had reneged on a negotiated pledge to cover the costs.[12] These are some illustrative examples of misery-inducing work—or more basically, life—in the phosphate basin.

Folk songs about the phosphate basin gave voice to the immense suffering of the region's people. A new "alternative poetry" was taking shape in the early 1980s, bypassing Arab traditions of long-winded flattery (*mujamalah*) to explore salient social issues and conflicts. A special issue of the journal *Alikah* spotlighted "mining poetry" by the likes of Ahmad 'Amir, Souilmi Boujum'ah, Salem Al-Sha'bani.[13] Musical metamorphosis kept apace. Sons of the Mines (*Awlad al-Manajim*), introduced in the vignette, and the Music Research Band (*Firqat al-Bahth al-Musiqi*) were among the few who dared to make "engaged music" (*al-musiqa al-multazimah*). Espousing and contributing to an "alternative" or counter-culture, they artistically broached issues of normative and human concern to Tunisians. Such engaged music is not unlike the "liberation musicology" of the Civil Rights Movement, with its reach to ordinary people and oral traditions, and its instrumental adoption as a medium for solidarity and strength (Reed 2019, 14–31). Room for maneuver, of course, was much narrower in Tunisia, driving bands underground. The choice of Tunisian dialect in

---

[8] *Al-Wad' Al-Thaqafi fi Gafsa* in *Al-Mustaqbal*, August 31, 1981, p. 13.
[9] *Rajjah Ardiyyah bi Redeyef,* in *Al-Mustaqbal*, September 21, 1981, p. 5.
[10] *Hawla Qurud Sharikat Fusfat Gafsa,* in *Al-Mustaqbal*, April 6, 1981, p. 2.
[11] *Al-Sahhah bi Manjam Al-Mdhila*, in *Al-Mustaqbal*, January 12, 1981, p. 12.
[12] *Hadhihi Ma'sati,* in *Al-Mustaqbal*, October 12, 1981, p. 13.
[13] Reviewed in *Madkhal ila Al-Shi'r Al-Jadid*, *Al-Mustaqbal*, December 22, 1980, p. 10.

at least some of their songs was deliberate. As the Gabes-based Music Research Band explained in an interview, they sang in "the language of the person on the street, the dialect of the human being who reversed the balance of power on 3 January 1984"[14] (see Khashanah 2021, 150–157). Invoking the bread riots is onto-epistemilogical, affirming affinity between music and oppositional politics, knowing and being.

Sons of the Mines propounded feelings and relayed stories of fractured or amputated limbs, lives lost in extracting the damned and damning phosphate. These renegade musicians "refused to submit" to new licensing requirements in 1979, as they explained in an interview. Band members were themselves miners. They literally sang in miners' tongues, "feeling what we sing, and seeking to outline an alternative future to which we aspire." Refashioning local musical traditions, they serenaded miners as well as wider Tunisian and Arab society, with its infinite tribulations including the Palestinian cause.[15] Social imaginaries are not exclusive to elites. In a region where "the company" or *kubbaniyyah*, was the main generator of income, failing to land a job at the phosphate company almost inevitably doomed one to unemployment writ large. Resistance was more than complaint, however. In the song *Al-Sha'b* (Nostalgia Adab 2014), Sons of the Mines fought back with their words and notes. They moved beyond the ambivalence of affect to articulate a cognitive awareness of oppression's transience and an agentic inclination to resist. Words are, like protest slogans, deeds—speech acts. "So what do we say, and what do we want?/We want life without oppressors." By declaring it so, the people could create "A renaissance, to break the chains of thieves/And push our banner forward/To reveal a new morning …" Uttering discontent and refusal switched on a light at the end of this phosphate tunnel. The recurring term "thieves" echoed the idea of "the right to have rights." Not only was phosphate "stolen." It also robbed locals of the right to "trickle-down" development.

The 1980 Gafsa Revolt

Winter seems to be protest season in Tunisia (see also Al-Taimoumi 2020, 41–44; and Ben Mim 2019, 12). The 1978 general strike-turned-Black Thursday and the 1984 bread riots (Chapter 3) both began in January, and the revolution (to come) would erupt in December 2010. Indeed, exactly two years after Black Thursday, Gafsa itself had been the site of an attempted coup in 1980, supported by neighboring dictator Muammar Qadhafi (Perkins 2014, 169–170). This self-proclaimed revolution waged by the Revolutionary Movement to Free Tunisia (*Al-Harakah Al-Thawriyyah*) sought to "incite the masses to enact a revolution in an organized fashion," for a complete social, political, and economic takeover of the country (*Al-Harakah Al-Thawriyyah* n.d., 5). Swiftly put down by Bourguiba, the movement that

---

[14] *Al-Ra'i,* March 9, 1984.
[15] "Ghannaina li Al-'Amil … Wa Intalaqna Ila Ma Huwa Arhab," in *Al-Mustaqbal*, March 16, 1981, p. 15.

invoked by name the known martyrs of 1978 (*Al-Harakah Al-Thawriyyah* n.d., 35–37) failed to rouse the broader public. The blow was jarring to the President who discovered that "a few people ... could shake the pillars of the regime," as noted by defected Destourian Mustapha Ben Jaafar. Bourguiba should take heed and solve mounting political crises, for instance Habib Achour and other UGTT leaders, also overcoming "hesitation" regarding the student movement. Political unanimity in "defending ... the threatened nation" was reassuring, however.[16] Witness to the occasion and even arrested briefly before his acquittal, veteran unionist Moncef Belhoula (2015) notes how the events imprinted on him personally and politically as an active UGTT member. He compares divergent assessments of the 1980 Gafsa insurrection. Some regarded it as an attempted invasion by Libya and Algeria, while others, viewed it as a "popular revolution ... to liberate Tunisia from the Bourguibist regime" (Belhoula 2015, 318). Student activists, for instance, were less likely to rally round the flag. Many Islamists and leftists both welcomed the challenge to the regime, considering the rebels "revolutionaries" and those slain "martyrs," according to Abdelaziz Tamimi and Issam Chebbi (in Al-Thabti 2017, 253, 282–284). Our own interviews confirm the mixed feelings surrounding these controversial events.

Predictably, Bourguiba's response was brutal. Long prison sentences and, in 13 cases, the death penalty were the fate of the dozens convicted on sedition charges. Intercessions by the Palestinian Liberation Organization (PLO) leader Yasser Arafat on behalf of those on death row, some of whom had apparently been revolutionary fighters (*fida'iyyin*), only further provoked the President (Belhoula 2015, 317). He hastened to implement the death sentence. Still, the attempted coup was of enormous political consequence, shaking up president and party. Rachid Khashana (of the Progressive Democratic Party or PDP) regarded the 1980 events in Gafsa to be a political "turning point." The thwarted coup was also an "alarm bell" sounded by the "deprived regions," prompting the government to upgrade development policy (e.g. a new secondary school in Gafsa, new administrative zoning for Tataouine and the Djerid palm oases).[17] These promises did not fully materialize, however. An anonymous letter to the editor complained that new secondary schools in Mdhila and Degueche generating so much fuss were ill-equipped to welcome a fresh crop of students: still under construction, lacking supplies—sometimes even teachers.[18] Surface-level changes fell short of mitigating the acute marginalization permeating the lives of residents.

Sparking Rebellion in 2008

Before and after 1980, the suffering of joblessness nurtured rage and rebellion. Notable is the "continuity" of popular contention in the phosphate basin from colonial times to the present day (Walsh 2021). Dreams of possible futures, the "new

---

[16] *1980: Sanat Gafsa; 1981: Al-Taghyir Al-Jihawi?*, in *Al-Mustaqbal*, December 29, 1980, pp. 1, 15.
[17] *"Gafsa" Wara'a Kulla Taghyirat Sanat 1980*, in *Al-Mustaqbal*, January 26, 1981, pp. 1, 7.
[18] *Gafsa: Min Waqi' Al-Hayat*, in *Al-Mustaqbal*, September 28, 1981.

morning," (akin to Arendt's rebirth) are cognizable among these downtrodden of "deep Tunisia," *Tunis al-aʿmaq*, in Tunisian parlance. That is, the hinterland, the strange territory of the other, *al-janub*. The space that is uncounted, unseen, and mute or muted, Rancière's "part that has no part". Hazardous employment, for musical and non-musical "sons of the mines," was better than no employment at all. Demanding jobs, in 2008 miners, prospective miners, unionists, and their families claimed the dignity that basic sustenance furnishes on human life (see Chebbi 2022, 138–140). They moved to break free from what Amartya Sen (1999) considers the un-freedom of deprivation. Our interviewees, young protestors, were consistent in explaining that long-standing protest demands (during and since 2008) involve jobs and better working conditions.[19] The Union of Unemployed Graduates found in the local UGTT leaders an organizational container and "rationalizer" of protests. Both mustered the audacity and the stamina to insist on "the right to have rights." These included the right to jobs, to organize, protest, demand humane treatment, and decry state violence. The phosphate basin uprising endured for six entire months until it was coercively aborted by security. Its leaders, including Bechir Laabidi and Adnan Hajji and members of the so-called "Gang" Committee (*lajnat al-wifaq*), were jailed, as the following section elaborates.

The 2008 uprising in the phosphate basin's mining quartet (Mdhila, Metlaoui, Redeyef, and Moularès) is commonly regarded as the "spark" of the 2011 revolution, *al-thawrah*. In his political memoir, the UGTT's Houcine Abassi (2023, 116) dubs it the "cradle of the revolution," an assessment the PDP's Nejib Chebbi (2022, 146) shares. Dozens of interviewees attest to as much. One man in his twenties suggested that the 2008 uprising "played an effective role in creating popular mobilization because when the residents . . . protested in the previous era [of Ben Ali], the people (*al-shaʿb*) sympathized with them."[20] The affect of solidarity rang forth. Another emphasized the shift in popular agency and cognition. He commented that the phosphate movement helped "create a syndicalist, popular *hirak*, such that the subjects rebel and take risks for the sake of achieving their demands, which . . . paved the way for 2011."[21] Transiting to peoplehood exacts a steep cost: injury, jail, torture, even death. Protestors summon deep courage from the depths of their emancipatory aspirations. Uprising leader, primary school teacher, and lifelong union member Bechir Laabidi sees the 2008 movement as a rehearsal if not more. For him, the 2011 revolution "was a copy of the phosphate basin movement."[22] As he elaborated to the director Sami Tlili in *Curse the Father of Phosphate!*: twin "slogans . . . same methods . . . same discourse . . . as though the movement was a model for the revolution later on." This appraisal of the uprising as "an example" disseminated among anti-regime activists such as the Workers' Party.[23] The problem, Laabidi added, is that post-2011

---

[19] Interviews with protestors in Gafsa, Metlaoui, and Moularès, 20–21 October 2020 and 11–12 October 2021.
[20] Interview, October 20–21, 2020, Gafsa.
[21] Interview, Gafsa, October 20–21, 2020.
[22] Interview, August 2, 2022.
[23] *Intifadat Al-Hawd Al-Manjimi Tabqa Al-Mithal*, in *Al-Badil*, July 22, 2009.

politicians "didn't recognize this." Like others dissatisfied with the list that has generated controversy for a decade, he expressed a heartfelt complaint that those killed in 2008 (Al-Hafnaoui Al-Maghzaoui, Hichem Alaymi, deliberately electrocuted by police,[24] Abdelkhaleq Al-Amaydi, and Nabil Shaqrah) have not been officially recognized among the martyrs of the revolution.[25] Martyrdom implies common sacrifice for a single, popular cause. Deferred since the Tunisian crucible, the burning quest for peoplehood had immortalized Ali Ben Ghedhahem as the first symbol of martyrdom. Gafsa's sons and daughters of the mines pulled closer the diachrony of a revolution over a century and a half in the making.

Mutiny of the Miners: January–June 2008

The phosphate basin uprising began in January 2008. Residents refused the results of the employment selection process (*munazarah*), which they found highly suspect.[26] The positions were distributed in what was seen as a corrupt fashion, between the UGTT (20 percent earmarked for the union, admits Houcine Abassi (2023, 166)), *Tajammu'* (RCD) partisans, and local tribes (e.g. Ouled Yahya, Ouled Obeid, etc.). That the scant spots in the CPG had, according to a May Day statement, been slashed from 14,000 to 5,000,[27] and "awarded" in such a manner only added insult to injury. Unfair hiring practices compounded grievances against handling (*munawalat*) companies awarded suspicious contracts. These companies are widely perceived to be part of the phosphate problem.[28] Corrupt schemes between the UGTT, the CPG, and businessmen generated huge sums of money but without completion of services workers were hired for. Precarious and casual employment were the result.[29]

Miners and their families thus rebelled in 2008. The South's marginalized moved to strike back against power-holders and wealth-distributors who left them "uncounted." As one sympathetic member of the Tajdid party commented, Metlaoui's

---

[24] '*Awdat Al-Tawattur ila Al-Hawd Al-Manjami*, in *Al-Mawqif*, May 9, 2008, p. 2.
[25] Ibid.
[26] *Ma Hiya Haqiqat Al-Munazarah Allati Kashafat Al-Mastoor? Ittihamat Mutabadilah bi Al-Mahsubiyyah wa Al-Muhabah*, In *Al-Tariq Al-Jadid*, January 2, 2008, p. 6.
[27] *Intifadat Al-Hawd Al-Manjimi: Muhawalah Taqwimiyyah*, in *Al-Badil*, May 2008, https://bit.ly/3T6fNvB (Retrieved: 20 March 2022).
[28] *Sharikat Al-Munawalah fi Al-Hawd Al-Manjimi: Hall Al-Azmah Am Juz' Minha*, in *Muwatinun*, March 5, 2008, p. 6.
[29] Changes in phosphate extraction methods led to new forms of corruption through these front companies. Outlawed for phosphate transport after the revolution, the practice was reinstated by fall 2013 (Laabidi 2015). Some post-2011 power-holders also seem to have been implicated. MP Lutfi Ali and a former Minister of Industry, Energy and Mines Selim Firyani, for instance, have been under investigation. Instead of shipping phosphate out of Gafsa via trains (less than half the cost of trucks, according to one investigation), trucking companies were hired but failed to transport millions of tons of phosphate (Ziyadah 2021). Over the last few years, some protests and disruption of shipping railways were orchestrated to the benefit of these *munawalat* companies, as a regional UGTT secretary general confirmed (Interview, 22 October 2022). Since 2008, *munawalat* have also been used in shell landscaping and environmental companies. "Trickery" by the CPG and government avoids addressing socio-economic demands, through companies offering precarious employment (Al-Tabbabi 2019). Hired to do "phantom" jobs, people are deprived of their "human dignity," receiving (minimal) salaries without producing or doing anything (Al-Tabbabi 2019).

residents were "identity-less." No trace of their lives or experiences was detected by Tunisian television or radio, let alone politicians, despite the much-vaunted contributions of phosphate to the national economy.[30] Yet it was not simply (aspiring) workers who took action. Longtime UGTT leader Sami Laakirmi, who hails from Mdhila, noted that the uprising was a family, and thus a societal, affair. A chronically unemployed, or casually employed, head of household (usually male) would have little means to provide for his wife and children. The same man was likely responsible for his parents' subsistence, his father having been forced by the CPG to retire early at age 50. Three generations were thus caught in the yoke of the indignity and destitution of joblessness. Thus, everyone took part in the uprising, says Laakirmi: "from the oldest to the youngest ... the entire region. ... It was a true popular uprising (*intifadah sha'biyyah*)."[31] To label the uprising a "unionist movement" (*harakah naqabiyyah*) would be to downplay its wide reach and significance, insisted Laakirmi. Still, unionists took the lead in terms of organization and mobilization. They coached residents to sit-in, demonstrate, and negotiate with the company and with local authorities. In his public testimony before the "Truth and Dignity Commission" tasked with post-revolution transitional justice, Bechir Laabidi pointed to the agency with which residents of the mining staged their uprising. It was "not spontaneous" but a deliberate repudiation of "policies that had failed," that were "anti-people" in the region (Instance Verité and Dignité 2016).

Over six eventful months, unionists Laabidi, Adnan Hajji, and others organized protests in Redeyef, Moularès, Mdhila, and eventually Metlaoui (see Al-Tabbabi 2012, 214–219). Locals blocked roads, workers went on strike, and residents formed a "Local Committee for the Unemployed." Ammar Amrousiyyah (2008) catalogued the creativity and organization of a panoply of protest forms. Public sit-ins,[32] tent sit-ins, demonstrations, hunger strikes, digging up train tracks to disrupt phosphate transport were some of the methods utilized. Most notable to him was the thwarting of police transgressions, including taking one hostage in Mdhila until seven arrested protestors had been released. As fire hydrants sprayed them with water, local lore has it that Redeyef's youth simulated showering under the downpour, some even applying shampoo for dramatic effect. Protestors thus provoked the police who turned off the water deployed for crowd control (Amrousiyyah 2008). Police and even army repression was rapidly employed, setting off a cat-and-mouse dynamic of advances and retreats by the protestors. Trekking to Mdhila, one correspondent for (the opposition party Ettakatol) newspaper wrote of the road obstructed by security, burning towers, and stacks of smoke visible from afar. Burning tires and flying rocks gave the impression that one was in "a flaming Baghdad neighborhood," invoking the contemporaneous peaking violence of the American war on Iraq.[33] Temporary lulls in

---

[30] *Al-Kadd wa Al-Shaqa' fi Al-Manajim wa Al-'Izz wa Al- Rakha' fi Al-'Awasim*, in *Al-Tariq Al-Jadid*, February 9, 2008, p. 11.

[31] Interview, October 26, 2022, Tunis

[32] *I'tisam 'A'ilat Umm Al-'Arais fi Al-Hawd Al-Manjimi bi Gafsa*, in *Al-Tariq Al-Jadid*, January 2, 2008, p. 7.

[33] *Gafsa: Al-Manatiq ... Al-Mushta'ilah*, in *Muwatinun*, January 16, 2008, p. 5.

the protest 50 days later, when RCD party officials visited the mining towns, did not spell the end of the uprising.[34]

Protestors in Redeyef formed a negotiating committee of five that pursued small gains such as the positions and conditions of casual workers in landscaping or phosphate transport. Protest did not rule out negotiations (even with a representative of President Ben Ali, Sami Jawahdu). Partial agreements (to reconsider the list of those hired, decrease overtime work hours, small loans, etc.) for a time led to an impression of stabilizing "détente" in the ongoing crisis.[35] That the respite was short-lived should not minimize the civic-ness of the protest movement, or the competencies its activists marshalled and honed. From his prison cell, Adnan Hajji penned a letter recalling these negotiating marathons. He reiterated "our belief that dialogue remains the best way to dissipate social issues [that are] stuck," calling for the release of prisoners and a "return to the negotiating table."[36] These activists, many whose union membership had primed them with prior protest competencies, thus socially acted and en-acted a practical, creative, dialogic, and argumentative agency. Ben Ali did sack the governor[37] and the head of the CPG. Was the government listening to the legitimate objections of "neglect" and marginalization in Gafsa? Ben Ali's critics were dubious.[38]

In early April 2008, leaders of the movement were arrested (Hajji, Laabidi, Adil Jayyar, Taieb Ben Othman, and Boujum'ah Al-Shrayti) along with over 100 others.[39] Charges included the suspicious burning of police headquarters. An enormous women's march, a sit-in at the municipality building, and negotiations with the mayor[40] in the days following their arrest brought enough pressure to secure their release. (Temporarily) exuberant residents celebrated in victory well into the night.[41] Here women especially flexed their protest competency muscles. Jail and torture, and even the deaths of three young men, were not strong enough deterrents. In May 2008, hundreds of families fled Redeyef, escaping punishing security measures that made daily life unbearable.[42] The crackdown's waxing and waning left many pondering the impasse. Opposition figures including Ahmed Ibrahim of the Tajdid Party wondered how national television and government propaganda could uphold "dialogue" with youth while refusing to dialogue with them in the (marginalized) regions (*jihat*), including besieged Gafsa.[43]

---

[34] *Hada'at Al-'Asifah wa Lam Yakhmud Al-Burkan*, in *Muwatinun*, February 27, 2008, p. 2.
[35] *Ay Nasib li Abna' al-Manajim fi Arbah Al-Mujamma'*? in *Al-Tariq Al-Jadid*, February 23, 2008, p. 8.
[36] *Al-Mawqif*, July 28, 2008.
[37] *Taghyir Wali Gafsa: Hal Yahill Azmat Al-Tanmiyah bi Al-Wilayah?* In *Al-Mawqif*, April 4, 2008.
[38] *Gafsa Baina Al-Tafawut Al-Jihawi wa Al-Ihmal*, in *Al-Mawqif*, February 22, 2008, p. 7.
[39] *I'tiqalat bi Al-Hawd Al-Manjimi Wa 'Azl Amni li Al-Jihah*, in *Al-Mawqif*, April 11, 2008, p. 2; see also, *Redeyef: I'tida'at wa Iqafat fi Sufuf Al-Ahali Al-Muhtajjin wa 'Adad min Al-Naqabiyyin!* In *Al-Tariq Al-Jadid*, April 12–18, 2008, p. 5.
[40] Interview with Leila Khaled, October 15, 2022, Redeyef.
[41] *Al-Hawd Al-Manjimi bi Gafsa: Madha Ba'd Al-Ifraj 'An Al-Mu'taqalin?* In *Al-Mawqif*, April 18, 2008, p. 4.
[42] *Ba'da Halak Al-Shabb Hisham fi Al-Manajim: Al-Niyabah Al-'Umumiyyah Taftah Tahqiq*, in *Al-Tariq Al-Jadid*, May 17–23, 2008, p. 7.
[43] *Hall Azmat Al-Hawd Al-Manjimi Mumkin, fa Ayna Al-Iradah Al-Siyasiyyah?* In *Al-Tariq Al-Jadid*, May 31–June 6, 2008, p. 3.

Unfazed by uncertainty, the protestors stayed the course. With a national (perhaps international) as well as local audience in mind, they amplified, defended, and explained their uprising through interviews with opposition newspapers.[44] The rebellion advanced. By early June, security forces had set in again, surrounding Redeyef. Their barricades circled the city, and piles of stones blocked surrounding roads.[45] Clear police targets, the youth in particular, exited, some to Tozeur, Nefta, and Degueche in the Djerid.[46] Others took to the mountains for sanctuary, as our interviewees recounted. Media blackouts reinforced the sense of willful abandonment by the authorities.[47] It was the opposition newspapers upon which we draw that reported on the uprising in detail. Unionist and rights activist covering the events for *Al-Tariq Al-Jadid*, Amor Qouidir wrote of being physically assaulted by a police officer, threatened with an ominous demise unless he ceased his excessively compassionate reporting.[48] Himself the son of a miner toiling in the *damus*, Qouidir was shaken but not daunted. He adamantly clung to his right—and duty—to convey "my people's ... voices to the authorities and to public opinion, calling for their rescue." Journalism here was an assertion of a solidarity, of peoplehood-in-the-making, beyond the confines of region or tribe. Qouidir further reflected on his chagrin at feeling the state's iron fist firsthand: "I realized that night how bitter it is for a person to be humiliated by his countryman." The episode of *hogra* seems to have triggered resilience and steadfastness in resistance. Submission to state bullying was not an option.

The "Wifaq" leadership was again arrested at the end of June 2008,[49] amidst army and security raids on the mining towns. Complaints of legal violations in the prosecution, such as moving prisoners without informing their attorneys, entrenched the perception of state vengeance against unruly peripherals.[50] Court hearings and sentencing took place over the next few months: Zakia Difaoui (a journalist/activist from Kairouan) in September[51] and other phosphate activists in December,[52] followed by an appeal in February 2009. "Harsh" sentences ranged from three to six years (eight for Bechir Laabidi), eliciting outcries from the families.[53] Opposition parties such as Ettakatol denounced the "oppressive" sentences.[54] National advocacy on behalf of

---

[44] For instance, *Adnan Al-Hajji: Nuridu Nasib Al-Hawd Al-Manjimi min Al-Tharwah*, in *Al-Tariq Al-Jadid*, June 7–13, 2008, p. 13.

[45] *Madha Hasala fi Redeyef…*, in *Al-Tariq Al-Jadid*, June 14–20, 2008, p. 8.

[46] *Ila Mata Halat Al-Ru'b Allati Ya'ishuha Ahali Redeyef?* In *Al-Tariq Al-Jadid*, June 21–27, 2008, p. 8.

[47] *Adnan Al-Hajji: Natamanna An Ta'ti Al-Sahafah Ila Redeyef li Tanqula Al-Haqiqata Kama Hiya*, in *Al-Tariq Al-Jadid*, June 14–20, 2008, p. 9.

[48] *Raddi 'Ala Risalat Al-Khamis*, in *Al-Tariq Al-Jadid*, July 5–11, 2008, p. 7.

[49] *Muhakamat Qadat Al-Harakah Al-Ihtijajiyyah fi Al-Manajim*, in *Al-Mawqif*, June 27, 2008, p. 1; also *Al-Sultah Takhtar Nahj Al-Tas'id fi Muwajahat Al-Harakah Al-Ihtijajiyyah Al-Silmiyyah bi Redeyef*, in *Al-Tariq Al-Jadid*, June 28–July 4, 2008, p. 7.

[50] *Hawla Muhakamat Nushata' Al-Hawd Al-Manjimi Al-Ta'assufiyyah*, in *Al-Tariq Al-Jadid*, June 28–July 4, 2008, p. 2.

[51] *Al-Tariq Al-Jadid* covered the trials in detail, September 13–19, 2008, pp. 6, 13.

[52] *Ahkam Qasiyah Didda Qadat wa Nushata' Al-Ihtijajat Al-Ijtima'iyyah fi Al-Hawd Al-Manjimi*, December 17, 2008, p. 3.

[53] *Al-Tariq Al-Jadid*, February 7–13, 2009.

[54] *Al-Takattol Al-Dimuqrati: Ahkam Ja'irah Didd Mu'taqali Al-Hawd Al-Manjimi*, in *Muwatinun*, December 17, 2008, p. 2.

the prisoners, including through the National Committee for Supporting Residents of the Phosphate Basin (Ben Yousef 2019, 85–87), resonated in and outside of Tunisia (e.g. Amnesty International 2009). Eventually, jailed activists were released from prison in stages, beginning in late October 2008.[55] Some (physically robust) remaining inmates waged a hunger strike and issued a statement from the Gafsa prison, demanding their own release.[56] Adnan Hajji and Bechir Laabidi's health meant they were too fragile to participate.[57] They resisted in other ways, however. Hajji refused to sign required paperwork as a way to boycott the "judicial theater" being staged, he wrote in a letter from jail.[58] Nor were the wives of the imprisoned idle during this time. In addition to ongoing advocacy, they attempted more protests, for instance in May 2009. Forty women congregated in front of the UGTT headquarters in Redeyef, harassed by security until they moved to Adnan Hajji's house, less central. They were forced to disband altogether.[59] About a year before Sidi Bouzid flared up in the impending inferno of revolution, the other Gafsa activists were released. They could not find employment, however, encountering new "retaliatory" measures by the authorities keen on depriving them of sustenance (*qat' al-arzaq*).[60] Environmental companies (*munawalat*) set up as a policy response to the 2008 uprising insulted residents' intelligence. They did no more than open up fake jobs, many without pay, for the unemployed, while lining the pockets of "crisis rich" (*athriya' al-azamat*) company owners, as one investigation revealed.[61] Marginalization still festered in the phosphate basin.

Speech Acts of Peoplehood

The phosphate basin uprising mastered the art and practice of composing and using slogans (see Table 5.1). All protests, whether one-time events or extended quasi-movements such as this one, are awash in slogans. Through these speech acts, protestors communicate their demands. Foremost among their appeals in 2008 was employment, which they constructed as a *right* to them as people of Tunisia. In so doing, they imbued their demands with normative substance. Their pursuit was not of narrow self-interest or greed. Rather, protestors sought their basic rights and the dignity with which (fair and adequate) employment clothes the human being. Moreover, protestors framed their predicament as (non)people shorn of dignity. They attributed the blame to a "gang of thieves": implying government, corporatist, and union culpability. Conspicuous was the advanced cognizing of a *people* (*sha'b*)

---

[55] *Al-Tariq Al-Jadid*, November 8–14, 2008, p. 3.
[56] *Al-Tariq Al-Jadid*, November 15–21, 2008, p. 7.
[57] *Mu'taqalu Al-Hawd Al-Manjimi Yashunnuna Idraban 'An Al-Ta'am*, in *Al-Mawqif*, November 14, 2008, p. 2.
[58] *Adnan Al-Hajji: Risalah Ukhra Min Wara' Al-Qudban*, in *Al-Mawqif*, October 17, 2008, p. 2.
[59] *Al-Tariq Al-Jadid*, May 16–22, 2009.
[60] As described in a letter signed by "Son of Redeyef," *Al-Tariq Al-Jadid*, April 11–17, 2009.
[61] *Al-Wajh Al-Akhar li Azmat Al-Hawd Al-Manjimi: Fasad Mali wa Athriya' Judud*, in *Muwatinun*, October 15, 2008, p. 5.

Table 5.1 Slogans of the Phosphate Basin Uprising

Slogan	Translation	Significance
Al-tashghil, al-tashghil, l-ibn al-'amil wa al-faqir	Employment, employment, for the (son of) the worker and the poor person	Conveys main protestors' main demand, the legitimacy of which is difficult to question. Normative impetus to protest (right to work, right from poverty)
Shughl, hurriyyah, karamah wataniyyah	Work, freedom, national dignity	Cognizes demand for employment as rights-based, emancipatory Links local demands (miners' employment) to a wider moral insistence on dignity of the Tunisian people
Al-shughl istihqaq, ya 'isabat al-surraq	Work is a right, you gang of thieves	Constructs employment as an inalienable right Implicates corrupt government (Ben Ali and Trabelsis), the CPG, and possibly (some) UGTT leadership in "stealing" people's rights
Iradatuna hurrah, hurrah, wa al-masirah mustamirrah	Our will is free, free, and the demonstration continues	Cognition of protest as a deliberate (agentic) practice Communicates patience and steadfastness as protest values
Ya muwatin, ya dahiyyah, ukhruj 'abbir 'al qadiyyah	Oh citizen, oh victim, come out and communicate the cause	Mobilizing slogan to expand the protest participant pool Mixes affective and cognitive appeals (victim of state *hogra*) to summon anger Implies shared responsibility by all residents (agency) to the protests
Na'am sanamut wa lakin sanaqtali' al-hurriyyah min ardina	Yes, we will die, but we will extract the freedom from our land	Accepts sacrifice required in pursuit of freedom, a lofty aim with moral content Frames movement as shared pursuit ("our land"), implying we-ness and requiring intense effort
Ya Hached, shuf shuf, al-khiyanah 'al makshouf	Oh, Hached, look, look! Betrayal is out in the open	Invokes union/national legend Farhat Hached, re-appropriating his legacy to legitimate workers' demands *against* the state (counter-memory) Reprimands union leaders for deviance from UGTT values (freedom, dignity emblematized workers' rights)
Ya nizam, ya jaban, sha'b Redeyef la yuhan	Oh regime, oh coward, the people of Redeyef cannot be humiliated	Cognizes a unified "people" in opposition to unjust regime Inverts affective dynamics of repression (regime unleashing security forces is afraid, not the people) Rejects humiliation and double consciousness of state *hogra*

Slogan	Translation	Significance
Al-sajin awwalan, wa al-hiwar thaniyan	First the prisoner, then dialogue	Conveys protest competency of negotiation (agency) Activation of repository (*makhzun*) of accumulated skills by unionist leaders
Ya 'Abbasi, ya mnawil ya khayin li-l-'ummal	Oh Abbasi, [owner] of the holding (*munwalat*) companies! Oh traitor to the workers!	Addresses Ammara Abassi, accusing him of corruption and aberrance from espoused UGTT mandate to protect workers

Source: Al-Tabbabi (2012, 222) and interviews. Some slogans are in the Tunisian colloquial.

joining the protest in pursuit of basic rights. The onus is on citizens (*muwatin* in the singular) to wrest these rights from a recalcitrant state and its (mal)distributive arm, the CPG. Here, the slogans indicate an agonistic understanding of state–society relations. Decades of counter-revolutionary oppression and marginalization taught Tunisia's uncounted that the state would not bestow freedom and dignity of its own accord. Conflict with the state was thus a necessity. To an extent, protestors renounce their right to life for the greater goal of freedom and *national* dignity. Risking their lives was a cost worth bearing. In a sense, they modeled their "cause" after the emancipatory career of national heroes such as Farhat Hached. He and others inflamed a social imaginary of selflessness for *the people* swindled and subjugated by their own compatriot leaders. From this shining precedent some local union officials had veered. The game is up, these protestors told what they considered to be a kleptocratic crew. We are onto your betrayal. We no longer accept your exploitation and humiliation. Together, we stand up to demand our rights, reclaim our dignity, recover our stolen freedom. We are a people, of Redeyef, and of Tunisia itself. We refuse to be forever "uncounted," even if the body count piles up. Such speech acts accompanied the embodied appearance of protest demonstrations and sit-ins. Residents of Redeyef (and the other mining towns) matched their words with deeds, and vice versa. Powerful words echoed but did not disappear. Some of these same (modified) slogans would return in the revolution of 2010–11. Protest competencies were passed on (learned, taught, and re-learned) partly through the rousing cries of a people in want, but not in oblivion.

Counter-Narratives of Revolt

How did activists "read" the Gafsa uprising? Our analysis dwells not in chronology but in (narrations of) the agency, affect, and cognition of social acts and en-actments of protest as peoplehood. Echoes of 1984, 1980, 1978, *fellaga* battles, and labor struggles before that reverberated in this, the longest uprising Tunisia had ever seen. Public testimony (including documentaries) is valuable insofar as it publicly shares the experiences of those who have been "historically invisible" (Wieder 2004). Activists' testimonies in this book help us to discover epistemic injustice. They span participation in the (controversial) Truth and Dignity Commission headed by veteran activist Sihem Ben Sidrine, documentary appearances, and even our own interviews, forms of oral history. It is as though Gafsa's protestors were afraid of double erasure. First, by the authoritarian regimes who trapped them in socio-economic and political misery, and second, by the post-2011 political establishment which sought to tie up the messiness of revolution in neat narratives and clean timelines. Leery of the transitional justice process, Bechir Laabidi admitted his hesitation to partake in the Truth and Dignity Commission's proceedings. He explained why he (and his wife) did ultimately opt to testify. It was because of

> ... my conviction, first, that history should not be written in courts (*al-bilat*).... Our history is falsified (*muzayyaf*), written on demand. ... Today ... we want to give our historical testimony so it remains [as] a testimony for our children, our [future] generations, researchers who want to know the truth of the Tunisian people, the suffering... during Bourguiba and Ben Ali's reign and even after the revolution ... Gafsa [and] the marginalized regions [have been victim to] deliberate, systematic marginalization. [It was] one of the governorates that rebelled against Bourguiba.
> (Instance Verité and Dignité 2016)

With gruff determination, Laabidi recounted the grotesque sadism of sexual threats, the anguish of hearing his son's tortured sobbing in the cell next door, the helplessness of languishing for four months without medical treatment for the tuberculosis that melted 30 kilos off his weakened body. He relived the physical and emotional pain without flinching. Leila haltingly told of how she did not recognize Bechir when at last she was allowed to see him, shrunken by illness. Their retelling elicits sympathy and sadness that borders on the physical, for both live and virtual audience—including us watching the testimony years later. Infusing the ordeal with political significance, Laabidi invoked Gafsa's unruly history. Individual distress melts into (spatialized, regional) group debasement by the state. Thus did Laabidi rebuff the claims of "mischief-making" by Ben Ali and his state-run media in 2008. He sought to establish a (pre)revolutionary credibility rooted in the normative morality of the uprising. A long lineage of protesting for peoplehood emerges in this counter-narration. The agency of pioneering rebellion coalesces with a cognition of people asserting self-presence, the right to have rights.

Storied sacrifice is significant to Tunisians as past and as future legacy. Even researchers seeking to understand the revolution's origins should pay close attention, Laabidi said. He dispelled any tempting notion of random raucousness or aimless anarchism. In this story, there are clear heroes vying with indisputable villains. The state was culpable for denying the people of Gafsa the basic material and resources required and offering only minimal opportunities to live and thrive as human beings. As a journalist for the Workers' Party publication put it, the accused activists upended the entire meta-narrative of the prosecution. They "transformed the trial into a prosecution of Ben Ali's regime, exposing its repressive, dictatorial nature, its backwards economic and social policies, and their impact on residents of the phosphate basin: unemployment, poverty, and marginalization."[62] Slogans chanted and scrawled on protest signs during the six-month uprising (Al-Tabbabi 2012, 222) rang with this normative content. They demanded social justice, emphasizing stubborn struggle and selfless sacrifice. "Employment, employment, for the poor worker," "work, freedom, national dignity," "o prisoner, rest, rest! We will continue the struggle," "Yes, we will die, but we will pluck the repression from our land," "the people's wealth is in castles, and the people's children and in tents." The contrast between exploitative, predatory power-holders and abused, destitute people was stark in these speech acts.

Sensory Rebellion and Becoming

Also central to the unfolding of the 2008 uprising, *and its retelling by activists*, was the affective glue of discourse and behavior. Activists unleashed rage not just against the state. They spat out angry epithets ("thieves and dogs") against the "union bureaucracy" of the UGTT leadership, including Gafsa Secretary-General Amara Abbasi, who had refused to embrace the uprising (see also Angrist 2013, 560–561). Adnan Hajji vocalized widespread accusations of corruption, hinting at Abbasi's reputation as owner of the notorious handling (*munawalat*) companies. Not shying from personal attacks, he wondered about Abbasi's daughter's Passat car and the whereabouts of funds raised for the children and for Palestine and Iraq.[63] (Alarmed at the trial and sentencing of the uprising's leadership, the central UGTT would finally come closer to the positions of local union branches. In September 2008, Houcine Abassi (2015 Nobel winner) traveled to Redeyef to visit unionists and families of the imprisoned in an visit conveying (at least partial) UGTT support (Al-Tabbabi 2012, 35). National Secretary General Abdelsalam Jrad finally entreated Ben Ali to release the prisoners and avoid "escalation."[64])

Even more drenched in affect were re-tellings of state repression and humiliation. Sharing their stories, activists and families feelingly set the record straight. They movingly pled their human suffering as a collective quest for dignity with painfully personal ramifications. They also wielded these tales as instruments of advocacy (and of recognition). In this way, public expression (verbal and non-verbal, through broken voices and tearful faces) was itself a form of protest. Along with other wives and mothers of the arrested uprising's leadership, Leila Khaled (namesake of the Palestinian freedom fighter) starred in the unvarnished, simple production of the documentary named for her: *Leila Khaled la Tunisienne*. In it, the wives laid out the events of the mining rebellion. They inhabited a zone of professed suffering by those left behind, husbands and sons unjustly taken away.

---

[62] *Adnan Al-Hajji wa Rifaqihi Yuhawwilun Al-Muhakamah Ila Muhakamah li Al-Nizam wa Jalladih*, in *Al-Badil*, February 22, 2009.
[63] *Adnan Hajji: Sa Uhaddithukum 'an Al-Liss wa Al-Kilab*, in *Al-Badil*, April 2, 2008.
[64] *Al-Sabah*, December 17, 2008 (see Al-Tabbabi 2012, pp. 140–141).

Leila Khaled detailed the emotional and physical exhaustion of visiting her husband (Bechir Laabidi) and teenage son (Muzaffar) in prison. They were thrown into far-flung jails, then moved to Al-Mornaguia and Rajim Maatoug. Squarely addressing her audience from behind the camera, she recalled repeatedly traveling thousands of kilometers to take each his basket of goods (*quffah*). This dutiful labor of love performed by prisoners' families—usually mothers and wives—is a standard, always moving, plotline in the Tunisian prison genre narrative. Khaled told of scorching 38 degree heat, feet sinking in the sand as she approached a prison adjacent to military barracks. Sometimes she simply could not stand up, she recalled. Impassioned anguish magnified physical exertion: husband and son taken, and 14 year-old daughter living with her aunt as Khaled scrambled across the country to visit Bechir and Muzaffar, to reassure and be reassured. The documentary included footage of Khaled as a guest at a UGTT Ben Arous chapter meeting. The solidarity is palpable, in words and tears male union members surreptitiously wiped from their eyes. "As families, we support our husbands, our sons . . . this is our obligation," Khaled told them softly, her voice breaking. Gafsa miners' families were "fragmented" unbearably. She and Jum'ah Jallabi, wife of Adnan Al-Hajji, also penned emotional pleas in leftist publications. They beseeched "the free people of Tunisia and those with live consciences" to pressure the authorities so their husbands could receive medical treatment.[65] Conscious but painful sacrifice here ties together agency, affect, and cognition of Khaled's, Jallabi's, and others' struggles. The twist comes in the anti-climactic aftermath of the revolution. Khaled, Bechir, and Muzaffar separately expounded in *Curse the Father of Phosphate* that the revolution failed to improve the daily lives of Gafsa residents. Worse still, her son Muzaffar continued to smart from his emotional-psychological scars. His trauma ran so deep that he fled Tunis for France. True, "in the old regime . . . you live freedom only on the run," he reflected. Chased by police, he hid with his father in the mountains surrounding Redeyef where they paradoxically relished a clandestine taste of freedom. Away from the gaze of the "police logic," they repatriated along feelings of affinity, solidarity, and sacrifice. In their mountainous hideout, they breathed not just short-lived freedom, but their sensory experience as "*ahrar*" (free beings), ephemerally divulging the taste of future becoming, beyond the territorialized reality of autocracy—"the promise of new life" (Rancière 2002). For, in that reality, Muzaffar seemed untouched by much-vaunted feelings of revolution. "I don't feel that [sense of] my homeland (*watan*)," he admitted bluntly. "Tunisia is a bitterness in my throat." For him, freedom without the dignity of restorative justice was hollow. His choice to leave Tunisia is one explored by many young people, including thousands who tragically embark on the perilous "death-boat" journey across the Mediterranean, what Tunisians call *harqah*. Such dissatisfaction with transitional politics that ignores material deprivation also motivates the Kamour protestors (Chapter 7).

---

[65] *Al-Tariq Al-Jadid*, November 22–28, 2008, p. 7; earlier, *Al-Tariq Al-Jadid*, September 27–October 3, 2008.

A Convergence of Activisms

Lopsided political maneuverings that left behind Tunisia's destitute do not detract from the revolutionary moment of 2011, the coalescing of peoplehood, however fleeting. In the 2008 phosphate basin uprising, cross-sectional cooperation among some of Tunisia's variously situated activists was also significant. This active solidarity, this recognition and participation of common plight and struggle, foreshadowed the convergence of protestscapes and forms of demos, along with their logoi, that would tip the scales into boisterous revolution in 2011. In the documentary *Leila Khaled la Tunisienne*, Khaled proffered appreciation for the UGTT and other friends who stood by her and other families, even offering financial support. She also mentioned the "amazing" team of attorneys and civil society.[66] Solidarity (*tadamun* or *luhmah*) was "very strong," she recalled, even between families of the imprisoned. "When I make the *quffah*, I make it not just for my son" but for sons of other women unable to make the arduous prison visit journey.[67] Altruistic generosity becomes mutual aid. Khaled acknowledged emotional and material solidarity and support from friends in the close-knit Redeyef community, to the local UGTT branches sprawled across the country, and civil society groups and opposition parties such as *Tajdid*,[68] *Al-Tariq Al-Jadid* journalist Omar Qouidir, the Tunisian League for the Defense of Human Rights (LTDH), the Tunisian Association Against Torture, the Tunisian Association for Democratic Women (ATFD), among others.

Bechir Laabidi estimated that 150–200 attorneys extended their services to the over 1,000 activists arrested, some prosecuted, from the six-month uprising.[69] Attorneys included Radia Nasraoui, wife of Hamma Hamami, Samir Dilou of Ennahda, noted leftist activist the late Chokri Belaid (assassinated February 6, 2013), and countless others—many of whom had cut their protest teeth on student activism (Chapter 4). Attorneys such as Ali Kalthoum told of police harassment and insults. Colleagues of theirs were prevented from visiting their clients Hajji and Laabidi in the Kasserine prison.[70] The Tunisian Human Rights League (LTDH) also expressed solidarity, issuing statements condemning repression and in the following year when prisoners were moved to the remote Rajim Maatoug.[71] It demanded release of Zakia Difaoui and all other phosphate activist prisoners (see Ben Yousef 2019, 82–83). The "Tunisian Association Against Torture" recorded testimony from Muzaffar Laabidi, Taieb ben Othman, and others arrested in late June and early July 2008. Its advocacy took the form of documenting activists' torture at the hands of security forces (some by name) (see Ben Yousef 2019, 40–46). The opposition party Ettakatol demanded

---

[66] Also reported in opposition newspapers. *Al-Tariq Al-Jadid*. See for instance *Muhakamat Masajin Al-Hawd Al-Manjami: Habbah Qawiyyah min Al-Mujtama' Al-Madani Li Musanadat Al-Manjimiyyin*, in *Al-Tariq Al-Jadid*, December 13–19, 2008, p. 3.
[67] Interview, October 15, 2022.
[68] One of their visits to families was reported in *Al-Tariq Al-Jadid*, October 4–10, 2008, p. 3.
[69] Interview, August 2, 2022.
[70] *Al-Tariq Al-Jadid*, November 15–21, 2008.
[71] *Al-Rabitah Al-Tunisiyyah li Al-Difa' 'an Huquq Al-Insan: Tawasul Manhaj Al-Qaswah Didd Qiyadat Al-Hawd Al-Manjami wa 'A'ilatihim*, in *Al-Badil*, May 22, 2009.

the release of prisoners. In a statement, it reproached Ben Ali's government for contradicting its own human rights rhetoric through repressing and imprisoning activists (see Ben Yousef 2019, 94–95). Similarly, the Democratic Work Party and the Socialist Leftist Party expressed "discontent" with state coercion against activists making "legitimate" claims on behalf of their "deprived" region.[72] A number of civil society groups issued a joint statement speaking out against the sentencing of arrested activists, calling for an investigation into the security treatment of the whole uprising.[73] It was upon their return from a visit to Tunis, in a solidarity event hosted by the ATFD, that Adnan Hajji and Adil Jayyar were arrested in April 2008, as they testified in their trial.[74] Signed by its president Sana Ben Achour, the ATFD again published a brief message verbalizing solidarity with families of the uprising's prisoners in May 2009. They had mobilized anew to demand improvement in detention conditions and release.[75] Lina Ben Mhenni, made famous during the revolution, recalls a budding network of clandestine bloggers who followed and wrote about the uprising (Aljazeera 2012). Even diaspora Tunisians in France protested against the crackdown (Ben Yousef 2019, 103). Civil society activists from Algeria and Morocco attended activists' trials in December 2008, as noted in a statement by the National Committee for the Support of the Phosphate Basin Residents (Ben Yousef 2019, 134). And so on.

We want to suggest here that this kind of civil society solidarity, garnered through often emotional appeals by Leila Khaled, Adnan Hajji's wife, and others, also produced learning dividends. Keeping the "cause" of the phosphate basin prisoners alive was more than just a personal, family, or town concern about their release. It was also a kind of oppositional alarm that Khaled and fellow activists kept sounding. Affective testimonies and appeals fed into continuous agentic discourses and practices (the documentary, newspaper interviews[76] and columns, meetings with unionists and other civil society members). These in turn emblazoned the notion of a repressive state wrongfully, violently prosecuting the Laabidis, Hajji, Jayyar, and others simply because they demanded rights owed to them as *people*, as human beings. Local unionists were steadfast in their insistence on the right to development and employment, unceasingly demanding that the unjustly incarcerated be released.[77]

Khaled demonstratively charted her continuous travel, not just to the (changing) remote prisons holding Muzaffar and Bechir, but also to Tunis,[78] Jendouba, Sousse, Kairouan,[79] Ben Arous, and (an impeded trip to) Siliana. She explained the twofold aims of this shuttle advocacy. "It was to spread information that Redeyef was

---

[72] *Al-Tariq Al-Jadid*, December 5, 2008.
[73] Ibid.
[74] *Muhakamat Al-Hawd Al-Manjimi: Kaifa Ajaba Qadat Al-Harakat 'Ala As'ilat Al-Muhakamah?* In *Al-Badil*, March 30, 2009.
[75] *Al-Tariq Al-Jadid*, May 11, 2009 (see Al-Tabbabi 2012, 132).
[76] *Al-Tariq Al-Jadid,* Sept. 20–26, 2008, p. 6.
[77] See their petition: *'Aridah Naqabiyyah Wataniyyah Hawla Ahdath Al-Hawd Al-Manjimi,* published in *Muwatinun,* July 2, 2008, p. 6.
[78] Khaled was sometimes stopped, "prohibited from traveling," according to security forces. See *Al-Tariq Al-Jadid,* November 1–7, 2008, p. 2.
[79] As reported in *Al-Tariq Al-Jadid,* Oct. 11–17, 2008, pp. 1, 7.

under siege," counteracting the government media blackout. Second was the objective of "pressuring the government" to release the prisoners, and perhaps improve employment and living conditions in the marginalized region. On the whole, "we succeeded in pushing the cause outside of Redeyef," to Tunisian and international cities from Paris to New York to Algiers.[80] Through this joint activism, Khaled, other family members, and the civil society activists (particularly local UGTT chapters who hosted them) all stretched the phosphate basin uprising beyond the six months (January–July 2008) of weekly (or more) protests. The phosphate basin "tragedy" resonated with activists and opposition parties calling on greater democracy in the country.[81] The state's security reflex, its court prosecutions, were no panacea for protracted social justice deficits such as unemployment and prohibitive prices on basic goods, as the PDP entreated.[82] "Solidarity" meetings were convened in Tunis into October 2008, gathering the Ettakatol and Tajdid (Communist) parties, the ATFD, and the Gafsa-based residents' committee.[83] Connections were forged and deepened. The denunciations of state repression, corruption, and human misery that echoed across the country were all notable, as was the central role played by unionists and even attorneys. It were these features that laid the learning and protest competency groundwork for the revolution of 2010–11.

Mobilizing beyond the Phosphate Basin

As the solidarity recounted above hints, brutal repression backfired on the regime. Moreover, sustaining ruly and unruly protest yielded a determination to persist with civil courage and disobedience. It was this determination that proved to be most impactful in three ways. First, the phosphate basin along with its besieged towns and communities became a symbol of anti-authoritarian defiance. State propaganda or silence on the 2008 rebellion failed to demonize the protestors. The phosphate basin carved out an intrepid spatiality that could no longer be ignored by the rest of the country. Second, thus, this symbol drew wider attention and rallied the support of civil and political societies, and dormant diverse publics kept in check by Ben Ali's repression. The phosphate basin activism of 2008 can be credited with re-igniting anti-authoritarian resistance and recharging demotic agency (see Table 5.2). In particular, syndicalists of the national but mostly the local (*asasi*) and regional (*jihawi*) UGTT offices mobilized for the cause. The local, then regional, syndicalists have a radical edge over the national leadership and executives working from Tunis.[84] They

---

[80] Interview, October 14, 2022.
[81] *Ma'sat Al-Hawd Al-Manjimi Wa Mahamm Al-Harakah Al-Dimuqratiyyah*, in *Muwatinun*, July 16, 2008, p. 4.
[82] *Al-Amn wa Al-Qada' La Yanfa'an li Tafkik Al-Ihtiqan*, in *Al-Mawqif*, June 6, 2008, p. 1.
[83] For instance: *Bi-Da'wah min Harakat Al-Tajdid: Al-Nukhab Al-Tunisiyyah Taqif bi Hazm Ila Janib Sukkan Al-Hawd Al-Manjimi*, in *Al-Tariq Al-Jadid*, June 21–27, 2008, p. 7; *Fi Ijtima' Tadamuni Ma'a Ahali Al-Hawd Al-Manjimi: Al-Hiwar la Yumkin An Yatawasal fi Zill Al-Tawattur* in *Muwatinun*, October 22, 2008, p. 4.
[84] Confirmed by interviewees, including Mehdi Abdeljawad, Abdelmajid Sahrawi, and Sami Laakirmi (October 26, 2022).

Table 5.2 Civil Society Mobilization in the 2008 Uprising

Group name	Date	Key phrases	Significance
Harakat Al-Hurriyyah wa Al-Insaf (Freedom and Equity Movement)	January 31, 2008	Describes "uprising" and demands: protestors "confirmed the justice of their demands"	Informative role disseminated online amidst official media blackout
Tunisian Human Rights League (LTDH)	August 15, 2008	Offers "sympathy and support" for prisoners Demands "immediate release and investigation of alleged torture" for all prisoners	Solidarity Informing public opinion Rights advocacy
Sectoral Council of UGTT +Higher Education and Scientific Research Union	December 14, 2008	"Condemns" prosecutions, security response to socio-economic demands "Affirms its support for the residents and its activists" "Demands release of all prisoners"	Solidarity Public recognition of legitimate rights (to development and employment) by reputed civil society group of national stature
Ettakatol Party	December 15, 2008	Denounces security response and sham prosecutions Demands release of prisoners Highlights "blatant contradictions" of Ben Ali regime that violates its own human rights discourse Calls for end to harassment of democratic political opposition parties	Solidarity with movement Escalation of criticisms to opposition against Ben Ali's regime itself Links between protest movement and democratic political opposition
Tunisian Observatory for Union Rights and Freedoms	December 4, 2008	Calls for release and pardon of prisoners Invites "dialogue" for de-escalation of unionist unrest, to arrive at "national solidarity"	Solidarity Rights appeals Union identification

LTDH+ National Council for Freedoms in Tunisia; International Association for the Support of Political Prisoners; Tunisian Association Working Against Torture; Hurriyyah and Insaf; National Al-Widad for Resistor Alumni	December 5, 2008	Denounces manipulation of court system Calls for cancelling sentences and investigation of uprising events, particularly killings and torture	Solidarity and rights appeals invoking UN Declaration for Human Rights Coalitional statement
Democratic Work Party + Leftist Socialist Party	December 14, 2008	Condemns "unjustifiably oppressive sentences" that aim to "punish activists" acting as "responsible citizens" Considers prosecutions+ sentencing a "real, direct threat to civil society" (associations and parties) that "brought to our minds dark days in our history" Calls for release of prisoners, social justice	Solidarity Recognition of legitimacy of socio-economic demands and activism Identification with protestors' activism as a manifestation of civil society Parallels to past state violence against protestors (e.g. 1978, 1984)
Committee to Support Residents of the Phosphate Basin in Paris	June 6, 2008	Denounces Ben Ali's "dictatorial regime" Condemns "barbaric violence" Calls for shows of support and Paris demonstration	Solidarity Attributing repression to nature of political regime (authoritarian) Appropriation of cause through (diasporic) protest
UGTT (Secretary General)	September 2008 (Eid Al-Fitr)	Eid greetings to families of the activists; expression of support Mentions efforts to secure release of prisoners and "appropriate, dignified employment for all Tunisian men and women"	Solidarity (Delayed) recognition of legitimate socio-economic demands in line with union's own mission

Continued

Table 5.2 Continued

Group name	Date	Key phrases	Significance
Regional UGTT in Kairouan	October 2008	Meeting and hosting family members of imprisoned activists UGTT "was not absent entirely… but did not lend the matter enough importance" Pledges to pursue release of prisoners, commission report on regional development in Gafsa, and work toward a "political solution"	Solidarity Response to criticisms of national UGTT for slow, limited response Reflection of multi-faceted national role (political negotiations, advocacy, public consciousness raising through knowledge production)
Tajdid Movement (Communist)	December 11, 2008	Expresses "extreme discontent" with sentences; calls for "reconsidering the case" and "working towards release" of prisoners Defends activists for "responsible role" in organizing protests Calls for "dialogue"	(Cautious) solidarity Recognizes legitimacy of protests Does not rule out compromise with regime
ATFD (Association of Tunisian Democratic Women)	December 4, 2008	Denounces "oppression" against protestors and region Calls for release of prisoners and lifting of security measures "Disaffection" with being prohibited from attending trial in Gafsa; questions motives: could they be "fear" of "mobilizing" power of women?)	Solidarity with protestors and women in particular Expression of a kind of "intersectional" feminism (cross-regional, cross-class) Implied criticism of regime patriarchy

Source: Authors' table based on primary documents in Ben Yousef (2019, 38–132).

are closer to the sites of struggle. They brush shoulders with the downtrodden. Primordial and other ties, make them the first port of call within the communities where they unionize. They organize local and regional protests, sometimes in defiance of the UGTT leadership. They protest to defend agreements with employers and government; they fight police and courts alike; they negotiate new bargains; and they mobilize their rank-and-file for the big stand-offs. In so doing, they draw solace from historic struggles that hardened and embittered them against all forms of centralized control, especially by the state. The cumulative repository of emotion-thought-action from continuous struggles and sometimes daily protests make them adept drivers of resistance in all sites of collective action. They mobilize around just causes not solely based on staging the actual acts of resistance. There is a relationality and intersubjectivity dynamic involved. This can be expressed by an "interiority" and "exteriority" juxtaposition (Butler 1988) that is in play in the rebellion of 2008. "The phosphate basin" is itself a representation that misrecognizes the dis-embodiment—at least discursively—of an entire community. It is as if the "body" of the communities, Southerners in the Gafsa region, is dis-connected from Tunisia's body politic. They come under the "Big Brother" gaze of the state, its spies and coercive apparatuses, the cameras of the media watching them, and the *beldi* onlookers who hail from the comfort zones of the capital city and other rich urban centers. The invocation of "phosphate" is the operative term. It mis-cognizes the human persons and the life-worlds *qua* cultural, historical, and Tunisian beings—irrespective of the spatiality of the injustice they undergo, the southern geography they inhabit and the raw material that has reshaped their otherness and exclusion in precolonial and postcolonial times. This is a quasi-racist misplacement that erases the humanity of citizens. Here the terrain of struggle is rendered through misrepresentations of the communities leading the protests in 2008. Social constructions of the protestors from the embattled phosphate communities are inevitable. Law and order, as shall be pointed out below, is, for example, disassociated from the "bodies" and lives of these communities. As if through phosphate, their situatedness in the South, and resistance to injustice are what determines their subjectivities. Their "Southern-ness" is coded and loaded with meanings and significations that the state-ruled Bourguiba's inheritors suffer: sedimentations of past rivalries (Habib Bourguiba vs. Salah ben Youssef) and defiant anti-colonial *fellaga*. This dis-embodiment points to socio-political properties that spell unruliness—a threat to rule and rulers.

It is not just spatiality, which constrains the emancipatory aspirations for these protestors. It is also, the "bodies" they live in, be they biological, territorial, or imaginary. The self-knowing protestors in these environs, perhaps unconsciously, resist contests to inner knowledge of who they are—as self-realizing, self-understanding, and self-knowing beings via interiority. This is also contested in the course of facing up to decades of marginalization and humiliation after independence. The spatial situatedness in the South, and defiance, become markers of negation—of exclusion. Under the gaze of the authoritarian state, acting and en-acting emancipatory norms of protest and in defense of rights, these communities cease to be "citizens" or even

"Tunisian." The construction of the protestors is couched within incommensurability with the "universal" goods (including identity) or rights expected from the state. If the exteriority of the authoritarian state's gaze and the othering and social constructions that it produces seek to dislodge these communities from their inner selves, it is the social doing and collective action via protests that return them to the comfort zone of their interiority. An interiority that finds anchorage in long-standing affective traces of *hogra*, *takriz*, kinship, defiance, and neglect that beckons their sense of pride and solidarity when standing up to injustice. These positive emotion-thought-action bundles sharpen their sense of community and belonging. This is what proved infectious in 2008. It moved many publics into feelings of guilt for their indifference to the plight of their fellow compatriots. The regime never allowed for the "boomerang effect" of state oppression in dealing with demands of social justice and the right to have rights. Lastly, the 2008 uprising widened the political, legal, syndicalist, and intellectual elites' own activism in solidarity with the protests. This engendered audacious subjectivities, norms, and defense of the protestors. The social learning this garnered in building momentum against systemic injustice was the start of a sharpening of the skills of resistance and self-knowing that broke south–north divisions, stimulating new demoi and logoi, and opening up an arch of new possibilities for peoplehood and freedom.

The regime downsizes protestors, using silence, force, and language, through state media propaganda. This downsizing is a form of categorization (Alim et al. 2016) in which protestors are exiled to a realm of social incongruity, almost outcasts guilty of anti-social behavior. The regime uses it to put the protestors in their place, as it were. Judgments handed down by courts scripted protestors as disruptive, destructive, offensive, and violent. They denigrated protestors and protest (see Table 5.3 for a sample of charges). This categorization—authoritarianism's nomenclature—represents a semiotic tool deployed by the state to rule by marking out political divisions (DuBois 1998) and reproducing social hierarchies—the counted and the discounted, for Ranciére. The semiotics of anti-systemic protest—in Tunisia and more broadly in the Arab world—is the elephant in the room. How categorized and stigmatized bodies (Fanon 1952) are constructed by authoritarian language is beyond the scope of our analysis. Sufficient to say that the signification involved articulates and disarticulates subjectivities. In this instance, Ben Ali's judges, privileged state employees, pronounced certain features and signs associated with protest and destabilized or mute others. "Protestor" as an indexical (Smith 1989) may disclose a variety of meanings, both positive (ruly, freedom-seeking, self-determining) and negative (unruly, violent, racist). A sample of language from court judgments against protestors from the 2008 uprising communicates fixed meanings and behaviors. Thus, the agency of en-acting emancipatory lives and subjectivities was itself interned by sentencing judges, and not just by the criminalization of actual protestors ordered to stand trial, to be convicted and imprisoned.

Table 5.3 Linguistic Features of Criminal Charges against 2008 Uprising Protestors

Case details	Date	Accusation	Significance
15536; 5 defendants	June 18, 2008	"membership in gang"* "premeditating vandalism and destruction of private property" "disrupting public traffic" "unlicensed possession of explosives [Malotov cocktails]" "throwing hard substances [rocks] on others" "disorderly conduct" "violence against a public servant"	Interprets protestors' behavior as gangster-like, violent, antisocial, inciting violence in public space Morally delegitimizes protest Reverses subject/object binaries and roles (aggressor/victim)
15534; 4 defendants	June 18, 2008	"destruction of private property" "obstructing public traffic" "verbal and physical assault against public servant [security official]" "throwing hard substances [rocks] on others" "unlicensed possession of explosives"	
3117; 8 defendants	June 26, 2008	"obstructing public traffic" "unlicensed possession of explosives" "destruction of private property" "violence against public servant" "creating chaos"	
3269; 1 defendant	June 12, 2008	"obstructing public traffic" "unlicensed possession of explosives" "destruction of private property" "violence against public servant" "creating chaos"	
3150; 8 defendants	June 27, 2008	"obstructing public traffic" "unlicensed possession of explosives" "destruction of private property" "violence against public servant" "creating chaos"	
959; 5 defendants	July 17, 2008	"obstructing public traffic" "unlicensed possession of explosives" "destruction of private property" "violence against public servant" "creating chaos"	
15509; 3 defendants	July 30, 2008	"arson" "destruction of private property" "creating chaos" "disorderly conduct"	

Continued

Table 5.3 *Continued*

Case details	Date	Accusation	Significance
3103; 14 defendants	July 3, 2008	"obstruction of public traffic" "verbal and physical assault on public servant" "creating chaos"	Focuses on social realities leading to protest
3102; 7 defendants	July 4, 2008	"obstruction of public traffic" "throwing hard substances [rocks] on others" "disorderly conduct" "unlicensed possession of explosives" [1 defendant]	
15515; 13 defendants	June 5, 2008	"laying materials [blocking] on train tracks" "verbal attacks and threats against public servant" "violating public morals" "creating chaos" "disorderly conduct" "obstruction of public traffic"	

* *Al-musharakah fi wifaq* is the legal term. On its own, the word *wifaq* translates as "accord."
Source: Collated from primary legal documents of the trials.

Embodied Resisters: Women in Protest

Punitive discourses and sentences denigrate rather than violate the uprising with its stunning community and extra-communal inclusiveness. Women prominently participated, presaging their presence in the 2011 revolution. Old and young, they are unmistakable in grainy documentary video footage. Widows of miners killed on the job pitched tents for an ongoing sit-in in Moularès, demanding jobs for their sons (Al-Arabi 2016). Maya Jribi, Secretary General of the opposition party PDP, visited the widows in their tents, assuring them of the party's "absolute support" for the movement, for "there is no dignity without work."[85] In addition to Leila Khaled, the now deceased Jum'ah Jallabi Hajji (wife of Adnan, also her kidney donor; assaulted by police and hospitalized in April 2008[86]), Afaf Bennaser Boukdous (imprisoned in her student activist days, and wife to Alfahem), Yamnah Shrayti (Workers' Party), and Ghazalah Muhammadi (Progressive Democratic Party) (Bouari 2019, 166–170) were among the well-known female faces of the uprising. Auntie (*Khalti*) 'Aljiah (deceased 2013), her wrinkled face wrapped in a paisley red bandana beneath a white scarf, was the memorable 74 year-old in the front lines, her picture and footage ubiquitous. Uprising leader Adil Jayyar noted in *Curse the Father*, "we discovered the role of women, their steadfast resilience (*sumud*)." Here he invoked a commonly used term in Arab struggles, especially Palestine.

[85] *Tawasul Al-Ihtijajat fi Zill Samt Al-Sultah*, in *Al-Mawqif*, February 8, 2008, p. 6.
[86] *Zawjat Adnan min Al-Masahhah ila Al-Mustashfa*, in *Al-Tariq Al-Jadid*, April 19–25, 2008, p. 5.

As this small sample reflects, Tunisia's female protestors have hailed from different protestscapes. Zakia Difaoui, a journalist, unionist, and member of the Ettakatol opposition party, plodded from Kairouan to observe the uprising. Demands in Gafsa echoed with the discontent of her own, peripheral, and marginalized region. She quickly found herself a participant, only to be jailed (and sexually threatened),[87] sentenced for over four months, and consequently expelled from her secondary teaching job. Wielding a defiant pen, Difaoui wrote a micro-story titled "The Wedding," describing brides (the four towns) who chose "freedom," "dignity," "justice" as their bridegrooms. Disgruntled wealthy barons kidnap the brides, break up the celebrations, make martyrs of young guests, and crowd others into jail cells.[88] The allegory is easy to decipher. Difaoui recalled the women's protest in April 2009. A discernible change was afoot in Gafsa. In describing the phosphate uprising, Difaoui used the term *al-shaʿb*. Whether deliberately or subconsciously, she transformed Gafsa into a metonym for the Tunisian people writ large:

> The people's consciousness began to increase, [regarding] the necessity of demanding [rights]. … I saw victory in the eyes of the female protestors [of which she was one]. It was a stand of pride (*ʿizzah*) and chivalry (*nakhwah*). … They arrested the men, the leaders, and the response of the women was majestic indeed. … This is not strange. … Tunisia was built by a woman. Its history is replete with resistance [of women], who etched fierce epics.[89]

In describing the "chivalry" of women, Difaoui re-appropriated a term often reserved for males, in English as well as Arabic. Referring to the Carthaginian Queen Dido (pre-Arab, pre-Islamic), she placed women, in the present as well as the past, on a par with men as builders of Tunisia, *as resisters*. Difaoui communicated a self-awareness common to Tunisian women across demarcations of ideology, class, or political affiliation. She confirmed and lent credence to the reputation of Tunisia as progressive in the Arab world. Activism in the (then) present day stemmed from a long pedigree of rebellious leadership (see Sadiki 2021, 576–578) in pursuit of rights, of equality, of freedom and dignity. Hers was a self-consciously and explicitly gendered cognition, atop the affect and agency as a participator and narrator, of Tunisia's peoplehood in formation.

Absorbing both women and men, the solidarity and consonance of similar suffering would expand in a confluence of existing protestscapes and the creation of new ones in 2011. Attorneys and opposition activists,[90] many of whom had been UGET or UGTE or university committee members in the 1970s and 1980s; unionists; bloggers and journalists including Alfahim Boukdous from *Alhiwar Altounsi* who was arrested;[91] women; and marginalized Tunisians, including many young people, with

---

[87] As she testified in court, *Al-Fajr News*, September 25, 2008.
[88] Published in *Muwatinun*, newspaper of Ettakatol, and the opposition magazine *Kalimah*, run by Sihem ben Sedrine and her husband.
[89] Interview, October 2, 2022.
[90] *Al-Tariq Al-Jadid*, December 21, 2008 (See Al-Tabbabi 2012, 142).
[91] *Al-Tariq Al-Jadid*, July 19, 2010 (see Al-Tabbabi 2012, 181–183).

no formal organizational membership, all enthusiastically joined in. Some ancillary protests, less well known in accounts of Tunisia's road to revolution, also erupted in nearby Fériana (in Kasserine governorate),[92] in unruly harmony with the phosphate basin. These mini-revolts were similarly repressed by security forces.[93] Arrests and security violence incited the ire of oppositionists including the Progressive Democratic Party[94] (to which Chebbi brothers Nejib and Issam, and Maya Jribi, belonged). The town of Skhira (in Sfax) rose up in February 2010, as young men protested about being passed over for employment in a fertilizer company. Security repression soon followed in this "additional nail in the regime's casket."[95] In the so-called "*Tarawih* uprising" in summer (Ramadan) 2010, residents (including local UGTT members) mobilized to protest the closing of a smuggling route into Libya. Outrage against a new customs duty eventually led to the government's cancelling of the tax (Laroussi 2018; see also Marzouki 2010). The phosphate basin miners had unleashed a new, fast-track round of Tunisia's protest ethos (*al-zakham al-ihtijaji*). It was the storm before the storm.

Conclusion

The phosphate basin uprising that raged between January and July 2008 was memorable for its popular (*sha'bi*) demotic reach, albeit spatially limited to the four mining towns in Gafsa. Regional underdevelopment and multiple marginalization, concentrated in the country's South, became untenable. Residents of the region rose up to vociferously reject the absurdities of immiseration and poverty under a corrupt and dictatorial system. Tunisia's structural and distributive maladies made contact with the individual-collective daily experiences, memories, imaginaries (frustrated anti-colonial dream of independence, freedom, and dignity; Southern rebelliousness), and repositories (protest competencies of local syndicalists) of residents. That even UGTT leaders (e.g. Ammara Abassi) were implicit in the "disappearance" of phosphate wealth was a cause for mobilization, further inflamed by unfair and non-transparent hiring practices. A strikingly organized and steadfast quasi-movement (*harakah*) was born. The periphery-within-the-periphery struck back at the state. We have sought to highlight the ways in which agency (demonstrations, sit-ins, public advocacy), affect (the double consciousness of *hogra*, the empowering strength of solidarity), and cognition (rejection of the indignity of a people robbed of the right to have rights) co-mingled. Residents of Redeyef, Metlaoui, Mdhila, and Moularès displayed remarkable stamina, within and without prison walls. For them, the vicious repression by Ben Ali's security forces indicated the regime's weakness and desperation. The smothering of an uprising in which entire families participated only deepened their resolve to resist. Support by rights activists and attorneys from outside

---

[92] *Haqa'iq Hawla Ahdath Madinat Firyana*, in *Muwatinun*, November 5, 2008, p. 5.
[93] *Musadamat 'Anifah Ithra Ihtijajat Silmiyyah*, in *Al-Tariq Al-Jadid*, June 7–13, 2008, p. 7
[94] *Al-Wasat Al-Tunisiyyah*, June 2, 2008 (see Al-Tabbabi 2012, 186).
[95] *Ahdath Al-Skhira: Mismar Akhar fi Na'sh Al-Nizam*, in *Al-Badil*, February 20, 2010.

Gafsa, including in the capital, they prefigured the kind of spatialized coalition-building that would be sustained and repeated more expansively in 2010–11. There is an aestheticizing effect, that humanizes suffering in a context of dehumanizing the "human condition." In the new genre of sensory narratives about feelings of hogra, kinship, solidarity, and resistance, mining communities freed themselves from the "police" order and logic Rancière condemns. In poetry, documentary-making, lyrical speech acts, and in music, the "part that has no part," lives moments of "dis-incorporating the king," or the autocrat. The uncounted de-link from authoritarian spatiality, materiality, and temporality. In so doing, it turns to sensory experiences as a terrain of new freedoms, a becoming of sorts, to de-police a "police order" of control, divisions, and hierarchies, of uncounting and discounting. Moreover, the phosphate uprising was an "alarm bell. But Ben Ali did not pay heed," as Abdelmajid Sahrawi, longtime UGTT leader, put it.[96] Parallel to months-long publicity and promotion of the phosphate "cause," were ancillary protests in Kasserine, Siliana, and Ben Guerdane (2008–0). These wove a link between the 2008 uprising and the December 2010 flare-up in Sidi Bouzid. As the next chapter details, that agentic event irreparably burst the dam of fear, unleashing a torrential downpour of protests across Tunisia. Activists from the phosphate basin would exuberantly join in. On the three-year anniversary of their uprising's launch, the Protest Movement of Redeyef reminded Tunisians that their 2008 uprising had been the "cornerstone for all social movements in Tunisia from Sidi Bouzid and Kasserine, and all the meadows that rose up yearning for freedom and justice."[97] Their own ongoing struggle inspired and was mirrored in resistance by all of Tunisia's uncounted, partial, and multiple demoi joining the cries of Sidi Bouzid's daring rebels. A revolution in miniature indeed. Revolution was in the works.

References

Abassi, Houcine. 2023. *Tunis wa Al-Furas Al-Mahdurah* [Tunisia's Lost Chances]. Tunis: Nirvana.

Al-Arabi, Huda. 2016. *Nidal Al-Mar'ah Al-Manjimiyyah Min Khilal Ahdath Al-Hawd Al-Manjimi* [Women Miners' Struggles Through the Phosphate Basin Events] *(Gafsa) Tunis (Janvier 2008). Insaniyyat* 74: 29–46.

Al-Hannashi, Abdellatif. 2005. "Aqsa Al-Janub Al-Tunisi: Min Al-Muqawamah Al-'Anifah Al-'Afwiyyah Ila Al-Muqawamah Al-Munazzamah (Aliyyat, Khususiyyat, Wa Hudu Al-Intiqal Wal Intishar). [The Deep Tunisian South: From Spontaneous to Organized Violent Resistance" In *A'mal Al-Nadwah Al-Duwaliyyah Al-Thaniyata 'Ashr Hawla Al-Janub Al-Tunisi min Al-Ihtilal Ila Al-Istiqlal* [Proceedings of the Twelvth International Symposium About the Tunisian South from Occupation to Independence] *1956–1881*, edited by Faisal Cherif. Manouba: University of Tunis, 241–270.

---

[96] Interview, October 26, 2022.
[97] *5 Janvi 2008: Hatta La Nansa . . .* in *Al-Badil*, January 6, 2011.

Al-Harakah Al-Thawriyyah li Tahrir Tunis [Revolutionary Movement to Free Tunisia]. N.d. *Wantalaqat Al-Thawrah min Gafsa.* Tunis.

Alim, Samy, John R. Rickford, and Arnetha F. Ball. 2016. *Raciolinguistics: How Language Shapes our Ideas about Race.* New York: Oxford University Press.

Aljazeera. 2012. *Witness to the Revolution: Lina Ben Mhenni (1).* https://bit.ly/3CGbItl

Al-Khashnawi, Naji, 2022. *Al-Majmu'at Al-Musiqiyyah Al-Multazimah: Min Al-Aghani Al-Muharrabah ila Al-Firaq Al-Muharrarah, Al-Sha'b News,* May 6, https://bit.ly/3M5V2hY

Al-Mahjoubi, Ali. 2015. *Al-Harakah Al-Naqabiyyah Al-Tunisiyyah Al-Shaghilah: Baina Al-Nidal Al-Ijtima'i wa Al-Nidal Al-Siyasi.* [Tunisia's Labor Union Movement]. Tunis: Nuzur.

Al-Mukni, Abdelwahed. 2005. *"Ahali Al-Janub Al-Tunisi bi Al-Hadarah Khilal Al-Fatrah Al-Isti'mariyyah: Al-Khasai'is wal Ishamat"* [Tunisia's Southerners]. In *A'mal Al-Nadwah Al-Duwaliyyah Al-Thaniyata 'Ashrah Hawla Al-Janub Al-Tunisi min Al-Ihtilal Ila Al-Istiqlal 1956–1881*, edited by Faisal Cherif. Manouba: University of Tunis, 21–41.

Al-Qasantini, Alkrrai. 2012. *Haqiqat Al-'Alaqah Baina Al-Hizb Al-Hurr Al-Destouri Al-Tunisi wa Jami'at 'Umoom Al-'Amalah Al-Tunisiyyah* [The Truth About the Relationship Between the Tunisian Free Destour Party and the CGTT] *(1924–1925).* Tunis: University of Manouba.

Al-Salehi, Al-Saghir. 2017. *Al-Isti'maar al-Dakhili wa Al-Tanmiyah ghair al-Mutakaafi'ah: Manzumat al-'Tahmish' fi Tunis Namudhajan* [Internal Colonization and Unequal Development: The Archeology of 'Marginalization' in Tunisia]. Tunis: Al-Sharikah al-Tunisyyah lil-Nashr.

Al-Shabbi, Mohamed Lutfi. 2015. *Al-Harakah Al-Wataniyyah Al-Tunisiyyah wa Al-Mas'alah Al-'Ummaliyyah-Al-Naqabiyyah* [The Tunisian Nationalist Movement and the Labor Union Issue], Part 1 1894–1924, 2nd edn. Manouba: Markaz Al-Nashr Al-Jami'i.

Al-Tabbabi, Hfayez. 2005. *"'Alam Yanhar wa 'Alam fi Tawr Al-Tashkil: Hawla Azmat Al-Mujtama' Al-Ra'awi Al-Taqlidi Khilal Al-Fatrah Al-Isti'mariyyah wa Masar Ikhda 'Al-Badawah (Mithal Jihat Gafsa)* [A World Disintegrating and Another World Taking Shape]." In *A'mal Al-Nadwah Al-Duwaliyyah Al-Thaniyah 'Ashar: Hawla Al-Janub Al-Tunisi Min Al-Ihtilal Ila Al-Istiqlal 1881–1956*, Compiled by Faisal Cherif. Manouba: Al-Ma'had Al-'Ali li Tarikh Al-Harakah Al-Wataniyyah.

Al-Tabbabi, Hfayez. 2012. *Intifadat Al-Hawd Al-Manjimi bi Gafsa* [The Phosphate Basin Uprising in Gafsa]. Tunis: Al-Dar Al-Tunisiyyah lil Kitab.

Al-Tabbabi, Khaled. 2019. *Al-Rihanat al-Ijtima'iyyah wa Al-Iqtisadiyyah li Al-tashghil Al-hash: Sharikat Al-bi'ah wa Al-ghirasah wa Al-bastanah bi Al-hawd Al-Manjimi Namoodhajan* [Social and Political Stakes of Precarious Employment: The Case of Environment and Landscape Company in the Phosphate Basin]. FTDES.

Al-Taimoumi, Alhadi. 2020. *Mawsu'at Al-Rabi' Al-'Arabi fi Tunis 2010–2020: Al-Juz' al-Awwal: Sanat Kul Al-Makhater* [Encyclopedia of the Arab Spring in Tunisia: Part One, The Year of All Dangers] 2nd edn. Sfax: Dar Mohammad li Al-Nashr.

Al-Taimoumi, Al-Hadi. 2021. *Tarikh Tunis Al-Ijtima'i* [Tunisia's Social History] 1956–1881. Sfax: Dar Mohamed Ali.

Al-Thabti, Adel. 2017. *Al-Ittihad Al-'Amm Al-Tunisi Li Al-Talabah: Khalfiyyat Al-Ta'sis Wa-Ma'alat Al-Masar* [The UGTE: Founding Background and Ends of the Journey]. Tunis: Maktabat Tunis Lil-Nashr.

Al-Yahyahoui, Jamal. 2005. "Mahattat min al-Muqawamah Al-Tunisiyyah fi Al-Janub Min Khilal Watha'iq Arshifiyyah [Milestones of Tunisia's Resistance in the South Through Archival Documents]." In *A'mal Al-Nadwah Al-Duwaliyyah Al-Thaniyata 'Ashrah Hawla Al-Janub Al-Tunisi min Al-Ihtilal Ila Al-Istiqlal 1956–1881*, edited by Faisal Cherif. Manouba: University of Tunis, 229–240.

Amin, Samir. 1997. Capitalism in the Age of Globalization. London: Zed Books.

Amnesty International. 2009. *Behind Tunisia's "Economic Miracle": Inequality and Criminalization of Protest*. https://www.amnesty.org/download/Documents/48000/mde300032009en.pdf

Amrousiyyah, Ammar. 2008. *Intifadat Al-Hawd Al-Manjimi*, 4 June, *Al-Hiwar Al-Mutamaddin*, https://www.ahewar.org/debat/show.art.asp?aid=136771

Angrist, Michele Penner. 2013. "Understanding the Success of Mass Civic Protest in Tunisia." *Middle East Journal* 67(4): 547–564.

Arfaoui, Khmayyes. 2020. *Al-Harakat Al-Ijtima'iyyah fi Tunis min Al-Ihtijaj ila Al-Thawrah* [Tunisia's Social Movements from Protest to Revolution]. Tunis: Dar Sihr lil-Nashr.

Bashir, Riadh. 2018. "*Al-Tafawut al-Tanmawi fi Tunis: Qabl al-Thawrah wa Ba'daha* [Economic Inequality in Tunisia: Before and After the Revolution]." *Al-Mustaqbal al-Arabi* 468(40): 80.

Belhoula, Moncef. 2015. *Mudhakkirat Naqabi: Al-Haqa'iq Al-Makhfiyyah fi Al-Tarikh Al-Mu 'asir li Al-Ittihad Al-'Amm Al-Tunisi li Al-Shughl* [Memoirs of a Unionist: Hidden Truths in the History of the UGTT]. Ariana: Al-Magharibiyyah Li Tiba'at Wa Ishhar Al-Kitab.

Ben Ali, Z. A. 2009. *Al-Tanmiyah al-Jihawiyyah Sanad wa Ithra' li Al-Tanmiyah al-Wataniyyah* [Regional Development: Supporting and Enriching National Development], *Turess*, October 15. Accessed November 3, 2018. https://www.turess.com/assabah/25525.

Ben Mim, Hammadi. 2019. *Asrar al-Thawrah al-Tunisiyyah: Qiyadatiha, Asbabiha, 'Awamil Najahiha wa Al-Durus* [Secrets of the Tunisian Revolution: Its Issues, Causes, Factors of Success, and Lessons]. Monastir: Al-Thaqafiyyah lil Tiba'ah wal Nashr wa al-Tawzee'.

Ben Yousef, Adil. 2019. *Al-Masar Al-Thawri wa Al-Intiqal Al-Dimuqrati fi Tunis (Min Khilal Al-Watha'iq)* [The Revolutionary Trajectory and Democratic Transition in Tunis (Through Documents)] *2008–2011*: Sfax: Maktabat Ala'eddin.

Bouari, Sakinah, Sulaima Majladi Mansouri, and Lutfi Al-Saddi. 2019. *Musharakat Al-Nisa' fi Al-Hayat Al-'Ammah wa Al-Siyasiyyah fi Wilayatay Gabes wa Gafsa: Mash Maidani* [Women's Participation in Public and Political Life in Gabes and Gafsa : A Survey]. Tunis: Kawthar.

Bourguiba, Habib. 1966. "The Tunisian Way." Foreign Affairs. Accessed May 18, 2018, https://www.foreignaffairs.com/articles/tunisia/1966-04-01/tunisian-way.

Bourguiba, Habib. 1974. *Speeches: Vol. 8* (Tunis: *Kitabat al-Dawlah lil-I'lam*.

Brahmi, Mohsen and Sonia Ghorbel-Zouari. 2012. "Historical Timeline, Global Positioning and Economic Performance: The Case of a Tunisia Public Mining Firm." *International Research Journal of Geology and Mining* 2(4): 88–102.

Butler, Judith. 1988. "Performative Acts and Gender Constitution: An Essay in Phenomenology and Feminist Theory." *Theatre Journal* 40(4): 519–531.

Casanova, Pablo G. 1965. "Internal Colonialism and National Development." *Studies in Comparative International Development* 1(4): 27–37.

Chebbi, Ahmed Najib. 2022. *Al-Masirah Wa Al-Masar: Ma Jara wa Ma 'Ara* [The Journey and the Path: What Happened and What I Believe]. Tunis: Mots Passants.

Della Porta, Donna, ed. 2017. *Global Diffusion of Protest. Riding the Protest Wave in the Neoliberal Crisis*. Chicago: University of Chicago Press.

DuBois, W. E. B. 1998. *Black Reconstruction in America, 1860–1880*. New York: Free Press.

Fanon, Frantz. 1952. *Black Skin, White Masks*. New York: Grove Press.

Ghilès, Francis and Eckwart Woertz. 2018. "Tunisian Phosphates and the Politics of the Periphery." In *Environmental Politics in the Middle East*, edited by Harry Verhoeven. New York: Oxford University Press, 53–74.

Gobe, Eric. 2010. "The Gafsa Mining Basin between Riots and a Social Movement: Meaning and Significance of a Protest Movement in Ben Ali's Tunisia." halshs-00557826

Gunder Frank, Andre. 1966. "The Development of Underdevelopment." *Monthly Review* 18(4). Accessed May 15, 2018. http://s3-euw1-ap-pe-ws4-cws-documents.ri-prod.s3.amazonaws.com/9781138824287/ch10/1._Andre_Gunder_Frank,_The_Development_of_Underdevelopment,_1966.pdf.

Haddad, Tahar. 2015 [1927]. *Al-'Ummal Al-Tunisiyyun wa Dhuhur Al-Harakah Al-Naqabiyyah* [Tunisian Workers and the Emergence of the Labor Movement]. Sfax: Dar Samed.

Harvey, David. 2006. *Spaces of Global Capitalism: Towards a Theory of Uneven Geographic Development*. Brooklyn, NY: Verso

Ibn Khaldun. 1984. *Al-Muqaddimah*, ed. J. Shaykhah. Tunis: Al-Dar Al-Tunisiyyah Lil-Nashr.

Instance Verité and Dignité. 2016. Testimoy of Bashir Laabid and His Wife: Public Listening Session 18 November. https://www.youtube.com/watch?v=pjLc0Rqgc4g

Khashanah, Rashid. 2021. *Maya Jribi: Ayqunah Tunisiyyah*. Tunis: Masarat.

Laabidi, Bechir. 2015. *Sharikat Fusfat Gafsa: "Riza Al-Bilik." Hal Yatawaqqaf Al-Nazif?* January 27, Nawaat, https://bit.ly/3VSOzLH

Laroussi, Kamel. 2018. *Al-Tijarah al-Muwaziyah wa Al-Tahrib fi Al-Fada' al-Hududi al-Tunisi-al-Libi (1988–2012): Tashkhis wa Afaq fi Zill 'Awlamah Mutakhafiyyah* [Parallel Trade and Smuggling at the Tunisian-Libyan Border Space (1988–2012): Status Quo and Prospects within a Hidden Globalization]. Doha: Doha Institute.

Lefebvre, Henri. 1971. *Everyday Life in the Modern World*. New York: Harper & Row.

Lefebvre, Henri. 1979. "Space: Social Product and Use Value." In *Critical Sociology: European Perspectives*, edited by J. W. Freiburg. New York: Irvington, 1979, 285–295.

Lefebvre, Henri. 1991. *The Production of Space*. Oxford: Blackwell.

Lefebvre, Henri. 2003. *The Urban Revolution*. Minneapolis: University of Minnesota Press.

Marzouki, Moncef. 2010. "Ben Guerdane: *Intifadah Muzaffarah*." August 21, Nawaat, https://bit.ly/3EuukxP

Murphy, Emma. 1999. *Economic and Political Change in Tunisia: From Bourguiba to Ben Ali*. New York: Mcmillan Press Ltd.

Nawaat. 2017. *Al-Talawwuth fi Redeyef : La'nat Al-Fusfat*. https://bit.ly/3CrWHtF

Nostalgia Adab. 2014. *Nashid Al-Sha'b: Firqat Awlad Al-Manajim*. [Song of the People: Sons of the Mines Band] https://www.youtube.com/watch?v=L_m1bSpHxz0

Perkins, Kenneth. 2014. *A History of Modern Tunisia*, 2nd edn. Cambridge: Cambridge University Press.

Guessoumi, Mouldi. 2012. "*Al-Mujtama' wa Al-Mujtama' Al-Muwazi: Shurut al-Talazum Al-Bunyawi wa Al-Infisal Al-Wazifi* [Society and Parallel Society: The Conditions of Structural Concomitance and Functional Separation]." In *Al-Mujatma' Al-Muwazi Baina Al-Hamishiyyah wa Al-Wazifiyyah* [Parallel Society: Between the Marginal and the Functional], Ed. Alkrrai Al-Qasantini. Tunis: University of Manouba Press, 29–68.

Radio Mines FM. 2011. *Awlad Al-Manajim: Shahadat Faqr:* Sons of the Mines: Degree in Poverty. https://www.youtube.com/watch?v=gQWKA7qzYjk

Rancière, Jacques. 2002. "The Aesthetic Revolution and its Outcomes: Emplotments of Autonomy and Heteronomy." *New Left Review*, 14(March–April): 133–150.

Rawa'i' Al-Fann Wal Adab Al-Multazim. 2019. *Al-Damoos…Awlad Al-Manajim*, https://www.youtube.com/watch?v=83bvhShzqOM

Reed, T. V. 2019. *The Art of Protest: Culture and Activism from the Civil Rights Movement to the Present*, 2nd edn. Minneapolis: University of Minnesota Press.

Riofrancos, Thea. 2020. *Resource Radicals: From Petro-Nationalism to Post-Extractivism in Ecuador*. Durham, NC: Duke University Press.

Sadiki, Larbi. 2019. Regional Development in Tunisia: The Consequences of Multiple Marginalization. Policy Briefing, Brookings Doha Center. https://www.brookings.edu/wp-content/uploads/2019/01/Regional-development-in-Tunisia-the-consequences-of-multiple-marginalization_English-Web.pdf.

Sadiki, Larbi. 2021. "Cascading Liberation and Renewal—Tunisia in History." In *The Oxford Handbook of Contemporary Middle Eastern and North African History*, edited by Amal Ghazal and Jens Hanssen. Oxford: Oxford University Press, 572–591.

Sen, Amartya. 1999. *Development as Freedom.* Oxford: Oxford University Press.

Smith, Quentin. 1989. "The Multiple Uses of Indexicals." *Synthese* 78: 167–190.

UGTT. 2010. *Al-Tanmiyah al-Jihawiyyah bi Wilayat Sidi Bouzid: Baina Al-Waqi' al-Mukabbal wa Al-Imkanat Al-Wa'idah* [Regional Development in Sidi Bouzid: Between the Limitations of Reality and Promising Capacities]. Tunis: UGTT Press.

Vanderwalle, Dirk. 1988. "From the New State to the New Era: Toward a Second Republic in Tunisia." *Middle East Journal* 42(4): 602–620.

Vatthauer, J.-P., and Weipert-Fenner, I. 2017. *The Quest for Social Justice in Tunisia: Socioeconomic Protest and Political Democratization post 2011.* (PRIF Reports, 143). Frankfurt am Main: Hessische Stiftung Friedens- und Konfliktforschung. https://nbn-resolving.org/urn:nbn:de:0168-ssoar-51866-3

Walsh, Alex. 2021. "The Contentious Politics of Tunisia's Natural Resource Management and the Prospects of the Renewable Energy Transition." February 15, *K4D Helpdesk Report.*

Wieder, Alan. 2004. "Testimony as Oral History: Lessons from South Africa." *Educational Researcher* 33(6): 23–28.

Zemni, Sami. 2017. "The Tunisian Revolution: Neoliberalism, Urban Contentious Politics and the Right to the City." *International Journal of Urban and Regional Research* 41(1): 70–83.

Ziyadah, Isa. 2021. *Qadiyyat Naql Al-Fusfat: 16 Muttahaman, 3 'Uqood wa Malayin Al-Atnan Ghair Al-Manqulah Sanawiyan* [The Phosphate Transportation Case: Sixteen Defendants, Three Contracts, and Hundreds of Un-Transported Tons Annually]. August 20, Inkyfada, https://bit.ly/3gEEgdS

6
Becoming in Diachrony
The Revolution of 2011

Ben Ali had fled, but the revolution was far from over. Taking off from Sidi Bouzid where it had all begun, activists marched towards the capital on foot, to Meknassy, to Regueb. In mid-January, a convoy set off from "deep Tunisia." The goal was to complete the revolution made by this indignant and determined people. Mohamed Ghannouchi's interim government must go, and so must Ben Ali's hated RCD party. Over the past few weeks, young Tunisians had marshalled their multidimensional agency: the persuasive force of voices crying out in unison, the energetic power of bodies congregating close together, differences momentarily melting away. These young men and women had overcome fear even when confronting the dreaded police. Arriving in the capital, joined by other young activists, they occupied Kasbah Square, literally staring down state power in the face. The symbolism of such "appearing" was unmistakable. "The people want the fall of the regime!" they chanted, setting up tents, sleeping under blankets in the cold air and the pouring rain. Volunteers passed out milk for breakfast, sandwiches for lunch. Crowds erupted into song, activists scrawled graffiti onto hallowed walls. Children climbed onto their parents' shoulders, women stood alongside men, and youth watched over the elderly. No political parties were allowed, no "bureaucratized" civil society. Premier Mohamed Ghannouchi reshuffled his cabinet on January 27. Just a partial victory. Military and security forces rolled in, deploying their handy tear gas.[1] But the job was not yet complete. Breaking through the police barriers, throngs of Tunisians again infiltrated Kasbah Square the following month. Their mission required more creativity, more of "the people" (al-sha'b). Activists from the interior and southern regions (jihat) remained. Some carried bullets fired at loved ones around their necks. Constant reminders of sacrifice in pursuit of peoplehood. This time, political parties were welcome. The UGTT and lawyers' syndicates flocked to Kasbah. Tunisia's own million-strong sit-in (malyuniyyah) was literally emptying out the center of authoritarian power. The people crowned themselves as sovereign. The Kasbah 2 ("departure sit-in") crowd formed committees, issued statements, agreed and disagreed over political futures and possibilities in hundreds of "discussion circles." On February 27, 2011 Ghannouchi resigned, and his transitional government collapsed. The protestors ended the sit-in, departing on buses made curiously, quickly available. Endlessly contested narratives complicate recollections and interpretations of those days. One thing is certain, however. The dogged determination of the Kasbah crowds catapulted Tunisia's demos into long-deferred peoplehood. If even for a moment, revolutionary rebirth was theirs.

---

[1] See *Al-Qanabil Al-Musayyilah li Al-Dumu' lam Tufarriq Al-Mutazahirin bal Qatalathum*, *Al-Sabah*, January 31, 2011.

Revolution and Democracy in Tunisia. Larbi Sadiki and Layla Saleh, Oxford University Press.
© Larbi Sadiki and Layla Saleh (2024). DOI: 10.1093/oso/9780192863997.003.0006

Introduction

The watershed Tunisian revolution is far too complex to be "written" as a simple chronology. In this chapter, we seek to explore the agentic, affective, and cognitive dimensions through which Tunisian peoplehood fulminated. The diachrony and synchrony of the country's revolutionary milieu, its protest ethos (*zakham ihtijaji*), came to a head in 2010–11. The chapter dwells on the ways in which the multiple streams of protest gradually merged in a single, popular torrent that in unison bellowed "Dégage!" to Ben Ali on January 14, 2011. We draw on original interviews and published Tunisian testimonies (*shahadat*). These are unique sources of oral history. The testimonies of revolutionaries and Kasbah participants, including but not limited to those orally delivered and recorded in print by the Tamimi Foundation, are significant as counter-narratives. Written archives of the revolution, digital and printed, are scattered across individuals, civil society, multiple government ministries, and even foreign embassies (Ben Yousef 2019, 394–395). Additionally, we refer to print media and social media sources, and the indigenous primary and secondary sourcing of Tunisian historiographers and sociologists. The oral history testimonies, whether the published *shahadat*, our own interviews, or (social) media accounts, do not adhere to the "stages" marked out by social scientists, however (revolution, then the takeoff of democratic transition). The roving restlessness of memory may jumble their recounting. Such jumps between the past and present, history and future of revolution are welcome. They enrich our re-ontologization and confirm the revolutionary sublimation of space and time.

Our approach to Tunisia's revolution is an open-ended one that shies away from sharp "start" and "finish" delineations. However, for the purposes of analysis and readability, we define a scope of events rendered as the protestscape, with its relational nature. After elaborating on the revolution's diachrony and its "carnivalesque" features, we begin with Mohamed Bouazizi's well-known self-immolation on December 17 that launched this synchrony. The chapter then moves through Ben Ali's departure on January 14, 2011, dwelling on marginalization and suffering as drivers of revolutionary counteraction. Next, the chapter lays out interpretations of the participation by the young and women. While analyses of the Tunisian revolution tend to stop at Ben Ali's night-stealth departure, we proceed to the Kasbah 1 and 2 sit-ins that drove out the interim government and solidified a rupture with the January 14, 2011 authoritarian era. There would be no winding back the clock of Tunisian history. It was at these junctures, we argue, that ongoing social doing entrenched both revolutionary release from authoritarianism and the crowning of peoplehood.

The revolution protestscape we attempt to concretize here is multiply "situated," an amalgam of existing dissentscapes joined by untethered youth joining the fray. We highlight three interrelated patterns in our analysis. First is the collapse of space and time in the revolution in a kind of Bakhtinian "carnival." It is the long-promised rendezvous between synchrony (both the disparate protestscapes visualized in previous chapters, as well as the spatio-geographic spread of the revolution from Sidi Bouzid to Tunis) and diachrony (temporalization of the historical footsteps echoed in the march of the revolutionaries: 1864, 1956, 1978, 1984, etc.). Second, the chapter relays the immense struggles for peoplehood spurred by and emanating from revolt. It was no revolution of a "jasmine"-scented (Omri 2011; see also Leisir 2012, 269–270), leisurely stroll. From the multiple marginalization of Gafsa mining towns and Sidi Bouzid to the repression protestors encountered in Redeyef, Menzel Bouzaiane,[2] or Mohamed Ali and Kasbah squares in Tunis, a series of "battles" is a more apt phrasing. The cost of shedding the "non-people" label is dear indeed, extracted most painfully from those imprisoned and tortured, injured and martyred. Lived trauma inhabits the vestiges of peoplehood, singed in revolutionary fires. Our critical-leaning analysis as scholars impels us to acknowledge and honor the suffering of Tunisians, in 2008, 2011, even decades before. Third, the various protestscape "estuaries" meeting like bodies of indignants in the sea of revolution. This was also the juncture at which "the people" provisionally coalesced in relational becoming. This is integral to re-ontologization. It is not just the "wall of fear" that protestors blasted asunder. Tunisia's revolutionaries also broke down the walls between them, if only ephemerally. The self folded into the other, and vice versa. Kasbah square, in particular, was the birthplace of a Tunisian demos that demanded, deliberated, contested, and distributed mutually conferred recognition. Intersectional links formed a coherent, if unwieldy, shape of an em-bodied people that, through performances and appearances of simultaneous and iterative social acting and en-acting, cognized themselves as such. Never complete, peoplehood is as messy, unsettling, and discordant as it is creative, invigorating and uplifting.

In this suspension of space and time, revolutionary protest summoned up the struggles, sacrifices, and insurrectionary savoire-faire that had wrestled with colonial and authoritarian powers since the Tunisian crucible of the 1860s. The social imaginaries (*mikhyal*) and repositories (*makhzun*) of a people-in-becoming, their dreams, counter-memories, learned protest competencies, imaginings and self-understandings, all exploded in this dramatic, stretched-out moment of rebirth.

Revolutionary Diachrony as "Carnival"

A Diachrony of Protest

We claim that protestscapes constitute the *sine qua non* of Tunisia's revolution. They form an epistemological toolkit for knowing the revolution, for interpreting it in the Tunisian context: the convergence of embodied experiences of protest-in-context,

---

[2] Yielding casualties or "martyrs." See *Shahid Akhar min Menzel Bouzaiane wa Tawasul Al-Ihtijajat Raghma Ihtidad Al-Qam*, in *Al-Badil*, Dec. 31, 2010.

insurgent subjectivities-in-context, and learning-in-context. The case made here is that revolution—not unlike language—evolves spatio-temporally. It is diachronic fruition. This does not imply pre-determinism. Rather, revolutionary diachrony is loosely incubated in the spatialities (Gafsa, Sidi Bouzid, Thela, Kasserine, Tunis) of synchronically recurring protests. What is implicit here is a synoptic grasp of the evolution of Tunisia's revolution over time that is based on extended protest activisms and repeated struggles, as elaborated in the diverse protestscapes at various times through history (1978, 1984, 2008, 2010–11). These are flashpoints in particular spaces (see Table 6.1) when social actors with multiple forms of demos and logos took to the public squares (Foucault's "other spaces") to "contest," "invert," and demonstrate. In so doing, at recurring points in time these actors sustained a revolutionary journey the end of which they neither fixed nor controlled. However, what they could control was keeping alive the moral flame of emancipatory becoming. Here lies diachronic unraveling in prior garnering of ontologically-driven wills to upgrade existence from subjection to peoplehood. To that end, revolutionary diachrony was embedded in the synchronies in which Tunisia's indignants sculptured agentic know-how and protest competency, centennial "reservoirs" of affect of indignation, solidarity, and sacrifice, matched by cognitive learning-in-context and self-understanding constitutive of peoplehood. The revolution happened. The protestors did not choose its timing. However, the horizon of revolution was plotted along static times in Tunisia's dynamic and evolving history, a history pulsating with a remarkable people's knack for defiance. An explosion of the aesthetics of rebellion known in all human revolutions descended upon Tunisians: clenched fists, cries of dignity and freedom, craving "the instigating call," and the tightening of hands at the jugular veins of oppression, misery, *hogra*, and the historical "miscounting" of "the part that has no part." It was an explosion of the groundswell emotion and motion of pent-up yearnings due to deterritorializing and reterritorializing.

Hence, the intermarriage between synchrony and diachrony in the Tunisian revolution is more than just a metaphor. What happened in 2011 surpasses a simple aggregative moment where various groups melded together, marching, chanting and demonstrating *en masse*. Rather, it is the overlapping experiences, skills, and memories, aided by the "learning loop" discussed in the student protestscape (Chapter 4), which converged in those fast-paced days of revolution. If the revolutionary spark lit by Mohamed Bouazizi on December 17 was spontaneous, its spread (spatially, temporally, geographically, popularly) was decades in the making. The interconnectedness of protestscapes is difficult to exaggerate. Unionists who taught high school students, who became university activists and then union members or high school teachers or both, went on to teach a new generation of Tunisian youth, taking them in at the UGTT headquarters when protests tore through the tribally linked, proverbial Southern "protest triangle": Sidi Bouzid, Kasserine, and Gafsa and then outward. Interviews[3] and other testimonies explored in this chapter corroborate

---

[3] Interview with Mehdi Abdeljawad, UGTT cadre, July 24, 2022, Tunis.

Table 6.1 Old and New Protest Geographies

Province/City	Pre-2011 Protests and Events	2011 Revolution Protests
BIZERTE	Battle of Bizerte 1961: anti-colonial protests and fighting	Anti-regime protests (Dec. 2010–Jan. 2011)
GAFSA	Miners' strikes (1920s–1930s) Anti-Colonial Battles (e.g. Djebel Orbata, 1954) Miners' strikes (1977) 1984 Bread Riots Phosphate Uprising (2008)	Anti-Regime protest (Dec. 2010–Jan. 2011)
KAIROUAN	Home to Ali Ben Ghedhahem, who launched revolt from Central-West (1864) Anticolonial battles (1881)	Anti-regime protests (Dec. 2010–Jan. 2011)
KASSERINE	Farashish Uprising (1905) Feriana protests (2008)	Protests in Thela and across the province (Dec. 2010–Jan. 2011)
KEBILI	Anti-colonial Maraziq uprising (1943–1944) Bread riots began in Douz, Dec. 1983	Anti-regime protests (Dec. 2010–Jan. 2011)
KEF	Anti-colonial Maraziq uprising (1943–1944)	Anti-regime protests (Dec. 2010–Jan. 2011)
MONASTIR	Anti-colonial battles (1950s) Ksar Hellal Protests (1977)	Anti-Regime protests (Dec. 2010–Jan. 2011)
MEDENINE	Ben Guerdane uprising (August 2010)	Anti-Regime protests (Dec. 2010–Jan. 2011)
SFAX	Anti-colonial protests (1951; 1954) 1955 Neo-Destour party: Ben Youssef expelled, prompting protest opposition among supporters Skhira protests (Feb. 2010)	Anti-Regime protests (Dec. 2010–Jan. 2011)
SIDI BOUZID	1864 Revolution (Mansour Ben Faraj Ben Mansour Ben Dahr jailed) Anti-colonial *fellaga* battles (e.g. Jebel Gebrar, 1954)	Dec. 17, 2010 self-immolation (Bouazizi) and protests
SOUSSE	Civil disobedience (not paying taxes) and armed rebellion by tribes and businesspeople, joining Ali Ben Ghedhahem's 1864 revolt	Anti-regime protests (Dec. 2010–Jan, including Jan. 14, 2011)
TATAOUINE	Anti-colonial Remtha battle (1915) Youssefist support (1950s)	Anti-regime protests (Dec. 2010–Jan. 2011)
TUNIS	Battle of Al-Jallaz (1911) Tramway protests (1914) Protests for parliament (1938) General Strike (1978) Bread Riots (1984)	Anti-regime protests (Dec.–Jan. 2011) Kasbah sit-ins (Feb.–March. 2011)

Sources: For Sidi Bouzid and Sousse: Al-Habbashi (2019, 47–49, 51); Al-Mahjoubi (1986, 43–58); see also Ben Salah (1989); for Sfax: Ben Abbas (2021, 209–220; 230–237; 315–339).

parts of this chain. *Links* (through memory, through protest pedagogy, through direct encounters) between "veteran" activists and first-time protestors shorten the distances between protestscapes, knitting them together. Such was the revolution constructed.

Another point bears stressing. There is a constitutive substance to protest as much as a normative content. All kinds of cognitive ontologies transpire and transmute throughout the revolutionary élan. So does the ethical compass ensconced in protest. Within that compass—morphing un-freedom into freedom, subjection into peoplehood, worthlessness into dignity, and inequity into equality—lie higher moral goals. Here we disagree with the abstractions offered by Yadh Ben Achour, who regards revolution as incommensurate with ethics (2023). Tunisians render their moral goals concrete. Ethical aims warrant sacrifice, suffering, and survival to sustain the agentic charge in order to fight another day, in another locale. Thus, an affective overload carries over across time and space, from generation to generation. In a constitutive sense, too, diverse social imaginaries and attendant speech acts keep the moral flame of protest alive. They relationally vie to interpret complex realities in postcolonial and authoritarian contexts through social doing, speaking, and writing back. Similarly, as we argued in Chapter 2, the protestscape features as an epistemology that interprets protests synchronically in ways that grasps their intersubjectivity, partiality, materiality, and locality. This is relevant for an understanding of the ontological connection with the spatiality and temporality of social acting and en-acting across political, ideological, regional, and socio-economic divides. Yet, one divide unites them: the colonizer–colonized tension that perennially implicates them in adventitious (imperialist structures of power) and nativist/authoritarian dyads (privileging of Euro-American-trained over religious elites, of rich regions over poor ones, and of certain discourses and imaginaries over others). Speaking and social acting across such divides in Tunisia's protestscapes is structurally rooted in postcolonizing and decolonizing (Tunisian–Tunisian) polarities. Thus, since independence, civic engagement, old and new, has engendered struggles intent on overcoming the distortions of both processes. That is, the right environment was created for refashioning an emancipatory cultural project the scope of which could not possibly be met by a single rebelscape, discourse, or lone political force.

Bakhtin in the Revolution

As synchrony and diachrony fused, Tunisia's diverse rebels flowed into the revolution's public squares. So did their sets of agency, affect, and cognition. A precedent arrived. The people were un-governed. The people briefly self-governed. The inherent complexities comprising the culmination of 2011, the spatio-temporal meeting-points of Tunisia's dissentscapes and the people who act and en-act them entered the revolutionary stage. Past and present, leftist and Islamist imaginaries, worker and (opposition) party leader, man and woman, young and old, *beldi* and *afaqi*, veteran and novice protestor, all collapsed into the dramatic moment of revolution. They came together in the decisive events of 2011 that unfolded in Habib Bourguiba Avenue, Kasbah Square, etc. Mikhail Bakhtin (1984) offers the useful and provocative analytic frame of "carnival" to unpack such generative, restorative contradictions and "ambiguity." His example of Renaissance festivals where "folk culture" was on full display inspires analysis of the similarly subversive occasion, albeit more serious and less fixated on laughter, that is the Tunisian revolution. Bakhtin explores "the experience of revolution, the swirling up of meaning that it brought forth, the experience of the plurality of worlds, of the intercrossing of cultures and languages, of texts, and genres" (Lachmann et al. 1988–89, 117). The embodied insistence on the people's will (*al-sha'b yurid*), the cacophony of coastal (*Sahel*) and Southern *(Janubi)* dialects, the multi-layered texts (slogans, songs, statements, YouTube video clips, graffiti), all "swirl up" dominant meanings. They invert the power arrangements where the singular ruler (Ben Ali and before him *al-za'im* Bourguiba) is king, his will the final word. Tunisians, like the medieval revelers Bakhtin considers, overturned and replaced the reigning narratives and power hierarchies (authoritarian state–rebellious society) not just with their tongues, but also with their bodies. What Lachmann et al. (1988–89, 151) call Bakhtin's "somatic semiotics" are central to carnival. People inscribed on and through their bodies their refusal to accept formidable authority, its symbols and even comportments implying deference and submissive order: the raucous crowds in Habib Bourguiba Avenue, the *malyuniyyah* in Kasbah, the stone-throwing youth in Menzel Bouzaiane or Thela with their full-throated calls ("Work, freedom, social justice!" or "Employment is an achieved [right], you gang of thieves!"). Defiance emanated from bodies marked by lived deprivation and mounting memories of misery. These examples all reflect the pivotal position of em-bodied acts and en-actments in the (many and diverse) appearances of protest.

In carnival's chaotic conflagration there is an all-consuming participation by the people with the full gamut of unruly aesthetics finding expression in the revolution. "Carnival is not a spectacle seen by the people; they live in it, and everyone participates because its very idea embraces all the people. While carnival lasts, there is no other life outside it. During carnival time life is subject only to its laws, that is, the laws of its own freedom. It has a universal spirit; it is a special condition of the entire world, of the world's revival and renewal, in which all take part" (Bakhtin 1984, 7). Time and space almost freeze, their respective linearity and distances subsumed under the haze of a people-making celebration. Carnival, continues Bakhtin, is the "feast of becoming, change, and renewal," stripping social order of "all hierarchical rank, privileges, norms, and prohibitions" (1984, 10). This festival of the people convolutes conventional wisdom and the authority of traditional power-holders. It oozes a "peculiar logic of the 'inside out' and the 'turnabout,'" or the "continual shifting from top to bottom, from front to rear ... . comic crownings and un-crownings" (Bakhtin 1984, 11). How Bakhtin's "folk" muster the audacity to "invert" all that is normal (and oppressive) is also worth noting. Laughter, for Bakhtin, chases away fear to wreak this "inside out" havoc. "Complete liberty is possible only in the completely fearless world," he adds (Bakhtin 1984, 47). Breaking the barrier of fear is a well-known sentiment, an internal affective leap turned outward by Tunisian (and later other Arab Spring) protestors. The contingency Bakhtin suggests between "complete liberty" and fearlessness squares with activist narrations of how and why they decided to act, join a protest, utter a revolutionary chant, confront security forces, participate in a sit-in adjacent to the Tunisian Prime Minister's quarters, etc.

In December 2011, a march (*zahf*) moved from the peripheries towards the center. The fire of rebellion flared up in the South, long-marginalized, long-muted, long victim to state (and social) *hogra*. Going rogue, the South's indignants drew the interest and attention of the North—paradox of paradoxes! Blogger/journalists (Rezgui 2012) such as Lina Ben Mhenni,[4] who had signaled virtual solidarity with the phosphate basin activists in their web diaries (see Lina Ben Mhenni and Aziz Amamo in Al-Tamimi 2012c, 75–87) trekked southward to observe first-hand the courageous, unfolding revolt of Southerners. They documented (again) the tragic violence unleashed on them by the state. Their journey followed the steps of former student dissidents of the 1970s and 1980s (Radia Nasraoui,[5] Chokri Belaid,[6] Samir Dilou[7], and others) who had plodded from Tunis in support (and awe) of the unruly unionists, laborers, and families demanding jobs and social rights in the 2008 phosphate uprising. In 2010–11, these same storied activists raised their voices and banners in protest against Ben Ali. Everywhere around the country, protestors took sanctuary in regional UGTT headquarters and advanced from them to protest in the streets. In the capital Tunis, the first major protests occurred in Mohamed Ali Square, UGTT general headquarters, watched over by drawings of anti-colonial and unionist leader Farhet Hached. Attorneys donning black robes, many of them human rights defenders (*huquqiyin*) in the Ben Ali years,[8] rendezvoused with unionized teachers in organized simultaneous protest across the street. School students went on strike.[9] An ashen-faced Radia Nasraoui protested in front of the dreaded Interior Ministry on

---

[4] The late Lina Ben Mhenni was one of the famous faces of the revolution's bloggers; she was nominated for the Nobel Peace Prize in 2011 for her courageous dissidence. The daughter of leftist Sadok Ben Mhenni, a former political prisoner and known student dissident in the 1970s–1980s, she died in 2020.

[5] A prominent human rights lawyer and activist (see Chapter 3).

[6] A proactive anti-Ben Ali dissident, also in the student movement of the 1980s. A leader within the leftist Democratic Patriots' (WATAD), he was assassinated on February 6, 2013.

[7] Former Ennahda member and human rights activist, and ex-Minister of Transitional Justice in the first Troika government.

[8] Ouled Carthage Facebook page, December 29, 2010, https://bit.ly/3ggbAI1

[9] For instance, *Idrabat Tullabiyyah fi Hayy Al-Riyad bi Sousse bila Isabat*, Alchourouk, January 11, 2011, p. 13; and *Sbikha: Masirah Hashidah, Matalib Mukhtalifah wa Muhafazah 'Ala Al-Mumtalakat Al-'Ammah wa Al-Khassah*, in *Alchourouk*, January 12, 2011, p. 3.

Habib Bourguiba Avenue, demanding her husband Hamma Hammami's[10] release.[11] Politically nondescript academics with no activist record rushed to Habib Bourguiba Avenue on January 14, 2011, if only to observe the uproar.[12] Having lain low for over a decade, some Islamists, active at the university and imprisoned in the 1990s, paraded in a procession of popular discontent in Sousse on January 14.[13] Fury (*ghadab*) against Ben Ali and his internal special forces (*al-bulis al-siyasi*) rolled upward and outward in an infectious elation. There is a joyous ring to mass defiance.

Abdelnasser Laouini, former WATAD student activist and attorney, memorably shouted *Ben Ali has fled* (*Ben Ali h'rab!*) piercing the night stillness in a cry stimulating tearful remembrances to this day (see Aljazeera 2022). Young people from the peripheral regions (*jihat*) such as Sidi Bouzid and Kairouan pitched tents in Kasbah square (January–February 2011). They huddled against the cold but also welcomed professors and civil society guests (including a would-be President of the country in 2019, Kais Saied), rubbing shoulders, debating their revolution, and exchanging ideas with intellectual-political elites. Underground, "engaged music" band Music Research (*Al-Bahth Al-Musiqi*), famous for having lyrically voiced popular woes and social injustice emblematized in the 1984 bread riots, performed at Kasbah Square.[14] "On the day of martyrdom, mother/Don't cry for me ... Say he has died, say he has died ... For the sake of the cause ..." the band sang before crowds whose mutinous bodies softened as they swayed to the mournful music. Martyrdom was declared by the people, the cause was their emancipation in this moving counter-narrative. Distinct snapshots and cumulative joinings of the revolution featured in these myriad contradictions. Encounters between people who would not otherwise come face-to-face, let alone dialogue and debate one another, defined this theatrical Bakhtinian spectacle. An upheaval of social and power relations recast meaning-making itself. For decades, loyalists and lackeys regurgitated political discourse formulated by Bourguiba and Ben Ali. Terms like *al-shaʿb* (the people), the republic (*al-jumhuriyyah*), even modernity (*al-hadathah*) were propagated from above to pin down Tunisians and smother peoplehood out of the people. In the carnival of revolution, the crossroads of all contradictions, the messy union of all protest reservoirs, people performed ultimate de-reterritorialization and reterritorialization. The people were no longer what Bourguiba envisioned them to be, or how Ben Ali in-/en-framed them. Having protested and demanded their right to have rights, they convened and in so doing, made themselves. Agency, affect, and cognition came full circle via the revolution. Tunisia's demos, for decades dangling in-becoming, through willful social acting and en-acting, *became*—a body of "dissensus."

---

[10] A communist dissident and head of the Workers' Party, also a student movement leader in the 1970s and 1980s.

[11] See image preserved on the Parti des Travailleurs official Facebook page, January 13, 2013, https://bit.ly/3eFYIdU

[12] For instance, Rachida Tlili (Interview, July 27, 2022, Tunis), Rawda Ben Othman (Interview, October 16, 2022, Tunis), and Lelia Chraibi (Interview, July 29, 2022, Tunis).

[13] For instance, Mounia Brahim, Interview, September 24, 2022, Tunis.

[14] See Parti de Travailleurs-Tunisie (Workers' Party) Facebook page, March 3, 2011, https://bit.ly/3s4OlDw

(Southern) Revolutionary Launch

Against this Bakhtinian backdrop, we begin with the heady days of the revolution demarcated as December 17, 2010 to January 14, 2011.

Table 6.2 charts the notable events in the timeline of the protestscapes we are considering in this and the previous chapter, from 2008 to 2011 (for a poorly referenced but descriptive overview, see also Al-Taimoumi 2020, 44–55). A northward procession from the peripheries to the center characterized the contours of this socio-political upheaval. Sidi Bouzid's eruption on December 17, 2010, protests in Kasserine within a few days, then the capital in the last week of December, the impressive crowds of the Sfax protest on January 13, 2011, the carnival-like gatherings filling Habib Bourguiba Avenue on January 14, all prompted Ben Ali to sneak away. It is difficult to clearly delineate the onset, build-up, escalation, climax, and dénouement of Tunisia's revolution, moving as it did at such breakneck speed. The following analysis is therefore not time-bound, even when it does break apart particular events and developments. The story of Mohamed Bouazizi of Sidi Bouzid is well-known. Stung by the humiliation and contempt of the police officer who confiscated his fruit cart, he doused himself in gasoline, setting himself alight in horrifying protest on December 17, 2010. The security crackdown on Sidi Bouzid was not surprising, mimicking repression of Redeyef and its sister mining towns in 2008, the 1984 bread riots, Black Thursday in 1978, and decades of student activism in Tunisia's yesteryears. Sometimes, protestors and students on strike engaged in counter-violence. Vandalism and looting of supermarkets, cars, and other property was reported in Beja,[15] Kairouan,[16] Jendouba,[17] and even the popular (and shabby) Ettadhamen neighborhood in the capital.[18] Some leading newspapers firmly denounced such mischief-making (*shaghab*).[19]

The 2011 revolution was a random explosion of the relationality of collectivity, locality, spatiality, and temporality. It fused together past struggles and sacrifices, subjectivities-in-context, protest-in-context, and learning-in-context. These embodied experiences of social doing and being were underpinned by concomitant affect and precepts dotting the quest for becoming by "*le peuple introuvable*," the "missing people," and "the part that has no part." Yet the actors, squares, names, faces, identities and consequent *demoi* and *logoi*, that traveled through times and spaces of struggle, were *not* random. Revolution threaded them all together, dissolving into an "epiphanic" moment. In Foucault's (2018, 336) words reflecting on a different setting, "when people went out into the streets [during the 1979 Iranian revolution],

---

[15] *Ahdath 'Unf Wa I'tida' 'Ala Matajir wa Sayyarat Khassah*, in *Alchourouk*, January 12, 2011, p. 13.
[16] *Tadarrur Munsha'at 'Umoomiyyah wa 'Ashrat Al-Jarha Natijat Al-'Unf*, in *Alchourouk*, January 11, 2011, p. 13.
[17] *Jendouba: Ihraq Maghaza wa Nahbiha wa I'tida' 'ala Maqarr Al-Baladiyyah*, in *Alchourouk*, January 12, 2011, p. 3.
[18] See *Alchourouk*, January 12, 2011, p. 11, including *A'mal Shaghab … Itlaf Al-Munsha'at Al- 'Umumiyyah wa 'Amaliyyat Nahb*.
[19] *Li-Naksir Da'irat Al-Shaghab Wa Al-'Unf!* in *Alchourouk*, January 10, 2011, p. 4.

Table 6.2 Revolution Timeline (2008–2011)*

Date	Event + Description
Jan.5, 2008	Launch of phosphate basin uprising
March 13, 2008	Security attacks on UGTT headquarters in Redeyef
April 6–8, 2008	Confrontations with security in Redeyef Arrests of uprising leadership
April 9, 2008	Huge demonstration and sit-in by Redeyef families; release of arrested unionists
April 10, 2008	Celebrations by Redeyef townspeople
May 6–7, 2008	Security raids in Redeyef
June 22–30, 2008	Security raids and arrests of "Wifaq" leadership committee
Sept. 18, 2008	Zakia Difaoui (journalist/activist) trial
Dec. 11, 2008	First trial of uprising activists
Late March–Feb. 2009	Appeal trial of uprising activists
October–November 2009	Release of phosphate activists
July 27, 2008	Demonstration by Redeyef families demanding release of prisoners
Feb. 2010	Skhira protests over phosphate/chemical hiring protests
August 2010	Ben Guerdane protests against Ras Jdir (Libya border crossing) closure
Dec. 17, 2010	Bouazizi's self-immolation in Sidi Bouzid
Dec. 22, 2010	Attorney protest in Kasserine
Dec. 26, 2010	Protests spread to Meknassy, Regueb, Bir El Hafey, Tunis, Kasserine, Thela, Gafsa, and other locales
Dec. 27, 2010	Teachers, postal workers, health workers, and others protest in the capital
Jan. 6, 2011-	Protest in Tunis
Jan. 12, 2011-	Nation-wide school and university closures after student protests
Jan. 12, 2011	General strike, large protest in Sfax (estimated at 100,000)
Jan. 14, 2011	Largest *Dégage* protest on Habib Bourguiba Ave. Ben Ali flees
Jan. 20–27, 2011	Kasbah 1 sit-in
Jan. 28, 2011	Kasbah 1 sit-in shut down by military
Feb. 20, 2011	Kasbah 2 sit-in
Feb. 25, 2011	"Great Friday" or "Friday of Rage"—Kasbah *malyuniyyah*
March 4, 2011	Kasbah 2 sit-in suspended
March 15, 2011	Higher Authority for Realization of the Objectives of the Revolution, Political Reform and Democratic Transition created
May 10, 2011	Adoption of Decree-Law 35 organizing the National Constituent Assembly elections
October 23, 2011	National Constituent Assembly elections

* This table is not exhaustive of all protests during this time.

they knew that they were doing something … that it was … a suspension of an entire part of their history". In Tunisia, such a "suspension" hung in the air in 2011. The revolution approximated a simultaneous suturing and unspooling of past and present.

As if the Khalduniyyah hall of historic meetings, the Burj Al-Rumi prison, among others, the Mohamed Ali Square, the maritime docks, the university discussion circles of the 1970s and 1980s, the dark *damus* phosphate caves, all forged into an undifferentiated socio-spatiality of emancipatory "cosmopolitanism," intersecting imaginaries and indeterminacy. The voices, forces, and drivers that had for decades toiled in resistance were all on full display at the moment of revolution—even if fleetingly. Their (re)appearance enabled deterritorializing and reterritorializing of (over) a century of pent-up urges. UGTT syndicalists, students, human rights activists, women dissidents, miners, old Perspectivists, LTDH lawyers and judges, Zaytuna pupils, prison inmates held in the Ministry of Interior, and even disparate rioters—all captured but were themselves captured by the revolutionary instant of moral concern, human depth, and emancipatory rapture. It was a moment to savor. The "headless revolution" had no single leader. Yet it was propelled by the gravitas of those who had variously and similarly been straddling numerous synchronies and temporalities. The revolutionary ferment and its slogan of "dignity, freedom" owed a great deal to knowing and learning-in-context, protest competencies (perhaps protest pedagogies) honed in the public squares—and "lyceums"—of anti-authoritarian resistance—located in past times and in other spaces. The revolution was not "mind-less." In 2011, it exuded the confidence, beneficence, and self-consciousness of peoplehood in a wayward unraveling of diachrony.

Notes from Kasserine

Before, during, and since 2011, the permanence of (Southern-instigated) protest owes as much to history as to materiality, that is, the atrophy of regional development and distributive justice in the South and Interior. This geography shares a sense of national pride in its anti-colonial resistance and its emancipatory imaginaries. Independence's advent introduced a new sequence of authoritarian oppression and marginalization but this time by national power-holders—Marcuse's "counterrevolution." These regions cradled the misery for which subsidized strategic foods (bread, flour, sugar, tea, etc.) and goods (kerosene) only just kept hunger at bay for the people. As for the government, subsidies kept these regions' famed popular rebellion in check. It was a policy of "basics." The "crumbs" of services in infrastructure, health, education, and employment were never going to ameliorate socio-economic strata. The subsidy of the proverbial "baguette" or loaf of bread (*khubzah*) framed both survival and conflict, for ruler and ruled. This moral implement of public policy defined a "red-line" as it were, tacitly and explicitly the contours of *what is* and *what should be*, that is, the terrain of the possible in Tunisia's politics. Consecutive prime ministers, from the Socialist Ahmed ben Salah to the liberal Hédi Nouira, Bourguiba's notable architects of socio-economic policy, had to jostle for control and survival, hegemony and legitimation. This they did by treading carefully around these contours. Both failed. They "lived by the sword" of subsidized bread. They died by the same sword. Both eventually crossed the bread red-line—the unwritten contract of providential politics. Subsidy policy was a double-edged sword of Damocles. In the hands of rulers, it was wielded to stay at the top of the game of power. When the rulers' grip on power loosened, that very blade cut short political careers, precipitating a fall from favor. Were the late Ben Salah and Nouira to recount their own testimonies of the fall from grace, in 1969 and 1980, respectively, that would have been an immaculate prosopopeia of political play in Bourguiba's Tunisia. The checkered nature of politics gave in to the rhythm of the December–January uprisings from the late 1960s (co-operatives rebellion) and throughout the 1970s–1980s. These events unevenly dotted the period's temporalities and scattered spatialities with multiple protest identities, practices, and moralities. Prime ministers came and went but what remained was the draconian stamp of counterrevolution. Neither the crackdowns nor the ad hoc quick fixes and blueprints geared to placating people in impoverished regions, urban outskirts, and rural peripheries, and their schools, did enough to rebuild state-society trust or regime capacity to gag critics or choke bottom-up activism. The rhythm of increased state securitization and policing was matched by the rhythm of rising fearless resistance, *al-zakham al-ihtijaji*, by the wider society, including unionists, teachers, and students. The socio-economic dead-end in the country's South and the Interior not only marginalized entire communities, but also spawned a supply (*khazzan*) of indignant have-nots. Many of these, across decades, were socialized into willing protestors or protest sympathizers. Many others became school dropouts, that is, readily available recruits for smuggler or contraband syndicates.

We use a focus group discussion to provoke tales and reflections on protest practices in Tunisia's South. Brainstorming sessions in February 2011 with participants, specifically teachers from Gafsa (a town in the Center-West, theatre of the phosphate basin protests), Kasserine, and adjacent Thela (also Center-Western towns, with modest agricultural activity, including of *halfa*, esparto grass) allowed for conversations over three separate gatherings. The aim was to gain first-hand accounts of the prevalence of protests by teachers and students, from the 1970s–1980s period through to the 2011 uprising. The discussions were conducted in informal settings (e.g. a café in Kasserine), drawing the interest of onlookers who sat around, happily listening and interjecting. This was very empowering for the teachers and the curious crowd, enthused in those early days of 2011 by their hard-won revolution. The flow of ideas was helped by a very free context, notable for the total absence of any agents of authority, with police disappearing from all public space. Emotions and ideas intermingled, enriching the exchanges. In that context of nation-wide euphoria, revolution tended to be bandied about frequently as an obvious synonym to protest (*ihtijaj*). For the speakers, references to 1978 and 1984 uprisings, for example, came naturally to mind. But so did memories of anti-colonial resistance and heroism. The feedback added nuance and historical texture. It cloaked protest in multiple correlations that evocatively tended to draw on firm repertoires with strong registers of agency (*nidal*, i.e. struggle), affect (pain, victimhood, humiliation, national pride, solidarity, and sacrifice), and cognition (deeply dyadic, self–other definitions, and a strong sense of belonging to the "people" and becoming).

"Those Farashish (al-Farashish)!"[20] Thus, descendants of Kasserine tend to be pejoratively lumped together into a single mass. Tunisians still use diverse labels to construct identity categories of one another. Some are defined according to the locale's nature (J'ridiyyah, named after the Djerid region, the date-rich oases). Some, like al-Farashish, are differentiated by their tribal or clan affiliation (Jlas, also known as Zlas, of Arab-Berber lineage, found largely in center Kairouan: see (Ayyari 2022)). Others are codified with an urban bourgeois "beldi" stamp (as opposed to "afaqi," the rural peripheries or hinterland). In any case, these socially constructed markers of identity created fixed and discriminate self–other demarcations, with residual inclusivity-exclusivity effects on the political, the social, and the economic. The focus group discussion with local teachers in February 2011 was held less than two months after the ousting of dictator Zinelabdine ben Ali. Talking revolution and protest with teachers reopened old and new wounds. When shared collectively, there is no complete record of words and phrases, which can do justice to describing crushed but defiant souls. Their pain is *sui generis*; in spite of expressive divergence, interlocutors left no doubt that their emotions of anger, disappointment, pride, struggles, and bonds of communal solidarity before and after independence were in a class of their own. Sami used a uniquely captivating word to sum up the "trauma": "*alhakim dagdag li'bad*" (Tunisian slang for "rulers crushingly quash people"). The verb "*dagdag*" has no equivalent in any Arabic dialects except in Algeria and Libya. The use of the word "*li'bad*" is as telling: "*Al-'ibad*," itself a Quranic term, a contraction of *'Ibadu Allah* ("God's servants"). The resonance in the political vernacular is pictorial: no bodies would survive the physical act of grinding, a cognate of "*dagdag*." The crushing is emotional. It transforms free human beings into *servants* of fellow human beings. Deleuze and Guattari's stress on the co-extensiveness of becoming and affect strikes a chord in this context. Like communities in the South and Interior, discussion of the revolution with people in Kasserine fan "backdrafts" evocative of humiliation or *hogra*, state neglect, and overall indignation about mediocre allocations of developmental resources.

Compounded Suffering

That Tunisia's revolution, the "protestscape of protestscapes," was instigated by indignant Southerners as indicated above is no coincidence. In this very initiation lies a gathering of synchronies: Ali Ben Ghedhahem's revolt, anti-colonial resistance, the first labor union's launch pad, countless student activisms, and the miners' uprising, etc. In this section, we turn to the weight of suffering borne by Tunisia's marginalized before and during the revolution. Over a century and a half of affective spurning breeds a defiant and demotic agency and a stubborn cognition of a form of a demos, willing to become. Sidi Bouzid residents articulate a searing affect that recalls the double consciousness of *hogra*. It was a "state of indignation" (*naqmah*) common

---

[20] Focus group discussions, February 9, 2011, Kasserine.

among the city's residents, says Jamal Saghruni (Al-Araby TV 2017). Bouazizi's death was "the drop that made the cup over flow ... a new thing, that one burn himself to relay a message." His painful sacrifice generated a kind of grim appreciation among his townsfolk. "Before that, we did not exist ... we were not on the map," adds Imad Nefti, a hospital worker (Al-Araby TV 2017). He enunciates a punctuated cognition of peoplehood. Not existing *before* suggests a change towards *existing now*, an insistent self-presence. In nearby Kasserine, where the protests spread next and where, as in Menzel Bouzaiane,[21] thug-like security forces killed people in Thela,[22] the refusal of state-imposed *hogra* resonated. A young female participant, Sabah Al-Chadhly recalls, "we have rights to this homeland (*watan*), we are Tunisian citizens... (*ahl*) [who belong] to this country" (Al-Araby TV 2018). She reiterates the cognitive messaging from Sidi Bouzid, the assertion of membership and presence. The tragic death of this fellow *Janub*-dweller recalled decades of multiple marginalization in the Tunisian south. The dramatic spectacle of his death not only inflamed anger and rebellion in Sidi Bouzid, but drew the attention of the security forces (repression) as well as Tunisians everywhere (solidarity in rebellion). Bouazizi's appalling death summons Bakhtin's "grotesque" body in all its ambivalences. A willful act of self-destruction set a whole country's determination ablaze. Death begets life, as in Bakhtin's (1984, 352) "pregnant death".

The violence with which Ben Ali's security foot soldiers assailed protestors raised the stakes of revolution. This battle with the state would wring sacrifices of life and limb from its daring combatants. Munia Bouali, attorney activist from Thela in Kasserine, noted in her television testimony that (like Sidi Bouzid 120 km away), her city has been historically "marginalized" (Aljazeera 2012). People still felt "colonized," she explains. Bouazizi's self-inflicted violence was doubly painful. It dredged up a collective memory of another young man from the area, who, "feeling that there was no hope," had burned himself in Monastir, coming home for his burial in nearby Zalfan. Describing the state of affairs on December 17 and afterwards as a "boiling point" (*ghalayan*), Bouali remembers different forms of protest. Not only did the youth rise up, but attorneys marched in Kassserine on December 22, 2010, donning their black robes as they would do later in the capital (see also Ben Yousef 2019, 179). "We coalesced (*iltahamna*)" with ordinary citizens, she says, connoting a kind of embodied solidarity. Her most vivid narration, however, is of security attacks on protestors in early January.[23] Thela's revolutionary "credibility" is associated in Tunisian revolutionary lore with its martyrs. Bouali remembers the advance and retreat (*karr wa farr*) between young protestors and the police. Police attacked crowds with tear gas and water. Angry protestors hurled stones in retaliation. Adamantly defiant young men pretended to shower under the hot water, enjoying its

---

[21] Tunisian Community Facebook Page, December 25, 2010 post, *"Ahdath Sidi Bouzid wa Menzel Bouzaiane,"* in https://bit.ly/3DJ3Ibm

[22] Tunisian Community Facebook Page, January 22, 2011 post, *"Ahl Thela Yatahaddathun,"* in https://bit.ly/3fiXm9i

[23] See *Qa'imah Awwaliyyah fi Al-Shuhada' Alladhina Saqatu fi Kasserine wa Thela wa Regab*, in *Al-Badil* online, January 9, 2011, which lists martyrs killed "within the last 24 hours."

warmth in the cold air. Tear gas and water would not suffice. Revolutionary fervor seemed to unspool time. "In that night ... you couldn't measure [time] the regular way. ... Everyone was in the street, or the hospital. ... Men, women ... I saw young children carrying stones." One 70-year old woman was hitting large rocks, splintering them into more wieldy stones for young people to throw. Snipers moved in, killing five protestors; a sixth later died (see also Al-Bouni 2013, 44–46). Four of them were her neighbors. In particular, Marwan Jemli's death detonated a desire for revenge, says this attorney.

Other revolutionaries have similarly mused over the paradoxical connection between repression and revolt. Remarking on his travels throughout the country, Marwan Hamri refused to glorify any one spatiality within it over the rest. He explains,

> When Kasserine revolted, they revolted because they saw on national television the ugly way in which the people of Sidi Bouzid were killed, and [then] Monastir and Sfax revolted, they revolted against their [socio-economic] situation and there are martyrs in Tunisia, they revolted not against hunger and unemployment ... they revolted because they saw the acts of violence and abuse as though we are in Gaza, these crimes that are perpetrated in our country, in Medenine, in Sidi Bouzid, in Sousse, in the [Tunis] Ettadhamen neighborhood. ... In the course of four days the country was turned upside down, it was no longer Tunis but it was as though we were in Palestine ... the entire people revolted for the sake of Tunisia, for the sake of its people. (in Al-Tamimi 2012b, 171)

The people revolted for others and themselves, Hamri says in this heartfelt rush of words. Anger and anguish for fellow human beings surpassed socio-economic want in pushing people to rise up. Grief over martyrs in Kasserine[24] and elsewhere was contagious. Solidarity born of shared pain has a mobilizing capacity, he implies. Stories like those of the seven-month-old baby killed by tear gas deployed by police who followed women into the socially sacrosanct public bath (*hammam*) on January 9, 2011 (Al-Bouni 2013, 43) cannot but horrify. Violence, the sharpest and most over-powering of state *hogra*, made one feel like a stranger in his own land, Hamri suggests. Tunis mutated into a country occupied by a foreign power, like Palestine under Israeli siege. The drive to reclaim one's country impels revolt. Inciting powerful affective reactions, state violence simultaneously activated a diffusing cognition that rejected alienation in the homeland. The travesty of violence paradoxically propelled the agency through which the people conjoined in confronting the state. Warding off the blows of batons, grieving over martyrs, the people rose up. Revolution is the people's rejoinder to unbearable repression.

Coercion can inspire solidarity. But the toll it exacts from survivors can also be ruinous. Muslim Qasdallah, testifying before the Truth and Dignity Commission,

---

[24] *Huzn, Hudu' wa Janazat Khashi'ah*, in *Alchourouk*, January 12, 2011, p. 12.

tells of being shot in the Wardanin affair (Instance Vérité and Dignité 2017). The importance of his proud sacrifice seems to have been banalized by state neglect and popular nonchalance, years after Ben Ali's departure. Before his own calamity, he witnessed others being shot. He and other young men in the neighborhood committees, *lijan al-ahya'*, attempted to thwart the escape of Ben Ali's nephew Kais.[25] One man was recording events with his phone. He was struck on the head, "such that his brain was stuck to the ceiling." Qasdallah himself was hit in the leg, immobilized. Transported to a hospital, he was comatose for three and a half months. He had a total of 32 operations on his leg, he says, and still his leg does not function properly. Shipped to Qatar, he was not treated there either. Worms infested his leg. He considers himself and others injured in the cause of the revolution to have been neglected by post-revolutionary governments.[26] "If they were stone, they would feel ... not human beings, but stone," the suffering of the injured. He resents people's censure of the injured as thieves (*surraq*), after handouts from the government. "They enjoy freedom, and curse us for being *surraq*. ... This flag, we have added blood to it." Still, he is willing to give more to Tunis, to its people. "Until now, I am willing to sacrifice my whole body ... my other leg," he declares. "Our revolutionary path continues." Testimonies like Qasdallah's bring to bear an ambivalent aspect of revolution and a nascent peoplehood. Unacknowledged, inadequately recognized, revolutionary sacrifice can breed acrid discord and ill-feeling between compatriot rebels. Shared cognition and agency do not necessarily override affect. Negative affect, rage, and *hogra*, can create a tenuous solidarity.

A Revolution in Travel

The (unpaid) collective debt to Tunisia's injured and martyrs would be a thorny matter for years to come. We now focus, however, on the rapid-fire advance of protests from South to North. Within mere days, Sidi Bouzid's revolt diffused to Meknassy, Menzel Bouzaiane, Regueb (Sidi Bouzid), Kasserine, Thela, Fériana (part of Kasserine),[27] Madinat Bou Abdallah and Douz (in Kbili), Hamma (in Gabes), Tataouine, Medenine, Zerzis, Ben Guerdane, Gafsa, Tozeur, Kairouane, and Siliana (Al-Bouni 2013, 37–54). The security forces cracked down; in some cases they went on looting rampages, or left a trail of martyred protestor casualties in their wake.[28] On January 12, 2011, enormous crowds rallied in Sfax, Tunisia's capital of the South.[29] Reflecting

---

[25] See *Echorouk Online*, January 23, 2011, Kais Ben Ali Mutawarrit fi Qatl Arba'at Abriya', https://bit.ly/3CQsNPZ

[26] Initial overtures to distribute financial compensation to the revolution's victims in the first Cabinet meeting post-Ben Ali were insufficient. See *Fi Awwal Majlis Wizari li-Hukumat Al Wihdah Al-Wataniyyah ... in Al-Tariq Al-Jadid*, January 22–28, 2011, p. 3.

[27] *Hasilat Usbu'ain min Al-Ghadab: Sidi Bouzid ... Al-Shararah Allati Awqadat Hariq Al-Ihtijajat*, in *Al-Tariq Al-Jadid*, January 1–7, 2011, p. 4.

[28] See for instance, *Ahali Al-Regab Yasrukhun: Lasna 'Isabat Mulathamin wa 'Anasir Shurtah Kharrabu Mahallatana wa Dasu Sharafana*, in *Al-Tariq Al-Jadid*, January 22–28, 2011, p. 10.

[29] See I "love" Sfax Facebook post, "Manifestation Sfax=12 Janvier 2011," January 12, 2011, https://bit.ly/3UdbfVv

the "carnivalesque" turbulence of revolution,[30] protestors set fire to the RCD headquarters and a store where liquor was sold. This vandalism prompted the army to move in to the city.[31] Still, Sfax was a major turning point. Its protests followed a January 10, 2011 decision by the UGTT national leadership to allow regional-level leaders to call general strikes in the region (Ben Mim 2019, 78–79).

Initially, the UGTT chimed in to reiterate demands for employment and development by Sidi Bouzid youth on December 21, 2010, calling for the release of prisoners, decrying the "security" approach but stopping short of affirming more than vague solidarity with the protests (see Ben Yousef 2019, 171). The union also pointed to a report (UGTT 2010) it had published on development in Sidi Bouzid,[32] defensively claiming the initiative in taking marginalization seriously there and in Gafsa.[33] The focus of a December 28, 2010 UGTT Executive Committee statement was on development, employment, prisoner release, de-escalation, and dialogue.[34] Nearly two weeks later, its National Administrative Body declared "principled solidarity with" residents of the areas in revolt. As in 1978, the union affirmed strikes as "the essence of union freedoms."[35] An exceptional statement published in the January 15 issue (likely drafted earlier) denounced the shooting of protestors and overall security measures, reiterated the "freedom of expression and peaceful protest," demanded the release of prisoners and participatory social measures mitigating marginalization, and berated the government for the media blackout.[36] Finally, the UGTT was changing tack, having initially dismissed unionist support for the budding revolution as reflecting individual opinions ("personal positions") but not being representative of the national leadership. Himself a protest enthusiast since 2008, Houcine Abassi (2023, 128) insists that the UGTT was keen to "avoid the same mistakes we made in dealing with the phosphate basin events" less than three years earlier.

However, Khamis Arfaoui attributes the incentive for the union to support and join the revolt that spread from Sidi Bouzid to the progressive positions of the short-lived Al-Liqa' Al-Naqabi Al-Dimuqrati Al-Munadil (the Democratic Militant Unionist Forum) coming from inside the UGTT. Established by members including Tawfiq Al-Tawati, Jilan Al-Hammami, Hussain Al-Rahili, Radi Ben Hussain, Zuhair Al-Jouini, Taieb Bouaishah, Uthman Belhadj Amor, and Faraj Shabah, this leftist-leaning group demanded greater internal democracy inside the union in accordance with its founding principles (Arfaoui 2020, 140–147). Al-Liqa' declared its solidarity with what we have dubbed ancillary protests in Fériana and Ben Guerdane in 2010. Two days into the Sidi Bouzid flare-up, they publicly backed the "struggles of

---

[30] See *Tawasul Al-Ahdath Al-Alimah fi Ba'd Al-Mudun*, Alchourouk, January 11, 2011; and "*Alchorouk Tuwakibu Aham Al-Ahdath Al-Alimah fi Al- 'Asimah wa Sfax wa Kasserine wa 'Adid Al-Mudun*," Alchourouk, January 13, 2011.
[31] "*Alchourouk fi Qalb Al-Ihtijajat bi Sfax: 13 Musaban … Harq Maqarr Lajnat Al-Tansiq wa Al-Mustawda' Al-Baladi…* in Alchourouk, January 13, 2011, p. 8.
[32] *Haqiqat Ma Hadatha fi Sidi Bouzid* in *Al-Sha'b*, December 25, 2010, p. 1.
[33] *Hatta Yatadhakkar Man Qad Nasiya Annana Dawman Ra'idun*, in *Al-Sha'b*, January 15, 2011, p. 16.
[34] *Bayan Al-Maktab Al-Tanfidhi li Al-Ittihad Al-'Am Al-Tunisi li Al-Shughl* in *Al-Tariq Al-Jadid*, January 1–7, 2011, p. 3.
[35] *Al-Hay'ah Al-Idariyyah li Al-Ittihad* in *Al-Sha'b*, January 8, 2011, pp. 1–4.
[36] *Al-Hay'ah Al-Idariyyah Al-Wataniyyah Al-Istithna'iyyah*, in *Al-Sha'b*, January 15, 2011.

the residents of Sidi Bouzid that seek to defend the rights of the region for social, economic, and cultural development and the rights of its youth to stable employment and a dignified life" (quoted in Arfaoui 2020, 157). Indeed, their Facebook page shared updates on Sidi Bouzid, police repression and retaliation (e.g. cutting off electricity), arrests, and subsequent protest.[37] This indicated that there could be productive tension within an organization as large, influential, and diverse as the UGTT. The union's trajectory in terms of its internal democracy and alternation of power is beyond the scope of our discussion here. Yet its dissenting factions, even if they did not much outlive the 2011 revolutionary events, contributed to mobilizing virtual and in-person support for the protests ripping through the country.

Veterans Support the Margins

Early awareness of Sidi Bouzid's revolt stirred the empathy and interest of some veteran oppositionists in the capital. The following snapshots do not lend exclusive or primary credit to Jribi, Khashanah, or any single other individual, movement, or force in the escalation of protest. Neither they, nor the bloggers who kept track and kept watch over the burgeoning protests (see Kerrou 2012)and what was viewed by many to be cold-blooded murder by security forces, nor the informal and formal networks within and between the hierarchy of the UGTT, nor the winter return of students from the regions to the capital Tunis, *alone* pushed protest over the edge in Tunisia. This snippet is significant rather for its content and cadres, emphasizing a synergy between socio-economic and political rights, demands, and solutions, as well as continuities over space and time in the muzzling of those who dared to move, speak, and write back to authoritarian domination. We also wish to stress the necessary concatenation of all rebellious actors and energies that made the revolution. It was not *solely* the "revolutionary youth," betrayed as they felt, who carried Tunisians into peoplehood. Neither did revolution simply flow from gesturing by renowned activists. Those who coalesced in the "October 2005" movement waging "the battle for freedoms and democracy," brought together such (formerly) discrepant ideological and political voices as Moncef Marzouki's Congress for the Republic, Islamist Ennahda, Hamma Hamami's Workers' Party, Mustapha Ben Jaafar's Ettakatol, Unitarian Nasserists, the National Council for Rights, Nejib Chebbi's Progressive Democratic Party (PDP) (Chebbi 2022, 126–137), and other independents (Nachaz 2022). Some of these names were to varying degrees at the vanguard of revolutionary change in 2010-11. Yet the gains in emptying out the authoritarian center were not the fruit of their labors alone.

Maya Jribi, a prominent leader of the Progressive Democrats—herself a former student activist—issued a statement on behalf of her opposition party. Offering support and condolences to Bouazizi's family over his "painful" death, the statement notes

---

[37] See, for instance, December 19, 2010 post, *"Al-Liqa' Al-Naqabi Al-Dimuqrati Al-Munadil"* Facebook page, https://www.facebook.com/allika.annakabi

prior similar self-immolations in Jendouba and Monastir that reflected the "feeling of oppression and social despair" for which the state was solely responsible.[38] Moreover, the Tunis-based militants in effect welcomed the uprising to the capital itself. Frustrated by the security siege that prohibited journalists from entering Sidi Bouzid, Rachid Khashanah, active in the same party and editor of their opposition newspaper *Al-Mawqif* recalls, the PDP organized a panel in their office in Tunis. Party activists invited eight activists from Sidi Bouzid (some from the Committee to Fight Marginalization). International journalists were also in attendance (Khashanah in Al-Tamimi 2015, 363). A journalistic thirst for "the forbidden story" augments an anti-authoritarian protest ethos. Like numerous others, the agentic decision to host activists also touches on affect (grief, sadness) and cognition (identification and appreciation of a common struggle for the right to have rights). The statement opening the press conference[39] rehearsed similar and preparatory events in Redeyef, Skhira, and Ben Guerdane. Together with Sidi Bouzid, they pointed to directionless futures and "feelings of injustice regarding the heightened imbalance between regions." The statement crosses over into political territory. True development to counteract marginalization can transpire only with "wide popular participation" through political parties, civil society, and the media. "Political and social reforms" were thus necessary, as is an end to the security crackdown, making way for "dialogue with unemployed youth and civic bodies" hastily formed in Sidi Bouzid.

Other declarations of solidarity came from veteran human rights and democratic oppositions groups and parties. In addition to Jribi's Democratic Socialist Party which issued statements on both December 17 and 19 (Ben Yousef 2019, 167–169), the Tunisian Human Rights League (LTDH) also spoke up. Recalling the 2008 phosphate uprising as a precedent of social discontent, the LTDH expressed its "sympathies" and "solidarities" with Bouazizi and similarly positioned young men. It called on the authorities to address unemployment and poverty, warning that exclusionary "monopolization" of political life would not solve trenchant problems (in Ben Yousef 2019, 170). Hamma Hamami and Radia Nasraoui's Workers' Party was more direct by January 3, 2011, pledging support for daily protests, exhorting the opposition to gather and brainstorm on the way forward, and stressing that the "Tunisian people is in need of a new [political] system, democratic, national, popular, emerging from its will and representative of its deep interests" (in Ben Yousef 2019, 192). By January 10, 2010, the Workers' Party cried *Dégage* with the Tunisians: "these protesting masses ... demand the departure of Ben Ali who took over power 23 years ago." Gesturing to the unity in the diversity of its ranks, the Party declared itself "with our people, with its laborers and workers and farmers and women and youth and intelligentsia and artists" agreeing on the "desire for change." Ben Ali must go, making way for the people to establish "a new and true democracy" (Hizb Al-'Ummal Al-Tunisi 2011). Upon Hamma Hamami's arrest on January 12, Moncef

---

[38] Re-published on the Facebook page of *Al-Mawqif* newspaper, December 14, 2021, https://bit.ly/3ETMlFS

[39] Republished in a Facebook post by Les Partisans du PDP, December 25, 2011, https://bit.ly/3ETMlFS

Marzouki's Congress Party called for his release, adding that "the end of the despot (*taghiyah*) is nigh" (in Ben Yousef 2019, 205).

The Democratic Progressive and Workers' Parties created its own political vanguard in support of the revolution. They were ahead of the Islamist Ennahda, for instance, whose leadership in exile did not officially weigh in until January 16, 2011, after Ben Ali's exit. Ennahda then celebrated the "success [of] our blessed people's revolution" and looked ahead to a "true democratic alternative that restores dignity to citizens, power to the people, and respect for the law" (in Ben Yousef 2019, 242–243). Before the fateful day of January 14, journalists, too, waged a battle alongside politicians. Covering protests to enlighten and mobilize the broader public, they decried state censorship. On behalf of her party, Maya Jribi condemned the confiscation of issue 574 of the opposition newspaper *Al-Mawqif*. This action was an "illegal and blatant attack on the freedom of expression, and the right ... to alternative media."[40] The same fate befell an issue of the opposition newspaper *Al-Tariq al-Jadid* covering events in Sidi Bouzid that had been largely sidelined by the official media.[41] Refusing such gag orders, a Tunisian journalism blog republished images of the censored issue 211 in its entirety (*Journaliste Tunisien* 2010).

Synchronies of Protests

The foregoing overview of elite statements, solidarity, and participation in protests is significant as we emphasize the convergence of protestscapes in a Bakhtinian-like chaos of revolutionary contingency. Activists who had opposed Bourguiba and Ben Ali, some for decades, at different moments and to varying degrees, threw their weight behind the people's uprising. Some revolutionary youth or *shabab al-thawrah* would later resent what they saw as elite domination of the fast-paced process of change. Aspirations for greater youth participation in the country's new politics[42] propelled some to the national stage, as the discussion of Kasbah later in the chapter will show. A people's revolution, after all, absorbs both elites and masses. The challenge is socially acting and en-acting a kind of dialogic ethos that practices as much as it preaches solidarity. This knotty issue has profound implications for democratization, as we hint in the concluding chapter.

As middle-aged activists well-versed in protest competencies joined the fray, the revolution continued to move *on the ground*. A video of a protest in Mohamed Ali Square, the first to reach Tunis on December 27, 2010,[43] carries important themes. The inkblot of rebellion expanded across Tunisia. The location of this daring and

---

[40] *Balagh Hizb Al-Dimuqrati Al-Taqaddumi Hawla Hajz Jaridat al-Mawqif*, in *Al-Mawqif* online, republished January 9, 2012.
[41] They re-published the article on Sidi Bouzid in the first week of the New Year. See, *Ahdath Sidi Bouzid: Kaifa Intalaqat ... Wa Ma Hiya Asbabuha?* In *Al-Tariq Al-Jadid*, January 1–7, 2011, p. 5.
[42] *Al-Shabab wa Thawrat Al-Sha'b*, in *Al-Sha'b*, February 12, 2011, p. 13.
[43] Tunisia New Today Facebook Page, October 2, 2013, https://bit.ly/3Dcp7cI

defiant gathering is significant. The spatiality of the UGTT (or Ittihad) headquarters is at once symbolic and tactical. The site bespeaks literally the centrality of the Ittihad as an opposition force fighting for the little guy, the downtrodden worker or unemployed. Union headquarters functioned as a kind of "free space" liberated by dissidents protesting against the regime. This particular location is also near Habib Bourguiba Avenue, the main thoroughfare traversed by everyone who approaches the capital from within and without. In Tunis as in Sidi Bouzid, Sousse,[44] and countless other locales around the country, the UGTT headquarters was the gathering point from which protests would take off. On this point there is consensus among interviewees, writers, and other participants. Mounia Obeid, longtime unionist and leftist activist remembers, almost tripping over her words in emphasis,

> [In] the revolution … it's true, the people [came out], but the unionists (*al-naqabiyyin*) … the local and regional union branches (*ittahadat*) … they were open … in all the (*jihat*) … they led the protests, they motivated the people to go out. … True, the people were fed up with Ben Ali, with the Trabelsi's [Ben Ali's in-laws] rule, the mafia … but a word of truth [must be uttered] … the unionist role was clear in the protests of 2011. … The slogans raised (and repeated) … were clear: dignity (*karamah*), freedom. … This was the demand of the unionists … unionist, political slogans [were] adopted by the people (*sha'b*) … because they expressed their suffering, their demands …[45]

From this perspective, foot-dragging by the central UGTT leadership did not overshadow the leadership role by other rank-and-file union leaders. The video of the December 27, 2010 protest depicts a crowded square, people stuffed into even the second floor balconies. A flag of Palestine, the (historically) uncontroversial, premier regional cause, hangs from one wall of the headquarters. Sami Tahri, at the time Assistant Secretary General of the UGTT, stands above the crowd, presumably carried on a comrade's shoulders. His impassioned speech demands "lifting the siege" off Sidi Bouzid, as well as "demilitarizing" the southern governorate. The movement there, he explains, "has demands that represent not only Sidi Bouzid," but the rest of Tunisians. He greets the wives and mothers in the crowd. In so doing, he and others tap into to a quasi-constant of Tunisian self-image that valorizes women's public presence (e.g. Debuysere 2016). For the crowd before him and for all Tunisians who watched or heard of this protest, he draws a direct link between the grievances of the rebellious, marginalized youth in Tunisia's forgotten periphery and the tribulations of people in the far-off capital. Sidi Bouzid had in this way come to Tunis. The solidaristic expansion of the revolt built momentum as through a diachronic confluence of past synchronies. Distant spatialities, the respective identities and (power,

---

[44] Interview with Tunisian academic Amor Boubakri, member of the "Higher Authority for the Realization of the Revolution's Objectives, Political Reform and Democratization," October 19, 2022, Sousse.

[45] Interview, July 28, 2022, Tunis.

social) relations that define them, moved closer. Time also began to "collapse." The protests in Sidi Bouzid "started in Redeyef," Tahri proclaims in the video. The crowd enthusiastically agrees. "From Redeyef to [Sidi] Bouzid!" they chant. Tahri continues, spewing a laundry list of problems "non-people" of Sidi Bouzid confront in the negligence of the state, familiar to Tunisians everywhere: marginalization, underdevelopment, corruption. "We don't accept painkillers!" he shouts. The people will not be placated by Ben Ali's cosmetic half-measures that aim to quell dissent. Slogans that become emblematic of the Tunisian revolution reverberate across the square: "Freedoms! Freedoms!" and "Work, freedom, national dignity!" As if to insist that by opposing Ben Ali's regime they are not casting off their national loyalty or membership, the crowd bursts into the national anthem, more than once. However, at this point there were still no calls for the downfall of the regime, or cries of "dégage!" Peoplehood's peaking, its complete revolt against the authoritarian regime, proceeded in fits and starts.

Protest momentum continued to build, in and outside the capital. Speeches and chants recorded in a video of an attorneys' protest before the Tunis courthouse on December 29, 2010 reiterated sympathy and identification with the marginalized and deprived.[46] "How many young men need to burn until you listen to the people?" Abdelnasser Laouini's question, addressed to Ben Ali through what he called the people's television (*talfazat al-sha'b*)—that is, Facebook—rang out across the crowd. Elderly women complained of their young sons, university graduates who could not find work. "Attorney and unemployed, one line [together] in the struggle!" Solidarity thus spanned regional and class divides. Like other protestors in Thela and elsewhere, anger at state violence pushed them to redouble their resistance. Affect bolstered agency and cognition. Protestors began to cognize themselves as "the people" in the battle against the regime. Laouini put Ben Ali and his regime on notice: "This people, once a drop of blood spills, will not retreat …" This and other protest gatherings lived up to the warning. The build-up continued over the next two weeks. The huge Sfax strike and demonstration on January 12 almost prefigured the breakthrough *dégage* protest that would chase Ben Ali out of the country the next day.

What is probably most memorable for many Tunisians (and observers) was the apex of the 2010–11 revolutionary protests on January 14, hours before Ben Ali's escape. Endless clusters of protestors descended upon the main street in Tunis, Habib Bourguiba Avenue. The tree-lined boulevard bulged with people who filled up every empty nook and cranny, carving it out as a new "freed space" at the heart of the capital city. More or less wresting it from police control took effort. Videos of that day show street battles with security officers. Through plumes of tear gas smoke, young men in jeans and dark leather or sports jackets pelt stones at helmeted police. Screaming, chanting, clapping, ululations, and the crack of rubber bullets fill the air. Swelling crowds chant, "Down with the people's executioner (*jallad al-sha'b*)! Down with the Destour party!"; "No Ben Ali," "With our souls and blood, we sacrifice to you, our

---

[46] Ouled Carthage Facebook page, December. 29, 2010, https://bit.ly/3ggbAI1

martyrs," and "Ben Ali, o coward! The people of Tunisia will not be humiliated!"[47] Bodies huddle together, some holding up signs emblazoned with *Dégage!* Sirens blare, people perch on top of cars and hang from the windows of buildings, many chanting "*sit-in, sit-in, until the regime falls!*"[48] One Tunisian academic present juxtaposed two recollected images of protest symbolism. Some demonstrators carried baguettes (representing socio-economic demands), while others carried cages which they opened to release the birds inside (representing political freedoms).[49] Dignity and freedom combined, their collected might formidable against authoritarian misery-making. Other protests took place in full force across the country. In Gafsa, people chanted "the interior ministry is a terrorist ministry!" referencing security violence, and "people, freedom, national dignity!"[50] Sfax protestors marched beside the city fortress dotted with palm trees, invoking the many martyrs who had lost their lives.[51] Numerous other displays unfurled in simultaneity. These and other scenes exemplified a Bakhtinian "ambivalence," unlikely encounters between people, contradictory emotional states, sights, and sounds.

Embodying the Bakhtinian notion of the carnivalesque absurd rendered meaningful was a mini-musical performance. Against the twilight sky, young singer Amel Methlouthi[52] serenaded the crowd, her dulcet tones momentarily stilling the boisterousness. Wearing a long red coat, her eyes glistening with emotion, Methlouthi sang in the Tunisian dialect:[53]

> I am the free people (*ahrar*) who are not afraid
> I am the secrets that never die
> I am the voice of those who did not submit
> I am meaning in the midst of chaos …
> I am free, and my word is free
>
> I am free, and my word is free
> Do not forget the price of the bread loaf (*khubzah*)
> Do not forget the planter of the lump in one's throat (*ghassah*)
> Do not forget the one who does not heed woes
>
> ….
> I am the secret of the red rose
>
> Beloved for years for its redness
> Its fragrance buried one day

---

[47] Kelibia Facebook Page, May 6, 2011 post, "*Li al-Tadhkir: Shariʿ Alhabib Bourguiba,*" January 14, 2011 https://bit.ly/3sGgUrp

[48] Roots TV Facebook Page, January 14, 2020 post, 13 et 14 Janvier 2011, Ben Ali Dégage!, https://bit.ly/3NlcQ9o

[49] Interview, Rachida Tlili Sellaouti, July 27, 2022.

[50] Gafsa Horra Facebook post, January 15, 2021, *Gafsa fi 14 Janvi 2011*, https://bit.ly/3WdgXbA

[51] I "love" Sfax, January 14, 2011 Facebook post, *Sfax: Yawm Al-Jumʿah 14 Janvi*, https://bit.ly/3Dpqt2y

[52] Methlouthi later performed at the 2015 ceremony for the Tunisian "Nobel Quartet" (see Elbousalmi 2017).

[53] Ghassan Boughanmi Facebook post, June 23, 2012, "Amel Methlouthi," https://www.facebook.com/ghassen.boughanmi.12/videos/113596532115902

> Then emerged in its blanket of fire
> Calling on the free people

Her lyrics are drenched in sensory language and wrapped in emancipatory aspirations (free/free people). They commiserate with the *hogra* of the poor (connoted by bread, *khubzah*), the miserable and frustrated, those suffocating under Ben Ali's rule. In the throes of a becoming peoplehood, individual and group become indistinguishable (I am the free people ... I am free). Word is deed, and deed re-territorialized as word (I am the secrets ... I am the voice ... I am free, my word is free ...). Speech acts come to life: singing and saying are social acts and en-actments insisting on freedom, on the right to have rights, declaring to and from within the congregating masses that here and now we liberate ourselves. Past sacrifices and pains liquefy into present protest demands. The rose in the song (perhaps dreams, futures, creative projects snuffed out) gives to the crowd. Its color erupts into flames of rage, illuminating the path to freedom by Tunisians discovering, creating, their peoplehood.

In Habib Bourguiba Avenue on January 14, as in prior protests including the phosphate basin, speech festivals (*mahrajanat khitabiyyah*) (Arfaoui 2020, 51) were also notable. It is impossible to reconstruct all that was uttered on that day. Limited samples offer clues to a maturing cognition, propelled by affect (rage, anguish, determination, solidarity, joyousness), in these disparate yet complementary individual-collective articulations of agency. Human rights activist and attorney Samia Abbou, member at the time of Moncef Marzouki's Congress for the Republic (CPR) party, addressed the surrounding crowd.[54] Her voice harsh, she mocked Ben Ali's speech the night before. Like him, she said, "I will speak in the dialect." Echoing the general revolutionary sentiment, Abbou rejected his promises of no more killing. "Liar!" The President, his wife, his inner circle must be held accountable. Abbou repeated a protest slogan, and the crowd joined in. "Bread and water, but no Ben Ali! *Khubz wa ma' ben Ali la',*" insisting on dignity and freedom with meager living standards if need be. "No to repression, no to despotism *(istibdad),*" she continued. "Enough (*yizzi*)! ... our main demand is his departure! We don't accept bread ... or milk [as distributive placations]. ... long live Tunisia, long live the people!" His signature cap covering his head, leftist politician and former UGET student activist Chokri Belaid,[55] emphasized that the people had acted decisively. Motioning to those beside him not to interrupt, he declared:

> The people have spoken. ... [I call for] a transitional national government with absolute powers because the dictator and the gangs of corruption who gave the orders

---

[54] CPR Facebook page, October 7, 2011 post, "*Munadilat Al-Hizb, Samia Abbou,*" https://bit.ly/3DNhudi

[55] His assassination, alongside that of Mohamed Brahmi in July, threw the country into a political crisis, forcing the resignation of the governing "Troika" coalition in 2013.

to ... kill ... have been [exposed]. ... No sound is louder than the sound of the people. ... And for those [afraid of a power void]: Tunisia has an elite of thousands ... that can manage the country and create a real democracy. ... Tunisia has its parties, its associations, its union, its students, its attorneys who have stood up and said their word [had their say] ... the dictator must leave ... the *Tajammuʿ* [Ben Ali's RCD] party ... must be dissolved ...

The social doing of Tunisian peoplehood could be no clearer. Their demands, even if controversial,[56] were explicit, forthright. Occupying Habib Bourguiba Avenue, they succeeding in emptying out the center of authoritarian power that other protestors, militants, and activists alive and deceased, had chipped at for decades. In Belaid's and Abbou's speeches, in Methlouthi's song, in the moving chants and the national anthem echoing across the street, on television and computer screens around the country and the world, Tunisians cognized themselves as the people, *al-shaʿb*. They had achieved the ultimate reterritorialization of the term that had been hollowed out and trivialized by Bourguiba and Ben Ali. They were able to finally proclaim: We are the people, all of us, and we will ourselves free, we will the dictator to leave. We activate the audacity to reclaim our right to have rights: freedom, dignity, social justice, employment, fearlessness. Following and completing the protest paths lit by the struggles and sacrifices of those before us, from Ben Ghedhahem to Al-Hammi to Hached to the unionists and miners and students and sundry oppositionists, we have demonstrated our will to life.

Fate did respond, in the words of Abou El Kacem Chebbi sung throughout. Ben Ali got the message, responding secretly and silently by jumping ship. (The UGTT's Houcine Abassi (2023, 135) assures us that "had Ben Ali not fled, the UGTT would have called a [nationwide] general strike" to push protests over the edge and the President out.) Having fought in vain to erase the myth and cult of Bourguiba his entire 23 years in office, Ben Ali lost yet again. Bourguiba would have the last laugh, an ironic gift bestowed by the people in a reversal of presidential patronage. That this remarkable turning-point in Tunisian history, when the people drove out their dictator, took place on Habib Bourguiba Avenue, will be forever synonymous with January 14.

We have persistently suggested that the revolution was not made on January 14, or even December 17. Rather, it was simply crowned during this brief period, having been "in becoming" for decades and decades back to the 1860s crucible. Yet the long diachrony of Tunisia's revolutionary milieu does not detract from the day's significance. Tasked with babysitting her friend's daughter, unable to reach her as telephone coverage was disrupted, Mounia Obeid ruefully lamented that despite having participated in all the Tunis protests after a long activist career, she was not physically

---

[56] The proposal to disband the RCD was controversial. Many defended its historical pedigree and rebuffed the notion that the party itself was culpable for Ben Ali's political oppression and corruption. See, for instance, "*Khawatir min Wahyi Al-Hirak Al-La Muntazar wa Sadmat ma Hadath*," *Al-Tariq Al-Jadid*, January 22–28, 2011, p. 11.

present that day. "Truly, truly, I have a *ghassah* in my heart [heartbreak] ... a big, big pain that in spite of everything ... every time I remember, that despite everything, truly, truly, that I did not participate in the [protest on the] 14th, in Habib Bourguiba Avenue ... after everything, I was deprived of that ... I was watching it on TV!"[57] Rawda Ben Othman struck a similar but inverted chord: had she not attended that day, she would have been "heartbroken" forever.[58] Post-revolution activist Leila Chreibi[59] shared with others the sense of heightened affect: "the chains [binding us] were broken, fear vanished ... [it was] a feeling we have never felt before ... so beautiful ..." She gestured toward a kind of ambivalence. "The nightmare [we were living] was cast aside," but she experienced "happiness mixed with fear ... as though we were taking the plunge from a high place ... toward the unknown." Free "to move" at last, Chreibi directed her energies and newfound buoyancy toward civil society. Exactly what Tunisians would make of the new void filled by people power, teetering on uncertainty and chaos, was an open question.[60] The Kasbah sit-ins would grapple with these puzzles soon after. For the moment, however, Ben Ali had fled. Tunisians had made a revolution. It was a common experience of equality, a reconfiguration of power by people, not kings.

Contemporaneous Revolutionary Narratives

The accelerated action of the 28 days it took for Ben Ali to pack his proverbial bags was remarkable. Revolutionary pandemonium did not, however, preclude reflective stock-taking as events unfolded. This section traces an additionally important dimension to the detonating revolutionary *hirak*: its continuous reading and re-reading by those at the heart of its most dramatic moments. The cognition of peoplehood took expressive shape not just in the protest slogans but also in the (re)interpretations of what was happening, how, and what was going right and what was going wrong. This reflexivity intensified as protestors moved into the Kasbah sit-ins (see next section). Early reactions to Sidi Bouzid protests drew almost automatic connections to the phosphate basin (2008) and Ben Guerdane (2010) unrest. Not too long ago were the bread riots of the late 1970s and 1980s—an arc of "deprivation, discrimination, and marginalization" exploding in rebellion, according to the late judge Mokhtar Yahyaoui (2010). He called for a national "listening" to the pain and anger of Sidi Bouzid's rebels. State policies could in theory restore the "dignity of the excluded," to become a "true revolution against deprivation and social injustice" (Yahyaoui 2010). The onus would be on Ben Ali's state to distribute fairly, not on the protestors to retreat for the sake of public order. The dispersion of protests initially began as "support" and "solidarity" with the indignants of Sidi Bouzid. The southern governorate

---

[57] Interview, July 28, 2022, Tunis.
[58] Interview, October 16, 2022, Tunis.
[59] Interview, July 29, 2022, Tunis.
[60] *Taghtiyah Kamilah li Ahdath Al-Ams bi Kamil Anha' Al-Bilad*, in *Alchourouk*, January 15, 2011.

was in some ways an extreme version of *hogra* and deprivation, the psycho-social-material misfortunes that to varying degrees afflicted *all* Tunisians, denying them little or no stake in their own socio-economic uplift. Solidarity with the downtrodden developed into identification that "he" or "she," *they* in the south, are *me* as well.

Youth in Act and Affect

A youth workshop organized by *Al-Adab* journal at April 9 College (University of Tunis) in January 2011, touched on similar themes of spatio-temporal coupling. Testimony and reflections by the leftist-leaning group of five provide clues about mindsets, feelings, and aspirations only days after Ben Ali had fled. There was no unanimity at this early stage about whether the tumultuous events had become a "revolution" or were still merely an "uprising." These activists expressed a shared recognition that those in the far-flung regions were the pioneers of the revolution, namely Sidi Bouzid and Kasserine. The pedagogical featured strongly in this narrative. "We learned from them [rebels in Sidi Bouzid, Kasserine, Thela, etc.] that the people can take down their regimes," says Mohammad Ali Ltayyef (quoted in Ben Khalifah 2011, 49). Ben Ali's young naysayers also learned from their own direct experiences. Layla Gayfa tells of the "accumulation of experience" countering internet censorship, including during the 2008 phosphate uprising (quoted in Ben Khalifah 2011, 47). Mohamed Ali Latayyef notes how Tunisians had "tried and accumulated [various] experiences: since the strike of 1978 [Black Thursday] ... the Bread Uprising of 1984, and the struggles of the 1990s, and then the phosphate basin struggle in 2008." Through these confrontations with the regime, people had "lost all trust in the police ruler of the Tunisian 'polity'" (quoted in Ben Khalifah 2011, 48). Malik Al-Sghayri looks another century further back, to Tunisia's crucible. He draws a parallel between 2011, where revolutionaries did not accede to power, and Ali Ben Ghedhahem's revolution of 1864 that lit up in the regions while stopping short of Kasbah or Carthage. "Our failure" then should not recur this time around, he adds (quoted in Ben Khalifah 2011, 50). These testimonies seem to confirm 2010–11 as a diachrony in which conjoined the memories, affect, built-up learning, and mutual trust of prior synchroniesconjoined. Past and present folded into each another, guided by a people's future outlook toward freedom and dignity.

His protest involvement interrupted by his arrest on January 10, Malik Al-Sghayri recounts the main mission he and his colleagues had set for themselves, once the uprising had spread to Kasserine: "What do we do so that we [make] the protests reach the capital?" (quoted in Ben Khalifah 2011, 48). This agentic insistence on expanding the geographic range of protests also speaks to the consciousness of a *nation-wide* demos. Lamin Bouazizi of Sidi Bouzid recounts months of interspersed protests: slogans against the "November 7" regime in August when Turkey's "Freedom Flotilla" headed to Gaza, farmers' uprisings over confiscated land, unruliness by a core group of 50 secondary school "troublemakers" insisting on the right to labor organization. We were "trying to accumulate anger," aggregating and escalating it through protest, he explains. When Mohamed Bouazizi burned himself on December 17, family and friends "searched for the group of 'troublemakers' to stage a sit-in," and the rest was history (quoted in Ben Khalifah 2011, 47). Affect, which permeated Sidi Bouzid's society widely, was thus directed agentically in representational, oppositional, agonistic acts against the regime.

Moreover, intentional invocations of affect were sometimes strategic mobilizing practices. The Student Union was central to university youth organization, across colleges, as Mohamed Ali Latayyef suggests. His references to the Student Union parallel the proactive, pioneering role the UGTT itself played in the evolution and travel of protests from Sidi Bouzid to the capital, discussed above. He recalls the Union's role in "framing people's consciousness," often through coining slogans and disseminating images. We "appealed to emotions through raising [in demonstrations] pictures of the martyr Mohamed Bouazizi and the other martyrs, for the sake of moving people to let go of their narrow thinking"—geographically, regionally narrow, perhaps. The approach was "successful," he recalls, indicated by the "great solidarity" it engendered. Cognitive and affective changes followed. Students grew to mock the notion of "supporting our people in Sidi Bouzid," he remarks. "We are not in France in order to support our people, but a part of it!" (quoted in Ben Khalifah 2011, 48). This fragment of activist memory implies a burgeoning consciousness of joint suffering that crowded out the "other." The "self" grew to envelope all Tunisians repressed, marginalized, deprived, and humiliated by the regime.

Gendering Revolutionary Diachrony

The ruminations above from Tunisia's youth reflect some ways in which Tunisians considered their differently positioned and situated roles in the revolution. We now examine women's involvement and post-Ben Ali prospects, which has similarly generated extensive argument and even controversy. Here, a reminder of epistemological and methodological proportions is in order. As we have repeatedly noted, we do not bracket off Tunisian women into a unique protestscape in this book. Instead, we have pointedly featured women's gendered participation—and the particular gains and constraints thereof—in each protestscape. Some, like the UGTT and to an extent, the Kamour uprising, and the ultras especially, are more masculine spaces than others. Our approach thus avoids flattening all Tunisian women across space and time into one unified grouping with identical demands and aspirations in their multifaceted confrontations with authoritarianism. Postcolonial feminism helps us avert such a simplistic analytical impulse. Competing visions and notions of "modernity," with its (patriarchal) bundles of state- and nation-building, class connotations, varied relationships to religious texts and traditions, and equivocal positions vis-à-vis (ex)colonial powers and the vestiges of European (then American) cultural evangelism are all "entangled" in Arab and Islamic feminist politics and practices (Abu Lughod 1998).

It is thus impossible to pin down one orderly set of social imaginaries, discourses, and behaviors by Tunisian women across the revolutionary milieu. We are, in fact, faced with a paradox familiar to observers and analysts of (always) gendered socio-political change. Our numerous interviewees from different protestscapes, in addition to reams of published Tunisian reporting and analysis, unanimously stress women's indisputable presence and participation in the 2010–11 revolution. As Chapter 5 demonstrated, women had assertively "appeared" in manifold modes of protest through the many months of the phosphate basin uprising and its aftermath. With its historical precedents and the "protest competencies" built up through the student movement and women's civil society formations (e.g. AFTURD and ATFD), such vociferous female involvement carried through into the revolution itself.

Here is where the consensus on women ends, however—like much else in Tunisian post-Ben Ali politics and society. Khalil (2014, 187) argues that while women's "partnership" in the revolution traversed ideological (secularist vs. Islamist) divides, "intense political competition" erected new/old barriers that stymied cooperation to counteract women's political exclusion. Charrad and Zarrugh (2014) consider the fierce debate about the clause on "complementarity" (which they translate as "integrat[ing] with one another"), as opposed to "equality," between men and women in the family, Article 28 of the draft 2014 Constitution[61] as a manifestation of a new "bottom-up" politics supplanting decades of "top-down" state feminism. With its contentious implications for male–female, state–society, and modernist–traditionalist power relations, this contest of language (Sadiki 2012), also fomented further protest in the post-2011 polity. (Many women interviewed for this book took part in the August 13, 2012 protests denouncing the "complementarity" wording.) Our interest here is in the "disagreement" on notions and directions for women in private and public life within the pulse of the 2011 revolution. Building on the struggles of their country-men and -women over the arch of Tunisian anti/postcolonial history, protestors from Sidi Bouzid to Tunis had de-crowned the head and symbol of authoritarian rule. The missing people were finding themselves as Tunisians-in-revolution. In so doing, they freed up not only the site of political power, but space for debate on the political[62] as well as personal significance and pathways for a post-authoritarian, democratic future.

It is in this vein that we briefly discuss reflections by women on the ramifications of (post)revolutionary politics in polity and society. One common trend, from interviews and published material, is a fixation on Bourguiba's 1956 personal status code (CPS) as a referential milestone for women's equal status (in theory, if not practice). Discomfort and outright refusal of "complementarity" wording in the draft Constitution (see also Marks 2013) can be read in this light. Anxiety over the possible reversal of the CPS is the subtext for some women's prognoses of their social

---

[61] The term "complementarity" was eventually dropped in the version of the Constitution passed in 2014. After his 2021 power grab, President Kais Saied replaced the democratically promulgated Constitution with his own version in July 2022, an issue to which we will return in the final chapter.

[62] One early but longstanding debate was over a parliamentary versus presidential system. See *Al-Islah Al-Asasi ... Ilgha' Al-Nizam Al-Ri'asi,* in *Al-Sabah,* February 4, 2011, p. 8.

and political futures. A well-known Tunisian feminist academic, Amel Grami, puts the dilemma in stark terms. She contends that constitution-drafting debates, including those pertaining to women and family roles, emanate from a conflict between those with "modernist" (*hadathiyyin*) and anti-democratic "Salafist" views. Awkwardly straddling these two camps, what she sees as Ennahda's[63] untenable position essentially discards the language and legislation of "equality," male/female and otherwise (Grami 2012, 28). As another academic, Hafidha Choukeir (2014, 20) put it, comparative readings across Islamic contexts hint that "this concept [of complementarity] is among the most important concepts that reverts us to the traditional distribution of roles within the family". That a revolution in which women had struggled alongside men could usher in such backward steps was thus unacceptable to many.

In Tunisia (as in other Arab states), it is not simply women's bodies but their cultural-social-political positioning that serves as a kind of ideological benchmark. Debates relating to distinctly women's issues (the CPS, inheritance laws, sometimes even lingering opposition to the veil) escalate into political flashpoints. The inextricable link between the personal and the political is an important embodiment of a new agonism *within* a burgeoning peoplehood since 2011. Here lies the crux of democratic politics, of course: managing conflict and disagreement among equal citizens, in matters of representation, policy-making, distribution, recognition. We will return to these prickly issues in the concluding chapter. For the moment, however, we wish to hint at nascent frictions relevant to women. One study commissioned and published by the official Center for Research, Studies, Documentation and Information on Women (CREDIF) on women in the Tunisian revolution exposes the chasm in understandings and imaginings of female futures. In this book, Al-Ammari and Chakroun (2013) aver in colorful language that women's revolutionary "presence was not a passing event but a crowning of a historical trajectory our country lived since the 20s of the last century" (2013, 6). A century of women's advancement parallels, then, the century of the union and student protestscapes. In the revolutionary aftermath, disagreement surfaces between (anonymized) women whose brief testimonies they record. Shared initial euphoria and exhilaration give way to diverging experiences and assessments. Spatialized class disparities (North/Coastal vs. Interior/South), typified by city-based, educated women's distance from rural women (*al-mar'ah al-rifiyyah*) are only one source of strain. One woman from Beja describes the revolution as one "I had been waiting for with extreme patience," jumping at the chance to participate as soon as it erupted. A proponent of "moderate Islam," she is confident that "there is no fear regarding women's rights today," doubting the possibility of dictatorial resurgence after "tongues have been unleashed and minds freed" (quoted in Al-Ammari and Chakroun 2013, 119–120).

Most other women whose testimony is featured in the study see matters differently. An attorney from Kef is torn "between happiness and fear, between sadness

---

[63] The leading party after the October 2011 elections of the National Constituent Assembly tasked with writing the constitution, holding 89 of 217 parliamentary seats.

and hope" (quoted in Al-Ammari and Chakroun 2013, 121–122). Her affective ambivalence is pronounced. As soon as Ben Ali had been deposed, men took over all transitional positions of power, beginning with the regional Committees to Protect the Revolution.[64] Even the parity law passed by the High Commission for the Realization of the Goals of the Revolution, Political Reform, and Democratic Transition (see Borsali 2012, 11–50) was insufficient to "safeguard the revolution" and specifically, women's socio-political place, adds the attorney. Some seem to confer a kind of blame on Islamist women. A teacher from Tunis who deplores the exclusion (*taghyib*) of women in new political formations and even in the new Executive Committee voted in by the 2011 UGTT Congress, discounts women's parliamentary gains. Implying the Ennahda women (who held 42 of the 49 female seats in the NCA), she is skeptical of how representative female MPs are of Tunisian women in general. "Most of them do not represent me," failing as they do to fight for women's rights, as she perceives it (R.B., quoted in Al-Ammari and Chakroun 2013, 124).[65] A cleaning worker from Tunis agrees: "the women of the NCA (*ta'sisi*) do not represent me, nor do they adopt any strategy to defend women, or protect their [rights achievements], nor do they even possess in my view the adequate consciousness" to deal with various socio-political problems that befall women (J.W., quoted in Al-Ammari and Chakroun 2013, 127–130).

Similarly, the head of a civil society organization in Mehdia expresses "fear of the group of women who choose acquiescence and do not defend their rights" (B.S., quoted in Al-Ammari and Chakroun 2013, 141). Some Ennahda-skeptics veer into nostalgia for Bourguiba (the authoritarian!). Even having just come out of a revolution, a journalist from Tunis fondly notes that "the leader (*al-za'im*) Bourguiba, when he awarded women freedom, aimed at building ... a balanced society" where each individual played their part (R.W., quoted in Al-Ammari and Chakroun 2013, 132). Her reverence for Bourguiba as a liberator of women contrasts with some other women's assessments (e.g. Perspectivists and student activists: see Chapter 3). Still, R.W. joins female compatriots in the CREDIF study's majority view that women's rights are endangered in the wake of revolution. Some are more vocal than others in asserting that Islamists, and Islamist women in particular, are obstacles towards "preserving advancements" in women's rights (*al-hifaz 'ala al-makasib*)[66]. In this narrative, one cornerstone of Tunisia's progressive reputation is in jeopardy. An inclusive peoplehood thus stands on shaky ground. It is wracked by indicative tensions, whether between women and men, or women and women. Such disputes, touched on in the CREDIF study, comprise merely the tip of the iceberg. Skirmishes over representation, democratic participation, inclusiveness, and popular sovereignty, so central to cognitive ontologies (in the plural) of peoplehood, would crack the veneer

---

[64] For the entire country, the National Council for the Protection of the Revolution brought together 28 parties and organizations. See *Ittafaqa 'Alaihi 28 Hizban wa Munazzamah... Majlis Watani li Himayat Al-Thawrah*, in *Al-Sabah*, February 15, 2011, p. 6.

[65] Arabic Initials are used in the original source.

[66] This is a recurring sentiment and phraseology. Najlaa Douiri, member of the National Office for Working Women in the UGTT, for instance, insisted on "preserving" *and building on* past national achievements in the case of syndicalist women (Lecture given to Demos-Tunisia Summer School, July 20, 2023).

of a people's unity against the dictator in the Kasbah sit-ins. Yet it was exactly those argumentative social acts and en-actments that would firm up the agency, affect, and cognition of a people in revolution, as the next section will show.

"Occupy" Kasbah

We have argued above the merit of incorporating rather than separating, youth and women's presence and participation into Tunisia's protest synchronies and diachronies. It might be simpler to end our attempt to re-ontologize the protestscape here, upholding the dictator's departure on January 14, 2011 as a clean boundary delineating the revolution's conclusion. However, the President's exit did not halt protests clamoring in the name of the revolution. The remaining sections delve into the Kasbah 1 (January 22–January 27) and Kasbah 2 (February 20–March 3) sit-ins (Ben Meem 2019, 150–155). We show that the Kasbah was the next consequential stop as the train of popular revolution lurched forward. The young were aghast that Fouad Mbazza, Ben Ali's Speaker of Parliament, was Acting President, and Mohamed Ghannouchi, Ben Ali's Prime Minister, remained in the same position. It is not clear that this transitional government, with Ministers holding over from Ben Ali's rule, would have budged had not these two youth-led protests insisted that they too, *dégage*. (The UGTT had vacated the first version of this transitional government days after the President fled.[67]) Largely under-explored, the Kasbah sit-ins have been dealt with journalistically as they took place (e.g. Coll 2011) and in more extended works (e.g. Wright 2012, 234–235). Some Tunisian scholars have briefly incorporated Kasbah into early examinations of the revolution (e.g. Ayeb 2011; Saidani 2012, 52–53). Consolidating our analysis of the revolution rebelscape, we draw largely on participant testimonies to explore the agentic, affective, and cognitive discourses and practices of the Kasbah youth (and those who gathered around them).

The Kasbah's significance is three-fold. *First*, through this creative initiative Tunisian youth further carved out "freed spaces" that unionists and student activists had chiseled (in UGTT headquarters, or the university) decades earlier. Literally occupying the site of government power where several ministries and the Premiership (*al-wizarah al-ula*) are located, was an assertion of peoplehood critically cognized as the source of sovereignty. Protestors also convened in front of the Interior Ministry on Habib Bourguiba Avenue.[68] Mohamed Ghannouchi's government should go out, so that we can be in, was the message. The Premier's eventual resignation (February 27, 2011) in response to this sustained protest pressure was the symbolic completion of the "de-throning" of authoritarian power. The most overt emblems of counterrevolution were kept at bay, for the time being. *Second*, in the Kasbah sit-ins, particularly Kasbah 2, protestors created a platform for speech acts,

---

[67] *Ittihad Al-Shughl Yansahib min Al-Hukumah Ihtijajan 'ala Musharakat Wuzara' Ben Ali*, in *Al-Wasat Al-Tunisi*, January 18, 2011, echoing a wider sentiment. See *Al-Shari' Al-Tunisi Yatazahar Didd Al-Hukumah Al-Jadidah Wa Thalathat Wuzara' Yastaqilun*, in *Al-Fajr News*, January 18, 2011.

[68] *I'tisamat Amama Qasr Al-Hukumah wa Wazarat Al-'Adl wa al-Naql wa al-Dakhiliyyah*, in *Al-Sabah*, January 25, 2011, p. 7.

public deliberation, and debate. Attempting rough representation (e.g. of Tunisian provinces), they administered sit-in logistics, dealt with officials and the media, and discussed and debated issues salient to a revolutionary vibe. Here protestors fashioned for themselves a mini *demos*, a seedling of democratic governance even as the institutional pathway was yet undecided. Cognition of *al-shaʻb* as willing and capable of self-rule began to mature. *Third*, the Kasbah sit-ins brought to the fore differences in how the newly emancipated polity should be run. How radical did revolutionary change need to be? What form of government could rise to the hopes and dreams of a people just found? The shared demand for a National Constituent Assembly (*majlis taʼsisi*) to write a new constitution did not equate with consensus on the pace and form of democratic change. Without romanticizing the Kasbah sit-ins, we emphatically claim that they tipped the balance in favor of the revolution. These protests propelled the country's (discordant) elites to move towards democratic transition. Whether or not the transitional trajectories were commensurate with the emancipatory expectations of freedom *and* dignity by Tunisia's downtrodden and marginalized is a question we take up in the coming chapters.

The Freedom Caravan: Kasbah 1 Sit-in

Fawzi Daas retells the origin story[69] of the Kasbah 1 sit-in (in Al-Tamimi 2012a). It was almost a "joke" that came up in a Publinet cafe in Sidi Bouzid. Activists there were furious that after they had ignited a revolution, Ben Ali's men stepped in to lead the country. Why not march to the capital in protest? As Daas narrates it, Sidi Bouzid youth decided that with no transportation, they would approach Tunis on foot: "How did Ali Ben Ghedhahem's revolution and people in the past, how did they used to transport themselves, are they better than us?" they asked each other. The diachrony rears its head again. Tunisia's (Southern) revolutionary hero animates the social imaginaries of rebellious youth in 2011. One was Hamza Nasri who had been shot in the leg, yet walked 34 kilometers on foot in defiance of his doctor's orders (in Al-Tamimi 2012a, 148–149). Determined agency here requires no explanation. Lutfi Al-Yaqoubi comments on the choice of Kasbah as the location for sit-in. The youth sought to "paralyze government work" carried out by the ministries housed there (quoted in Al-Tamimi 2012a, 152). The "freedom caravan"[70] of 18 people that had set off on January 22–23 from Menzel Bouzaiane in Sidi Bouzid, walking to Meknassy, then Regueb, eventually riding to Tunis, multiplied in size until 800 people arrived at the capital, as Taieb Bouaisha tells it. Infiltrating Kasbah was no easy feat. The youth had to shove past the army which had closed off the square (in Al-Tamimi 2015a, 162). Slogans included "from Bouzid on foot, until the toppling of the regime!" "Oh people, revolt against the remnants of the dictator!"; "The right to protest is an

---

[69] Disputed in the testimonials at the Tamimi Foundation, where Fawzi Daas and others rejected Meqdad Majri's Tunis-based account (in Al-Tamimi 2012a, 119–120, 148–150).
[70] *Qawafil Al-Hurriyyah Tatazahar fi Qalb Al-ʻAsimah … in Al-Sabah*, January 25, 2011, p. 6.

obligation, the right to free speech is an obligation!" (in Al-Tamimi 2015a, 162–3). Protest was a conscious exercise of the just-won, fragile right to have rights. Faouzi Daas notes that he and other Tunis-based activists met this group from the South through UGET and other student activists (in Al-Tamimi 2012a, 149). Abdelkhaleq Bouiqqah remembers a short-lived "national popular harmony" (*wifaq*) characterizing the political void, before the political parties re-organized. In fact, political parties were not allowed into the Kasbah 1 sit-in. We were "sweeping away the regime" (*taknis*), as he puts it (quoted in Al-Tamimi 2012a, 137). Bouaisha remarks on the level of consciousness (*wa'y*), a frequently circulating term. Facilitating the endurance of the protest was "an entrenched idea among the protestors that their shared enemy is the remnants of the existing regime," to be ousted in order for the revolution to succeed (quoted in Al-Tamimi 2015a, 164). Moreover, Kasbah 1 was a microcosm of Tunisian society, with people from

> Bizerte [north] to Ben Guerdane [south], rich and poor, the politicized and apolitical, men and women, the educated and illiterate, the sons of the popular neighborhoods and sons of the posh neighborhoods … some members of parties and associations (as individuals) … the sit-in was truly a real society and what was astonishing was how everything proceeded without problems worth mentioning.
> (quoted in Al-Tamimi 2015a, 163–164)

Despite their large numbers, protestors were able to administer themselves. A sudden visit by General Rachid Ammar raised questions.[71] Protestors' rejection of the army's potential tutelage confirms their cognition of emancipation as civic rather than military. Food, blankets, a minimal level of security, and media contacts, were all arranged by the Kasbah youth. Their primary demand was the resignation of Ghannouchi's government, to be replaced by one representative of the people, in the spirit of the revolution. Graffiti, songs, chants, discussion circles all signaled the seriousness of this popular take-over of government space. Smaller protests against the interim government tore through other regions, from Bizerte to Zerzis.[72] By January 27, Ghannouchi gave in partially, instituting a cabinet reshuffle. On January 28, the military moved in, invading even the Great Mosque (Zaytuna), as Turkiyah Alshaybi remembers (in Al-Tamimi 2015a, 169–170). Yet even after Kasbah 1 was shut down forcefully (see Leisir 2012, 220–222), according to Tareq Karim, "we emerged repressed but happy that we had not despaired … and we began to think of a way to return to Kasbah" (quoted in Al-Tamimi 2015a, 188). The youth's agency was undeterred, their affect jumbled (outrage and relief at their own persistence), their cognition beaming (they were the people who would see their revolution to the end).

---

[71] *Tawasul Al-I'tisam fi Sahat Kasbah Wa Itlalah Mufaji'ah li Rachid Ammar*, in *Kalimah Tunis*, January 25, 2011.
[72] *Al-Shabab Yuqidun Al-Shumu'—Tawasul al-Intifadah al-Sha'biyyah*, in *Al-Sabah*, January 25, 2011, p. 7.

Kasbah 2 Sit-in

The foregoing discussion suggests that disparate *demoi* had banded together after the President had been made territory-less. The simulated deterritorialization of Ben Ali's ousting was not enough to empty the seat of power, so Tunisian youths moved to occupy that very seat in Kasbah 1. There they extended an embodied de/re-territorialization of power and sovereignty worthy of a revolution, only to be interrupted. This section expounds on the political and symbolic significance of the next iteration, Kasbah 2 (see Leisir 2012, 222–224). Coercively dispersed by the military and the police, Tunisia's revolutionary youth would make a comeback only days later. Seeking clarity in the midst of rampant uncertainty,[73] youth organizers would try to compensate for the shortcomings of the rudely aborted Kasbah 1. In the interim, protests continued unabated across the country. Youth railed against governor appointments (for instance, because of RCD membership in Kasserine[74] and general incompetence in Kebili[75]) and unemployment, sometimes degenerating into violent unruliness.[76] The sit-in eventually re-ignited by February 22 would be more organized, more inclusive, more crisp and clear in its demands, by the activists' own telling.[77] In preparation and solidarity, Sfax youth embarked on their own "Kasbah 1" sit-in to coincide with Kasbah 2 in Tunis. This "parallel sit-in" aimed at becoming "a life artery" to the one in the capital, according to Mohamed Alkhalfi, one of its coordinators (Diwan FM 2014). As in the revolutionary protests, the Sfax youth also launched their demonstration at the UGTT headquarters, heading as did the Kasbah 1 youth to protest in front of the French consulate. Revolutionary agency, affect, and cognition had an unmistakable postcolonial ring: the former colonial power was perceived as meddling to prop up Ghannouchi's decidedly counter-revolutionary government. In Sfax, youth from all ideological stripes (leftists to Salafis) congregated, set up tents, blared music, chanted slogans, and released statements with the same demands sought by the Tunis sit-in that would begin two days later. The cross-regional complementarity (Sfax/Tunis) kept up the symbolic march from South to North begun in the Sidi Bouzid December 2010 protests and picked up in the Kasbah "freedom caravan" the month before. Participant leader Mohamed Alkhalfi paints a picture of simple but powerful solidarity in Sfax's own Kasbah: "we used to split the loaf of bread, the cup of tea … and [even] our blankets" in the days-long sit-in. Still, tensions over partisan balances of power and influence, the choice of wording and demands espoused in statements, were perhaps unavoidable. A general youth mistrust of political elites (even veteran anti-authoritarian militants) hangs over the testimonies of all Kasbah youth sit-ins. Yet peoplehood was at its finest. Its social acts

---

[73] *3 Sinaryuhat Siyasiyyah li Tunis Ma Ba'da Ben Ali*, in *Al-Sabah*, February 20, 2011, p. 5.
[74] *Kasserine: Al-Muwatinun Yarfuduna al-Wali Al-Jadid … wa al-Jaish Yarfa' Al-Nifayat*, in *Al-Sabah*, February 5, 2011, p. 8.
[75] *Ihtijajat wa Masirat li Tanahhi Al-Wali Al-Jadid,* in *Al-Sabah*, February 5, 2011, p. 9.
[76] *Tawasul Al-I'tisamat li al-Mutalabah bi Tanhiyat Ba'd Al-Wullat* in *Al-Sabah*, February 5, 2011, p. 8.
[77] *Afwaj … Amwaj min al-Jamahir … wa Jumlah min Al-Shi'arat*, in *Al-Sabah*, February 26, 2011.

and en-actments repelled the double consciousness of *hogra* and even, if temporarily, ideological abrasions.

In the carnivalesque commotion, graffiti slogans, posters, and banners vied with chants, singing, arguments, and the overall bustle of large crowds. Featuring black lettering against the background of the Tunisian flag, a large sign hanging on the brown, curved ministry wall listed protestor demands with precise clarity:

> Dissolving the temporary government; activating a constituent assembly; declaring a public pardon; dissolving the parliament and the council of advisers; suspending and reconstituting the Committee for Investigating Truths so it is independent and trustworthy to the people; dissolving the RCD … dissolving the … Constitution; forming a temporary national salvation government; holding accountable remnants of the previous regime; purifying associations and [civil society] groups of … those implicated in [working with] the previous regime …; delaying responses to popular social demands except in emergency situations; re-drafting the journalism law; working towards a new judicial law; working towards a new electoral law.
> (see Alabadli 2011)

Turkiyah Alshaybi attributes the more exacting organization of Kasbah 2 to lessons activists gleaned from the first sit-in. "We overcame chaos and learned from Kasbah 1," she remembers, indicating a continually, quickly developing protest competency. Fawzi Daas elaborates: "We learned from Kasbah 1," forming committees for defense and organization, media, supplies and logistics (*tamwin*), and statement-drafting (quoted in Al-Tamimi 2015a, 175). Statements such as the one issued on February 20, listing the basic demands of the sit-in, were addressed to the "sons [and daughters] of our great people," he remembers (quoted in Al-Tamimi 2015a, 176). More than organization and logistics, learning entailed "elevating [the] level of [political] consciousness" outlining what the people gathered wanted and how they could best articulate it (Alshaybi quoted in Al-Tamimi 2015a, 172). Daas explains how the blossoming cognition of a people in revolt perceived itself and its authoritarian adversaries: "the revolutionary *sha'b* was conscious since 14 January that there is no meaning to freedom and dignity in light of the existing regime's [Ghannouchi government] continuation" (quoted in Al-Tamimi 2015, 162). Freedom and dignity must be put into practice, as in the praxis of Freire's pedagogy of freedom. Slogans could not be demoted to empty words, without corresponding political deeds.

Revolutionary Movement for Democracy

Relative inclusiveness was notable in Kasbah 2, which unlike Kasbah 1, was open to civil society groups, political parties (excepting the RCD), and the UGTT. Like the heady revolutionary days of December and January, women were ever-present. They wore multiple hats: "in the media and in the kitchen and even in the defense committee; they used to write the slogans and participate in the discussions and in [politically and intellectually] framing the sit-in, and cleaning" (quoted in Al-Tamimi

2015a, 174). Abdelslam Haidouri recalls the "Committee for Representing the Kasbah delegations" of about four dozen members. Its operation was a "small democratic practice," he says. "Each group went to its tent ... and each tent elected a person whom they sent to the large tent," although not without some disagreements about regional representation (quoted in Al-Tamimi 2015a, 182). The repository of protest competencies that activists had developed over the diachrony and across protestscapes had merged with a roughly democratic social imaginary and its relevant procedures (e.g. in syndicalist bodies). This accumulated democratic learning was put into practice in new ways. The miniature demos materializing stood in stark contrast to the Ghannouchi government. The latter included ministers from Ben Ali government and even veteran student and opposition party activists such as Najib Chebbi, Minister of Local and Regional Development in Mohamed Ghannouchi's second government. Chebbi maintains in his memoir that Ghannouchi's plan (National Unity Government, Ben Ashour's High Commission, and elections in six months to be monitored by international observers) appealed to him as a way to "safeguard the state." "This roadmap [was in] agree[ment] with [the PDP's] most important demands to liberate political life and open the horizon for democratic transition" (Chebbi 2022, 151–152). He vocally opposed the Kasbah sit-in[78] but had decried the violent shutdown on January 28 (Aljazeera 2011). Its band of mini-publics was led by rash youth who, at least in Abdelsalam Hamdi's view, "want[ed] the marginalized and the impoverished to be the power-holders" (quoted in Al-Tamimi 2015a, 203). Many who joined the sit-ins were newcomers who "did not have any political membership, or any political background," recalls Nouman Alqadri (quoted in Al-Tamimi 2015a, 193). Some, like Haidouri, expressed suspicion of the Bar Association led by Abderazak Kilani and the UGTT for their role in encouraging the eventual suspension of the sit-in (in Al-Tamimi 2015a, 182). Others like Rida Ben Issa were more approbatory towards the union. He recounts that leftist attorney and rights activist Radia Nasraoui was the one who had suggested to him that a sit-in should be a sustained stay in Kasbah. Here the protest competencies of an earlier generation were passed on, learned by a new crop of activists. The mammoth centenarian opposition body, too, played a supportive role (at least to an extent). Ben Issa approached Noureddine Tabboubi (Secretary-General of the Tunis regional UGTT at the time; now national Secretary General). He donated the first 360 dinars, which they used to buy 30 mattresses, water, and sandwiches. Mustapha Ben Jaafar's Ettakatol Party also sent two of its female cadres to make and distribute sandwiches, according to Ben Issa (in Al-Tamimi 2015a, 194–195).

Activists embellished the serious political demands of the Kasbah 2 sit-in with their creative, cacophonous imprints. Hatem Laouine comments on the artistic side of the gathering: drawings, celebratory songs, especially revolutionary ones, including *Mahla Al-Qaʻdah ʻal mayyah* ("How Lovely the View on the Water") (Leisir 2012, 240–241). There were folklore songs (*aghani shaʻbiyyah*) performed by "competing" regions, dancing, veteran bands such as Al-Bahth Al-Musiqi noted earlier, and even

---

[78] See, for instance, his comments to Aljazeera, republished on *"Dahn wa Taslih al-Parachut."* Facebook page, December 9, 2011 post, *"Al-Chebbi Yatahaddath ʻan al-Kasbah 1,"* in https://bit.ly/3Fzzjxv

skits. "The form of the sit-in … was a kind of symphony, or a kind of artistic portrait, or an artistic epic," he recalls (quoted in Al-Tamimi 2015, 196), struggling to settle on the most fitting metaphor. Indicating a keen awareness of the imperative for a people's historiography (history from below), Alshaybi bitterly recalls that they asked the army to

> preserve the writings on the walls of Kasbah square; there were people who wrote on them with their blood, there were very distinctive writings and everything was documented and photographed. We believe this is part of the [people's] heritage and the archive of the revolution, … but the [army] refused and this refusal, we consider it a transgression against the right of the people to document the history of its revolution.
>
> (quoted in Al-Tamimi 2015a, 173)

In this narrative, a people's historiography is an intangible but imperative "right" of a people, among their hard-won right to have rights. That the army rebuffed this demand reinforced the notion that freedom was not quite within the people's grasp.

Many activists tell of the discussion circles (*halaqat niqash*) they held at the sit-in. These deliberative mini-forums recall the ones held by students in university free spaces decades earlier. Instead of heated intellectual debates referencing key texts in competing anti-authoritarian ideologies, however, discussions centered around reading the past, and concocting the political way(s) forward. Laouine describes the discussion circles as ways to intellectually "frame" (*ta'tir*) the sit in, a "contribution to the elevation of political consciousness (*wa'y siyasi*)" (quoted in Al-Tamimi 2015, 195) two frequently invoked terms. Innovative, curious agency buttresses a growing cognition of the responsibilities, challenges, and even disagreements of a new peoplehood. One academic who frequented the Kasbah 2 sit-in remembers some of the topics discussed in these circles, not formal lectures but a kind of political "chit-chat": the workings of the former despot's rule (*hukm al-taghiyah*); international indebtedness; Tunisia's natural resources such as hydrocarbons; and citizens' rights to information.[79] She recalls that speakers included Kais Saied, Radia Nasraoui, Safi Said, feminists from the ATFD, unionists, university professors,[80] and rights activists.

Activists were also hyper-conscious of media coverage that demonized them as destructive ruffians, scarcely taking their demands seriously and allowing them scant air time. Some note the contrast with reporting on the parallel sit-in at the Menzah Dome (*Qubbah* or Cupola), in support of the transitional government.[81] Demands at the Qubbah concerned the "return to work."[82] Maher Al-Khashnaoui refutes

---

[79] Interview with Rawda Ben Othman, October 16, 2022.
[80] At the law and political science faculty, academics also deliberated on a "political roadmap" toward a new constitution. See *Jami'iyyun Yarsumuna Kharitat Al-Tariq: Hakadha Yaqa' Tajawuz Al-Inflat Al-Dusturi*, in *Al-Sabah*, February 26, 2011, p. 4.
[81] *Al-Wasat Al-Tunisiyyah*, Tunis: *I'tisama Al-Kasbah wa Al-Kubbah Yakshifan Madamin Jadida lil Al-Thawrah*, March 6, 2011.
[82] See, *Baina Kasbah wa Al-Qubbah: al-Khafaya al-I'lamiyyah li al-Taharrukain fi Hiwar Ma'a Amin Barakallah wa Altayyeb Bouaisha*," in *Al-Tariq Al-Jadid*, March 12–18, 2011, p. 6, which visually juxtaposes the views of one Qubbah and one Qasbah protestor in a split page layout.

accusations that Kasbah youth were no more than rag-tag, barefooted good-for-nothings. In response, the youths demonstrated their "level of sophistication," he notes. "They [skeptical onlookers] saw how we carried out cleaning sessions in Kasbah, and we raised slogans [in banners] in a civilized, unprecedented way, because it [Kasbah] belongs to us, it is not the possession of [Mohammad] Ghannouchi" (quoted in Al-Tamimi 2012a, 163). Despite being sidelined by the media and vilified by many, the physical occupation of the center of power did translate into a further erosion of authoritarianism. On the "Great Friday" of February 25, what activists exaggeratedly refer to as Tunisia's million-strong protest (*malyuniyyah*), the multitude expanded to tens of thousands. This time under a blue sky warmer than the December/January gray of the revolution, people filled the square, the streets, and the balconies across from the Defense Ministry.[83] Some young men hung from the French-style iron lampposts to declaim to the crowd. "Tunis, land of the free!" "Constituent Assembly ... an obligation (*wajib*)! A new constitution ... an obligation (*wajib*)!" "The people want to topple the regime!" and "O Ghannouchi, o coward, the Tunisian people will not be humiliated!" were some choice slogans. The vastness and momentum of the crowds seems to have made a turning point of that day. Two days later, Mohamed Ghannouchi resigned. By March 3, activists decided to suspend the Kasbah sit-in. Had they achieved their goals? Evaluations were mixed, just as they had been of Kasbah 1.[84] Turkiyah Alshaybi regards it as a "relative success in toppling the Ghannouchi government" (quoted in Al-Tamimi 2015, 172). For Abdelsalam Haidour, the sit-in's goals "were circumvented" (quoted in Al-Tamimi 2015, 184–185). Adel Ben Ghazi drives home the disagreement and further affective ambivalence that gripped them:

> There were those among the protesters who cried from extreme happiness, and those who cried of heartbreak. I personally cried for both reasons, because this was the first time I [was] with my people saying their piece, and from heartbreak because the essential goals of the revolution hadn't been achieved. I wish the protesters could have remained [there] (*murabitin*) until they see what happens, and continue their sit-in until all the goals were achieved because their exit will create a void for the enemies of the revolution to regroup.
>
> (quoted in Al-Tamimi 2015, 199)

In mixed tenses, he weaves in and out of temporalities (the sit-in and his retelling of it) in a tangle of emotions. The elation of becoming a "part that *has* a part" alongside his compatriots descends into grief at the carnival's end, and fear of a future run by kleptocrats of a revolution too easily lost. One commonly used phrase by those disgruntled by the pursuant political transition, whether Kasbah activists or interviewees, is "circumventing" or "manipulating" the revolution, *iltifaf 'ala al-thawrah*.[85] The formal political outcomes of Kasbah were ambiguous, but they did tilt in favor

---

[83] See for instance, Facebook post by Mourad Boubaker, February 26, 2011, "*Al-Kasbah, Al-Jum'ah Al-'Azimah* 1/2011-2-25," https://www.facebook.com/mourad.boubaker.7/videos/1,297,406,850,993
[84] *Madha Jara fi Sahat Al-Kasabah wa Limadha?* in *Al-Sha'b*, February 5, 2011.
[85] *Wa Khashyatan min al-Iltifaf 'Alaiha* in *Kalimat Tunis*, January 14, 2011.

of protestors' general demands. Ghannouchi's abdication (replaced by Beji Caid Sebssi, who would eventually be democratically elected in 2014); dissolving the RCD; election of a constituent[86] assembly; a new constitution; a new electoral law; even a recasting of the revolution-era committees in the High Commission discussed briefly below. Activists' demotic agency, affect, and cognition had in fact fended off the counterrevolution in the leaps and bounds, the social acting and en-acting, of a fledgling peoplehood. Augmented protest competencies evolved into nascent democratic practices. Kasbah as a free space, "the people's ministry," as one sign labeled a corridor of power, transformed into a site for displaying creative aggregation of demands, and quasi-democratic rites of decision-making.

However, disagreement broke through the veneer of a popular "unity" coercively imposed by Ben Ali and Bourguiba before him. Discord that had simmered in contained freed spaces, in the underground or exile of activists on the run, began to break through the surface of a demos operating in public. Some recall that altercations between Islamists/secularists sped up ideological polarization, to the detriment of the "revolutionary pathway" demanding some level of common ground (Chennaoui 2015; see also Zghal 2015 et al.). Interpreting and managing the substance and pitch of disagreements is an open-ended task, entwined with democratization itself. Whatever level of accord or discord pervaded the revolutionary political climate, one achievement is certain. The High Commission would usher in an assortment of laws and institutions, eventuating in an entirely new political system. Who populated the new void of power, how the "missing people" would be (self)represented, and to what extent they could marshal democratic learning to confront trenchant inequalities, were pressing questions deferred to Tunisia's "transition." For now, the people had reterritorialized the "revolution." Bourguiba's claim to anti-colonial fame was traded in for a popularly won "second independence."

Conclusion

The legacy of the Kasbah sit-ins, its leaders and participants, has been generative even if controversial.[87] The High Commission for the Realization of the Goals of the Revolution and Political Reform[88] and Democratic Transition,[89] headed by legal

---

[86] *I'tisam Al-Qasabah Yattasi': Al-Sha'b Yurid Majlisan Ta'sisiyyan,* in *Al-Sabah*, February 26, 2011.
[87] For instance, *Musharik fi I'tisam Kasbah 2 li Alchourouk*, in *Alchorouk*, October 24, 2012; and more recently, *Ahdath February 2011 Kama Yarwiha Al-General Ammar, in Al-Sabah*, January 3, 2022.
[88] Early versions included the Political Reform Committee also headed by Yadh Ben Achour. Against criticism, he insisted on its "advisory" role. See, *Yadh Ben Achour fi Nadwah Sahafiyyah,* in *Al-Tariq Al-Jadid,* February 26–March 4, 2011, p. 4.
[89] This "bi-cameral" commission was comprised of an "Expert Committee," composed of twenty legal scholars and practitioners, and the "Council," representing political parties, civil society associations, important political personalities, and even representatives of the "regions" and martyrs' families. The convoluted name, as Yadh Ben Achour tells it, was cobbled together as three expert committees (for investigating reported crimes during the revolution, for investigating bribery and corruption, and for political reform), were merged. Ironically, these committees had been instituted by Ben Ali on January 13, desperately seeking to "rescue his regime" (Guessoumi 2022, 66–67, 102). The "Council" sought to replace the "Council for the Protection of the Revolution" in which the spectrum of (former) opposition

scholar Yadh Ben Achour,[90] was a direct political outcome. It took on the daunting task of instituting the legal foundations for the country's democratic transition. The quasi-representative body deliberated intensely, its members reaching agreements in this veritable "cookhouse of consensus," as one member of the Expert Committee describes it.[91] The Commission[92] did produce the election law and elections for a National Constituent Assembly, which took place in October 2011. From the first, the Commission was riddled by disagreements even among its legal experts, over its legitimacy, its makeup, its legislative output, even its head (Guessoumi 2022, 191). Kais Saied's[93] testimony to the Al-Tamimi Foundation at the height of the Commission's work reveals the rancor of public debate over the electoral system being hammered out at the time. Party lists and other archaic modes of decision-making should be tossed in favor of "voting for individuals" and even public referenda, given the gaping "trust crisis in the entire political society," distant from the "people" (quoted in Al-Tamimi 2012e, 230). Audience interventions at the session included one interlocutor bemoaning the "legally consultative, but in practice binding, commission that controls us despite everyone['s will]" (quoted in Al-Tamimi 2012e, 223), reflecting the resentment of some at the far-reaching powers of the High Commission. Yet these mechanistic debates (e.g. parliamentary vs. presidential,[94] closed vs. open party lists) seem anticlimactic after the revolutionary momentum that had arguably brought this very process into being. The Kasbah protesters had called for a constituent assembly. Was the revolution already being tamed, or were the fruits of the people's agentic, affective, and cognitive labor simply being institutionalized in a long-awaited democratic transition? We return to this formidable question at the book's conclusion.

This chapter has mapped the crowning of Tunisian peoplehood as the diachrony of Tunisia's revolutionary milieu, inaugurated in the 1860s crucible a century and a half before, exploded through an amalgamation of its protestscape synchronies. In it, universal values (freedom, dignity) were localized within the Tunisian socio-economic and cultural setting (Guessoumi 2020, 8–9). The revolution thrummed with normative content inspirational for the region and the world (Al-Soudani 2015). On the back of the 2008 phosphate uprising and the ancillary protests threading the Gafsa protestscape with the flare-up in Sidi Bouzid, Tunisia's revolution was a long time coming. By charting out the unfolding of the revolution, we have in this chapter disputed some mistaken assumptions about Tunisian's mis-named "Jasmine

---

parties, the LTDH, the Bar Association, the Judges' Association, and other civil society groups were represented, amidst fears of "two states" creeping into existence (Yadh Ben Achour, in Al-Tamimi 2012d, 182–185).

[90] Accused of nepotistic nominations. See for instance *Mahzalah fi Tarkibat Al-Lajnah Al-'Ulya li al-Islah al-Siyasi*, in *Al-Sabah*, February 4, 2011, p. 6.

[91] Interview with Amor Boubakri, October 19, 2022, Tunis.

[92] Established on March 15 after extensive debate between Fouad Mbazza's government and the National Council for the Protection of the Revolution. See for instance *Al-Sabah Tanfarid bi Nashr Fahwa Mashru' al-Hay'ah Al-'Ulya Li Himayat Al-Thawrah*, in *Al-Sabah*, February 20, 2011.

[93] He did support the notion of a new constitution and constituent assembly type-body. See *Ustadh al-Qanun al-Dusturi Kais Saied li al-Sabah*, in *Al-Sabah*, February 25, 2011, p. 7.

[94] The Islamist party Ennahda was an early proponent of a parliamentary system. For instance, see *Hadith fi al-Siyasah Faqat Ma'a Za'im Harakat al-Nahdah*, in *Al-Sabah*, February 15, 2011, p. 6.

revolution." *First*, the revolution was not devoid of a knowledge base. It was far from united under a single ideology, but multiple, competing logoi–social imaginaries, carried on from student activism in the 1960s–1980s, were alive and well in the cadres and repositories of the revolution's participants. Many figures from the student movement would reappear during the revolution and in post-2011 Tunisian politics. They and other syndicalists had built up protest competencies, much learning-in-context, with a lasting impact among young, first-time activists themselves honing their own skills of revolt. *Second*, the revolution was not simply a spontaneous outburst that began in December 2010. We have shown the diachrony "coming home," as it were. Tunisians had constructed this revolution over decades of anti-authoritarian protest struggles, by adamant discounted multitudes and publics, caught between absence and presence: absent as citizens, present in many a temporality and spatiality or through a credo of resounding defiance. The resonance of such a credo was drawn in protest protraits which intersect time and space, but also individual actors and collective social doing, feelings, and cognizance. Thus, the protestscapes of the preceding chapters sought to re-ontologize situated protest and consequent embodied knowing, being, acting, and feeling. *Third*, the revolution was not made exclusively either by oppositional elites (e.g. from political parties or the activist intelligentsia), or only by the enthused youth, the downtrodden with nothing to lose—the part that has no part. It is a simplification and over-gerneralization to claim, as Ben Achour suggests, that Tunisia's was a "revolution without a revolution and without revolutionaries" (2023, 330). The situated partiality of respective protestscapes and the expansiveness of mass mobilization, aided by the UGTT's well-oiled protest machinery, disperses the credit to be awarded to any particular collectivity, demographic, region, class, or ideological membership. It was indeed a people's revolution (*thawrat shaʻb*) *Fourth*, the revolution did not "end" when Ben Ali fled on January 14, 2011. The Kasbah sit-ins proceeded in emptying out authoritarian centers of power in a time-space expansion of "freed spaces." Mohamed Ghannouchi's resignation in early 2011 was a major milestone that arguably staved off an impending counterrevolution. How effective the subsequent High Commission and its successors in Parliament and government would be in living up to the work, freedom, and national dignity demanded from Bizerte to Ben Guerdane was unclear in mid-2011. Tunisia's youth and marginals never stopped protesting. In Southern Tataouine, they embarked on an entire social movement. How few "goods," and how many protest competencies, they had reaped from the revolution! The next chapter explores a new kind of dissentscape that took shape within a democratic start, disrupting the existing hierarchical order.

References

Abassi, Houcine. 2023. *Tunis Wa Al-Furas Al-Mahdurah* [Tunisia's Lost Chances]. Tunis: Nirvana.

Abu-Lughod, Lila. 1998. "Feminist Longings and Postcolonial Conditions." In *Remaking Women: Feminism and Modernity in the Middle East*, edited by Lila Abu-Lughod. Princeton, NJ: Princeton University Press, 3–32.

Alabadli, Imed. 2011. *La Yajib an Yafshal I'tisam Al-Kasabah Hadhihi Al-Marrah* [Kasbah Sit-In Should Not Fail this Time]. 22 February, *Nawaat*, https://bit.ly/3Fz83PH

Al-Ammari, Saniyya bin Jami' and Hanan Chakroun. 2013. *Tunisiyyat wa Masar Al-Thawrah* [Tunisian Women and the Revolution's Trajectory]. Tunis: CREDIF.

Al-Bouni, Afif. 2013. *Al-Thawrah Al-Tunisiyyah: Al-Nusus al-Marji'iyyah 'an Yawmiyyat al-Ahdath bi Al-Jihat wa Asmaa' Al-Shuhadaa' wa Al-Jarha* [The Tunisian Revolution: Documents of Reference Regarding Daily Events in the Regions and Names of the Martyrs and Injured]. Tunis: Dar Sihr Li Al-Nashr.

Al-Habbashi, Mohamed Ali. 2019. *Al-Sawahliyyah: Zaman Al-Bayat… Wa Al-Dawlah Al-Bourguibiyyah* [The Sahel-ites: Time of the Beys…and the Bourguibist State]. Tunis: Sotumedia.

Aljazeera. 2011. *Hudu' bi Tunis Ba'da Fadd I'tisam Al-Kasbah.* 29 January, https://bit.ly/3U5PlmW

Aljazeera. 2012. *Munia Bou 'ali Tarwi Ahdath al-Thawrah al-Tunisiyyah wa Qisas al-Shuhada' min Madinat Al-Kasserine wa Thela* [Mounia Bouali Narrates Events of the Tunisian Revolution]. 24 June, *Shahid 'Ala Al-Thawrah* https://www.youtube.com/watch?v=RchICbkpvEU

Aljazeera. 2022. *Ya Twensa Ma'ash Khuf … Ben Ali H'rab.* https://www.youtube.com/shorts/EBuG85XLK3A

Al-Mahjoubi, Ali. 1986. *Ma Yajibu An Ta'rif 'An Intisab Al-Himayah Al-Faransiyyah* [What You Should Know About Establishment of the Tunisian Protectorate]. Tunis: Ceres.

Al-Soudani, Hussain. 2015. "Al-Thawrah Al-Tunisiyyah: Amalan Akhiran lil al-Shu'ub Al-Mudtahadah." *Akademia* 37: 20–23.

Al-Taimoumi, Alhadi. 2020. *Mawsu'at Al-Rabi' al-'Arabi fi Tunis 2010–2020: Al-Juz' al-Awwal: Sanat Kul Al-Makhater* [Encyclopedia of the Arab Spring in Tunisia: Part One, The Year of All Dangers] 2nd edn. Sfax: Dar Mohammad lil Nashr.

Al-Tamimi, Abdeljalil, ed. 2012a. "Al-Tada'iyat Al-Siyasiyyah li I'tisamayy Al-Kasbah 1 wa 2 fi Masirat Al-Thawrah Al-Tunisiyyah ma'a Al-Sayyidayn Miqdad Al-Majri wa Abdelkhaleq Bouqaah. [Political Implications of Kasbah 1 and 2 Sit-ins …]" In *Marsad al-Thawrah Al-Tunisiyyah* [Observatory of the Tunisian Revolution], Vol 1. Tunis: Tamimi Foundation, 115–158.

Al-Tamimi, Abdeljalil, ed. 2012b. "*Mabadi' wa Tumuhat Shabab Thawrat Al-Karamah wa Al-Dimuqratiyyah* [Principles and Ambitions of Youth of the Revolution for Dignity and Democracy]." In *Marsad al-Thawrah Al-Tunisiyyah*, Vol 1. Tunis: Tamimi Foundation, 153–180.

Al-Tamimi, Abdeljalil, ed. 2012c. "*Dawr al-Mudawwinin al-Tunisyyin fi Thawrat Al-Karamah wa Al-Dimuqratiyyah Ma'an: Lina Ben Mhenni wa Salim Amamo wa Aziz Amami.* [Bloggers' Role in the Revolution of Dignity and Democracy…]" In *Marsad al-Thawrah al-Tunisiyyah*, Vol. 1. Tunis: Tamimi Foundation, 73–114.

Al-Tamimi, Abdeljalil, ed. 2012d. "*Al-Nadwah Al-Sadisah Ma'a al-Ustadh Yadh Ben Achour Ra'is Al-Hay'ah al-'Ulya li Tahqiq Ahdaf Al-Thawrah wa al-Intiqal Al-Dimuqrati wa al-Islah al-Siyasi* [Political Symposium with Prof. Yadh ben Achour]." In *Marsad Al-Thawrah Al-Tunisiyyah*, Vol. 1. Tunis: Tamimi Foundation, 181–207.

Al-Tamimi, Abdeljalil, ed. 2012e. "*Al-Nadwah Al-Sabi'ah Ma'a al-Ustadh Kais Saied Ustadh Al-Qanun Al-Dustouri bi al-Jami'ah al-Tunisiyyah* [7th Political Symposium with Kais Saied]." In *Marsad Al-Thawrah Al-Tunisiyyah*, Vol. 1. Tunis: Tamimi Foundation, 209–246.

Al-Tamimi, Abdeljalil, Ed. 2015a. "*Al-Nadwah 28…Al-Halaqah Al-Thaniyah Mukhassasah li-I'tisam Kasbah 1 wa 2 wa 3* [Symposium 28…Part Two, Concerning the Kasbah 1, 2, and 3 Sit-ins." 2015. In *Marsad Al-Thawrah Al-Tunisiyyah*, Volume 3, Ed. Abdeljalil Al-Tamimi. Tunis: Tamimi Foundation, pp. 159–203.

Al-Tamimi, Abdeljalil, ed. 2015b. "*Ma'a al-Sahafi Rachid Khashanah Hawla Dawr Al-I'lam fi Muqawamat Al-Istibdad 1987–2011* [With Journalist Rachid Khashanah About the Media's Role in Resisting Authoritarianism]." In *Marsad al-Thawrah Al-Tunisiyyah*, Vol 3. Tunis: Tamimi Foundation, 335–390.

Arfaoui, Khmayyes. 2020. *Al-Harakat Al-Ijtima'iyyah fi Tunis min Al-Ihtijaj ila Al-Thawrah* [Social Movements in Tunisia from Protest to Revolution]. Tunis: Dar Sihr lil-Nashr.

Ayyari, Najat. 2022. *Jlas Wa Awlad 'Ayyar: Baina Al-Tahaluf Al-Tawattur* [Jlas and the Sons of 'Ayyar: Between Alliance and Tension] *1864–1881.* Tunis: Dar Nuqush 'Arabiyyah.

Ayeb, Habib. 2011. "Social and Political Geography of the Tunisian Revolution: The Alfa Grass Revolution." *Review of African Political Economy* 38(129); 467–479.

Bakhtin, Mikhail. 1984. *Rabelais and His World*, Trans. Helene Iswolsky. Bloomington: Indiana University Press.

Ben Abbas, Abdeljalil. 2021. *Al-Harakah Al-Wataniyyah bi-Jihat Sfax* [The Nationalist Movement in the Sfax Region] *(1920–1955)*. Sfax: Maktabat Alaeddine.

Ben Achour, Yadh. 2023. *L'éthique des revolutions*. Tunis: AC Editions.

Ben Khalifah, Ghassan ed. 2011. "*Al-Shabab Al-Tunisi Yatahaddath 'An Thawratihi* [Revolutionary Youth Talk About Their Revolution]." Majallat Al-Adab 1-2-3: 47–54.

Ben Meem, Hammadi. 2019. *Asrar al-Thawrah al-Tunisiyyah: Qiyadatiha, Asbabiha, 'Awamil Najahiha wa al-Durus* [Secrets of the Tunisian Revolution: Its Issues, Causes, Factors of Success, and Lessons]. Monastir: Al-Thaqafiyyah lil Tiba'ah wal Nashr wa al-Tawzee'.

Ben Salah, Mohamed Al-Hadi. 1989. *Mi'at 'Am Min Al-Qaryah* [One Hundred Years of the Village]. Tunis: Dar Al-Wataniyyah.

Ben Yousef, Adel. 2019. *Al-Masar al-Thawri wa al-Intiqal al-Dimuqrati fi Tunis (Min Khilal Al-Watha'iq)* [Revolutionary Trajectory and Democratic Transition in Tunisia (Through Documents)]: *2008—2011*. Sfax: Maktabat Alaeddine.

Borsali, Noura. 2012. *Al-Tanasuf fi al-Qanun Al-Intikhabi wa fi al-Mujtama' wa Kitabat Nasawiyyah* [Parity in the Election Law and in Society and Feminist Writings]. Tunis: Arabesques.

Charrad, Mounira M. and Amina Zarrugh. 2014. "Equal or Complementary? Women in the New Tunisian Constitution after the Arab Spring." *The Journal of North African Studies* 19(2): 230–243.

Chebbi, Ahmed Najib. 2022. *Al-Masirah Wa Al-Masar: Ma Jara wa Ara* [The Journey and Trajectory: What Happened and What I Believe]. Tunis: Mots Passants.

Chennaoui, Henda. 2015. *Kasbah 1 wa 2: 'Awdah ila Asbab Intikasat al-Masar Al-Thawri* [Kasbah 1 and 2], trans. Mohamed Samih Beji Okkez, 10 February, Nawaat, https://bit.ly/3UcjmS2

Choukeir, Hafidha. 2014. "*Huquq al-Mar'ah Asas al-Dawlah al-Hadithah* [Women's Rights are the Foundation of the Modern State]." *Akademia*, 29: 20–22.

Coll, Steve. 2011. "The Casbah Coalition." March 28, *The New Yorker*, https://www.newyorker.com/magazine/2011/04/04/the-casbah-coalition

Debuysere, Loes. 2016. "'La Femme' Before and After the Tunisian Uprising: (Dis)continuinities in the Configuration of Women in the Truth Regime of 'Tunisianité." *Middle East Law and Governance* 8: 201–227.

Deleuze, Gilles and Felix Guattari. 1987. *A Thousand Plateaus*, Trans. Brian Massumi. Minneapolis: University of Minnesota Press.

Diwan FM. 2014. *I'tisam Al-Kasabah 1 bi Sfax …. Wa La Yazal Al-Hulm Mustamirran*. March 6, https://www.youtube.com/watch?v=lCoEm6GNSns

Elbousalmi, Diyaa. 2017. "'*Umrak ma Tqool Fadait*," *Tughanni Amel Al-Methlouthi*, April 11, Raseef 22, https://bit.ly/3Dp1ht8

Grami, Amel. 2012. "*Dustoor Yata'arjah Baina Marji'iyyatain* [A Constitutions Swings Between Two References]." *Akademia*, 10, 28–29.

Hizb Al-'Ummal Al-Tunisi. 2011. "*Bayan Hizb al-'Ummal Ila al-Sha'b Al-Tunisi wa Qiwah Al-Dimuqratiyyah* [Statement of the Tunisian Workers' Party to the Tunisian People and Democratic Forces]." *Al-Hewar Al-Mutamaddin*, January 12, 2011, https://www.ahewar.org/debat/show.art.asp?aid=241429

Instance Vérité & Dignité. 2017. *Shahadat Jarih Al-Thawrah Muslim Qasdallah* [Testimony of Muslim Qasdallah: Injured in the Revolution]. January 15. https://www.youtube.com/watch?v=PgzAHlVJhnQ

Kerrou, Mohamed. 2012. "Les nouveaux acteurs de la revolution et de la transition politique." In Hamadi Redissi, Asma Nouira and Abdelkader Zghal (eds.), *La Transition Démocratique en Tunisie: Etat des lieux*. Tunis: Diwen, pp. 218–234.

Khalil, Andrea. 2014. "Tunisia's Women: Partners in Revolution." *The Journal of North African Studies* 19(2): 186–199.

Lachmann, Renate, Raoul Eshelman, and Marc Davis. 1988–89. "Bakhtin and Carnival: Culture as Counter-Culture." *Cultural Critique* 11: 115–152.

Leisir, Fethi. 2012. *Mu'jam Al-Thawrah Al-Tunisiyyah* [Compendium of the Tunisian Revolution]. Sfax: Dar Mohamed Ali.

Marks, Monica. 2013. "Women's Rights before and after the Revolution." In *The Making of the Tunisian Revolution: Contexts, Architects, Prospects*, edited by Nouri Gana. Edinburgh: Edinburgh University Press224–251.

Nachaz. 2022. *Watha'iq Hay'at 18 October li al-Huquq wal al-Huriyyat bi Tunis* [Documents of the 18 Oct. Committee for Rights and Freedoms in Tunisia]. https://bit.ly/3MOU9L1

Omri, Mohamed-Salah. 2011. "Tunisia: A Revolution for Freedom and Dignity that Cannot be Colour-Coded." TNI, Jan. 29, http://bit.ly/3E2xiYp

Guessoumi, Mouldi. 2020. *Mujtama' Al-Thawrah wa Ma Ba'd Al-Thawrah* [Revolutionary and Post-Revolutionary Society]. Sfax: Dar Mohamed Ali lil Nashr.

Guessoumi, Mouldi. 2022. *Fi Muwajahat Al-Tarikh: Sada Al-Hay'ah Al-'Ulya li Tahqiq Ahdaf Al-Thawrah fi Masar al-Islah Al-Siyasi wa Al-Intiqal Al-Dimuqrati fi Tunis* [Facing History: the High Commission for Achieving Goals fo the Revolution…in Tunisia]. Sfax: Dar Mohammad Ali li al-Nashr.

Rezgui, Aymen. 2012. *"Les jeunes facebookeurs de la revolution du 14 Janvier."* In Hamadi Redissi, Asma Nouira and Abdelkader Zghal (eds.), *La Transition Démocratique en Tunisie: Etat des lieux.* Tunis: Diwen, pp. 235–258.

Sadiki, Larbi. 2012. "Tunisia: Women's Rights and the New Constitution." September 21, *Aljazeera* https://bit.ly/3DMQyu7

Saidani, Mounir. 2012. "Revolution and Counterrevolution in Tunisia: The Forty Days that Shook the Country," trans. R.A. Judy. *Boundary 2* 39(1): 43–54 [pp. 52–53 on Kasbah]

Sassine, Fares and Michel Foucault. 2018 [1979]. "There Can't Be Societies without Uprisings." *Foucault Studies* 25: 324–350.

UGTT. 2010. *Al-Tanmiyah Al-Jihawiyyah bi Wilayat Sidi Bouzid: Baina Al-Waqi' Al-Mukabbal wal Imkanat Al-Wa'idah* [Regional Development in Sidi Bouzid]. Tunis: UGTT.

Wright, Robin. 2012. *Rock the Casbah: Rage and Rebellion Across the Islamic World.* New-York: Simon and Schuster.

Yahyaoui, Mokhtar. 2010. *Al-Ihtijajat Al-Ijtima'iyyah fi Tunis: Al-Dalalah wa Al-Rihanat* [Social Protests in Tunisia: Stakes and Implications]. December 25, *Nawaat*, https://bit.ly/3aIOkQx

Zghal, Abdelkader, Abdelhamid Hénia, Fatma Ben Slimane, 2015. *Révolution Tunisienne: Compromis Historique et Citoyenneté politique.* Tunis: Arabesques.

7
"Kamour"

A Periphery Uprising

In the tale of Tunisia's own "lion heart," a certain Mohamed Daghbagi,[1] anti-colonial freedom fighter, memory meets identity. In his struggle, Tataouinians and, perhaps most of the protestor-indignants of the south, hear echoes of all manner of shooting, fire exchange, the cracks of rifles. His humble roots as a son of farmers and shepherds in Al-Hamma (Gabes) forced the young Daghbaji into conscription by the French. The humiliation of serving under the enemy, fortifying foreign occupation of his own land and murder of his own brethren, was intolerable. His sharp shooting earned him a place warring alongside the Libyan Ben 'Askar. He led fierce battles (Khanqat 'Isha, Mahfoura, Al-Jilbaniyyah, Al-Mghadhiyyah) celebrated across Tunisia. The people, resisting, were not dead. After his capture, the austere-looking Daghbagi was dragged into a town square in Al-Hamma. His fate was sealed by a French firing squad. The public spectacle sought to replace defiance with fear, to snuff out the whiff of freedom-in-the-making. Yet the execution would immortalize the martyr. Unafraid to stare down death, legend has it that Daghbagi refused the blindfold offered him. Shots bore into his body, which slumped to the ground in a pool of blood. His step-mother's mournful and celebratory ululations reverberated. They rang out as a resonant reminder of a dignified people's will. Her cries would meld with forlorn elegies and soulful ballads that carried over the decades to fill the ears and psyches of Daghbagi's self-styled Tataouine progeny. Echoes that murmur faint recollections of an unsung hero and mythologized attachment to a locale, bringing up a whole people to life. Dead but endowed with rebirth in the admiration of Kamour protesters, for whom Daghbagi's resistance serves to inspire and edify anew.

---

[1] Born Mohamed ben Salah Al-Zaghbani (nicknamed Al-Daghbagi) in 1885, four years after Tunisia's colonization by France. He hailed from the South, Wadi-Zitoun, a Bedouin village in the governorate of Gabes. In 1907, he was among the indigenous conscripts mobilized by the French army in Tunisia. He was involved in anti-Italian army resistance in Libya, whilst still leading sniper-teams against the colonial forces in Southern Tunisia. By executing him, the colonists set out to teach a lesson to the *fellaga* who infested vast geographies of guerilla struggle on behalf of independence. See Marzouki (1979) for a full account of Daghbagi's life.

Introduction

Deterritorialization-reterritorialization equates with revolution. They constitute a historic equalizer. That is, gateways that are supposed in this book to level the playing field, and create openings and possibilities for being equal. The crux of the Kamour 'story' is that revolution has not ushered in equality. Against such a backdrop, this chapter showcases the Kamour protestscape, dwelling on how issues of the social question and social injustice hang together. Reference to affective elements (feelings of anger, humiliation, solidarity, and defiance) continue to reflect inner conflicts of nascent peoplehood. Tunisian Southerners find it challenging to bind themselves to a clear-cut designation that Tunisia's 2011 revolution is "whole." The cries of dignity and freedom deployed to stage the dreams, myths, and morality of the revolution still mobilize them. In the Kamour's local universe of deprivation, degradation, and marginalization, perhaps there is nothing left of the revolution but agentic immanence. That is, immanent problems of their existence, even after the 2011 revolution, animate a quest for Rancière's (2002) "promise of new life" and "new possibilities," and the much vaunted Arendtian "rebirth." Their only "lines of escape," so to speak, manifest in practices of protest with deterritorialization inscribed through agentic, affective, and cognitive experiences. Thus, the Kamour dissentscape reconstructs and re-ontologizes one of the "revolutions-within-the-revolution": its contextual, experiential, ideational, and relational intersections, inevitably inflected by forms of embodied knowing, language, aesthetic experiences, and ideological symbolism. This is at the heart of how protest still moves whole locales, rekindling the moral flame lit by centuries-long dreams (noted in the vignette above) of dignity and equality, even in a revolutionary context. Second, this protestscape opens up a vista for "re-staging" lived experiences of protest by the insurgent identities collective social doing has engendered. Interpretively, this rebelscape enables us to capture the ongoing dynamic between ("post")revolution and peoplehood once democratization was launched in the country. How do the Kamour activists see themselves and their cause in relation to the 2011 revolution? To what extent is their protest against the state a series of continuing—or shifting—acts and en-actments of the peoplehood that, as we have argued, crested in the 2011 revolution? Kamour, a site in which a form of demos appears, offers a "subversive space" within which we examine—"read"/write—acting and enacting of "becoming," and of "finding," of a "part that has no part," within a dynamic setting of democratization. This space can be slotted, a Foucault (1986, 22–27) puts it, among "other spaces". A space, that is, as a "counter-site," engaged in "contests" and "counteraction" (Foucault 1986, 24), against visions, realities, choices, attitudes, movement, etc. … among multiple spaces of oppositions and incompatibilities, seeking change. An investigation of the unruly activisms in this "periphery-within-the-periphery" points to the unevenness, indeterminacy, and non-linearity of both peoplehood and revolution. It shows that the concrete fruits of peoplehood, driver of revolution, are *not* bestowed equally upon all. Distributional gains remain out of reach for these doubly colonized, extreme subalterns of the South. Thus, these peripheral "doldrums" propel continual acting and en-acting of that very peoplehood, the embers of a revolution. Facing off against the "counter-revolutionary" tenor of the newly democratizing state's policies, in this protestscape we stitch together the agentic, affective, and cognitive threads of the Kamour youth's peoplehood *still* in-becoming. A bidirectional *hogra* feeds into a hard-forged (regionalized) solidarity. Vocalized and embodied refusals of individual-turned-regionally collective multiple marginalization bespeak an enduring agonism vis-à-vis the state. Burgeoning democratic and legal institutions raise expectations and intensify disappointments. They furnish the Kamour activists' critical consciousness with a new vocabulary that facilitates social and normative learning, linking them to Tunisia's other peripheral geographies.

A note about methodology is in order. The chapter weaves together original interviews (anonymized for the protection of our interlocutors, given the imprisonment of some activists after 2021), local media sources, and social media, subjecting them to critical discourse analysis. The purpose is to piece together technologically-mediated "thick descriptions" spanning language, symbolism, and practices. Thus, we can understand the peoplehood–revolution dyad in the Kamour protestscape, as Tunisia's revolutionary élan stretches out beyond 2011. Why are Facebook posts (textual, photographic, or video) on the group's official page, with over 207,000 followers at the time of writing, so telling? The Kamour campaign is not unlike Indigenous activism in Latin American countries such as Bolivia, Chile, and Ecuador that, as Lupien (2020) charts, has shifted online in recent years. The Kamour protestscape is more hybrid, combining online and offline unruliness. Social media use is of course an important contemporary mode of mobilizing protest among activists, Kamour included.[2] In addition, it is a platform for generating outside support. Potential sympathizers, detractors, powerbrokers, and policymakers are all possible audience members. Thus, social media discourse is a meaningful re-presentation by activists of themselves and their cause as they would like it to be understood, within and without Tunisia. Decrying their demonization in the media and by political elites, the Kamour activists display a persevering agency through the creation and maintenance of their Facebook page. It has become the go-to source for their "official" positions on the latest developments. Wrestling with revolutionary letdowns and democratic disappointments, they assert themselves and their demands within this virtual space. Somewhere between spontaneity and rehearsed oration, the live feed filmed against a blank wall, the post published in haste after a demonstration, the photo uploaded in the thick of a march, are noteworthy mediums for protestors' voice and argumentation on their own terms.

The chapter begins with an overview of major events in the Kamour timeline, from 2017. It moves to notable features of the protestscape, before exploring the dynamics of self–other relations, state *hogra* and counter-*hogra*, and solidarity within and with the protestors. The chapter then turns to the question of (social) rights under democratization. It demonstrates how "social learning" shapes the contours of the Kamour campaign, diffusing to other partial demos still "othered" in the unsteady new democracy. The chapter closes with a discussion of dappled Southern self-hoods in which the regional and national conflate and collide.

---

[2] Interviews, August 25–27, 2021.

The Kamour Protestscape

Like Gafsa and the phosphate basin, Tunisia's peripheral, southern-most governorate of Tataouine has been weighed down by multiple marginalization since independence, and perhaps before that time. Even its history has been sidelined. Efforts to reverse a "systematic blackout" in the remote province's anti-colonial historiography subsequent to Bourguiba's victory over Ben Youssef arose in the years before the 2011 revolution (Mousa 2018, 16–19). Parallels emerge with indigenous protest movements fighting for the marginalized in Latin America. Brazil's Landless Poor and Chile's Mapuche use tactics such as blocking roads or occupying land to oppose neoliberal reforms (Rice 2012, 8–15). Our attention in this chapter is on the Kamour campaign, reminiscent of the revolution and its immediate aftermath (Hanin 2017). This extended moment of "unruliness" has been waged by disenchanted young activists since 2017, demanding a share of the country's natural resource wealth (oil, gas, gypsum). Tataouine is resource-rich, but its residents are among the poorest in Tunisia. Its unemployment rate is around 32 percent since 2016, twice the national average, according to the National Institute of Statistics (Radio Tataouine 2018). Unemployment in the Tataouine town Dehiba was the highest in the country, 40 percent in 2021. The skewed map of Tunisian deprivation also reveals Tataouine's lack of sewage infrastructure, alongside six other interior or southern governorates (Mzalouat et al. 2021).

In late March 2017, some of the region's youth began protesting for jobs in the governorate's capital city of Tataouine. A month later, they decided to undertake more drastic measures. Spokesperson for the *Tansiqiyyat I'tisam al Kamour* (Coordination Committee of the Kamour Sit-in, hereafter referred to as "Kamour"), Tarek Haddad, patiently explained the logic of their sit-in (Attessia TV 2017). To get the government's attention, they decided to "escalate" by driving 100 kilometers into the desert, the closest point to the oil fields. The movement transformed Tunisian popular understandings of the word "Kamour." Instead of connoting a mafia-like group, the term now indicates the oil facilities occupied by protestors.[3] Flanked by surveilling army and security vehicles, the activists pitched dozens of tents in the unsteady sand. In each one squatted a representative from an area within Tataouine, as 1,200 young men camped out in Tunisia's remote desert, added fellow Kamour leader Dhaou Elghoul. The harsh climate paled in comparison to the marginalization and deprivation resulting from six decades of government "kleptocracy," Haddad insisted (Attessia TV 2017). Their popular slogan (No relenting!) *al-rakh la,* expanded to (No relenting! No pumping!) *al-rakh la! al-dakh la!* The catchphrase reinforced the earlier 2015 activist slogan "Where's the oil?" (*waino al-bitrol?*) (FTDES 2020). It also recalled anti-colonial mottos from the 1950s and before,[4] indicating the continuity of resistance against (colonial, then postcolonial) domination in the local social imaginary. From its earliest days, residents of Tataouine

---

[3] *Laisa Man Sami'a Kaman Ra'a … Mawsim Al-Hijrah Ila "Al-Kamour"!* in *Al-Sabah,* April 29, 2017.
[4] Interview with Amor, Kamour activist, June 2021.

demonstrated in support of the sit-in.[5] Soon after, the regional UGTT organized a sectoral strike: petroleum workers ceased production for one day in April 2017.[6] Union solidarity and mobilization lived up to the best of its reputation, cemented in the 2011 revolution.

A cat-and-mouse game has unfolded over five or more years. Contesting narratives to elicit sympathy (towards protestors) as opposed to deference (to the state) complement altercations over public space and amenities. "Escalation" is a frequent rallying cry among protestors.[7] Flare-ups and ultimatums[8] are punctuated by appeasement and promises by successive governments. Movement leaders have experimented with tactics, including hunger strikes.[9] Repression by security forces has (allegedly) taken the lives of three protestors. Kamour activists first disrupted oil production—closing the *vana*—in May 2017 (Derbali 2020). The bold move, which did not garner consensus within the movement, cost the government millions of dinars a week.[10] Some reports suggest that those who turned off the tap, so to speak, flouted the result of a movement vote to suspend the sit-in.[11] It prompted urgent government meetings about security in Tataouine.[12] Pressure from the *vana*'s closure eventually brought the government to the negotiating table in June 2017. Intense consultations generated a list of written activist demands presented to the government.[13] Roughly a century after Tunisian students, workers, and others had inaugurated a range of anti-colonial protest modalities, the Kamour protestors displayed a combination of radical (disruption, sit-ins) and more moderate (negotiation) protest competencies.

Called in to facilitate negotiations, the national UGTT marshaled its historical pedigree to "bring opinions closer together," between protestors and government.[14] This mobilization across old (union) and new (Kamour activists') protestscapes was striking, indicating a kind of learning from and through Tunisia's long protest centenaries. Negotiations were not completely smooth, even with the UGTT embroiled in talks. The Union wondered how seriously the government welcomed its involvement.[15] The eventual agreement was ratified by a majority vote (60, according to reports) among the Kamour ranks.[16] The government promised work for the

---

[5] *Mutasakinu Wilayat Tataouine Yunaffidhun Waqfah Ihtijajiyyah Li-Musanadat Mu'tasimi "Al-Kamour,"* in *Al-Sabah*, May 7, 2017.
[6] *Tataouine: Idrab Qita'i fi Qita' Al-Nift Ma Iqaf Al-Intaj*, in *Alchourouk*, April 5, 2017.
[7] *Tataouine: Al-Muhtajjun Yulawwihuna Bi Al-Tas'id*, in *Alchourouk*, April 20, 2017.
[8] *Al-Kamour: Idrab Ju' Wa Muhlah bi 48 Sa'ah li al-Hukumah*, in *Al-Sarih*, May 18, 2017.
[9] *Al-Natiq Bi Ism Tansiqiyyat I'tisam Al-Kamour li "Al-Sabah News": Dukhul 7 Min Tansiqiyyat I'tisam Al-Kamour fi Idrab Ju' Wahshi*, in *Al-Sabah*, March 6, 2018.
[10] *Wazarat Al-Taqah Tuhadhdhir Min Tawasul Tawaqquf Intaj Al-Nift bi-Tataouine Wa Kebili*, in *Al-Sabah*, June 1, 2017.
[11] *Tataouine: Al-Mu'tasimun Yuhaddiduna bi-Ghalqi Tariq "Al-Kamour" Al-Mu'addiyah Ila Huqul Al-Nift fi Al-Sahra*, in *Al-Sabah*, April 20, 2017.
[12] *Ijtima' Tari' bi Al-Kasbah Hawla Al-Wad' Al-Amni bi Tataouine*, in *Alchourouk*, May 21, 2017.
[13] *Tansiqiyyat I'tisam Al-Kamour Tuhaddid Qa'imat Matalibaha Al-Niha'iyyah min Al-Hukumah*, in *Alchourouk*, May 8, 2017.
[14] *Noureddine Tabboubi li "Al-Sabah Al-Usbu'i": Tharwatuna Khatt Ahmar ... Wa Hadhihi Hululuna li-I'tisam Al-Kamour!* In *Al-Sabah*, June 12, 2017.
[15] *Hal Qasada Wazir Al-Tashghil Istib'ad Al-Ittihad Min Malaf Al-Kamour?* in *Al-Sha'b*, June 7, 2017, p. 1.
[16] *Bi-Aghlabiyyat Al-Aswat ... Tansiqiyyat "Al-Kamour" Tuwafiqu 'Ala Muqtarahat Al-Hukumah*, in *Al-Sabah*, May 16, 2017.

families of two young men killed in the protests.[17] Sit-ins at tent encampments and demonstrations were to stop in return for immunity from prosecution. An 80 million dinar ($32 million) development fund was pledged for Tataouine, along with 1,500 jobs in 2017 -18. Tahar al-Skrafi, father of Anwar killed by security (see below), signed the agreement, representing Kamour, as did Secretary-General Noureddine Tabboubi, on behalf of the UGTT.

Youssef Chahed's government (August 2016–February 2020), followed by Fakhfakh's (2020) and then Mechichi's (2020–21) short-lived administrations, were all slow to implement the terms. Ten months into the agreement, in April 2018, protests flared up again in Tataouine. Activists who blocked roads were arrested, inciting further protests by the townspeople.[18] Delays (read: foot-dragging) were due to insufficient state resources, according to the province governor's justifications.[19] Some observers have faulted (consecutive) governments and MPs for pledges that the empty state coffers can ill afford.[20] Shortly after his election, in January 2020 new President Kais Saied hosted the young activists in Carthage. He vaguely pledged to honor the agreement, coaxing the Kamour delegation to end their renewed sit-in. The period of calm was brief: impatience propelled a return to (months of) protest in the summer of 2020. Even landscape workers whose jobs had been "created" in the 2017 Kamour agreement—not unlike the handling (*munawalat*) companies in Gafsa, noted in Chapter 4—protested over their missing salaries.[21] Residents stepped up their protest momentum through a general strike called by the regional UGTT in June 2020. Altercations between protestors and police broke out again.[22]

Once more, the government was forced to negotiate over the Kamour's disruption of oil production. No matter what the government's financial woes, exhorted Haddad, Tataouine's oil wells were not (merely) the state's property.[23] They allowed the government a three-day grace period before the next escalation.[24] Clearly cognizing their legally guaranteed rights, the Kamour activists remained steadfast in their insistence on implementation of the 2017 agreement. This time, Head of Government, Hichem Mechichi, sent a government delegation to sit across the table from the regional delegation *(al-wafd al-jihawi)* representing Kamour activists, the UGTT, UTICA (Union Tunisienne de l'Industrie, du Commerce et de l'Artisanat, Tunisian Union of Industry, Trade and Crafts), and other community members in Tataouine. After numerous

---

[17] *Nanshuruhu ... Tafasil Mahdar Al-Ittifaq Baina Mu'tasimi Al-Kamour wa Al-Hukumah*, in *Al-Sabah*, June 16, 2017.
[18] *Tataouine: Masirah Sha'biyyah Li Al-Mutalabah Bi-Itlaq Sarah Al-Mawqufin wa Tatbiq Ittifaq Al-Kamour*, in *Alchourouk*, April 3, 2018.
[19] *Wali Tataouine Al-Jadid: Usanidu Matalib Al-Shabab Al-Muhtajj Lakin Fi Hudud Imkaniyyat Al-Dawlah*, in *Al-Sabah*, April 30, 2017.
[20] In *Al-Maghreb*, September 11, 2021.
[21] *Tataouine: Tajammu' Wa Masirat Li-'Ummal Wa A'wan Sharikat Al-Bi'ah wa Al-Ghirasah Wa Al-Bastanah*, in *Al-Sabah*, June 16, 2020.
[22] *Tataouine: Tajaddud Al-Muwajahat Baina Quwwat Al-Amn Wal Muhtajjin wa Tajawub Nisbi Ma'a Al-Idrab Al- 'Amm*, in *Alchourouk,* June 22, 2020.
[23] *Ba'da An Awdaha Al-Tawajjuhat Al-Jadidah: Al-Mechichi: Al-Murur ila Tatbiq Al-Qanun bi-Quwwat Al-Dawlah, Al-Haddad: Al-Dakh La Wa Al-Rakh La!* in *Al-Sha'b*, November 5, 2020, p. 8.
[24] *Tataouine Al-Kamour ... Ihtijaj Jadid Wa Imhal Al-Hukumah 3 Ayyam*, in *Alchourouk*, November 19, 2021.

false starts, they jointly worked out a *new* agreement affirming government provision of employment positions and small loans for unemployed youth to be staggered over the coming months (Shems FM 2020). In COVID-laced heat, protests rebounded in 2020 (Chibani 2020), escalating once again by November 2021 (Jawhara 2021). Congregating in "People Square," they blocked roads once again.[25] Their threats to Saied's new Head of Government, Najla Bouden, indicated that they would readily disrupt oil production again.[26] Their demands included dropping all criminal charges against activists, as stipulated in the original 2017 agreement.[27] In January 2022, a military court reportedly sentenced the three most prominent faces of the movement to prison: Tarek Haddad and Dhaou Elghoul (five years), and Khalifa Bouhaouach (one year), the three most prominent faces of the movement (Al-Ikhbaria Attounsia 2022). Haddad was arrested in December 2022, eliciting angry outcries from the movement.[28] Kamour's restlessness persists, and the campaign continues at least virtually.

Notable Features

Protest since the revolution is not unique to Kamour. Nevertheless, some specific features of this campaign stand out. First, it is very localized, devoid of significant participation even from other parts of Tunisia. Second, the activists frame their movement in moral terms across Tunisia's revolutionary élan, often in self–other binaries against various powers of domination. Thus, their impetus is anti-colonial—still a pressing mandate six decades after independence: "Tataouine is the citadel of struggles against colonialism."[29] From anti-colonialism emerges anti-authoritarian resistance of the most recent 2011 revolution that waged combat against an overly encroaching state. Years later, a new class of politicians incited dissent: "We are the original revolutionaries ... all politicians can go to hell for they are passing and we are the lasting ones."[30] Third, the Kamour protests are still inconclusive, enduring for over six years. They are intermittent, propelled by their continual charge against the state that it neglects the region, perhaps deliberately. Hence, activists consider their movement an extension of the revolutionary *hirak*.

Fourth, the protestors themselves hail from a social-cultural background of deprivation, lingering tribalism, and religious conservativism. They are for the most part without university education. Reflecting these roots, their discourse is often unpolished. It contrasts in syntax and tone with much of the political

---

[25] *'Adu ila Al-Shari' min Jadid ... Shabab Al-Kamour Yaqta'una Al-Tariq*, in *Al-Sabah*, November 21, 2021.
[26] *Al-Maghreb*, November 22, 2021.
[27] *Fi Khutwah Tas'idiyyah ... Mu'tasimu Al-Kamour Yughliquna Kull Al-Manafidh Al-Mu'addiyah Ila Al-Sharikat Al-Niftiyyah*, in *Al-Sabah*, November 21, 2021.
[28] *Ba'da Iqaf Al-Natiq Bismiha ... Ahad A'da Tansiqiyyat Al-Kamour Yatahaddathu li "Al-Sabah News" 'An Matalibihim Wa- Al-Ahkam Al-Sijniyyah Didda Tariq Haddad*, in *Al-Sabah*, December 29, 2022.
[29] Kamour Facebook page, November 1, 2020, https://www.facebook.com/elkamour/
[30] Kamour Facebook page, November 16, 2020.

class—notwithstanding the rowdy 2019 parliamentary term cut short by President Saied's power grab in July 2021. Tataouine seems to them a dynamic revolutionary hub, and they are not shy to say so. Perhaps this orientation is itself an implicit refutation of multi-layered, long-term exclusion and exploitation by the state and *Sahel* residents and interests. The tone of Kamour activists is often bracing, their use of language resorting to curses. They hurl (counter) insults like "dogs," "mercenaries," and *tahhan* (colloquial for traitor) at security officials who attack and humiliate them, politicians occupying the seats of power, media personalities spurning the movement, or oil companies refusing to hire enough local employees. The "live" videos, and to a lesser extent their interventions in television and radio media, sound like rants more than studied and planned speeches. This is even outside the boisterous protest setting where improvised messaging is to be expected.

The affect of *hogra* in all its anger, frustration, and humiliation thrust back upon the state, and sometimes the solidarity, animate their speech most clearly. Tataouine or "the South" seems to crowd out Tunisia, which comes in second at times. Undergirding their rage and their demands is the spatialized discrimination of multiple marginalization. The confluence of geography and economic poverty in the South (Bardi 2023, 474–475) is a recurring theme. Soja's "spatial (in)justice" (2010) carries over into Tunisia's democratization, with explosive results. Fifth and relatedly, Kamour's discourse is vocally conscious of Tataouine's spatialized political location. The governorate's population (157,000), number of municipalities (8), number of seats in Parliament (4: we "gave" 3 to Ennahda and 1 to Nidaa Tounes) come up in their discourse every so often. In so doing, they highlight various manifestations of geographic, (sub)cultural, and political presence. They crash up against the litany of the state's forgetfulness as neglect (*nisyan*) of the region despite all these concrete numbers that should render such disregard impossible (See Table 7.1 for the language of the Kamour).

Thus, it can be said that within this protestscape, the Kamour appears to represent a "socio-political structure": male, labor-providers with little or no tertiary education. (Womens' protest participation is regular in the city,[31] but the sit-in at the Kamour oil wells is a mostly male space—although still a form of "other space"). To an extent, this dissentscape's specificity imbricates the Kamour protestors in a process of deterritorialization and reterritorialization in which they are institutionally presupposed as equals after the 2011 revolution. Thus, their protestscape qualifies as:

1. Driven to a revolutionary end via *affect* of *hogra*, indignation and group solidarity, but also *cognitively* through self–group knowledge (e.g. self-consciousness of victimhood due to inequality), interactively, feeding off plural, relational, experiential modes of struggle.
2. Performed through social acts and en-actments of resistance: protestors reconstruct and are re-constructed in the socio-political moment, its attendant morality, and spatialized practices of subversive, emancipatory identities.

---

[31] Interview with Heba, female Kamour activist, June 2021, Tunis.

Table 7.1 The Language of Kamour

Term	Meaning-in-context	Significance
Hogra	Humiliation by state, counter-acted in turn by resistance or spurning	Vocalized, lived experiences of neglect and marginalization become an effective "engine": anger, frustration propel unruly discourses and practices of peoplehood
Al-rakh la	"Relent not!" the slogan of the Kamour movement	Agentic determination to wage struggle for extracting "the people's" rights "stolen" by the state
Al-dakh la	"No to pumping!" addendum to Kamour slogan, referring to disruption of oil/gas production	Escalation and development of tactics in contest with the state, a forceful "counter-strike" to repression and indifference
luhmah	Affinity and solidarity between Kamour activists and with the people of Tataouine	Positive affect underpinning peoplehood, inflected with spatialized and even tribal (sub)identities that may emanate outwards to Tunisia's "people"
Al-Janub	Literally, "the South," the (marginalized) southern parts of the country including Tataouine	A spatialized identity constructed through shared historical (anti-colonial) and contemporary (marginalization, socio-political exclusion) experiences across revolutionary élan
Al-tahmish	Marginalization of *al-Janub*	Common elsewhere among Tunisia's subalterns, the term indicates a kind of "critical consciousness" that *names* and *refuses* non-peoplehood
Vana	The pump, from the French word *la vanne*: the sites of gas or oil production	Subversive resistance through *language* (word); Arabized adaptation buttresses real-life resistance practices (world), disrupting production
Ahrar	"Free people," used to address fellow activists:Tataouine residents and Tunisians (potentially) sympathetic to Kamour	Invokes parlance of the 2011 revolutions (freedom and dignity), which in turn recalls anti-colonial struggles for independence.
Faz'ah	Call to rescue Tataouine brethren in peril or under attack	Solidarity (sometimes through blood ties): actions of support in which Tunisia's marginalized come to each other's aid in the face of the state and its *hogra*.
Mafiat	Arabization of "mafias," in reference to either the state or corporations	Accusation against political or corporate elites who plunder and transgress the Othered people's rights.
Mawt bati'	Slow death, referring to life in Tataouine	A life of *hogra* is no life at all: Deprivation and indignity are a gradual death sentence by the state—even after democratization

3. Dynamic: ever-evolving *hirak*, iconizing a history of struggle and its heroes, with implications for knowledge production as situated, partial, and subjective.
4. Reset of deterritorialization and reterritorialization.
5. Accordingly, the rebelscape seems to depart from an underlying assumption of protest being a civic duty: upholding the right to have rights long denied, by (re)claiming a pressing moral mandate inherited from Tunisian rebels for justice and freedom which can be traced back to the crucible of the 1860s.

"We Are Tunisians, Too": Affect and Precept of *Hogra*

The Kamour movement disseminates much material through which to understand their motivations, grievances, and (self–other) identifications. Over the last six years, there has been no shortage of communications on their part: to the government, to the oil companies, to Tunisians, to fellow residents of Tataouine. Within this fecundity of discourse, further enriched by our own interviews, one key motif has been a troubled relationship with the state, and sometimes even the rest of Tunisian society. The have-nots in these parts, stand apart from the Tunisia of the beldis and the power-holders, the more advanced infrastructure, and areas with lower unemployment: one manifestation of "the part that has no part." Within this already poor country, these are among the poorest. Yet the problematic extends beyond joblessness and social injustice, the "plague" of Tunisia's South. As they always do, the material and immaterial reinforce one another. Distributional *neglect* by the state seeps into states of mind, modes of being. Having been passed over for development projects, public investment, and any circulation of (their own) natural resource wealth amounts to no less than humiliation by a state that repeatedly strips them of dignity *on purpose*. This is the complicated dynamic that is *hogra*. It is not just a term we and others (see Hanin 2019, 110) impose externally as researchers in this and other contexts, but one that permeates Kamour discourse, often unprompted. Their assessments stem from personal experience, inward-turned-outward, individual-turned-collective, combat with a state that has all but cast them out. "The government doesn't care about our city," a female protestor says bluntly.[32] One Kamour leader describes *hogra* as a "deliberate policy" for decades, put in place by Bourguiba. It involves experiences of "neglect, lies, not providing employment opportunities" and poor infrastructure. Thus, *hogra* lights the destructive force of "divisions (*fitan*, plural of *fitnah*) in the South," he continues.[33] Another Kamour leader agrees. He (and the leadership is all-male) considers *hogra* to be "marginalization, lies, procrastination," the "apartheid" between the Sahel and the South, instituted by Bourguiba, "may God not have mercy on his soul."[34] The doldrums in which Tataouine residents wade are neither incidental nor accidental. The state seems to be at fault, and has been since independence. Inequality in development translates into abhorrent separation akin

---

[32] Interview with Maha, December 24, 2019, Tataouine.
[33] Interview with Ahmed, August 25, 2021, Medenine.
[34] Interview with Taieb, August 26, 2021, Tataouine.

to that of South Africa's, on this reading. Except here, the boundary is spatial, not racial. On top of under-investment in development and infrastructure, manifestations of *hogra* include what these indignants read as the state's intention to "steal" the region's wealth from them. Driving home the point, one interviewee freely admits that fifty years of being "forgotten" has brought on a simmering "hatred" for all that is related to the state.[35] *Hogra* is an emotional-psychological state, an affective motor for protest and revolution. More than one interviewee complained that they feel as if "we are from another country."[36]

The larger Kamour group echoed this very language on social media at the apex of the COVID-19 pandemic. Some things are more deadly than coronavirus. "Unemployment, marginalization, *hogra* are the biggest viruses," as even "foreigners" live better with "[o]ur livelihood while [we] are in a state of slow death."[37] Even if they are not literally starving, they might as well be. It is as though the state that does not recognize even their right to have rights, drives them out of their own homeland, like Arendt's stateless. Some await an opportunity to leave Tunisia altogether, preferring to take their chances on the perilous death-boat (*harqah*) journey[38] to unwelcoming European shores. They have already witnessed friends and family members exit thus. Such deep collective anguish illuminates the ways in which Kamour activists lash out against the state, or give up on it altogether by undertaking the "unorganized" migration Tunisian governments work so hard to fend off at European behest.[39]

Thus, *hogra* can be deadly. In May 2017, 23-year old protestor Anwar Al-Skrafi from Bir Lahmar in Tataouine was run over by a security official's car ("the machinery of injustice," according to a May 2020 Facebook post) as the National Guard sought to disband the Kamour sit-in.[40] Tataouine's governor insisted that most of the protestors agreed to suspend the demonstration.[41] Yet the forced shutdown of the tent site remains a contentious point between activists and the state. Deadly violence is difficult to bypass. The young man was killed in the melee of security forces burning tents and pelting the Kamour activists with tear-gas (Abdelmoula 2021). In addition to frequent posts memorializing Al-Skrafi, the movement's official Facebook page is adorned by a smiling picture of the "martyr." The words *Ziffu al-'Aris* (march in the groom, as to a wedding procession) and "martyr of Kamour, son of the South" precede his name at the bottom of the image. He has become a symbol of the movement's deadly struggle with the state. His death—and narrations

---

[35] Interview with Kais, August 26, 2021, Tataouine.
[36] Interview with Lutfi, August 26, 2021 and Interview Ahmed, August 27, 2021, Tataouine.
[37] Kamour Facebook page, March 3, 2020, Tataouine.
[38] Interviews with Kamour activists, December 21–23, 2019, Tataouine.
[39] Tunisia cooperates closely with Italy to both block undocumented migrants from reaching Europe and to repatriate those taken into custody across the Mediterranean. Meetings with Italian diplomats often hinge on this issue, for instance between Tunisian Interior Minister and the Italian ambassador on September 22, 2022 (*Al-Sabah*, 22 September 2021).
[40] Other "martyrs" mentioned on the group's Facebook page are Taher Flammari and Said Aroud (November 21, 2021 post).
[41] *Fadd I'tisam Al-Kamour: Wali Tataouine Yuwaddih,* in *Haqaiq Online,* May 17, 2017.

thereof[42]—epitomize the recurring violence directed at the marginalized. Disembodied, they are stripped of their people status by a state lashing out with impunity. The thousands attending Al-Skrafi's burial ceremony did not include any politicians or officials (Eljimei 2017), much to the chagrin of the Kamour activists. (A parliamentary committee did hear the testimony of his brother Moncef days later.[43]) A short video of Anwar Al-Skrafi's funeral procession conveys the affective climate of the event.[44] Young men clad in T-shirts hang out of beeping car doors and crowd into pickup trucks. Others march alongside vehicles in the sunny street. The trills of ululating women dressed in long dresses and headscarves fill the air. Cries of "with our souls and blood, we sacrifice ourselves to you, oh martyr!" (*bi-l-ruh, bi-l-dam, nafdika ya shahid*) and "there is no God but God, and the martyr is the beloved of God!" (*la ilaha illallah, wi-l shahid habibullah!*) are reminiscent of wartime lamentations in Palestine or Syria. Tataouinians chant meaning into murder at the hands of police through these emotive yet highly stylized, religious ritual-like reactions of kinfolk and townspeople, an extended family of "subalterns." The mourners declare: *our* Anwar Al-Skrafi was killed by *them*, the enemy, the state. Is there any more stark rightlessness of a non-people? If Hached is Tunisia's historical martyr, then Al-Skrafi is Tataouine's present-day martyr. His father is even signatory to the 2017 agreement with the Chahed government, indicative of the politicized weight his sacrifice and his family's forbearance carry. Photos of the father's visit to the Kamour camp less than six weeks later[45] is the *tansiqiyyah*'s way of claiming his death and his legacy for the movement. Posing for the cameras, a faint smile on his lined, bearded face; flashing the victory sign; sharing a meal with the activists: reassuring with visual evidence that the sacrifice was meaningful, not in vain. Moreover, we have the Al-Skrafi family's blessing, the Kamour activists imply. He encourages us to soldier on. We in turn commemorate him and his tragic death. Anwar's killing is the ultimate *hogra* that animates relentless stamina in confronting the state to secure the region's rights. As in the funeral chants, mourning and loss are indistinguishable from anger and frustration, fearlessness and tenacity—a powerful mix in the cauldron of affect. "We are all your sons, Uncle Tahar. We are all Anwar Alskrafi. We are all *al-rakh la*."

Anwar Alskrafi's ghost breathes sacrificial life into subsequent Kamour discourse and practices. The Facebook page raises his specter periodically to haunt the state and the "fat cat" oil companies. They thus seem to read Tunisian politics through the loss of Al-Skrafi. Kamour activists gave their opinion about the Parliamentary Committee's visit, led by Abir Moussi, to inspect the new Nawwara gas plant. Invoking a prophetic *hadith* that is part of everyday Arabic parlance, they proclaimed: "If you

---

[42] In January 2021, a Sfax court dismissed the case against the National Guard member accused of intentionally murdering Al-Skrafi. The Tansiqiyyah mocked the "just judicial system" in a January 30, 2021 post, sharing a short video clip of the security car in question, visibly speeding in the direction of the protestors. The case was being appealed, according to the family's attorney (Kapitalis 2021).

[43] *Shaqiq Anwar Al-Skrafi Yatahaddath 'An Tafasil Da's Akhihi wa 'An Isti'mal "Al-Rash,"* in *Alchourouk*, May 29, 2017.

[44] Kamour Facebook page, May 23, 2017.

[45] Kamour Facebook page, June 2, 2017.

have no shame, then do what you will."[46] The MPs are "shameless" in their indifference and perhaps exploitation of the site where Anwar Al-Skrafi's "soul ... fell." They have come not to pay their respects, but to "inspect the livelihood of your masters," presumably the state. Brazen parliamentarians can "play" however, they wish, the activists warned, since the "real playing" will come soon. The implication was that (representatives of) the state should not celebrate prematurely: further disruption of the shiny-new Nawwara plant was just around the corner. That is exactly what activists did not long afterward. Foreign oil companies OMV (Romanian), ENI (Italian), and ATOG (Anglo-Tunisian) penned an appeal to the President to take action and re-open Pump 4, threatening to close the fields entirely should the disruption continue.[47]

Counter-*Hogra*

Obstructing oil and gas production has been the sharpest weapon in the activists' arsenal. Against tear gas and security force vehicles, Tataouine's multiply marginalized are not idle. Thus, one activist bristles at the notion that *hogra* is a one-way street.[48] His comrade elaborates: *hogra* is the "magic motive for confronting the [very] machinery of *hogra*."[49] This powerful affect is a circular relation of being humiliated only to spurn the very state in return. Conflictual activism—the *agon* of Tunisian politics—apathy, and the rejection of formal politics are some modes of counter-*hogra*. Hurriedly published as a photo of a typed document marked up in blue pen, a founding statement is telling. It unequivocally lists "putting an end to *hogra* which we have been subjected [to] for sixty years" as a principal motivation.[50] Clear demands launch this bottom-up refraction of humiliation: "no to unemployment, no to marginalization, [no to] expensive living standards, and [no to] deep inequalities between cities."[51] The objections embodied in the appearances of protest, sit-ins, blocking roads,[52] and production disruptions are driven by psychological devaluation *and* a simultaneous response by citizens: a counter-*hogra*. Tataouine's residents are not simply on the *receiving end* of the state's indignities that force so many residents, prominent Kamour activists included, to engage in smuggling for subsistence. While some ponder (or actually attempt) a Tunisia-less alternative through 'illegal' migration, *harqah*, many Kamour activists choose what they call "confrontation" personified, organized, and mobilized. One leader thus advocates "confrontation" as the sole way to "claim our rights." (Both are recurring terms in interviews and social media.) Through iterative tussles, he has thus learned

---

[46] Kamour Facebook page, February 28, 2020.
[47] *Al-Maghreb*, August 29, 2020.
[48] Interview with Kamel, August 27, 2021, Tataouine.
[49] Interview with Hedi, August 25, 2021, Medenine.
[50] Kamour Facebook page, May 3, 2017.
[51] Interview with Hedi, August 25, 2021, Medenine.
[52] *Tataouine: Al-Mu'tasimun Yuhaddidun bi Ghalqi Tariq Huqul Al-Nift fi Al-Sahra',* in *Alchourouk*, April 20, 2017.

techniques and strategies through which to "tire the state,"[53] as though engrossed in an ongoing war of attrition. If the state is seeking to *tame* the peoplehood-in-becoming—the revolutionary fervor—of protestors, they in turn engage in a counter-taming. Another speaks of gaining skills in "mobilizing tribes against the regime" so as to "weaken security forces."[54] A third proudly mentions practical knowledge gained in "irritating the power[s that be]."[55] Protest activity is about securing distributional demands, but can additionally be motivated by the satisfaction of getting back at the state, the marginals' other, even when the policy dividends have proven to be minimal. Their defiant agency is forthcoming. Agonistic practices also demonstrate an unwillingness to be erased from the political cartography of the country, despite compounded neglect. Through protest, Kamour activists show that "we are citizens who belong to this country and we will not bow down [surrender] until we wrest our rights." Protesting in the street exhibits to the state that they exist, while they await the state starting to "listen."[56] By making noise, so to speak, the activists prove to the state, other Tunisians, and perhaps themselves, that they are in fact members of "the people." This renders situated and embodied protest a medium of "representational play," and of "communicative/speech play," co-emergent with both construction of forms of demos and logos—by "the part that has no part." Thus, the Kamour insurgent spatiality with its alienated history and muted existence introduces the means of deviating from the space-time social logics of domination. A domination that, in the Rancière scheme of things and under the "distribution of the sensible," decides the "sayable and unsayable," the doable and un-doable, and the "visible and invisible." This deviation from the social orders of dominant consciousness and practice of authoritarian politics opens up "new possibilities," reinforcing escape along the lines of deterritorialization—reterritorialization. Notwithstanding the unruly nature of protest, the legitimacy of the demands, and the historic injustice have empowered the Kamour activists and supportive communal networks as self-knowing voices. That is, voices enabling speech acts and social doing seeking to empty (deterritorialize) spatiality and temporality from state transcripts and practices of domination. Through Kamour protestors' new-found interactivity, and learning-in-context (with their own socio-political memory), from embodied practices of protest, new meanings, language, imaginaries, and forms of affect and cognition are unraveled to fill spatiality and temporality (reterritorialize).

Does an assertion of presence through protest always remain within the confines of the law? This question preoccupies scholarship on social protest, and concerns the protestors themselves. Clearly, the state has considered camping out in the desert, blocking roads, taking over other public amenities, and eventually disrupting oil and gas production, as outside the remit of the law. The indignants themselves do not seem to agree whether showdowns are in line with a peaceful civic attitude. One

---

[53] Interview with Ahmed, August 26, 2021, Tataouine.
[54] Interview with Tawfik, August 26, 2021, Tataouine.
[55] Interview with Kais, August 26, 2021, Tataouine.
[56] Interview with Hedi, August 26, 2021, Tataouine.

Kamour leader, who has called for "direct confrontation" with the state, sees it as the opposite of "peaceful solutions" to problems of underdevelopment and marginalization.[57] Another concludes after over four years of activism that protesting in the street is "not enough," as the state only budges when its property or resources are targeted.[58]

Yet in its more public discourse on social and traditional media, the group insists they are "peaceful." They are aware that such "civility" (ruliness) may defy wider cultural and political expectations of the *Janub* as a "periphery-within-the-periphery"; this may be why they emphasize it so persistently. Reminiscent of 2011 revolutionary mantras across the Arab geography, they call for and insist on peaceful protest, *silmiyyah* (Saleh 2017). Basking in the victory of a new agreement with the Mechichi government in November 2020,[59] Kamour spokesman Tarek Haddad reiterates, "… as we always say, closing the *vana* is not an end [in itself] but a means to achieving our goal … we are not what they say about us … we are not a gang" (Mosaique 2020b). In the early weeks of their sit-in, they are aghast that Essebsi's government had sent security forces to Kamour.[60] "Our protest is constitutional and peaceful … we will not burn or destroy our nation. …To the army and the security [forces], we say you are of us and we are of you." They then draw a parallel to Ben Guerdane,[61] where "the people protected your back." Tataouine can do the same. Moreover, dying to "reclaim the rights of Tataouine" is not beyond the realm of possibility, but would be an "honor." In this narrative, the Kamour youth invert the civilian–military balance in favor of the people, of whom they assert themselves to be a representative part. It is we who will protect you, they maintain. Attacking us with tear gas not only appalls, it violates our envisioned order of things, they imply. Far from a recognition of the "just cause" they consider theirs to be, the security crackdown is a refusal to acknowledge their right to have rights.

This tension between civility and perceived in-civility (unruliness), lawfulness, and lawlessness, reaching out to the state and pulling back from its control, is inescapable. As the Kamour protests recommenced after a hiatus in summer 2020, movement leader Khalifa Bouhaouach records a direct address[62] to fellow Tataouinites, Tunisians, and civic-political elites (Tabboubi, Saied, Fekhfekh, and Ghannouchi). His language vacillates between reassurances of "civility" and loyalty to the nation, reminders of decades-long discrimination and victimhood at the hands of the state and nonchalance by fellow Tunisians, and warnings that the *tansiqiyyah* could escalate matters if their demands remain unheeded. Underlying the impassioned exhortations seems to be the double-consciousness of being aware of how others—compatriots and governing officials—regard those from Tataouine. Outlaws, gangs, uncivilized, not loyal enough to the state: a subtext of spoken and unspoken accusations that Bouhaouach, face glinting under a sheen of summer sweat, is, like

---

[57] Interview with Kais, August 26, 2021, Tataouine.
[58] Interview with Lutfi, August 26, 2021, Tataouine.
[59] *Al-Kashf 'An Tafasil Al-Ittifaq Al-Niha'i li-Malaff Al-Kamour*, in *Alchourouk*, November 7, 2020.
[60] Kamour Facebook page, May 22, 2017.
[61] A Tunisian town bordering Libya attacked by ISIS fighters in 2016, only to be put down by the military and local population in an "epic" battle. See Sadiki (2020, 89–90).
[62] Kamour Facebook page, July 4, 2020 post.

Haddad, eager to repudiate. There is moreover a dual use of such portraits by the Kamour collective. They wish to refute them: we are "civilized," the "flag" is sacred to us. However, they simultaneously play into this narrative: "beware," ours is a "border region" and we can allow matters to get out of hand. Through the Facebook videos and posts, the Kamour insist that they are indeed members of the people, bonded in solidarity, unstoppable, and defiantly present. They belong to Tunisia. They insist that protests, sit-ins, strikes, and hydrocarbon destruction are no more than frustrated responses (after years of "patience") to being denied legitimate rights. Theirs is not merely criminal behavior. This is likely why Haddad, for instance, rages against accusations that Kamour is a ragtag group of gangs.[63] "We are not savages (*hamajiyyin*). ... We [merely] demand our rights ... we don't burn our country. ... Five years and we have not ... broken [into] any stores, or attacked any houses. To the contrary, [people in] the houses serve us couscous, give us milk!" he elaborates. In fact, they attempt to distance themselves from vandalism against security headquarters, denouncing lone acts for which the Coordination is not responsible (Mosaique FM 2017). To accept the "gang," "savage," or "spoilers" (*mukharribin*)[64] labels is to succumb to the status of "non-people". By freely using such invective, government officials or media personalities abstract the Kamour activists of agency, of rights worthiness, in addition to smearing them. Reminiscent of Bourguiba and Ben Ali's language about "*agents provocateurs*," it reflects a consistent state mindset in dealing with the collective social doing of protest.

The Defense Minister's ominous warning that terrorists might "exploit the unruliness"[65] communicates the same notion. Securitizing dissent dismisses the underlying political nature of protestors' claims and their selfhoods. A *people* can legitimately object to state policies; non-people can only destroy, lash out mindlessly, or loot greedily. Haddad and his Kamour comrades seem to have got this message, dismissing it summarily. Additionally, protestors reject labels that castigate them on regional lines. Security forces fling verbal abuse like the term *jabburah*, an offensive version of "country bumpkin," popularized during the Bourguiba era to refer to Tunisians of the interior or the South. Bouhaouach publicly repudiated the security official: "this is the language of *hogra*," and a verbal apology did not go deep enough to repair the damage (Carthage Plus 2020). If the denunciations of "gangs" or *mukharribin* strip the Kamour youth of their political agency, *jabburah* and similar language inflicts psychological harm, reifying social-cultural exclusion. (Such double consciousness occasionally emerges in media coverage, as in a colorful editorial noting that Kamour elicits a rhyming word for cow feces used as fuel.[66]) It reinforces self-styled hierarchies (beldi vs. afaqi) and the alienation of multiple marginalization. By vocalizing their displeasure in public, Kamour activists expose *hogra*, countering

---

[63] For instance, Kamour Facebook page, November 19, 2021.
[64] For instance, by the army warning that it will not allow any destruction of public amenities such as the oil pump. See *Wizarat Al-Difa'*: "*Al-Jaish Ta'amala Ma'a Muhtajji Al-Kamour* ...," in *Alchourouk*, July 16, 2020.
[65] *Al-Sabah*, January 20, 2021.
[66] *Awwalan Wa-Akhiran ... Al-Kamour Liman La Ya'rif Al-Kawamir*, in *Alchourouk*, November 3, 2020.

it and rejecting this humiliation. The frustrations and anger of *hogra* foment a further determination to protest.

'United We Stand': Kamour Solidarity and Kinship

Affect works in more than one way. There is a communal feel to the Kamour's Facebook page. It evinces identifications that begin with Tataouine and *Al-Janub* but do not stop there. The solidarity is local/regional: fundraising efforts (a mother stricken with illness, unable to work),[67] obituaries and funeral announcements (the uncle of a member of the regional delegation); national pride (cheering on Tunisia's team in the Africa cup); and international Islamic communion (Palestine, the defense of the Prophet against cartoon abuse). This solidarity is on the one hand the bitter fruit of state *hogra*. Shared misery and deprivation, humiliation and indignity, gives rise to a "we-ness" against the state other. Yet solidarity is also the positive vindication of collective struggle and the agency of action. Raising money for the group—tents, food and drink, eventually the smartphone(s) and laptop(s) through which they maintain Kamour social media presence—is one material manifestation of such solidarity among Tataouinians, including, as in other Arab geographies (see Moss 2020) those in the diaspora.[68] The latter, also play a role here, in raising money, say Kamour leaders. Tataouinians in Canada, for instance, announced a drive to raise $50,000 for a regional hospital.[69] Tangible support emanates from deep wellsprings of solidarity as "one [unified] determination, one heart, one pocket," that is, pooling resources.[70] Stirred by the affect of collective concern and mutual recognition born of *hogra*, a common cause forms among the marginalized who may be further linked by "primordial" ties, namely clans and tribes. The notion of unity arises as a consistent theme. Phrases such as "one hand" (*yad wahidah*) or "one row" (*saff wahid*) are sprinkled throughout their mobilization discourse urging, for instance, the larger Tataouine populace to join in a general strike.[71] Pleas for cooperation indicate the two-way relation of solidarity that is neither *natural* nor incidental but carefully crafted. Kamour needs Tataouine for the strike's success, while Tataouine, they argue, needs them. Partake in the strike, they admonish, otherwise "you leave these young men to 'commit *harqah*' ... that's it ... sick of everything, he says so be it, that's enough for me ..." There is no choice *but* to defy the state, and no choice *but* to stand with Kamour, in this narrative.

Examining Kamour discourse closely, we detect the contours of a three-fold sense of solidarity. This multilayered *tadamon* or *luhmah* spans the common psychological-socioeconomic-political hurt of multiple marginalization; a shared will in pursuit of a joint cause by activists who take matters into their own hands; and

---

[67] Kamour Facebook, January 19, 2022.
[68] Interviews with Tawfik and Kamel, August 26–27, 2021, Tataouine.
[69] Kamour Facebook page, January 26, 2021.
[70] Interview with Taieb, August 26, 2021, Tataouine.
[71] Kamour Facebook page, February 22, 2021.

a spatialized regional identity of *Al-Janub* interlaced with tribal affiliation. Through the prism of Kamour activism, we may have in Tataouine a close approximation to Ibn Khaldun's '*asabiyyah* as he conceived it. Group ties are forged to repel marginalization and deprivation as the state's other. However, such a collective identification and struggle are stitched over existing layers of sanguine ties, of blood (tribe, as interviewees mention) and region (the South). What is important is that *luhmah*, as the activists often call it, between the activists is nested within the Tataouine community. Sometimes, it materializes in coming to the rescue (*faz'ah*) *of* fellow activists nearby. One such example is a call to *faz'ah* "for our brothers in Remada … Remada is Tataouine, Tataouine is Remada," when they were under attack by security forces.[72] Solidarity is in this case making the trip to *appear* in supportive physical presence. Kamour activists tend to stress this point in refuting accusations of gangster-hood or unfettered, mindless destruction where they prey on the local community. This is why, in a quote mentioned earlier, Haddad reminded audiences that locals welcome and feed the Kamour collective. They are not parasites taking advantage of local goodwill or meager resources. In turn, the Kamour activists speak of "representing" the entire state of Tataouine. They often begin exhortations with, "Oh people of Tataouine!" (*ya sha'ba Tataouine!*), from Bir Lahmar to Remada to elsewhere.[73] Yet this bond or *luhmah* is not a static, permanent feature of Kamour's relations with local communities. Localized, regionalized solidarity sometimes seems to be crushed by the weight of the state's non-cooperation, its neglect and broken promises. Dual addresses on Facebook illustrate this complicated web of interactions and expectations. Activists speak to fellow Tataouinians, to explain, justify, mobilize; and to the government to demand, cajole, warn. In one video,[74] after Haddad and Bouhaouach speak, other community members take their places before the camera. An "Uncle" that looks like an Imam, dressed in the traditional red cap *shashiyyah* under a white shawl encircling his head, chimes in to defend the *tansiqiyyah*. The group are seen to be standing (physically and morally) with the Kamour, to prop up flagging trust and confidence in the activists across Tataouine. This message is directed toward the "inside" of this periphery-within-the-periphery. Community elders remind Tataouinians that the Kamour leaders are simply doing their best for the collective good of residents. One middle-aged man upholds the activists as reincarnations of a larger, unfinished struggle. They are "a recreation of the Tunisian revolution and the Arab revolution" of 2011. A continuous thread ties Kamour to the popular uprising ousting Ben Ali, and even the Arab-wide mobilization against dictatorship and deprivation, for dignity and freedom. In their minds and from their mouths, revolution is not over. Support should be given freely. Solidarity should be airtight.

---

[72] Kamour Facebook page, July 9, 2020.
[73] For instance, Kamour Facebook page, July 4, 2020.
[74] Kamour Facebook page, April 3, 2021.

This *luhmah* is a serious business. It is the glue that holds together the pledge *al-rakh la*. With the gravity of self-assigned religious obligations to God before countryman, Haddad and a throng of activists around him swore an oath on the Qur'an not to betray Tataouine.[75] To God they are accountable, to humans they bear witness. The implication is that countless others have already sunk to treachery, starting with the politicians who did not activate the 2017 agreement. "I will not forgive" *mish msameh*, he intones. (Deliberately or not, the phrase brings to mind the 2017 campaign against the Administrative Reconciliation Law, *manish m'sameh* (El-Hemmi 2017)). Forgiveness has both a normative, moral quality and an affective ring. We forgive those who have done wrong against us, deserving and undeserving. To forgive is to exercise moral judgment that reaches into the heart. We cannot forgive if we are not ready, if the wrong is too heinous, if the object of potential forgiveness is not worthy. "We will not forgive" betrays an intentionally conveyed anger: the wrong is too egregious, still ongoing. Forgiving means abandoning our claim to legitimate rights, guaranteed by the constitution, or a legal contract, in this new democracy. The dramatic vow sensationalizes the Kamour activists' commitment to their movement, to one another, and to their rundown region. At the same time, it draws a hard affective boundary between them and those who let Tataouine down, whose policies marginalize and deprive. The pledge flows into a threat that is emotional, steeped with religious and political righteousness.

Solidarity against the State

The state can weaken group solidarity, however. Interspersed with the inward communication is an external entreaty to the government. Stop breaking the ties that bind us, the activists suggest.[76] As one puts it, *luhmah* is the "safety valve" for the Kamour cause. The government's flouting of the ubiquitously named "agreement" puts in-group solidarity at risk. In turn, compromised solidarity throws the web of relations and responsibilities into question, casting doubt on the "just cause" as they call it elsewhere. Thus, group solidarity exhibits a complex relation with the "outsider" (state/government's) action. If Mechichi's administration keeps its end of the bargain, the Kamour activists might maintain their hold when they are losing credibility among those they claim and aim to represent. For the time being, the reverse holds true. Activists and elders make a second point, this one made to state officials is an apology for "transgressions" by young teenagers. Here they demonstrate solidarity with the state's newest victims. They ask for the release of adolescents arrested for burning rubber tires. The minors got carried away and let frustration get the best of them. "Deep wells of anger" (again, affective motivations) are drivers of such unruly yet understandable behavior, says one elder. These very young youth should not languish in prison.

How this kind of solidarity refracts into the self (-other) identifications of this partial demos is an important question. A sometimes uneasy relationship seems to link

---

[75] Kamour Facebook page, July 4, 2020.
[76] Kamour Facebook page, April 3, 2021.

the residents of Tataouine with the rest of Tunisia. On the one hand, they constantly reach out to fellow compatriots, implying: Oh people of Tunisia! We are like you, we are a part of you, we belong to the same nation, suffer under the same state. On the other hand, Kamour activists express dispirited feelings with respect to fellow Tunisians. One interviewee went so far as to distance himself from those outside Tataouine or the South: "we don't care about the other regions,"[77] because they don't care about us. As with the state, *Hogra* for *hogra*, he seems to say. It is noteworthy that many of the Kamour activists protested for the first time in 2010–11, participating in the revolutionary *hirak*. The contrast between the social doing of peoplehood of the revolution 12 years ago and more regionalized Kamour protest, is striking. There is an unresolved tension here, between "the people" as Tunisians outside and inside Tataouine or the South. Snubbed again and again, some of these activists do not seem to be above intimations of separatism, using terms like "state of the South" (*dawlat al-Janub*). Yet what exactly that implies politically is unclear. Its prevalence and depth are difficult to ascertain. This insularity contradicts much of Kamour's public face, declared positions and leanings. The activists constantly rebut attacks against them—of terrorism, of a penchant for violence, of refusing the Tunisian umbrella identity, of flouting the loyalty of citizenship. In a telling example, Haddad angrily responds to a social media accusation that he and his movement seek to "break up the state," since they harbor no allegiance to Tunisia, instead forging connections with Libyan militias.[78] The President himself hosted us in his palace, he reminds his accuser. Are you aware that we present some ominous threat that has escaped the notice of the President *and* "protectors of the nation" (the army), (*humat al-watan*), he mockingly asks. This forceful repudiation seems underwritten by a yearning for acceptance as part of "the people," and rage at the lack of lack of recognition and equality supposed to be heralded by the revolution.

Tunisian Solidarity, *Fellaga* Legacy

Does being among the "people" sow the seeds of a *Tunisian* affinity? To some extent, the *luhmah* of Kamour spreads outwards to a nation-wide solidarity. This is a qualified identification, however: conditional support requested and given. Language used and history re-narrated offer clues about this intricate (agentic, affective, and cognitive) assemblage of subaltern peoplehood. Free to join those "othered" by *colon*, dictator, and even democratic government, are all those Tunisians similarly challenging oppression in the manner of their revolutionary forefathers. A mutual recognition of (former or lingering) non-peoplehood and its discontents ensues. An early declaration and quasi-manifesto by the group is telling.[79] They write of "honoring" not only their region, but also the entire nation. Their demands for the region are only a "first step," after which all Tunisians can "unlock the puzzle of their stolen national resources" by following Kamour's example. "There is no difference among

---

[77] Interview with Kais, August 26, 2021.
[78] Kamour Facebook page, January 25, 2022.
[79] Kamour Facebook page, May 3, 2017.

us from Bizerte [north-most Tunisia] to Borj El-Khadra." Here is a hand extended to the entire people, and especially to all who will recognize Tataouine's suffering that echoes their own. Yet it is a particular appeal, to the *non-people* seeking to become *people*. The Kamour activists claim the mantle of the exploits of early anti-colonial heroes. *Fellaga* legacy, experienced and embodied in everyday speech and memory, accrues legitimacy. They are descendants of Ben Ghedhahem and Daghbagi. "We are the grandsons of Ali Ben Ghedhahem," says one Kamour leader, likening his example and others to a "candle lighting our path."[80] Yet in time-tested tales, these mythic figures in popular Tunisian history were halted in their tracks. Ali Ben Ghedhahem "led a revolution against the Bey, whose kindling was the poor and the oppressed."[81] His victory nearly within reach, he was "tricked" by the Bey and "the revolution ended" (just as Daghbagi was executed by the French). Drawing on this social memory, the Kamour activists narrate counter-stories, to adapt Smith's (2003) "stories", that spur action. "Does it please us to end mid-way in our journey?" The rhetorical question provokes a resounding *no* for a response. Revolution to the very end, until all of Tunisia is liberated from the dictatorship of marginalization. That is the meaning of *al-rakh la*. Solidarity among and with the people of Tunisia is standing with the downtrodden, the *zawawla* (singular, zawwali),[82] and mutual support between them.

The power stirred up by a rebellious use of history and language itself is stirred up by the term *fellaga*. The echo of the term and the memory it evokes are ineffable. Tataouine's anti-colonial struggle in the "Youssefist revolution" has been documented by historians (Belsoud 2017). We are "the grandsons of resistors of *fellaga*, sons of the revolutionary South," says a Kamour leader proudly.[83] Another adds that they are "sons of the desert" that was the *fellaga*'s arms smuggling route from Libya.[84] The Arabic term *fellaga* (which we have encountered in other protestscapes), literally from the word "split" or *falaqa*, indicating those who veer from the main path, may connote bandits (Dhouib 2017, 137). In French colonial usage, the word stood for mountain-dwelling resistance fighters, casting a negative aspersion on those who defy their mandated rulers (Evans and Phillips 2007). Its wider circulation included not just mobilizing Tunisians, but also Algerian anti-colonial combatants (Elsghayer 2020). Instead of taking offense, some Tunisians came to "own" the label, referring to resistance fighters *fellaga* to this very day (see for instance Zartman 2019, 140). Exercising a kind of counter-power through language, they transformed the vituperative term into a signifier of fighting oppression, bravery, and honor.

The postcolonial era brought with it another plot twist. The anti-colonial political movement, led by Habib Bourguiba and others, worked in parallel (not always in agreement) with armed freedom fighters to secure, albeit gradually, Tunisia's full independence in 1956. To an extent, Bourguiba's popularity and legitimacy sprang

---

[80] Interview with Lutfi, August 26, 2021.
[81] Kamour Facebook page, May 3 2017.
[82] See for instance Kamour Facebook page, July 4, 2020.
[83] Interview with Hedi, August 25, 2021, Medenine.
[84] Interview with Tawfik, August 26, 2021, Tataouine.

from these very anti-colonial credentials. However, as recounted in earlier chapters, he himself was not above denigration and repression of the very people the nationalist campaign had sought to emancipate. Hence, Bourguiba ultimately quashed the peoplehood-in-becoming that had energized the *fellaga*'s revolution against the French. None of this history is lost on the people of Tataouine or the rest of *al-Janub*.

At the same time, Bourguiba's power consolidation did not swallow up every pocket of resistance in the country. Dictatorships seldom do. In turn, bottom-up defiance, nurtured for decades, *including under the new democracy*, has as this chapter demonstrates turned against the (coastal/capital) machinery of dictatorship and its security apparatus. In a similar vein, Kamour protestors proudly declare they are sons and grandsons of anti-colonial challengers who took up arms against the French, including Libya's Omar Al-Mukhtar.[85] Historically, this is of course true. Renowned fighters such as Misbah Al-Jarbouʻ hailed from Tataouine, fighting from Bir Lahmar to Remada where he was killed in a French airstrike in 1958 ('Ariq 2020). Additionally, Kamour activists draw parallels between the domination of the *colons*, of dictators Bourguiba and Ben Ali, and even of the unrestrainable security arm of the democratizing polity after 2011. Revolution or *thawrah* against the French glides smoothly into *thawrah* against dictatorship, subsequently propagated by Kamour activists and others against the resurgent remnants of the "*ancien regime*." In this way, they restore popular depth to the term *fellaga* and to revolutionary heroes such as Ben Ghedhahem. Just as rebellious Tunisians, armed and unarmed, subverted French labels, claiming them as their own to communicate proud revolt against colonial oppression, these Kamour activists reclaim the moniker for the marginalized (non)people. Mythological courage, an assertion of *presence*, a refusal to be cowed by sheer force, a willingness to sacrifice—all fan the moral flames of these three iterations of rebellion. The revolutionary élan, from Ben Ghedhahem's crucible to *fellaga* to the Kamour, is kept alive by this chain of unruliness and a solidarity that transverses time.

Protesting (under) Democracy

Legitimate Rights

Tunisia's democratization launched in 2011 shaped the contours of the Kamour movement in novel ways, differentiating it from the earlier protestscapes. Among other things, democracy plays an identitarian function in their discourse. In addition to invoking their anti-colonial pedigree, Kamour activists emphasize their membership within the people by sprinkling their video monologues and Facebook posts with references to the constitution, democracy, its norms and procedures, and legal rights. Like all Tunisians, we have internalized the civic-legal discourse of the post-2011 political order, they intimate. We are good, law-abiding citizens. The inverse

---

[85] Interview with Ahmed, August 26, 2021, Tataouine.

holds as well: because we belong to the Tunisian body politic, our region is as deserving of legal-constitutional rights to development, employment, and overall equality. We have remained steadfast and forbearing in withstanding multiple marginalization. *Hogra* has outstayed its welcome. Enough is enough. Pleas for acceptance blend with defiant challenges to the state. Even border security is not out of bounds. Tataouine is "the den" in your backyard, bordering Libya and Algeria, says one activist, implicitly invoking images of sleeping lions in addressing the government and Interior Ministry upon the targeting of Kamour leaders.[86] The interweaving of threats and entreaties seems to be spontaneous, not rehearsed. It is reflective of the affective impetus of what is clearly meant to convey bravado and confidence. Desperation mingles with insubordination. This audacity, built on the determination to break the ongoing cycle of victimhood, misery, and apathy, is threefold. It involves i) people seeking to change their fate through protest (agency); ii) sublimating pent-up humiliation and anger delivering solidarity (affect); and iii) making use of the solid ground of new constitutional equality putatively within reach to all Tunisians and regions (cognition).

Thus, the language of rights permeates the vocalized demands and the Facebook declarations of Kamour activists. "Oh people of Tataouine! Oh people of Tunisia! ... we are ... defending legitimate rights and demands, transparency in dealings, and dealings [by the state] with all [actors] via the same distance [equally] ... what is called the founding of democracy ... the language of rights ... [ours is] a message the world ... we are sure that God will make the cause of Tataouine victorious, because it is a just cause."[87] Note they do not simply petition for the more abstract "human rights" appeals to which the oppressed resort under dictatorial regimes. Rather, they point to very specific rights within a broader political context of *democracy*. The audience cannot feign misunderstanding or irrelevance. The state cannot wriggle free of an acknowledgment that Kamour activists' demands are in fact drawn from the 2014 constitution's provisions for employment, development, and allocation of the wealth from natural resource (Articles 12, 40, 136, 14). Bourguiba's and Ben Ali's grand projects for, but unfinished, regional development will no longer suffice. Instead, the parlance of democracy frames the *argumentation* in which Kamour activists socially act and en-act their agency. All the leaders interviewed in the focus group mentioned some version of the mandate to "wrest our rights" or "claim our rights" from the state.[88] Gushing upon the "Kamour 2" agreement wrangled out of the Mechichi government, Haddad extoled the breakthrough. He magnanimously gave credit to the Head of Government (Prime Minister). These decisions spearheaded by the Prime Minister "allow Tataouine to [be] like the other governorates, to achieve its rights in development, in employment ... [so it can be] *la bes* [literally, "not bad," a term used for "doing well"]" (Mosaique 2020b).

---

[86] Kamour Facebook page, June 22, 2020.
[87] Kamour Facebook page, July 4, 2020.
[88] Interviews, August 26–27, 2021.

Protesting an "Extractivist" Depletion of Rights

There is a global context for the family of rights to which Kamour activists diligently aspire. Once again, Tunisia is in good company with similarly underdeveloped, formerly colonized, globally dependent societies around the world. Natural resource extraction commandeered by multinational corporations inspires protest in Tunisia. Global extractivism inordinately impacts the world's marginalized—disadvantaged by spatialized, class, race, and gendered positionality—who in turn fight back (Villarreal and Munoz 2020). Staging protests and sit-ins, creating resistance art, and envisioning alternatives, women and peasants object to encroaching mining projects across Latin America and the Caribbean that imperil the environment, homes, and ways of living (Villarreal and Munoz 2020). Tataouine's Kamour have admittedly taken a different approach in terms of their means and tactics,[89] attempting to force the state's hand to employ them rather than seeking to drive out the mining companies. Environmental concerns may seem far off the radar for some. Still, civil society groups are vocally cognizant of the environmental disasters ensuing from effectively unregulated (or poorly regulated) oil drilling by the multi-national/national, unequally partnered oil companies. What Bebbington et al. (2008) label "ambivalence towards mining" (or in this case, hydrocarbons) surfaces. Objections to the drawbacks (pollution, problematic distribution) coincide with the potential for employment and development. As an FTDES (2021) report notes, the "natural resource curse" in Tataouine is the infliction of environmental damage—polluting soil, war, and consuming excessive amounts of water—by the petrochemical companies in Al Burma and Dehiba. Residents complain that local authorities are deaf to environmentalist groups' warnings. This is all despite Tunisia having signed up to the Extractive Industries Transparency Initiative, as well as Article 44 in the 2014 Constitution protecting citizens' environmental rights. At hand is another example of poorly thought-through policies by the state. A project to improve the water quality and supply signed by then PM Youssef Chahed, to which a 650 thousand dinar budget was allocated, has reached a dead end (FTDES 2021). A *Meshkal* investigative report found that foreign oil and gas companies to whom Tunisian state energy companies have made huge concessions are dumping "sludge" in the desert in violation of proper waste procedures, as activists (including Kamour) and farmers testify. Combined with over-extraction of water, this waste is ruinous to the health of camels and thus farmers' livelihoods. Further complicating the exploitation is the military cover. Most of Tataouine is designated as a "military zone" requiring special permission ("desert cards") to access. This limits the mobility of workers, residents, and even government officials tasked with oversight (Ben Mbarek and Aliriza 2022). Environmental injury exacerbates underdevelopment mediated by dependence on foreign corporations.

---

[89] *Tas'id Jadid Li-Mu'tasimi "Al-Kamour 2,"* in *Haqaiq Online*, March 3, 2018.

These negative externalities mirror other resource extraction afflictions from around the world. Like hydrocarbon drilling, mining dries out and pollutes local water resources ultimately detracting from development and contributing to "unfreedom" rather than "freedom," à la Sen (Arellano 2011). Forced displacement of local populations by large Canadian international mining companies in Marmato, Colombia goes against the grain of the Northern country's declared democracy promotion policies (Arellano 2011). How much of a say do locals have in the manner, environmental effects, and profit distribution of natural resources buried under the very land they inhabit? These conundrums resonate, from Colombia to Tunisia, from Tataouine to the phosphate basin. They perplex the socio-political consciousness of citizens, detracting from un-kept revolutionary promises of democratization, namely the institutionalization of freedom, dignity, and equality.

Since June 2017, however, the biggest sticking point for the activists has been what they see as a reneging on the agreement they signed with the government. The negotiated, documented settlement with Chahed's government, representative and executive administrator of the state that had spurned them for decades, validates their demands and compounds them. It is not just historical marginalization to which they are urging an end, as citizens craving equality, as non-people having "found" themselves and made their way toward "the people." They have, moreover, entered into a *contractual* relationship with the Chahed government. The government's failure to implement the agreement (first Chahed with "Kamour 1," followed by Mechichi with "Kamour 2") is still relegation to "non-people" status after the 2011 revolution. In fact, at least one Kamour leader construes *hogra* to be the state's "procrastination"[90] and "lies"[91]—the latter referring to broken promises such as the 2017 accord. In dodging its pledges, the Tunisian state is recreating erasure of Southerners as full and equal members of the people. What makes this revamped *hogra* insufferable is that it unfolds in this presumptively new age of democratic egalitarianism, of rights and recognition. The Kamour activists refuse to accept this. Through protest and sit-ins, by shutting off the *vana* pump, they are socially acting and en-acting peoplehood, swooping into new conflict with the Tunisian state. But this *agon* for the democratic age is framed by certain restrictions. Even with their anger unleashed, legal rights, constitutional responsibilities, and peaceful protest circumscribe and signpost the discourse and practice of Kamour's activists. Responding to arrests or court sentencing, they insist that their only crime is that of peaceful assembly, which is no crime at all! Again, the slogan that has endured for over five years resounds so powerfully. *Al-rakh la*. We will not relent, and the law is on our side. Is this not a revolutionary moment, an equalizing reset?

---

[90] Interview with Taieb, August 26, 2021, Tataouine.
[91] Interviews with Ahmed and Taieb, August 26, 2021, Tataouine.

Disaffection with Democracy

Since 2011 and 2014, when a new democratic constitution (revoked in the wake of the July 25, 2021 coup) was promulgated, one new question has arisen, regarding the precise channels and the types of political behavior through which marginalized people in the peripheries such as Tataouine can express discontent with unfulfilled pledges. Protest activity has been one preferred method, as we have demonstrated. This indicates the vivacity of an agonistic peoplehood that came to fruition in 2011, stretching out the revolutionary élan even after the rupture effected by Ben Ali's stealthy departure. It is important to consider, however, the activists' own assessments of their new democracy and its trappings: free and fair elections, revitalized parliaments, and power-sharing executives. In Tataouine as elsewhere, discontent with these institutional pillars of democracy deepened noticeably after the delayed implementation of the 2017 agreement. However, the election of independent populist Kais Saied in October 2019 seemed to have temporarily raised expectations among Kamour protestors, most of them among the young (Sadiki 2020, 91). "We place all our trust in President Kais Saied, the level-headed, informed, professor," noted one protestor.[92] The hope was that Saied would usher in a new era of change. In January 2020, he hosted youth representatives from the Kamour protests at the presidential palace in Carthage. They aired their grievances to the new president. Speaking shortly after the meeting, one Kamour leader described Saied as "the truthful and trustworthy" (*al-sadiq wa-l-amin*), descriptors commonly associated with the Prophet Mohamed. The young man noted that he felt he had been listened to for the first time by the authorities. The president, it seemed, was concerned about problems of employment and development in Tataouine, and the Kamour protest movement initially chose to cooperate (Presidence TN 2020). After exercising the agency of voice and argumentation, that is, they felt acknowledged. A brief respite from the affect of *hogra* turned out to be no more than a short episode of "decompression," however. After giving up their protests and sit-in, the Kamour group appears to have concluded that the President's overtures were superficial rhetoric. As recounted earlier in the chapter, March 2020 saw the renewal of protests and sit-ins, responses to government "procrastination" (Nessma TV 2020). Accompanying the renewed protest in what proved to be a (politically) hot summer were retorts of "escalation" (*tas'id*). "The government doesn't listen except to escalation!"(Mosaique FM 2020a).

This fighting stance, its unmistakable discontent with the democratic transition, is the result of more than government evasion of signed agreements. Those driven to protest see that marginalization has not abated in any meaningful way since the revolution (see Sadiki 2020). Many flatly state that the socio-economic situation in Tataouine "had not changed"; it was either "the same as before" or had even become "much worse."[93] Harsh evaluations of each Tunisian government since 2011

---

[92] Interview with Salem, December 2019.
[93] Interviews, December 2019.

level the charge of inaction against a successive set of ruling elites. This inertia is read as indifference to a worsening marginalization of their communities: more of the same! *Hogra* proves to be the stubborn affective ligament binding "non-people" with those who govern them—even when the latter are elected. Anti-establishment sentiments are not uncommon. Appraisals of the post-2011 political establishment use descriptors such as "not effective in dealing with problems," "very bad," "very weak," "not good," and having "done nothing." One evaluation, not meant to be hyperbole, was that "90 percent of politicians made marginalization worse."[94] Several protestors regard politicians as kleptocrats or simply "thieves" (*surraq*), echoing the revolutionary chant "employment is an entitlement, you gang of thieves!" (*al-tashghil istihqaq, ya 'isabat al-surraq*) (see Chapter 6). "They come to get our votes and then go back to parliament and steal from us," accused an unemployed university graduate from Tataouine.[95] Viewed thus, the center merely deploys the implements of democracy to exploit or ignore the periphery. In their elite game of democracy, mistrusted elected officials (McCarthy 2022) merely toy with Tataouine's subalterns and the South's downtrodden. They are stuck in "non-people" status, as ballots become hollow stand-ins for "the people" actually deserving the right to development, the right to dream of a dignified life and a sunny future. Some do not even attempt revolutionary optimism, going so far as to say life was "better under Ben Ali." One protestor mused that during Ben Ali's rule, "marginalization was just intellectual [and political]; now it is also material."[96] Many admitted they "do not care about [formal] politics." A significant number of those interviewed have stopped voting,[97] confirming national trends. Marginalization, interviewees said over and over, had given rise to "political apathy" in the face of government "negligence." Many dismiss elections as ineffective in mitigating the marginalization that perpetually puts their lives on hold. Post-revolution, they expect government in democratizing Tunisia to address people's basic needs, their dignity and equality. Failing that, what kind of democracy takes shape? Thus the stony judgment that Tunisia's "dictatorship is not yet gone."[98] For them and others, democratic institutions are meaningless in the absence of an equitable distribution of wealth. Voting does not put food on the table. Deprivation—the antithesis of freedom, according to Amartya Sen (1999)—leaves people in the peripheral *Janub* bereft of the means of emancipation as free and equal citizens. Dual peripheries like Tataouine thus appear distanced from peoplehood, despite the string of elections in 2011, 2014, 2018, 2019, 2021, and 2022.

A related and constant mantra of the Kamour collective is that they are not party adherents and bickering in Bardo (seat of parliament) does not concern them. (However, they are widely reputed for their affinity with Ennahda and the short-lived party Itilaf Alkarama (Dignity Coalition), as interviews confirm.[99]) Haddad points

---

[94] Interview with Gassem, December 23, 2019.
[95] Interview with Bilel, December 23, 2019.
[96] Interview with Karim, 23 December 2019.
[97] Interviews, December 2019.
[98] Interview with Osama, December 22, 2019.
[99] Interviews, August 2021.

out the contradictions of the naysayers, noting that Kamour closed the *vana* twice during Ennahda's rule, and stood accused of being followers of Kais Saied. Since July 25, 2021, as they press the President with a singular hold on power to stick to the 2020 agreement, the Kamour is tagged with the "Ennahda" label[100] (implied as a liability). There is a certain disingenuousness to this complaint, however. More than once, the Kamour activists admonished the government that Tataouine "gave three seats to Ennahda and one to Nidaa."[101] The grievance projected here is that they are not getting their share of representation. During the 2019 election season, they organized what seem to be modest campaign-style events for candidates including for the Amal wa 'Amal list.[102] On social media, they express support for Itilaf Al-Karama's Saifeddine Makhlouf, calling him a "symbol of the revolution" and thanking him for publicly mentioning Kamour.[103] These opinions do not seem to square with the declaration that "We are the party of *al-rakh la*," not Ennahda or Nidaa or any other party" (Nessma TV 2017). Dissimulation of partisan leanings aside, however, Kamour activists are consistent in their argument that their demands defy party-level categorizations and platforms. Perhaps that is the penultimate idea they vouch for. No citizens, no regions, should be subject to state *hogra* distributing neglect and indignity instead of employment, infrastructure, and a reasonable standard of living. Especially under democracy.

Cognizing "*Al-Rakh La*"
Social and Normative Learning

Peoplehood, like all socio-political phenomena, is not static in its manifestations and expressions. It travels across spatio-temporal contexts in response to various structural or environmental situations and changes, sometimes even within the same territorial state. Nestled within a nascent democratizing state and its fledgling institutions, the Kamour campaign was to some extent made possible by the changing structures of a new democracy. Once the rights to assembly and protest as discussed above were enshrined in the Constitution, much of the oppositional, unruly activity of the Kamour activists was in effect made *legal*. Not all their practices were sanctioned by law, of course. Sealing the *vana* at Nawwara and disruptions prior to that are tantamount to the destruction of public property, according to the state. We have seen that from the movement's earliest months in summer 2017, the state responded with repression and full force, evacuating the tent city. (The clearing out of New York's Zucotti Park where the Occupy Wall Street movement had squatted in fall 2011, comes to mind (Crabapple 2021).) The codification of laws (constitutional) and inauguration of institutions (elections) has been far-reaching. One consequence has been the patterning of expectations vis-à-vis the state, among even the most marginalized

---

[100] Kamour Facebook page, November 21, 2021.
[101] Kamour Facebook page, May 22, 2017.
[102] Kamour Facebook page, October 1, 2019.
[103] Kamour Facebook page, September 10, 2019.

in Tunisia. Kamour's have-nots came to anticipate their rights to employment, clean water, dignified living, and basic public amenities as promised in the 2014 democratic constitution. They internalized, in other words "the right to have rights"—an important cognitive element of the self-consciousness of peoplehood. Here, then, we can tentatively point to the kinds of learning at play by Kamour's vociferous indignants. We observe in their (social) media discourse and interviews material references to democracy as a system under which they *should* but *have not* acquired or received the basic building blocks of a dignified life. In the absence of that, *hogra* recreated itself, this time donning the accoutrements and the language of democracy. Democracy is a "two-way street," between electors and the elected, representatives and the represented. Thus, protest is now stressed as a *democratic right* and a *democratic practice*, as is accountability to constituencies and to legal documents such as the 2017 and 2020 agreements. Barring that, an aggravated unruliness may border on the illegal, as in the disruption to oil and gas production.

An additional aspect of social learning in relation to the Kamour movement is noteworthy. In fall and winter of 2020, protests and sit-ins sprang up across Tunisia's "regions," (*jihat* usually referencing those outside the North or Sahel) such as Beja and Gabes. Seemingly encouraged by the November 2020 Kamour–Mechichi agreement, other activists tried similar tactics. Marginalization and deprivation had been their experience, too, worsening since the 2011 revolution.[104] Social acts and enactments of peoplehood in Kamour were more or less mimicked by the comparably destitute, the comparably frustrated who had come to expect more from the state. The outcomes of such bottom-up pressure may not always have been in substantive favor of the unruly. Media disparagement was widespread. Accusations circulated of national divisiveness, for which the Kamour agreements set an unhappy precedent. Even the Kamour activists were cautious as they lent their solidarity. "We are with you, but please not in this manner ... you will set this country back" through resorting to vandalism and the destruction of property. "Demand your rights in the light of day and we will be with you in the front lines," they instructed the rioters.[105] Despite dubious tactics, the lesson had been learned after a fashion. Tataouinians suggested more than once that Kamour would be immortalized in the history books, and would "remain a part of Tunisia's history."[106] The activists proclaim their presence as part of the people not just in the present, but for the future. Tunisian history-as-past-present is not, and will not be, complete without consideration of Kamour's imprint, the path its activists have trodden in the scorching desert. (Such acknowledgment includes due homage to the movement's martyrs. As do many others, the post begins with the common Muslim prayer for the soul of the deceased: *rahimahu Allah*.) Consistently and eloquently, the Kamour activists uphold themselves as an example for other Tunisians. They are "teaching lessons" in "sacrifice ... steadfastness (*sumud*) ... challenges [against the odds] ... steadfastness/persistence ... achievement ..."[107]

---

[104] *Al-Maghreb*, November 26, 2020.
[105] Kamour Facebook page, Jan. 2021.
[106] Kamour Facebook page, May 22, 2019.
[107] Kamour Facebook page, November 22, 2020.

If the Kamour collective swiftly learned democratic norms, labeling marginalization as a transgression of rights, en-acting protest as constitutional freedom of assembly, demanding accountability of elected MPs as representatives, the marginalized in other regions seem to have engaged in a similar kind of learning.

Learning the Identities of Peoplehood

When viewed South-side, what do the identities of peoplehood outline themselves to be? This question is important to the re-ontologization of this protestscape. It discloses ontological and cognitive capacities of being as subaltern, Southerner, protestor, etc. We can point to a Southern subculture with its own linguistic distinctiveness. A contrast is observable with the more Francophone capital and Sahel regions, as Tataouine and its sister governorates retain the Arabic language as spoken or displayed in public spaces, local media, and advertisements (Ben Khalifa 2017). An undaunted expression of identity leans more toward Arabic, staving off French linguistic-cultural leanings in the Northern part of the country and among its elites. The Kamour activists weave in and out of concentric circles of identity (regional–national): skillfully turning the "double consciousness" of *hogra* on its head by adapting discourse depending on the context and occasion. Sometimes, Al-Janub/Tataouine takes precedence (*faz'ah* for those in Remada, addresses to "O people of Tataouine!"). At other times, they activate the national self-identification, eager for the "Tunisian" people to understand their cause. In so doing, the Kamour activists are adamant regarding self-representation. The subaltern will speak, does speak. They wield words, images, videos, and symbolism through their Facebook page, through countless appearances in the media, and by maintaining their specific manners of speech and even attire. For instance, the Kamour delegation sported the *shash*, depicted in a group picture (self-portrait) of them wearing the camel-colored head turban to some meetings of their fall 2020 negotiations with the Mechichi government.[108] This made for a striking contrast with the business suits of government officials, as desert Arab sat opposite Western(ized) forms, each evocative of an entire cultural repository. This resolute fidelity to visible styles of Southern afaqi custom does not melt away in the repeated calls for recognition, as Tunisians and as people with rights. Similarly, there seems to be a discriminating identification with various national heroes across Tunisia. As though the national identity houses all these larger-than-life figures, and various sub-groups selectively invoke those that ring relevant to their cause or align with their sense of self. In Southern Tataouine, the Kamour activists conjure the spirits of Ali Ben Ghedahem and Daghbagi. Others do the same with Bourguiba or Hached, as explored in previous chapters.

Furthermore, we can discern in Kamour an element of social movement "prefiguration," cognitively understood. A means–ends synergy can help effect political alternatives to the status quo through group practices of "experimentation," the

---

[108] Kamour Facebook page, October 11, 2020.

cultivation of critical political viewpoints, and the development of "new collective norms," followed by their "demonstration and diffusion" (Yates 2015, 12–15). The Kamour campaign's arrival at two negotiated agreements with the government more than three years apart emerged from a chain of practices. They repeatedly emphasized their *hogra* and marginalization as governments failed them for decades. Demonstrating (i.e. "teaching") other Tunisian subalterns by example, through (social) media, they solidified bonds and passed the torch on to various protesting cohorts across the country. Social doing by the demos is no pre-molded enterprise; it is the fashioning within the community of individual-made-collective connections, political demands, identities, and selfhoods. The experiential practice of protest offers cognitive possibilities that re-purpose knowing through learning and teaching (Freire's critical pedagogy). Additionally, learning is socially embedded, recalling the evolution of linguistic abilities among human beings from birth through adulthood (Vygotsky 1986). The spark of peoplehood simultaneously shoots through people's actions (agentically), hearts and bodies (affectively), and minds (cognitively), running from individuals to groups and back.

Interactions nurture solidarity as well as learning. The pedagogical is dispensed into socio-cultural imaginaries and value-practice repositories that can engender civic identities and democratic sensibilities (Sadiki 2015). Iterative experiences, from the 2011 revolution to the campaign of 2017 and onward, sharpen the skills of organization, mobilization, argumentation, and even elocution. Shared time in the trenches, so to speak, seems to burnish the we-ness of marginalized, deprived, spatialized self-hoods agonistically juxtaposed with the state robbing subalterns of both dignity and equality. Sometimes, such learning becomes parochial. Sub-state identities rear their rebellious heads. One Kamour leader spoke of "learning how to mobilize tribes against the regime."[109] At other times, the cognitive takes shape as an adaptation of discourses and practices, the repertoires of protest as peoplehood. "Escalating" as far as shutting off the *vana* when demonstrations proved fruitless is one example. Modulating *Janub*-centric oratory to summon Saied's words from their trip to Carthage verbatim ("you hold the embers in your hands," confirming the group's righteousness) and insisting that Kamour is a "national cause"[110] is another. The seamless transition from learning to teaching follows a quasi-prefigurative intent to diffuse (restrained) unruliness. Copying Kamour can help to widen the circumference of becomings of peoplehood to encompass all of the land.

Conclusion

This chapter has re-ontologized the Kamour protestscape, still in existence even if deflated since 2021. The campaign has granted the analytical leverage through which to examine protest activism within a changing (democratizing) political context.

---

[109] Interview with Tawfiq, August 26, 2021, Tataouine.
[110] Kamour Facebook page, January 25, 2022.

Note that this is not identical to the explanation from resource mobilization and political opportunity (McAdam et al. 2001) whereby structural conditions flowing from democratization make (more) protest possible. Rather, our tryptic of agentic, affective, and cognitive peoplehood is understood here as an extension of the 2011 revolution when authoritarian structures were far from propitious. In the revolutionary élan, it is this same sub-group of the spatially marginalized who seem to "appear" repeatedly. Social doing by those kept at arm's length from polity, economy, and society since postcolonial independence, perhaps before, upturns this partial demos from the object to the subject of *hogra*. The chapter has examined the specificities of these interlocking elements of peoplehood in the Tatatouine setting where decades of spatialized marginalization and deprivation form the bedrock of psyches, livelihoods, and restless aspirations. Scrupulous attention to pedagogies of self-representation in Kamour's written and spoken discourse sheds light on the vernacular of the indignant: protest in its online and offline forms.

This rebelscape captures a fascination with the possibilities of protest for thrusting non-people onto the political stage. It entails the convergence of both state distributional deficiencies falling short of restorative justice *and* the agency, affect, and cognition kindled in the 2011 revolution, not so far in the recent past. Through Tunisia's "part that has no part", peoplehood is (re)enacted piecemeal under the canopy of a newly democratizing state. By and large, ruling parties and elites ignored these alarm bells. Certainly, the revolution that shook Tunisia in 2011 has struggled to break free of inequity and fashion, much less sustain, a democracy in which the social question was to reterritorialize being and acting. Kamour's dramatically publicized discourse and actions, and "copycat" sit-ins, disruptions, and protests across the country in winter 2021, arguably helped to pave the way for Kais Saied's July 25, 2021 power grab. (Some Kamour leaders expressed opposition to the July 25 trajectory, however.)[111] The populist president played on legitimate anger and frustration by many of the marginalized who felt that the 2011 revolution and the new democratic system had failed them. A(n) (re)ignited peoplehood need not always bend toward liberal or representative democracy, as the concluding chapter will hint. Democracy may not kill the revolution or terminate the revolutionary élan. In Tunisia, however, democratization has tried its hand at counterrevolution to tame a peoplehood constantly in becoming.

References

Abdelmoula, Mohamed Rami. 2021. *I'tisam al-kamour: Nisf Intisar wa Ba'd Hazimah* [The Kamour Sit-In: Half a Victory and Some Defeat]. Legal Agenda. 10 April. https://bit.ly/2SUDNs9

Alikhbaria Attounsia. 2022. *Hakatha 'Allaqa 'Udu Tansiqiyyat Al-Kamour*. January 11. https://bit.ly/45nChPY

---

[111] Interviews, August 26–27, 2021.

Al-Sabah News. 2017. ["We publish it: Transcript details from the agreement between El Kamour protesters and the government"], Al-Sabah News, June 16, 2017, www.turess.com/assabahnews/153048

Arellano, Juan M. 2011. "Mining in Latin America: The Interplay between Natural Resources, Development, and Freedom." *Inquiries* 3(8): 1. http://www.inquiriesjournal.com/articles/559/mining-in-latin-america-the-interplay-between-natural-resources-development-and-freedom

'Ariq. 2020. "Misbah Al-Jarbou'. https://bit.ly/3uSe4BG

Bardi, Houcine. 2023. *Difa'an 'An Al-Sha'bawiyyah: Kais Saied, Al-Islam Al-Siyasi, wa Mustaqbal al-Yasar*. [In Defense of Populism]. Tunis: Arcadia Editions.

Bebbington, Anthony, Leonith Hinojosa, Humphreys Bebbington, Denise Burneo, Maria Luisa, and Ximena Warnaars. 2008. Contention and ambiguity: Mining and the possibilities of development. *Brooks World Poverty Institute* (BWPI Working Paper 57).

Belsoud, Daou. 2017. *Ma'arik Al-Tahrir fi Al-Janub Al-Sharqi: Al-Thawrah Al-Yusifiyyah* [Liberation Battles in the South-East: The Youssefist Revolution] *1956*. Gabes: Matba'at Salam Rajeh.

Ben Khalifa, Ghassan. 2017. *I'tisam al-Kamour wa- al-harakat al-ijtima'iyyah wa Afaq al-Sira' al-tabaqi fi Tunis* (File 1) [Kamour Sit-In, Social Movements, and Horizons for Tunisian Class Conflict]. *Al-Adab*. August 14. https://bit.ly/3oqZvkq

Ben Mbarek, Ghaya and Fadil Aliriza. 2022. "The Cost of Oil in Tunisia's Desert." February 17, *Meshkal*, https://meshkal.org/the-cost-of-oil-in-tunisias-desert/

Carthage Plus. 2020. *Mawqif Tansiqiyyat al-Kamour min Ahdath Tataouine* [Kamour's Position Regarding Events in Tataouin]. June 23. https://www.youtube.com/watch?v=l0y9InDe8zg

Chibani, Achref. 2020. *I'tiqalat, Muwajahat, wa Wabil min al-ghaz al-musayyil li al-dumu'* [Arrests. Confrontations, and a Barrage of Tear Gas]. June 25. https://bit.ly/3obUfkD

Crabapple, Molly. 2021. "Occupy Memory." The New York Review of Books, September 16, https://www.nybooks.com/online/2021/09/16/occupy-memory/

Derbali, Manel. 2020. *I'tisam Alkamour: Al-Sullam Al-Zamani* [Kamour Sit-In: Timeline]. Nawaat. https://bit.ly/35uhOi5

Dhouib, Mohammad. 2017. *Al-Fellaga wa- Al-Yusfiyyah Min Khilal al-Masadir al-Shafawiyyah* [Fellaga and Youssefists through Oral Sources]. Tunis: Sotimidia.

El-Hemmi, Neila. 2017. *'Ala Lisani Nushata'iha ... Ma La Ta'rifunahu 'an "Manish Msameh" Al-Tunisiyyah* [In the Words of Its Activists…What You Don't Know About Manish Msameh]. UltraTunisia. http://bit.ly/3icJk64

Eljimei, Mazz. 2017. *Anwar Al-Skrafi ... Hilm Shabb Tunisi Da'asathu Sayyarat Amn* [Anwar Al-Skrafi…Dream of a Young Tunisian Man Trampled By a Police Car]. Aljazeera, May 24. https://www.aljazeera.net/news/reportsandinterviews/2017/5/24/%D8%A3%D9%86%D9%88%D8%B1-%D8%A7%D9%84%D8%B3%D9%83%D8%B1%D8%A7%D9%81%D9%8A-%D8%AD%D9%84%D9%85-%D8%B4

%D8%A7%D8%A8-%D8%AA%D9%88%D9%86%D8%B3%D9%8A-%D8%AF%D8%B9%D8%B3%D8%AA%D9%87

Elsghayer, Umairah Alyah. 2020. *Min 1881 ila 1956* [From 1881 to 1956=. *Jomhouria*, May 31. https://bit.ly/3uXodxf,

Evans, Martin and John Phillips. 2007. *Algeria: Anger of the Dispossessed*. New Haven, CT: Yale University Press.

Foucault, Michel. 1986. "Of Other Spaces." Diacritics 16(1): 22–27.

FTDES. 2020. *'Ala Abwab al-Dhikra al-'Ashirah li A l-Thawrah: Al-Kamour: Wiladah 'Asirah li Harakah Ijtima'iyyah Qawiyyah wa Fa'ilah* [On the Eve of the 10th Anniversary of the Revolution: Kamour…]. https://ftdes.net/ar/kamour

FTDES. 2021. *Naqmat Al-Mawarid fi Sahra Tataouine: Talawwuth Bi'i wa Istnizaf li Al-Tharwah* [Resource Curse in the Tataouine Desert]. February 12, 2021. https://ftdes.net/ar/tataouine/

Hanin, Maher. 2017. *Bardo wa 'Al-Kamour': I'tisaman Dimn Masar Wahid*. FTDES, May 17. https://bit.ly/3spUNVn

Hanin, Maher. 2019. *Mujtama' Al-Muqawamah: Ma Ba'd Al-Islamawiyyah, Ma Ba'd Al-Bourguibiyya, Ma Ba'd Al-Marksiyyah* [Resistance Society]. Tunis: Nachaz.

Jawhara FM. 2021. *Tansiqiyyat al-Kamour Tuqarrir al-Tas'id* [Kamour Decides on Escalation]. November 17. https://bit.ly/3s4b0PP

Kapitalis. 2021. http://www.kapitalis.com/anbaa-tounes/2021/01/30/%D9%82%D8%B6%D9%8A%D8%A9-%D9%85%D9%82%D8%AA%D9%84-%D8%A3%D9%86%D9%88%D8%B1-%D8%A7%D9%84%D8%B3%D9%83%D8%B1%D8%A7%D9%81%D9%8A-%D8%A7%D9%84%D9%86%D9%8A%D8%A7%D8%A8%D8%A9-%D8%A7%D9%84%D8%B9%D9%85%D9%88/, accessed January 26, 2022.

Lupien, Pascal. 2020. "Indigenous Movements, Collective Action, and Social Media: New Opportunities or New Threats?" *Social Media + Society* 6(2): 1–11.

McAdam, Doug, Sidney Tarrow, and Charles Tilly. 2001. *Dynamics of Contention*. Cambridge: Cambridge University Press.

McCarthy, Rory. 2022. "Transgressive Protest After a Democratic Transition: The Kamour Campaign in Tunisia." *Social Movement Studies* 21(6): 798–815.

Marzouki, Mohammad. 1979. *Mohamed Al-Daghbagi*. Tunis: Maktabat al-Manar.

Mosaique FM. 2017. *Khalifah Alchibani: Sahib Sharikah fi Jerba Waffara 44 Sayyarah li Mu'tasimi Tataouine* [Khalifah Alchibani: Company Owner in Djerba Provided 44 Cars to Tataouine Protestors]. June 24. https://bit.ly/3Ho4sSM

Mosaique FM. 2020a. *Shabab Al-Kamour Yahtajj Mujaddadan Wa Yuhaddid Bi Al-Tas'id*. [Kamour youth protest anew and threaten escalation]. March 9, https://youtu.be/aNhUDLkwIjE.

Mosaique FM. 2020b. *Malaf Al-Kamour: Tansiqiyyat I'tisam Tumdi al-Ittifaq al-Niha'i Ma' Al-Hukumah* [Kamour File]. https://www.youtube.com/watch?v=GITRbPJ_9D8

Moss, Dana M. 2020. "Voice after Exit: Explaining Diaspora Mobilization for the Arab Spring." *Social Forces* 98(4): 1669–1694.

Mousa, Aldaoui. 2018. *Adwa' 'Ala Al-Harakah Al-Yusifiyyah bi-Jihat Tataouine* [Spotlight on the Youssefist Movement in Tataouine Region] *1955–1956*. Sfax: Matbaat Al-Tasfir Al-Fanni.

Mzalouat, Haifa, Malek Khadhraoui, and Monia Ben Hamadi. Inkyfada. 2021. *Inkyfada*, 23 September. *Al-'Aish bi Aqal min 5 Dananir fi Al-Yawm: Kharitat Al-Faqr fi Al-Bilad Al-Tunisiyyah* [Poverty Map in Tunisia]. https://bit.ly/3gwQ5j1

Nessma TV. 2017. *Nahnu Hizb Al-rakh la* [We are the Party of Al-Rakh La]. July 6, https://www.youtube.com/watch?v=qRFJoLsYJb4

Nessma TV. 2020. *Shabab Al-Kamour Yahtajj Mujaddadan wa Yuhaddid bi Al-Tas'id.* https://bit.ly/3P9a6yv

Presidence TN. 2020. *Ra'is Al-Jumhuyriyyah Kais Saied Yajtami'bi Mumathilin 'an Mu'tasimi Al-Kamour.* [President Kais Saied meets with representatives of the Kamour protesters.] January 16, https://youtu.be/lzCOxxuDQnA

Ranciere, Jacques. 2002. "The Aesthetic Revolution and Its Outcomes: Emplotments of Autonomy and Heteronomy." *New Left Review* 14:133–151.

Radio Tataouine. 2018. "The National Institute of Statistics: Tataouine Is Ranked First in Unemployment, Reaching 32.4 Percent in the Third Quarter of This Year." August 29, 2018, www.radiotataouine.tn/

Rice, Roberta. 2012. *The New Politics of Protest: Indigenous Mobilization in Latin America.* Tuscon: The University of Arizona Press.

Sadiki, Larbi. 2015. "Towards a 'Democratic Knowledge' Turn? Knowledge Production in the Age of the Arab Spring." *The Journal of North African Studies* 20(5): 702–721.

Sadiki, Larbi. 2020. "Tunisia's Peripheral Cities: Marginalization and Protest Politics in a Democratizing Country." 2021. *Middle East Journal* 75(1): 77–98.

Saleh, Layla. 2017. *US Hard Power in the Arab World: Resistance, the Syrian Uprising, and the War on Terror.* London: Routledge.

Sen, Amartya. 1999. *Development as Freedom.* Oxford: Oxford University Press.

Shems FM. 2020. *Ittifaq al-Kamour: Ba'd Al-Tafasil Hawla al-Ta'dilat allati Tamma Idkhaluha 'ala Al-Ittifaq Al-Sabiq* [Kamour Agreement]. November, 7. https://bit.ly/33NowMt

Smith, Rogers. 2003. *Stories of Peoplehood: The Politics and Morals of Political Membership.* Cambridge: Cambridge University Press.

Soja, Edward W. 2010. *Seeking Spatial Justice.* Minneapolis: University of Minnesota Press.

Tansiqyiyyat I'tisam al-Kamour: Al-Safhah al-Rasmiyyah. [Kamour Coordination Committee Official Page]. Facebook. 2022. https://www.facebook.com/elkamour/

Villarreal, Maria and Enara Echart Munoz. 2020. "Extractivism and Resistance in Latin America and the Caribbean." Open Democracy, February 6. https://www.opendemocracy.net/en/democraciaabierta/luchas-resistencias-y-alternativas-al-extractivismo-en-am%C3%A9rica-latina-y-caribe-en/, [Retrieved: January 28, 2022].

Vygotsky, Lev. 1986. *Thought and Language*, Trans. Alex Kozulin. Cambridge, MA: The MIT Press.

Yates, Luke. 2015. "Rethinking Prefiguration: Alternatives, Micropolitics and Goals in Social Movements." *Social Movement Studies* 14(1): 1–21.

Zartman, I. William. 2019. *I William Zartman: A Pioneer in Conflict Management and Area Studies: Essays on Contention and Governance.* Cham and Washington, DC.: Springer and Johns Hopkins.

8
Tunisia's Ultras

The "Freeplay" of Resistance

*In the haunting lyrics of 'Ya Hyatina' (O, Our life),[1] Club Africain (CA—Al-Nadi Al-Ifriqi) ultras movingly deplore the "hole that they called our country", where "we do not live like our peers." These insolent football fans speak in the voice of Tunisia's excluded and downtrodden. The demand to live their passion (*gharam*) for football transcends the limited calling of a few. It comes to stand in for a dogged pursuit of freedom (*hurriyyah*)*, in the "country that forgot us." Here the pronoun "us" embraces ultras Africain and Tarajji (Espérance Sportive de Tunis—EST), but also wide-ranging Tunisian suffering. "Marginalized" "hoods" (*hooma*) are teeming with unemployed youth. The defiance of drug addiction bespeaks the hopelessness of a future-less generation: "you have nothing to wait for." Memorializing their martyrs, they remind listeners of Omar Laabidi (killed by cops), a young drowned girl Maha Al-Qadqadi, the 30 young people who perished in a bus accident in Amdoun (Beja).[2] State repression and negligence are to blame. "Ya Hyatina" mourns the risk-taking agony of youth "thrown" into death boats (*harqah*). This song that went viral[3] pumps out affect by the line: grief, pain, despair, love, and passion. Indignation and rage, too, blare from the rhythmically intoned words. A consciousness emerges, of wealth snatched, peoplehood pilfered. Powerful politicians exploit and dupe. Stealing from Tunisians, "they want immunity"?! Incredulousness descends into the most negative affect of all. "We hate you," the system (*al-manzumah*). Rage incites bold commitment and will. Since "the end is death" for everyone, no confrontation is too perilous. "We fight the system, as we did in the past." Before the revolution, after the revolution. Africain ultras chant for themselves, and for Tunisian peoplehood. No rest for these football aficionados. No truce with the state. Resistance sings and cheers onwards.*

---

[1] The song was published by 'African Winners' (2019) on their YouTube Channel. Their logo, a rendering of Club Africain, features a turbaned man of the hardy desert Touareg, twisted cloth covering his half-shadowed face. The juxtaposition of Tunisian and foreign is typical of ultras insignia and discourse: image of a local tribal figure wearing a *shashiyyah* headcovering, with an English name rendered in Arabic and English lettering.

[2] For an explanation of some events to which the song alludes, see Mosaique (2019).

[3] Reaching over 9 million views on YouTube.

Introduction

The vignette above points to the powerful pull of frustrations and complaints emotively expressed by a specific subset of Tunisia's demos. Extreme football fans give voice to anger and a pain that radiates across the stadium, through cyberspace, into the vocal cords, hearts, and minds of the wider Tunisian populace. Practiced on a miniature scale, aspirant peoplehood explodes outward, its angst not to be subdued or silenced by censors, police, or those complacent in the face of counterrevolution. The elasticity of this protestscape extends spatially as well as temporally. This protestscape re-ontologizes football fans via their own brands of protest-in-context and knowing-in-context. It privileges aesthetic experiences, seemingly disembodied politically and yet filters self-reflexivity, subjectivity, consciousness via marginalized bodies, emotions, and thinking. Their own brands of logos, speech acts, and imaginaries (of anti-politics) tend to allegorize a kind of alienation (*ghurbah*) through their presence via absence in public space, and literally in Rancière's "police order" that has discounted them—as a "part that has no part" (Rancière 1999). In this protestscape rebellion manifests as a disconnect with the myths of existence (*hyatina*) in an authoritarian order. The disruption they live and speak through embodied experiences and rebellion against the "distribution of the sensible," as it were, points to internal "dissensus," relentlessly sustaining external recalcitrance in politics and vigorous contestation of injustice and exclusion. The world of ultras is itself a space of "exile" where social acting/en-acting is counteraction, and affect and cognition, nonetheless, have deterritorializing effects.

Derrida's notion of "freeplay," not just as metaphor and a "pun," springs to mind in relation to Tunisia's football ultras. Derrida's formulation is quasi-tangential to the main puzzle in this dissentscape, except in one aspect that recurs throughout the book: presence–absence. "Freeplay" here features in contexts of revolt and protest as "disruption" and in terms of a de-centering movement—akin to "derritorialization." Derrida elaborates: "Freeplay is the disruption of presence. … Freeplay is always an interplay of absence and presence … being must be conceived of as presence or absence beginning with the possibility of freeplay and not the other way around" (Derrida 1978, 292). This movement between presence (as locus, structure, and center) and absence favors the absence of presence—the Derridean notion of trace. Activism through discourse, allegory, words, and the aesthetics of protest through the absence of presence in the rupturing of structure of authoritarian rule (in the form of police brutality) and of a decaying locus of power (Ben Ali's regime) warrants the invocation of "freeplay." This hints at the permutations of dissidence by a group whose own mutiny defies conventional social doing. A spatialized presence–absence interplay (Meyer and Woodthorpe 2008) is at work. For, where the ultras are concerned, affect is central to their own interiority tied to a spatiality (stadiums) and temporality (football derbies). Thus, affect not only shades their own social construction of time and space, but also tends to be geared towards rupturing the system by absence: escaping the body politic's own form of social order. Intermittently, they choose to reconnect with that social order only to disrupt it in the time-space of collective protest.

We have argued throughout this book that revolution is not made in a day. Neither is it suddenly undone. Like wars that "don't just end," but "fizzle and sputter," and "sometimes ... reignite" (Enloe 1993, 2), revolution does not expire mid-protest as soon as the dictator is deposed. Tunisia's revolutionary élan stretches from the 1860s crucible into the present day, even after President Kais Saied's power grab on July 25, 2021. The last five chapters have attempted to open up a portal onto hidden struggles, by "archiving" and re-ontologizing protestscapes at various synchronic points in the twin ferment of ongoing revolution-peoplehood. In this chapter, we close the series of situated dissentscapes by turning to Tunisia's football ultras, noteworthy for their always latent, sometimes "present–absent" protest capacity prior to, during, and since the 2011 revolution. Anti-systemic orientations and practices appear to be constant but malleable prior to and after the *thawrah*. Defying "pre" and "post" labels, the motor of young super-fans' rebelliousness runs strong over a decade after they mobilized throngs demanding freedom, dignity, and Ben Ali's departure. Relatively diminished repression has not given way to ultras' acceptance of the system, *al-manzumah*. Nor do the system's foot soldiers (police) of the ultras. Yet these football "rogues" do not simply remain in their own pitches. They tap into and sometimes stir up popular anger and identification. Here lies their unique significance.

The chapter proceeds with an overview of the ultras protestscape: its notable features and a sketch of the main events in Tunisia. Next, it locates Tunisia's ultras within the global ultras "culture," focusing particularly on protest and spectacle. Visual methods and multi-modal discourse analysis are vital for the embodied and spatialized, situated knowledge of this protestscape: its affect, resistance competencies, and belonging. Tunisia's ultras enact spectacles with a very local ceremonial (*hadrah*) twist, we suggest, moving to analyze songs and choreographies (*dakhlah*) with special emphasis on the affect they elicit as agentic performances cognizing a peoplehood yearned for but unfulfilled. The chapter closes with an exploration of the *T'allam 'Oum* ("learn to swim") campaign that demonstrates conflict with police, in online and offline protest. All the while, as is our wont in this book, we pay close attention to the *language* of the ultras and the vocabulary they bring to Tunisia's protest-revolution lexicon. Table 8.1 lists and briefly explicates main terms in the ultras parlance, used throughout the chapter.

Charting the Ultras Protestscape

Football is one important progenitor of youth protest politics. Novel ways of organizing and objecting dig deep into the reservoir of group membership, identity, and a resistance pedigree dating back to anti-colonial times—protest momentum-ethos, or *zakham ihtijaji*, enhanced by cumulative protest competency. Football protest is an important kinetic synchrony along the diachrony of Tunisia's revolutionary milieu. Protest is constructed in embodied experiences and in speech acts embedded in and embedding spatial and temporal contexts. Thus, the empirical analysis below makes use of original interview data from four focus groups, comprising six interlocutors

Table 8.1 Language of the Ultras

Term	Meaning-in-Context	Significance
MUWAJAHAH	Refers to protest practices, especially vis-à-vis police	Agonistic interactions with the state; resistance mindset and behavior
GHARAM	Love-passion for football and/or one's club	Affect underlies ultras' group identity and behavior
VIRAGE	Football stadium (from the French)	Cultural cross-pollination; localization of European/Latin American language, ultras' culture
AL-HAKIM	The ruler, referencing formal political (and club) authority	Signals distaste, skepticism, and overall negative affect towards powers-that-be
DAKHLAH	Literally, entrance: the choreographic spectacle ultras stage before a match (also called *tifo* among transnational ultras)	Visuality, orality central to resistance practices: creative and expressive of identity
AL-SYSTAM	"the system" against which the ultras consistently situate themselves (*didd al-systam*)	Rebelliousness characterizes the affect, agency, and cognition of ultras' individual and collective discourse and practices
T'ALLAM 'OUM	Since 2018, "learn to swim," referencing Omar Laabidi's death and subsequent campaign	Resistance against police repression through slogan that connects "peoplehood" struggles from narrow (ultras) to broader (subaltern Tunisians)
ISTIFZAZ	Provocation, usually of police	Agentic intent behind ultras' resistance practices; feeds into agonism, sometimes cycles of violence, with police
AL-IFLAT MIN AL-'IQAB	Impunity, usually referring to police, against which ultras vocalize and mobilize dissent	Ultras are still "anti-system" after 2011 revolution, but democratization has brought some openings to confront worsening police lawlessness: a paradox
AL-QAM' AL-BOLISI	Police repression, which ultras blame for their problems with the state and its security forces	Power asymmetries (state vs. marginalized, smeared ultras) propels cycle of mutual distrust and "baiting" by police and ultras

each, with ultras supporters of Al-Tarajji and Club Africain. These were conducted between August and October 2021 and are anonymized out of respect for a strict culture of secrecy within the ultras. It also draws on an indicative sampling of social media discourse, and media accounts. A few salient features distinguish the ultras from sister protestscapes:

- Uniting ultras groups—diverse in their (non)ideological leanings, intellectual achievements, and even socio-economic backgrounds—is an overarching commitment to the club and to football as a sport. Adherents display a close-knit identity linked to the specific football club, replete with shared practices—including protest—values, and symbolism, slightly differentiating adherents of one club from another. Self/other demarcations ensue. Ultras membership becomes a mantle of belonging, further charging unruly youth with a sense of purpose they may not find outside their club.
- Ultras spout rebellion (an internal posture), partially expressed or made public through protest (external performance). Kristeva's (2014) suggestion that revolt is as much private and psychological as it is extraneous collective behavior reverberates once again. The underlying attitude of rebellion is anything but apathetic. Our analysis below thus probes its *appearances* through protest, violence,[4] boycotts, etc., also digging beneath the surface to uncover the interior humiliation (*hogra*) and double consciousness that impels such embodied practices.
- The primary cohort active in the ultras are young men, roughly aged 15–34. Rebellion is not surprising among this demographic. It takes the form of protest in and outside the stadiums, sometimes veering into violence. Moreover, ultras' modes of expression reflect the tools and ambience of this generation: YouTube videos, songs, *dakhlah* choreographs, etc.
- Wary of the media, ultras rail against security forces and the police, in a pattern not uncommon among youths on the margins of society. Ultras are regularly imbricated in conflict with the police, but these animosities are not unique to Tunisia (e.g. George Floyd's murder in the US and the Black Lives Matter Movement (Honwana 2019; Hill et al. 2020).
- A presence/absence dynamic dwells in the ultras protestscape. The super-fans' professed non-membership (*la intima*) in anything except the football club itself, is only part of the story. Ultras youth are *absent* from the body politic, from political participation, from investment in political machinations and goings-on, even after the revolution. At the same time, however, they are *present* through their (latent) protest activism. Non-membership becomes a kind of membership (and sometimes leadership) of an aspiring peoplehood, as in their revolutionary participation. Thus, the ultras do not seem to actually be divorced from the concerns, aspirations, and frustrations of peoplehood.
- Affect itself is very important, particularly in its *intensity*: love and passion for the game and the club, embodied responses and practices that run like an electric current through seated or standing spectators, infectious rage against the state and against police. Songs such as "Ya Hyatina" in the opening vignette demonstrate that in their own way, the ultras are expressing the concerns and

---

[4] Estimated in 2018 at 600,000 cases of sports-related violence over six years, mostly in football. See, "Arqam Mufzi'ah Kashafaha Al-Multaqa Al-Watani Hawla Zahirat al-'Unf fi Al-Mala'ib," *Al-Sabah*, March 23, 2018.

pain and anger of the larger Tunisian populace, making affect partly constitutive of their subjectivities. Affect cannot be reduced to a sensory continuum comprising a range of emotions existing between dysphoria and euphoria. Rather, affect is enmeshed with cognition and behavior, for instance in liberal politics (Nussbaum 2001) and broader human psychology (Joseph Forgas 2001). "Ya Hyatina" is an allegory of existence in the doldrums. Its affective register is powerful. A small subset of Tunisians who claim they are non-political actually seem to give voice to the misery, suffering, and disaffection of many Tunisians—even though they themselves may almost be social outcasts. The anodyne appeal of the song is likely to lie in the substance of the lyrics. Its words are a play on absence–presence, expressing direct messages that are also laced with "hidden" meaning (e.g. against corruption or violence) addressed to power-holders.

In the ultras protestscape, the affect of humiliation, deprivation, and solidarity are compounded by the sensory resources that emanate from sport and its spectatorship. Thus, this chapter features a heightened sensitivity to affect, with epistemological and methodological implications. We attempt to work through our own affective impressions as well as the affective "vibes" given off by the ultras' (online and offline) multi-modal discourse (see Jakimow and Yumasdaleni 2016). Ultras notoriously revel in their anonymity. They seem to wear their enigma as a cloak of (non)identification. We seek to understand their protestscape and share it with others, without compromising the social obscurity draping their identity and their operation. However, we are aware that our interpretations as researchers are only just that, interpretations. The analysis is based on the evidence we have observed and collected, churned through the theoretical framework we have constructed in Chapter 2. Our "writing" of the ultras protestscape in Tunisia is far from a definitive account. Its situatedness, in Haraway's terms, makes the chapter a "partial" and "positioned" exploration. We take seriously, here as elsewhere throughout the book, her warning against smugness and over-confidence even when seeking to write "from below." The ultras protestscape, like the others, is not above "critical reexamination, decoding, deconstruction, and interpretation" that Haraway (1988, 583–584) advises. We modestly approach ultras as peripheral "objects" of study with an agency of their own, aware of the limitations and specific slant of our vision (Haraway 1988, 592–593). Our interpretation is an ongoing reflexive endeavor, tentatively scripted in the words that follow.

Staging Protest … Pre- to Post-Revolution

Anti-colonial and Postcolonial

The foregoing pages have identified the main features of the ultras protestscape, centering, and the presence–absence "freeplay" it engenders in anti-systemic protest. This section briefly maps how, historically, protest and football are intertwined. The founding of the two earliest football clubs in Tunisia, "brother rivals" (Hazgui 2018) Al-Tarajji Al-Riyadi Al-Tunisi (1919) and Al-Nadi Al-Ifriqi (1920), is coterminous with that of the Tunisian nationalist movement (Daifallah 2023, 31–33). As Ben Rajab (2021) implies, defeating European-Christian *colons* in sport became almost an end in itself: the football pitch simulated the battlefield. Anti-colonial protests would rage in stadiums, especially after the French limited or banned public gatherings in public spaces. Independence did not eliminate the impetus for protest in the stadium. The March 5, 1961 match between Tarajji and Sousse's Najm Al-Sahili elicited outcries over referee calls, which turned into protests and "mischief" (Hazgui 2018). President Bourguiba's response was to temporarily disband the team. Directing but taming the passions inspired by sport had long been part of the President's authoritarian cultural playbook. One reviewer of the movie "Football and Dreams" celebrating Tunisia's 1978 World Cup participation (the same year as Black Thursday) reminded readers that the "Tunisian regime lends great importance to the sport of football" and sports to "distract" people and dampen "their talk about politics." Tongue in cheek, he wonders when films would be made about events of greater (political) significance: January 26 (Black Thursday 1978, discussed in Chapter 3), Gafsa 1980 (Chapter 5), and "political prosecutions" over the decades.[5] Reviewing Bourguiba's sports policy over two decades, one opposition newspaper called for an overhaul to disentangle the physical-psychological-ethical domain from political manipulation. Sport should not be "exploited politically to anaesthetize social tensions in one stage, then to protect [nationalist] fanaticism in the next stage."[6] Bourguiba instrumentalized sports in exhorting the masses, only to suppress any potential unruliness against the state (Sadiki and Saleh 2021, 479–481). Yet football fans are notoriously difficult to control completely. In 1971, at the infamous Menzah stadium conflagration (*mahraqat al-manzah*), trouble broke out after Al-Tarajji was banned from playing in the wake of altercations with the Sfax team (Karshaoui 2021). Livid fans rioted and eventually sought Bourguiba's intercession. Connoting its untouchable grandeur, Bourguiba famously said, "Club Espérance is a country" (*al-tarajji dawlah*). The phrase has stuck, even making its way into the club's ultras songs to be examined below. Club Africain or *Al-Nadi Al-Ifriqi* on the other hand, is dubbed the people's club (*nadi al-sha'b*). From colonial times to the present, "stadiums [have been] a platform for political criticism," sometimes even rioting and protest (Ben Rajab 2021).

Tunisian football fans have organized for decades in precursors to the ultras. Collectivities of supporters for Al-Najm Al-Sahili (Étoile Sportive du Sahel (ESS), 1947) and Bizerte (1950) formed as early as 1947 and 1950, respectively (Bouyahya 2019, 114). Fans founded the group known as the Tarajji devotees (*Muhibbi al-Tarajji*), producing a magazine *Al-Tarajji* among other sources of club encouragement. However, ultras as such came to Tunisia in 1995, through the group Africain Winners,

---

[5] *Kurah wa Ahlam: Ahla Al-Dhikrayat* in *Al-Mustaqbal*, January 5, 1981, p. 10.
[6] *Ithra In'iqad Al-Nadwah Al-Wataniyyah li Al-Riyadah: Siyasah fi Hajah ila Islah Jawhari*, in *Al-Mustaqbal*, September 7, 1981, pp. 1, 16.

followed by Tarajji supporters Ultras Mkashkin in 2002 (Atmah 2017; see also Daifallah 2023, 50–51). Even in football fandom Tunisia has been a pioneer, its ultras being among the first in the Arab world. Like their European counterparts, ultras maintain a hierarchical structure headed by a *capo* under whom regular members operate (Zaghdoudi 2020). One investigation places the number of Tunisian ultra groups at roughly 50, scattered across the country from Tunis and Ariana to Gafsa and Gabes, forming a "society within a society" that rebuffs state, media, and club administrators at the same time (Zaghdoudi 2020). Table 8.2 breaks down some known ultra groups by name (usually English, Spanish, or French), club and/or governorate. European and Argentinian influences penetrate deeply into the practices, names, and overall culture of Tunisian ultras. "Zapatista," "North Vandals," and "Brigade Rouge," are group names that connote a fighting spirit and rebellious outlook (Bouyahya 2019, 119–120). Competitive showmanship, from the spectacle of the entrance (*dakhlah*) to catchy songs written, performed, and recorded, knits together a club-specific identity. Yet, club rivalries can be superseded by a constant (ant)agonism against the state.

Table 8.2 Geographic and Club Distribution of Tunisia's Ultras

Name	Governorate/Region	Sports Club
UM05 (MARINES)		
UCA06 (CAPISTE)	Bizerte	
BJ09 (PANTHER SIGNOROS)		
COM07	Beja	
UGG01 (GREEN GLADIATORS)	Kairouan	
UGW08 (GREEN WARRIORS)		
ULGMD01 (LOS MAGICOS)		
IF11 (FRACCISE)	Kasserine	
UG13	Gafsa	
UM13 (METLAWI)		
LB09	Gabes	
V.V12		
RED AND BLACK		
UGB07 (GREEN BOYS)	Djerba	
BWF03 (BLACK AND WHITE FIGHTERS)	Sfax	
LOS7 (LYONS)		
RB07 (RAGGED BOYS)		
US07 (SFAXIAN)		
DI10 (DIABOL)		
D'13 (D'ROUGE)		
PM03 (POWER MARINES)	Monastir	
SP08 (SPARSITAS)		
PR12 (PARTISON)		
FA03 (FANATICS)	Sahel	
SAH07 (SAHELION)		

Continued

Table 8.2 *Continued*

Name	Governorate/Region	Sports Club
UA12 (ARIANA)	Ariana	
LA12 (LA PANDA)		
AW95 (WINNERS)	Tunis	Africain
LC037 (LEADERS CLUBBISTS)		
DC07 (DODGERS CLUBBISTS)		
KG07 (KOWTECH GROUP)		
NV07 (NORTH VANDALS)		
UC08 (CLUBBISTS)		
CL08 (CHICOS LATINOS)		
YC08 (YANKEE CLUBBISTS)		
LB09 (LOS BORAJOS)		
SC10 (SOLDADO)		
USW11 (S. WARRIORS)		
ULEO2 (MKASHKHIN BAB SOUIKA)		Tarajji
BLB11 (BLUE BOYS RADES)		
LG10 (LIBERTE BOYS)		
FIDA'IYYUN		
TE08 (TOR SIDA)		
MD08 (MATADORS)		
ZE07 (ZAPATISA ESPERENZA)		
BG05 (BLOOD AND GOLD)		
SS04 (SUPRA SUD)		
BB02 (BARO BOYS BARDO)		

Source: Authors' table constructed based on information drawn from Zaghdoudi (2020).

Ultras' Uprising

After they infiltrated Tunisian society by the early to mid-2000s, some joined a rare anti-systemic group called *Takriz*.[7] A major ultras event transpired a mere few months prior to the 2011 revolution. The rise of ultras is more or less parallel with the onset of the anti-systemic dissidence of the 2000s, culminating in the 2008 phosphate basin protest. Some consider the "spark of the revolution" to have been lit in the Menzah stadium on April 8, 2010. Others refer to it as a "turning point" in the relationship between the security machinery of the state and rebellious, "anti-systemic" youth (Zaghdoudi 2020). A grainy Facebook video uploaded to YouTube shows roaring crowds throwing objects into the stadium, rushing down and then up the stairs (Esperanza News 2014). Spectators are singing and chanting. Some appear to be clashing with security, others congregating in a huge mass near one side of

---

[7] Takriz means "anger" in the Tunisian dialect. This "street resistance network" was established in 1998, according to its Facebook page, a quasi-anarchist citizens watchdog that calls out, in sometimes vulgar terms, politicians and policies since and after Ben Ali's dictatorship. See https://www.facebook.com/takrizo/

the steps. It was during this match between Tarajji and Hammam Lif (*Hammam Al-Anf*) that a fan made his way onto the field, instigating "epic" skirmishes with security forces that escalated when fans cut the electricity for a full 14 minutes.[8] Impassioned Tarajji supporters also charged towards security forces and destroyed parts of the stadium (Aljazeera 2016). At this point, police reportedly attacked fans, attempting to repress the raging crowds that had gone off-script in a public space. Surely alarming to Ben Ali's regime, it was no surprise that the uproar prompted the closure of the stadium for a long period after these events (Aljazeera 2016). One blog relays a statement made by the Ministry of Youth, Sport, and Physical Education denouncing the "acts of mischief and violence" (terms still commonly used by the authorities) that violated "the honor code" of sports. The Ministry vowed to institute new restrictions (e.g. prohibiting pyrotechnics) and mete out punishment to those involved (see Zitoun 2010).

A month before the 2010 protests broke out in Sidi Bouzid, Tarajji fans and ultras rioted at the stadium yet again. Angry at losing the title in the Rades stadium, they threw bottles at the head of the African Union Issa Hayato and at journalists, prying seats out of their orderly rows. "Chaos," "destruction" and the "Tarajji spectators' hysteria … touched everyone."[9] Players *and* their coaches were to blame for the violence resulting in $20,000 worth of damage, added another assessment.[10] The affect stimulated by sport (adoration, belonging, rage, disappointment) alarms authoritarians in its potential for unruliness. Ben Ali may not have been incorrect. The Menzah confrontation roused anger and helped mobilize the "first cell" of the 2011 revolution, where ultras were reportedly "in the front lines" (Atmah 2017). Ultras participated and helped mobilize revolutionary protests "as individuals" and not in a declared, collective fashion (Ben Rajab 2021).

Soon after Ben Ali's departure, stadium violence among ultras (and with the police) became more than a rare occurrence.[11] In the years since Tunisia's revolutionary breakthrough, ultras confront the Tunisian state and other football authorities on at least two fronts. First is the perennial battle over the "sacred" and aspirational "free space" that is the stadium. Putative efforts to prevent violence take the form of banning ultras from attending their matches.[12] Officials justify these prohibitions on the basis of "ensuring citizen safety."[13]

Sometimes, political events emerge from the cauldrons of regional conflict, spilling into the rules governing ultras, which they in turn attempt to flout. In April 2014, Maher Al-Maqmaqi was killed in Syria. Investigations revealed that he had been an avid Brigade Rouge (ultras group for Sousse's ESS) member who penned the song

---

[8] *Fi Dhikra Ahdath 8 Avril 2010 Bi Mal'ab Al-Manzah*, in *Achahed*, April 9, 2019
[9] *Qawarir 'Ala Ru'us al-Sahafiyyin, Qita' Naqdiyyah fi Wajh Hayato … Wa Damar fi al-Mal'ab: Hysteria Jumhur Al-Tarajji*, in *Alchourouk*, November 15, 2010.
[10] *La'ibun wa Mudarribun Wara'a Tazayud al-'Unf Wa Tahwil Dawri Tunis ila Sira' Damawi*, in *Al-Wasat Al-Tunisiyya*, December 4, 2010.
[11] *Hiwar Hawla Al-'Unf fi Al-Mala'ib: Da'wah Mulihhah li-Ijad Hulul*, in *Koorah*, September 17, 2011
[12] For instance, "*Minha Ghalq al-Virage: Ijra'at Jadidah li Al-Hadd Min Al-'Unf fi Al-Mala'ib,*" *Business News Arabic*, March 20, 2019.
[13] *Wali Bizerte Yaghluq Mal'ab Hmaied al-Mujahid Bi-Manzal Abdelrahman*, in *Al-Shari Al-Magharibi*, April 23, 2018.

"Love Letter" (*Kitab Gharam*) (Zaghdoudi 2020). Some ultras reportedly became worthy recruits to extremist Islamist fighters. This exacerbated their targeting by security forces and deepened the stigma against them. Multiple pairings of antagonists can result in violent showdowns: ultras vs. police, ultras vs. ultras of different teams, and ultras vs. ultras of the same team (Bouyahya 2019, 128–129). Repeated incidents at stadiums reinforced state (and often, media) treatment of these fans as mischief makers. An Africain–Tarajji match in May 2017[14] and a Tarajji game with a team from Angola in October 2018 (Assabeel 2018) are two examples where security forces and fan injuries were followed by arrests. Injunctions against fans attending matches were preemptive, a harsh sentence for crimes most ultras have not committed. The prohibition robs them of the "freed space" within which their *raison d'etre* is rooted, the soil upon which their group identity sprouts and is (re)produced. It reinforces the "anti-systemic" stance, feeding into the agentic, affective, and cognitive practices underlying their protest activities. Objecting to police violence, Club Africain ultras Curva Sud, for instance, have engaged in a (counter) boycott of football matches (Hazgui 2018). From the perspective of the power-holders, such as the Interior and Youth and Sport Ministries, fan–police clashes exemplify the disturbing phenomenon of uncontrollable, insubordinate youth.[15]

A second front for anti- or extra-systemic practices through which ultras lash out against authority concerns football clubs' struggle for survival. Once again, ultras resist control of power-holders from the national football association in Tunisia or FIFA, or the state of Tunisia itself. In 2019, Club Africain's fans launched a campaign to save their club which was at the time facing fines of millions of dinars from FIFA (reportedly 20 million dinars, or over 6 million dollars), due in large part to mismanagement by new owner Slim Riahi (once an aspiring politician) (Ben Rajab 2021). They raised close to 6 million dinars through a mobilization that drew upon ultra cadres and organizing skills, including 5-member teams and a publicized Facebook campaign that prioritized openness and trust and transparency, Ben Rajab adds. The Tunisian football association even opened a special bank account for the money raised by the fan base. The campaign to save Club Africain comprised of "shocking appearances," (*latkhat*), a term inspired by the skyrocketing dark horse popularity of (then candidate) Kais Saied in 2019 term (Ben Rajab 2021). High levels of fan "commitment" translated into Facebook pages, organizing by neighborhood, and the involvement of all four Africain ultras groups (Dodgers Clubistes, North Vandals, Leaders Clubistes, and African Winners) to raise millions of dinars (Ben Rajab 2020, 93–105.) A four-year contract with Qatar Airways announced in August 2020, reportedly worth 24 million dinars, helped further rescue Club Africain from its financial woes.[16]

---

[14] 'Isabat Rijal Shurtah Wa Mushajji'in fi 'Derbi' al-Ifriqi Wa al-Tarajji…'Innaha Fadiha,' in *Annahar*, May 1, 2017.

[15] See for instance, Hal Tu'ashshir Thawrat 'Al-Virage' Ila Huduth Infijar Shamil? in *Al-Shari Al-Magharibi*, March 23, 2019.

[16] Bi-Wasatah min Ra'is Al-Jami'ah … Al-Ifriqi Yazfar Bi-'Aqd Ishhari Qimatuhu 24 Milyar, in *Alchourouk*, August 17, 2020.

In 2020, the Hilal Echebba club in Southern Mahdia was also prevented from playing by the Tunisian football association, for failing to submit the required paperwork on time. Fans went on strike, rioted, protested in front of the headquarters, and then threatened a midday publicized collective *harqah* to Italy, which they announced on Facebook (Radio Med 2020). Here they rejigged conventions of covert, perilous journeys across the Mediterranean. Several prominent attorneys, athletes, and academics published a petition that expressed solidarity with banned footballers. "We understand popular protest in the city," they proclaimed, puzzled over punitive measures targeting the players.[17] In this case, the Tunisian football association was repressing football fans, whereas it had stood by Club Africain (Ben Rajab 2020). Regional (spatialized and geographic-turned cultural) biases may implicitly play into Association decisions. Tribal solidarity and regionalist (Sahel/Janub) solidarities and animosities rear their head among football authorities as well as fans (Ben Rajab 2020). This coincided with the spike in the number of protests ripping across Tunisia in Fall/Winter 2020 and 2021 (Umairah 2020). Sometimes spilling into larger protest mobilization, the ultras football prostestscape simmers on years after the 2011 revolution.

Tunisia's "Ultras Culture"

The above section mapped out the ultras' history in Tunis, as well as their main protest junctures before and since 2011. We now showcase distinctive elements of ultras' social being and doing, highlighting the prominence of spectacles. Ultras are of course not a uniquely Tunisian phenomenon. Relatively recent in Tunisia, these overwhelmingly masculine (Doidge et al. 2020, 4) super-fans of football have proliferated across the world over the past 50 years. Doidge and Lieser (2018, 838) stress the interplay of global and local dynamics that combine in a "global ultras culture," or "*mentalitas ultras*". Its main features, they note, involve extreme-fandom, rebelliousness, social media use, spectacle, showmanship, and self/other identification by a football club. Superimposed onto these globalized characteristics are local dynamics, cultural expressions, socio-political concerns, and modes of participation. Ultras are known for "disruptive and antisocial activities," often communicated and enacted through performance (Doidge and Lieser 2018, 833–835). Performances that demarcate "we-ness" comprise "clapping, chanting, pyrotechnics, banners and choreographies" (Doidge and Lieser 2018, 836). Other visible aspects of these ritualized performances include music and songs, signs and banners, flags and shared outfits, often disseminated through social media (Doidge et al. 2020, 2–16). For this reason, we dip into multi-modal analysis of visual politics.

Affect stands out as an immaterial, intangible, and invisible adhesive that binds ultras. Their feeling feeds into social doing and knowing. How ultras act and en-act dissent, for example, and relate to political debates and big questions or withdraw,

---

[17] *Al-Bayan Al-Ta'sisi li Al-Lajnah Al-Wataniyyah li Da'm al-Hilal Al-Shabbi Wa Musanadat Al-Taharrukat Al-Silmiyyah*, in *Al-Sha'b*, October 29, 2020, p. 23.

is inseparable from how they feel about the questions and challenges that populate their spatiality and flow out of their temporality. Uniting ultras is a spatialized "emotiona[l] attach[ment]" to team, such that the club or stadium may be a "sanctuary of passion, identity and memory, also engendering a sense of territorial belonging" (Scalia 2009, 45). Tunisian ultras additionally exhibit a kind of "tribal," perhaps parochial, territoriality centered around the "virage" or stadium and different locations within it (Bouyahya 2019, 124). However, at times "intense rivalries" can be overcome through necessary cross-club alliances (Doidge et al. 2020, 83). In Tunisia, such cross-club solidarity was most prominent in the revolution, surfacing again in the T'allam 'Oum movement against police brutality, somewhat the bane of the ultras' existence, in socio-political terms, as a dissenting group.

In addition to its expression through music and spectacle, affect is thus spatially rooted. Each club becomes a microcosm of belonging. It simulates the nation in a partial demos. Bourguiba's legendary phrase "al-tarajji dawlah" (Espérance is a country) conveys this very notion of invested membership undergirded by outsize affect. Ultras already possess the built-in "glue" of collective identity that overrides the individual (Doidge et al. 2020, 2–3), making them a unique synchrony among the protestscapes we investigate in this book. This entails deep membership that casts a collective glow over passions, dreams, and concerns. Ultras possess a group identity that is already strong even before ritualistic performances take a protest turn, a cohesiveness that precedes the social acts and en-actments of peoplehood. These rituals give rise to a "collective emotional energy" the intensity of which (to adopt a Deleuzian notion) flows at the spatio-temporal sites of matches, also extending outside the actual play time to create "emotional belonging" (Doidge et al. 2020, 16). It is almost as though the stadium is a practice run for developing protest competencies stemming from group identity, organization, and collective action. Affect at this point becomes a locomotive of resistance against authorities. The targets of ultras' ire are often the police (Scalia 2009, 43–45) with whom interactions are conflictual (Doidge and Lieser 2018, 836–837). Reflecting relations of ambivalence, sometimes ultras beam their anger towards club owners or managers, who capitalize on the former's frenzied fandom to generate interest in and spectators for the club, at times switching to reining in and constraining them (Doidge et al. 2020, 3). In the wake of violence by some ultras, a generalized "feeling of persecution" permeates ultras' circles and practices, fomenting the "ACAB (All Cops are Bastards) syndrome" signaling revolt (Doidge et al. 2020, 3). Indeed, the walls of Tunisian cities and suburbs are "desecrated" by the acronym ACAB in graffiti. Since ultras repeatedly have face-to-face scuffles with the police, they have acquired "strategies to evade, confront and challenge" the security forces (Doidge et al. 2020, 147). As the empirical analysis will show, Tunisian ultras have thus learned and developed not just *protest competency*, but a broader *resistance competency* through their antagonistic dealings with police.

Ultras, Tunisian groups included, often declare themselves to be apolitical (Doidge et al. 2020, 7–8). This does not necessarily make them so. Our exploration of ultras as a rebelscape clearly imbues their discourse and practices with a political hue. One question to broach, then, is what triggers protests by ultras? Oftentimes, issues relate to the politics of the club itself: its ownership (Daifallah 2023, 36), threats of expulsion or not being allowed to play, prohibitions around attending matches. The commercialization of football and various stadium policies have elicited ultras' protests in Poland (Kossakowski 2021, 191–206, 104–106). However, as Scalia (2009) suggests, based on the Italian pioneers of ultra-dom, football protest is also related to wider socio-political conflicts and national developments. Grievances range from the transformation of the football economy towards more professionalization to mafia interference to party politics and campaigns (Scalia 2009, 43–57). We plot the case of Tunisian ultras as a synchrony of social acts and en-actments of peoplehood in struggles against domination. French-dominated football leagues a century ago gave way to a post-revolutionary political system where police impunity ran rampant. Particular events may provoke specific protests, such as the financial hardship of Club Africain or Chebba. We chart these proximate causes within ultras' underlying rebelliousness that is activated by occasions local and specific, national and regional. A paradox arises from the amorphous "claims" made by ultras. In their quest for liberation from "regulati[on]," this unruly "persona invites [more] regulation" (Doidge et al. 2020, 174). Perhaps they will always be in this bind. In our analysis, ultras' inherent spirit of revolt can keep the resistance edge of peoplehood alive. They are oppositional for the sake of being rebellious, speaking to the (ant)agonistic thread running through Arab politics and social relations. Such bellicosity may be just the touch required for activating and mobilizing wider anti-authoritarian, or anti-counterrevolutionary, dissent.

Visualizing Peoplehood?

Affect and Visual Politics

As the previous section has shown, spectacle in and around the stadium stands out in ultras' protest behavior and self-conceptions. All protest activity is performative, as we argued in Chapter 2. This section demonstrates how the public rites of Tunisian football "ultra" super-fans are unique sets of performances. Distinct visual displays span the *dakhlah* that opens a football match, matching the outfits of ultras gathering to sing, dance, and cheer hours across town before the game, and songs released on YouTube. William Callahan's notion of "sensible politics" is an entry to exploring ultras' highly visual, anti-systemic practices. The concept refers to sensory encounters consequential to daily individual experiences as well as collective creations and understandings of "social ordering," both "what can be sensed" and "what makes sense," all carried on the wings of *affect* (Callahan 2021, 37). In our case, affective dynamics underlie (challenges to) power relations and tensions between Tunisia's haves and have-nots, people and the state, marginalization and participation. Ultras move themselves and others through affect (*hogra*, anger, solidarity, joy, etc.). The visual does "affect-work," the investigation and interpretation of which is crucial to our "post-literate age," Callahan argues. This is fitting for a protestscape whose young protagonists are adept in the latest technological manners of expression and being. "Visuality," says Callahan (2021, 35, 44), is "what images can do and what they can make," in a mode of power that shapes and subverts what "can…be seen, said, thought, and done." Here Callahan borrows from Ranciere (2004), suggesting that the potency of visuality strikes by stimulating "new affective registers" or creating "affective communities of sense" (Callahan 2021, 36–44). Shared ideas, feelings, embodied ways of being, and practices are incited by the affect flowing from "visual artifacts" such as documentary films and other videos, art exhibits, gardens, or even culturally-politically charged clothing choices, Callahan contends.

Active spectatorship can ensue from engaging with outputs and performances of visuality (Callahan 2021, 139). Affective responses are indicative of the "shimmer-value" that Callahan highlights as a feature distinguishing visual from verbal/written discourse (2021, 44). Song-making and video-making, the theatricality of elaborate pre-game performances, are recorded in the accumulating ledger of peoplehood's social doing. In the case of the ultras' protestscape, then, stress is on the affective, which we proceed to interpret. Such emphasis befits the comparative value of music, whose meaning generates powerful emotions (McKerrell and Way 2017, 8–9). The agentic and cognitive remain important, however, lending the affective significance and enveloping it within a platform.

Performative Acts of Protest

Enhancing the emphasis on visuality, multi-modal discourse analysis is appropriate to the task of explicating the songs, videos, and performances populating the ultras' protestscape. Particularly in music, "lyrics, written text, image, color" multi-modally combine with the specific features of sound ("rhythm, instrumentation, pitch," etc.) to create meaning (McKerrell and Way 2017, 8). These we seek here to deconstruct in our examination of ultras' protest through "visuality." We approach cautiously, though. Listening to and watching music lends itself to variable interpretations, since "music's meanings are emergent and performative," provisionally unlocked by the listener and watcher (McKerrell and Way 2017, 13). Police officers may hear ultras' songs as rebellious provocation, prompting harassment or arrest. Other ultras or Tunisian sympathizers may respond to songs as legitimizing or giving voice to their own *hogra*, playing into Callahan's "affective communities of sense." We supplement our analysis of musical performances through corroboratory evidence, from interviews, and written discourse in (social) media. Analysis of video songs and their "semiotic resources" involves attention to lyrics, background music, and visual presentations (Way 2017, 98–100). Scrutiny of the values espoused, (self/other) identities constructed, actors and their roles, implications of bodily movement, song structure, and even mode of dissemination all facilitate deciphering the sociopolitical messaging and the power relations it upholds or seeks to overturn (Way

2017, 100–111). Methodologically, then, we deploy critical multi-modal analysis to interpret ultras' songs, a specific kind of "visual artifact."

Ultras' songs and videos, *Hyatina* among them, arguably create an "affective community of sense" that resonates with Tunisians, and even other Arabs (and social scientists!). The lyrics and acoustics (further analyzed below) give voice to and inflame familiar experiences of rage, frustration, and despair at mounting transgressions against people's rights and dignity. Visual, musical modalities may permeate psyches differently from the stilted declarations of political parties or civil society groups, even when the subject matter is similar—for instance, socio-economic disparities or corruption. However, to an extent we depart from Callahan. Visual artifacts need not cobble together *new* "affective registers" or always create *new* communities. Rather, a Club Africain song or video might exude affect hearkening back to pedigrees of rage. It may foment embodied emotions such as *hogra* that has historically bred resistance since Tunisia's precolonial crucible. These songs release what we might term "affect hooks" drawing from the local repertoire of Tunisia's political vernacular. Invoking such terms or experiences can stimulate responsiveness by the broader populace, extending their reach beyond fellow club super-fans. *Hogra*, colonialism, marginalization, and the struggle for Palestine all resonate with fellow Tunisians, (re)creating meanings already embedded in a collective ethos of struggle. To *activate* (rather than Callahan's "*create*") "affective communities of sense," visual artifacts must signal to an existing cognitive and affective register. In addition to tone, rhythm, and multi-modal visual/sound cues, a deliberate choice of words is an *agentic* social act and en-actment comingling with the cognition and affect of peoplehood-in-becoming.

Football's "Hadrah"

There is a risk of over-emphasis on contemporary, millennial or Gen. Z, modes of visual expression and communication. Even if social media technology that lowers the barriers to production and circulation did not exist, indignants such as the ultras or fellow Tunisian subalterns might invent something similar. Centuries-old local repertoires, the cultural *makhzun*, contribute to the accretion of a lively, learned protest competency. We suggest that Tunisian *hadrah* performances celebrating the Prophet Muhammad, articulated and embodied longing for his company, exhibit features similar to ultras' flashy performances. Ritualized spectacles are necessarily embedded in cultural registers and repositories. The seemingly disparate worlds of Sufism and soccer may collide. Sufism's long history and popularity in Tunisia is well-known. The capital is "guarded" in each direction by a saint (*wali salih*): Mihriz Ibn Khalaf, Abu Al-Hasan Al-Shadhli, Abu Said Al-Beji, and the female Al-Sayyida Al-Mannubiyyah (Al-Haidari 2021). Even as their monastic centers of learning and worship (*zawiyah*) suffer neglect, Sufi orders are not without political significance. Many engaged in historical, albeit disputed anticolonial resistance (e.g.

Clancy-Smith 1997) and *rabat* (literally, tying up the holes, an Islamic term akin to border patrol) (Qarrah 2012). Tamed and dis-armed over the centuries, such active socio-political roles have given way to a reputation for "moderation," marshalled and instrumentalized by some politicians to offset youth recruitment to violent, "extremist" ideologies and groups since the revolution (Al-Haidari 2021). Refashioned after Ben Ali's days and increasingly since 2011 as the face of "official Tunisian Islam," Sufism is cast as "moderate," neither Brotherhood Islamist nor Salafi (Ben Brik 2016).

Even hollowed out as mere ritual, the stuff of annual festivals, Sufism's cultural influence supersedes the doctrinal or the organizational. This multi-order[18] modality of Islamic being is of interest here for its *appearances* in the public domain, memory, and imaginary. The *hadrah*, for example, is a Sufi ritual of chanting prayers and singing lyrics, accompanied by music and dance, often enacted to mark occasions such as the Prophet's birth (*mawlid*). The name *hadrah* comes from "presence," indicating a presence with God through utterances and bodily gestures in the presence of a holy man or shaykh, leader of a Sufi order (*tariqah*) (Damaq). *Hadrahs* are associated with particular Sufi orders and their *wali salih*. Rooted in religious-cultural practices of listening (*al-sam'*) with origins in the orality of Qur'anic recitation and singing without musical instruments (*anashid*), it varies in execution from one order to the next (*Leaders Arabic* 2018). The 'Issawi *hadrah*, deriving its name from the order nestled near Bab Souika in Tunis, is particularly elaborate. As the pace of singing and chanting picks up, participants gesticulate wildly, imitating the movements of lions, ostriches, or cats (*Leaders Arabic* 2018). Other more violent displays include swallowing glass or thorns, or even licking hot iron (*Leaders Arabic* 2018). Over the top, creative theatricality is not a specifically secular mode of cultural expression. Nor is it simply imported from Italian or Latin American ultras practices. Sfax's Sidi Bou'akkazan *hadrah* is among the famous performances of the city. A band of Sufi brothers, clad in white, red caps (*shashiyyah* or *kabbus*) perched atop their heads, tap the orb-like hand drums (*daff*) and other instruments such as the *bandir*. They sing and chant, dancing in rhythm with the drumbeats. Starting off slow, the gesticulation and whirling speeds up with the singing and chanting, reaching a point of "drunkenness" (*takhmirah*)—a kind of ecstasy and rapture borne of union with the divine. Audience members join in, too. Their singing and dancing climax in almost a "hysteria," whereupon band members and even spectators begin to walk on coals or dance precariously near blazing *halfa* grass, adroitly avoiding the fire (Damaq n.d.).The *hadrah* spectacle is shot through with religious affect. The embodied performances are visually and orally acted out and transmitted, in rituals linked to legends of the saint, his Godly-bestowed miracles, and powers to mitigate mundane suffering. More modern renderings of centuries-old *hadrah* keep the ritual alive for contemporary times in stylized productions broadcast on television or even YouTube.

---

[18] Heterogeneity characterizes the Tunisian Sufi landscape. Residents of Southern Douz in Kebili, for instance, clamor for the blessings of two saints (Al-Ghouth and Al-Mahjoub), rather than the customary sole saint. No single order dominates the *zaway*a in this tribal locale where city and country intermesh at the portal to the Sahara (see Lahoual 2009).

Tunisian director Al-Fadil Al-Jaziri's version, acted out by a 100-man ensemble in the Cultural City, adds saxophones and electric guitars, for instance (Babnet 2022).

Our suggestion here is that the *dakhlah* performances choreographed and orchestrated by ultra fans are not borrowed from Europeans in their entirety. They are in tune with indigenous cultural spectacles brimming with similar, familiar religious affect. Here, we contend, lies the dual power of the ultras' *dakhlah*. Rebellious, they dazzle in their politically subversive and flashy excess, simultaneously evoking the *hadrah* well-known to all Tunisians. The question (and the danger, for power-holders wary of restive masses) is how such affective excitability can be "triggered" among the crowds-in-waiting (Sadiki and Saleh 2021). It is apt to ask: How do the sleeper cells of anti-authoritarian resistance, local cultural repositories (*makhzun*) of spectacle tinged with globalism (ultras' *tifo* or *dakhlah*), converge in the knowledge of a resistance competency? Corroborated by interviews, an examination of ultras' music and *dakhlah* samples below, speaks to the affective, cognitive, and agentic muscles flexed and capacities honed.

Inaugurating a Resistance Competency

From the *dakhlah* recalling the *hadrah* to shuttling between cities to attend matches, Tunisia's ultras have been serious about their game for years. We now broach the issue of deliberate ultras resistance against the state. One notes that unlike Morocco (*Al-Maghrib Al-Aqsa*) where ultras have vocalized their opposition to political authority only in the last three years, in Tunisia their overt resistance preceded the 2011 revolution.[19] In fact, some members of the relatively older cohort interviewed for this book—now in their thirties—consider themselves to have had a clear hand in leading open defiance to Ben Ali's regime and to socializing other Tunisians to follow suit. Along with the phosphate basin protestors (explored in Chapter 5),

> We [ultras] became a problem for them [*al-hakim,* the ruler]. … The ruler became conscious that there is something "simmering" inside ultras youth, during a period when the country was stable, without chaos, and political authority was in control of everything. … Tunisia witnessed only the phosphate basin events in Gafsa [in 2008]. Other than that, there was no movement [against the regime]. There were only the stadium events and the confrontations (*muwajahat*) of the ultras against the political authorities. You can consider them to be confrontations with the system.[20]

Confronting the system in 2008 or before, of course, meant taking a great risk to enact dissent against Ben Ali's ill-famed police state. Mohamed describes the "system," embodied in its police officers, coming to a realization that some youth exhibited

---

[19] Interview with Bilal, October 18, 2021.
[20] Interview with Mohamed, October 18, 2021.

a willingness and a capacity to revolt, even in the stadiums. Such an awareness—of a potential threat to untrammeled authoritarianism and stability—was instigated by a budding consciousness among these youth, of police repression that violated their dignity. In turn, the free hand granted to the police was linked to Ben Ali's dictatorship. There was no automatic understanding among ultras, but one arrived at through repeated experiences and exposure. It is part of a *cognitive* self-consciousness of the ultras as (non)people up against a coercive apparatus seeking to keep them in their place. Mohamed considers the revolution to have been launched from the *virage* by the ultras. Youth "began to demand [their] freedom, who began to feel [their] own worth. [Their] main question became: You, oh police, why do you repress me?"[21] Sami concurs, highlighting the affective undertones behind this cognitive self/other awareness. He adds that an "individual feeling of repression became the feeling of a group," framed within the ultras. Thus, each repressed individual "began to turn to his [ultras] group, and the groups began to unite against repression ... all the groups from Club Espérance and African, and since 2008 until 2010, the confrontations between the police and ultras groups occurred almost weekly."[22] Even under the iron grip of Ben Ali's regime, all was not quiet on the stadium front. Prompting these confrontations was an understanding that in Tunisia, police repression of ultras was much worse than that in Europe, for instance.

Tunisia's dreaded police, their repression symbolized in their instantly recognizable "*beja*" car,[23] did not simply act of their own accord. At least, they had the implicit backing of an authoritarian state. Bilal notes the relative political maturity of the ultras active before the 2011 revolution. "Unlike the ultras [who joined] after ... we were conscious that we live in a big dictatorship, and that the system will show us no mercy ... so we were driven, but also cautious, and we lived a strong solidarity with one another."[24] Alaa concurs: "we began to realize that something was bothering [and constraining us] ... it was the dictatorship."[25] For ultras, encounters with dictatorship were personal, up-close, but also shared. More than one ultra recounted experiences of being stripped of his shirt, sometimes his pants, by callous police. Such humiliation engendered a determination not to tolerate violations of bodily dignity (*al-karamah al-jasadiyyah*). The negative affect of anger and *hogra* spurred a solidarity of shared repression, not unlike that in other protestscapes we examine throughout the book. The difference may be the quasi-communal living and "way of life" inherent in ultras' identity, which we explore in the next section. By 2008, six or seven years after the first ultras groups formed in Tunisia, songs and slogans became more politicized, clearly calling for freedom, these veteran ultras say. Two years or so before the revolution, "we united around the idea that the police repress us, all of

---

[21] Interview with Mohamed, October 18, 2021.
[22] Interview with Sami, October 18, 2021.
[23] From the French baché, alternatively referred to in slang as *naqah* (camel), *shmat*, or *combie*, the police car can be either a dark blue van or a smaller, square black vehicle with metal-latticed windows. Police officers are often called "vipers" (*ahnash*, plural of *hnash*) in slang. Ultras are not the only Tunisians spiteful toward police, but may be one of the few groups who consistently attempt to strike back at them.
[24] Interview with Bilal, October 18, 2021.
[25] Interview with Alaa, October 18, 2021.

us different [ultras] groups, without exception."[26] This unity across disparate ultras groupings began internally, then manifested in altercations with the police. Clashes were not random or aimless. Instead, they were deliberate reactions to the political suffocation under which Tunisians and specifically this young cohort lived. "We were repressed in the street, and we would respond in kind inside the stadium, because when *al-hakim* grabs a hold of you in the street, he will show no mercy. But when you are with your [ultras] group, and your friends, and you feel your unity [with them], you see that you become strong, and that we became peers to the ruler."[27] Strength in numbers, protection through the group, is a recurring theme in all the interviews. Deriving from and generating such collective power is the exercise of agency, a studied "response" to police violence on the ultras' own turf. From the microcosm of the stadium, the ultras' alternative world and dream of freed space, through protest, they came to view themselves as *equal to* police implements of power and repression. A nascent awareness, and subsequent practice, of popular sovereignty—socially acting and en-acting peoplehood—seems to underlie a newfound, learned protest and resistance competency.

Ultras fight for "freedom" inside and outside the stadium. Prior to the revolutionary protests of 2010–11 (in which several of our interlocutors confirm taking part), showdowns with the police crested in the April 8, 2010 Espérance–Hammam Lif match mentioned above. Bilal recounts this event as his initiation into protest. Being present with his ultras group, observing the signs they carried with oppositional slogans, listening to them singing brazenly, their hands locked together in a show of togetherness, all imbued him with a newfound courage. At that point, "I did not hesitate in [joining] the confrontation and protest."[28] In contrast to the media and government portrayal of "mischief," for ultras turning off the electricity and attacking the police was a purposeful rejoinder to incessant harassment, humiliation, estrangement, and anger. Agency, affect, and cognition combined in the voice and the fist of a protest that descended into violence. The April 2010 game may have been the most dramatic pre-revolution event. The ultras interviewed suggest a cumulative effect of becoming battle-hardened through iterative encounters with police in those two years ("the golden years") before 2011. Moreover, the new increasingly defiant posture diffused throughout their neighborhoods to non-ultras, as they tell it. The "ultras mentality" made its way through the "hoods" (*ahya' sha'biyyah*) from which many of the ultras hailed. These neighborhoods "broke the barrier of fear and meek submissiveness, and [residents] began to hit back at the police that beat them."[29] Inspiring in their courage, emboldening in their resistance practices, the ultras seem to have energized propensities and practices of defiance in some poor, urban neighborhoods. Ultras thus played both a direct and indirect role in the coalescing and converging of Tunisia's various demoi in the 2011 revolution. Their leadership and

[26] Interview with Sami, October 18, 2021.
[27] Interview with Alaa, October 18, 2021.
[28] Interview with Bilal, October 18, 2021.
[29] Interview with Mohamed, October 18, 2021.

example in this extended synchrony of protest clings to the ultras' reputation over a decade later.

Ultras as Identity and Belonging

Resistance and protest, whether against the police or the larger *system* headed by Ben Ali or post-revolutionary governments, is not an individual enterprise. However, the depth and intensity of the group may distinguish the ultras from other protestscapes we explore in the book. This section shifts to ultras' understandings and practices of identity that interweave with protest. In focus group interviews, songs, and social media messaging, they consistently invoke their collectivity as super-fans who are not just "regular spectators" of football. Rebelliousness is their hallmark. One picture posted on the Zapatista Facebook page, for instance, shows what appears to be a photo of a graffiti mural that features a cigar-smoking Castro to the right and a masked rebel to the left. The Arabic phrase at the bottom drives the point home: " '*aqliyyah mutamarridah*." For the benefit of non-Arabic speakers, the post comment translates: in Spanish*, mentalità ribelle*, in English, "rebel mindset."[30] Pictures and drawings, sometimes Guy Fawkes-style masks, of the group named for Mexican revolutionary Emiliano Zapata (see Brunk 1995) appear throughout the Facebook page. Joining an ultras group is like finding a family. Solidarity, protection, support, companionship, even counsel, follow. Quasi-communal living springs from a group identity that supersedes individual self-interest, giving shape, purpose, and meaning to youth who otherwise feel adrift. Spurned, humiliated, even targeted by a state in which misery crowds out hope, ultras come into their own through involvement in a group that effectively takes over their life. Many refer to the ultras mentality (*'aqliyyat al-ultras*) that orders their daily living, their (non)political outlook, and their fandom prioritized over anything else. "Youth are by their nature lost. ... Yes, we are this youth. We live together as brothers ... each one lives crisis-ridden on his own, but the friendship inside the ultras fills the void."[31] Being part of these super-fan groups grants to youth a sense of value they lack, a worthiness the state refuses to confer upon them: "Ultras contributes to giving you a sense of worth in society."[32] Many ultras are high school dropouts who, according to Ahmed, became bored ambling from one café to another, day after day without direction. Finding the ultras adds spice to their bland lives, and becomes an "opportunity to change our daily habits" towards a more fruitful, purposive existence.[33] Friendship and brotherhood are additionally strengthened by localized ties. Ultras group together at the neighborhood level: "we all know the details of each other's lives, which makes the solidarity

---

[30] Zapatista Esperanza 2007 Facebook Page, June 15, 2022.
[31] Interview with Idriss, Zapatista member, September 7, 2021.
[32] Interview with Helmi, Zapatista member, August 18, 2021.
[33] Interview, September 4, 2021.

between us stronger."³⁴ As it does for Kamour activists, solidarity takes both material and immaterial forms. A collective willingness to brave danger together affords logistical and emotional support as ultra members travel from city to city, attending their teams' games. Ali gives the example of traveling from Tunis all the way southward to Gabes, "broke," in a laborious journey lasting three whole days!³⁵ Immense effort and time reflect the ultras' commitment to their team, revealing their passion (*gharam*) for the sport. Affect feeds into identity: of the group, of the role they play encouraging their team, of the sacrifices they endure to express themselves as ultras. Indeed, most interviewees referred to "values" inherent to the ultras way of life: sacrifice, loyalty, and generosity.

Protection

Further, ultras membership offers protection. "We travel as one group, facing danger together, so how can we leave one another?"³⁶ Police danger lurks behind every corner. Ultras expect to be accosted, humiliated, stripped of the regalia in which they invest money they do not have. Their artistic creativity is unappreciated. They seem always prepared to be robbed by police of the fireworks (*shamarikh*) they carry and hope to light. Thus, many ultras interviewed mentioned the sense of "security" their group offers. On their own, they would be unable to "confront" the police, left more vulnerable to their attacks. Nader puts it eloquently: to be an ultra is to be "protected [within] a network of relations in different neighborhoods, to be part of an active group of hundreds, where you are kind of protected from the state. In the end you live your life, but you know that you are not alone."³⁷ If youth as an age group search for themselves within peer groups, ultras are doubly in need of the warmth and security of collective association, especially since they are more or less "marked" by police officers. The life of an ultra is one of constant peril, as they tell it: for the sake of the group, the team, the sport. Ahmed recalls a traumatic experience when he was merely thirteen. Vulnerable due to his "weak" appearance and build, two police officers beat him to the ground, kicking and striking him repeatedly in the head. By joining the ultras, he preempts such attacks. He no longer cowers in fear when he frequents the stadium. Along with his colleagues in the group, he feels himself to be a "peer" of the police, an equal rather than a subordinate.³⁸ Protection derives not just from numbers, but also from skills acquired through involvement with the ultras. Some speak of learning from one another, especially from members who are educated or cultured (*muthaqqafin*). They pick up

---

[34] Interview with Helmi, Zapatista member, August 18, 2021.
[35] Interview with Ali, September 7, 2021.
[36] Interview with Firas, Zapatista member, August 18, 2021.
[37] Interview with Ahmad, September 4, 2021.
[38] Interview with Ahmad, September 4, 2021.

skills useful for survival, including negotiations with police. Direct (possibly violent) confrontations are not always suitable or smart.[39] Such learning is complementary to the overt resistance of protest practices (discussed below), acquired know-how relating to social and political issues, or navigating the street and neighborhood as (anti)police patrol.

Solidarity

Solidarity between ultras also encompasses everyday life. The affect of support, *luhmah*, and togetherness play out in practices that enrich their often difficult reality. These veritable bands of brothers celebrate weddings and mourn at funerals together. They split the cost of coffee when they lounge in cafes. Many spoke of a common practice of "circulation" (*tadwirah*), where the group raises money for a member in need, or even their families in the diaspora. Sometimes, this internal "crowd-sourcing" is the only way that members languishing in prison can afford a defense attorney to represent them in court.[40] In addition to money, ultras provide in-kind aid to one another. Putting together the sturdy hand-woven basket (*quffah*) filled with foodstuffs, cigarettes, money, and other essentials, delivered to ultras in prison by their family members, is another such operation. "They did not leave me in my calamity (*mihnah*)," Nabil narrates of his time in jail, brightened by the solidaristic assistance of his fellow ultras.[41] "If one of us falls, it is as though all of us have fallen," explains Bilal.[42] Helping an ultra comrade is akin to helping oneself. These examples that ultras generously supply indicate the comprehensiveness of their group membership perforating stadium boundaries, pervading both lives and identities.

Another striking feature of ultras membership is the substitutability of the fan group for a homeland in the minds and hearts of youth affiliates. It is almost as though the solidarity and identity of ultras (Zapatista, Mkashkhin, etc.) comes to stand in for a kind of small-scale peoplehood. These young men falter in their connectedness to the state from whom they encounter mostly *hogra*: of being strip-searched and beaten by police, of being cast out of the stadium, of (some) living in slums beset by poverty. They sound alienated from their own country, many noting they live in a "different" or "separate world."[43] Instead of asking more from a state that has failed them distributionally and politically, they create an alternative space in which they (ideally) practice freedom and love for the game amidst the community they construct. In place of a Tunisia that offers them nothing, they make the ultras group (*jam'iyyah*, as they call it) their home. Ali puts the case simply: "If you ask every person here from the ultras, he will tell you my country is Tarajji or Club Africain."[44] Ghassan chimes

---

[39] Interviews, September 4, 2021.
[40] Interview with Nader, September 4, 2021.
[41] Interview, August 18, 2021.
[42] Interview, August 18, 2021.
[43] For instance, interviews on August 18, 2021.
[44] Interview, September 7, 2021.

in, "His country is his *jam'iyyah* ... nothing [else] matters to him ..."⁴⁵ Sami denies the state's existence completely: "There is no state; we live on our own ... the state is [just] empty talk."⁴⁶ Where many people may speak earnestly of living in freedom simply as Tunisians, ultras search for liberty in their club, in the stadium, with their group, as well as outside it: "We love the *jam'iyyah* and we love to be free in the stadium and outside it. ... The stadium and the ultras are the world (*mondo*) that we live in."⁴⁷ Bassam confirms the sentiment, suggesting, "The sports stadium is our country, which is why we say, the stadiums are our property, we youth."⁴⁸ Inadvertently almost alluding to the freed space concept, some posit that it is only inside the stadium that they feel truly liberated. Such freedom allows them to resist "the system" even violently: "There, inside the stadium, we are free, and there we strike the police if need be."⁴⁹ Ultras invert Bourguiba's famous quip *al-tarajji dawlah* such that it becomes the country of Tarajji, *dawlat al-tarajji*. Attachment to the club or the ultras group helps explain the enormous commitment ultras demonstrate: raising money, traveling long distances to matches, braving police brutality, confrontations with the police.

It is because of this affective identification that being banned from the stadium⁵⁰ grates at the ultras so harshly. Blocked from entry, they face a kind of exile. "We don't own anything, all we own is the 90 minutes in the stadium, which is the most important thing in our lives," explains Nader.⁵¹ Thus, for them marginalization (*tahmish*) and deprivation (*hirman*) take on immaterial tones, possibly in addition to the material manifestations of structural poverty and socio-political exclusion. Marginalization prevents them from observing their embodied and practiced passion for the game (*gharam*).⁵² Deprivation is not just limited subsistence means, but a kind of deprivation from freedom to attend and support matches, to feel truly alive and part of their stadium community. "We protest the *hirman* from entering the stadium" in addition to "mistreatment by the police," clarifies Salim.⁵³ Several interviewees mentioned the 2017 decision to ban ultras under 18 from entering the stadium (Mosaique FM 2017) as an unforgettable episode that fomented their indignation (*naqmah*) against the state. Here, a forced literal absence (from the stadium) incites a (protest) presence (see Meyer and Woodthorpe 2008). We do not ask for much, ultras seem to say. Our way of life, our passion, does not encroach upon the rights of others. Unlike the unending quest for employment that defines the Kamour protestscape, ultras do not request special accommodation, or demand state largesse. They merely

---

⁴⁵ Interview, September 7, 2021.
⁴⁶ Interview, September 4, 2021.
⁴⁷ Interview, September 4, 2021.
⁴⁸ Interview, October 18, 2021.
⁴⁹ Interview with Ahmad, September 4, 2021.
⁵⁰ Sometimes the ban does not apply to local audiences, for instance in 2019. See *Li-Muhasarat Al-'Unf wa Al-Fawda fi Al-Mala'ib ... Ghalq "Al-Virage" wa Kull Al-Mubarayat bi Al-Jumhur Al-Mahalli Faqat*, in *Alchourouk*, March 20, 2019.
⁵¹ Interview, September 4, 2021.
⁵² Interview with Nader, September 4, 2021.
⁵³ Interview, September 4, 2021.

yearn for the freedom to be and to live in the moment of the match, in the spirit of their team.

Protest Practices
Anti-"Political"

How does the pursuit of freedom that is the crux of ultras' self-identification, as illustrated above, spill into their protest practices? We now take up this question. When the freedom of the stadium and access to it are curtailed, ultras activate their anti-systemic proclivities and go on the offensive. They do so within the protection and fellowship of their groups. Solidarity and its practices help to hold together ultras within and across their *jam'iyyat* (plural of *jam'iyyah*), indicating the holism of the "ultra mentality" and "ultra way of life," reinforcing their strong group identity. The affect of solidarity casts its protective warmth over ultras' resistance against "the system." Solidarity makes protest possible. Ultras' modes of protest, and their orientation toward protest in general, call for specific attention to how it is distinct from other protestscapes we have examined. First, most ultras interviewed initially chafed against the term *ihtijaj*, protest rendered in Arabic. Only once they understood that our questions concerned their practices and performances resisting authority did they themselves begin to use the term in their answers. The exception was the more experienced group of Tarajji fans, some of whom had protested before and during the 2011 revolution.[54] We have used this term throughout the book and in our fieldwork, asking (former) student activists, unionists, miners, and unemployed from the Kamour region about their various protest endeavors. Among all our interlocutors, the ultras have been unique in repudiating *ihtijaj* as such, because they associate it with formal politics. They are forthcoming in their disavowal of politics, repeating the phrase, "we don't care about politics." More specifically, "We are always against, against them, any authority, and we search for [ways to] provoke it."[55] There was consensus in the four different focus groups that politics—which they understood as the machinations of politicians and political parties—was a domain of exclusive self-interest, far removed from the concerns of regular people including themselves. Ayman ventures that any ultra would insist that they "don't care about politics, but we understand politics as ultras, in our daily lives."[56] The implication is that ultras are quite familiar with the political realm through their experiences of incessant victimization and marginalization. Wael adds more dramatically, "we are in a rupture or boycott (*qati'ah*) with the political system," a complete break[57] in which they abjure voting, for example. Abhorrence for politics is clearly tied to the rejection of the state itself, discussed above. Ali expounds on exactly why the

---

[54] Interviews October 18, 2021.
[55] Interview with Nader, September 4, 2021.
[56] Interview, September 7, 2021.
[57] Interview, September 7, 2021.

state and its politics are not for them: "I tell you, what is the state? It is lies and bias toward the powerful and an instrument to protect the wealthy. As for the regular people, they have [only] God... . Nobody among the ultras trusts in the state."[58] Even over a decade after the revolution in which many ultras took part—they still feel more like non-people than people. Politics is for a select, privileged few.

Moreover, many ultras distastefully label politics as a system and structure of "lies" with which they wanted to have no association. Like Holden Caulfield's youthful, idealistic authenticity that writes off "phonies" he encounters at every turn in *The Catcher in the Rye*, ultras seem to revel in their disgust for a domain far removed from their own commitment to truth, sincerity, loyalty, and love (for the game, for one another, perhaps for Tunisians). In fact, the ultras' community seems to offer far more than does formal politics. Bilal explains that ultras "feel superior to the intelligentsia (*muthaqqafin*) and the politicians, who live in lies, and the state does not provide anything" to the people.[59] Nader even balked at being "compared" to political players. "The political circuit is lies and hypocrisy. We are the opposite of them: we trust in each other as members of groups, even without knowing one another, we hug [one another] when our team excels, we [stand in] solidarity when we go on the offensive" against other teams, or perhaps even the police.[60] Feelings of trust are embodied in the physicality of team and group embrace. He juxtaposes this positive affect with the corruption, fragmentation, and atomization of the self-interested individualism rampant in politics. Clearly, despite their statements to the contrary, the ultras *are* political in the sense of resisting formal and institutional authority, exercising agency to relay pointed messages about socio-political developments, clamoring for freedom and dignity, conscious of the power disparities they attempt to thwart.

Moreover, it may be that a self-imposed, mandatory distance from partisanship or ideology protects the ultras from being dragged into some trends. For instance, Alaa admits that a very small number of ultras were recruited into "jihadism" pulling them to Syria, but they did so as individuals. "Nobody tried to put forth these ideas, or any other, inside the ultras, because they know very well that the ultras have their own principles and do not accept politics or any school of thought (*madhab*)."[61] Sami added that "deviant cases" do not make the rule that shields ultras from adopting any political line of thought, hardline Islamist or otherwise, despite the "turbulence" of the post-2011 period.[62] Based on the focus group interviews, ultras seem more tolerant of internal ideological heterogeneity than Tunisia's notoriously polarized politicians and parties—so long as diversity of thought and practice stops short of evangelism within the fan groups. Formal politics sometimes incites ambivalence, however. During one interview, three ultras disagreed over President Kais Saied. Two of them, Ayman and Wael, stated that if the President requested their support through protest, they would congregate quickly, supporting him to "the last drop of

---

[58] Interview, September 7, 2021.
[59] Interview, October 18, 2021.
[60] Interview, September 4, 2021.
[61] Interview, October 18, 2021.
[62] Interview, October 18, 2021.

blood." The President (who had campaigned on the slogan *the people want*, paying lip service to the revolution and Tunisia's forgotten youth), might be an "opportunity" for ultras, for young people. Ali begged to differ. "Do you think that Kais Saied will [work for] the development of the youth? Of course not! He will increase our marginalization. … He will drown us even more."[63] Here Ali stayed true to the ultras' jaded anti-systemic pledges, while Ayman and Wael were swayed by Saied and his populist discourse.

Anti-Systemic Confrontation

Common among all interviewees is a predilection for the term "confrontation" (*muwajahah*), which ultras adopt to "differentiate themselves from political protests."[64] Underlying this agency of resistance is the affect of *hogra* and *naqmah*, combined with the cognitive self-awareness that the group is being oppressed by the state, metonymized in the personhood of police. Freedom inside and outside "free space" of the stadium is the ultimate end game for ultras. The two feed into each other. To achieve this freedom for themselves and others, ultras are engaged in a running battle with the police. Only when they are no longer banned, no longer suffer ordeals to purchase tickets, no longer strip-searched, no longer have their fireworks and banners confiscated, no longer see their elaborately expensive choreographies cancelled, will they feel free. Only then will this "part that has no part" enjoy the status of "people," even if ephemerally, on a par with the police and politicians, the club administrators, and the wealthy. Their social doing translates into both affective and cognitive resonance with a quest for autonomy and peoplehood more generally. To this end, somehow, confrontation features as a weapon in their inventory. Through confrontation, ultras unceasingly "provoke" the police through protest. Some view such confrontation as a spontaneous, permanent state of affairs: "Naturally, our life with them [the police] is [one of] protest."[65] Others disagree, pointing out that sometimes, ultras actually plan protests. For instance, various ultras groups organized through their Facebook pages, gathering at their respective clubs to renounce the bans on match attendance.[66]

Interestingly, by some of their accounts, ultras did come out strongly (70 percent of participants, according to one!) during the protests on July 25, 2021, when President Kais Saied set in motion his power grab.[67] For some, July 25 felt comparable to the 2011 revolution. They reference their mounting impatience with the "lies" of politics as motivation. Nader goes further, speaking of a "longing" for Tunisia their country despite swearing off politics. Both Nader and Ahmed insist that no prior organization, whether on Facebook or otherwise, spurred this mass participation

---

[63] Interviews with Ayman, Wael, and Ali, September 7, 2021.
[64] Interview with Ahmed, September 4, 2021.
[65] Interview with Bilal, August 18, 2021.
[66] Interview with Firas, August 18, 2021.
[67] Interviews, September 4, 2021.

on that scorching summer day. An unavoidable paradox presents itself. Ultras who are highly organized into clear hierarchical structures, who discuss and deliberate major activities such as the *dakhlah* (below), simply joined the July 25 protests as "individuals." Groups where individuality melts away, disappearing into a tight-knit solidarity and collective behavior, as they tell it, suddenly faded into the background of a rambunctious political scene.

As the ultras interviewed put it, however, for them protest is not confined to demonstrations in the street. Rather, protest encompasses announcing their presence clearly, visually, in public space and to the police specifically. Wearing the colors of one's team—Tarajji's crimson and gold, Africain's red and white—itself is an assertion of fearless identity and existence as super-fan youth for whom football and the team take precedence over all else in life. Ali explains: "Protest is to confront them with the colors of your team … protest is to not be afraid."[68] Even group gatherings in the middle of the street are something the "police can't stand," a "provocation" which prompts ultras to exaggerate their public appearances, hurling curses at the police.[69] It is provocation to be felt and seen. Ultras seem to delight in provoking the police with whom relations are consistently acrimonious. They sing their songs out loud, also bandying about their ritualistic regalia in visual displays such as igniting fireworks, further irking the police. The visual and the discursive combine in graffiti they splash on city walls. Group names (e.g. Zapatista), for example, adorn surfaces across the capital. More pointed graffiti slogans such as "learn to swim" (*T'allam 'Oum*, the campaign we discuss later) and "the resistance continues" (*al-muqawamah mustamirrah* seemingly adopted from the Palestinian struggle), are a "constant protest against repression." These doodles are artistic works by "skilled and creative" youth.[70] While the artwork of graffiti and banners is designed to inflame the police, the illustrations are also a sore point for the ultras themselves. Several interviewees discuss their creative expressions with pride, complaining bitterly that aesthetic talent and creativity among ultras are un-appreciated by the police and larger Tunisian society. We are more than just agitators, they maintain. Yet all the police see in us is trouble.

Protest (Non-)Violence

Within this explosive cycle of mutual suspicion, ultras do not deny the engagement by some in illegal activity, or their preparedness for violence. Smoking the hashish drug *zatlah* (including during the interviews) is one not uncommon practice.[71] In addition

---

[68] Interview, September 7, 2021.
[69] Interview with Wael, September 7, 2021.
[70] Interview with Wael, September 7, 2021.
[71] Denied by the Interior Ministry, Facebook rumors circulated in early 2021, that all youth would be subject to drug tests and offenders would be sacked from government jobs. Yet the "fake news" points to the controversy of sentencing for drug (especially *zatlah*) use, which can since 2011 be years in prison. Thousands of Tunisians have reportedly been sent to jail on drug charges. Many youth protestors view the laws governing drug convictions as archaic (Law 52, dating back to 1992), see their implementation as targeting those engaged in protest activity, and push for further reforms than those undertaken in May

to vandalism, sometimes looting invites police "anger," such that at times "confrontations erupt for the slightest reason."[72] Affect and its incitement are a two-way street: *hogra*, anger, and provocation are lockstep in an ongoing dance. Yet ultras vary in where they locate violence in the repertoire of protest activity and practices, their *muwajahat*. Whether personal proclivities or situational, circumstantial factors push them towards violence (offensive or defensive) is not always clear. They may go on the attack and pelt police officers with stones. While some of Tunisia's ultras carry simple weapons, such as knives and razors, to the football stadium, this light ammunition pales in comparison to the guns with bullets that their Latin American counterparts wield, or the (presumably more elaborate) fireworks of European ultras. "Each country has its specificities," says Ahmed.[73] He adds that some, but not all, ultras resort to violence against the police; others deploy more creative and "intellectual" protest practices. Graffiti, songs, and the *dakhlah* choreographies likely fall into the latter category. Sami casts ultras' violence against the police, not a first choice, in a defensive light: "We defend ourselves and our bodily dignity."[74] Whether preemptive or not, this perspective sees ultras striking back to waylay assuredly violent police officers from further denigrating the right to dignity. Through such violence, ultras defend their turf (literally: the stadium as freed space), also sending a message that while they may be the underdogs, they are neither passive nor meek toward the state and its police. They are certainly not silent. The point here is not to romanticize ultras' violence.[75] Rather, it is to situate such protest practice within their mindsets and affective dispositions, etched through accumulating experiences into song, artwork, and psyches. The ultras' resistance competency, and its performance through protest, is neither spontaneous nor coincidental. It is a form of experiential knowledge. While our twenty-first-century sensibility may shudder at the veneration of violence, history might furnish the contextualized perspective necessary for interpreting physical unruliness.

It is not just English football hooligans who fall into violence (Frosdick and Marsh 2005). More resolutely political movements, such as radical student activism of the "global 1968" and the subsequently stormy 1970s (Chapter 4), teetered at the brink of violence. Third World anti-colonial movements certainly did not drive out the *colons* waving olive branches or scattering fragrant roses. Italian militant insurrectionism-terrorism perpetuated by the Red Brigade and other groups, for instance, emitted an "aura of a fantasy of revolution as armed struggle" in the manner of outsize personalities such as Che Guevara (Passerini 1996, 138–140). The violence of the Black Power movement that "scandalize[d]" the US from the 1960s into the 1970s, catapulting figures such as Stokely Carmichael, Malcolm X, and Angela Davis into

2017 (see Ben Salah 2022). Qasem (2022) bemoans rising drug and *zatlah* addiction in Tunisia, the latter estimated at 400,000 people (70 percent of them youth). These statistics have generated discussion over whether strict laws can best tackle the problem.
[72] Interview with Hilmi, August 18, 2021.
[73] Interview, September 4, 2021.
[74] Interview, October 18, 2021.
[75] Fights break out not infrequently in Rades stadium, first between ultras and then with the police, as in October 2018. See for instance *Al-Dakhiliyyah Tanshur Tafasil wa Adrar Ahdath Al-'Unf Allati Jaddat Ams fi Mal'ab Rades*, in *Alchourouk*, October 24, 2018.

(inter)national notoriety, coincided with and possibly complemented the nonviolent civil rights movement (Joseph 2009). Absent the compass of clear demands or grievances, the puzzle of the ultras protestscape remains: what sets their (non)violent protest conflagration alight and how?

Detecting the struggle for ultras "peoplehood" on its own terms calls for considering the full panoply of their protest practices. Color-coded clothing, irreverent singing, full-bodied group presence, playful or raging pyrotechnics, head-turning artwork and graffiti, and intricate choreographies overlap with violence against police *or* protest as demonstrations. Yet the ultras interviewed were rather coy in describing the impetus for protest participation. Aside from the 2011 revolution and the nation-wide street protests on July 25, 2021, several noted that they only stage protest demonstrations when *football* issues are at stake. Sometimes, riotous violence sharpens these flare-ups. A few interviewees mentioned a 2018 demonstration on Mohammad V Street, parallel to Habib Bourguiba Avenue in the capital. The cancellation of a friendly match against a visiting Palestinian team, Wad Al-Nais, infuriated the ultras and elicited sympathy from football fans and ultras (Nessma 2018), descending into a violent showdown with police. "We did not accept the cancellation of the match, and went out in the thousands, confronting the police in total violence."[76] The agency of defiance, the affect of rage, and the cognition of group victimization by the state indicate how perceived breaches of freedom ignite protest fervor. Even, that is, when the ultras presume to be apolitical.

Singing and Choreographing Protest

As we have been signaling, ultras' protest practices in their confrontation with the state and provocation of its security appendages (police) takes forms unique to this dissentscape. It would be difficult to abstract the basis of the January 2018 cancellation of the game with the Palestinian team from its political undertones—or audacious political content. This section explores the aesthetics of ultras protest through analyzing a sampling of their songs and *dakhlah*. A flair for the dramatic characterizes sports in general. The *dakhlah* (ultras' opening choreography and its attendant singing and visual exhibits) is even more decidedly dramatic, often peppered with political messaging. Alongside *dakhlah*, songs such as *Ya Hyatina* sketched in the opening vignette are a connection between ultras and the broader Tunisian peoplehood-in-becoming. Eliciting affect, ultras cross protestscape, gender, class, regional, and urban divides in their invocation of recognizable suffering. Interviewees uniformly point out that their choreographies are carefully planned, subject to (quasi-democratic) deliberation. One idea might be collectively chosen among a number of suggestions put forth by group members.[77] Like ultras across the

---

[76] Interview with Nader, September 4, 2021.
[77] Interviews, August 18, 2021.

world, videos of these spectacles are then published online, to attract as many "eyeballs" as possible. Global websites such as Ultras-Tifo also disseminate some Tunisian *dakhlah*, showing crowds of shirtless youth waiting in the wings beneath the stadium stairs. They leap up and down and pump their fists in the air, singing and chanting in close physical proximity. Some twirl their shirts above their heads. The energetic intensity is almost palpable, even filtered through years-old videos. Scenes of billowing, colorful smoke and yellow balls of fire floating in arches across the pitch (see Ultras-Tifo 2021) are evocative of wildfire disasters, or war zones. Even some high school students construct elaborate *dakhlah*. A lycée in Nabeul painted a banner featuring unlucky players running across stacked brown stones to reach a golden throne, only to fall into a pit of fire. Topped by an English lettered slogan taunting, "You guessed you could beat the greatest? You guessed wrong!", the second scene features a hoodie-donning football player hoisting up a fluttering blue and white flag (see Ultras-Tifo 2018). Red smoke and flames follow, as the students fire up coruscating pyrotechnics. Ultras' protest creativity begins quite young.

"Dakhlah": Between Sports and Politics

Even when deprived of their free spaces to carry out *dakhlah* in person, cyberspace transmits the messages anyway. The circulation of a banner painted by the ultras, one they planned to hold up in the 2018 Palestine match they had dubbed "martyrs of the nation" (*shuhada' al-ummah*), gave the Interior Ministry pause. They banned the banner, and the Tarajji, sensing mounting unrest among ultras ranks, aborted the match (Ultra Filastine 2018). Divided into four panels,[78] the banner featured a group "portrait" of Ahmed Yassin, Saddam Hussain, Yassir Arafat, and Abu Jihad[79] peering over the Dome of the Rock mosque, enveloped in ethereal, shimmering clouds. The second panel from the left was a close-up of Yassir Arafat donning the familiar black-and-white checkered *kuffiyyah*. Next to Arafat lay Ahmed Yassin peacefully on a slab of concrete as though in his grave, an uncanny rendering of his snowy white beard almost matching the blanket enrobing him from head to toe. The final, right-most panel shows, against the backdrop of the Dome, more recent legend Ahed Tamimi,[80] recognizable by her long blond curls as she firmly grasps the Palestinian flag like a weapon. Her sideways glance seems to scan the horizon for advancing Israeli troops. In this case, the political substance and slant of the *dakhlah* was regional: support for the Palestinian cause. (Recall that Kamour activists, unionists, and students have in various ways expressed solidarity with the Palestinian struggle.) The ultras might feign political dis-interestedness. Backing Palestinian rights to self-determination,

---

[78] See *Al-Dawlah Al-Tarajjiyyah* Facebook page, January 13, 2018: https://www.facebook.com/Adawla.Atarajjia/photos/a.159139664118221/1,746,023,528,763,152/?type=3
[79] The alias of Khalil Al-Wazir, PLO co-founder assassinated in Tunis in 1988. Recent Israeli accounts confirm the widespread attribution of the operation to Israel (Watad 2020).
[80] Club Africain gifted Ahd an honorary jersey lettered with her name. See *Hay'at al-Ifriqi Tukarrim Al-Filistiniyyah Ahed Al-Tamimi*, in *Al-Sabah*, October 3, 2018.

celebrating its martyrs, transcends the "political" in its normatively and ethically quasi-consensual, principled urgency. Yet by outlawing the banner and cancelling the match, Tunisian political and club authorities threw the game and its parade squarely into the political domain. "They refused the message of the *dakhlah* because it reminds them of the [leaders] of the Muslim nation (*ummah*), and our leaders today don't like them because they are ... not [true] men." (Ironically, the ascription in this case of honor and bravery is to masculinity, despite Ahed Tamimi being a young woman.) Moreover, because of the ban and cancellation, ultras' time, effort, creativity, and hard-saved cash—nearly 50 thousand dinars—was squandered.[81] This at a time when "the politicians were negotiating towards normalization" with Israel, Wael adds in disgust.[82] Solidarity with Palestine—an affective disposition towards a fellow people pursuing sovereignty and liberation—is at once a political act *and* a declaration of identity.

Displays and the songs that accompany them are not always overtly political. They might be addressed to the other team. Mohamed recalls one such *dakhlah* that portrayed Tarajji as a "Roman Caesar," implying unassailable strength and splendor that effectively belittled and "dwarfed" the other team.[83] Another Club Africain *dakhlah* featured a banner lettered with the slogan, "Football was made by the rich and stolen by the poor."[84] If one positive development can be seen since the 2011 revolution, it is the relatively freer expressiveness of the ultras in their songs and spectacles, several interviewees stated. Within the tangle of ultras' multi-modal discourse, however, songs and the *dakhlah* are most likely to impart either identifiable or "coded" political positions and repudiations of political or club corruption, self-interest, repression, and treachery (Nawaat 2022).

Performance Features

The discussion above, along with the chapter's opening vignette, illustrates several characteristics of ultras' performances, be they songs or the *dakhlah* replete with banners, fireworks, and jumping fans. First, songs and choreographies traverse the narrow concerns of a partial Tunisian demos—football fans keen to attend matches and cheer on their teams—to other national and even regional protestscapes. A common quest for peoplehood animates ultras music and lyrics. The *dakhlah* conveys a "message" relating to recent developments that afflict either ultras themselves or the broader people (*sha'b*), ultras explained in several interviews. The performance is "your point of view ... it could even be your position with respect to a new president ... if he doesn't convince you."[85] Nabil concurs that *dakhlah* might relate to Tunisian

---

[81] Interview with Nader, September 4, 2021.
[82] Interview, September 7, 2021.
[83] Interview with Mohamed, October 18, 2021.
[84] Interviews, October 18, 2021.
[85] Interview with Ahmed, September 4, 2021.

issues or "matters of [Arab] public opinion, such as Palestine."[86] Second, songs and *dakhlah* are necessarily oppositional, in line with other ultras' practices and symbolic expressions. Several interviewees used the Arabized term *clashes* (rendered *clashat*, pluralized in the Arab feminine form) in referring to the *dakhlah*. Firas describes one scene choreographing a confrontation with the police:

> Take as an example … a police [officer] holding [a canister of] tear gas, trying to hit you with it, but you grab onto him and land a punch [on his face] … the image would be like this. This means that the police have lost their respect. They appear as though they have no power…. So are the police going to agree to allow this *daklhah*? Of course, they won't let it go on, especially because the world and all people watch it.[87]

The content of *dakhlah* and songs is itself (anta)agonistic, from attacking a police officer to castigating Arab regional leaders. This hostile, "provocative" messaging as they call it, sets up renewed conflict with the police, or the Interior Ministry, or the sports club administration. Rebuffed or confiscated by the authorities, the contentiousness of ultras' performances doubles. The vicious cycle between the ultras and the state in particular seems unstoppable. Third, through their songs and *dakhlah*, ultras self-consciously gear up for a fight, the shape of which is malleable. It could be an altercation with police, or a professed willingness to take on regional hegemons, but the hostile stance is the same. "When we write 'fight for the sake of glory,' it is a message that motivates the players but at the same time reminds them that there is no room for letdowns," says Bilal, commenting on combative slogans.[88] Ultras' songs are not a post-revolutionary phenomenon, even if they have multiplied in popularity since then, aided by Facebook and Youtube. Mohamed[89] recounts the lyrics of a song titled "Every Week," which he says was banned under Ben Ali. Like other songs, its words are a jumble of the Tunisian dialect and Tunisified French words (e.g. terminer, mentalité, limiter). It headlines a fourth feature of ultras' songs and *dakhlat*, unequivocally sounding a clarion call for freedom in the stadium and outside of it. The ballad-like style evidences a fifth feature of ultras songs and *dakhlah*, triggering a spectrum of affect (grief, anger, solidarity) the way music easily does:

> And every week, how many of us
> Are jailed, leaving his mother sad
> Making his friends who love him cry
> They swear to God they won't leave him [alone]
> He joined his group, and left his life [behind]
> ….
> …

[86] Interview, August 18, 2021.
[87] Interview, August 18, 2021.
[88] Interview, August 18, 2021.
[89] Interview, October 18, 2021.

The traitors were no match for us, those who love appearing on television
They accuse us of [being] gangs, and said we are limited [in number]
And forgot what we did
They said the ultras' story has finished
The ultras is a tale whose end is impossible
A strong mentality, the weapon of freedom
God willing, we will live [freedom], if death does not take us
…

You took our belongings, our caps, our slogans
You all control and impose what clothes we wear
…

Unfortunately, you forced us [to these confrontations]
Freedom, by God, I will gain
Power-holders intervene even in football

Lamenting the recurring ("every week") jailing of ultras, in addition to the theft of their regalia ("our belongings, our caps"), the song strikes a sharp tone of *pathos*. Mothers' hearts are torn asunder, friends shed tears. Solidarity of the group crops up through an oath that fellow ultras members "won't leave him alone." The community of football lovers is juxtaposed with "traitors" in politics and the media who hurl accusations, falsely declaring an "end" to the ultras' run. Yet these premature obituaries only nurture ultras' determination: another oath vows to attain freedom. Rebellious youth resist the "control" and "intervention" of the authorities in their professed way of life, hinting that confrontation may be necessary for liberation. From the messages communicated in such a song, ultras' leap into the 2011 revolution seems logical, or at least affectively consistent. Indeed, the song that Basem summons from the recesses of his memory, "You Saw with Your Own Eyes, Police," unflinchingly spells unruliness. Spreading after the 2010 Tarajji–Hammam-Lif match and riots discussed earlier in the chapter, the tone is one of bravado and unbridled rebelliousness. It boasts of killing two police officers: "We came to you, charged, even taking drugs/we caused chaos/It is the revolution, the revolution of the capital's youth/An uprising, and we want freedom/You cannot govern me, oh government."[90] "Chaos" is their specialty, these ultras sing. The violent victory of the match is a precursor of more to come. Revolution, uprising, confrontation, are all around the corner. In fact, the revolution took off in Sidi Bouzid a mere eight months later. Songs and *dakhlah* proved then to be, as they still are, resistance performances. These social acts and en-actments of a denied or deferred peoplehood burgeon to encompass the cares and pursuits of countless Tunisians.

[90] Interview, October 18, 2021.

T'allam 'Oum (Learn to Swim)

One recent and memorable *dakhlah* spotlighted a cause that has pushed the ultras out of "absence" and into "presence" as they protested a gross injustice against one of their own. This section examines the "Learn to Swim" campaign which has been close to ultras' hearts, and formed a springboard for their targeted defiance in recent years. In a June 2022 match against Monastir United, Club Africain paid tribute to their slain martyr, Omar Laabidi (Sans Gants 2022). The deafening boisterousness of a bouncing, cheering crowd, sometimes breaking into song, was the soundtrack for a striking visual display. Red and white ran through the Africain side of the stadium, the Curva Nord architects of the *dakhlah* unmistakable in a huge horizontal banner. In the middle of the white lettering against the red was sketched a faceless head, its identity marked by the Arabic rendering of Omar Laabidi. Perhaps in keeping with the color scheme, a shield of gray ivy outlined in black framed Laabidi as if to honor him. Inside the block letters of CURVA NORD were scribbled other phrases in English and Arabic: a common expression, with our souls and blood, we sacrifice for you, [Club] Africain (*Bil-ruh, bil-damm, nafdik ya Ifriki*); the dear quartet, *al-ruba'iyyah al-ghaliyah*, referring to the four-time champion club; "living within us" (*saknah fina*); a heart; a pumped, upward-facing fist; Ultras Commandos (name of another group); 1920 (the date of the Club's founding); created by the poor stolen by the rich; justice (*al-'adalah*); freedom (*huriyyah*); and the slogan that has become the catch-phrase of a budding quasi-movement: *t'allam 'oum*. Love and sacrifice for the club and the game are fueled by the pain of losing a fellow ultra. Yet those Omar left behind were undeterred in their quest for freedom and dignity—slogans of the 2011 revolution. They would not allow his memory to shrivel and die after his body and soul departed this earth. Provocation, memorializing, shared grief, collective struggle all played out in the opening minutes of the match, perhaps becoming more significant than the outcome of the game itself.

The *t'allam 'oum* campaign started as a hashtag over five years ago, and is an almost para-ultra phenomenon. It is a synchrony-within-a-synchrony of this protestscape. The story of 19 year-old Omar Laabidi is well-known in Tunisia. He was chased by police officers after a match in the Rades stadium spiraled into altercations with ultras in April 2018. Cornered in the nearby Oued (Valley) Meliane, Laabidi reportedly pled with the police to let him go, as he could not swim. According to the widely-circulated story, one of the officers taunted him: learn to swim. Just weeks away from his secondary school graduation, the young man perished that day (Laabidi 2018). Fellow ultras, family, and friends adopted the slogan *t'allam 'oum* to inscribe his tragic story into collective counter-memory. Many ultras interviewed mention him as a quintessential instance of state violence, and an example of ultras solidarity, even across club lines.[91] One Facebook clip featuring jumping, chanting fans in their Esperenze (Tarajji) red and gold singing

---

[91] Interviews, 18 August 2021, October 18, 2021.

for Omar at a handball match speaks to the point.⁹² The caption reads, "Tarajji fans sing for the departed Omar Laabidi." Our departed is also their departed, they seem to suggest. We stand united against police violence.

The rage and grief of his death (murder) has prompted the campaign to pursue justice for Omar as a launch pad for a wider fight against police impunity, led in part by Ayub Amarah. The campaign was re-reinvigorated again in 2022, as ultras and other supporters staged protests during the trials of 14 police officers charged in the case. It plugged into resurgent tensions between security officials and sports audiences (Tunigate 2022). Demonstrators gathered in front of the courthouse, even setting up a tent on Habib Bourguiba Avenue in the capital (Mosaique FM 2022). Officers' failure to appear in court only further perturbed participants and sympathizers of *t'allam 'oum*. A Tarajji–Africain handball match became one site of violence. Additionally, ultras (including the group Vandals) did not hold back. They popularized the slogan "justice or chaos" (*al-'adalah aw al-fawdah*), lettered in white on a black banner as hooded ultras, faces disguised in balaclavas, lit their trusty pyrotechnics to discharge plumes of smoke (Nawaat 2022). The provocation did not go unnoticed. Police seemed to go on the attack against ultras, arresting over a dozen, some on terrorism charges. Alarmed by what they observed as the lengthening arm of police violence, the Tunisian National Human Rights League, a civil society organization with a long pedigree, began to send monitors to sports matches (Nawaat 2022). The League has controversially begun to document cases of police violence against ultras and other civilians. At least partly to blame for spiking police violence may be the ascendancy of over 100 police unions since a law allowing their organizing was passed in 2011. Watchdogs consider their thuggery (*"baltajah"*), evident in violence, online spying, threats to protestors and even politicians, as a reincarnation of the Ben Ali era police state (Al-'Ush 2021).

A Virtual and Embodied Campaign

T'allam 'oum has become a prominent online–offline campaign against police violence. In it we see a protest multiplier effect. Ultras' protest practices—their dress, songs, fireworks, and goading of police—coincided with the death of a young superfan. The affect of loss flooded into further protest *as demonstrations* and ongoing ultras' *muqawamah*. This amplified second round of protest has also ricocheted outward to the wider Tunisian demos, recruiting activists and sympathizers to the cause. The online group *Takriz*, for instance, shared news of Laabidi's death by "police monkeys," promising a new revolution.⁹³ Protestors often chant the slogan *t'allam 'oum*, even in demonstrations not explicitly calling out police violence. This

---

⁹² *T'allam 'Oum* Facebook page, https://www.facebook.com/profile.php?id=100066628300205, April 20, 2022 post.
⁹³ Takriz Facebook page, April 1, 2018.

example of how the ultras' protest echoes back and forth is anchored in the campaign. The Facebook page uploads plenty of affective fodder (anger, grief, solidarity) that buttresses the cognitive consciousness of rights transgressed by police, also propelling the agency of online and offline mobilization. Like the Kamour page, signage and images stand out.[94] In May 2022, the page's profile banner featured a drawing of a recognizable Omar Laabidi, with his scarred eyebrow, combed-up bangs, face half in shadow, the glint of white teeth dimmed by a life snuffed out too early (1998–2018). To the right of his drawing is a request to sign (in Arabic) a change.org petition and *"justice pour* Omar Laabidi" (French). The Arabic explanation reads, "for the declaration of 31 March of every year as a national day for fighting impunity from punishment (*al-iflat min al-ʿiqab*)." The message here is one of recruitment. Online public support (signing a petition) can make Omar's death an annually memorialized reminder for all Tunisians. The unnamed perpetrators (police) will not be let off the hook. Accountability beckons.

The *t'allam ʿoum* campaign seems to be led by an activist (Ayub Amarah) who emerges in the public eye, forsaking the anonymity and media-shyness for which the ultras are known. (This has not stopped police from harassing journalists reporting on *t'allam ʿoum* protests.[95]) Yet the Facebook page reflects the anti-systemic stance of the ultras themselves. One post[96] proclaims to "public opinion" that the protest planned for May 15, 2022 (the largest anti-Saied protest up to that date) was "not [their] concern." The "system" is one. Legitimacy derived from the family of Omar Laabidi (a martyr legitimacy charged with social movement energy) who has "authorized" them and them only to speak on behalf of the group. Thus, the campaign wishes to "avert ... political wrangling and conflicts." This position is not unlike what the Kamour protesters (Chapter 7) sometimes declare. Rather, the page notes that "police repression and the policies of impunity from punishment" have been the "tools" of consecutive governments, "past and present." The revolution was no rescue from unjustified police wrath, the violence of batons, a chokehold or a night chase that might turn deadly. In the same way as Anwar Al-Skrafi's ghost for Kamour, Omar Laabidi's spirit breathes life into this campaign, and the ultras' anti-systemic posture.

No Revolutionary Rupture

The "Learn to Swim" group pursues "justice" for "the martyr of the stadiums, Omar Laabidi," and critics working against police violence "in all eras."[97] This seems to be an implicit reference to a commonly upheld revolutionary rupture that they do not accept. There is almost a contemporary timelessness to their strife with the police or what they call the "repressive police apparatus." The simmering conflict did not cool

---

[94] T'allam 'Oum Facebook page, https://bit.ly/3ACPvM2
[95] *Iqaf Muswawwirin Sahafiyyin Athna'a Taswir Taharruk Mawatini li-Hamlat 'T'allam 'Oum,'* in *Alchourouk*, March 23, 2022.
[96] T'allam 'Oum Facebook page, May 13, 2022.
[97] T'allam 'Oum Facebook page, April 21, 2022 post.

with the socio-political avalanche that deposed Ben Ali. Police brutality, for them, has remained a stifling, stubborn fact of life in the years since the revolution, exemplified by the killing of Omar Laabidi. The "volunteers" waging this campaign reiterate dispositions of the "diverse" football fans whom they thank for support. They point to detractors who "demonize" or defame them, who cast suspicious aspersions over their sources of funding and their memberships. They seem eager to allay the fears of potential sympathizers, framing themselves as unpaid, voluntary soldiers of justice whose cause was born upon Laabidi's death. The declaration (*bayan*) deploys a specific usage for the term *hogra*. It refers to "the power/authority of repression and *hogra*" and its attempts to "bury justice" and distort the "purveyors of truth." By vilifying them and their campaign, the police, media, and power-holders are acting in character, they imply. For these ultras or ultras affiliates, *hogra* is embodied in police violence and related antics, including the rumor-mongering of police unions.

The T'allam 'Oum Facebook page disseminates collages of multi-lingual multimodal discourse. One example seems to have been designed by a "Fighters" ultras group, based on the coat of arms logo on the top right.[98] Large, jagged red and white letters demand in Spanish, "Liberta per GU Ultras": Freedom for Gabes Ultras, arrested for graffiti and inciting police. Political claims and demands are wrapped in mourning garb. The more delicate Arabic script at the bottom reads, "Our brother (*khuna*, in the Tunisian dialect) Omar inshallah in Heaven." Sanguine solidarity surpasses mere group membership. To the right is an angled image, as though displayed on a concrete wall, of a fan marker (Black and White Fighters Territory). Under it hangs a cartoon depicting a judge declaring in Tunisian Arabic, "Whoever killed Omar will face accountability." (No last name is necessary. All sympathizers are on intimate, first-name terms with Omar.) A presumably disgruntled police officer, spewing French into his speech bubble (the words difficult to make out in this digital artwork), sits to the judge's right. Below the image, in a jarring contrast a quadruplet of Arabic poetry is set:

> By God, injustice is fatal
> And the perpetrator remains the unjust "one"
> To the settler of debts we proceed on the day of religion [judgment]
> And before God, the rivals gather
> #God_bless_Omar

Below this rendering in Standard Modern Arabic proceeds a narrative in slang dialect. It tells the tale of the "child" Omar, an undeserving innocent killed by police and whose death was still pending investigation, let alone sentencing and punishment. Four years later, repression breeds more repression. Fans at a "match" (in Arabic letters), sang about the "freedom they wished to wrest" and prayed for "our brother Omar" (*khuna* Omar). "As usual" their words were read as provocations,

---

[98] T'allam 'Oum Facebook page, April 19, 2022 post.

prompting "force and barbarism (hitting, repression, [tear] gas)." Their only crime "singing for freedom," a few bore the brunt of police violence. Yet this *hogra* would not mute a determination to resist. The ultras' slogan interviewees mention is: "*almuqawamah mustamirrah*." In the same vein, "injustice will meet its downfall, if at a later time …" Here the Facebook admin and the indignant sports fan it claims to represent reiterate a zeal for fighting back. They reproduce acts of solidarity and refusal of authority against a long string of police abuse. Resistance in its various forms includes (peaceful) singing that may have sounded like taunts to the ears of police who in turn may have developed solidarity in their animosity with ultras. Police unions may be one frame for solidarity within the system. The hashtags in Arabic #resistance and #t'allam 'oum close the post.

One final note is in order. Significant in the *t'allam 'oum* discourse is a kind of conflation between violence against ultras and infractions against the disempowered Tunisians writ large. Stories of suffering create a bridge of kinship. One post[99] condemns recurring police "attacks" first in Tataouine, then in Sfax, on football fans blessing the dead memory of *khuna* Omar. How does the campaign portray "the people"? The cause of Omar Laabidi is "the cause of all Tunisian youth, the cause of an entire generation raised on confrontation and resistance." *Al-sha'b* seems to be the unfairly castigated youth. Divisions crop up along generational lines, but so does (presumed, or pleaded) solidarity. Again, the recurring theme of perpetual injustice, pre- and post-revolution: "the regime is the same for decades." They will not sit idly by, however: "the resistance continues, either us or you." Invoking Tunisian and Arabo-Islamic luminary Ibn Khaldun's views on "justice as the basis of building civilization (*'umran*)," they declare the same phrase carried in demonstration banners: #justice_or_chaos."[100] The ethos is one of non-submissiveness, of fighting back. It lends their discourse a derisive, almost menacing edge. Seemingly itching for a fight, these may not be simply peaceful chanters in the streets. The ultras' "provocation" resistance replicates itself online, speaking to the fellow downtrodden, struggling for peoplehood.

Conclusion

Organizing and mobilizing less explicitly for political ends than syndicalists, students, miners, or the unemployed, Tunisia's ultras nevertheless comprise a compelling and consequential protestscape. Its embodied, spatialized, and situated knowledge lend a very specific (and necessarily partial) vision of protest in the country. Diverse groups of football fans form bonds, construct identities, and practice resistance in overtly anti-systemic ways, including violence up to the time of writing.[101] With its "freeplay" of presence and absence, their protest spans more than

---

[99] *T' allam 'Oum* Facebook page, April 18, 2022 post.
[100] In November 2022, 12 officers were sentenced to two years in prison for Laabidi's murder. See *Fi Qadiyyat Muhibb Al-Ifriqi Omar Laabidi … 'Aman Sijnan li 12 Amniyyan*, in *Alchourouk*, November 4, 2022. Specifics of the appeal process were unclear at the time of writing.
[101] *A'mal 'Unf Wa Shaghab fi Rades wa Al-Amn Yukhli Al-Qa'ah Min Al-Jumhur* in *Business News Arabic*, May 11, 2022.

demonstrations. Yet localized riots and skirmishes in and around the stadium make ultras memorable, often disparaged, by the state[102] and sometimes in the public eye. Ultras began to hone their protest and resistance competencies years before the revolution, bringing a youthful, rebellious momentum to the *hirak* of 2011. It is significant that democratization has not cooled the intensities of embodied feelings. *Al-hakim*'s infringements still call for resistance in pursuit of peoplehood.

This chapter has shown how the ultras have, on their own terms, perfected the art of miming power via presence–absence. They disembody ("disincorporate the King," as it were) authoritarian power by dis-authorizing it, by acting and en-acting absence via escapades and exits from the seen, the sites and scenes of domination. They stage a kind of Foucauldian "other spaces"—for the counteraction, inversion, and contestation of authority. This freeplay of presence–absence is a tool of counter power, through which they efface authoritarianism from their spatiality and temporality. The stadiums are their own deterritorializing response to police brutality, in which they exit the regime's territory and enter an a-territory quivering with agentic, affective and cognitive self-presence. Within affect, they draw sensory boundaries of immateriality of time, space, and expression that the regime's police logics and orders (as per Rancière's formulation) are unable to subdue, much less grasp. The freeplay of presence–absence is a potent toolkit the ultras deploy as their own "Plato's Cave." They enact a game of shadows (Derrida's trace: smoke curtains and fireworks of the *dakhlah*, songs with their double meanings) that allegorizes their self-other cognition and ontological condition as belonging to "the part that has no part." Through this presence–absence split, they invert the "play" of power through the devotion to their own game, football. They sideline and 'absent' the state that sidelines them. It is a game in which they free body, emotion, and sense of self, and restrict the powers that be, committing them to an endless chase of shadows and allegories. These tell stories of defiance etched in the psyche of ultras, as individuals and embodiments of higher forms of reality, outside the game and the stadium.

The challenges of writing about this very distinctive protestscape jump out from every corner. We have tilted the analysis towards affect, both political and emotional. Affect's intensities tie us to the ultras as we respond to their words, their music, their choreographed spectacles. Have our affective registers matched up? We hope to have relayed the anger and the passion, the solidarity and the loyalty, and the politics in which they are draped and embedded. We have attempted to portray the cognitive and agentic, rebellious flaunting of identity and presence that rails against the "system" stacked against them, a rejection and *hogra* they in turn do not accept. We have gleaned these ideas, feelings, and practices from the multi-modal discourse and performances of the ultras. The ultras protestscape leaves a continual imprint on Tunisians' ongoing, active yearning for peoplehood. Ultras exhibit a spirit of revolt: the demotic agency, the resistance and protest competencies synchronically polished

---

[102] Even in Saied's so-called "new republic," the government conjures up methods to forestall stadium violence. See *Al-Lajnah al-Amniyyah Takshif 'An Abraz Mahawir Muqarabatiha fi Muqawamat al-'Unf*, in *Alchourouk*, September 29, 2022. Perhaps Europeans have crowd control answers. See *Anis Ben Meem, Mukafahat Zahirat Al- 'Unf fil Mala'ib*, in *Alchourouk*, September 24, 2022.

and fed into the diachrony of Tunisia's revolutionary élan. Moreover, ultras' inclinations towards confrontation complicate a linear march from protest and revolution to democracy. The support of at least some for Kais Saied and the July 25 "corrective" takeover disrupts a presumed transition from revolution and peoplehood into democratic participation and legitimation. We will return to this last theme in the concluding chapter.

References

Al-Haidari, Sghayyir. 2021. "Al-Turuq al-Sufiyyah fi Tunis Turassikh Nafsaha Mu'assasah Li al-Tadayyun al-Munfatih fi Muwajahat al-Fikr al-Mutatarrif" [Tunisian Sufist Trends Entrench Themselves as an Institution for Open-Minded Religiosity to Combat Extremist Thought], *Al-Arab*, September 2, https://bit.ly/3y4QxP4

Aljazeera. 2016. "Ultras Tunis…Kabus Yu'arriq Amn Al-Mala'ib" [Tunisian Ultras…Nightmare that Makes Stadium Security Sleepless], June 20, https://bit.ly/44tEQhP

Al-'Ush, Mehdi. 2021. "Tunis: Min Al-Dawlah Al-Boolisiyyah Ila Dawlat Al-Naqabat Al-Boolisiyyah?" [Tunisia: From a Police State to a "Police Union" State?] *Legal Agenda*, February 15, https://bit.ly/3PfVA4W

Assabeel. 2018. "Isabat 51 Shakhsan wa Tawqif 12 Mushajji'an fi Tunis" [51 People Injured and 12 Fans Arrested in Tunisia], October 24, https://bit.ly/3yhR7cE

Atmah, Ahmad. 2017. "Al-Ultras fi Tunis" [Ultras in Tunisia], *Aljazeera Blogs*, June 19, https://bit.ly/3Qxo8bE

Babnet. 2022. 'Ard Al-Hadrah li-l-Fadil Aljaziri…April 18, https://www.babnet.net/cadredetail-244767.asp

Ben Brik, Yasin, 2016. "Al-Sufiyyah fi Tunis … Raqam Bila Ma'na?" [Sufism in Tunisia … A Number without Meaning?] *UltraTunisia*, January 28, https://bit.ly/3O6KzCV

Ben Rajab, Sheyma. 2020. "Al-Iltizam wa Fakk al-Iltizam: Fi Kurrasat Al-Muntada 3" [Discipline and Undoing Discipline, In Forum Notebooks 3] Ed. Riyadh Ben Khalifa, FTDES, pp. 76–106, https://ftdes.net/ar/le-numero-3-des-cahiers-du-ftdes-des-engagements-2/

Ben Rajab, Sheyma. 2021. "Al-Riyadah Maidan Li al-Ihtijaj: Hina Takhruj al-Kurah Min al-Mal'ab Ila al-Shari" [Sport is a Protest Field: When Football Exits the Stadium into the Street], *Legal Agenda*, March 3, https://bit.ly/3OuJQeH

Ben Salah, Najla. 2022. "Isthilak al-Mukhaddarat: Hal Sayakhda' Kul Shabb Tunisi li Al-Tahlil Intilaqan Min Fivri Al-Qadim?" [Drug Consumption: Will All Tunisian Youth Be Subject to [Drug] Tests Beginning Next February?] *Nawaat*, January 20, https://bit.ly/3NKk0Cy

Bouyahya, Usama. 2019. "Majmu'at Al-Mushajji'in Wa Thaqafat al-Ultras: Majmu'at Al-Utras Fi Tunis Namuthajan" [Fan Groups and Ultras' Culture: The Example of Tunisia's Ultras Groups], *Afaq Fikriyyah* 5(10): 113–132.

Brunk, Samuel. 1995. *Emiliano Zapata: Revolution and Betrayal in Mexico*. Albuquerque: University of New Mexico Press.

Callahan, William A. 2021. *Sensible Politics: Visualizing International Relations*. Oxford: Oxford University Press.

Clancy-Smith, Julia A. 1997. *Rebel and Saint: Muslim Notables, Populist Protest, Colonial Encounters*. Oakland: University of California Press.

Daifallah, Mohamed. 2023. *Mawsu'at Al-Tarajji Al-Riyadi Al-Tunisi fi Mi'at 'Am (1919–2019)* [Encyclopedia of Tunisian Sports Tarajji in One Hundred Years (1919–2019)]. Tunis: Sotomedia.

Damaq, Ali. N.d.. *Al-Mawruth Al-Musiqi Al-Sha'bi Wa 'Alaqatuhu bi Al-Turuq Al-Sufiyyah fi Tunis Min Khilal Namoothaj Al-Thaqafah Al-Sha'biyyah* [Musical Folk Heritage and its Relationship to Tunisian Sufi Orders: An Example], Issue 38.

Derrida, Jacques. 1978. *Writing and Difference*. Chicago: University of Chicago Press.

Doidge, Mark and Martin Lieser. 2018. "The Importance of Research on Ultras: Introduction." *Sport in Society* 21(6): 833–840.

Doidge, Mark, Radoslaw Kossakowski and Svenja Mintert. 2020. *Ultras: The Passion and Performance of Contemporary Football Fandom*. Manchester: Manchester University Press.

Enloe, Cynthia. 1993. *The Morning After: Sexual Politics at the End of the Cold War*. Berkeley: University of California Press.

Esperanza News. 2014. *Video Hasri Yuwaddih Ahdath 8 April 2010* [Exclusive Video Shows the Events of April 8, 2010]. https://www.youtube.com/watch?v=7SDqmOdpWAE

Forgas, Joseph P. ed. 2001. *Feeling and Thinking: The Role of Affect in Social Cognition*. Cambridge: Cambridge University Press.

Frosdick, Steve and Peter Marsh. 2005. *Football Hooliganism*. London: Willan.

Haraway, Donna. 1988. "Situated Knowledges: The Science Question in Feminism and the Privilege of Partial Perspective." *Feminist Studies* 14(3):575–599.

Hazgui, Haikel. 2018. *"Kurat Al-Qadam Al-Tunisiyyah: Al-Shuhnah Al-Siyasiyyah Wa Inhiyar 'Al-Shaqaf'"* [Tunisian Football: Political Tension…] Nawaat, June 29, https://bit.ly/3nbMfPZ

Hill, Evan, Ainara Tiefenthäler, Christiaan Triebert, Drew Jordan, Haley Willis, and Robin Stein. 2020. "How George Floyd Was Killed in Police Custody." *The New York Times*, https://www.nytimes.com/2020/05/31/us/george-floyd-investigation.html

Honwana, Alcinda Manuel. 2019. "Youth Struggles: From the Arab Spring to Black Lives Matter & Beyond." *African Studies Review* 62(1): 8–21.

Jakimow, Tanya and Yumasdaleni. 2016. "Affective Registers in Qualitative Team Research: Interpreting the Self in Encounters with the State." *Qualitative Research Journal* 16(2): https://doi.org/10.1108/QRJ-04-2015-0026

Joseph, Peniel E. 2009. "The Black Power Movement: A State of the Field." *The Journal of American History* 96(3): 751–776.

Karshaoui, Nazih. 2021. *Ba'da Ahdath Mal'ab Rades*: "'Unf Al-Mala'ib Safhah Sawda' fi al-Kurah al-Tunisiyyah," Winwin, June 8, http://bit.ly/3hEEHFE

Kossakowski, Radoslaw. 2021. *Hooligans, Ultras, Activists: Polish Football Fandom in Sociological Perspective*. Cham: Palgrave Macmillan and Springer.

Kristeva, Julia. 2014. "New Forms of Revolt." *Journal of French and Francophone Philosophy*. XXII(2): 1–19.

Laabidi, Asmaa. 2018. *#T'allam_'Oum: Sarkhat Tunisiyyin Didda Zulm Al-Bolis*. April 12, *OpenDemocracy*, https://www.opendemocracy.net/ar/tunisia-police-violence-campaign/

Lahoual, Mohamed. 2009. *Al-Zawaya Wa Al-Turuq Al-Sufiyyah Bi Al-Bilad Al-Tunisiyyah Mantiqat Douz 'Ayyinah, Al-Thaqafah Al-Sha'biyyah* [Sufi Shrines and Trends in Tunisia: The Example of the Douz Region] (4): 52–69, https://bit.ly/3HBoYQA

Leaders Arabic. 2018. *Min Taqalid Al-Inshad Al-Dini Wal Hadrah Al-Sufiyyah Al-Tunisiyyah*, May 16, https://bit.ly/3beW3G4

McKerrell, Simon and Lyndon C.S. Way. 2017. "Understanding Music as Multimodal Discourse." In *Music as Multimodal Discourse: Semiotics, Power and Protest*, edited by Lyndon C.S. Way and Simon McKerrell. London: Bloomsbury Academic, 1–20.

Meyer, Morgan and Kate Woodthorpe. 2008. "The Material Presence of Absence: A Dialogue Between Museums and Cemeteries." *Sociological Research Online* 13(5): 127–135. https://doi.org/10.5153/sro.1780

Mosaique FM. 2017. *Man' Dukhul Man Hum Aqall Min 18 Sanah Al-Mala'ib: Ila Mata?* March 9, https://bit.ly/3NAYq3k

Mosaique FM. 2019. *Ya Hyatina: Ughniyah Jadidah Li-Virage Al-Ifriqi La Tatahaddath 'An Al-Kurah (Video)*, [Our Life … A New Stadium Song that Does Not Discuss Football] December 24, https://bit.ly/3RgOcbC

Mosaique FM. 2022. *Hamlat T'allam 'Oum: Ila Mata Yaflat Al-Amniyyun min al-'Iqab?* ["Learn to Swim" Campaign: Police Immunity Until When?] March 29, https://bit.ly/3aoAEKp

Nawaat. 2022. *Nawaat fi Daqiqah: Rasa'il Al-Ultras Al-Mushaffarah* [Nawaat in a Minute: Ultras' Coded Messages] June 24, https://bit.ly/3yL02Dy

Nessma TV. 2018. *Ba'idan 'An Al-Intima'at Al-Dayyiqah: Al-Jamahir Al-Riyadiyyah Tata'ataf Ma' Ahibba' Al-Tarajji* [Far from Narrow Memberships: Sports Audiences Sympathize with Tarajji Fans], January 13, https://bit.ly/3AqzqJf

Nussbaum, Martha. 2001. *Upheavals of Thought: The Intelligence of Emotions*. Cambridge: Cambridge University Press.

Passerini, Luisa. 1996. *Autobiography of a Generation: Italy, 1968*, Trans. Lisa Erdberg. Middletown, CT: Wesleyan University Press.

Qarrah, Fatima. 2012. *Mawqif Al-Turuq Al-Sufiyyah Al-Tunisiyyah Min Al-Himayah Al-Faransiyyah1881–1939 (Al-Tariqah Al-Qadiriyyah Wal Tijaniyyah)* [Tunisian Sufi Turuq and the French Protectorate], Masters Thesis, University of Algeria, see: https://bit.ly/3tMM1Cm2

Qasem, Rawah. 2022. *Intishar Al-Mukhaddirat fi Tunis: Zahirah Tu'riq Al-Mujtama' fi Intizar Al-Hulul Al-Najihah*, *Al-Quds Al-Arabi*, April 9, https://bit.ly/3nBi6JM

Radio Med. 2020. *Harqah Jam'iyyah min Al-Shabbah Ila Italya* [Group Harqah from Chebba to Italy], November 12, youtube.com/watch?v=Kl_vCO37cSI

Rancière, Jacques. 1999. *Disagreement: Politics & Philosophy.* Minneapolis: University of Minnesota Press.

Rancière, Jacques. 2004. *The Politics of Aesthetics: The Distribution of the Sensible.* London: Continuum.

Sadiki, Larbi and Layla Saleh. 2021. "Playing Ball: Crowd and 'Contre-Crowd' in the Politics of Egyptian and Tunisian Football." In *Routledge Handbook of Sport in Asia*, edited by Fan Hong and Dr. Zhouxiang Lu. London: Routledge, 473–490.

Sans Gants. 2022. *Shahid Dakhlat Umar Laabidi Wa Junun Jamahir Al-Ifriqi fi Mubarat Al-Ittihad Al-Manastiri* [Watch the Omar Laabidi Dakhlah and the Africain fans go Wild in the Monastir Game], June 17, https://www.youtube.com/watch?v=HuA9yHZmMiw

Scalia, Vincenzo. 2009. "Just a Few Rogues? Football Ultras, Clubs and Politics in Contemporary Italy." *International Review for the Sociology of Sport* 44(1): 41–53.

T'allam 'Oum [Learn to Swim] Facebook Page. 2022. https://www.facebook.com/%D8%AA%D8%B9%D9%84%D9%85

Tunigate. 2022. *Baina Al-Amn Wa Al-Jamahir fi Tunis ... Qissat Sira' Ta'ud Ila Al-Mala'ib* [Between Police and Audiences in Tunisia ... The Story of Conflict Returns to the Stadium], April 12, https://bit.ly/3GoPGO0

Ultra Filastine. 2018. *Ghadab fin Tunis Ba'da Ilgha' Mubarat Wadi Al-Nais Ma' Al-Tarajji* [Anger in Tunisia after Cancellation of the Wadi Nais Game with Tarajji], January 15, https://bit.ly/3OIgvOd

Ultras-Tifo. 2018. "Youths Make Tifo for Their High School." December 23, https://www.ultras-tifo.net/photo-news/5563-youths-make-tifo-for-ther-high-school.html

Ultras-Tifo. 2021. "Es Tunis-Al Ahly 19.06.2021." June 22, https://www.ultras-tifo.net/photo-news/6456-es-tunis-al-ahly-19-06-2021.html

Umairah, 'A'id. 2020. *Tawa'ada Bibast Sultat Al-Qanun: Hal Yaqdir Al-Mechichi 'Ala Waqf Ihtijajat Tunis?* Noonpost, December 3, https://www.noonpost.com/content/39097

Watad, Mohamed. 2020. *20 Musallahan wa 8 Rasasat fi Khams Daqa'iq Lightiyal Abu Jihad ... Kitab Isra'ili Yakshif Kawalis Al-Ightiyalat Al-Isra'iliyyah* [20 Armed Men and 8 Bullets in 5 Minutes...], Aljazeera, June 26, https://bit.ly/3urmlvz

Way, Lyndon C. S. 2017. "Authenticity and Subversion: Articulations in Protest Music Videos' Struggle with Countercultural Politics and Authenticity." In *Music as Multimodal Discourse: Semiotics, Power, and Protest*, edited by Lyndon C.S. Way and Simon McKerrell. London: Bloomsbury, 95–117.

Zaghdoudi, Malek. 2020. *Al-Ultras fi Tunis: Sarkhah Azaliyyah fi Wajh Al-Systam* [Ultras in Tunisia: Eternal Cry in the Face of the System], *Al-Katibah*, September 17, https://bit.ly/3xQ373C

Zapatista Esperanza 2007/ Page Officielle. 2022. https://www.facebook.com/zapa.2007

Zitoun, Lotfi. 2010. *Tunis...Wa Al-Hariq Al-Qadim* [Tunisia...and the Coming Fire]. Al-Hiwar.net, https://www.turess.com/alhiwar/5842

9
Conclusion

Taming the Revolution?

Ali Belhouane's Tunisia in Revolt locates revolution in precolonial and colonial histories of lives, sacrifices, emotions, and thought. Collectively, they challenge the prevailing orders and logics of domination. By ontologizing struggles for a free Tunisia, Belhouane adds to the toolkit of social scientists. He deftly switches spatial, temporal, and intellectual registers as if writing his own protestscapes. He moves between canonical events, actors, emotions, imaginaries, and speech acts. His words depict the will to strike back at the colons, despite a wave of repression in the 1940s. Protestors had marched in the famed April 1938 demonstration to reject the colonizers' shrinking of local sovereignty and to call for the creation of a Tunisian parliament. A strike took place that crippled all activity in the Beylicate. It was in response to "a call by the [Neo-Destour] politburo" (Belhouane 1954, 49). More than one million Tunisians took part. "This is a huge number in a country of no more than three million people" (1954, 49). Belhouane captures the sensory experiences of revolution in the courage to face bullets. "As the striking workers in the Sfax train station maintained their picket line, armed forces attacked them in the early morning, without prior warning. They unleashed upon them a barrage of bullets; the workers rushed from everywhere to the battlefield and they waged battle shorn of their weapons, storming the tanks, and capturing from them the machine guns." Noting their steadfastness, he adds, "Th[e workers] did not retreat until soldiers outnumbered them from all sides. Thirty-three died as martyrs, and one hundred fifty were injured" (1954, 81). Nothing describes the agony of exile, like the colonizer banishing the colonized overseas. Belhouane personally experienced along with Bourguiba the ignominy of revolutionists' imprisonment for six months in the dark and humid dungeons of Marseille's Saint-Nicolas Fort in May 1940 (1954, 54). He was in awe of the epic struggle of the people despite the ferocity of colonial violence. Habib Thamer's role in bolstering defiance, with the fellaga's armed resistance (1954, 51), reflected the resolve of a people "thirsty for freedom" (1954, 41), steadfast in its "self-presence" and "ethos of sacrifice" (1954, 62).

Tunisia in Revolt

The years 1864, 1896, 1907, 1911, 1924, 1938, 1954 all mark some examples of salient dates in Tunisia's annals of socio-political history and resistance. These synchronies demarcate spatialities of resistance and punctuate temporalities that offer to forecast the future victory of a subjugated people and revolutionary moments. Just as the Beylicate quivered at Ali Ben Ghedhahem's cry for justice in 1864, so did the French colons at the Khalduniyya group (1896) and the Young Tunisians (1907), both of which quickly rose to embody emancipatory activism advocating greater Tunisian political, civil, cultural, and intellectual rights. In 1924 Mohamed Ali launched Tunisia's syndicalism, 100 years ago. He dreamed of equal pay, self-presence, and justice for dockworkers and miners, among others, whose conditions were a living hell. His work and that of others after him represented an emancipatory activity whose spirit was to rule over the agentic, affective, and cognitive energies that defied ignorance, colonialism, and poverty and sought to determine the face of freedom in Tunisia. Ali Belhouane's (1909–58) book, indicated in the vignette above, is a quintessential example of a historiography that ontologizes "Tunisia in revolt" (*Tunis Al-Tha'irah*). Belhouane writes a rousing defense of revolution qua war of liberation against the French colonizers, celebrating a phalanx of nationalist revolutionaries from across the intellectual and socio-political spectrum. From the "Fundamental Pact" of 1857 (precursor of Tunisia's 1861 constitution) to Khayr al-Din's (Ahmed Bey's Grand Vizier, 1873–77) reforms, Belhouane finds "traces" of rebirth aplenty. The genealogy of rebirth is embedded in traditions of sacrifice, protest, and resistance by singularities and collectivities. Belhouane refuses to allow endless names of freedom fighters and leaders to fade into oblivion. Equally, he celebrates unsung heroes: Ali Bach Hamba (d. 1918), founder of Young Tunisians (Belhouane 1954, 40); Abdelaziz Thaalbi (d. 1944), co-founder of the Destour Party(1954, 42–43); Mohamed Snoussi (d. 1900), vociferous objector against colonialism (1954, 40); Bourguiba's founding in 1932 of his newspaper "Al-'Amal Al-Tunisi" (1954, 45); and Mohamed Ali, the father of Tunisia's trade union movement in 1924 (1954, 80). Belhouane finds revolution, zooming in on the Jallaz uprising (1911). The compelling references to these revolutionaries and emancipatory ethos of Tunisia's eventual independence in 1956, a revolution by any standards, demonstrate how knowledge, affect, and defiance in the face of colonial subjugation formed part of the inventory of struggle. Never did such cataclysmic events, within a protracted time-span across 160 years, determine the fate of a colony (1956) and an authoritarian postcolony (2011). If they all belong to the province of revolution, it is thanks to the magnitude of unforeseen and contrived forces, voices, precepts, concepts and emotions that intersect to project moral power into the quest for peoplehood, freedom, and dignity.

The revolutionary drama unfurls via uprisings of words, worlds, being, speaking, and thinking. Our protestscape formulation problematizes the profiling, mapping, and parsing of Tunisia's revolution. It gestures to an "inter-protest"—synchronies, as it were, interwoven temporally by uprisings over a period of a century. Revolution, no matter how fleeting, is transversal. As a disappearing diachrony, it erupts only through a chain of links of spatialites and temporalities populated by embodied experiences of knowing, learning, living, acting, and feeling resistance. The idea of revolution as a wave of protests steeped in such histories, stacked with more than a hundred years of grassroots' struggles, brands of affect, and cognition, each coded by the meanings, significations, imaginaries, kinship, toil, battles, and sacrifices across time and space, rejects revolution as autonomous. Luminaries who have studied revolution before us, the likes of Moore, Skocpol, and Tilly, aver (each in their own way) its entanglement in economic structures, state arrangements, or power dynamics.

Demos and Rebirth in Protestscapes

Tunisia's 2011 "revolution" remains misconstrued. It defies neat interpretation, construction, and deconstruction. Writing it in this book has meant assigning agency to protest and protestscapes. By studying revolution through spatiotemporal, situated, and relational lenses and through context-specific formulations, the book addresses questions about imaginings of peoplehood. The dissentscapes re-ontologize Tunisian revolutionaries across spatial and temporal sites of resistance and struggle. While this innovative approach is deployed for the sake of a "panoptic" account, the resignification of revolution in this way, over a long timespan, attempted by focusing the analysis on agency, affect, and cognition, yields only a "partial" reading—in line with Haraway's "situated knowledges."

Epistemologically, a rebelscape is a kaleidoscope revealing the active, performative, creative, discursive, affective, and cognitive layers that dynamically construct and reconstruct situated protest. It speaks to the question of how to know revolution. The methods of knowing revolution are multiple. Within this book, "protestscape" is one medium for unlocking revolution's historically dynamic ontogeny in Tunisia. It is challenging to assume that revolution is not a problematic formulation with a single lifeline. It is not "whole" and complete in itself. It is even more audacious to attempt to study revolution wholly. If revolution is an assemblage, protestscapes allow for situating protest in a single locale at a fixed point of time. It is an exercise of quasi-aggregation of revolution into its constitutive sites of action-emotion-thought, across time and space, to understand how they commonly build-up revolutionary momentum. In protestscapes, Tunisia's revolution is not a sudden twister of polity, society, economy, culture, or history. It has hundred-year-old roots in all of them. In this book, revolution is considered within long time scales. Protestscapes bring to life, synchronically and diachronically, the effervescence of struggles that have since 1864 sought to subvert pre-colonial, colonial, and postcolonial hierarchies.

Situated protest, thus, interrogates the cliché of protest and revolution being whole and ahistorical. In it, the reshaping of becoming and being travels through those who resist as knowing subjects whose action, emotion, and cognition are imbricated with past and present struggles that make revolution: deterritorialization and reterritorialization. Syndicalists, students, miners, marginalized men and women, all tried to sow the seeds of resistance and renewal, socially, politically, and culturally. In tandem, situated protest opens onto struggles bent on deterritorializing the "Bourguibist complex" with its supportive normative, affective, and cognitive structures that have combined to reproduce authoritarianism (Ayari 2017). (De/re)territorialization processes are not devoid of thought and of norms.

Tunisia's January 14, 2011 is such an example. Prior protest competencies, learning, knowing, and knowers all collapse into a moment of revolution. Many a January of revolt passed before the one of January 2011. On January 13, 1952 pupils and students protested in Le Cap Bon, Bizerte and Menzel Bourguiba, then across the entire country in the protests of January 26, 1978, January 3, 1984, and of January 14, 2011. Therein dissolve learned and inherited knowing, social doing, and social doers. Moreover, situated protest is made up of knowledge publics. Daifallah records the numerous publications, for example, created by student struggles representing pan-Arabists, leftists, and Destourians: *Ibn Khaldun* (1957), *Jeunesse* (1959), *Al-Ittihad* (1961), *Al-Talib Al-Destouri* (1962), and *Perspectives* (1963) (Daifallah 2016, 166). He notes that "the students of the new left launched in October 1963 the publication, *Perspectives*, which will have a huge impact on the future of the Tunisian political landscape" (Daifallah 2016, 167). Amongst its leaders were Aziz Krichen (future advisor to President Moncef Marzouki), Noureddine Ben Khedher (d. 2005) and Mohamed Mahfouz.[1] Many of the voices and leaders who populated the public squares of revolution, ranging from the Bourguiba Boulevard to Kasbah 1 and 2, were schooled in one situated protest or another across a century of defiant struggles for freedom and dignity.

Convergence of Theories

Grappling with this hundred-year pedigree, writing revolution in a postcolonial context cannot be anything other than a diffuse enterprise. It syncretizes diverse knowledge practices. It engages postcolonial, critical, and feminist theories. It converses with "metropolitan revolution," identified here as the Euro-American corpus on the subject. Postcolonialism is akin to a critical theory of the "subalterns," as they struggle to have a voice and write back the nature of the encounter with the ex-colonizers. That is, it records how the ex-colonized still struggle to decolonize sociality (language, mind, culture, identity, knowledge) and materiality (power relations, economic structures reproducing domination). Departing from Tunisia, our analysis interprets 1956, independence, as a "counterrevolution," adapted from Marcuse. In the spirit of Adorno and Horkheimer's *Dialectic Enlightenment*'s disillusionment with the irrationality of "rational" modernity, and

---

[1] Noureddine Ben Khedher's father was himself a victim of the enmity between Bourguiba and his rival Salah Ben Youssef (assassinated in Germany in 1958). He hails from the town where Mohamed Al-Hammi, the syndicalist leader, was born. Ben Khedher along with leftists such as Ahmed Smaoui, Khemaïs Chammary, and Mohamed Charfi, etc., in 1963 in Paris who created the movement *Afaq* or Perspectives. As Chapter 4 recounted, the movement shaped the nature of student protest and struggles well into the 1970s–1980s.

late capitalism's "barbarism," as evidenced by the "human condition" under fascism, we pinpoint parallel hierarchical orders of authoritarianism in a postcolonial non-Western society. An "instrumental" rationality, as it were, geared towards the domination of humans and their nature. The type of "one track mind," Adorno and Horkheimer mention, is intent on amassing power. The resulting domination, they critique, is not unlike socio-political processes that subdue and exclude, including coercively, thus routinizing authoritarian politics in decolonizing societies as standards of a new normativity. Feminist knowledge making de-authorizes silences on and the omission of women, refashioning epistemologies into knowing that enables speaking back. It reconfigures knowing and knower through attention to issues of epistemic in/justice, positionality, and situated and embodied knowledge. Epistemically, our analysis advances in appreciation of the convergence of these theories around emancipatory possibilities and becomings, partial knowledge that does not avail outside context, history, language, or power structures and relations.

It is appropriate here to briefly reiterate the distinctiveness of our analytical approach to Tunisian revolution. We draw on the fine body of knowledge of "metropolitan revolution" (Chapter 1). This critical, dialogic engagement does not exclusively favor any one particular structure (Barrington Moore, Theda Skocpol) individualized, behaviorist-type agency (Gurr), contestation over state power (Tilly 1978), nor the rationalist-turned-relational advances of social movement theory and contentious politics (McAdam et al. 2009). These largely Euro-Centric theories that neglect most of the Arab setting, even in their Third World variants, fit awkwardly against the postcolonial, dependent, Arabo-Islamic Tunisian context. No universality or objectivity in knowledge-making stands the test of diversity, as in situated protests globally. The centrality of metropolitan revolution's tenets and approaches, then, prompts a creative accounting for protests within a postcolony, through a localized lens leaning towards a decolonizing knowledge practice (Wa Thiong'o 1986; Smith 1999). Whilst in terms of positionality, we are integrated in the ways of Anglo-American epistemologies and methodologies, we have attempted to optimize local inputs and representations. Due attention to life stories and memory, to oral history and testimonies centers indigeneity within an overall research orientation that is dialogic and interdisciplinary. In addressing issues of social justice in the contest of histories of protest, our analytical trajectory seeks to de-totalize the identities, ideologies, and verities of coloniality in the practices of power (authoritarian, and/or neocolonial), knowledge (Eurocentric or neocolonial), and hegemony (with subaltern logics). It is no longer sufficient to echo the poignancy of Spivak's question: "Can the Subaltern Speak?" What is integral to the critical and creative take followed in this book is arriving at further questions that scream for attention. Can the indignant rebel? Can "the part that has no part" have a part? Can the "uncounted" be counted? Can the missing come to hand? Can "the unfound people" be situated? Weaving these questions' underlying messages of people's indigence, absence, and silence necessitates not only Kristeva's intertextuality, but also multimodal textuality. These questions hint at methodologies, and also genres of problems in the lifeworld that work syntagmatically, so to speak. The momentum of memory and social imaginaries (*mikhyal*), the accumulation of resistance practices and competencies (*makhzun*), dives deeper than time-bound, linear, neat accounts of social movement theory analyses that may take 2011 as a starting-point.

From Post-colony to Post-Structure

By situating protest as a core dynamic of change in Tunisia, our approach does not derogate from appreciating the full gamut of the complexities involved. It implicates sociality and materiality of resistance, recognizing them as interlocking (Kirby 2017). The analysis has largely leaned towards the discursive. Social imaginaries, speech acts, language, and ideology all provide evidence for interpreting the recurrence of protest within the book's six (partial) protestscapes. They are vivid cases, demonstrting situated knowledge at work. Disassembled, multiple dissentscapes showcase their utility in affirming Haraway's situated knowledge. The "knowing self... [is] partial in all its guises, never finished, whole" (Haraway 1988, 586). The reductive parts do not diminish how protest, as *hirak*—self-regenerating and self-determining motion—is irreducibly multiple and unstable. Each describes how protest touches central nerves in an agentic, affective, and cognitive sense. Situated knowledge allows interpretation within and across the co-experiences of motion-emotion-thought. The combination of these protestscapes facilitates a firmer grip over revolutionary becoming. A diachronic collapse of experiences (synchronies/spatialities), fusing separate segments of protest, facilitates a critical reading of revolution—as in Tunisia, January 14, 2011.

Protest politics of resistance, in mines, university campuses, or stadiums, is not only about the carving of "freed space," but also about the non-carved space of authoritarian domination that the state monopolizes through a variety of tools, including the ideational (read propaganda) and the political (including coercion). Here we have invoked Rancière's dissensus, bringing to the fore a presence–absence duality: "the counted" and "the uncounted." As the book suggests, the Bourguibist endeavor (also taken up by Ben Ali) to routinize consensus was reproduced via an exclusionary power equation that relegated the uncounted to the margins of politics, and whence the people honed the skills to resist, to rise up in revolution.

Embodied Knowledge and Dis-Embodied People

The interpretations we present in this book have sought to highlight the rebellious content of the struggles, lives, temporalities, spatialities, imaginaries, intellectual repository, forces, and voices behind the 2011 revolution. It is one example of an Arab revolution aiming at its core for the emancipation of shackled lives—from the multiple oppressions of histories, geographies, modernities, ideologies, personalities, personal cults, and structures of power. Through rebelscapes, an analysis of the vicissitudes of socio-political existence across a 160-year time-span has allowed us to depict a multilayered "panorama" of key material and immaterial drivers of protest, noting the contexts in which they arise. The book has recorded the dynamism of thought and practice, and attendant meaning-making and becoming of peoplehood. The analysis similarly embedded in a normative agenda that favors a notion of epistemic in/justice. Scholarly discussion and conversation within our protestscapes valorize a condition of moral engagement. Our approach opens up a vista for a thorough grasp of the human person's summoning of memory, agency, affect, and cognition on the path to emancipation—the quest to empty all centers of oppressive power. In this vein, the discussion reveals the insurrectionary spirit in its tenacity to de-totalize the foundations of authoritarian nation- and state-building. The "uncounted" of Tunisia across time and space build and harbor revolutionary desires and aspirations. These desires are matched by a dogged determination to sacrifice self and freedom in a long and arduous journey to prevail over successive orders of authoritarian stasis, causing exclusion. As the late Ahmed Ben Salah noted in an interview, "Leaders of the post-independence period thought they could forever delay the explosion Tunisians witnessed many times from the early 1960s."[2] His remarks ring true in light of the marginalization and exclusion that have precipitated the kind of counter-politics, counter-imaginaries, and counter-values of the authoritarian postcolonial order within which the January 14 revolution was incubated.

Revolutionary Becomings

Bringing revolution into dialogue with Deleuze's becomings, our book has also made use of deterritorialization and reterritorialization. Nothing captures revolution more than the idea of seepage, escape and flows of (socio-political) subjectivities, bodies (agentic, affective, cognitive, or corporeal) between and within a-territory and territory of fluidity. Revolutions are political and take place in social contexts—and in territories crowded not just with power, but also with the desire to defy power, escape it, transform it, emancipate it, and be emancipated by it. Tunisia's revolution is animated by a quest, a will and desire for becoming, to enter the realm of the "visible," "sayable," and "audible," to paraphrase Rancière. Thus, protestscapes have attempted to re-ontologize the journey to draw lines of escape, as it were, from rigid, single, fixed, and domineering socio-political fields of social doing—protest—that best capture the crux of revolution. Through Deleuze's concepts, our book tells one story of peoplehood in diverse spatialities and temporalities fighting the fight of becoming, via countless *demoi* and *logoi*, that is, resisting permanent institutional and structural erasure and miscounting as "non-people," "missing people," or "the part that has no part." Creatively, Deleuze's questions about the becoming in art strike a strong

[2] Interview, 12 February 2011, Tunis.

chord about revolutions—in our case, Tunisia's revolution, its potential and limits *qua* liberation and transformation.

As in the becoming of art, Deleuze and Guattari reflect on the making of revolutions. They pose a question about the potential of art revolutions to "survive their victory" (Deleuze 1994, 177). Their answers befit the interplay of synchrony and diachrony proposed in the book: they reject teleology. Becoming is ceaseless. Thus, an ontology of becoming permeates this book. First, they note that "the success of revolutions resides only in itself, in the ... openings it [gives] to men and women at the moment of its making and that composes in itself a monument that is always in the process of becoming ..." (Deleuze and Guattari 1994, 177). Second, they add: "The victory of a revolution is immanent and consists in the new bonds it installs between people, even if these bonds last no longer than the revolution's fused material and quickly give way to divisions and betrayal" (Deleuze and Guattari 1994, 177).

Taming the Revolution

Complicating such becoming are the aforementioned divisions and betrayal that seem to constantly chase revolution, seeking to tame if not abort it. Our excursion into Tunisia's revolution has attended to the nationalist counterrevolution (à la Marcuse), set in motion by the always present, even when absent, first President. How did a revolutionary change into the country's supreme counterrevolutionary? Bourguiba emblematizes the postcolonial condition, its im/possibilities and contradictions. Tunisian, North African, Francophile, Arab, and Muslim, an avid secularist modernizer and a dictator, by any standards. The much famed and celebrated June 1, 1955, a national day in the Tunisian calendar, the day of Bourguiba's heroic return from exile, remains etched in national memory. Bourguiba disembarked in La Goulette; he waved a white handkerchief at tens of thousands of Tunisians cheering him. Crowds gathered as he sat astride a white horse. Tahar Belkhodja, one of Bourguiba's ministers in the 1970s–1980s, was among the crowd. He reflected on that picture-perfect portrait of the return of Tunisia's prodigal son and future first president after independence. "We were in the hundreds of thousands atop [human] waves of cheers, in a frenzy of ecstasy. Then Bourguiba mounted a horse and made his way through the crowds. He had planned his return very meticulously. Edgar Faure, [the French] Prime Minister, had organized, during the negotiations [for independence] in Paris, horse riding classes [for Bourguiba]" (Belkhodja 1999, 3). How can one disentangle the colonial from the de-colonial? Bourguiba's anti-colonialist consciousness did not prevent him from accepting the colonizers' aid to stage and presage a postcolonial moment, in 1955, less than one year before full independence! It is within the crevices of these performative acts that sub-texts of neo-colonialism and counterrevolution lurk. Taming the revolution, independence, seemed already under way.

However, protest opens up spatialities of resistance steeped in historicity, enabling demotic self-presence, self-determination, and self-understanding. Tunisia's politics and history effuse rebellion. The "missing people" behind rebellion cannot be forever absent. Mohamed Ali Al-Hammi, Ali Belhouane, Bechira ben Mrad (Tawil 2021, 117–124), Farhat Hached, Salah Ben Youssef, Habib Achour, Noureddine Ben Khedher, Radia Nasraoui, Zakia Difaoui, Lina Ben Mhenni, Ajmi Lourimi, and Mohamed Bouazizi are all protestors. In different contexts, they generate environments of meaning-making with agentic, affective, and cognitive implications for rethinking the human condition in Tunisia, across different spatialities and temporalities. Protest is a kind of language of political struggle, a medium of social doing, ruly and unruly, as well as a method to talk about social change. Yet in Tunisia's remarkable history of social doing, deliberative politics via "discussion circles" and mural newspapers by students were criminalized. So were whole movements, the leftist Perspective, and meeting of the union of students in 1971, the famous Korba Congress (Al-Tamimi 2008). In 1956 Bourguiba, the protestor of yesteryear, was the leader of an independent Tunisia. Belkhodja, a Secretary-General of the union in 1957–59, explained the change of heart. The students' recalcitrance and protests did not fit with Bourguiba's new predilection for consensual politics under his leadership (Bouguerra 2015). The building used by the students as headquarters was reclaimed by the state (Belkhodja 1999, 7). Furthermore, soon after independence, in a Tunis meeting with students Bourguiba reminded them all of his own struggle as a student in France. Yet, Belkhodja adds, Bourguiba, in the same breath, "sought to coopt our student body and win its loyalty" (1999, 8).

Dictator's Learning Curve

Whether by students or other protestors, learning (e.g. through protest competencies) is a consistent thread running through the book's protestscapes. As we close, the revolution–counterrevolution dynamic propels us to reflect how dictators, too, recruit and draw on knowledge publics and elites. Thus, Bourguiba managed to stay in power for 18 years after Ahmed Ben Salah's "cooperativization" debacle of 1969. The convergence of dictator and intellect, though intended to ease the excesses of coercive and ideological control, never challenged the mythologizing of Bourguiba. The distortions this causes to the collective repository of knowledge (*makhzun*) are huge. But huge, too, are the sophistication of protest competencies, which included an epistemic determination to resist with speech acts, writing back, publications, etc. Under Bourguiba and Ben Ali, coercion targeted publications, mural newspapers, orators, recordings of speeches, and union newsletters and pamphlets. However, cognitively, awareness begets more resistance, which, in its turn, breeds norms of defiance, sacrifice, and solidarity.

Bourguiba counted amongst his ministers some of the luminaries of knowledge-making in Tunisia. Mahmoud El Messadi (d. 2004), Tunisia's top novelist,[3] and

---

[3] Mahmoud El Messadi was among the nationalist generation that resisted colonialism. Sadiki College and Sorbonne-educated, he served as Minister for Education (1958–68) and then Culture (1973–76),

Mohamed Mzali (d. 2010) illustrate the point.[4] Mohamed Charfi (d. 2008) served under President Zinelabedine Ben Ali. He was a leader in the Union Générale des Étudiants Tunisiens (UGET) and in the leftist movement, *Afaq*, in the 1960s and 1970s, later jailed. He was among the intellectuals who co-founded the Ligue Tunisienne des Droits de l'Homme (LTDH) in 1976.[5] These literati lacked neither intelligence nor a record of their own activism, anti-colonial and in the postcolonial period, within unions, the student movement, etc. Mzali's testimony in his work titled *Un Premier Ministre de Bourguiba Témoigne* (A Prime Minister of Bourguiba Attests, 2010) claims he was a made a scapegoat for Bourguiba's decision to raise the price of bread (Mzali 2010, 287–309). More important, is the top-down staging of democracy, namely, after Bourguiba's approval to hold multiparty elections in 1981. Mzali recounts his liberalizing moment. "Along with my liberal colleagues, I decided to hold free and democratic elections to replace the [National] Assembly voted after the January 1978 events. ... The poll was fixed to take place on the 1st of November 1981, and the electoral campaign between 18–29 October" (Mzali 2010, 267). Mzali, not insincerely, celebrated this political feat, which he realized against all odds. He recounts how TV screens flashed with the faces of infamous opposition figures, including the heavyweights: Ahmed Mestiri, Mohamed Harmel, and Mohamed Bel Hadj Amor, etc. (Mzali 2010, 267). Mzali, in this memoir, gives vent to his frustration at the incessant meddling to fix the electoral lists. "Bourguiba, for example, imposed, Habib Ben Ammar, brother-in-law of Wassila [the First Lady] for the Tunis [electoral] list. The first Lady, also, wanted Hassib Ben Ammar,[6] activist and director of an independent newspaper of the opposition, *Al Ra'i*" (Mzali 2010, 268).

The 1981 elections are a critical example of voices aspiring for emancipation that did not die despite Bourguiba's counterrevolution. Two clashing orders are identifiable, emphasizing how revolutions-in-the-making play out agonistically in real life. This event constitutes a watershed in Tunisia's protest and *democratic* movements, which had built momentum since the late 1970s. Here we use *Al-Mustaqbal*, a leading newspaper of the opposition to record two things:

1. A brief qualitative analysis to interpret the view from below regarding the November 1981 elections tolerated by Bourguiba and promoted by Mzali. We do this with the benefit of hindsight of the massive rigging of those elections—affirmed by many ex officials, including Tahar Belkhodja (1999).

---

before becoming House Speaker (1981–86). His philosophical novel *Al-Sadd* (1955) has been translated into several languages.

[4] Mohamed Mzali founded the journal *Al-Fikr* in the 1950s and served in numerous ministries in the 1970s. He started a slight liberalization, in 1980–1986, when he was Prime Minister. During his premiership excessive force by the army in the 1984 bread riots resulted in dozens of deaths, the worst in Tunisia's history (see Chapter 3).

[5] Minister of Higher Education and Scientific Research, 1989–94.

[6] Hassib Ben Ammar (d. 2008) was Mayor of Tunis, 1963–69, then served as Minister of Defence, 1970–71. He was endorsed by Wassila, Bourguiba's wife. He helped launch the first opposition newspapers in the late 1970s, especially *Al Ra'i* in Arabic (see Khashanah 2021) and the magazine *Démocratie*, in French

2. It woud be reasonable to ask whether it is sound methodological practice to rely on newspapers articles to analyze a dimension of written protest (writing back) and political opposition and civic engagement (Oliver and Maney 2000). However, issues of bias should not arise here as this method is specifically intended to record the opposition's discourse of the event: what kind of civic mobilization did the opposition execute in its activism in favor of the elections, prior to the event, and in rejection of the results, after the event? There is no alternative source, which gives such an insight. *Al-Mustaqbal* (in tandem with *Al Ra'ï* and *Al-Sha'b*, both used in the empirical analysis) was representative of the view from below, a kind of contemporary record.

We have used a dozen weekly issues of *Al-Mustaqbal*, selected from the period between August and November 1981. True to Mzali's words, the opposition mobilized massively to contest the elections. Recurring terms in the editorials and articles by key figures such as Ahmed Mestiri, Mohamed Moada, Mohamed Harmal, Ismaïl Boulihia, and Mustapha Ben Jaafar include "the people," "democratic process," "democracy," "popular sovereignty," "participation," "rule of law," "elections," "opposition," "legitimacy," "consensus," and "dialogue." The newspaper's coverage is loaded with language that paints Mzali in a non-democratic light. In one article, Mohamed Moada, a leader within Mestiri's Socialist Democrats Movement (Mouvement Démocratique Socialist—MDS) is scathing of Mzali's November 18 speech on national TV to defend the (rigged) elections.[7] He points out that Mzali changed his usual open and liberal rhetoric to exactly the opposite, especially, with reference to Mzali's idea that "the people stand as a judge between the government and the opposition." Moada's retort reads: "how could that be when popular will and people's votes were usurped," through rigged elections? In a feature article, the issue of Week 30 November 1981, Hammouda Ben Slama, an MDS leader, criticizes the electoral fraud.[8] He reminds readers that the opposition's participation in the election was based on good will to help advance the democratic process and help "decompress the crisis of trust" between state and society. He regrets what he calls "the electoral farce," *al-mahzalah al-intikhabiyyah*, which made mockery of people's rights. The same issue records the return to politics of Habib Achour as UGTT president leader.[9] It stresses that his return should be used to boost the democratic process and inquiry into the rigging of the elections. Going back as far as October in the election campaign, one opening article takes up electoral integrity.[10] The issue has the opposition's "Green List" in which its candidates contest the poll in 20 districts. It mentions political responsibility as binding on both opposition and government. One interesting note links the practice of politics to the "moral commitment" by cadres who represent popular "consciousness."

---

[7] "The People 'An Arbiter' How?" *Al-Mustaqbal*, November 23, 1981, 1–2.
[8] "No Escape from Reality," *Al-Mustaqbal*, November. 30, 1981, 1–2.
[9] *Al-Mustaqbal*, November 30, 1981, 1–2.
[10] "The Administration's Neutrality: An Entitlement and an Assurance," *Al-Mustaqbal*, October 5, 1981, 1–2.

Moreover, issues for the weeks of August, 3, August, 10, August 17, and August 24, 1981 covered the trials of Ennahda, stressing their right to fair trial and the injustice of the Islamists' case. *Al-Mustaqbal* ran articles on reconciling Tunisia with its Islamic heritage and issues of religion and politics. Multiple articles in the four issues focus on prospects of genuine "political pluralism," creating suspense for the much awaited political opening started by Mzali. One issue elaborates the role of opposition in a democracy, stressing that democracy requires it—as a criticism of the state's practice of marginalizing its political opponents.[11] As a medium of peaceful activism that benefited from the capital of social doing and protest competency accumulated over decades of popular resistance, *Al-Mustaqbal* runs articles on syndicalist strikes, students' meetings and protests, political trials of dissidents, etc. It highlights regional discrepancies, shedding light on a town in the governorate of Kasserine where the annual income was at the time 36 Tunisian Dinars per year (nearly $20).[12] The same issue carries an article signaling the opposition's intention to participate in the November 1 elections, if the right conditions prevail. The stress is on "political struggle," the rights to "democracy" and to "opposition." Ahmed Mestiri and others, such as Aldali Aljazi, are adamant that political struggle is inseparable from the people. Editorial titles such as "Political Pluralism Thought and Practice" are telling.[13] The following issue contains good coverage of the electoral campaign in different districts and towns.[14] It refers to democratic preconditions in a country like Tunisia, namely separation of state and ruling party. The cover page for the last issue before the end of the electoral campaign, is splashed with a big title: "Vote Green" [*Sawwitu li Al-Khadhra*]—with an element of double speak and tongue-in-cheek.[15] The Green—or land of verdure—being a nickname for Tunisia.

Safeguarding the Revolution

The "Greens" did not prevail, of course, and neither did democracy in 1981. Bourguiba's counterrevolution won that round, too. Over four decades later, the problematic of taming revolution—not against the colons, but against authoritarianism—is more than a truism. Seeing the fruition of a century of protests leading to revolution is at first sight the true end of historic struggles. One puzzle, however, regards the uneasy dance between democracy and contemporary revolution. Revolution may connote chaos and radicalism in the eyes of power holders. Democracy may be read as a medium for normalizing politics with all its faults and contradictions (Rosanvallon 1998). Emancipation via revolution from the shackles of exclusion, marginalization, oppression, and the bigotry of prejudice could prove short-lived.

---

[11] *Al-Mustaqbal*, August 24, 1981 issue.
[12] *Al-Mutaqbal*, August 31, 1981 issue.
[13] *Al-Mustaqbal*, October 19, 1981, p. 1.
[14] *Al-Mustaqbal*, October 26, 1981 issue.
[15] *Al-Mustaqbal*, November 2, 1981, p. 1.

Is there an intrinsic relationality between protest (turned revolution) and democracy? In theory yes. As per our usage of deterritorialization-reterritorialization, our definition foregrounds a co-extensive ontology in which revolution means a moment of rebirth: an equalizing reset for kings and peoples. The public squares of resistance do not only summon the people. They also convoke thinking about the becoming of a demos, the space for the people to stake all kinds of claims—agentic, affective, cognitive—both representational and distributive. That is, engendering possibilities for the "missing people," "the part that has no part," and "le people introuvable"—for decades excluded from the political, the public, and the collective of peoplehood—finding self-determination, becoming, and being in a perennially "missing democracy." The late Maya Jribi, a prominent figure in the rebuilding of the political system after the revolution, states that "a revolution is a stage. It is not a permanent state of affairs. ... Yes, the people have earned this moment, and this is their revolution. ... However, the remaining work must now be delegated to political parties and the institutions of the democracy we want to create in the new Tunisia."[16] Mustapha Ben Jafar, Ettakatol's leader, concurs. He states that "there is no permanent revolution. ... We all know what permanent revolution did during the French revolution, disorder, violence and destruction of the state ... The Tunisian people have chosen through revolution a new order. Now comes our role as politicians, political parties and civil society to complete the task."[17] Hamma al-Hammai and Rachid Ghannouchi, more or less, beg to differ. Ghannouchi notes that "no politicians can today authorize politics without recourse to the people. ... The lived experience of protest include the brave youth of Tunisia. This is their revolution. It is their gift. ... Building new Tunisia must be founded on popular sovereignty. Without the people, we will lose our revolt."[18] Hamma Al-Hammami, a key dissident and leftist leader states that "No serious democracy will emerge if the Tunisian people do not lead ... supervise ... and protect it."[19] On the subject of marginalization, Ahmed Ben Salah reminds us that "a people can make a revolution, and even a democracy. Tunisians are capable. The challenge will remain social justice and a democracy of opportunities for all people and all regions."[20] This is echoed by Ebeid El-Briki, UGTT Deputy Secretary-General at the time, who points out that "the revolution belongs to the ordinary people, many of them permanently unemployed. No can take that from them. ... What is needed now is to go back to the struggles of workers for nearly 100 years and draw lessons. ... The lesson for me is that we need social justice, equality. ... With social justice there will be no democracy in Tunisia nor in other Arab countries."[21] Hossein Dimassi, a former syndicalist and government minister, concurs, saying: "Tunisia needs an economic democracy to secure the gains of this glorious revolution."[22]

---

[16] Interview, Maya Jribi, February 2, 2011, Tunis.
[17] Interview, Mustapha Ben Jafar, February 10, 2011, Tunis.
[18] Interview, 30 January, 2011, Tunis.
[19] Interview, 9 February 2011, Tunis.
[20] Interview, 9 February 2011, Tunis.
[21] Interview, 31 January 2011, Tunis.
[22] Interview, 14 February 2011, Tunis.

Protest: Learning "Counter-Democracy"

The interviews reported above gesture towards the challenging fruition of revolutionary becomings through an expansive understanding of democracy. We wish to tentatively suggest here that "protecting" Tunisia's revolution has (and must continue to) involve the long agentic adamancy of protest in a new democratizing setting. A return to the concepts of the "missing," *introuvable* people, the part that has no part, is fitting here. These terms coined by leftist French intellectuals Deleuze, Rosanvallon, and Rancière emerge in a different context of (an already democratic) setting, of course. In a (post)revolutionary setting still confronting the vestiges of authoritarian rule, "permanent protest" is essential to the actualization of the demos within and beyond the procedural implements of democracy (constitution, elections, etc.). If popular sovereignty is always tinged with doubt when the people are "missing" and "introuvable," it follows that existing democracies suffer fundamental pathologies. Rosanvallon (2008, 4) explores how mounting public distrust in democracies is channeled as "social counter-powers," to counteract flagging "confidence" in formal institutions and their performance. Importantly for our purposes, the appendages of counter-power can be "pre-democratic," a "first step toward human emancipation" through critique and resistance of the authorities (2008, 24–25). Manifestations of counter-democracy are stops on the pathway of the "testing ground" that is democracy, across time and space, Rosanvallon (2008, 26) contends. The union, student, and phosphate protestscapes showcased in Chapters 3, 4, and 5 attest to the richness of protest counter-power prior to Tunisia's democratization. Counter-power seems to reside in the blurring of authoritarianism and democracy in the contemporary context. Through its various protest expressions, vivacious *demoi* develop and hone their skills and practices of appearance, its agency, affect, and cognition. Revolution, according to Rosanvallon (2008, 165) is the "most radical" and "most effective" brand of "critical sovereignty" animating democratic "vigilance," a bridge into the world made anew—what we view as a type of rebirth.

The Kamour protestscape (Chapter 7) suggests that absent effective policymaking attention to people's material needs (jobs, adequate infrastructure, clean environment, etc.), the narrowness of procedural, nominally representative democracy has amounted to a "taming of the revolution" for the democratizing age. Both the Kamour and ultras protestscape (Chapter 8) additionally show in different ways that some level of state acceptance of Tunisia's marginalized citizens (the Janub, or delinquent football super-fans) is necessary for the full engagement of the *demos* in the country's new formal politics. Here, then, the classic critical theory debate about distribution and recognition (Fraser and Honneth 2003) speaks to the sustainability of Tunisian democratization that flowed from the 2011 revolution. In his exploration of "organized distrust" that stretches the scope of citizenship in democracies, Rosanvallon rebuts the idea of "political apathy." Against the onslaught of the "economization" of democratic politics detrimental to the demos itself (Brown 2015), Rosanvallon sees citizens moved to oppositional action. He notes a "simultaneous diversification of the *range*, *forms*, and *targets* of political expression" through collectivities alternative to political parties (2008, 19, original emphasis). What happens in between electoral cycles, in the years between the parade of ballot boxes? Voting is not the only way for the people as citizens to sound displeasure and discontentment (Rosanvallon 2008, 19). Instead, political participation is three-dimensional. The people interface with the political realm through "expression" (or "voice"), "involvement" (working in common), and "intervention" ("collective action" toward a particular ends) (Rosanvallon 2008, 20). He conceptualizes "counter-democracy" as complementary to "the usual electoral democracy ... a democracy of indirect powers disseminated through society." Bottom-up action intersperses periodic elections, "to shore ... up" existing legal and electoral institutions (2008, 8). On the one hand, this counter-power positively features a "growth in social powers," a "positive" development. At the same time, counter-democracy can veer towards populism and more "problematic[ally]," result in "fragmentation and dissemination" at the expense of "coherence and comprehensiveness" (2008, 23)—as Deleuze warns of revolution itself. On the whole, protest and social movements in Rosanvallon's estimation serve a *democratic* function (2008, 62).

Rosanvallon's bottom-up nodes of politics are often "post-democratic" reactions to broken pledges by power-holders. Increasingly, "counter-powers" avoid formal political institutions. Hence, counter-democracy has a prominent "protest dimension" (Rosanvallon 2008, 303). As Rosanvallon recounts, social protest originating in the late 1800s was steeped in moral indignation. (Here is a different take on Tilly's repertoires of contention in parliamentary contexts.) People compounded their "'refusal to suffer a debased existence" with attempts to nurture a "true critical sovereignty," to keep democracy democratic through social protest (2008, 153). While rebels and dissidents are key vectors of "critical sovereignty," for Rosanvallon revolution outstrips them both. Rosanvallon adds that protests and strikes, making demands and voicing critiques of governments are a type of "civic vigilance" (2008, 39). His propositions, and their very language, are redolent of the diachrony of Tunisian and Arab protests calling for rights, freedom, and dignity prior to and since 2011. It is almost as though the people practice their sovereignty through staging protests, including in what we have referred to as the "civic lyceums" of public squares. This social doing does not suddenly halt with revolutionary rupture, as our book has argued.

If protest is a manifestation of "counter-democracy," it also accrues learning dividends. In the post-2011 age, the uneasy embrace between protest and democracy/democratization foments a new kind of learning where bottom-up practices entwine with formalized politics. Democratic learning and skills acquired in the protest squares can be buttressed by legal codification. As Brunkhorst (2014) argues, to become "activated" in a manner conducive to democracy's perpetuation, legislation must be more than ink on paper. Social and "normative learning," according to him, are the internal (individual and collective) processes through which the law can give rise to democratic and civic *norms*. This kind of learning shapes what comes to be perceived as appropriate behavior by both "people" (as citizens) and state. When (popularly legitimate) law takes root, the cognition of peoplehood also precipitates Brunkhorst's (2014) "normative learning." Propped up by the law, this kind of pedagogy is spurred on by "crisis," in some cases instigating revolution or new social movements. Normative learning is an ongoing process that tends towards values including egalitarianism, reciprocity, justice, inclusiveness, etc. (Brunkhorst 2014, 50–51). It intertwines with the "cognitive learning of the political system" (2014, 288), almost as though people demand its more complete implementation. Denied the rights of peoplehood—institutionalized as citizens' rights in a new democracy—indignants still reeling from *hogra* cognize what the (new, democratic) system is meant to offer (employment, water, healthcare), through its absence. Elsewhere, Brunkhorst indicates democracy as a kind of crowning of normatively-hued, "process of continual [political] learning," enshrined through a melding of practice and law to actuate people's sovereignty (Brunkhorst 2005, 99; 170–171). Indeed, political but also democratic learning is relevant for post-2011 Tunisia. The equalizing capacity of revolutions demands (implementable) constitutionally codified rights (distribution, recognition) for the people previously neglected by elected governments of the state (Chapters 7–8), including the right to publicly protest as such, especially since July 25, 2021.

Branching out of Revolution

The quasi-permanence of protest in Tunisia since 2011 only confirms the indeterminacy of revolution that we have emphasized throughout this book. The "twin ferment" of revolution and peoplehood that reached its apex on January 14, 2011 was a fleeting moment, as it turns out. Deleuze's "divisions and betrayals" lurked in the chasms between popular expectations of equality and poor elite performance. A commensurability between acting and en-acting revolution and staging democracy is yet to be consummated. The "clamor of being" and/or of peoplehood qua subjectivizing (Rancière 1992) the "part that has no part", even if dynamically imagined, constructed, and defended in Tunisia's protestscapes, is not a straightforward story. Tunisia's revolutionary pathway was not linear, but choppy, its peoplehood not unified, but given to splintering. This even though Ben Ali's overthrow by the revolutionary masses set in motion a much-vaunted democratic transition that was for a decade the pride of the Arab region. Through constitutionally executed democratic transition, aided by a robust civil society, Tunisia became mired in a hit-and-miss process of dually "pacted-revolutionary transition" (Sadiki 2021). Pacted because it bore the imprimatur of constitutionality and democratic rules of engagement. Revolutionary because democratization tried but failed to tame the revolution. Contests and protests were instead continuous. Still, elections were not sufficient to routinizing politics and normalizing state–society relations on the basis of popularly democratic processes, cadres, and institutions. Complacency inspired by institution-building provided a sense of false security to post-2011 elites who sought to close the door on revolution, deemed at odds with the stability required by democratic transition. Moreover, the state of acrimonious political play among post-2011 governments made both revolution and democracy look suspect to some (Allal and Geisser 2018). The failure to activate parallel processes of transitional and distributive justice was likely the gravest error of the post-2011 political establishment. Thus, Tunisia's political elites endangered both the revolution and democratization. Enter Kais Saied, the relative unknown personality elected by 72 percent of voters in 2019 simply for being outside the political fray. Less than two years into his surprising election, he tore down hard-won democratic institutions beginning on July 25, 2021. For Manser, this has not been a "revolutionary turn" but "an authoritarian turn" (2023, 264) that "dismantles democracy" (2023, 335–360). Al- 'Ush regards these developments as a pathway towards an a-republic, even (2022, 123–172). Saied's freezing of Parliament, rule by decree, cooptation of the judiciary, eventual promulgation of a new constitution by (a widely boycotted) referendum, the installation of a rubber-stamp Parliament by (even more widely boycotted) elections in December 2022/January 2023, and imprisonment of critics from the media, civil society, and the political opposition (by the time we completed writing this book) are just some markers of what Redissi (2023) considers a return to singular rule. Despite three consecutive constiutions, Tunisia returned to rule by one one man (Ben Achour 2023). The latest constitution is akin to "de-democratization" (Klibi 2023). These regressions all pose serious questions (normative, theoretical, empirical) for researchers. They may dampen enthusiasm about the emancipatory rebirth of revolution.

When they rejected Mohamed Ghannouchi's governments in early 2011, did the Kasbah youth foresee this hijacking of their revolution? Figure 9.1 succinctly indicates this and other disruptions along a revolutionary momentum that diverged and branched off. Precise interpretations of the near-inscrutable puzzle of Tunisia's "democratic degeneration" (Sadiki and Saleh 2023), still in the works, are beyond the scope of our book. However, the question of Saied's counterrevolution, or "correction movement" (*harakah tashihiyyah*) as his supporters call it, warrants some tentative musings. How might we provisionally consider the July 2021 power grab, within the diachrony of Tunisia's revolution–counterrevolution dynamics? Perhaps the fragmentation of which Deleuze wrote is not random. (What complex socio-political occurrence ever is?) Dissatisfaction with broken revolutionary pledges, distasteful parliamentary antics, and un-bridgeable political polarization did not bode well for a newfound peoplehood. Saied was a President without a clear program. His speech act utterances of the slogan "the people want," familiar to all Tunisians (and the entire Arab Spring generation) stirred many voters, however. That his supporters (and campaigners) included some of the Kasbah youth recounted in Chapter 6 and other participants in the 2011 revolution, calls for pause. Perhaps it was here that Tunisia's revolution branched out, eventually giving rise to a one-man phenomenon whose counter-revolutionary trajectory was at the time difficult to predict. Streams of the 2011 revolution/peoplehood's actors and en-actors were dissenting and dissatisfied, discontent with Ben Achour's High Commission, the election of the National

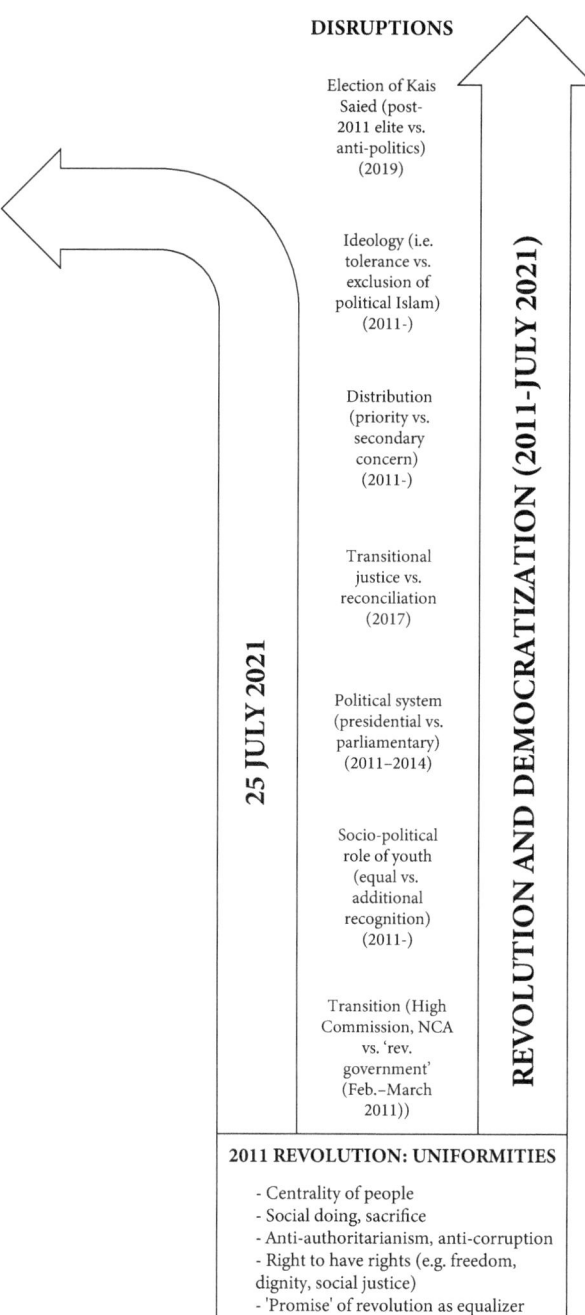

Figure 9.1 A Branching of the 2011 Revolution?

Constituent Assembly in October 2011, and perhaps even the resulting Constitution ratified in 2014. Historian (and President Moncef Marzouki's former Chief of Staff) Adnan Manser recalls the heady Troika[23] era as "years of sand" that slipped away faster than the new political class could effect revolutionary and democratic change (2014). Disappointment piled up. The "consensus democracy" engineered by Ennahda's Rached Ghannouchi and President Beji Caid Sebssi in 2015–16 was read by many in Tunisia's irate publics as peacemaking with the ancien regime. The "Administrative Reconciliation Law" of 2017 assassinated transitional justice. Meanwhile, unemployment soared, poverty deepened, prices skyrocketed, and COVID mismanagement appalled the population. Tunisia's disaffected carried conceptions of what peoplehood and equalizing revolutionary achievements should look like, but that departed sharply from those of elected, fast-rotating governments and their respective supporters. Naysayers boycotted elections, or stretched their vocal cords in protest, or both. The bitterness of exclusionary ideological discourse (e.g. anti-Islamist, or anti-elitist, or both) further stoked notions of a revolution wronged, a revolution to be reclaimed (even if for some, paradoxically, by one man). This rancor was on full display in the buildup (e.g. anti-Parliament protests) and immediate celebration of the President's late-night announcements on July 25, 2021. Claims to represent or enact "the true" revolution clashed interminably, in variably populist discourse (see Krichen 2023). Such language veers from the "affirmative" potential of affect, as Brian Massumi (see Evans and Massumi 2017) might put it.

The above narrative is admittedly a simplification of a complex series of events. Importantly, "competing ontologies" (Wight 2006) of revolution and peoplehood are not a problem in themselves. Revolutionary indeterminacy unfolds in practice, not just in theoretical tomes. At a normative level, this kind of dissensus does not necessarily spell disaster. So long, that is, as disagreement is enveloped within democratic institutions. So long as such divergent conceptions coincide with distributional justice that mitigates marginalization (the right to have rights) *and* are nurtured by normative, democratic learning engendering civic identities. Here is where Tunisia's revolutionary becomings, its democratic transition, have stumbled badly. Competing ontologies, after the 2011 revolution, were quickly evident in the "conflicting narratives" spanning even the origins of the state itself (e.g. Bourguibist vs. Youssefist) (Manser 2021). These contests lapsed into interactions closer to those of Mouffe's "enemies" than "rivals" operating under shared (democratic) rules of the game. It is as though the moment when "revolution" was declared in 2011 marked the beginning of its atrophy. No state, no political system, valorizes revolution continuously as it happens. Lending primacy to erecting democratic institutions, new governments sought to tame the revolution, which continued to rear its rebellious head in post-2011 protestscapes such as the Kamour. Tunisia's experience (vs. theory) of democratization seems to have been at odds with its revolutionary ethos and the

---

[23] The ruling Troika (2011–2014) is the name given to a tripartite coalition between Rachid Ghannouchi's Islamist Ennahda, Mustapha Ben Jaafar's Ettakatol Party and Moncef Marzouki's Congress for the Republic.

social doing of protestors. Instead of Rosanvallon's counter-democracy, how was a counterrevolution born? A man suffering from a "crisis of imagination," its latest ruler contorted into a "Frankenstein" nightmare, as one writer recently put it (Riahi 2023).

"Useless to Revolt?"

Where will Tunisia's renegade President take its revolution next? As democratic prospects dim by the day, an inevitable question might be: was the 2011 revolution, the toil and sacrifices, all worth it? Or, as Foucault once asked in a different revolution gone awry, is it "useless to revolt"? We offer here a defense of revolution. To reiterate, the practice of revolution is neither single, nor fixed. Revolution relates to "power over" practices found in all societies. In reflecting on Islamic Iran, Foucault brings back the question of power in an article about the 1979 revolution: "The power that one man exercises over another is always perilous" (Foucault 1999, 134). He considers the complex roles of power, ethics, knowledge, and religion in revolution. Revolution is not the exclusive bastion of one civilization, class, religion, or region. In seeking to answer his own question about the utility of revolution, Foucault does not fault the oppressed for rebelling or sacrificing their lives for higher values of emancipation. "One does not make the law for the person who risks his life before power. Is there or is there not a reason to revolt? … It is through revolt that subjectivity … introduces itself into history and gives it the breath of life" (Foucault 1999, 133). It is a form of quasi-self-transcendence in which revolutionaries risk life in the quest for revered dreams such as freedom. In this way, the relationship between revolution and freedom unravels, even in a religious settings such as Iran at the time of the Islamic revolution. Past eschatology plays a role (Foucault 1999, 131–134). In seeking to understand the "enigma of revolt" (1999, 132), Foucault finds explanations that relate to the human condition, in Iran or elsewhere, when "traumatized" by " censorship and persecution, years of marginality" and failed governance in terms of "…'development,' 'reform,' 'urbanization,'" etc. (1999, 132). However, Foucault plants an epistemic role for affect in highlighting the practice of resistance and revolution by the oppressed. Emotions deriving from "hunger … humiliations … hatred of the regime and [the] will to overthrow it" (1999, 132) are not to be underestimated as pivotal in generating moral awareness, popular association, and mobilization on behalf of higher values such as emancipation.

Here we might recall Belhouane, who reads from a letter sent on October 1, 1951, by Bourguiba from his exile in La Galita, the rocky islands adjacent to Bizerte in the north of Tunisia. "No sooner than I came to the last line in your letter did my eyes well up in tears. Tears of joy, pride, and gratitude to God the Almighty who graced this blessed, righteous, and sincere movement … whose members toil night and day with all their wisdom, devotion and know-how to uphold God's religion … and to deliver an abode of Islam from the abyss of humiliation and enslavement" (Belhouane 1954, iii). It is the affective dimension that, even in a religious context, reconfigures acting, feeling, and knowing differently and defiantly in ways that "overthrow a regime which seemed to be amongst the best armed in the world" (Foucault 1999, 132). It is within this reconfiguration of acting/en-acting, feeling and knowing that "reterritorialization" is set in motion. Thus unhinge existing police orders and logics whereby "distribution of the sensible" (and its implication for miscounting "the part that has no part") is disturbed. This signals the start of a politics of "dissensus," a site for sharpening civic courage, social doing, and re-associating via emerging revolutionary *demoi* and logoi. As in Iran, Ben Ali's powerful police apparatus caved in, forced out by a crowning revolution-peoplehood. The catastrophic blunderings of post-2011 governments, the jubilant festivities that greeted Kais Saied's July 25 proclamations, arguably smoothing the way for his power grab, however, imperiled revolutionary becomings and democratization. Was Tunisia's revolutionary dream overblown?

Both conceptually and empirically, revolution promises only to disappoint, and to break its promise. The grandees of revolution from Brinton to Tilly know this all too well. Frustrations and regressions have left the revolution's "promise of spring" unfulfilled, but Tunisians must "resume the journey," to restore democratic imaginaries and inspire a broken region anew (Krichen 2016, 399–401). So much for revolution. Within dissentscapes, revolution is epistemic, animated by an intertwining of spatial and temporal registers. Its study, through re-ontologization, opens up the possibility of accessing lives whose triad of agency, affect, and cognition are constituted by the biggest predicament of all: a human condition still captive to various patterns of pre-colonial, colonial, and postcolonial domination. Delivery from this predicament within Tunisia's protestscapes involves oscillation between past knowing, learning, feeling, and doing and future possibilities of revolution, that is, a rupture with captivity.

Protest is an art of adapting captivity of being (including to space and time). This means accessing inner capacities for transporting self and community towards habituation with free becoming. That is, entering a revolutionary experience in which freedom and dignity are contemplated as worthy ends, for their own sake; and social doing, feeling, and knowing are deflected onto deterritorializing and reterritorializing, equalizing trajectories. These possibilities of imagined options for free imaginings of being, feeling, and knowing, carry their own promises and frustrations. The inherent normativity of rebellion to construct free peoplehood and rescind un-freedom and inequality should not inhibit asking questions about the utility of revolution or its promise. For, in 2011 Tunisia, a people rose up against their oppressors to affirm revolution's promise. From the foregoing, the 'multitudes' law' seems to be that *Tunis Al-Tha'irah* has staying power. Long live the revolution!

References

Allal, Amin and Vincent Geisser. 2018. *Tunisie: Une Démocratisation au-dessus de Tout Soupçon?* Paris: CNRS.

Manser, Adnan. 2021. *Sanawat Al-Raml: Tafakkur fi Ma'arik Al-Intiqal Al-Dimuqrati fi Tunis* [Years of Sand: Reflecting on the Years of Democratic Transition in Tunisia] *2011–2014*. Tunis: Sotomedia.

Al-Tamimi, Abdeljalil. 2008. *Siminar al-Dhakirah al-Wataniyyah wa Al-Tarikh: Hawla al-Dawr Al-Siyasi wa Al-Thaqafi li Barsbaktif wa Al-Barsbaktifiyyin fi Tunis Al-Mustaqillah* [On the Political and Cultural Role of Perspective and Perspectivists in Independent Tunisia]. Zaghouan: Mu'assassat Al-Tamimi.

Al- 'Ush, Mehdi. 2022. *Nahwa Al-La-Jumhuriyyah: Maqalat Hawla Al-Intiqal Min Dimuqratiyyat Maridah Ila Hukm Al-Fard* [Toward an A-Republic: Articles On the Transition From a Sick Democracy to One-Man Rule]. Tunis: Nashaz.

Ayari, Michaël. 2017. *Le prix de l'Engagement Politique dans la Tunisie Autoritaire: Gauchistes et Islamistes sous Bourguiba et Ben Ali*. Paris: Karthala.

Belhouane, Ali. 1954. *Tunis Al-Tha'irah* [Tunisia in Revolt]. Cairo: Lajnit Tahrir Al-Maghreb Al-'Arabi.

Belkhodja, Tahar. 1999. *Al-Habib Bourguiba: Sirat Za 'im* [Habib Bourguiba: A Leader's Biography]. Tunis: 'Alamat li Al-Tiba'ah wa Al-Nashr.

Ben Achour, Sana. 2023. *Trois constitutions, un seul pouuvoir*. In Redissi, Hamadi, Editor. 2023. *Le Pouvoir DÚn Seul*. Tunis: Diwen Editions: pp. 65–84.

Bouguerra, Abdeljalil. 2015. *Al-Yasar Amam Mahkamat Amn Al-Dawlah* [The Left before the State Security Court]. Tunis: Dar Afaq Tunis li Al-Nashr wa al-Buhuth.

Brown, Wendy. 2015. *Undoing the Demos: Neoliberalism's Stealth Revolution*. Brooklyn: Zone Books.

Brunkhorst, Hauke. 2005. *Solidarity: From Civic Friendship to a Global Legal Community*, trans. Jeffrey Flynn. Cambridge, MA: The MIT Press.

Brunkhorst, Hauke. 2014. *Critical Theory of Legal Revolutions: Evolutionary Perspectives*. New York and London: Bloomsbury.

Deleuze, Gilles and Félix Guattari, 1994. *What is Philosophy?* Trans. H. Tomlinson and G. Burchell. New York: Columbia University Press.

Daifallah, Mohamed, 2016. *Al-Talabah Al-Tunisiyyun wa Makhadhat al-Watan fi Muntasaf Al-Qarn Al-'Ishrin* [Tunisian Students and the Travails of the Nation's Birth]. Tunis: Maktabat Tunis.

Evans, Brad and Brian Massumi. 2017. " Histories of Violence: Affect, Power, Violence—The Political is Not Personal." Los Angeles Review of Books, November 13, https://bit.ly/44CmeO8

Foucault, Michel. 1999. *Religion and Culture*, selected and edited by Jeremy R. Carrette. Manchester: Manchester University Press, 131–134.

Fraser, Nancy and Axel Honneth. 2003. *Redistribution or Recognition? A Political-Philosophical Exchange*, Trans. Joel Golb, James Ingram, and Christiane Wilke. London: Verso.

Haraway, Donna. 1988. "Situated Knowledges: The Science Question in Feminism and the Privilege of Partial Perspective." *Feminist Studies* 14(3): 575–599.

Khashanah, Rachid. 2021. *Hassib Ben Ammar wa Hilm Al-Mashruʻ Al-Islahi* [Hassib Ben Ammar and the Dream of the Reformist Project]. Tunis: Simpact.

Kirby, Vicki, 2017. "Matter out of Place: 'New Materialism' in Review." In *What if Culture was Nature all Along?* edited by Vicki Kirby. Edinburgh: Edinburgh University Press, 1–25.

Klibi, Salsabil. 2023. *La Constitution du 25 Juillet 2022, constitution de la dé-démocratisation*. In Redissi, Hamadi, Editor. 2023. *Le Pouvoir DÚn Seul*. Tunis: Diwen Editions: pp. 85–102.

Krichen, Aziz. 2016. *Waʻd Al-Rabiʻ* [Spring's Promise]. Tunis: Script Editions.

Krichen, Zyed. 2023. *La paradoxes dún pouvoir populiste autoritaire et solitaire*. In Redissi, Hamadi, Editor. 2023. *Le Pouvoir DÚn Seul*. Tunis: Diwen Editions, pp. 33–44.

Manser, Adnan. 2023. *Sanawat Al-Tin: Tunis Min Al-Dimuqratiyyah Al-Kasihah Ila Al-Istbidad Al-Shaʻbawi*. [Years of Mud: Tunisia Between Shaky Democracy to Populist Authoritarianism] 2019–2023.Tunis: Sotumedia.

McAdam, Doug, Sidney Tarrow, and Charles Tilly. 2009. "Comparative Perspectives on Contentious Politics." In *Comparative Politics: Rationality, Culture, and Structure*, Edited by Mark Irving Lichbach and Alan S. Zukerman. Cambridge: Cambridge University Press, 260–290.

Mzali, Mohamed. 2010. *Un Premier Ministre de Bourguiba Témoigne* [A Prime Minister of Bourguiba Attests]. Tunis: Sud Editions.

Oliver, Pamela E. and Gregory M. Maney. 2000. "Political Processes and Local Newspaper Coverage of Protest Events: From Selection Bias to Triadic Interactions." *American Journal of Sociology* 106(2): 463–505.

Rancière, Jacques. 1992. "Politics, Identification, and Subjectivization." *October* 61: 58–64.

Rancière, Jacques. 2011. "The Thinking of Dissensus: Politics and Aesthetics." In *Reading Rancière: Critical Dissensus*, edited by Paul Bowman and Richard Stamp. London: Continuum, 1–17.

Redissi, Hamadi. 2023. "*Une dictature bien singulière*". In Redissi, Hamadi, Editor. 2023. *Le Pouvoir DÚn Seul*. Tunis: Diwen Editions, pp. 45–64.

Riahi, Kamal. 2023. *Frankenstein Tunis*. Tunis: Dar Al-Kutub.

Rosanvallon, Pierre. 1998. *Le Peuple Introuvable: Histoire de la Représentation Démocratique en France*. Paris: Gallimard.

Rosanvallon, Pierre. 2008. *Counter-Democracy: Politics in an Age of Distrust*, Trans. Arthur Goldhammer. Cambridge: Cambridge University Press.

Sadiki, Larbi. 2021. "Sculpting the Statue of Revolution and Democracy: Tunisian Ten Years On." *Al-Sharq Strategic Research*, February, 3. https://research.sharqforum.org/2021/02/03/tunisia-ten-years-on/

Sadiki, Larbi and Layla Saleh. 2023. "Degeneration and the Demos in North Africa: Towards a 'Critical' Study of Democratization?" *The Journal of North African Studies,* https://doi.org/10.1080/13629387.2023.2207227.

Smith, Linda Tuhiwai 1999. *Decolonizing Methodologies: Research and Indigenous Peoples.* London: Zed Books.

Tawil, Ahmed, 2021. *Zu'ama' Khalidun fi Tarikh al-Harakah Al-Wataniyyah Al-Tunisiyyah* [Lasting Leaders in the Tunisian Nationalist Movement]. Tunisi: Al-Magharibiyyah li Al-Tiba'ah.

Thiong'o, Ngugi Wa. 1986. *Decolonising the Mind: The Politics of Language in African Literature.* London: James Currey; Nairobi: Eastern African Educational Publishers

Tilly, Charles. 1978. *From Mobilization to Revolution.* New York: Random House.

Wight, Colin. 2006. *Agents, Structures, and International Relations: Politics as Ontology.* Cambridge: Cambridge University Press.

Index

Tables, figures, and boxes are indicated by an italic *t*, *f*, and *b* following the paragraph number. References to notes are indicated after the paragraph number by 'n', followed by the note number.

For the benefit of digital users, indexed terms that span two pages (e.g., 52–53) may, on occasion, appear on only one of those pages.

1864 Revolution 25*t*, 67–73, 232–234*t*, 256, 357
1896 Khaldounia (Khalduniyyah) foundation *See* Khaldounia (Khalduniyyah) foundation (1896)
1907 Young Tunisians, foundation of *See* Young Tunisians
1911 Jallaz protests *See* Jallaz protests (1911)
1924 General League for Tunisian Labor, foundation of *See* General League for Tunisian Labor
1938 pro-"Tunisian parliament" protests 55, 67–68, 232–234*t*, 357
1954 anti-colonial resistance *See fellaga*
1969 collapse of Ben Salah cooperativization policy *See* cooperativization policy, collapse of
1978 General Strike ("Black Thursday") 198–199
1984 bread riots *See* bread riots (1984)
2008 Gafsa Revolt *See* Gafsa phosphate basin uprising (*intifadah*) 2008
2011 Revolution *See* revolution; namings and narratives (2011 Revolution)

Abassi, Houcine 106*t*, 125, 200–201, 209, 246, 254
"Absent People" concept *See* people and peoplehood
abstract space 193
Achour, Habib 52–53, 104, 105–107, 105–107*t*, 108–109–CP36, 111–113, 115–119, 121–126, 120*t*, 146–147, 363–364, 366
action *See also* violence
    collective action 7*t*, 11, 13–14, 76, 103, 193, 213–218, 324, 369–370
    speech and 43
afaqi (see also *beldi*) 2–3, 7, 75, 192–194, 213–217, 234–235, 241, 285–286, 291–292
affect
    "affect hooks" 327
    counter-*hogra* and 288
    direction of 177, 313, 332–334, 344, 351–352, 361–362
    double consciousness 189
    emotions arising from 71–72, 99, 109–110, 146–147, 156–157, 159–160, 164, 231–232, 241, 242–243, 247–248, 253, 263, 317, 321, 330–331, 334, 337, 341, 344
    emphasis on 314
    experience of 254–255
    hogra and 242–243, 283, 285, 301, 338–340
    language of 121–123*t*
    origin of 324
    peoplehood, and 44, 325
    religious affect 328–329
    role of 7*t*, 38*f*, 375
    significance of 283*t*, 314–315, 323–324, 334, 336–337, 315*t*, 357–358
    source of 177
    visual politics, and 325
    youth activism, and 256
agency, peoplehood and 43
agon 48, 76–77, 288–289, 300
agonism, protest as 48
Ahmad II, Bey of Tunis (Ahmed Bey) 25*t*, 40, 67–72, 76, 295–296, 357
Al-Daghbagi, Mohamed C9 (p. 276), 295–296, 305
Al-Hammi, Mohamed Ali *See also* General League for Tunisian Labor 90–98, 100–103, 105, 108–109, 125–126, 120*t*, 162, 190–191, 195, 359, 363–364
Al-Jallaz cemetery *See* Jallaz protests (1911)
Al-Khaldounia (Al-Khalduniyyah) foundation (1896) *See* 1896 Khaldounia Foundation
Al-Materi, Mahmoud 69
al-mujtama'al-muwazi ("parallel society") 191
Al-Mustaqbal (newspaper) 27–28, 99, 123–124, 140–142, 146, 148–149, 155–156, 160–161, 175, 178–179, 195, 196–199, 318–319, 365–367
Al-Ra'i (newspaper) 27–28, 105–107, 113–114, 118–124, 120*t*, 122*t*, 141, 160–161, 197–198
al-rakh la! (slogan) 279–280, 283*t*, 286–287, 294, 295–296, 300, 302–303
Al-Salehi, Al-Saghir 191
Al-Sha'b (newspaper) 27–28, 99, 101, 107–126

Index   **381**

Al-Shammari, Khamis 149, 155–156
Al-Skrafi, Anwar 280–281, 286–288
Al-Taimoumi, Alhadi 51, 55, 67–68, 74–75, 194–195, 198–199, 238
Al-Tamimi, Abdeljalil (*see also* Tamimi Foundation) xviii, 27–28, 230, 262–263, 269–270, p. 272
Al-Thabti, Adel 149–150, 159–165, 171, 174, 198–199
Ammar, Rachid 263
April 9 College 140–143, 153–154, 161–162, 177, 239*t*, 256
"Arab Spring" 13–15
Arendt, Hannah. 7*t*, 25, 41, 42–43, 64–65, 38*f*
Aristotle 63
Arundhati, Roy 18–21*t*
'asabiyyah 46, 48–49, 292–293
Association of Tunisian Women for Research on Development (AFTURD) 178–179
Austin, John L. 171–174
authoritarianism *See also* counterrevolution 3, 23*t*, 39*f*, 46, 49–50, 60, 65–67, 78, 104, 133, 139, 143–145, 149, 157–158, 161, 174–176, 180, 218, 230, 257, 267–268, 329–330, 358–360, 367–369
  anti-authoritarian ideology 165
  counterrevolution, and 29–30, 51–52
  protest as dissent against domination 69
  student "protestscape," and 134–135

Babeuf, François-Noël (Gracchus Babeuf) 30–31
Bailyn, Bernard 7*t*
Bakhtin, Mikhail 30–31, 230–231, 234, 238, 245–246, 252, 265, 268–269
Bayat, Asef 14–15
Bebbington, Anthony 299
"becoming"
  behaviour and consciousness of 209
  counter-consciousness, growth of 197
  diachrony, and 229
  people and peoplehood, and 41
  protestscapes, and 41
  revolution, and 229, 362
  "social imaginaries" 169
"being"
  genius loci concept, and 63
  genius mazes concept, and 63
  intersectional 62
beldi (*see also afaqi*) 2–3, 7, 75, 192–194, 213–217, 234–235, 241, 285–286, 291–292
Belhouane, Ali 96, 356, 357, 363–364, 375
Belkhodja, Tahar 105, 109–110, 112–113, 363–365
"belonging," ultras as 332
Ben Achour, Sana 212, 371–372
Ben Achour, Yadh 69–71, 234, 269–270

Ben Ali, Zine El Abidine
  "Ben Ali generation" of students 151
  Counter-*Hogra* 290–293, 297, 298, 301–302
  Democratic Constitutional Rally (*Hizb Al-Tajammu'*) (RCD) 139, 254n56, 265–266, 268–269
  National Compact 124–125
  regional activism, and 192–193, 203, 208–209, 213–218, 222–223
  revolutionary language against 25*t*
  revolutionary synchrony-diachrony, in 69–71*f*
  Revolution of 2011, and 236–237, 243–245, 248–249, 251–256, 259–261, 269, 270–271
  student activism, and 134–135, 149–151, 164–165, 171–174*t*
  Tunisian People, and 51–53, 124–125, 241, 361, 364–365, 371–372, 375
  UGTT activism, and 101–103
  ultras, and 313–314, 321, 327–330, 344, 348–349
Ben Ammar, Habib 364–365
Ben Ammar, Hassib 118–119, 364–365
Ben Ammar, Wasila (Wasila Bourguiba) 105
Ben Ghedhahem, Ali 2–3, 5, 25*t*, 38, 43, 66–73, 95, 200–201, 232–234*t*, 242–243, 255–256, 295–296, 305, 357
Ben Jaafar, Mustapha 198–199, 247, 265–266, 366, 367–368, 372–374
Ben Jannat, Mohamed 155–156
Ben Mhenni, Lina 175–177, 211–212, 236–237, 363–364
Ben Mhenni, Sadok 175–176, 180–181
Ben Mrad, Bechira 363–364
Ben Salah (ben Saleh), Ahmed 77, 89–92, 98, 101, 104, 105–107*t*, 136, 155–158, 164–165, 168, 170–171, 192–193, 240–241, 361–362, 364, 367–368
Ben Younes, Kamal 148, 174
Ben Youssef, Adel 75
Ben Youssef, Salah 66, 72, 75, 77, 96–98, 109–110, 139, 145–146, 151–154, 213–217, 233*t*, 296, 359, 363–364, 374–375
Beylicate, Bey of Tunis, *See* Ahmad II
Bishara, Azmi 14–15
"Black Thursday" *See* General Strike 1978
Blili, Leila 155–156, 159, 177–178
Bouazizi, Mohamed, death of (2010) 75, 151, 232–234, 238, 242–244, 247–248, 256–257, 363–364
Bouguerra, Abdeljalil 60, 69–71, 76, 77, 139, 153–156, 168, 363–364
Boulihia, Ismaïl 366
Bourdieu, Pierre 16, 42–43

Bourguiba, Habib 374–375
  1911 Jallaz protests, and 69–71
  1938 pro-democracy protests, and 67–68
  authoritarian regime 21–22, 52–53, 59–60, 358–359, 361, 364
  Bourguibism 51
  Bourguibists 66
  economic development 7
  fellaga, and 72
  foundation of *Al-'Amal Al-Tunisi* (newspaper) (1932) 357
  foundation of Tunisian Republic (1957) 25–26, 40, 73
  Hogra 285–286, 290–292, 296–298, 305
  nationalism 4–5, 50
  opposition movements, and 76–77
  Orientalism 18
  political language 237
  regional activism, and 196–199, 213–217
  return from exile (1955) 363
  Revolution of 2011, and 237, 240–241, 254, 258–261, 269
  Salah Ben Youssef assassination (1958), and 359n1
  student activism, and 134–135, 139–140, 142–147, 149, 151–160, 167–168, 170–174, 178, 189–193
  trade union activism, and 89–91, 95–99, 101, 102–105, 108, 109–110, 112–116, 118–123
  ultras, and 317–318, 324, 334–335
Brahim, Mounia (Munia) 175–176, 236–237
bread riots (1984) 43, 55, 69–71*t*, 102–103, 121, 125–126, 143–145*f*, 151–152*t*, 198–199, 207–208, 232–234*t*, 241
Brinton, Crane 6, 376
Brown, Carl L. 38
Brunkhorst, Hauke 370–371
Butler, Judith 42–44

Callahan, William 290, 325–327
capitalism
  capitalist class 167
  revolution, and 7
Carroll, David 54–56, 38*f*
Casanova, Pablo G. 191
Center for Research, Studies, Documentation and Information on Women (CREDIF) 259–261
Chabuto, Munira 153–154
Charfi, Mohamed 153–154, 170, 364–365
choreographies *See dakhlah*
class
  capitalist 167
  concept of 174
  conflict 7, 44
  consciousness 91–92, 94–95
  counter-revolution by 10

  cross-class 195, 213–217*t*, 221, 251
  hegemony 167–168
  identification with 109
  interests 168–169
  middle-class 13
  political class 180–181, 282–283, 372–374
  second-class 135–136
  spatialized disparities 259
  structures 10
  subordinate 168
  working-class 62–63, 97, 99–100, 113–114, 123–124
Club Africain Ultras *See* ultras
cognition of people and peoplehood, and 46
collective action 7*t*, 11, 13–14, 76, 103, 193, 213–218, 324, 369–370
collective violence, theory of 11
colonialism *See also fellaga*; postcolonialism
  anti-colonial protest 317
  "decolonization" of revolution 21
  people and peoplehood, and 57
Communism and Communist movement 7*t*, 154–156, 170, 178, 213–217*t*
Communism, Communist movement 212–213
complementarity 123–124, 192, 258–259, 264–265
constructivism 64
contentious politics 8*t*, 11–13, 22, 27, 42–44, 47, 193–194, 360–361
contested knowledge 66
contest (political or cultural) 48
convergence of theories 359
critical positioning 65–66
critical theory 4, 62, 359–360, 369–370
Chebbi, Abou El Kacem 254
Chebbi, Issam 150, 161–162, 198–199,
Chebbi, Nejib (Ahmed Najib) 150, 153–154, 157–158, 175–176, 199–201, 247, 265–266
Compact, university (1986) 160–161
consciousness, double *See* concepts and theories
constructivism, protestscapes and 64
contentious politics *See* concepts and theories
contentious violence, theory of 11
contested knowledge *See* concepts and theories
contest (political or cultural) *See* concepts and theories
cooperativization policy, collapse of (1969) 55, 89–90, 98, 240–241
counter-*hogra* *See hogra*
counterrevolution
  authoritarianism, and 29–30, 51–52
  nationalism, and 50
  people and peoplehood, and 29–30, 53
  postcolonialism, and 38*f*
  revolution and 4–5, 10, 25*t*, 52
  societal and cultural effects 51–52

CPG *See* Gafsa Phosphate and Chemical Company
critical theory *See* concepts and theories

Daifallah, Mohamed 133, 138–142, 148, 153–154, 157–161, 163–165, 171, 179–180, 317–319, 324–325, 359
dakhlah (choreographies) 342
   aesthetics of 325–326
   choreography of protest 338
   competence for 329
   empowerment by 314
   expression through 314–315, 318–319
   meaning of 314–315*t*
   performances of 325–326, 329, 339–340, 351
   preparation for 338–339
   sports and politics in relation 326
   t'allam 'oum ("learn to swim") campaign 346–347
decontested political concepts 168
Deleuze, Gilles 40–41, 44, 56, 71–72, 38*f*, 94–95, 241, 362–363, 369–374
democracy p. xv, 23*t*, 29–31, 40, 41–42, 48, 49–50, 57, 58–60, 76, 101, 107–108, 110–113, 116–119, 120*t*, 132, 140–141, 143–145, 163–165, 167, 172*t*, 212–213, 246–247, 253, 265, 278, 294, 297, 301, 303–304, 307, 351–352, 364–374
   inclusive communicative democracy 174
   revolution, and 5
   revolution as "counter-democracy" 369
democratization 5, 12–14, 25, 31, 76–77, 91–92, 249, 269, 277–278, 283, 284*t*, 297–298, 300, 306–307, 315*t*, 350–351, 369–374, 373*f*, 374–375
Democratic Constitutional Rally (RCD) 139, 254n56, 265–266, 268–269
Democratic Patriots' Unified Party (WATAD) 150, 161–163, 171–175
deprivation theory 11
Derrida, Jacques 3, 40, 46, 313
description *See* language
Destour *See* Neo-Destour
De Tocqueville, Alexis 6, 7*t*
Dhouib, Mohamed 67–68, 72–73, 75, 296
diachrony
   alliance of new and veteran protesters 247
   Bakhtinian "carnival," as 30–31, 230–231, 234, 238, 245–246, 252, 265, 268–269
   "carnival," as 231
   contemporaneous revolutionary narratives 255
   diachronic analysis of revolution 5
   diachronic collapse of experiences 361
   disappearing diachrony 357–358
   Kasbah 1 sit-in, and 261–262
   Kasbah 2 sit-in, and 261, 264

Kasbah sit-ins, legacy of 269–270
Kasserine, events in 240
people and peoplehood, and 26, 38, 53, 125–126, 270–271
protest, of 48, 60, 67, 72, 231, 370
protestscapes, and 2, 15, 25*t*, 53, 56, 60–61, 73, 78, 314–315, 358
protests, places/times of (table) 232–234*t*
revolution, and 2, 25–26, 29, 30–31, 63, 69–71*f*, 55, 238, 357–358, 361, 363, 372–374
revolutionary diachrony, introduction to 230
spread of revolution, and 245
student activism 131–132, 141, 152–153, 156–157
suffering as a gathering of synchronies 242–243
suffering as seedbed for protest 242
synchronies of protests, and 249
synchrony within a diachrony 156–157
Ultras, and 314–315, 324–325, 351–352
women, and 257
young protesters, and 256
dictatorship *See* authoritarianism
Difaoui, Zakia 204–205, 211–212, 221, 239*t*, 363–364
discourse analyses of revolution 29
dissent *See* protest
dissentscape 15, 43–44, 56, 65, 73, 78, 104–105, 130–131, 134–135, 140–141, 166, 180–181, 230–231, 234–235, 270–271, 277–278, 283, 313–314, 341–342, 358, 361, 376
double consciousness 46, 109, 189, 197, 222–223, 242–243, 264–265, 305
Dubois, W.E.B. 46
Durkheim, Emile 46

economic regional underdevelopment as cause of revolution 191
Eisenstadt, S.N. 6
Ekiert, Gregorz 59–60
Elections 41–42, 60, 107–108, 165, 172*t*, 239*t*, 265–266, 269–270, 301–304, 364–367, 369, 371–374
Embodied protest 149, 161, 288–289
Ennahda 159, 161–162, 164, 171–174*t*, 247, 249, 259–261, 269–270n94, 283, 302–303, 367
epistemic injustice 2, 16, 176–177, 207–208
epistemic justice 17–18, 66, 133

false needs 51–53
fellaga (anti-colonial armed resistance movement, 1954) 72, 89–90, 99–100, 102–103, 132, 135–136, 145–146, 190–191, 207–208, 213–217, 232–234*t*, 295, 356
feminist political theory 176–177
football fans *See* ultras

Foucault, Michel 16–17, 21, 168–169, 238–240, 277–278, 375
Frank, Gunder 191
Freeden, Michael 167
free(d) spaces 132, 140–146, 149, 150, 154–155, 164, 176–178, 261–262, 267, 269–271, 342–343
Free Destour *See* Destour
"freeplay" concept (Derrida) 313
Freire, Paulo 47, 133–134, 141, 170, 257
Fricker, Miranda 16–18

Gafsa Phosphate and Chemical Company (CPG) 62–63
Gafsa phosphate basin uprising (*intifadah*) 2008 *See also* Gafsa Phosphate and Chemical Company
  behaviour and consciousness of "becoming" 209 "being" and 62–63
  civil society mobilization during (table) 213–217t
  convergence of activisms 211
  counter-consciousness, growth of 197
  counterrevolution, and 53
  current book's analytical approach 4–5, 12–13, 189
  dissent, as 69–71
  distinctive features summarized 222
  exploitation of miners 194
  Gafsa Revolt of 1980 198
  hogra and 189, 197, 204, 205–207t, 217–218, 222–223
  inspiration for wider mobilization, as 211
  language of 25t, 30–31
  linguistic features of criminal charges against protestors (table) 218t
  miners mutiny (Jan-Jun 2008) 201
  plurality of participations in 76–77
  prelude to 2011 Revolution, as 199
  protestscape 60, 189
  regional underdevelopment as cause of 191
  slogans of 205
  southern Tunisia's revolutionary tradition 190, 193
  student activism, and 135
  UGTT, and 102–103, 108–109, 113–114, 125–126
  understandings of 207
  women's participation 220
Gafsa Revolt of 1980 198
General League for Tunisian Labor (Founded 1924) *See also* Union Générale Tunisienne du Travail 89–90
  foundation of (1924) 93
  labor mobilization 89, 92, 125–126, 195
  Mohamed Ali Al-Hammi's vision for 90

  revivals and re-creations 95
General Strike 1978 ("Black Thursday") 43, 47, 55, 69–71t, 102–104, 118–121, 124–126, 143–145f, 151–152t, 207–208, 232–234t, 241
General Tunisian Students' Union (UGET) *See also* student activism 139–140, 149, 151–153
genius loci concept 63
genius mazes concept 63
Gerring, John 167–169
Ghannouchi, Mohamed 261–263, 265–271, 367–368, 372–374
Ghannouchi, Rached 164–165, 372–374
Gill, Jungyun 132
Gluck, Sherna 28, 133
Goldstone, Jack A 7t
Gonzalez, Hector M. 145, 149–150
Goodwin, Jeff 7t, 10, 12–13
Grami, Amel 258–259
Gramsci, Antonio 149–150, 167, 168, 170
Guattari, Felix 41, 44, 71–72, 38f, 241, 363
Guessoumi, Mouldi 53, 191–192, 269–271,
Guevara, Ernesto (Che) 340–341
Gurr, Ted 7t, 10–11, 13, 360–361

Habermas, Jurgen 51–52
Hached, Farhat 41–42, 52–53, 75, 90–91, 96–97, 99–103, 105, 106t, 107–110, 113–115, 120t, 125–126, 206t, 205–207, 236–237, 254, 286–287, 305, 363–364
Haddad, Tahar 88, 90–95, 190–191, 195
hadrah performances 327
Hamma, Hammami 211–212, 236–237, 247, 248–249, 367–368
Havel, Vaclav 7t, 13–14
Heidegger, Martin 64
hirak (*see also* al-hirak) 2–3, 15–16, 23t, 25, 40, 200–201, 255–256, 282, 283, 294–295, 350–351, 361
Hirschman, Albert 43–44
history
  oral histories of revolution 28
  oral histories of student activism 133
Hobsbawm, Eric 6–7, 7t, 10
hogra
  affect and 242–243, 283, 285, 301, 338–340
  concept of 45
  counter-*hogra*, affect and 288
  double consciousness 46, 109, 197, 222–223, 242–243, 264–265, 305, 314–315
  Gafsa uprising, and 189, 197, 204, 205–207t, 217–218, 222–223
  Kamour movement, and 277–278, 283, 285–288, 292, 294–295, 297–298, 301, 303–307
  protest, and 71–72
  solidarity, and 46, 292, 294–295

Index   385

state, of the 283t
student activism, and 135–137
Horkheimer, Max 62, 359–360
human rights, Tunisian Human Rights League (LTDH) 121–123, 211–212, 213–217t
human security 116–117

Ibn Khaldun   See also 1896 Khaldounia foundation 2, 48–49, 190–191, 292–293, 350
identity, ultras as source of 332
ideology
   anti-authoritarian ideology 165
   'clamor of being' 105
   contestation as to 167
   identity, and 105
   interpellation and 134–135
   localized ideological understandings 168
   "one-dimensional man," of 51–52
   perspectivism and 153–154n34
   revolution of 2011 372–374f
   "social imaginaries," and 171–174t
   speech-based protest, and 174
   student activism See student activism
   trade union (UGTT) 100–101, 105–107t, 105
inclusive communicative democracy 174
industrialization, revolution and 7
injustice See justice
interdisciplinary study of revolution 16
Interpellation 134–135
interpretative approaches to revolution 27
intersectional "Being" 62
Islamic Tendency Movement (MTI) See Ennahda

Jallaz protests (1911) 25t, 43–44, 55, 69–71, 232–234t, 357
"Jasmine Revolution" 230–231, 270–271
Jlassi, Abdelhamid 180–181
Jouhaux, Léon 93–94
Jribi, Maya 178–179, 220, 247–249, 367–368
justice
   epistemic injustice 2, 16, 176–177, 207–208
   "epistemic injustice" as target of revolution 16
   epistemic justice 17–18, 66, 133

Kamour movement
   al-rakh la! (slogan) 279–280, 283t, 286–287, 294, 295–296, 300, 302–303
   counter-hogra 288
   current book's analytical approach 277
   democracy in relation 297
   disaffection with democracy 301
   distinctive features of protest 282
   distinctive features summarized 306
   fellaga 295
   hogra and 277–278, 283, 285–288, 292, 294–295, 297–298, 301, 303–307

   identities of peoplehood, learning of 305
   language and terminology associated with (table) 283t
   learning, social and normative as to 303
   protestscape 277–279
   resistance to reduction of resources rights 299
   rights-related language of 297
   solidarity against the State 294
   solidarity and kinship in relation 292
Khaldounia (Khalduniyyah) foundation (1896)
   See also 1896 Khaldounia foundation 55, 96–97n7, 238–240, 357
Khaled, Leila 209–213, 220
Khayr Al-Din 38, 43–44, 357
khubz   (see also khubzah) 23t, 121, 122t, 240–241, 252, 253
knowledge
   "contested" knowledge 66
   "partial" knowledge 65
   protestscapes, and 65–66
   "situated" knowledge 65–66
Korba Congress See student activism
Krichen, Aziz (Aziz Krishan) 149, 155–157, 359, 376
Kristeva, Julia 27, 44, 314–315, 360–361
Ksar Hellal 92–94, 112, 233t
Kubik, Jan 60

Laabidi, Bechir 199–205, 207–212
Laabidi, Muzaffar 210–213
Laabidi, Omar 312 (p. 312), 346–351
Laabidi, Samir 118, 145–146, 150, 159
labor activism See Union Générale Tunisienne du Travail
Labyad, Salem 138–139, 149, 153–154, 158, 179–180
language
   affect, of 121–123t
   al-rakh la! See al-rakh la!
   dakhlah See dakhlah
   discourse analyses of revolution 29
   Gafsa uprising 25t, 30–31
   hogra See hogra
   interpretative approaches to revolution 27
   intertextual study of 27
   Kamour movement 283t, 297
   linguistic features of criminal charges against protestors (table) 218t
   linguistics theory 53
   oral histories of revolution 28
   power, and 22
   slogans See slogans
   "thick description" of revolution 29
   ultras 314–315t
"learn to swim" (t'allam 'oum) campaign 346–347

Index

Lefebvre, Henri 193–194
LeFort, Claude 41–42, 38f
Lenin, Vladimir 149–150
Lourimi, Ajmi 146–150, 159, 161–162, 363–364
Luxembourg, Rosa 44

Madrasa Al-Khaldounia (Al-Khalduniyyah) foundation (1896) *See* 1896 Khaldounia foundation
Manser, Adnan 97–98, 104, 371–375
Manouba campus (university) 152t, 153, 161–162
Mao Zedong 151–152, 180
Marcuse, Herbert 2–3, 25, 38, 38f, 50–53, 62, 240–241, 359–360, 363
Marx, Karl 7, 25–26, 44, 149–152, 154–155, 165, 167–169, 174, 180
Marzouki, Moncef 221–222, 247, 248–249, 253, 372–374
Mbazza, Fouad 261, 270–271
Mdhila 195–203, 222–223
Mekki, Abdellatif 145–146, 160–161, 164–165
Mestiri, Ahmed 99, 118–119, 364–367
Metlaoui 95–96, 195, 196–197, 200–203, 222–223, 319t
"metropolitan revolution" 5–7, 8t, 10, 13–17, 21–22, 38, 48, 55–56, 62, 78, 133, 359–361

middle-class *See* class
mineral resources, resistance to reduction of rights related to 299
miners *See also* Gafsa phosphate basin uprising (*intifadah*) 2008
    exploitation of 194
    miners mutiny: January-June 2008 299
"Missing People" concept *See* people and peoplehood
Moada, Mohamed 366
mobilization, revolution and 11
modernization, revolution and 7
modernization theory 7t, 13
Moore, Barrington Jr. 6–7, 7t, 10–11, 14–15, 17, 25–26, 46, 357–358, 360–361
Mouffe, Chantal 48–49, 38f, 167, 374–375
Moularès 188, 196–197, 200–203, 220, 222–223
Mouvement Démocratique Socialist (MDS) 366
music *See* ultras
Mzali, Mohamed 121, 123–124, 164–165, 170–171, 364–367

namings and narratives (2011 Revolution)
    Arab Spring 13–15
    Jasmine Revolution 230–231, 270–271
Nasraoui, Radia 117–118, 211–212, 236–237, 248–249, 267, 363–364
Nasser, Abdul Gamel 18, 165, 167, 180
nationalism, counterrevolution and 50

National Union of Tunisian Women (UNFT) 192
Neo-Destour *See also* Destour 90–95, 97, 104, 114, 118–119
nonviolent protest and revolution 13, 339
Norberg-Schulz, Christian 63–64, 170
Nouira, Hedi 89–90, 95–96, 113–115, 117–118, 157–158, 240–241

online-offline campaign against police violence 347
oral histories 28, 133
Orientalism 2–3, 5–6, 18–21, 49–50, 66, 67–68, 77

"parallel society" (*al-mujtama'al-muwazi*) 191
"part that has no part" 57–60, 38f, 123–124, 130–131, 191, 199–200, 222–223, 231–232, 238–240, 270–271, 277–278, 285–286, 288–289, 313, 338, 351, 360–363, 367–369, 371–372, 375
Pei, Minxin 8t, 13
people and peoplehood
    "Absent People" concept 40
    affect, and 44
    affect and 44, 325
    agency, and 43
    agonism, protest as 48
    "becoming," and 41
    "becoming" a people 41
    cognition, and 46
    concept map of 38f
    constructivism, and 64
    counterrevolution, and 29–30
    creative forces for peoplehood 78
    dimensions of peoplehood 43–44
    "double consciousness" concept, and 45
    four-dimensional analysis of protestscapes 60
    hogra, concept of 45
    interpretation of 26
    intersectional "Being" 62
    "Missing People" concept 3, 38f, 40–41, 56, 94–95, 238–240, 258, 269, 362–364, 367–368
    people as makers of revolution 78
    "politics of the people" concept 4
    positionality 17–18, 66
    postcolonialism, and 50
    precolonial-to-postcolonial development of 57
    protest, and 2
    protest as agonism 48
    protestscapes, and 38–40
    revolution, and 2
    solidarity, and 46
    workers' syndicalism, and 40, 99
performance
    protestscapes, and 42
    ultras *See* ultras

Index   387

Perspectives (*also* Afaq; *also* Perspectivists) 69–71, 152*t*, 143, 150, 152–158, 165, 172*t*, 178, 180–181, 238–240, 260–261, 359
phosphate basin uprising *See* Gafsa phosphate basin uprising (*intifadah*) 2008
Plato 58–59, 63
police violence, online-offline campaign against 347
political parties
 Communism and Communist movement 7*t*, 154–156, 170, 178, 212–213, 213–217*t*
 Democratic Constitutional Rally (*Hizb Al-Tajammu'*) (RCD) 139, 254n56, 265–266, 268–269
 Democratic Patriots' Unified Party (WATAD) 150, 161–163, 171–175
 Destour *See* Destour
 Ennahda 159, 161–162, 164, 171–174*t*, 247, 249, 259–261, 269–270n94, 283, 302–303, 367
 Islamic Tendency Movement (MTI) *See* Ennahda
 Neo-Destour 90–95, 97, 104, 114, 118–119
 Progressive Democratic Party (PDP) 199, 212–213, 247–248
political process theory 12–13
politics *See also* concepts and theories
 contentious politics 8*t*, 11–13, 22, 27, 42–44, 47, 193–194
 contest (political or cultural) 48
 political class *See* class
 political process theory *See also* concepts and theories 12–13
 protest and revolution in relation 342
 radical change of political power arrangements 22
positionality *See* concepts and theories
postcolonialism *See also* colonialism
 counterrevolution and 38*f*
 people and peoplehood, and 50, 57
 postcolonial analyses of protest and revolution 18
postcolonial theory 18–21*t*, 21–22
power, protest and revolution in relation 22
Progressive Democratic Party (PDP) 199, 212–213, 247–248
protest *See also* revolution
 agonism, as 48
 Bourguiba counterrevolution as preliminary for protest 77
 conflicts generated by 75
 counterrevolution, and 4–5
 counter to established historical-political narratives, as ("counter-logos") 73
 crucible of nineteenth century 71
 current book's analytical approach 2

 current book's main aims and arguments summarized 2, 4
 diachrony, and *See* diachrony
 dissent against domination 69
 empirical studies of, absence of 21
 history of Tunisian grassroots protest 67
 introduction to Tunisia's political history of protest and revolution 2
 language and power in relation 22
 nonviolent protest and revolution 13
 peoplehood, and *See* people and peoplehood
 performative practice, as 78
 places/times of protests (table) 232–234*t*
 pluralism of 75
 postcolonial analyses of 18
 revolution, and 2
 social activity, as 4
 sociology of "Protest Momentum/Ethos" 72
 synchrony, and *See* synchrony
protestscapes *See also* dissentscape; rebelscape; diachrony; synchrony;
 "Absent" People, and 40
 "becoming," and 41
 concept of 15, 78
 constructivism, and 64
 four-dimensional analysis of 60
 genius loci concept, and 63
 genius mazes, concept, and 63
 introduction to 38
 labor *See* Union Générale Tunisienne du Travail
 "Missing" People, and 40
 "partial" knowledge, and 65
 people and peoplehood, and 38
 performance, and 42
 positionality, and 66
 "situated" knowledge, and 65–66

radical change of political power arrangements 22
Rancière, Jacques 38*f*, 57–60, 65–66, 77, 94–95, 168–169, 171–174, 191, 218, 222–223, 277–278, 313, 351, 361, 362–363, 369, 371–372
rebelscape 15, 30–31, 38, 52–53, 58–59, 62–63, 66, 76–77, 90–91, 131, 189, 234, 261, 277–278, 283, 307, 324–325, 358, 361–362
reality 25–26, 62, 63, 134–135
Redeyef 95–96, 195–198, 200–207, 206*t*, 209–213, 222–223, 230–231, 238, 239*t*, 247–248, 250–251
Redeyef Uprising (2008) 200–207, 209, 238–240
regional underdevelopment as cause of revolution 191
relationality 42–43
re-ontologize p. xiii, p. xiv, p. xvii, 56–59, 62, 104, 131–133, 180, 189, 261, 270–271, 277–278, 306–307, 313, 358, 362–363

representation 21, 49–50, 162, 213–217
revolution *See also* counterrevolution; protest
  capitalism, and 7
  collective action *See* action
  collective violence, theory of 11
  contentious violence, theory of 11
  counterrevolution, and 4–5, 10, 25*t*, 52
  current book's analytical approach 2
  current book's content and structure 30
  current book's main aims and arguments summarized 2, 4
  "decolonization" of 21
  discourse analyses of 29
  empirical studies of, absence of 21
  "epistemic injustice," against 16
  histories of *See* history
  hogra and 71–72
  industrialization, and 7
  interdisciplinary study of 16
  interpretation of 26
  intertextual study of 27
  introduction to Tunisia's political history of protest and revolution 2
  "knowing" revolution, ways of 25
  language in relation 22
  mobilization, and 11
  modernization, and 7
  namings of 2011 Revolution *See* namings and narratives (2011 Revolution)
  nonviolent protest and revolution 13
  peoplehood, and *See* people and peoplehood
  postcolonial analyses of 18
  power in relation 22
  protest, and 2
  statist metropolitan revolution, limitations of 10
  storytelling approaches to 25
  structures of state and international systems, and 10
  "thick description" of 29
  tradition of 5
  Western social science perspective on 6
revolutionary situation 11, 14–16
revolutionary theory 2, 5, 6, 14–15
Ricoeur, Paul 54–55
Rohrschneider, Robert 143–145
Rosanvallon, Pierre 39*f*, 40, 369–370
Roucek, Joseph S. 167
Rowbotham, Sheila 6
Rushdie, Salman 18–21*t*

Sahraoui, Abdelmajid 105, 109–110
Saied, Kais 5, 11, 161–162, 237, 258–259, 267, 269–270, 281–283, 290–291, 301, 302–303, 306, 307, 314, 322, 337–339, 348, 350–352, 371–374, figure 9.1 (page 373), 375

Sassi, Fadhel 160–161
Sebssi, Beji Caid 268–269, 372–374
Sartre, Jean-Paul 53
Saussure de, Ferdinand 38*f*, 53
Sayyah, Mohamed 72, 105, 109–110, 115
Scott, James C. 43
security (human) *See* concepts and theories
selfhood *See* "being"
Sen, Amartya 43–44, 199–200, 301–302
sensible politics 325–326
Sfar, Rachid 67–71
Skocpol, Theda 7*t*, 10–11, 46, 357–358, 360–361
slogans
  al-rakh la! 279–280, 283*t*, 286–287, 294, 295–296, 300, 302–303
  use of 205
social imaginary 73, 100–101, 169
social movement theory 12, 360–361
social theory 50, 58–59
society and culture
  counterrevolution, and 51–52
  localized ideological understandings 168
  protest as social activity 4
  "social imaginaries" of "becoming" 169
  Western social science perspective on revolution 6
solidarity
  hogra and 46, 292, 294–295
  people and peoplehood, and 46
song 341
space *See* concepts and theories
speech
  action and 43
  acts 30–31, 64–65, 205
  "ideal speech situation" 48
  "inner speech. 64–65
  oral speech 64–65
  "social speech" 64–65
  speech-based protest, and 174
  synchrony of 54
  test of 59–60
  written speech 64–65
Spivak, Gayatri 19*t*, 360–361
sports in relation to protest 342
the state
  building of 192
  counter-revolution by 10
  destruction of 367–368
  face of 283*t*
  forgetfulness of 283
  gaze of 213–217
  hands of 290–291
  hogra of 283*t*
  implements of 52
  indignities inflicted by 288–289
  marginalization by 367

narratives of 114, 374–375
negligence by 250–251, 292–293, 370–371
non-cooperation of 292–293
"occupiers" of 52–53
others of 65–66
"part that has no part" of *See* concepts and theories
pillars of 114–115
place of 141–142
rejection of 336–337
representatives of 300
reproduction of 51–52
security machinery of 320–321
subalterns of 65–66
statist analysis of revolution 10
Strauss, Levi 53–55
structural systems-related analysis of revolution 10
student activism
    18th extraordinary UGET Congress 1988 159
    1968 protests 155
    affect and 256
    anti-authoritarian ideology 165
    current book's analytical approach 130, 133
    diachrony of student protestscape (table) 151–152*t*
    distinctive features summarized 180
    early history of university syndicalism 138
    "embodied" protest 161
    events leading to 151
    Gafsa uprising 2008, and 135
    General Tunisian Students' Union (UGET) 139, 149, 151–153
    hogra and 135–137
    ideological controversies 167
    ideology 165, 169
    ideology and protest in speech 174
    introduction to 130
    Islamist students 162
    Korba UGET 18th Congress 1971 146, 157
    localized ideological understandings 168
    oral history of 133, 146
    "pedagogy" of oppression and of freedom 141
    perspectivist protest 153
    political and union recruitment of students 151
    "social imaginaries" and ideologies of student protestscape tendencies, 1963–1991 (table) 171–174*t*
    student protestscape 131, 133
    student publications 359
    students' stories of protest 146
    student–teacher learning loop 142
    teachers as fellow-protesters 137
    universities as centers of 138, 149
    universities as "free spaces" 149
    violence 149

women's discussion groups (e.g. Club Tahir Haddad) 178
women's inclusion or exclusion 176
women's participation level assessed 177, 179
student movement 132, 140–141, 170
suffering
    gathering of synchronies, as 242–243
    seedbed for protest, as 242
synchrony
    diachrony, and 156–157, 230, 232–235, 240–241
    people and peoplehood, and 26, 38, 41, 53
    protestscapes, and 2, 15, 25*t*, 53, 56, 60–61, 78, 358
    protests, of 48, 67, 249, 283, 314–315, 361
    revolution, and 2, 25–26, 29, 40, 69–71*f*, 55, 314, 357
    student activism 131–132, 143, 147, 152–153, 156–157
    suffering as a gathering of synchronies 242–243
synchronic analysis of revolution 5
synchrony-within-a-sync 346–347
Ultras as 324–325, 329–332, 346–347, 351–352
syndicalism 93–94, 98, 101–102; *see* General League for Tunisian Labor; Union Générale Tunisienne du Travail

t'allam 'oum ("learn to swim") campaign 346–347
Tarrow, Sidney 7*t*, 12–15, 22, 42, 46, 47
Taylor, Charles 169
teachers *See* student activism
Thaalbi, Abdelaziz 357
thawrah (*see also al-thawrah*) *page xii*, 2–3, 23*t*, 25, 37, 122*t*, 200–201, 249, 268–269, 297, 314
Thompson, E. P. 2–3
Tilly, Charles 6–7, 7*t*, 10–15, 17, 22, 38*f*, 42, 47, 357–358, 360–361, 376
time *See* diachrony; synchrony
trace 25–26, 313
trade unions *See* General League for Tunisian Labor; Union Générale Tunisienne du Travail
Trotsky, Leon 149–150, 165
Trouillot, Michel-Rolph 21
Tunisia
    current book's analytical approach 2
    current book's main aims and arguments summarized 2, 4
    foundation of Tunisian Republic (1957) 25–26, 40, 73
    introduction to Tunisia's political history of protest and revolution 2
    regional underdevelopment as cause of revolution 191

Tunisia (*Continued*)
   southern Tunisia's revolutionary tradition 190, 193
   tradition of revolution 5
Tunisian Association of Democratic Women (ATFD) 211–217
Tunisian personality 75

UGET *See* General Tunisian Students' Union
ultras
   anti-colonial protest 317
   anti-"political" stance of 336
   anti-systemic confrontation by 338
   arising of 320
   "belonging," as 332
   choreography of protest 338
   culture of 323
   current book's analytical approach 314
   dakhlah 342
   distinctive features summarized 350
   football protestscape 313–314
   "freeplay" concept (Derrida) 313
   hadrah performances 327
   identity, as 332
   language and terminology associated with (table) 314–315*t*
   musical performances by 326
   non-violent protest 339
   online-offline campaign against police violence 347
   people and peoplehood, and 325
   performance and visual politics by 325
   performances, features of 343
   protectiveness of 333
   protest practices of 336
   protests 317
   protests, places/times of (table) 318–319*t*
   resistance competency of 329
   revolution, and 314, 348
   solidarity, and 334
   songs of protest 341
   sports and politics in relation 342
   t'allam 'oum ("learn to swim") campaign 346–347
   violence 325
   violent protest 339
Union Générale Tunisienne du Travail (UGTT) *See also* General League for Tunisian Labor
   Habib Achour's leadership 109
   Habib Achour's re-election 124
   "associative cooperation" with Ben-Ali regime 125
   beginnings of worker activism 92
   Ben Ali's National Compact, and 124–125
   "Black Thursday" protests 104
   bread riots 1984, and 118
   characteristics of Tunisian syndicalism 100
   congresses 105–107*t*
   creation of 96
   current book's approach to study of 4, 30, 89
   formation of General League for French Labor 93
   Gafsa uprising 2008, and 125–126
   General Strike 1978, background to 104
   General Strike 1978, events of 117
   government's portrayal of 114
   Al-Hammi's vision for 90
   historical background to creation of 90
   identity and ideology of ('clamor of being') 105
   ideology 100–101, 105–107*t*, 105
   introduction to 89
   legitimacy of strikes 113
   media usage by 115
   National Compact 1977, withdrawal from 111
   Neo-Destour, and 90–95, 97, 104, 114, 118–119
   people and peoplehood, and 40, 99
   political opposition ("democratic" and "socialist") support for 118
   protest slogans, meanings of 121–123*t*
   public reputation and relations 115
   revival and re-creation after 1929 ban 95
   Revolution of 2011, and 125–126
   secretary generals 105–107*t*
   syndicalist traditions and values 102
unity 292
universities *See* student activism

vana 62–63, 280, 284*t*, 290, 300, 302–304
violence
   collective violence, theory of 11
   contentious violence, theory of 11
   non-violent protest and revolution 13, 339
   police violence, online-offline campaign against 347
   student activism 149
   ultras 325
visual politics 325
Viswanathan, Gauri 18–21*t*
void of power 40–42, 58–59, 254–255, 269
Vygotsky, Lev 64–65, 143–145

Wacquant, Loic J.D. 42–43
Way, Lyndon C. S. 326–327
women
   Association of Tunisian Women for Research on Development (AFTURD) 178–179
   Center for Research, Studies, Documentation and Information on Women (CREDIF) 260–261
   diachrony, and 257
   discussion groups 178
   Gafsa uprising 2008 220

student activism *See* student activism
Tunisian Association of Democratic Women (ATFD) 211–217
workers' syndicalism *See* General League for Tunisian Labor; Union Générale Tunisienne du Travail
working-class *See* class

Working Group for Socialist Studies and Work (GEAST) 153–154

Young, Iris Marion 174–176
Young Tunisians (Founded 1907) 51–52n10, 55, 67–68, 357
youth activism *See* student activism